Secretaries and Statecraft in the Early Modern World

Secretaries and Statecraft in the Early Modern World

Edited by
Paul M. Dover

EDINBURGH
University Press

Edinburgh University Press is one of the leading university presses in the UK. We publish academic books and journals in our selected subject areas across the humanities and social sciences, combining cutting-edge scholarship with high editorial and production values to produce academic works of lasting importance. For more information visit our website: www.edinburghuniversitypress.com

Edinburgh University Press Ltd
The Tun – Holyrood Road
12(2f) Jackson's Entry
Edinburgh EH8 8PJ

First Published in hardback by Edinburgh University Press 2016

Typeset in 10/12pt Times New Roman by
Servis Filmsetting Ltd, Stockport, Cheshire, and
printed and bound in Great Britain by
CPI Group (UK) Ltd, Croydon CR0 4YY

A CIP record for this book is available from the British Library

ISBN 978-1-4744-0223-1 (hardback)
ISBN 978-1-4744-2844 6 (paperback)
 ISBN 978-1-4744-0224-8 (webready
PDF) ISBN 978-1-4744-1588-0 (epub)

Contents

Contributors

Rayne Allinson is Assistant Professor of History at the University of Michigan-Dearborn. She is the author of *A Monarchy of Letters: Royal Correspondence and English Diplomacy in the Reign of Elizabeth I* (Palgrave Macmillan, 2012), and is currently researching a biography of William Maitland of Lethington.

Rebecca Ard Boone (PhD Rutgers, 2000) is Professor of History at Lamar University in Texas. She has published two books examining the relationship between information and state power in early modern Europe: *War, Domination, and the Monarchy of France: Claude de Seyssel and the Language of Politics in the Renaissance* (Brill, 2007) and *Mercurino di Gattinara and the Creation of the Spanish Empire* (Pickering and Chatto, 2014). Her current project, *Sixteenth Century Lives: Leadership, Love, and Loss in the Early Modern World*, looks at state consolidation in the sixteenth century from a global perspective.

Paul M. Dover (PhD Yale, 2003) is Associate Professor of History at Kennesaw State University. He has published widely on the diplomatic and cultural history of late medieval and early modern Europe. He is the author of the textbook *The Changing Face of the Past: An Introduction to Western Historiography* (Cognella, 2014) and of the forthcoming *The Information Revolution of Early Modern Europe: A Reign of Paper* (Cambridge University Press).

Rajeev Kinra (PhD University of Chicago, 2008) is Associate Professor of South Asian and Global History at Northwestern University, where he currently serves as director of the Asian Studies Program and co-director of the newly launched Global Humanities Initiative. He has written extensively on early modern Mughal and Indo-Persian cultural history, and is the author most recently of 'Cultures of Comparative Philology in the Early Modern Indo-Persian World' (*Philological Encounters* 1.1 (2016)) and *Writing Self, Writing Empire: Chandar Bhan Brahman and the Cultural World of the Indo-Persian State Secretary* (University of California Press, 2015).

Isabella Lazzarini is Associate Professor of Medieval History at the University of Molise, Italy. Her research interests focus on the political, social and cultural history of late medieval Italy, with an emphasis on Renaissance diplomacy and the growth of different political languages in documentary sources. Her most recent books are *The Italian Renaissance State*, edited with Andrea Gamberini (Cambridge University Press, 2012), *Communication and Conflict: Italian Diplomacy in the Early Renaissance, 1350–1520* (Oxford University Press, 2015) and the forthcoming sourcebook *Italian Renaissance Diplomacy: Texts in Translation*, edited with Monica Azzolini (Durham Medieval and Renaissance Texts in Translation).

Russell E. Martin is Professor of History at Westminster College and Associate Editor (Editor in 2017) of *Canadian-American Slavic Studies*. He is the author of *A Bride for the Tsar: Bride-Shows and Marriage Politics in Early Modern Russia* (Northern Illinois, 2012), which won the 2014 W. Bruce Lincoln Book Prize. His articles have appeared in *Slavic Review, Russian Review, Russian History, Manuscripta, Kritika, Journal of Medieval and Early Modern Studies, Harvard Ukrainian Studies, Forschungen zur Osteuropäischen Geschichte* and elsewhere.

Colin Mitchell is Associate Professor of History at Dalhousie University. He is a specialist of early modern Iran, with an emphasis on literature and politics. He has published *The Practice of Politics in Safavid Iran: Power, Religion, and Rhetoric* (I. B. Tauris, 2009) and *New Perspectives on Safavid Iran: Empire and Society* (Routledge, 2011). He is currently working on a project entitled *Ruling from a Red Canopy: Princely Cities and Governates in the Turco-Persianate World, 1000–1650*.

Toby Osborne is Senior Lecturer in History at the University of Durham, having studied for his undergraduate and graduate degrees at Balliol College, Oxford. He is a specialist on early modern diplomacy and court history, with a focus on the Italian duchy of Savoy. His publications include *Dynasty and Diplomacy in the Court of Savoy: Political Culture and the Thirty Years War* (Cambridge University Press, 2002).

David Parrott is Fellow and Faculty Lecturer in History at New College, University of Oxford. He is the author of *Richelieu's Army* (Cambridge University Press, 2001), articles on many aspects of early modern military and political history, and most recently a study of military entrepreneurship: *The Business of War: Military Enterprise and Military Revolution in Early Modern Europe* (Cambridge University Press, 2012). His current research project focuses on France in the 1650s.

Daniel Riches (PhD Chicago 2007) is Associate Professor of History at the University of Alabama. He is the author of *Protestant Cosmopolitanism and Diplomatic Culture: Brandenburg-Swedish Relations in the Seventeenth Century* (Brill, 2013), as well as numerous articles, essays and reviews on early modern European history.

Franz A. J. Szabo is Professor Emeritus of Austrian and Habsburg History at the University of Alberta and was the founding Director of the Wirth Institute for Austrian and Central European Studies from 1998 to 2011. He has published widely in Europe and in North America on the subject of Austrian history and culture, and is the author of the award-winning *Kaunitz and Enlightened Absolutism, 1753–1780*

(Cambridge University Press, 1994) and of *The Seven Years War in Europe, 1756–1763* (Pearson-Longman, 2008).

Erik Thomson is Associate Professor of History at the University of Manitoba. He researches the intersection of commerce and government, primarily in early modern Europe, and has published articles in *French History*, *The Journal of the History of Ideas*, *Sixteenth Century* and *Histoire, Economie & Societés*, among others.

Megan K. Williams (PhD Columbia, 2009) is Assistant Professor in Early Modern History (Diplomatic History) at the University of Groningen in the Netherlands. Her current research, funded by the Netherlands Organisation for Scientific Research (NWO), examines the adoption, use and management of paper as a new communications technology in early modern diplomacy, c.1460–1560. This project has resulted in a number of recent and forthcoming publications, including the chapter in this volume.

CHAPTER 1

Introduction:
The Age of Secretaries

Paul M. Dover

Across Eurasia, the early modern period was the age of secretaries. These figures, while not always identified by this particular name, became proverbial in society, pen in hand, surrounded by paper, the custodians of institutions that sought to capture the world in writing. Merchant companies, universities, religious foundations and, above all, governments were replete with such secretaries, deemed essential for the effective functioning of these bodies. The enhanced role of the secretary was especially manifest in the operation of diplomacy, where the increasingly complex conduct of foreign affairs saw the emergence of officials tasked with managing the growing number of tasks and personnel involved, as well as the expanding paper trail that they produced. Such figures – secretaries, chancellors and ministers – assumed central roles in a broad range of regimes – small and large, monarchies and republics. The current volume brings together studies that seek to elucidate the roles of these individuals, with a view to increasing our understanding of how foreign policy was made and implemented in the early modern world.

The period starting in the fifteenth century was marked by an intensification of contacts in international affairs, evidenced in a notable rise in the frequency of exchange of diplomatic personnel and in the volume of correspondence that they generated.[1] Increasing numbers of these diplomats were resident ambassadors who spent long periods of time at a single court. Hence the need for dedicated diplomatic personnel (if not diplomatic professionals strictly defined) both at home and abroad, as well as institutions, such as diplomatic chanceries and archives, dedicated to the support of such activity. Foreign policy (a term one uses guardedly when the lines between foreign and domestic policy were not at all finely drawn) was increasingly multifaceted and complex, involving the dispatch and oversight of numerous ambassadors and relations with multiple states. Most importantly, diplomacy was no longer spasmodic and episodic but rather a seamless activity of the state, a means of tending to bilateral relations and maintaining vigilance through intelligence gathering.[2] These demands stretched the limits of the personal rule that characterised most states. Such pressures enforced a widening of the circle of those involved in the formulation of foreign affairs, in some cases begetting the rise of prime ministerial offices, state secretaries and royal favourites as figures of central importance in early modern government. The waxing influence of these figures in the exercise of state power is one of the most notable features of early modern statecraft and is a central theme in this volume.

The studies presented here span the length of the early modern period, from the Renaissance to the French Revolution, and include regimes stretching from England to Mughal India. The inclusion of two exemplars from the Muslim world (Colin Mitchell on Safavid Persia and Rajeev Kinra on Mughal India) alongside a number from Christian Europe is especially gratifying, as the two sides of the confessional divide are usually considered in isolation from, and not infrequently in opposition to, one another. The evidence presented in this volume suggests, in fact, that there are important similarities amid the cultural differences, and that the early modern period was just as much an age of secretaries in the Islamic empires as it was in Europe. Indeed, the Islamic secretariat and the Persianate tradition of the *munshi*, if anything, had deeper roots in a rich medieval history of administrative practices.

This volume takes shape at the intersection of two prominent historiographical trends. First, it shows how the 'new diplomatic history' that has emerged in recent years has reshaped our understanding of early modern politics in significant ways.[3] This work, in particular, has been leavened by the insights of social and cultural historians. In keeping with the thrusts of this historiography, the authors in *Secretaries and Statecraft in the Early Modern World* have sought to understand their subjects against the backdrop of their political and social milieus and their personal, familial and cultural formations. The state and statesman cannot be regarded as autonomous actors, but rather must be seen as subject to a great variety of social, cultural and institutional forces. The importance of the ritual and ceremonial features in mediating diplomatic exchanges has recently received considerable attention. Diplomats have also been examined as agents of cultural exchange, of items and ideas.[4] A genuine historical understanding of inter-state relations in this period must take these various social forces and facets of diplomatic activity into consideration.

Thus the negotiations studied in this volume are not simply those that resulted in treaties and alliances, but also the great many social negotiations that underlay the making of policy: the negotiation of the interests of various stakeholders within early modern societies, the negotiation of authority and influence (in council, at court and with the head of state) among those involved in decision-making, and the ongoing negotiation of the personal interest and ambition of secretaries and ministers that went hand in hand with their service to state and sovereign. The history of statecraft presented here, therefore, is a layered one. Many of the individuals described in this volume played multiple roles: they occupied influential positions in government councils, at court and in society. They were not only operatives of government, but also scions of families, representatives of social classes, and cogs in the machine of patronage, both as distributors and as recipients. Statecraft, while ultimately formulated by individuals, is regarded here as the product of a complex set of interactions shaped by various overlapping and intermingling social, political and institutional settings.

The second historiographical area of emphasis is the role of information in the early modern world. These may have been information-poor societies in comparison with our own, but this was a period of important transitions in attitudes and practices concerning the generation, transmission and storing of information of all types.[5] Abetted by the wider availability of paper, people in a broad array of human activities generated a voluminous paper trail and exhibited a zealous instinct for record-keeping and preservation. Chanceries and archives proliferated as locales for this 'info-lust'.[6] When these developments are considered alongside the broad-reaching repercussions of the printing press, the accounting innovations and enhanced numeracy of merchants and financiers, and the growing empirical spirit of natural philosophers, some scholars have been inclined to locate an 'information revolution' in the early modern period.[7] In all of these areas, the desire for information and the resultant volume of collected data meant that the task of information management took on unprecedented importance. This was especially true in diplomacy, and secretaries and ministers tasked with foreign affairs expended much of their time in the control and supervision of the documentary record of statecraft.

In his 1594 treatise *Il Segretario*, Giovanni Battista Guarini wrote that the secretary

> must be intelligent and have a very versatile and well-mannered style, full, with a rich vocabulary and abundance of forms, and he should be able to do with his pen what Proteus did with his body, contorting it into every possible form, and varying it according to need.[8]

Such virtuosity was in wide demand in the early modern centuries – not only were written records of the secretary supposed to supply a written representation of reality, but they could also create a reality of their own. A 1689 treatise by Michele Benvenga of the tasks of the secretary was tellingly entitled *Proteo il segretario*.[9]

This chiefly rhetorical challenge to imitate Proteus was married to the considerably more prosaic requirement of hard work. Paperwork was the demon of early modern statecraft. Not every state, of course, was Habsburg Spain, where Philip II famously found himself vexed by the challenges of managing an empire virtually by paper. But even small states could find themselves inundated with paper generated by their statecraft. The astonishing explosion of records that we witness in fifteenth-century Italian states, even in small polities like Mantua under the Gonzaga and Ferrara under the Este, are illustrative.[10] These principalities produced archives bulging with materials generated from the administration of their territories and their diplomatic relations with their neighbours in the tightly packed and politically fraught Italian peninsula.[11] Although the name secretary suggests the centrality of secrecy to their work, that they were to keep their papers in the recesses of office and archive, the role of the early modern secretary encompassed the mediation of public transactions. Indeed, rather than being cloistered, secretaries occupied some of the most visible and important offices within the regimes of the period. The stewardship of the state, of course, was the business of the prince, but there was a universal recognition, in theory and in practice, that the prince required informed and capable assistance, ideally from a trusted councillor or secretary. The numerous mirrors of princes that appeared in both Christian and Muslim contexts were insistent on this point: the prince was only as good as those who advised him and assuring that he received prudent advice should be among his chief concerns. Statecraft was thus a corporate venture, with prominent secretaries and councillors assuming leading roles. Political writers of the day often used corporeal language to describe their duties: they were the prince's head, eyes and ears, or feet and hands. They were, also, importantly, his pen.

Most of what coursed through this 'government by paper' were letters. Across Eurasia, the rise of the secretaries in the early modern period reflects how government became what we might call a 'letterocracy', whereby it was chiefly correspondence that mediated the relationships between sovereign and subjects, between centre and periphery, and between metropole and diplomatic agents abroad. Much of the power vested in secretaries and chancellors flowed from their access to, and shepherding of, the correspondence of the sovereign and the agents of his government. That correspondence could be vast. Historians of Spain, most comprehensively Geoffrey Parker, have shown how richly Philip II deserved his moniker of *rey papelero*. Philip oversaw a vast empire which, on a day-to-day basis for the king, existed chiefly on paper, embodied in reams of correspondence, reports and instructions flowing in and out of the Escorial.[12] Rayne Allinson has elsewhere demonstrated the great importance that Elizabeth I placed on her own correspondence as a means of shaping English policy abroad.[13]

Nowhere was this 'letterocracy' more evident than in the arena of foreign affairs, where an ambassador was only as good as the letters that he produced. It is striking how much of the statecraft conducted by the figures studied in this volume was transacted predominantly through the exchange of letters. This was chiefly a function of the increasing importance of ambassadors, who, among other things, were expected to maintain a regular flow of correspondence. Although written correspondence did not displace entirely the importance of oral communication and face-to-face exchanges were deemed essential for particularly important or extraordinary negotiations, statecraft largely came to be an activity governed by epistolary exchanges: instructions from the metropole, dispatches from the ambassadors stationed abroad, and direct communication between sovereigns and other important figures inside regimes.

Early modern diplomacy, therefore, was increasingly practised as 'diplomacy at a distance', conducted at a geographic remove. We can see an example in the chapter in this volume by Rayne Allinson, who reconstructs the personal and political relationship of William Cecil and William Maitland through their correspondence. Although these two men did meet each other several times, and these face-to-face encounters were important in cementing their relationship, as state secretaries, their stewardship of their ships of state was in many ways a virtual one, and their friendship, repeatedly expressed in the florid phraseology of Renaissance rhetoric, unfolded in the pages of their correspondence. In a similar vein, the attempts of Richelieu and Mazarin to control affairs in Italy at a distance, treated in this volume by David Parrott, were mediated almost entirely through long-range correspondence.

Consequently, in many locales, effective statecraft now required the management of correspondence: drafting, reading, sorting and filing. The states of fifteenth-century

Italy provided numerous bureaucratic models to handle this paper that to greater and lesser degrees were adopted subsequently across Europe. Gregorio Dati in the mid-fifteenth century wrote that the chancellor of Florence 'stays in the palace during the day and writes all the letters which are sent to the princes of the world and to any person on behalf of the commune'. He described his work as collecting and recording the outpourings of the Florentine state as if he were a 'drain'.[14] It is not surprising, then, that in the states of Renaissance Italy, and especially in seigneurial regimes that pursued a particularly activist diplomacy, such as Milan, Mantua and Ferrara, there was significant interchange between service in the chancery and active diplomatic service abroad. There was a pragmatic recognition that familiarity with the operation of the former was valuable for application to the latter.[15]

The explosion of paper that characterised diplomacy in fifteenth-century Italy soon became a reality in sixteenth-century European regimes. As Meghan Williams shows in her chapter, Bernhard Cles' role as imperial chancellor required 'continuous writing' to run his 'chancellorship by correspondence', governed by the rhythms of the drafting of letters, the dispatch of the post and the filing of letters. A number of the authors in this volume reference the phrase, coined by David Dery, of 'papereality'.[16] In Dery's formulation, bureaucracies, in their circulation of paper, end up relying on official written documents to represent the world. In this sense, the pursuit of statecraft becomes a virtual activity, whereby the reality perceived by secretaries and diplomatic agents is encased within their correspondence, and the management of that material is central to the construction of what is deemed 'real' within diplomatic institutions. Much of this paper of statecraft would find its way into diplomatic archives, reflecting a widely shared instinct to preserve and a determination to establish a database of precedent.[17]

This activity points up the emergence of an early modern secretarial culture that departed from the chiefly notarial culture of the Middle Ages. Already by the end of the fifteenth century in Italy, a common vocabulary and set of practices governing diplomatic exchanges within the secretarial bureaucracies of its city-states were emerging.[18] The enhanced focus on writing, facilitated by the tendency of early modern courts to be sedentary rather than itinerant as they had been in the Middle Ages, fostered a close relationship between secretarial work, systematic thinking about politics and the state, and Renaissance humanism. Most of these Italian secretaries had been trained in the humanistic curricula predominant in Italy at the time, and Marcello Simonetta has shown that many of the most important Italian humanists had roots in the secretariat of Italian city-states, where they oversaw the drafting, copying, receipt and archiving of correspondence and other written products of government.[19] Humanistic training became *de rigueur* for the secretariat in Europe and a very close and deepening relationship developed between paperwork and politics in general, and diplomacy in particular.

Mitchell and Kinra, in their chapters in this volume, make it clear that a similar relationship existed in Islamic South West Asia. The work of the *munshi* as managers of bureaucracies was married to expertise in a rich Persianate epistolographical tradition. Aesthetics and rhetoric were thus central to the work of these imperial secretaries – components that are deeply reminiscent of the humanist formation of many secretaries and ministers in Europe. Indeed, 'government by paper' had a history that stretched considerably farther into the past in Islamic lands, where the ready availability of paper meant that by the tenth century in Baghdad the Abbasids ruled via the use of a wide array of paper instruments and officials in the regime were penning books of advice with titles such as *The Education of the State Secretary*.[20] Across Eurasia, therefore, the conduct of active and effective diplomacy required competent secretaries who could manage the flow of correspondence generated, and translate the 'virtual' policy of paper into real, implemented, statecraft.

The emergence of the office of secretary of state and its various analogues, as well as of numerous other lesser offices concerned with affairs abroad, coincides with the much remarked-upon 'rise' of the modern state, during which the state centralised and expanded in scope and complexity. The challenges of carrying out all of the resulting tasks were substantial and nowhere was this more evident than in the area of foreign affairs. A famous and oft-cited invocation of these demands of govern-ment is a remark attributed in 1667 to Louis XIV:

> It is hard to see everything at once! He who is charged with a private affair often blames the sovereign for not furnishing him with everything he desired for his purposes. But he does not consider how many things there are to do at once, that it is necessary to take care of all of them, and that whoever would give too abundantly to one, would inevitably be lacking toward the others.[21]

Louis XIV famously chose, on reaching his majority, not to appoint a first min-ister, electing instead to divide authority among a number of ministers. But in his instructions to the dauphin, Louis tellingly insists that in matters of foreign affairs (which he calls 'interests of the state and for secret affairs'), it is better to rely on a small number of voices in order to clarify what needs to be done.[22] It was clearly beyond the capacity of a single individual, even an informed and involved monarch like Louis, to master all of foreign affairs. In the latter years of his reign, Louis entrusted foreign affairs to the hands of a singular secretary of state, first Croissy, and then Colbert de Torcy.[23]

Leading secretaries and ministers frequently arose out of the practice of conciliar government, which was increasingly common in early modern regimes. A wide array of states (and not just the monarchies of the proto-absolutist variety) embraced such forms, with various councils (called *juntas* in Spain) allotted to different areas of governance, with a specific council often dedicated to foreign affairs. It is true that monarchs accepted the input of such councils reluctantly, especially if they were seen to circumscribe their own capacity for action. Kossmann has noted that monarchs in the sixteenth century ruled with these councils only when they duly expressed their will and ambition, after which time they resorted to the input of particularly trusted and prominent members within the councils, or convened a nar-rower council of ministers (often referred to as 'high' or 'privy') for consultation over the 'great affairs' of the prince, which almost always included issues of war and diplomacy.[24] The sixteenth century witnessed a roughly contemporaneous establish-ment of ruling councils in many locales. The Council of State was established in

Spain in 1522, and Privy Councils formalised in England (1540), Scotland (1545) and France (1557). Individuals or small cadres of ministers, secretaries or (in some cases) favourites often dominated the agendas and decision-making within these councils and assumed the leading roles in dictating policy. In practice, then, conciliar government tended to revert to consultation with men in whom the monarch had confidence, brought together in a group that may or may not have enjoyed official standing as a government institution. Such practices embodied the advice offered by Jean Bodin in his *Six Books of the Commonwealth*: 'the council must necessarily be small in numbers in view of the rare qualities requisite in a councilor . . . it should be chosen solely with regard to the virtue and wisdom of those who merit such a responsibility'.[25]

Of particular importance, especially in the years after 1500, was the office of secretary of state. In England, France and Spain, the secretaries of state were among the most important figures of authority within their respective regimes. Their authority rested not only in their proximity to and intimacy with the prince, but, as has been suggested above, in their access to and control of documents. Such activity, for example, was at the core of the power exercised by Francisco de los Cobos, the secretary of Emperor Charles V. Cobos, like many secretaries in this period, had his clerks make summaries of important news coming in, such that the business that was presented to Charles had essentially been pre-sifted by Cobos himself. The emperor's ambassadors, aware of Cobos's vital role, often sent a copy of their correspondence to the emperor directly to Cobos. In most cases, Cobos would have seen the letter before the emperor. The Venetian ambassador Bernardo Navagero remarked of Cobos: 'when he is with the Emperor, everything goes through his hands, and when the Emperor is absent, in all important matters he is the ruler through the Council and his own judgment'.[26] The secretary's power, therefore, flowed from his management of both relationships and of correspondence; that is, of people and of paper.

The sixteenth-century or seventeenth-century monarch sought to project the universality of personal rule, but also needed to delegate decision-making wisely. He had to do so without compromising his own authority. One oft-celebrated solution to this quandary was the rise of royal favourite, whereby a single, well-placed individual aggregated authority over royal policy and patronage and through whom nearly all the important business of governing passed. Richelieu (in France), Olivares (in Spain), Buckingham (in England) and Khlesl (in the Empire) are the paradigmatic figures of this phenomenon, although analogous figures could be found in smaller states as well.[27] Even with the emergence of collective decision-making in which the heads of various ministries offered their viewpoints to the prince, the top-down nature of rule in most early modern regimes meant that authority accreted instead to a single favourite, who was empowered to make decisions on behalf of the prince. To a large extent the favourite emerged to spare the king from many of the bothersome and undignified minutiae of governance. As Philip IV of Spain remarked: 'The task could scarcely be performed by the king in person, since it would be incompatible with his dignity to go from house to house to see if his ministers and secretaries were carrying out their orders promptly.'[28] Instead it would be the task of the favourite to oversee this enforcement.

A. Lloyd Moote has differentiated three types of favourite: the personal favourite, the political favourite and the minister-favourite.[29] Some, like Richelieu, straddled these categories. Some held important offices of state and wielded the authority vested in those positions, while others were essentially ministers without portfolio. Dudley, the Earl of Leicester, for example, never held an administrative office of any importance in Queen Elizabeth I's government. But he was widely regarded to have his 'finger in every pie' and was the most important figure in shaping English diplomacy (other than the queen herself) for over a decade.[30] In isolated cases, favourites effectively ran governments, such as the Duke of Lerma in Spain under the uniquely ineffectual Philip III ('a monarch who never became a real king', per Francisco de Quevedo[31]), or Concini in France following the assassination of Henri IV in 1610. But most so-called favourites wielded far less power, regardless of contemporary perceptions.

The 'age of the favourite', in fact, only lasted a century or so, peaking in the first half of the seventeenth century. This period was one of widespread, and near constant, warfare across Europe, and the concomitant demands on the sovereign and the state helped encourage the emergence of such figures. By 1700, however, it was rare to find single figures wielding as much authority as had these royal favourites in the preceding century. The distorting effects of their roles, and their routinely dramatic falls, mitigated against their re-emergence. By the eighteenth century, as Hamish Scott has demonstrated, the European state had undergone sufficient bureaucratisation that there was no longer really a niche for the favourite; his role was replaced by the first minister, a defined position within the government. We might look to the figures of Wenzel Anton Kaunitz in Austria (the subject of Franz Szabo's chapter in this volume) or of Maximilian Montgelas in Bavaria, as representative of the changed landscape.[32]

Although it does include David Parrott's chapter on Richelieu and Mazarin, the present volume is not primarily concerned with the phenomenon of the royal favourite. That topic was ably explored in a collection of studies, *The World of the Favourite*, edited by John Elliott and Laurence Brockliss and published in 1999.[33] The figures represented in this volume are a more varied lot than the catalogue of favourites covered in Elliott and Brockliss's book. They encompass minister-favourites such as Richelieu and Mazarin, but also chancellors such as Bernhard Cles, Mercurino Gattinara, Kaunitz and Axel Oxenstierna; secretaries of state like William Maitland and William Cecil; chief ministers such as Eberhard von Danckelman and Afzal Khan Shirazi; the grand vizier Hatim Beg; the long-serving and influential ambassador Alessandro Scaglia; and even a mid-level chancellery clerk, Grigorii Karpovich Kotoshikhin. All of these men had a hand in shaping foreign policy in their particular roles and contexts. Their roles demonstrate that a wide range of individuals beyond the sovereign were involved in the making of foreign policy in the early modern world. Thus we have the likes of Mazarin, the indisputable architect of state policy in the kingdom of France, but also a Foreign Office functionary like Kotoshikhin, who, as Russell Martin demonstrates, made important contributions to the development of the Muscovite wedding ritual, so essential to Russian matrimonial strategy and relations with the outside world.

This volume is not designed to be strictly comparative, as the diversity of the case studies brought together confounds direct comparison. Instead, in seeking to characterise the outlook of this volume, I find appealing the formulation of Cédric Michon in his recent edited volume, *Conseils et conseillers dans l'Europe de la Renaissance*.[34] Michon, aware of the pitfalls of direct comparison and of seeking to match apples and oranges, describes his approach as *croisée* rather than strictly comparative. In this vein, I believe it more profitable to identify the important areas of overlap, points of contact and genealogies of change shared by this volume's chapters, and what they suggest about the conduct of early modern statecraft.

The period covered in this volume witnessed the emergence of recognisably modern diplomatic institutions and practices. All the same, diplomacy did have different connotations in the early modern world. The chief architect of policy abroad in the early modern period was still assumed to be the prince, regardless of who and how many were involved in its formulation. The burnishing of the prince's honour and prestige, through the pursuit of advantageous war, was the chief expectation of policy. Diplomacy and war, today generally considered as the two opposing poles of international relations, were not regarded as such in the early modern period. Diplomacy was a means by which to position oneself favourably for the next outbreak of hostilities. In the medium term, the advent of resident embassies and permanent diplomatic institutions, as well as of secretaries of state and foreign ministers, did not change this fundamental fact.

Given such fundamental differences, we might be led to ask just how 'modern' was early modern statecraft. These studies provide ample evidence that this remained a very different political world to our own. In a political landscape populated almost exclusively by monarchies, which were, after all, dynastic enterprises, the pursuit of advantageous marriage remained an important facet of international relations. Shared norms of practice in international relations were only beginning to emerge and were far from universally acknowledged or practised. Formal praxis existed side by side with the informal, the impersonal beside the personal, and non-state actors alongside state functionaries. While in the modern world, we are accustomed to departments, secretariats and personnel dedicated solely to the business of foreign affairs, such stark distinctions were rarely so straightforward in this earlier period. But with greater institutionalisation, the enhanced importance of ambassadors and growing emphasis on the expertise of individuals in the area of diplomacy, as well the widespread ideological articulation of the early modern state and its theoretical underpinnings, certain sectors of government came to be dedicated chiefly to the pursuit of relations abroad. The prosecution of foreign policy was more and more differentiated. Again, there are early examples of such differentiation in Renaissance Italy. A division between internal and external affairs was made in the chancery of Cicco Simonetta in ducal Milan in the middle of the fifteenth century, and reforms in Florence in the 1480s gave autonomy in the field of diplomacy and foreign affairs to the Florentine chancellor, who was now in charge of the registration of all incoming and outgoing correspondence having to do with relations with other states.[35]

By the time of Kaunitz in the mid-eighteenth century, as Franz Szabo's treatment of the long-standing Austrian minister makes clear, the differentiation of, and specialisation in, foreign affairs is that much clearer. While domestic and foreign policy could never be entirely divorced from one another, the states of the eighteenth century, even before the French Revolution, increasingly employed staff and supported institutions that were committed exclusively to foreign affairs. The distinctions that were hinted at in statute and practice in the Renaissance Italian states could increasingly be seen as codified in early modern regimes. Numerous early modern individuals had long careers acting essentially as specialists in diplomacy. This is the case for several of the figures highlighted in this volume: not only Kaunitz, but also Alessandro Scaglia in Savoy (examined here by Toby Osborne) and Eberhard von Danckelman in Brandenburg (Daniel Riches). We would not be risking too much to call these men diplomatic professionals.

In fact, emphasising the pre-modern aspects of the institutions and practice of statecraft and the extent to which the actors under consideration operated under conditions inherited from the Middle Ages can be somewhat misleading. In considering the making of foreign policy in the early modern world, I am drawn to the analytical model employed by John Rule and Ben Trotter in their remarkable recent study of the Louis XIV's foreign ministry under Colbert de Torcy.[36] Rule and Trotter have provocatively suggested that the bureaucracy under Torcy was considerably more modern than we might suppose and, complementarily, that the modern state is quite a bit less 'modern' (in the Weberian sense) than we might assume. Within Torcy's bureaucracy, there was a recognised a distinction between foreign and domestic policy, even if in practice, then as now, the two zones of activity proved impossible to disentangle entirely. Torcy himself operated in a deeply pragmatic fashion, paying particular attention to the flow and management of information, for example in his organisation of the diplomatic archive founded under Croissy. In addition, the Louisquatorzian ministries were largely staffed by competent, well-trained functionaries with specific tasks within the organisation, and who advanced within the organisation chiefly on merit according to a reasonably well-defined *cursus honorum*. Even the so-called creatures of Torcy were likely to be men of some talent. There were exceptions, of course, concessions to the exigencies of patronage, but both Torcy and Louis recognised the dangers of placing incompetents in positions of influence. This twin emphasis on professionalism and information is what we expect to see in the modern bureaucratic state.

For Rule and Trotter, however, the reverse is also true. We fundamentally mischaracterise the nature of modern bureaucracies if we depict them in a rationally institutionalised and mechanistic fashion. Modern bureaucracies rarely operate as meritocracies and are full of beneficiaries of nepotism and favouritism. This is perhaps especially the case in foreign policy establishments, where ambassadorships are regularly distributed among political friends and donors and a cohort of patronage appointments exists alongside the bulk of diplomatic 'professionals'. Many of the top officials and cabinet secretaries in contemporary foreign policy bodies did not follow a familiar process of sequential promotion to their exalted ranks, but instead owe their position to long-standing personal relationships, networks of patronage and trading of favours. It is also evident that the architects of foreign policy continue to pay heed to stakeholders beyond merely the state and sovereign, among them corporations and entities of finance, lobbying groups and prominent non-state actors. Today, as in the early modern world, the stakeholders within regimes and societies in the making of policy are many, and their interests and concerns have to be calibrated in the decision-making process.

In a similar vein, the history of the twentieth century holds many notable examples of 'personal' rather than 'official' diplomacy, and of consequential statecraft transpiring through non-institutional channels. In the Cold War, for example, we might point to the Cuban Missile Crisis, during which the secret, face-to-face encounters between Bobby Kennedy and Anatoly Dobrynin were essential in diffusing tensions; or to the back-channel diplomacy of Kissinger, without which the détente between China and the United States in the early 1970s would not have been possible.[37] All of this is to say that modern diplomacy is not nearly as contained by institutions and conventions as we might assume it to be. A possible implication, therefore, is that we can learn more that is apposite to the present day from the study of early modern statecraft than we might at first assume. Certainly that is my hope as editor of this volume.

It is inevitable that a collection such as this one, despite the diversity of individuals and regimes represented in its pages, has lacunae that the editor regrets. Ideally the collection would have included a chapter on papal statecraft, which remained important and influential but in many ways unique throughout the early modern period. As participants in international politics, pontiffs felt the need to balance ideological imperatives and strictly pragmatic concerns particularly keenly. The editor would also have liked to include a study of a representative figure from a republican state, such as Venice or the Dutch Republic. These states were important diplomatic players in the early modern period and their distinctive forms of government were reflected in their statesmen and statecraft. A chapter on the statecraft of early modern China would have also been welcome, and would have served to produce a volume genuinely 'upon which the sun never sets'. A chapter on the Duke of Lerma, one of the favourites of Philip II of Spain, was slated to be included, as was one on Nasuh Pasha, the minister-favourite of the Ottoman Sultan Ahmed I, but unfortunately neither of these made it to publication. These omissions are regrettable, but I hope that the diversity and quality of the chapters that have been included will leave the reader with a deeper understanding of statecraft in the early modern world.

Anyone who has edited a scholarly volume like this one will tell you that it inevitably ends up being a lot more work than envisioned at the outset. And such was the case with this one. One of the themes that recurs in this volume is that in the early modern period, diplomacy and statecraft invariably involved ploughing through huge quantities of paper – in working on this volume, there were times when I sympathised with the complaint of Jacopo Trotti, the Ferrarese ambassador in Milan in 1489, that his paperwork was turning him *mezzo orbo*, 'half blind'.[38] Luckily, the advice and guidance of many generous scholars helped light the way that led to the completion of this volume. These include Ali Anooshahr, Lisa Balabanlilar, Paul Bushkovitch, Jane Dawson, Munis Faruqui, Paula Fichtner, Catherine Fletcher, Linda Frey, Marsha Frey, Robert Frost, Thomas Kaiser, Michael Levin, Rudolph

Matthee, Brian Maxson, Ali Azfar Moin, Geoffrey Parker, Kaya Sahin, Vanessa Schmid, Hamish Scott, Jacob Soll, Edward Tenace, Matthew Vester, Gerrit Voogt, John Watkins and Christopher Whatley. At Dundee University Press, and then Edinburgh University Press, I would like to thank Anna Day, Jen Daly, Joannah Duncan, Michelle Houston, Ersev Ersoy, Rebecca Mackenzie and Eliza Wright, for guidance and (I confess) patience. I would also like to acknowledge the support of Kennesaw State University's College of Humanities and Social Sciences, which extended me a summer grant to pursue work on the book.

NOTES

1. The term 'intensification of contacts' I take from Isabella Lazzarini, *L'Italia degli stati territoriali. Secoli XIII–XV* (Rome-Bari: Laterza, 2003). John Headley, in *The Emperor and His Chancellor: A Study of the Imperial Chancellery under Gattinara* (Cambridge: Cambridge University Press, 1983), labelled the sixteenth century the 'age of secretaries'. This volume expands the chronological and geographical reach of that label.

2. The classic treatment of these developments is Garret Mattingly, *Renaissance Diplomacy* (Boston: Houghton Mifflin, 1955). See also, generally, Lucien Bély, *L'Art de la paix en Europe: Naissance de la diplomatie moderne XVIe–XVIIIe siècle* (Paris: Presses universitaires de France, 2007) and M. S. Anderson, *The Rise of Modern Diplomacy, 1450–1919* (Harlow: Longman, 1993). For a concise summary of the historiography since Mattingly, and a bibliography, see Paul Dover and Hamish Scott, 'The Emergence of Diplomacy, c. 1450–1815', in Scott (ed.), *The Oxford Handbook of Early Modern European History, 1350–1750.* Vol. 2, *Cultures and Power* (Oxford: Oxford University Press, 2015), pp. 663–95. For the crucial changes first seen in Italy, and so influential in the rest of Europe, see Isabella Lazzarini, *Communication and Conflict: Italian Diplomacy in the Early Renaissance* (Oxford: Oxford University Press, 2015). And for the later period, see Hamish Scott, 'Diplomatic Culture in Old Regime Europe', in Scott and Brendan Simms (eds), *Cultures of Power in Europe during the Long Eighteenth Century, 1680s–1815* (Cambridge: Cambridge University Press, 2007), pp. 58–85.

3. For a sense of the scope and shape of this work, see the special issue of the *Journal of Medieval and Early Modern Studies* 38 (2008), edited by John Watkins, on the 'new diplomatic history'.

4. See, for example, the essays in Robyn Adams and Rosanna Cox (eds), *Diplomacy and Early Modern Culture* (Basingstoke: Palgrave Macmillan, 2011).

5. Among a growing literature, see the special issue of the *Journal of the History of Ideas* 64:1 (2003) on early modern information overload, edited by Daniel Rosenberg; Ann Blair, *Too Much to Know: Managing Scholarly Information before the Modern Age* (New Haven, CT: Yale University Press, 2010); Michael Hobart and Zachary Schiffman, *Information Ages: Literacy, Numeracy and the Computer Revolution* (Baltimore: Johns Hopkins University Press, 1998); Jacob Soll, *The Information Master: Jean Baptiste Colbert's Secret State Intelligence System* (Ann Arbor, MI: University of Michigan Press, 2009); Robert Darnton, 'An Early Information Society: News and the Media in Eighteenth-century Paris', *American Historical Review* 105:1 (2000), pp. 1–35; Arndt Brendecke, Markus Friedrich and Susanne Friedrich (eds), *Information in der Frühen Neuzeit: Status, Bestände, Strategien* (Berlin: Lit, 2008); Paul Dover, 'Philip II, Information Overload and the Early Modern Moment', in Tonio Andrade and William Reger (eds), *The Limits of Empire. European Imperial Formations in Early Modern World History: Essays in Honor of N. Geoffrey Parker* (Farnham: Ashgate, 2012), pp. 99–120.

6. This term is from Ann Blair and Peter Stallybrass, 'Mediating Information 1450–1800', in Clifford Siskin and William Warner (eds), *This Is Enlightenment* (Chicago: University of Chicago Press, 2010), pp. 139–63.
7. For an admirable summary of the relevant historiography, see Ann Blair and Devin Fitzgerald, 'A Revolution in Information?', in Hamish Scott (ed.), *Oxford Handbook of Early Modern European History, 1350–1750*. Vol. 1, *Peoples and Place* (Oxford: Oxford University Press, 2015), pp. 244–67.
8. Giovanni Battista Guarini, *Il segretario. Dialogo do Battista Guarini* (Venice: Ruberto Megietti, 1594), p. 65: 'gli bisogna haver un ingegno, & uno stile molto versatile, & maniroso, ricco di termini, & abbondante di forme, & quello sappia fare della sua penna, che della sua persona faceva Proteo, in tutte le forme possibili tramutandola, & variandola secondo che ricerca il bisogno.'
9. Michele Benvenga, *Il segretario del Sig. Abbate Michele Benvenga* (Bologna: Pier Maria Monti, 1689). This treatise is examined in Salvatore Nigro, 'The Secretary', in Rosario Villari (ed.), *Baroque Personae*, trans. Lydia Cochrane (Chicago: University of Chicago Press, 1995), pp. 82–97, at pp. 96–7.
10. Isabella Lazzarini, *Fra un principe e altri stati: relazioni di potere e forme di servizio a Mantova nell'età di Ludovico Gonzaga* (Rome: Instituto storico italiano per il Medio Evo, 1996); Marco Folin, *Rinascimento estense: politica, cultura, istituzioni di un antico Stato italiano* (Rome-Bari: Laterza, 2004).
11. See Franca Leverotti (ed.), *Cancellerie e amministrazione negli stati italiani del Rinascimento*, special edition of *Ricerche Storiche* 15:2 (1994); Paul Dover, 'Deciphering the Diplomatic Archives of Fifteenth-Century Italy', *Archival Science* 7:4 (2007), pp. 297–316; Filippo De Vivo, 'Ordering the Archive in Early Modern Venice (1400–1650)', *Archival Science* 10 (2010), pp. 231–48. De Vivo is overseeing a long-term research project at Birkbeck College, University of London on the comparative history of archives in late medieval and early modern Italy, which promises many new insights into early modern archival development.
12. Geoffrey Parker, *The Grand Strategy of Philip II* (New Haven, CT: Yale University Press, 1994), esp. pp. 11–110. See also Arndt Brendecke, '"Diese Teufel, meine Papiere . . ." Philipp II. von Spanien und das Anwachsen administrativer Schriftlichkeit', *Aventinus nova* 5 (Winter 2006), available at <http://www.aventinus-online.de/no_cache/persistent/artikel/7785> (last accessed 18 December 2015).
13. Rayne Allinson, *A Monarchy of Letters: Royal Correspondence and English Diplomacy in the Reign of Elizabeth I* (New York: Palgrave Macmillan, 2012).
14. Alison Brown, *Bartolomeo Scala, 1430–1497, Chancellor of Florence: The Humanist as Bureaucrat* (Princeton: Princeton University Press, 1979), p. 135.
15. For the Mantuan case, see Lazzarini, *Fra un principe*. For Milan, see Franca Leverotti, *Diplomazia e governo dello stato: i 'famigli cavalcanti' di Francesco Sforza (1450–1466)* (Pisa: GISEM-ETS Editrice, 1992). It was also customary in fifteenth-century Venice for high-ranking staff in the ducal chancery to undertake periodic service on overseas diplomatic missions. See Andrea Zannini, 'L'impiego pubblico', in Alberto Tenenti and Ugo Tucci (eds), *Storia di Venezia. Dalle origini alla caduta della Serenissima*. Vol. IV, *Il Rinascimento. Politica e cultura* (Rome: Istituto dell'Enciclopedia italiana, 1997), pp. 415–63.
16. David Dery, '"Papereality" and Learning in Bureaucratic Organizations', *Administration and Society* 29:6 (1998), pp. 677–89.
17. See the works in note 11, as well as Markus Friedrich, *Die Geburt des Archivs. Eine Wissensgeschichte* (Munich: Oldenbourg, 2013).
18. See Daniela Frigo, 'Prudence and Experience: Ambassadors and Political Culture in Early Modern Italy', *Journal of Medieval and Early Modern Studies* 38:1 (2008), pp. 15–34.

19. Marcello Simonetta, *Rinascimento segreto. Il mondo del segretario da Petrarca a Machiavelli* (Milan: Franco Angeli, 2004). See also Vanna Arrighi and Francesca Klein, 'Dentro il Palazzo: Cancellieri, Ufficiali, Segretari', in Maria Augusta Morelli Timpanaro, Rosalia Manno Tolu and Paolo Viti (eds), *Consorterie politiche e mutamenti istituzionali in età laurenziana* (Florence: Silvana, 1992), pp. 77–102; and Isabella Lazzarini's chapter in this volume.

20. Alexander Monro, *The Paper Trail: An Unexpected History of the World's Greatest Invention* (London: Allen Lane, 2014), p. 212. For the role of paper in Islamic governance more generally, see Jonathan Bloom, *Paper before Print: The History and Impact of Paper in the Islamic World* (New Haven, CT: Yale University Press, 2001).

21. Louis XIV, *Mémoires for the Instruction of the Dauphin*, trans. Paul Sonnino (New York: The Free Press, 1970), p. 9.

22. Ibid. p. 33.

23. John Rule and Ben Trotter, *A World of Paper: Louis XIV, Colbert de Torcy, and the Rise of the Information State* (Montreal: McGill-Queen's University Press, 2014).

24. E. K. Kossmann, 'The Singularity of Absolutism', in Ragnhild Hatton (ed.), *Louis XIV and Absolutism* (Columbus: Ohio State University Press, 1976), pp. 3–17. Similar points are made in Antonio Feros, *Kingship and Favoritism in the Spain of Philip III, 1598–1621* (Cambridge: Cambridge University Press, 2000), pp. 32–47.

25. Jean Bodin, *Six Books of the Commonwealth*, abridged and trans. M. J. Tooley (Oxford: Basil Blackwell, 1955), p. 78.

26. Quoted in Howard Keniston, *Francisco de los Cobos: Secretary of the Emperor Charles V* (Pittsburgh: University of Pittsburgh Press, 1958), p. 348.

27. See, for example, Michael Kaiser and Andreas Pečar, *Der zweite Mann im Staat: Oberste Amtsträger und Favoriten im Umkreis der Reichsfürsten in der Frühen Neuzeit* (Berlin: Duncker & Humblot, 2003).

28. Francisco Tomás Valiente, *Los validos en la monarquía española del siglo XVII* (Madrid: Instituto de Estudios Políticos, 1963), p. 181.

29. A. Lloyd Moote, 'Richelieu as Chief Minister: A Comparative Study of the Favourite in Seventeenth-Century Politics', in Joseph Bergin and Laurence Brockliss (eds), *Richelieu and His Age* (Oxford: Clarendon Press, 1992), pp. 23–35.

30. See Wallace McCaffrey, *Queen Elizabeth and the Making of Policy, 1572–1588* (Princeton: Princeton University Press, 1981).

31. 'de una monarca que acabó de ser rey antes de empezar a reinar' (cited in Feros, *Kingship and Favoritism*, p. 1).

32. See Michael Kaiser and Andreas Pečar, 'Reichsfürsten und ihre Favoriten. Die Ausprägung eines europäischen Strukturphänomens unter den politischen Bedingungen des Alten Reiches', in Kaiser and Pečar, *Der zweite Mann im Staat*, pp. 9–20; Hamish Scott, 'The Rise of the First Minister in Eighteenth-Century Europe', in T. C. W. Blanning and David Cannadine (eds), *History and Biography: Essays Presented to Derek Beales* (Cambridge: Cambridge University Press, 1996), pp. 21–52.

33. J. H. Elliott and L. W. B. Brockliss, *The World of the Favourite* (New Haven, CT: Yale University Press, 1999).

34. Cédric Michon (ed.), *Conseils et conseillers dans l'Europe de la Renaissance v. 1450–v. 1550* (Tours: Presses universitaires François Rabelais de Tours; Rennes: Presses universitaires de Rennes, 2012).

35. For Milan, see Francesco Senatore, *'Uno mundo di carta': forme e strutture della diplomazia sforzesca* (Naples: Liguori, 1998); for Florence, see Brown, *Bartolomeo Scala*, pp. 177–85; and Riccardo Fubini, 'La figura politica dell'ambasciatore negli sviluppi dei regimi oligarchici quattrocenteschi', in Sergio Bertelli (ed.), *Forme e tecniche del potere nella città (secolo XIV–XVII). Annuario della Facoltà di Scienze Politiche dell'Università di Perugia. 16 (1979–1980)* (Perugia: Università di Perugia, 1982), pp. 33–59.

36. Rule and Trotter, *A World of Paper*.
37. On the Dobrynin–Kennedy back channel, see Aleksandr Fursenko and Timothy Naftali, *One Hell of a Gamble: Khrushchev, Kennedy and Castro, 1958–1964* (New York: Norton, 1997); on Kissinger's secret diplomacy, see Margaret MacMillan, *Nixon and Mao: The Week that Changed the World* (New York: Random House, 2007) and Chris Tudda, *A Cold War Turning Point: Nixon and China, 1969–1972* (Baton Rouge, LA: Louisiana State University Press, 2012).
38. Jacopo Trotti to Ercole d'Este, Milan, 15 March 1489, Archivo di Stato di Modena, Archivio Segreto Estense, Carteggio Ambasciatori – Milano, b.4.

CHAPTER 2

Records, Politics and Diplomacy: Secretaries and Chanceries in Renaissance Italy (1350–c. 1520)

Isabella Lazzarini

INTRODUCTION

In August 1458, the Duke of Milan Francesco Sforza wrote in his own hand a letter to Cardinal Capranica, one of the potential candidates for the papacy, to reassure the prelate of his support. At the end of a letter both long and politically explicit, Sforza concluded that 'I have been the chancellor of myself in writing all this letter: if the letter is bad, I am sorry, but soldiers write badly, as your Lordship knows.'[1] A few years later, and still in Milan, a charter of privilege granted to the Milanese chancellor Cicco Simonetta by Francesco's widow Bianca Maria and his eldest son Galeazzo Maria Sforza shortly after the death of Francesco summarised the secretary's tasks in an impressive list of gerundives connected to the main duty of actively mastering the spoken and written word: Simonetta deserved the duke's gratitude for his restless activity of 'conferendi, proponendi, tractandi, ventilandi, discutiendi et concludendi [. . .] faciendi, agendi, procurandi, exequendi et executioni mandari faciendi [. . .] committendi, imponendi, dictandi, conficiendi, ordinandi, residendi, signandi, scribendi, subscribendi, ac rogandi'.[2] Astute political reasoning, a particular attitude to writing, secrecy, professionalism: the words of a duke renowned for both his unconventional education and his strategic use of the written and spoken word, and this extended sequence of chancery gerundives define the daily work of one of the most famous secretaries of fifteenth-century Italy. In these words we can see laid out the broad scope and blurred boundaries of the world of Renaissance chancellors and chanceries, and catch a glimpse of their immense influence and potential.

In recent years, as research on both literacy and power in Renaissance Italy has focused on the development of the larger territorial powers, chancelleries and public written records have increasingly attracted scholarly attention. The process of territorial growth stimulated the formalisation and diffusion of shared political languages that required novel written forms and innovative documentary practices. During a long Quattrocento that stretches roughly from 1350 to 1520, almost everywhere in Italy the central chancery – as the most important centre for the production of public written records – also became the heart of public authority, power and legitimacy, monopolising more and more the decision-making process. At the heart of such loci of power were the lay professionals of written communication: chancellors, secretaries and notaries. The specific roles, competences and social profiles of those men were variable but crucial: in between the multilayered world of the Italian chanceries and the deep cultural change brought in by humanism, chancellors and secretaries multiplied, and their influence grew amidst technical and lexical ambiguities, and amid a difficult balance of functions, personal influence, intellectual charisma and specific skills. Internal politics, diplomatic interactions, documentary production and preservation were the main fields of action of chancellors and secretaries. Reliability, communication skills, political knowledge, technical know-how and cultural finesse were all increasingly required for a job that was at once crucial and dangerous, visible and invisible.[3] Prominently portrayed in the frescoes in the heart of their lords' palaces, like Marsilio Andreasi in the *Camera Picta* by Andrea Mantegna or Cicco Simonetta in the Red Room of the Castle of Pavia,[4] secretaries could parlay their service into social advancement, or end up marginalised, as was Machiavelli in the 1510s. Some might even end their career on the gallows, as did Antonello Petrucci in Naples or Cicco Simonetta in Milan.[5]

CHANCERIES AND CHANCELLORS: CONTEXTS AND TITLES

Chanceries

The major changes in Italian governmental structure and practice in the fourteenth and fifteenth centuries stemmed from a complex political process of concentration of power deeply connected to the conflicts of the late fourteenth century and the related processes of territorial expansion. Prolonged territorial wars – and the increasing financial pressure which came with them – pushed the Italian powers towards oligarchic channels and autocratic innovation. The resulting efficiency in political decision-making and the concentration of authority and power in the hands of princes and narrower elites were nonetheless often accompanied by a lack of internal legitimacy and external recognition.[6]

Chanceries were central to these changes almost everywhere in Italy.[7] This was a process common across Europe; in fifteenth-century Italy, however, it was linked to the particular problem of political legitimacy. Chanceries were responsible for producing acts of authority – that is, they daily elaborated on the formal foundations of power – on behalf of regimes with questionable legitimacy and partial autonomy.[8] These polities were either republican governments formally but vaguely subservient to the Empire (the regimes in both Florence and Venice tried at the beginning of the fifteenth century to be recognised by the emperor as collective imperial vicars) or princely or royal polities governed by the vulnerable heirs of imperial or papal princes or vicars, as in Milan and Naples.[9] Chanceries actively aimed to compensate for the lack of legitimacy of their rulers by defining the quality and nature of their political authority and sovereignty through the employment of documentary resources.

Within a state, there was often more than one chancery, and their composition and functioning reflected the various constitutional and institutional frameworks of the states, their size and their historical evolution.[10] Despite such variety, the chanceries day by day developed a similar range of governmental practices by combining various technical competencies, documentary strategies and political traditions. The result was a coherent and largely homogeneous complex of public written records that were organised and preserved thanks to a growing and widespread documentary consciousness. The lay professionals of written communication – chancellors, secretaries, notaries – experimented with a wide array of practices and techniques in order to build, maintain and refine an approach that could already be considered 'archival' in the modern sense of the word.[11] The simultaneous drive to standardise praxis and the need for flexibility resulted in a fragmented and variable landscape of changing men and techniques. The Italian chanceries at the end of the Middle Ages were a place where authority and legitimacy, as well as authenticity, were defined and formalised: they were also places open to experimentation at the very heart of the decision-making process.[12]

Multiple origins, various competences: notaries and chancellors, *referendari* and secretaries in the Italian chanceries

Late medieval and early Renaissance chanceries were complicated structures, deeply grounded in a thirteenth-century communal, imperial and papal past: in the long Quattrocento different functions emerged at a variable pace, and these corresponded with the different competences and various social and professional profiles of those involved. Starting at the end of the fourteenth century, chanceries were subject to an intermittent process of definition of roles, personnel and internal hierarchies. Moreover, local developments were influenced by a high level of circulation of men and practices, and lexical calques and institutional imitations surfaced periodically. Roles and names whose origins, development and proliferation have never been systematically investigated – for example, the chancellor or secretary – defined the main functions of the chancery. These functions related on the one hand to the production, registration and preservation of the public records and to the legitimating process that went with them, and on the other to the crucial and flexible daily work of mediating between the various actors of a given body politic, and then between them and an increasingly dense and interconnected international network of polities. Chancellors, notaries, *referendari*, *protonotari*, *protocancellari*, secretaries: these were recurring words, some of them related to specific responsibilities, some indicating hierarchies within the government or among the chancellors themselves. The offices and names used to describe them reveal an ongoing and often contested process of internal definition.[13]

The relationship between the chancery and the notariate was a dynamic one, and a crucial consideration here.[14] Notaries and chancellors did not necessarily share the same cultural background, and often had different careers: at some point, and in some contexts, the same men could be both, but the two worlds were different, and the process of adaptation by urban notaries to the increasingly autonomous sphere of the seigneurial and princely chancery or the emerging republican chanceries were crucial steps in the documentary evolution of late thirteenth- and fourteenth-century Italy. In the thirteenth century, in communal northern and central Italy notaries provided the documentary and juridical expertise needed to produce legally binding acts for the commune. In a long and varying process that witnessed many twists and turns, they gradually transferred their competences to the service of the *signori*, whose acts at first they signed as *cancellarius domini atque imperiali auctoritate notarius*.[15] This shift not only related to the status of the notaries, and the concomitant relationship between the communal elites and the *signori*, but also innovated and transformed the documentary record by absorbing into the notarial tradition many characteristics of the royal, imperial and princely chanceries, particularly in the broad domain of *littere*, both *clausae* (internal and diplomatic correspondence) and *patentes* (concessions, appointments, privileges).[16] On the other hand, in 1261 Corrado, a non-Venetian notary in the service of the Venetian chancery, was appointed as chancellor, then *cancellier grande* (the chronicler Martino da Canal called him *maistre canceler*).[17] In fourteenth-century Florence, meanwhile, it became increasingly common for one of the notaries of the *podestà*, who, because of his ability in the *ars dictandi* (the art of writing letters), had previously been called *dictator* or *cancellarius*, to be appointed for an indefinite period in order to provide some stability to a system that had been previously based on rotation, at least in the domain of the external politics.[18] In the thirteenth and fourteenth centuries, the role played by notaries was also crucial in the southern kingdoms: even though the Swabian, then Angevin and Aragonese chanceries did not need to assert any external legitimacy, and had models of their own to draw upon, notaries were at the very heart of the activity and documentary creativity of the chancery because of their mastering of the *ars dictaminis*.[19] Since the end of the fourteenth century, and with an increasing pace during the fifteenth century, however, the link between the chancery and the notaries became less and less fundamental, even though it never really disappeared. In fifteenth-century Florence, and particularly after Bartolomeo Scala's reforms in 1483, notaries were confined to secondary roles in the chancery, while in fifteenth-century Venice the notarial qualification was no longer necessary to be appointed to the chancery.[20]

A second crucial issue that accompanied the evolution of chanceries was the internal definition of the various roles played by their members. The words employed are here clues to change, adaptation and imitation. Apart from the distinctive case of the Roman curia, whose nature will not be considered here but which exercised a huge influence all over medieval Western Europe,[21] the Italian late medieval chanceries present two main patterns of development, which converge at the end of the fifteenth century. On the one hand, the southern kingdoms and the principality of Savoy followed, with their own particularities, a 'royal' model combining a central chancery (eventually divided into branches or subsections devoted to fiscal or juridical affairs) directed by a chancellor (in Savoy), a great chancellor or a *protonotaro* (in Angevin Naples), with one or more personal functions related to the letter-writing monopolised by a secretary closely linked to the prince, whose role became increasingly relevant and prestigious.[22]

On the other hand, the republican regimes that emerged from the thirteenth-century communes developed one or more chanceries that controlled the production of most political records, such as internal and diplomatic letters and the minutes of the temporary and powerful small assemblies that monopolised the key decisions within the republics. The adoption of the title of chancellor by the officers of these bodies derived both from the original link between them and the activity of letter-writing, and from a conscious imitation of princely models. In Florence, beside the notaries of the *Reformagioni* (the normative acts of the Commune) or of the *Tratte* (appointments to state offices), in the mid-fourteenth century we see the emergence of the 'chancellor of the people and the commune and *dictator* of the letters'. From 1353 Ser Niccolò di Ser Ventura Monachi, chancellor of the letters, started to register the minutes of the *Consulte*. The chancery appointment of Coluccio Salutati in 1375, and his subsequent nomination as chancellor in 1380 saw the consolidation of most Florentine public records under the chancellor's control.[23] After a series of false starts and dead ends, Bartolomeo Scala brought discipline to the Florentine chancery in 1483 by dividing it into two separate organs, and by specifying the competences and roles of chancellors and secretaries.[24] The emergence of the republican chancer-ies was rarely straightforward: many offices continued to rely on their notaries, and the chanceries themselves alternated between periods of great influence and phases of decline.[25] The use of the title of chancellor was the rule, while secretaries emerged slowly, and during most of the fifteenth century retained a chiefly subject and tech-nical role, even though in the age of Machiavelli, the secretaries of both the first and second chanceries assumed tasks that were increasingly political in nature.[26] In Venice, where the articulation of the chancery into superior (then ducal) and inferior units took place as far back as the thirteenth century, and was further complicated by the creation of a secret political sub-chancery at the heart of the ducal chancery in 1402, the subordination of the secretaries to the chancellors was balanced by the formal creation of a body of secretaries chosen from among Venetian citizens (*cit-tadini originari*), who retained a monopoly over the office.[27]

The *signorie* that emerged from communal regimes represent a very interesting combination of the 'royal' and 'republican' models. They adapted the original col-legial structure of their cities, rooted in councils and magistracies, to the increasingly autocratic governments of dubious legitimacy that proliferated in the fourteenth century. In so doing, they increasingly adopted royal and princely habits in the production and preservation of records that aimed to strengthen their new lords' authority in their recording of internal and external interactions. The chancellor was generally the main figure, and secretaries were second-rank *scribi*. At the end of the fourteenth century, in Mantua and Ferrara the main chancellor assumed the title of *referendarius*, often adding to his chancery duties the function of councillor.[28] While in Ferrara the *referendarius* remained at the head of the chancery until the end of the fifteenth century, after the 1450s in Mantua – as in Milan – the chancellors were slowly overtaken in rank and responsibilities by the secretaries. Marsilio Andreasi, the most influential chancellor in Ludovico Gonzaga's chancery, at the end of his life was defined – in an interesting neologism – as *prothocancellarius et secretarius*, while his son Jacopo, just starting in the chancery, worked as *subcancellarius*.[29]

At the beginning of the sixteenth century the main chancellors were all secretaries, and among them the most influential was sometimes called *primus secretarius.* The establishment of such hierarchies went together with the articulation of the chancery into branches, with a 'secret chancery' in the most exalted position.[30]

ISSUES AND CONTEXTS

As seen above, chanceries and the professionals of written communication who worked in them – whether chancellors or secretaries, notaries or humanists – were increasingly involved in the central decision-making process. By elaborating, authenticating, circulating, collecting and preserving the acts of authority and politics, chanceries became more and more the political centre of government, at the same time developing their own increasingly articulated and nuanced vision of history and political thought. Chanceries were at the heart of the theoretical and practical definition and redefinition of the framework of power required by the simultaneous growth of these governments and their enduring fragile legitimacy: in the chanceries, chancellors and secretaries applied their ability and know-how to articulate practices and languages of power that suited a volatile political system.[31]

Politics: internal and international interactions

A crucial characteristic defined the role of the chancery within the government. As producers and preservers of the acts of political authority and power – whether the power of a prince or of a republican regime – the chanceries were two-faced from the outset, monopolising both the internal and external affairs of the power they served. As the Florentine case clearly shows, chancellors and secretaries were in charge of the redaction and preservation of diplomatic letters as well as of internal correspondence and the minutes of central political debates. In some cases, chancellors were not only responsible for the production of texts but were themselves also on the front line of the political interactions, especially in the area of diplomacy: as Leverotti argues, in fifteenth-century Milan 'the diplomatic corps had its origin, developed and came to fruition in the lord's chancery'.[32] Occupying such a central role, chanceries became the workshops in which crucial cultural and political transformations took place. They established and maintained a multilayered process of negotiation, created new ways of conceiving politics, and above all pioneered a new attitude towards the management of political interactions through communication. The long-lasting tradition of relying on the spoken and written word to articulate the public political debate, and to govern internal and external interactions, prompted the emergence of a rhetoric of political discourse that became a prominent feature of Italian polities. The last – and most effective, or at least most long-lasting – of those rhetorical arsenals is what we are now accustomed to calling 'humanism'. Classical Latin, and classical antiquity more broadly, provided chancellors and secretaries with many necessary tools and models: the refinement of a methodology for examining political problems and issues; the introduction of Ciceronian rhetoric and a sense of history into the political discourse; crucial ideas on history, politics and human behaviour; and a treasury of stories with which to compare, classify and define contemporary events.[33] Such tools helped define the political languages of authority and resistance, which were moulded to suit, describe and influence an array of political interactions. Moreover, such a political discourse – and such a way of thinking about politics – had to be 'translated', codified and fixed in a written form in order to be transmitted and preserved. This process, emphasised also by a growing obsession with information gathering, generated an impressive explosion of written sources cataloguing political interactions, transforming a documentary landscape that had been composed chiefly of series of deliberation registers (that is, a 'communal' topography of records) into a 'mundo de carta', a world of letters whose extreme detail and flexibility deeply influenced ways of thinking and talking about politics.[34]

Florence in the age of Coluccio Salutati and his successors at the chancery provides an excellent case study: Salutati was responsible for the writing of both the diplomatic and internal letters, as well as the minutes of the *Consulte e pratiche*. We will come back to the documentary side of this phenomenon in due course; here, the focus is on the elaboration of a new language of power. From Salutati's analytical but dry summaries of the debates of the *Consulte e pratiche* to the much lengthier and elaborate reports of the new rhetorical speeches of the following decades, the trend towards a more narrative style paralleled the consolidation of an innovative form of political debate.[35] In this evolution, Ciceronian rhetoric played a crucial role: what Witt defines as 'oratorical humanism' entered into 'diplomacy, statesmanship and political ritual' with 'its strategic and dialectical approach to argument and its attentiveness to psychological gamesmanship'.[36] A classical Latin education enhanced awareness of 'the intricate layering of human events in time' and provided to the political discourse the capacity to express complex temporal sequences through a sophisticated use of the period and subjunctive verbs.[37] This process implied the emergence of particular textual, lexical and linguistic resources that '[can] contribute to the way in which individuals perceive issues, frame their language and evolve systems of interpretation'.[38] It was a process long in the making: evident in literary and rhetorical texts composed by humanists (Bruni, Alberti), this change gradually influenced the daily public speeches pronounced by the political elites and ambassadors, and their records, written and often transformed – when not conceived directly – by chancellors and secretaries.[39]

Action and thought

A side-effect of the centrality of the chancery in the construction of a distinctive political language of Renaissance Italy was the passage from politics and diplomacy to contemporary history writing and political thinking. The socio-professional groups that monopolised the production and use of public records and the building of orderly archives were in fact composed by men who were often also at the front line of historical writing and political thought.[40] The many biographies of the Florentine chancellors from Salutati to Machiavelli or Ianziti's magisterial research on history writing in the Sforza age have made abundantly clear the deep link between the chancery and the highest rank of Italian political culture.[41] Men like Salutati, Biondo

Flavio, Lorenzo Valla, Giovanni Pontano, Giovanni Simonetta, Pier Candido Decembrio, Francesco Barbaro or Leonardo Bruni, as Ronald Witt ironically wrote (describing Salutati), 'lived with split personalities'. They not only used 'humanist language in their personal writing, *dictamen* in their public letters, and either *ars predicandi* or an adaptation of *ars arengandi* [. . .] in their speeches', or adopted different scripts (*cancelleresca*, *umanistica* or even *mercantesca*) for different texts, but also switched from chancery practices to writing on history and politics with great fluency.[42] Such a phenomenon, well known for the likes of Bruni or Machiavelli, was not confined to the highest levels of culture and politics: it was a much more widespread process, involving a whole group of professionals of written communication for whom the chancery was a pivotal institution.[43] Ianziti himself in his most recent monograph on Bruni offers an analysis of the daily 'mechanics and processes of history writing', inviting investigations of a wider group of professionals of written communication, and putting on the literary historian's working table a much broader range of texts.[44] Taking Ianziti's methodological suggestions a step further, one can posit that the increased availability of news and information pushed a diverse group of men towards a daily investigation of historical events and human behaviours.[45] By including daily recording practices and writing habits, the 'practicalities' of history writing extend into the increasingly common adaptation and reworking of documentary sources for both personal and public purposes. The widespread attention given to contemporary history paralleled the massive growth of written records, mostly diplomatic letters, reports and summaries, and in some way prepared the way for an outpouring of systematic writings on political thought.[46] The link between government and history writing deepened towards the end of the century, influencing a broadening range of public officials and statesmen on all levels of administration and their institutional routines.[47] As a consequence, and in response to the increasingly detailed attention paid to daily events, the recourse to public records – and particularly to diplomatic letters – as sources for historical writing became a best practice for minor and major 'historians' of humanist or notarial education and ambition. These included humanists and chancellors like Giovanni Pontano (author of *De bello Neapolitano*) and Giovanni Simonetta (*Rerum gestarum Francisci Sfortiae Commentarii*), as well as first secretaries like Cicco Simonetta and ambassadors like Francesco Contarini, who chose Latin commentaries to tell the story of his embassy in Siena in 1455.[48] These men transferred their professional attitude towards the gathering and handling of information quite naturally to the composition of history. The urge to control information for historiographical purposes, even more than the search for authenticity or credibility, represents a prominent feature of this intellectual cross-fertilisation between daily political practices and vocabularies and the more theoretical level of history and political thought. The growing obsession with keeping information under control created a shared hunger for news that documentary sources could easily fill day by day.[49] In this sense, Machiavelli becomes less exceptional: he was preceded and surrounded by secretaries, chancellors and humanists who worked in the Italian chanceries and wrote about history and politics in many different ways and with varying degrees of intellectual awareness. This group of professionals has scarcely begun to be investigated.[50]

RECORDS AND ARCHIVES: ORDER AND MEMORY

The role of chancellors and secretaries in expanding and defining the public authority of princes and regimes was an important one. I will now focus on an aspect of that influence, the world of records and archives, having considered the contexts of the activity of chancellors and secretaries above. Obviously, the distinction is somewhat artificial: political functions, documentary outcomes, and systems of memory and identity are inescapably interconnected, and I consider them separately here only for the sake of clarity.

Italy at the end of the Middle Ages was a highly fragmented political space, and what unity it had rested on shared languages and practices of power, human mobility and a common cultural identity rather than on unitary political forms. Despite the diversity of constitutional frameworks and territorial domains among the Italian polities, the public written records produced and preserved by the central chanceries exhibited striking homogeneity in both form and content. All of the major forms of documents produced – registers of the acts of authority, like letters patent and decrees (*litterae patentes* and *clausae*); the registers that collected and organised governmental, military or fiscal data; the letters and dispatches sent and received from abroad or within the different states – were still evolving from documents with chiefly legal content (*Urkunden*) to records primarily administrative in nature (*Akten*). This move was embodied in the linguistic shift from Latin to the vernacular, which opened up a new range of models and solutions. At the same time, the strategies and practices of government were recorded in similar, recognisable and legitimised written texts, which were then organised into coordinated documentary systems that increasingly served as archives of memory and identity. The chancery was not the only laboratory for such a process, but it was undoubtedly the crucial one, and because of its centrality to governments and polities, it is the best preserved.[51]

Records

The many innovative steps that transformed thirteenth-century series of acts and registers into late medieval archives responded to the need to control larger and more composite dominions. Documentary variety was forced into typological homogeneity thanks to the diffusion of records and documentary practices from the political centre to the newly consolidated regions of composite states. Moreover, common needs stemming from similar governmental responsibilities – fiscality, war, justice, diplomacy – elicited similar responses in different political and institutional contexts, due both to the growing interconnection of the many states, and to the similar educational formations and experiences of their chancellors and secretaries. By working on written communication, and on its relationship with the spoken world of politics and diplomacy, chancellors and secretaries daily produced innovative texts, elaborated new political languages merging classical traditions and medieval thinking, and recorded and organised growing amounts of data and information.[52]

The merging of the *ars dictaminis* with the rediscovered classical and Ciceronian epistolary style, combined with the growing proclivity of urban elites to keep records, served to create a standard model of chancery letter whose structural flexibility and formal linearity were perfectly suited to contain almost every kind of written communication or act of authority.[53] While the letters patent could include the whole array of appointments, privileges, concessions and dispositions, the letters *clausae* became the ideal instrument with which to record sophisticated narrative of increasingly complex diplomatic interactions, as well as to display the highly literary tone of the familiar and personal 'letters between friends', as Najemy defines the epistolary exchange between Machiavelli and Vettori.[54] Chancellors and secretaries – both ordinary officers with notarial backgrounds like Marsilio Andreasi in Mantua and highly respected intellectuals such as Giovanni Pontano in Naples – mastered the recording techniques and the many styles and lexeis available in order to define, adapt and customise the standard framework of the letter. Their control over written communication, combined with their rhetorical fluency, put them at the heart of diplomacy and political negotiation in the Italian states.

Participation in such spheres of activity allowed the likes of Coluccio Salutati and Leonardo Bruni to construct, write and diffuse new languages of power. What matters most here, however, is that in doing so, they also created an entirely new group of documentary techniques and instruments in the course of recording the activities of councils, *balìe*, and diplomats. Coluccio Salutati was responsible for composing both the diplomatic and internal letters and the minutes of the political meetings called *Consulte e pratiche*. In expanding, in scope and detail, the reports of the deliberations, Salutati started to change the nature of these minutes by inserting into the political narrative an argumentative attitude that he derived from his conscious recovery and use of classical Latin and texts, and from the deliberate appropriation of a Ciceronian rhetoric designed to mediate conflict and debates.[55]

Finally, the need to master growing amounts of data and information pushed the chanceries towards the expansion of inherited instruments like lists and communal registers. The urgency to classify and keep on hand documents of all sorts produced a system of different chancery registers whose interconnection and internal coherence became increasingly evident. In Milan under the Sforza the process of definition of the different series of chancery registers, each one devoted to a specific issue and often produced by a newly separated chancery branch, became a guiding consideration. From a documentary point of view, the specialisation of chancellors, *scribi* and secretaries generated different kinds of registers devoted to the daily management and ordering of the increasing amounts of paper arriving into the chancery: the hundreds of volumes preserved among the *registri ducali* and the *registri delle missive* in the Milanese archives are the outcome of such a process of experimentation and the development of new or revised documentary instruments designed to control the growing complexity of political realities.[56]

Archives

All these records were components of multifaceted documentary systems: that is, they grew in quantity and quality as elements of a functional complex of written products that were increasingly focused on managing and providing data for governments and rulers rather than being mere autonomous clusters of texts. Contemporarily, if not at the same pace everywhere, they also started to be organised within archival systems, as basic elements of a written memory of power. Records were materially described, counted, classified, inventoried and collated in rooms and corridors, armoires and shelves, coffers and chests, according to an increasingly sophisticated logic of preservation and use. The basic idea of preserving records in order to use them generated numerous solutions and outcomes, on at least three levels. The first was related to the creation of techniques for ordering the records: numbers (Arabic and Roman), alphabetical letters (majuscule and minuscule), images and full words were employed to govern an increasingly detailed system of classification.[57] Second, by using these techniques daily, chancellors and secretaries also flexibly defined their offices, the extent of their duties and the limits of their respective action: in a word, they held up a mirror to the institutions that produced and preserved specific groups of documents, relating them to the other offices and organs of the state. In doing so, they not only described but actively transformed and defined still largely inchoate public institutions, offices and functions.[58] Finally, by specifying the rank, relevance and antiquity of the records, and by distributing and organising them hierarchically in different spaces, chancellors and secretaries not only established a documentary *ordre du discours* but also shaped new political identities rooted in a selective memory of power.[59]

Such a process did not necessarily imply the exclusivity and indivisibility of archives: on the contrary, the dynamic relationship between unity and plurality, between documentary centralisation and dispersion, added to the overall complexity of the evolution of late medieval archives, reflecting the superimposition of offices and the variety of choices made within each institutional framework. The political choices in preserving records merged in this case with the spatial and material dimensions of power: in redefining the spaces of authority in princely and republican palaces increasingly attentive to monumentality, the location of archives had to engage the competing demands of daily use and symbolic representation.[60]

The increasingly detailed and technical archival inventories were the result of a complex process that involved issues of order, hierarchy, geography, and memory of power and authority. From the Sabaudian Jean Balais and Henri de Clairvaux to the Mantuan Marsilio Andreasi, from the Ferrarese Pellegrino Prisciani to Cicco Simonetta in Milan and to the Venetian great chancellor Andrea Grandi, the leading figures among the chancellors and secretaries of the various states generally monopolised the function of redacting, updating and preserving inventories and lists. These became increasingly detailed and technically refined. This process was not limited to documents but also entailed books and even *mirabilia* like relics or jewels. The same men who classified and reordered records also often catalogued books, sometimes – as in Ferrara – keeping them in the same rooms and vaults where they preserved the documents, sometimes – as in Mantua – organising separate spaces for libraries and documentary archives. In the castle of Pavia, the renowned Visconti library was put alongside the archive and not far from the famous ducal collections of relics.[61]

All this does not mean that the decision to preserve records was automatic. On the contrary, chancellors and secretaries intentionally applied specific *stratégies de la mémoire* to preserve, order and classify a variable range of writings and/or *mirabilia*, in a process still mostly uneven, and never definite.[62] A man like Cicco Simonetta was obsessed with bringing some order to the events, personnel, records and books of the ducal regime. But even in lower-profile cases, the chancery was deliberately brought to the heart of such processes.[63] Apart from being the main producer of public written records, the chancery in fact rapidly monopolised the task of putting them in order, a role that had political implications. The production and availability of records were in fact both a pragmatic tool of state and a means of legitimation for regimes. They also played a role in promoting identity, as elites, political actors and subjects recognised themselves in the collective memory produced and preserved by the public writing power of the state, and could themselves respond to it with a paper trail of their own.[64]

SOCIAL PROFILES AND POLITICAL IDENTITIES

A final subject to be considered is the social profile of chancellors and secretaries: their familial and personal status, education and training, career paths and mobility in fact combined in many ways to define the political and social identity of this new crucial group of men.

Social status and education

The chancery was at the heart of political power, but was not at the top of the social ladder: a common character of the Italian chancellors and secretaries was their membership in the notarial or intellectual milieu. Across Italy, chancellors and secretaries were characterised by a 'low' social profile among the political elites; their skills (both notarial and political) and their reliability and fidelity to the prince or the regime were the keys to their professional success. A crucial role was also increasingly played by humanism: Brian Maxson has recently emphasised the role of an 'established reputation for humanist letters' in Florence as a 'ladder against the wall of the Florentine social hierarchy'.[65] While for prestigious diplomatic missions the ambassadors were generally chosen from among the lay and ecclesiastical aristocracy, daily diplomatic practice was a job for professionals, chosen from among the members of the chancery. The *famigli cavalcanti* that formed the core of Francesco Sforza's diplomatic service, for example, were first and foremost men of the duke, long-time servants and personal clients.[66] The same was true of the men leading the different branches of the Milanese chancery: few were Milanese, even fewer had any previous contact with the social elites of the duchy. This combination of metic and non-noble status – clearly influenced by the outsider origins of the duke himself – did not disappear with the death of Francesco Sforza, even though in the age of Galeazzo Maria (1466–76) and Ludovico il Moro (1480–94) a slow process of integrating chancellors into Milanese political society – both aristocratic and mercantile – is visible not only at the top of the hierarchy (Cicco Simonetta married a Visconti, his brother Giovanni a woman from the aristocratic Milanese family of the Barbavara) but at lower levels as well.[67] In Gonzaga Mantua the chancellors were mainly chosen from middle-rank families of Mantuan or Lombard origin and rarely from the aristocracy. To a core of families who supplied chancellors across generations – like the Andreasi, the Arrivabene and the Bonatti – a few foreigners were added in the second half of the fifteenth century, like the Pisan Zaccaria Saggi and the Neapolitan Jacopo Probo d'Atri. They mainly married into the local princely political society, and only in the sixteenth century did they rise to the top of the Mantuan aristocracy.[68] The same pattern was common also in Ferrara: the chancellors and diplomats of the 1450s were still known as *quilli de Borso* – Duke Borso's men – in the age of Duke Ercole, some twenty years later. The powerful Ludovico Casella, *referendarius* from 1450 to 1469, was of humble origins and known as a 'homo de villa'.[69] In the republics the status and social standing of chancellors and secretaries were even more rigidly limited to the lower level of the urban elites, despite the fact that some were renowned humanists.[70] In Florence, secretaries like Machiavelli could not aspire to the highest public offices and functions. As Andrea Guidi argues, at the end of the fifteenth century secretaries and chancellors (apart from the first chancellor Marcello Virgilio Adriani) were men in marginal positions among the republican elites.[71] In the age of Lorenzo (1469–92), moreover, the Medicean regime opened the way to a group of *uomini nuovi* personally trusted by him, whose favour granted them substantial influence. But such favour did not necessarily mean a formal career among the offices and honours of the Florentine republic. Bartolomeo Scala was exceptional in his appointment to the highest ranks of the government, a result of him being a trusted man of Lorenzo and a renowned humanist.[72]

Almost everywhere, the training of a chancellor was pragmatic and experiential. The exception is Venice: here a chancery school was founded in 1446, and in general the education and cultural background of chancellors and secretaries were crucial issues very early on.[73] Elsewhere, a notarial background or a humanist education were both a good start, and a combination of the two was even better (as in the case of the Florentine Alessandro Braccesi), but a professional attitude to mastering the written and spoken word, and a demonstrated competence in politics – however acquired – were more important than one's academic profile, and became increasingly crucial towards the end of the fifteenth century, when chancellors and secretaries developed a growing political autonomy in both internal and international matters.[74]

Career paths and mobility

A career in the chancery could be life-long, as it was for many who served Sforza Milan, and normally ended in the same milieu in which it started: chancery notaries, *scribi*, secretaries, and chancellors of various standing and responsibility did not normally change their professional setting, even though they could switch between different branches of the same chancery, or scale the career ladder within the chancery.

These men might eventually change lord or regime, still continuing to work as chancellors: such flexibility, however, seems particular to the principalities, where a previous engagement with another prince was not necessarily a barrier to a successful career elsewhere.[75] Humanists were particularly prized, and therefore their tendency to move between different courts and regimes tended to be greater: men like Francesco Filelfo or Pier Candido Decembrio switched – or tried to switch – employers and locales by emphasising their intellectual profile or their experience as professionals of written communication.[76] A specialisation in diplomacy could also help with mobility, aiding the assimilation of a chancellor into a different political milieu and affording him a back-up plan in case of emergency: the Milanese Antonio da Trezzo, ambassador on behalf of Francesco Sforza to the Aragonese kings of Naples, transferred to Ferrante his loyalty after Francesco's death because of his hostile relationship with Francesco's son and heir, Duke Galeazzo Maria.[77]

A career in the chancery could thus help a man and his family to enter the world of public offices and assignments, but it did not normally allow for regular father–son succession, particularly in republics but also in principalities. The exception is the Mantuan marquisate, where Alessandro Arrivabene in 1476, listing himself as the seventh to be appointed as a secretary in the Arrivabene family, could define the office a 'magistratus Arrivabenorum familiae peculiaris'.[78]

CONCLUDING REMARKS

The Italian chanceries of the end of the fifteenth century were the product of a complex process of adaptation among the many groups of notaries and professionals of written communication to the changing nature and the many needs of the Italian regimes that emerged from thirteenth-century communal and royal governments. In this sense, the evolution of the main models and their variants out of a web of imitation and diffusion involving the Swabian, Aragonese and Angevin (as well as papal) documentary and institutional cultures converged at the end of the fifteenth century with the appearance of multilayered structures that were internally stratified, staffed by personnel with expertise in different sectors of government, and increasingly political in their outlook.[79]

Obviously, chanceries were not the only workshops of power, nor were central chanceries the only chanceries at work. In those integrated socio-political systems, however, an increasingly prominent and well-defined group of professionals created, modified and maintained political functions and languages, administrative techniques, documentary outcomes, and systems of memory and identity. Humanists like Giovanni Pontano, Giovanni Simonetta, Pandolfo Collenuccio and even Machiavelli; statesmen like Cicco Simonetta and Antonello Petrucci; and lesser-known notaries and chancellors like Marsilio Andreasi, despite their differences in status, education and wealth, all shared political and diplomatic know-how and technical skills, as well as a hunger for the preservation of memory and writing of history. Their high ambitions in some cases might even lead them to the gallows. Their role in the chancery and in the internal and external politics of their states had multiple origins, and varied according to the constitutional, political and diplomatic contexts in which they worked. But their emergence proved to be one of the most important and influential developments in late medieval Italian statecraft.

NOTES

1. 'Io son stato el cancellero mi stesso de tucta questa littera: si la littera è trista, mi rincresce, ma li soldati sanno mal scrivere, come la signoria vostra sa' (Francesco Sforza to Domenico Capranica, Milan, 2 August [1458], Archivio di stato di Milano, Potenze Estere, Roma, b. 1303, quoted in Marcello Simonetta, 'Il duca alla dieta Francesco Sforza e Pio II', in Arturo Calzona, Francesco Paolo Fiore, Alberto Tenenti and Cesare Vasoli (eds), *Il sogno di Pio II e il viaggio da Roma a Mantova* (Florence: L. Olschki, 2002), p. 252, n. 15 (pp. 247–85)).

2. Integrally edited in Carlo Rosmini, *Dell'istoria di Milano* (Milan: Manini e Rivolta, 1820), vol. IV, pp. 106–8; Marcello Simonetta, *Rinascimento segreto. Il mondo del segretario da Petrarca a Machiavelli* (Milan: Franco Angeli, 2004), p. 129: 'to confer, propose, negotiate, consider, discuss and conclude [. . .] to do, act, manage, execute, and make executed [. . .] to commit, impose, dictate, prepare, order, reside, sign, write, subscribe, and ask'. On Simonetta's grants, Nadia Covini, 'La patente perfetta. I privilegi accordati ai Simonetta dagli Sforza', in Beatrice Del Bo (ed.), *Cittadinanza e mestieri: radicamento urbano e integrazione nelle città bassomedievali (secc. XIII–XVI)*, (Roma: Viella, 2014), pp. 181–208.

3. Isabella Lazzarini (ed.), *Scritture e potere. Pratiche documentarie e forme di governo nell'Italia tardomedievale*, Reti Medievali 9 (2008); Gian Maria Varanini, 'Public Written Records', in Andrea Gamberini and Isabella Lazzarini (eds), *The Italian Renaissance State* (Cambridge: Cambridge University Press, 2012), pp. 385–405; Isabella Lazzarini, 'De la "révolution scripturaire" du Duecento à la fin du Moyen Âge: pratiques documentaires et analyses historiographiques en Italie', *Cahiers électroniques d'histoire textuelle du Lamop* 5 (2012), available at <http://lamop.univ-paris1.fr/IMG/pdf/article_Isabella_Lazzarini.pdf> (last accessed 30 December 2015).

4. Roberto Signorini, *Opus hoc tenue. La camera dipinta di Andrea Mantegna: lettura storica, iconografica, iconologica* (Mantua: Sintesi, 1985); Simonetta, *Rinascimento segreto*, p. 131; Isabella Lazzarini, *Communication and Conflict: Italian Diplomacy in the Early Renaissance, 1350–1520* (Oxford: Oxford University Press, 2015).

5. Andrea Guidi, *Un segretario militante. Politica, diplomazia e armi nel Cancelliere Machiavelli* (Bologna: Il Mulino, 2009); Elisabetta Scarton, 'La congiura dei Baroni del 1485–87 e la sorte dei ribelli', in Francesco Senatore and Francesco Storti (eds), *Poteri, relazioni, guerra nel regno di Ferrante d'Aragona* (Napoli: ClioPress, 2010), pp. 213–90; Simonetta, *Rinascimento segreto*.

6. Isabella Lazzarini, *L'Italia degli Stati territoriali. Secoli XIII–XV* (Rome-Bari: Laterza, 2003); Gamberini and Lazzarini, *The Italian Renaissance State*.

7. Franca Leverotti (ed.), *Cancelleria e amministrazione negli stati italiani del Rinascimento*, Ricerche storiche 24 (1994), pp. 277–424; Guido Castelnuovo and Olivier Mattéoni (eds), *Chancelleries et chanceliers des princes à la fin du Moyen Âge ('De part et d'autres des Alpes' II)* (Chambéry: Université de Savoie, 2011).

8. Marie-Louise Faverau-Lilie, 'Reichsherrschaft im Spätmittelalterlichen Italien. Zur Handhabung des Reichsvikariat im 14./15. Jahrhundert', *Quellen und Forschungen aus Italienischen Archiven und Bibliotheken* 80 (2000), pp. 53–116; Riccardo Fubini, '"Potenze grosse" e piccolo stato nell'Italia del Rinascimento, Consapevolezza della distinzione e dinamica dei poteri', in Laura Barletta, Franco Cardini and Giuseppe Galasso (eds), *Il piccolo stato: politica, storia, diplomazia* (Città di Castello: AIEP, 2003), pp. 91–126; Jane Black, *Absolutism in Renaissance Milan: Plenitude of Power under the Visconti and the Sforza, 1393–1535* (Oxford: Oxford University Press, 2009).

9. Gamberini and Lazzarini, *The Italian Renaissance State*.

10. Isabella Lazzarini, 'Le Pouvoir de l'écriture. Les chancelleries urbaines et la formation des États territoriaux en Italie (XIVe–XVe siècle)', in Elisabeth Crouzet-Pavan and Élodie

Lecuppre-Desjardins (eds), *Les Mots de l'identité urbaine à la fin du Moyen Âge*, *Histoire Urbaine* 35 (2013), pp. 31–50.

11. Lazzarini, *Scritture e potere*.

12. Isabella Lazzarini, 'Power beyond the Rules. Formalism and Experimentation in the Italian Chanceries (1380–1500 ca.)', in Christina Antenhofer and Mark Mersiowsky (eds), *Negotiating Rules: Platforms and Exchanges. The Role of Medieval Chanceries* (Louvain: Brepols, forthcoming).

13. The only recent general overview of the phenomenon, Simonetta, *Rinascimento segreto*, does not tackle the problem of qualifications and definitions.

14. Attilio Bartoli Langeli, *Notai: scrivere documenti nell'Italia medievale* (Rome: Viella, 2009); Giuseppe Gardoni and Isabella Lazzarini (eds), *Notariato e medievistica. Per i cento anni di* Studi e ricerche di diplomatica comunale *di Pietro Torelli* (Rome: Istituto storico italiano per il Medioevo, 2013); Andrea Giorgi, Stefano Moscadelli and Carla Zarrilli (eds), *La documentazione degli organi giudiziari nell'Italia tardo-medievale e moderna* (Rome: Ministero per i beni e le attività culturali, Direzione generale per gli archivi, 2012).

15. Bartoli Langeli, *Notai*; Gian Maria Varanini, 'Notai trecenteschi tra tradizione comunale e cancellerie signorili. Appunti', in Antonio Rigon (ed.), *Cecco d'Ascoli. Cultura, scienza e politica nell'Italia del Trecento* (Rome: Istituto storico italiano per il Medioevo, 2007), pp. 289–300; Gian Maria Varanini, 'La documentazione delle signorie cittadine tra Duecento e Trecento e l'*Eloquium super arengis* del notaio veronese Ivano di Bonafine *de Berinzo* ', in Castelnuovo and Mattéoni (eds), *Chancelleries*, pp. 53–76; Gian Maria Varanini, 'I notai e la signoria cittadina. Appunti sulla documentazione dei Bonacolsi di Mantova fra Duecento e Trecento (rileggendo Pietro Torelli)', in Lazzarini, *Scritture e potere*, available at <http://www.rmojs.unina.it/index.php/rm/article/view/96> (last accessed 30 December 2015).

16. See note 14 and Attilio Bartoli Langeli, 'Cancellierato e produzione epistolare', in Paolo Cammarosano (ed.), *Le forme della propaganda politica nel Due e nel Trecento* (Rome: École Française de Rome, 1994), pp. 251–61.

17. Marco Pozza, 'La cancelleria', in Girolamo Arnaldi and Giorgio Cracco (eds), *Storia di Venezia. Dalle origini alla caduta della Serenissima.* Vol. III, *La formazione dello stato patrizio* (Rome: Istituto dell'Enciclopedia Italiana, 1997), p. 365 (pp. 365–86).

18. Demetrio Marzi, *La cancelleria della repubblica fiorentina* (Rocca San Casciano: Cappelli, 1910); Riccardo Fubini, 'Classe dirigente ed esercizio della diplomazia nella Firenze quattrocentesca. Rappresentanza esterna e identità cittadina nella crisi della tradizione comunale', in *I ceti dirigenti nella Toscana quattrocentesca* (Florence: Olschki, 1987), pp. 117–89; Riccardo Fubini, 'Dalla rappresentanza sociale alla rappresentanza politica. Sviluppi politico-istituzionali in Firenze dal Tre al Cinquecento', in Fubini (ed.), *Italia quattrocentesca. Politica e diplomazia nell'età di Lorenzo il Magnifico* (Milan: Franco Angeli, 1994), pp. 41–61; Francesca Klein, *Scritture e governo dello stato a Firenze nel Rinascimento. Cancellieri, ufficiali, archivi* (Florence: Edifir, 2013).

19. Bartoli Langeli, 'Cancellierato', p. 253; Roberto Delle Donne, 'Le cancellerie nell'Italia meridionale (secoli XIII–XV)', in Leverotti, *Cancelleria*, pp. 361–88; Benoît Grévin, *Rhétorique du pouvoir médiéval: les lettres de Pierre de la Vigne et la formation du langage politique européen* (Rome: Ecole Française de Rome, 1994); Guidi, *Un segretario militante*, pp. 79ff.; Ronald Witt, 'Medieval "Ars dictaminis" and the Beginning of Humanism', *Renaissance Quarterly* 25 (1982), pp. 1–35.

20. Robert Black, 'Machiavelli, Servant of the Florentine Republic', in Gisela Bock, Quentin Skinner and Maurizio Viroli (eds), *Machiavelli and Republicanism* (Cambridge: Cambridge University Press, 1990), pp. 82–3 (pp. 71–99); Guidi, *Un segretario militante*, pp. 48–50; Giuseppe Trebbi, 'Il segretario veneziano. Una descrizione cinquecentesca della cancelleria ducale', *Archivio Storico Italiano* 144 (1986), pp. 37–8 (pp. 35–73).

21. The papal chancery could in fact scarcely be defined as an 'Italian' chancery: its uses and practices – such as the combination between a chancellor/vice-chancellor and the secretaries – were much more European than Italian. For a useful survey, however, see Thomas Frenz, *I documenti pontifici nel medioevo e nell'età moderna* (Città del Vaticano: Scuola Vaticana di Paleografia, Diplomatica e Archivistica, 1989), pp. 61–70.

22. Guido Castelnuovo, 'Cancellieri e segretari fra norme amministrative e prassi di governo: il caso sabaudo', in Leverotti (ed.), *Cancelleria*, pp. 291–304; Bernard Andenmatten and Castelnuovo, 'Produzione documentaria e costruzione archivistica nel principato sabaudo, XIII–XV secolo', *Bullettino dell'Istituto Storico per il Medio Evo e Archivio Muratoriano* 110 (2008), pp. 279–348; Pietro Corrao, 'Mediazione burocratica e potere politico: gli uffici di cancelleria nel regno di Sicilia (secoli XIV–XV)', in Leverotti, *Cancelleria*, pp. 389–410; Delle Donne, 'Le cancellerie'.

23. Marzi, *La cancelleria*; Ronald Witt, *Hercules at the Crossroads: The Life, Works and Thought of Coluccio Salutati* (Durham, NC: Duke University Press, 1983); Daniela De Rosa, *Coluccio Salutati: il cancelliere e il pensatore politico* (Florence: Olschki, 1980); Fubini, 'Dalla rappresentanza sociale'; Klein, *Scritture e governo*, pp. 115–26.

24. Paolo Viti (ed.), *Leonardo Bruni cancelliere della repubblica di Firenze* (Florence: Olschki, 1990); Robert Black, *Benedetto Accolti and the Florentine Renaissance* (Cambridge: Cambridge University Press, 1985); Alison Brown, *Bartolomeo Scala, 1430–1497, Chancellor of Florence: The Humanist as Bureaucrat* (Princeton: Princeton University Press, 1997).

25. Fubini, 'Classe dirigente'; Klein, *Scritture e governo*.

26. Guidi, *Un segretario militante*, pp. 47–8; Francesca Klein, 'La riforma del 1483 e l'istituzione dei segretari', in Maria Augusta Morelli Timpanaro, Rosalia Manno Tolu and Paolo Viti (eds), *Consorterie politiche e mutamenti istituzionali in età laurenziana* (Florence: Silvana, 1992), pp. 92–108.

27. Pozza, 'La cancelleria', p. 370; Giuseppe Trebbi, 'La cancelleria veneta nei secoli XVI e XVII', *Annali della Fondazione Luigi Einaudi* 14 (1981), pp. 65–125; Mary Neff, 'Chancellery Secretaries in Venetian Politics and Society, 1480–1533' (PhD thesis, UCLA, 1985); Trebbi, 'Il segretario veneziano'; Andrea Zannini, *Burocrazia e burocrati a Venezia in età moderna: i cittadini originari (sec. XVI–XVIII)* (Venice: Istituto veneto di scienze, lettere e arti, 1993), pp. 119–81; Filippo De Vivo, 'Coeur de l'état, lieu de tension. Le tournant archivistique vu de Venise (XVe–XVIIe siècle)', *Annales HSS* 68 (2013), pp. 699–728.

28. Isabella Lazzarini, '"Peculiaris magistratus". La cancelleria gonzaghesca nel Quattrocento (1407–1478)', in Leverotti, *Cancelleria*, pp. 337–50; Teresa Bacchi, 'Cancelleria e segretari estensi nella seconda metà del secolo XV', in Leverotti, *Cancelleria*, pp. 351–60; Marco Folin, *Rinascimento estense: politica, cultura, istituzioni di un antico Stato italiano* (Rome-Bari: Laterza, 2001), pp. 156–70.

29. Lazzarini, '"Peculiaris magistratus"', p. 343.

30. Franca Leverotti, '"Diligentia, oboedientia, fides, taciturnitas . . . cum modestia." La cancelleria segreta nel ducato sforzesco', in Leverotti, *La cancelleria*, pp. 305–36; Lazzarini, '"Peculiaris magistratus"'.

31. Lazzarini, *Communication and Conflict*.

32. Franca Leverotti, *Diplomazia e governo dello stato: i 'famigli cavalcanti' di Francesco Sforza (1450–1466)* (Pisa: GISEM-ETS Editrice, 1992), pp. 99–101: 'il corpo diplomatico dimostra di avere origine, transito e sbocco nella Cancelleria del signore'; Fubini, 'Classe dirigente', p. 125; Lazzarini, '"Peculiaris magistratus"'; somewhat different is the Ferrarese case: Folin, *Rinascimento estense*.

33. Ronald Witt, *In the Footsteps of the Ancients: The Origins of Humanism from Lovato to Bruni* (Leiden: Brill, 2000); Virginia Cox, 'Ciceronian Rhetoric in Late Medieval Italy', in Cox and John O. Ward (eds), *The Rhetoric of Cicero in Its Medieval and Early Renaissance*

Commentary Tradition (Leiden: Brill, 2006), pp. 109–35; Robert Black, *Humanism and Education in Medieval and Renaissance Italy: Tradition and Innovation in Latin Schools from the Twelfth to the Fifteenth Century* (Cambridge: Cambridge University Press, 2001).

34. Lazzarini, *Communication and Conflict.*

35. Gene Brucker, *The Civic World of Early Renaissance Florence* (Princeton: Princeton University Press, 1977); Dale Kent, *The Rise of the Medici: Faction in Florence, 1426–1434* (Oxford: Oxford University Press, 1978); Witt, *In the Footsteps*; Isabella Lazzarini, 'Argument and Emotion in Italian Diplomacy in the Early Fifteenth Century: The Case of Rinaldo degli Albizzi (Florence, 1399–1430)', in Andrea Gamberini, Jean-Claude Genet and Andrea Zorzi (eds), *I linguaggi della società politica* (Rome: Viella, 2011), pp. 339–66.

36. Witt, *In the Footsteps*, pp. 338–9; Cox, 'Ciceronian Rhetoric', p. 127.

37. Witt, *In the Footsteps*, esp. pp. 443ff.; quote on p. 501. See also, for a more theoretical approach, Kenneth Gouwens, 'Perceiving the Past: Renaissance Humanism after the "Cognitive Turn"', *The American Historical Review* 103 (1998), pp. 55–82.

38. Benjamin Stock, *The Implications of Literacy. Written Language and Models of Interpretation in the 11th and 12th Centuries* (Princeton: Princeton University Press, 1983), p. 5.

39. Lazzarini, 'Argument and Emotion'; Stephen Milner, 'Political Oratory and the Public Sphere in Early Quattrocento Florence', *New Reading* 1 (1995), pp. 41–64; Brian J. Maxson, 'The Many Shades of Praise. Politics and Panegyrics in Fifteenth-Century Florentine Diplomacy', in Georg Strack and Julia Knödler (eds), *Rhetorik in Mittelalter und Renaissance: Konzepte – Praxis- Diversität* (Munich: Herbert Utz Verlag, 2011), pp. 393–412; Fubini, 'Classe dirigente', pp. 134–5; Klein, *Scritture e governo*, pp. 129–43, esp. pp. 135–6. According to Brucker, 'the refinement of the methodology for examining problems and issues was quite as significant as the introduction of rhetoric and a sense of history into Florentine political discourse' (Brucker, *The Civic World*, p. 294).

40. Riccardo Fubini, *Storiografia dell'Umanesimo in Italia da Leonardo Bruni ad Annio da Viterbo* (Rome: Edizioni di storia e letteratura, 2003); Witt, *In the Footsteps*; James Hankins, 'The "Baron thesis" after Forty Years and Some Recent Studies on Leonardo Bruni', *Journal of the History of Ideas* 56 (1995), p. 321 (pp. 309–88).

41. Eugenio Garin, 'I cancellieri umanisti della Repubblica fiorentina', in Garin, *La cultura filosofica del Quattrocento italiano* (Milan: Bompiani, 1994), pp. 3–37; Witt, *Hercules*; Black, *Benedetto Accolti*; Brown, *Bartolomeo Scala*; Brian J. Maxson, *The Humanist World of Renaissance Florence* (Cambridge: Cambridge University Press, 2014); Gary Ianziti, *Humanistic Historiography under the Sforza: Politics and Propaganda in Fifteenth Century Milan* (Oxford: Oxford University Press, 1988); Gary Ianziti, 'Pier Candido Decembrio and the Beginnings of Humanistic Historiography in Visconti Milan', in Nicholas Baker and Brian Maxson (eds), *After Civic Humanism: Learning and Politics in Renaissance Italy* (Toronto: Centre for Reformation and Renaissance Studies, 2014), pp. 153–72.

42. Witt, *In the Footsteps*, p. 443. Coluccio Salutati the chancellor had to adapt to the traditional *cancellarie florentine stilus*, even if Salutati the humanist defined that same tradition as *irrationalis et corrupta*: Attilio Bartoli Langeli and Mario Bassetti, 'Scrivere "all'antica" Firenze, 18 ottobre 1402', in Amedeo De Vincentiis (ed.), *Atlante della letteratura italiana. Vol. I, Dalle origini al Rinascimento* (Turin: Einaudi, 2010), pp. 304–5 (pp. 304–12).

43. Isabella Lazzarini, 'A "New" Narrative? Historical Writings, Chancellors and Public Records in Renaissance Italy (Milan, Ferrara and Mantua, 1450–1520 ca.)', in Baker and Maxson, *After Civic Humanism*, pp. 193–214.

44. Gary Ianziti, *Writing History in Renaissance Italy: Leonardo Bruni and the Uses of the Past* (Cambridge, MA: Harvard University Press, 2012), p. 3.

45. Ianziti, *Humanistic Historiography*, pp. 11–12; Lazzarini, 'A "New" Narrative?'.

46. John Hyde, 'The Role of Diplomatic Correspondence and Reporting: News and Chronicles',

in Daniel Waley (ed.), *Literacy and Its Uses: Studies on Late Medieval Italy* (Manchester: Manchester University Press, 1993), pp. 217–60; and now Varanini, 'Public Written Records'; Lazzarini, 'Le Pouvoir de l'écriture'.

47. Ianziti, *Humanistic Historiography*; Marco Folin, 'Le cronache a Ferrara e negli Stati estensi (secoli XV–XVI)', in A. Prosperi (ed.), *Storia di Ferrara*. Vol. VI, *Il Rinascimento: situazioni e personaggi* (Ferrara: Il Corbo, 2000), pp. 459–92; Riccardo Fubini, 'Cultura umanistica e tradizione cittadina nella storiografia fiorentina del 400', *Atti e memorie dell'Accademia toscana di scienze e lettere 'La Colombaria'* 56 (1991), pp. 67–102.

48. Lazzarini, 'A "New" Narrative?'; Margaret King, *Venetian Humanism in an Age of Patrician Dominance* (Princeton: Princeton University Press, 1986).

49. The same urge for a systematic collection of authors and texts can be seen also on the 'humanist side' of this story: Cristopher Celenza argues that 'beyond certain fifteenth-century writings that can be considered masterpieces, there are innumerable works that, collectively, bring later figures like Machiavelli, Castiglione, and many others into clearer view, as well as offering other stimuli for further thought' (Celenza, *The Lost Italian Renaissance: Humanists, Historians and Latin's Legacy* (Baltimore: John Hopkins University Press, 2004), p. xix).

50. For a recent survey, see De Vincentiis, *Atlante*. Machiavelli himself has been recently analysed with much closer attention to his chancery experience, and his professional letters and texts. See Jean-Jacques Marchand (ed.), *Machiavelli senza i Medici (1498–1512). Scrittura del potere/potere della scrittura* (Rome: Salerno edizioni, 2006); Andrea Guidi, '"Esperienza" e "qualità dei tempi" nel linguaggio cancelleresco e in Machiavelli (con un'appendice di dispacci inediti di vari cancellieri e tre scritti di governo del Segretario fiorentino)', in Christian Del Vento and Xavier Tabet (eds), *Les Écrivains italiens des Lumières et la Révolution française, Laboratoire italien. Politique et société* 9 (2009), pp. 233–72; Robert Black, *Machiavelli* (London: Routledge, 2013).

51. Isabella Lazzarini, 'Materiali per una didattica delle scritture pubbliche di cancelleria nell'Italia del Quattrocento', *Scrineum* 2 (2014), available at <http://scrineum.unipv.it/rivista/2-2004/intro-lazzarini.html> (last accessed 30 December 2015); Lazzarini, 'Registres princiers dans l'Italie septentrionale aux XIVe–XVe siècles: une première enquête (Milan, Ferrare, Mantoue)', in Olivier Guytojeannin (ed.), *L'Art du registre en France, XIIIe–XVIe siècle*. Vol. II, *Registres princiers du Moyen Âge* (Paris: Bibliothèque de l'École des Chartes, forthcoming); De Vivo, 'Coeur de l'état'; on local chanceries, see Francesco Senatore, 'Sistema documentario, archivi ed identità cittadine nel regno di Napoli durante l'antico regime', *Archivi* 10 (2015), pp. 33–64.

52. Isabella Lazzarini, 'Introduzione', in Lazzarini, *Scritture et Potere*; Varanini, 'Public Written Records'.

53. Fubini, *Italia quattrocentesca*; Francesco Senatore, *'Uno mundo de carta'. Forme e strutture della diplomazia sforzesca* (Naples: Liguori, 1998); Lazzarini, 'Materiali'.

54. John Najemy, *Letters between Friends: Discourses of Power and Desire in the Machiavelli–Vettori Letters of 1513–1515* (Princeton: Princeton University Press, 1993).

55. Witt, *Hercules*; Cox, 'Ciceronian Rhetoric'.

56. Leverotti, '"Diligentia"'; Leverotti, 'La cancelleria'; Nadia Covini, 'La trattazione delle suppliche nella cancelleria sforzesca: da Francesco Sforza a Ludovico il Moro', in Cecilia Nubola and Andreas Würgler (eds), *Suppliche e "gravamina": politica, amministrazione e giustizia in Europa (secoli XIV–XVIII)* (Bologna: Il Mulino, 2002), pp. 107–46; Nadia Covini, *'De gratia speciali*. Sperimentazioni documentarie e pratiche di potere tra i Visconti e gli Sforza', in Massimo Vallerani (ed.), *Tecniche di potere nel tardo Medioevo: regimi comunali e signorie in Italia* (Rome: Viella, 2010), pp. 183–206; Andrea Gamberini, *Lo stato visconteo: linguaggi politici e dinamiche costituzionali* (Milan: Franco Angeli, 2005), pp. 35–67; Lazzarini, 'Registres princiers'.

57. Peter Rück, *L'ordinamento degli archivi ducali di Savoia sotto Amedeo VIII (1398–1451)* (Rome: Arti grafiche Panetto e Petrelli, 1977); Olivier Guyotjeannin, 'Les Méthodes de travail des archivistes du roi de France (XIIIe–début XVIe siècle)', *Archiv für Diplomatik* 42 (1996), pp. 295–373; Axel Behne, 'Geschichte aufbewahren: zur Theorie der Archivgeschichte und zur mittelalterlichen Archivpraxis in Deutschland und Italien', in Peter Rück (ed.), *Mabillons Spur: zweiundzwanzig Miszellen auf dem Fachgebiet für historische Hilfswissenschaften der Philipps-Universität Marburg zum 80. Geburstag von Walter Heinemeyer* (Marburg an der Lahn: Institut für historische Hilfswissenschaften, 1992), pp. 277–97; Lazzarini, 'Materiali'; Filippo De Vivo, Andrea Guidi and Alessandro Silvestri (eds), *Archivi e archivisti in Italia tra medioevo ed età moderna* (Roma: Viella, 2015).
58. Lazzarini, *Scritture e potere.*
59. Guido Castelnuovo, '"Contra morem solitum": un conflit d'archives savoyard en 1397. Quelques réflexions sur l'écrit, ses pouvoirs et les pouvoirs dans une principauté du bas Moyen Âge', in Lazzarini, *Scritture e potere*; Randolph Head, 'Knowing Like a State: The Transformation of Political Knowledge in Swiss Archives, 1450–1770', *Journal of Modern History* 75:4 (2003), pp. 745–82; De Vivo, 'Coeur de l'état'.
60. Franca Leverotti, 'L'archivio dei Visconti signori di Milano', in Lazzarini, *Scritture e potere*; Gamberini, *Lo stato visconteo*, pp. 35–68; Lazzarini, 'Registres princiers'.
61. Rück, *L'ordinamento*; Axel Behne, 'Archivordnung und Staatsordnung im Mailand der Sforza-Zeit', *Nuovi Annali della Scuola per Archivisti e Bibliotecari* 2 (1988), pp. 93–102; Axel Behne, *Antichi inventari dell'Archivio Gonzaga* (Rome: Ministero per i beni culturali e ambientali, Ufficio centrale per i beni archivistici, 1993); Filippo Valenti (ed.), *Archivio segreto estense. Sezione 'Casa e Stato'. Inventario* (Rome: Pubblicazioni degli Archivi di stato, 1953); Lazzarini, 'Materiali'.
62. Guyotjeannin, 'Les Méthodes'; Lazzarini, 'Materiali'.
63. Simonetta, *Rinascimento segreto*, p. 133; Enrico Fumagalli, 'Appunti sulla biblioteca dei Visconti e degli Sforza nel castello di Pavia', *Studi petrarcheschi* 7 (1990), p. 136 (pp. 93–211); Leverotti, 'L'archivio'.
64. Lazzarini, *Scritture e potere*; Varanini, 'Public Written Records'.
65. Maxson, *The Humanist World*, p. 84.
66. Leverotti, *Diplomazia e governo.*
67. Gabriele Pagliari married a daughter of the rich Milanese merchant Simone Meraviglia, while Giacomo Alfieri married Orsina, of the noble Anguissola kin, and Giovanni Molo was brother-in-law of the powerful feudal lord Luchino Rusca of Como. See Leverotti, '"Diligentia"', pp. 325–8.
68. Lazzarini, '"Peculiaris magistratus"'.
69. Folin, *Rinascimento estense*, pp. 156–60.
70. For Venice, see note 27 and De Vivo, 'Coeur de l'état', pp. 719–25.
71. Guidi, *Un segretario militante*, pp. 106–7.
72. Alison Brown, 'Lorenzo de' Medici's New Men and Their *mores*: The Changing Lifestyle of Quattrocento Florence', *Renaissance Studies* 16 (2002), pp. 113–42; Brown, *Bartolomeo Scala*; Klein, *Scritture e governo*, pp. 143–56; Maxson, *The Humanist World*, pp. 63–84.
73. De Vivo, 'Coeur de l'état'.
74. Black, *Humanism and Education*; Isabella Lazzarini, 'Renaissance Diplomacy', in Gamberini and Lazzarini, *The Italian Renaissance State*, pp. 425–43; Alessandro Fontana, 'Les Ambassadeurs après 1494: la guerre et la politique nouvelles', in Adelin Charles Fiorato (ed.), *Italie 1494* (Paris: Presses de la Sorbonne nouvelle, 1994), pp. 143–78; Guidi, *Un segretario militante* (on Braccesi, pp. 100–2; on secretaries' education with a specific focus on Machiavelli, pp. 48–90).
75. Leverotti, '"Diligentia"', p. 327 (Sagramoro da Rimini); Lazzarini, *Communication and Conflict* (Pandolfo Collenuccio).

76. Simonetta, *Rinascimento segreto*, pp. 37–64; Amedeo De Vincentiis, *Battaglie di memoria: gruppi, intellettuali, testi e la discontinuità del potere papale alla metà del Quattrocento* (Rome: Roma nel Rinascimento, 2002).

77. Leverotti, *Diplomazia e governo*, pp. 247–50; Senatore, '*Uno mundo de carta*', ad indicem; Paul Dover, 'Royal Diplomacy in Renaissance Italy: Ferrante d'Aragona (1458–94) and His Ambassadors', *Mediterranean Studies* 14 (2005), pp. 57–94.

78. Lazzarini, '"*Peculiaris magistratus*"', pp. 346–7.

79. Guidi, *Un segretario militante*, pp. 104–5; Franco Angiolini, 'Dai segretari alle "segreterie": uomini e apparati di governo nella Toscana medicea (metà XVI secolo–metà XVII secolo)', *Società e Storia* 15 (1992), pp. 701–20; John Najemy, 'The Controversy Surrounding Machiavelli's Service to the Republic', in Bock, Skinner and Viroli, *Machiavelli and Republicanism*, pp. 101–17.

CHAPTER 3

Mercurino di Gattinara (1465–1530): Imperial Chancellor, Strategist of Empire

Rebecca Ard Boone

In 1565 an agent of the Spanish empire in Italy complained about imperial over-reach: 'There are old men in Castile who believe we were better off when we had no more than that realm.' He confessed that if the political situation had reverted to

> that time when there was a king in Aragon and another in Naples, and a lord in Flanders, and another in Burgundy, and a duke in Milan [. . .] it would be better for the kingdoms, although not for the authority and greatness of the kings.[1]

Almost fifty years earlier, Mercurino di Gattinara (1465–1530) had helped to create this empire by orchestrating the Spanish domination of Italy. As grand chancellor of Holy Roman Emperor Charles V, Gattinara directed policy at the Spanish court from 1518 to 1530 and helped to construct the ideological foundations of a world empire.[2]

Gattinara provided the Spanish empire with a cohesive vision of 'universal monarchy', a world united under the authority of one ruler. Fortified with source material from a variety of genres and historical eras including medieval biblical prophecy, Roman law and Christian humanism, he sounded an almost revolutionary call for peace, justice and religious reform. The ideological underpinning of empire complemented an active political agenda aiming toward one overriding goal: the military conquest of the Italian peninsula. This chapter examines the relationship between ideology and action as the grand chancellor guided the policy of Charles V. His combination of utopian idealism and raw power proved irresistible both to his ruler and to the subjects of the numerous domains he sought to bring into the Spanish empire.

As one among many chancellors working to consolidate state power in the early sixteenth century, he played a role similar to that of Antoine Du Prat (1463–1535) in France, Matthew Lang (1469–1540) in the Holy Roman Empire and Thomas Wolsey (1473–1530) in England. Enlarging the territories and military grandeur of their rulers, these men gained reputations as ruthless diplomatic negotiators and efficient administrators. They devoted their attention to the endemic warfare which dominated European affairs at that time. During the Italian Wars (1494–1559), sporadic battles, brutal sieges and rapidly shifting alliances erupted endlessly throughout the Italian peninsula, a period skilfully (and cynically) recounted in Francesco Guicciardini's *History of Italy*.[3] Amid this turbulence, Gattinara sought to consolidate power through administrative reform. His exceptional bureaucratic skills were supplemented by an intellectual training and emotional intelligence that enabled him to read the motives of his subjects and adversaries. Gattinara's 'predatory empathy' and belief that everyone in the political arena could be bought, persuaded, coerced or conquered positioned him well to serve his emperor in the enterprise of conquest.

Born into the minor nobility of Gattinara, a small city in the Italian piedmont in the territory of the dukes of Savoy, Mercurino Arborio di Gattinara studied law at the University of Turin. His successful legal practice there won him the attention of Duke Philibert II of Savoy, who appointed Gattinara as legal advisor to his wife, Margaret of Austria. After the death of her husband, she moved her court to the Low Countries. Gattinara remained with her as main advisor and diplomatic liaison with the court of her father, Holy Roman Emperor Maximilian I. In 1508 she rewarded her advisor with the presidency of the parliament of Dôle in the Franche-Comté of Burgundy. Feigning Burgundian ancestry, and purchasing a castle, the new president clashed with the local nobility in the territory, fighting them in a legal dispute over the castle with such tenacity and ill will that Margaret relieved him of his position. It nearly ruined him.[4]

His prospects appearing bleak, the unemployed advisor retreated to a Belgian monastery in 1516 to fulfil a religious vow. He composed a short treatise intended for Margaret's nephew, Charles Habsburg, who had recently acceded to the Spanish throne. *A Supplicatory Oration including a Dream of the Last World Monarchy and the Triumph of Christianity, Broadly Stated, with the Means of Accomplishing it* had been composed as a rather elaborate mirror-for-princes based on biblical prophecy, ancient history and philosophy, as well as acute observations of contemporary politics. In the 'dream of world monarchy', Charles appeared as a saviour-emperor destined to pacify Italy, reform the Church, unite all of Christendom, liberate Jerusalem, and usher in an era of peace and justice on earth. Never published, the work had been lost until John Headley discovered the manuscript in the British Library in the 1990s.[5] After several months in the monastery, Gattinara returned to his native land to seek employment at the court of Duke Charles II of Savoy. While there he received word that Maximilian I intended to make him grand chancellor of the newly crowned Charles I of Spain. Gattinara set off for Charles's court in 1518.

Charles of Burgundy (1500–58), as the grandson of Maximilian I as well as of Ferdinand of Aragon and Isabella of Castile, inherited the largest collection of domains in Europe since the time of Charlemagne.[6] In 1519 he became Charles V, Holy Roman Emperor. The young ruler faced several pressing problems in the first decade of his reign. As a foreign prince raised at a Burgundian court in the Low Countries, he faced much opposition in Spain when his Flemish advisors refused to respect the myriad of customs, rights and interests of the local population. Resentment intensified into open rebellion in the Comuneros revolt of 1519. In the German lands of the empire, the religious movement initiated by Martin Luther threatened social and political turmoil, culminating in the Peasants' Revolt of 1525. Although the new colonies established in America held the promise of gold and silver, reports from the New World hinted that Cortés might seek to establish a rogue feudal domain. On the eastern frontier, the Ottoman Turks pushed into Habsburg territory, winning a stunning victory at Mohács in 1526, which killed the king of Hungary and divided the country. It was a daunting list of challenges, encompassing much of the geographical expanse of the empire and demanding a subtle and multifaceted imperial strategy.

Although Gattinara's tenure as chancellor spanned only twelve years, his work defined the direction of Spain's empire in difficult times. Despite the challenges enumerated above, his own interests ensured that the major policy objective of Charles V remained the fight against France for pre-eminence in the Italian peninsula. The grand chancellor had convinced the emperor that the domination of Italy would enable him to unite Christendom under his authority and successfully defeat the Turks. Of course, the papacy and Italian states had no desire to become satellites of the Spanish empire; neither Henry VIII of England nor Francis I of France wanted to see the enlargement of Charles's empire. The Habsburg–Valois rivalry over Italy was long-standing and would continue until 1559. Despite a great deal of rhetoric directed against the Turks, the real enemy of Charles V was France. The more the emperor appeared to be consolidating power in Italy, the more easily the French could portray themselves as a bulwark against imperial hegemony.[7]

Gattinara coordinated the diplomacy, finance, military recruitment and propaganda supporting the enterprise of Italy, which saw periodic campaigns there and culminated in the invasion of the peninsula in 1529, followed by the coronation of Charles V in Bologna the next year. A few months after he witnessed in person the coronation that stood as the symbolic accomplishment of Italian hegemony, the grand chancellor died at Innsbruck. Following his death, Charles redirected his resources to the fight against Protestantism in the German lands. But Italy remained a cornerstone of the first great European empire of the global age, a legacy of Gattinara's priorities as imperial chancellor.

A MYSTICAL PERSONA

Gattinara cultivated a persona infused with mystery and prophetic idealism. All of his works expound his conviction that the emperor was destined for world domination. He synthesised various traditions to provide a coherent and persuasive argument for empire, while buttressing his authority by claiming supernatural powers to interpret heavenly signs and predict the future. In his *Supplicatory Oration* (*Oratio Supplicatoria*), he included a short Italian sonnet outlining the foundation of his beliefs:

> If one can have knowledge of future things
> If divine secrets may be known
> If by prophecy they can be believed or revealed
> If by the images in dreams, or preoccupations
> If by revelation, or by scripture

> If by nocturnal voices, or unknown spirits
> If by wisdom infused in the foolish
> If by planets, signs, or even stars,
> If by calculations of true science
> If by living reason and right conjecture
> If by speculation or experience,
> One can have information or understanding
> About the Predestination or Prescience
> Of him who from the beginning was chosen
> To accomplish the fulfillment
> Of true universal monarchy
> Here within you will find the doctrine.[8]

Although the sonnet mentions reason and experience as foundations for political knowledge, its overall tone betrays a desire to place the political discussion on a supernatural and mystical plane of comprehension. The *Oration* contained a vision based on a dream. Gattinara had been contemplating the evil in the world, such as the 'overthrow of restraint, perversion of customs, desertion of virtue, abhorrence of good arts, exuberance of wickedness, the growth of all evils'. A voice in the night, perhaps a ghost, whispered the solution to all of the world's problems. It said that such evils arose from a 'plurality of princes'. Only a universal monarchy, in which Charles would 'congregate his flock under one shepherd' could reduce the calamities engendered by constant warfare. The work continued with a vision of the End Times, purportedly taken from Methodius, that depicted 'the king of the Romans' ascending the mountain of Golgotha and placing his crown on the true cross. At that point, 'stretching his hands to the sky, he will hand the kingdom of the Christians to God the Father'. Although he claimed to be using biblical prophecies from the early Middle Ages, much of the prophecy in the *Oration* had been lifted word for word from Annius of Viterbo and Johannes Lichtenberger. Both of these authors published prophetic works in the late fifteenth century during the reign of Maximilian I, who also claimed a right to world monarchy.[9] The early sixteenth century witnessed a proliferation of such biblical prophecies used for political purposes, and Gattinara might have consulted them during his extended stay at the Belgian monastery.

The kingdom of Aragon had its own tradition of political biblical prophecy which left its mark on Gattinara. Originating in the *Reconquista*, a common prophetic narrative held that a Spanish king would defeat the Muslims in Iberia, continue the fight across North Africa, unite all of Christianity and liberate Jerusalem from the infidels. A prophecy of the Catalonian mystic Arnau of Villanova, a fourteenth-century physician and advisor, exists among the grand chancellor's personal papers with marginal notes in Gattinara's distinctive handwriting. Known as the *Vae mundo in centum annis*, from 1315, the prophecy includes the following verses:

> The nest of donkeys, Italy, will be bitten by lions and wolves, born in its own woods, and the blood will run from the nails torn from the thumbs, and having experienced the earthly chasm, will learn to recognize the medicine for its thirst.

Germany will be crowned with sadness, and with its neck broken, will drink from the heat of its fury with gigantic priests, in whose sea a multitude of beasts will stir up a storm exposing the navigators to dangers. Now the confusion of the princes will put the tranquility of the people at risk.

Spain, nurse of the Mohammedan perversity, will be butchered by a fury ebbing and flowing, for its kingdoms rise up one against the other. And when the colt of the mare will reach twenty-one years, the devouring fire will multiply, until the bat devours the ashes of Spain and subdues Africa, crushes the head of the beast, and accepts the monarchy.[10]

The prophecy must have seemed eerily relevant to the political situation facing Europe two hundred years after it had been written. The *Vae mundo* of Villanova had also influenced Christopher Columbus, who, like Gattinara, portrayed himself as a prophet and described Ferdinand of Aragon as a saviour-emperor destined to establish world monarchy.[11]

Gattinara's embrace of prophecy seemed remarkable to many of his fellow diplomats and advisors. The Polish ambassador, Joannes Dantiscus, remarked on this tendency in a letter to his king:

War is made on the basis of predictions, and they believe in them, especially the grand chancellor, who sometimes speaks of them proudly at the table. He said that many years ago there was a hermit from around Constantinople who pronounced a prophecy that began, 'rise, bat, rise, rise'. He attributes and applies this phrase to the emperor. Among many other words, this prediction contains these: 'You will humble all the tyrants and the three kings with your own blood.'[12]

The quote refers to the Valencian astrologer Jeroni Torella's *De rege valentine*, written about Ferdinand of Aragon in 1496.[13] The Catalonian reference to the Spanish king as a bat, *vespertilio*, refers both to Spain as the land of the setting sun and to the animal as a devourer of mosquitoes, a play on the word *mesquita*, meaning mosque in Spanish. Clearly, the grand chancellor was able to fuse a number of messianic imperial prophecies to support his interpretation of Charles V as a saviour-emperor and universal monarch.

Gattinara's penchant for prophecies coincided with a deep interest in astrology and other esoteric knowledge. In the early sixteenth century, many scholars sought to harness the power of the heavens to influence political reality on earth. Perhaps the most famous of these, Cornelius Agrippa von Nettesheim, author of *De occulta philosophia* (1517), had close ties with the grand chancellor. He met Agrippa at Dôle in 1508–9, and had secured for him the position of imperial archivist and historiographer in 1529. Agrippa's work described how one might use magical forces to draw down celestial influences such as angels or demons. Inspired by Neoplatonism, the Cabala and the Hermetic tradition, he built on the occult philosophy pioneered by Marsilio Ficino in fifteenth-century Florence. In Agrippa's funeral oration for Gattinara, the occult philosopher referred to him not as Mercurino, a name meaning 'little Mercury', but as 'Hermes', the Greek messenger god.[14] Undoubtedly, he wanted to connect him to Hermes Trismegistus, a mythical figure related to the Egyptian Thoth who had brought humans the arts of communication, knowledge and magic. One might even speculate that the grand chancellor linked in his own mind the role of messenger to the role of prophet, both of whom are charged with bringing heavenly knowledge to humans on earth.[15]

The aura of magic and mysticism failed to gain Gattinara much credit among his fellow counsellors. He related in his autobiography that many at court criticised him for devoting himself to 'vain astrological predictions' and trusting in 'apocryphal prophecies'. In his defence, he stated, 'True astronomy and prophecy is what prudence produces, the elements of which should be the memory of past events and the consideration of present affairs. This results naturally in foresight into the future.'[16] Whether or not the grand chancellor believed in his own supernatural powers is impossible to discern, but they were remarked upon by his contemporaries. During negotiations for peace in 1528, the Venetian ambassador Andrea Navagero related one of the chancellor's mysterious visions:

> The Chancellor (Gattinara) said he had discovered a remedy for everything, and that thereby peace would be made. That on the Sunday of the Epiphany he had a vision of this device (*venne in visione questa cosa*), which would resemble the star, whereby on that day the Magi were guided on the straight road; and thus would this contrivance lead the Kings and Princes of Christendom to peace. All men marvelled what a grand project this could be, put forward by so great a personage as the Chancellor Gattinara.[17]

It is not clear what effect such visions had on the young emperor. Charles V did not profess any interest in the occult tradition or Hermeticism. However, he remained profoundly influenced by Gattinara for almost a decade. In their dispatches, foreign diplomats remarked on the strange power that he wielded over the emperor. In 1527, Dantiscus related, 'It is admirable that not even the Emperor will dare to take any decision against his disposition. The Chancellor asserts that he is captivated (*hechizado*) by him.'[18] Did the advisor mean that he had his ruler charmed or enthralled? Or did he believe himself capable of a sort of *hechicería*, or wizardry? Either way, Gattinara recognised the intensely personal nature of his authority. His special capacity for persuasion rested on an ability to see what others could not.

THE HUMANIST

Gattinara supplemented the signs, dreams and prophecies that supported his providential view of world history with numerous arguments extolling the benefits of universal monarchy for humanity. Availing himself of fourteenth-century sources such as Dante and Bartolus as well as contemporary Christian humanism and Renaissance Platonism, the former lawyer constructed an argument supporting the benefits of conquest for the emperor's new subjects. Gattinara clearly outlined the goal of empire: human flourishing. In this light, he appeared as an idealist and an ardent champion of peace, justice and reform.

In the early fourteenth century, Dante proposed that only an all-powerful emperor could guarantee peace. *De Monarchia* argued from history and scripture that human flourishing required peace, and only a universal monarch could end all of the terribly destructive political squabbles that erupted between states. Dante asserted that 'Universal peace is the best of those things which are ordained for our human happiness', and from this it followed that

> the whole of mankind is ordered to one goal [. . .] there must therefore be one person who directs and rules mankind, and he is properly called 'monarch' or 'emperor' and thus it is apparent that the well-being of the world requires that there be a monarchy or empire.[19]

De Monarchia was a classic expression of the filo-imperial ideology of the Ghibellines. Dante not only argued that God had established the Roman Empire to bring peace to the world, but also that it did not owe its authority to the Church, because the empire predated it.[20] The controversial book had earned a ritual burning in 1329, and would be placed on the Index of Forbidden Books in 1554.[21] *De Monarchia* greatly influenced the grand chancellor, who asked Erasmus to edit and publish it in 1526. Erasmus, aware of the controversies, chose to turn down the offer.[22]

Gattinara also found support for universal monarchy in the tradition of Roman law. Trained as a jurist at the University of Turin, he claimed in his autobiography to have memorised the entire *Code of Justinian*.[23] The body of Roman law had been codified under the emperor Justinian in the late Roman Empire. In the fourteenth century, interpreters of Roman law such as Baldus and Bartolus argued that, in a legal sense, the empire remained unified. Indeed, Bartolus suggested that to deny the Holy Roman emperor the title of 'Lord and Monarch of all the world' was blasphemy.[24] Gattinara asserted the emperor's legal right to universal rule, stating:

> the sovereignty of Roman Law attests to the overriding supremacy of the imperial jurisdiction from which all jurisdictions derive. And the superiority of the emperor endures irrespective of existing political contingencies even if it may not be recognized for over a thousand years.[25]

Following the interpreters of Roman law, the emperor acted as the guardian of the law, the *dominus mundi* who upheld justice and order so that peace could prevail.[26]

Although often used to support tyrannical claims, Roman law as interpreted by Bartolus proposed a loose imperial hegemony that provided ample room for local customs and self-government. In the *Oration* he qualified his messianic vision of world domination:

> I do not mean that Caesar should be given ownership of everything in particular, nor that each and every kingdom and domain be put in his hands, nor that kings and princes should be robbed of their kingdoms and domains. But I think that

all kings and princes ought to recognize the superiority of the empire, and they should agree to it as they are legally bound. And their disputes, which are the cause of so many wars, will dissolve under the authority of the monarch.[27]

This softer hegemony, based more on *auctoritas* than direct *dominium*, allowed a greater, potentially limitless expansion of empire, one that included non-European subjects.[28]

Roman law provided Gattinara with an impersonal model of power that served as a counterweight to his portrayal of Charles as a messianic saviour-emperor. As he strove to refute accusations that Charles was acting as a tyrant, he worked with and through local powers and strengthened judicial administrations from Milan to Mexico. He supported public institutions such as representative assemblies and courts. His embrace of the Western legal tradition, which focused on the peaceful reconciliation of human interests rather than war, reflected a high-mindedness that set him apart from the warrior ethos that dominated the Spanish court in the early sixteenth century.[29]

The grand chancellor further softened the imperial message by appealing to humanist values. Thoroughly cosmopolitan, he seemed immune to small-minded or provincial bigotry. Understanding differences in culture, he advised Charles to hire local jurists to administer justice in their own regions.[30] Under his direction, the advisory council of the emperor included advisors from almost all regions of the European empire. Not surprisingly, he regarded the indigenous peoples in the New World as fully human and deserving of rights. As will be shown below, the grand chancellor had practical motives to support this open-minded and inclusive position.

The grand chancellor's openness extended to those with unorthodox religious beliefs. With his protection, Christian humanists at the University of Alcalá freely debated new directions in spirituality. Adherents of the *alumbrado* movement fused Platonic ideals with Christianity, emphasising harmony, brotherhood and a personal experience of God's love. Their criticism of the role of ritual in worship led to accusations of heresy by the Inquisition. However, as long as the grand chancellor remained powerful at court, they enjoyed protection. He was well disposed toward Christian humanism. He encouraged the press at Alcalá to publish many works by Erasmus in both Latin and Spanish.[31] Gattinara had strategic reasons to take an accommodating stance toward scholars and theologians, but his support reveals a view of politics as consensus-building rather than simple conquest or domination. He understood soft power as an important complement to military force.

Gattinara was not the first to enlist humanist scholars in support of political power. Humanism as an *instrumentum regni* had its origins in fifteenth-century Florence. Platonism, which encouraged the utopian values of peace and harmony, favoured monarchy as the most rational form of government.[32] As scholars in Italy revived antiquity, many focused on the model of ancient Rome. Although some revered the example of the Roman republic, others sought to revive the dream of Julius Caesar. This vision, which inspired rulers well into the eighteenth century, concentrated on the military glory of the ruler who enlarged his territory and organised it under one, centralised government. Scholars who wrote in the genre of 'Imperial Humanism' tended to expend more energy exalting the grandeur of the monarch than thinking about the well-being of his subjects.[33] Gattinara, as a scholar and a policy-maker, appeared to excel at doing both. An analysis of his effective political strategy, however, reveals a darker side to the image of a humane and cosmopolitan statesman.

IMPERIAL STRATEGIST

As grand chancellor, Gattinara worked systematically to consolidate state power in the face of numerous challenges. Charles had inherited the largest amalgam of lands since Charlemagne, but he ruled over a composite monarchy, rather than a unified empire. An enumeration of his titles suggests the complexity of his domains:

> Charles, Always August Emperor, king of Germany, of Castile, of Aragon, of the two Sicilies, of Jerusalem, of Hungary, of Dalmatia, of Navarra, of Granada, of Toledo, of Valencia, of Galicia, of Seville, of Mallorca, of Cerdaña, of Córdoba, of Murcia, of Jaén, of the Algarbes, of Algeciras, of Gibraltar, of the Canary Islands, of the Indies, islands and terra firma of the Ocean Sea; Archduke of Austria, duke of Burgundy, of Brabant, Lotharingia, Carinthia and Carniola, of Luxembourg, of Limburgh, of Guelders, Athens and Neopatria; Count of Brisna, of Flanders, of Tirol of Habsburg, of Artois and Burgundy; Count Palatine of Hainault, of Holland, of Zeeland, of Ferut, of Fribuque, Amuque of Rosellón and Cerdaña; Landgrave of Alsace, Marquis of Burgundy and of the Holy Roman Empire, of Oristan and Gociano; Prince of Catalonia and Swabia; Lord of Frisia, of the Marcas, of Labono, of Puerta, of Viscaya, of Molina, of Salinas and of Tripoli.[34]

Charles V ruled as emperor over German lands, but only as king in Castile and Aragon. In addition, he carried the titles of duke, archduke, count and margrave. Each title represented specific customary rights and duties which forced him to recognise particular liberties and legal customs of the states and kingdoms he governed.

Maximilian I had appointed Gattinara grand chancellor of all the 'kingdoms and states' of the emperor, but that office had been defined differently in various jurisdictions. Having served Margaret of Austria in Burgundy, Gattinara adopted the Burgundian interpretation of the office of chancellor. He held the seals of the ruler, and all important documents relating to policy, finances, salaries and foreign affairs went through him. He also served as the head of the numerous councils of the judiciary, and as spokesman for the ruler. Interestingly, Gattinara acted as chancellor in Aragon but not Castile. Traditionally, Aragon had a strong chancellery, and the Council of Aragon administered the emperor's Italian possessions. In Castile, the business of government was handled by secretaries rather than a chancellor. Francisco de los Cobos, the most important secretary for affairs relating to Spain, headed a faction that often opposed Gattinara at court.[35]

Although generally charged with foreign affairs, the grand chancellor also handled domestic issues. By 1520, he was composing numerous *consulta*, or reports, intended to reform the administration of the realm. He advocated the creation of a financial controller-general to regulate finances, urged the abolition of unnecessary offices, and recommended the appointment of secretaries with distinct geographical jurisdictions.[36] Working to coordinate symbolic forms of power such as seals, titles, heralds and coats of arms, he was the first to refer to Charles V as 'His Majesty', a title with divine pretentions that upset many of his Spanish subjects.[37] His eye for detail combined with his larger vision of universal monarchy set him apart from many of his fellow courtiers. At a time when government offices were largely distributed according to patronage, he was capable of seeing administration as a rational system. His thinking in this area was informed by his training as a jurist and his extensive reading in ancient history. Moreover, his political experience in Savoy, a multilingual duchy that had consolidated only in the fifteenth century, was undoubtedly valuable. His fellow Savoyard and former professor at the University of Turin, Claude de Seyssel, provided the first institutional analysis of the French monarchy in 1515, the *Monarchie de France*.[38] Neither Seyssel nor Gattinara took political legitimacy for granted, having both experienced life in northern Italy, which had been subject to frequent warfare and social conflict. This background helps to explain their concern with justice and stability. Gattinara's sophisticated understanding of the structure of political institutions provided much-needed direction for a young ruler more interested in Burgundian chivalry and the quest for personal glory than in the mundane concerns of administration.[39] This was the formation that shaped Gattinara's approach to the management of empire. Let us now see how Gattinara's imperial vision was brought to bear in the various challenges that faced the empire in Charles's first decade as ruler of this complex polity.

THE COMUNEROS REVOLT

Gattinara's appreciation of efficient administration and fear of social conflict impacted his response to the first major crisis of the regime, the Comuneros revolt. This political rebellion in Castile erupted over fears that Spanish resources would be diverted to fund not only the imperial election, but the military engagements necessary to defend numerous lands outside Spain. The advent of empire signalled a movement of the centre of power away from Spain and towards northern Europe. The announcement in November 1519 of the king's voyage to Germany was the spark that started the civil war. The question of imperial election exacerbated the tensions between cities and the Crown that had been simmering since the death of Isabella of Castile in 1504, after which Castile endured six changes of leadership in fourteen years.[40] Rival jurisdictions and courts had been helpless to stop aristocrats from enriching themselves in flagrant disregard of the traditional constitutions of the cities, or *comunidades*. Although the towns sought a legal remedy for these confiscations, neither the regency under Francisco Jiménez de Cisneros, nor the court in Flanders (from the death of Ferdinand in 1516) implemented the rule of law. This was the major complaint of the leaders of the revolt according to the petitions to Charles in the *cortes*, the representative assemblies of the Spanish kingdoms. The monarchy, dominated by Flemish courtiers, disparagingly termed 'flamingos' by the Spanish, was incapable of preventing and containing social conflict.[41] By 1520, fourteen cities had banded into a *Sacra Junta* in Valladolid that acted as the administrative authority for all aspects of the government in Castile. They won several military victories, but divisions arose within their coalition. Juana, the mother of Charles and under whose authority they ruled, failed to support them. Moreover, when the common people rose up in the cities, the urban elite began to fear them. At first, the aristocrats had supported the petitions of the *cortes* of Castile. They were infuriated because the Crown had granted benefices they considered their own to members of the Flemish entourage. However, when it became clear that many in the rebellion insisted on radical land reform and a reduction of aristocratic privileges, many nobles joined the royalist side. With the mercenary armies of the aristocrats now in the service of the Crown, the royalists won a series of military victories in 1521 that definitively crushed the rebellion.[42]

With Castile in flames, Valencia also erupted in a rebellion known as *Las Germanías*, or the Revolt of the Brotherhoods. The *germanías* were local guild militias authorised by the Crown to bear arms to protect the coastal cities from corsairs. Led by a mysterious and prophetic figure known as *El Encubierto*, or the 'hidden one', the militias demanded the wealth of the aristocracy for a crusade to aid the poor, reform the clergy and take Jerusalem. *El Encubierto* envisioned an egalitarian society without royal power, but the social rebellion he incited ended with his capture, decapitation and burning in 1522.[43]

Gattinara's policy decisions regarding these revolts were most likely informed by intelligence provided by Peter Martyr d'Anghiera (1457–1525). Originally from Piedmont, but educated in Milan, Anghiera moved to the Spanish court in 1487. He served as a soldier, confessor, advisor, counsellor, ambassador, mediator and historian. Most famous as the author of the first history of the Indies, the *Eight Decades of the New World*, or *De Orbo Novo*, he also left to posterity over eight hundred letters covering Spanish politics.[44] Almost fifty of his letters to the grand chancellor address the subject of the revolts in Valencia and Castile. In a letter from Valencia in December 1519, Anghiera discussed the social and political structures of the realm which included three estates (*brazos*): the Church, Military and People. He informed Gattinara that the people of the popular estate resented the king for not appearing in the *cortes* according to ancient custom. He also highlighted the threat of social disorder: 'The artisans have already expelled the nobles who dare not live in the city.' He added, 'The people are claiming their liberties, they will not submit to the magistrates. So if you do not bring Caesar here, you will lose this kingdom with great ignominy, and this contagious plague will infect the neighboring kingdoms.'[45]

A month later, Gattinara wrote a lengthy report to Charles V advising the emperor to put the Spanish kingdoms in order before he departed for the German lands. Concerning the popular uprisings, he suggested Charles employ 'justice and rigor as well as gentleness and friendship, using authority where needed'. He added that the emperor should 'have regard that each land ought to be governed according to its laws, constitutions, and customs' and warned that 'abrogating these would engender trouble'.[46] More specifically, he suggested sending representatives from each estate (*bras*) to court to address the situation. The report included nearly a dozen pages on clear policy objectives including the regulation of finances and the concession of offices, the mismanagement of which had played a large role in generating the rebellion. It is unclear whether Charles heeded his advice. At that time his main advisor was Guillaume de Croy, lord of Chièvres, a close companion from the Burgundian nobility who wielded great influence with the emperor until his death in 1521. He had gained a reputation among the Spanish for reserving important offices and benefices for members of his own Burgundian entourage.

In his autobiography, Gattinara blamed Chièvres for the uprising, describing the rebellion as a popular revolt against taxation. In the following paragraph, he portrays himself as opposed to the excessive burden posed by the *servicio*, an extraordinary tax paid mainly by the lower orders and subsidised by the clergy. Not surprisingly, he predicted that it would cause disorder:

> Diverse opinions divided the *cortes* as Chièvres wanted to require a new *servicio* from them. Mercurino opposed it. He pointed out that the *servicio* from two years ago had not yet been collected, thus it did not make sense to require a new one. He predicted that doing so would provoke a popular rebellion, which happened just as he said it would. On the advice of Chièvres, the representatives of the realm consented to an additional tax of 500,000 ducats. However, this resulted in nothing but a revolution, which threatened to exterminate all the kingdoms. They could not collect the *servicio*, and the popular unrest consumed the remaining royal revenues.[47]

This passage indicates that Gattinara lamented the expenditure of resources that might have been avoided had the other counsellors taken account of the interests of the Spanish people. There is a notable and significant difference in the way he describes the revolt in his autobiography and in his private report to the emperor. In the report he stressed that procuring sufficient resources required the respect and cooperation of representative institutions such as the *cortes*, which demanded responses to popular appeals for justice. The report acknowledged the reality of social conflict. In contrast, his autobiography never addressed the existence of social divisions or demands for traditional liberties among the Spanish people. This might be explained by a difference in intended audience. His autobiography was written for posterity and designed to cast Gattinara in the best possible light. In this context, recognising divergent social interests would have undermined the overall theme of unity and social harmony that animated his imperial ideology. A conflict of motives is also evident in the passage just cited. Did the counsellor oppose the tax as a champion of the poor, or did he oppose it as a prudent administrator trying to conserve resources? His writing leaves his motivations unclear. Nevertheless, it is evident that he took the motivations and interests of the rebelling subjects into account when deciding policy. His insight into, and concerns for, the interests of the emperor's subjects, as well as the ambiguity of his own motives, can also be discerned in his decisions concerning the indigenous peoples of the New World.

AMERICA

Gattinara kept himself well informed on affairs in New Spain. Having served on the *Consejo Real y Suprema de las Indias*, which handled all affairs relating to the New World, he had presided over the case that determined Cortés's legal right to the conquest of Mexico. Luigi Avonto has argued that Gattinara's humanitarian impulses in the Americas offer a contrast with his interests in state centralisation and economic exploitation, as well as with his dedication to the ideal of universal monarchy. Here I attempt to reconcile this contrast by arguing that Gattinara's support of social justice in America served the economic and political interests of the Spanish empire. I want to suggest that, although he played a pivotal role in establishing the administrative structures of New Spain, the grand chancellor viewed America predominantly as a source of revenue for the invasion of Italy, a concern that, indeed, hung over all of Gattinara's calculations.[48]

   In the 1520s, two main problems undermined the interests of Charles V in America: the mistreatment of the king's new subjects, and the possibility that Hernán Cortés would take Mexico under his own authority. News of Spanish atrocities reached the court through Bartolomé de Las Casas, the 'Apostle of the Indies' most famous for his work, *A Short Account of the Destruction of the Indies*, published in 1552.[49] From July 1519 to January 1520 Las Casas presented to the court of Charles V his proposal for peaceful conversion of the indigenous people of America. He argued against the *encomienda* system of forced labour which effectively enslaved the inhabitants. Rather, he advocated a system in which inhabitants settled into villages, converted peacefully, and paid tribute directly to the Crown.[50] Las Casas promoted his plans for more humane treatment for the indigenous peoples chiefly because it offered a more effective way for Spain to collect revenue. Indeed, some contemporaries criticised the commercial nature of his plan and questioned whether a clergyman should use the lure of profit to promote his project. He replied that if he had to 'buy' Jesus Christ in order to protect Him from abuse and to love, serve and cherish Him, he would do so.[51]

   In his *History of the Indies*, Las Casas described Gattinara as a 'modest and kind man' who did much to aid his plans for the Americas.[52] The grand chancellor requested two official reports addressing the mistreatment of the Indians and provided him with land with which to pioneer a more humane approach to colonisation. He also shared Las Casas's view of the indigenous peoples of America as fully human and true subjects of the Spanish empire.

   Gattinara understood that treasure rested on human resources. The Crown had no interest in a policy of annihilation. His personal papers include a report from Tenochtitlán written immediately after the conquest that estimated the subject population of the Aztec empire at 1.6 million inhabitants. On the left side of this report, marginalia in his hand shows that he had carefully added up the populations of every province, town and village.[53] While recognising the humanity of these new subjects, he also regarded them as exploitable resources. Observing the situation from the standpoint of efficiency, Gattinara sent a letter to a Spanish official in the New World providing instructions to determine whether it would be 'more convenient to have the Indians pay tribute to the Crown, as they had done under Montezuma, or be entrusted in *encomienda* to local Spanish residents'.[54] He entertained either option, slavery or tribute, if it proved profitable to the Crown.

Independent conquistadors posed a real threat to the effective collection of resources in the New World, and Gattinara's efforts to contain the ambitions of Hernán Cortés reveal his anxieties regarding this matter. After the conquest of Mexico (1519–21), the court had appointed Cortés governor and expected him to act as a loyal administrator with the interests of the Crown foremost in his mind. By 1525, however, officials began to suspect his motives. Rumours circulated that he intended to break Mexico off from Spain and rule the newly conquered territories himself.[55] When Cortés left Tenochtitlán to lead an expedition to Honduras, dissension and turmoil among his appointed magistrates in the capital encouraged conspiracies among the local inhabitants. The Crown was in real danger of losing the whole territory.[56] The grand chancellor discussed the conquistador in a long report from September 1525 to Charles V about the expedition to Italy. The report included specific advice on the preparation for the Italian invasion, and the necessity for a powerful fleet of ships. It was in this context that Gattinara brought up the subject of Mexico and Cortés. He suggested that Charles V prepare the fleet destined to invade Italy under the false pretence of using it to consolidate power in Mexico:

> The decision about the voyage [needs] to be secret, and the preparations for it should be made under false pretenses. I think you can hide it very well by indicating that your Majesty wants to make a powerful armada to seize and reduce the land discovered by Cortés to true obedience to you, and you want to put it in order so that you can enjoy the great riches in it. Because once Cortés's departure [to Honduras] is known, as well as other news already made public that requires you to give prompt remedy to the malice of Cortés, everyone will believe that such an armada was disposed for this reason, and not for your Majesty's voyage to Italy. From this pretext, you will also derive another benefit, because you will put fear into the relatives, allies, and friends of Cortés. They will leave, and by such means, without even launching the armada you will bring Cortés around with great advantage to your majesty. He will be reduced to being a good administrator, and more amenable to reason.[57]

The above passage makes clear that the primary goal of Charles V should be to bring New Spain into obedience to the emperor, so that he could exploit its enormous resources. Interestingly, he does not actually advise the use of the armada for this purpose: the fear of its use would suffice. In a sort of psychological game, the grand chancellor seems to have put himself in the mind of Cortés and his supporters. Gattinara did not attempt to use the fear of force to gain the obedience of Cortés. The conquistador had shown exceptional courage in his ruthless conquest of an entire civilisation. He was not likely to fear any Spanish army. On the other hand, the advisor realised that his relatives, allies and friends might be swayed by fear to abandon the conquistador. If Cortés was truly seeking to establish his own feudal domain, he would need his supporters. These associates of Cortés were the intended targets of the armada rumour. Here was a classic illustration of Gattinara's use of predatory empathy.

It is quite possible that the conquest of Mexico transformed an abstract ideology of universal monarchy into a concrete plan for world domination within the mind of Gattinara. Given that his signature appears on around 450 cargo reports from treasure-laden ships arriving at Seville, it is clear that he understood how much gold and silver was coming in from America. Historians have estimated that around 17,000 kilograms of gold had come in by the 1520s.[58] These funds would secure the necessary loans from Genoese bankers needed for the invasion of Italy. Although his imperial rhetoric provided a framework for thinking about global empire, and his policy decisions helped to create a foundation for its administrative structure, nevertheless his primary concern regarding New Spain was to secure resources for an invasion and conquest of Italy.

THE LUTHERAN REVOLT

In a lengthy report from July 1526, the grand chancellor alerted the emperor, 'The empire remains in much confusion and in the greatest danger because of the revolts and disorders of the cursed sect of Luther.'[59] By 1525, the grand chancellor was addressing the destructive potential of the social unrest Luther's movement had unleashed in Germany. Gattinara understood the personal appeal of Martin Luther as a revolutionary figure, and told an English ambassador that in his estimation a hundred thousand Germans were prepared to sacrifice their lives for Luther.[60] But here, too, the grand chancellor understood the tumult of the Lutheran revolt in terms of its impact on Italian affairs.

In his pursuit of his political strategy, Gattinara had many reasons to urge Charles V to make accommodations with the Lutherans. Primarily, he needed to recruit German soldiers, especially the fearsome *Landsknechts*, for an invasion of Italy. The grand chancellor believed he could placate those among them drawn to Luther's message with the hope of an ecumenical council. The Lutheran heresy presented a strategic opportunity for Gattinara, who sought to capitalise on the alarm of the papacy. The Spanish needed the support of Pope Clement VII to dominate the peninsula. When the pope opposed the emperor's designs on Italy, the grand chancellor sought ways to menace and threaten him by enticing Lutherans with the call for a church council. These two aims, stated plainly in a report to the emperor, are also reflected in a war of propaganda between the Spanish and papal court in 1526-7.

Gattinara began the secret report with an appeal to the emperor to 'satisfy the charge that God has given him' to invade Italy and bring universal peace to Christendom. The report contained practical advice concerning the preparation of an invasion including the provision of a powerful army, a large fleet of ships, money from Genoese bankers, and aid from the emperor's brother, Ferdinand, who ruled over the German lands. Gattinara discussed the Lutheran uprising in this context, and proposed a remedy that would 'have a great impact and cost nothing'. He urged the emperor to publish a new edict expressing his desire for universal peace, and for uniting the armies against the Turk in Hungary for the benefit of the *Republica Christiana*. This edict would promise full amnesty to all Lutherans willing to abandon the errors of Luther and return to the bosom of the Catholic Church. He advised the emperor to 'publish, proclaim, and declare' his pardon of anyone, irrespective of condition or estate, who wanted to return to the Church and 'submit to the truth of evangelical doctrine to be determined by the first universal council of Christians'. He then explained the reason for such a wide amnesty. While stating his concern for the well-being of both the Lutherans and the mother Church, he made clear the strategic purposes of the plan. The relevant passage is worth including in full, as it shows the progression from idealism to practical objectives so characteristic in the chancellor's counsel:

> With clemency and amnesty from penalties we can secure them and more easily draw them from their errors. In particular, we can give them the right way to determine the truth of the evangelical doctrine upon which the sect is principally founded. With their conversion and quick submission we can aid and remedy this sect. I believe we can gain some good support from cavalry and infantry who can join with the *infante* for whatever you want to do, whether to aid Hungary or move forward to help the situation in Italy, appearing to act for the public benefit [*con color del beneficio public*] of Christianity. And this can be a torment [*torcedor*] for the pope to lead him more easily to reason, fearing lest bringing them back and joining with them would hasten the calling of the council which is the thing he fears most.[61]

Of all the possible solutions to the Lutheran question, Gattinara did not seriously consider military force. As in his approach to the new subjects in America, he chose persuasion and enticement over armed warfare. He realised that soldiers could not subdue the hundreds of thousands of Lutherans willing to die for their cause. However, they might be persuaded with mercy, kindness and the 'truth of evangelical doctrine'. The next few statements clearly expose his real purpose: not conversion but recruitment. The grand chancellor seems to allow the emperor to decide between two courses of action, sending soldiers to Hungary or Italy. A Hungarian expedition would make more sense, considering the terrible defeat at Mohács that led to the division of that country and the death of the king, as well as the Turkish threat to Eastern Europe. However, Gattinara clearly wants the emperor to send the troops to Italy. Surely in the mind of the emperor providing aid to Hungary or Italy would serve the common cause of Christianity, so why did he use a Latin idiom indicating a pretext or appearance of the common good? Using the phrase '*con color de*' added a hint of guile to the discussion. The next sentence mentions another reason for the edict of amnesty. By joining the Lutherans in the call for a council, the Spanish court can frighten the pope into 'seeing reason'. By this he means supporting Spanish claims in Italy, a complicated problem discussed at length below. As with the report cited earlier regarding Cortés, this passage sheds light on Gattinara's statesmanship. From a rhetorical standpoint, the counsellor has changed his tone three times in this one passage. His argument progresses from comity, to deceit, to intimidation. Once again, it illustrates the predatory empathy of the grand chancellor, who put himself in the mind of his adversaries to imagine their interests. In his view, the Lutherans wanted truth and justice, while Clement VII wanted a unified Catholic Church. He used this insight to devise a strategy and determined that a council to address Church reform could entice the Lutherans while coercing the pope to support the imperial cause.

In order to understand why Gattinara so opposed the pope, one must take into account the context of diplomatic politics. The battle of Pavia in 1525 greatly transformed the balance between the European powers. In this remarkable victory, the imperial army destroyed their French opponents and took the French king, Francis I, prisoner. The outcome stunned the Italian states, which feared that a major invasion of Italy would soon follow. Several Italian states entered into an alliance with France and England, both of which pledged money and arms to secure the 'liberation of Italy'. Led by Pope Clement VII, this League of Cognac, or Holy League, demanded that the emperor cease military operations in Italy and work towards a universal peace in Christendom. Facing an alliance of all the major powers in Europe against his Italian agenda, Gattinara sought to place pressure on the papacy and to detach the pope's allies from the league.

Amnesty for Lutherans and the threat of a council were only two aspects of Gattinara's multipronged challenge to Clement VII, one that blended centuries-old anticlerical themes with contemporary Christian humanism. The Holy Roman Empire and the papacy had battled over temporal and spiritual powers for centuries. European rulers had routinely used the threat of a council (and the doctrine of conciliarism) to pressure popes who stood in the way of their military conquests. For example, Louis XII of France had supported the second council of Pisa in 1511 against Pope Julius II.[62] In this light, Gattinara's call for a council was not a new political tool. But now he employed evangelical overtones reminiscent of Luther and Christian humanism, and employed the printing press to do so.

In 1526–7, the imperial court and the papacy engaged in a bitter propaganda battle over the League of Cognac. Gattinara enlisted the support of his personal secretary and celebrated Spanish humanist, Alfonso de Valdés. Closely linked to Erasmus and Christian humanism, Alfonso and his brother Juan published strongly imperialist literary works.[63] Alfonso de Valdés was listed as the author of a work of propaganda drafted by Gattinara, *Pro Divo Carolo eius nominis quinto Romanorum Imperatore Invictissimo*. It contained an appeal for a council that echoed the humanist themes of transparency, spiritual equality and optimism. According to the author, 'At this assembly Christ, the Best and Greatest, shall preside, the freest opinions are spoken.' With open dialogue as the key to truth, and the good will of the participants, the author inquired, 'Who may doubt that Christ will be present, if he shall see all come together there for the supreme improvement of the Christian commonwealth?'[64] The pamphlet, published quickly and widely, sought to connect the emperor with anticlericism to gain popular support for his aims in Italy.

With Gattinara's consent, Valdés also penned a controversial humanist dialogue, *Dialogue of Lactancio and an Archdeacon*, concerning the sack of Rome in 1527. In May of that year, imperial armies invaded Rome and subjected its residents to five months of rape, slaughter and famine. Some of the soldiers, including Lutherans Gattinara had expended so much effort to recruit, destroyed and desecrated religious images, relics and sacraments. Valdés asserted that the sack was divine retribution for a corrupt clergy. In the dialogue, the courtier Lactancio argues, 'God permitted the robbing of His churches to show us how worthless He considered all things that can be stolen or corrupted [. . .] so that we might offer Him our wills rather than gold and silver.'[65] At the end of the work, one of the speakers in the dialogue made the extraordinary statement, 'To the end of time people will say that Jesus Christ founded the Church and that Emperor Charles V restored it.'[66]

It is not clear whether Gattinara himself saw the sack as divine punishment or military excess. In his autobiography, he rather coldly recounted his advice to Charles V about a proper response to the horrible event. He proposed two possible strategies:

> [Charles] had two choices. He could approve the actions of his men and contend that they took up arms not against a pastor, but a predator, a disturber and usurper of Christianity. It was a necessary act of defense to protect himself and his clients against such a scandalous and incorrigible pope, who had upset the whole state of the Christian religion by avoiding the universal council that had so often been implored of him. Or, if Caesar did not want to embrace this rigid stance himself, nor approve of the actions of his men, he might announce these deeds in writing and explain how bitterly he bore such a terrible event without, however, taking blame for it.[67]

One wonders how the grand chancellor could see the disaster as both an unfortunate accident and divine punishment at the same time. Although he never mentioned the Lutheran movement by name in his autobiography, he strove to portray himself as a prophet of reform. But as the above passage indicates, he also wanted his readers to see him as a practical and savvy political strategist.

THE INVASION OF ITALY

In the last five years of his life, racked with gout and bedridden much of the time, the grand chancellor truly revealed his diplomatic expertise. With energy, organisation and unwavering conviction, he enabled the Spanish court to defeat a coalition that included every other major power in Europe. All others united to demand peace, while Gattinara pressed for a war of conquest. Among the most illuminating sources for his statesmanship in these years are the writings of his fellow Italians from 1525 to 1529. With their astute and insightful consideration of the personalities involved in policy-making, two Venetians, Gasparo Contarini and Andrea Navagero, and one Florentine, Francesco Guicciardini, provide a fascinating view of Gattinara as he orchestrated the invasion of Italy.

In his *relazione*, or comprehensive report, on the affairs of Spain to the Venetian senate in 1525, Contarini provided a detailed portrait of Gattinara, explaining his method of conducting state business as well as his vision of empire. He described the grand chancellor as being of 'sanguine complexion, cheerful, prudent, an experienced negotiator, somewhat quibbling, animated, and so hardworking that one could hardly believe it'.[68] According to the Venetian, Charles V directed all foreign correspondence to him. Gattinara then distilled the information into a summary report given to the emperor, who responded to it in writing. After this, Gattinara's report and the emperor's response were read out loud in the council chamber. Although the council discussed the matter, Contarini remarked that it always reached the conclusion that Gattinara had 'contrived' for it. He reported that Gattinara 'treated, devised, and put in order' everything essential to foreign affairs. This included both finances and the securing of soldiers and arms. According to Contarini, Gattinara's incredible capacity for work made him indispensable at court.[69]

The Venetian diplomat also outlined the chancellor's larger view of empire. Gattinara wanted an empire resembling that of Persia or Rome, where kings and republics ruled their own people, while favouring and enjoying the fraternity of the imperial hegemon. He viewed the *monarchia* as a loosely ruled regime that respected the rights and privileges of the local rulers and institutions of the conquered subjects.[70] This is the carefully crafted vision Gattinara presented to Italian diplomats in order to reassure them that they would maintain their autonomy in the face of imperial conquest.

Many Italians feared the coming invasion as the 'ruin of Christianity and the papacy'.[71] Some considered imperial conquest as tantamount to slavery. Gattinara understood this perspective and looked for ways to assuage this fear. This provides one explanation for Gattinara's resistance to the punitive terms of the Treaty of Madrid. While his Burgundian counterpart, Charles de Lannoy, had sought immediate and overwhelming military force as the means to subdue Italy, the grand chancellor urged the emperor to tread lightly and use finesse. Francesco Guicciardini provides an interesting set of speeches outlining these contrasting positions in his *History of Italy*. After introducing Gattinara as 'a man who, although born of humble origins in Piedmont, by much reputation and experience, had for many years sustained all the important business of the court',[72] he depicted the grand chancellor giving a speech against the treaty. With vehemence, he urged the court to see the situation from the perspective of its adversaries, the French king and the Italians:

> Does he [Francis I] not know, and everyone else, that [the treaty] gives consent for you to enter armed into Rome, that it will give you a bridle over Italy, that you will reduce to your will the spiritual and temporal state of the Church, and the reason of redoubling your power, that never more would you lack money or arms of offending it, that it will be necessary to accept all the laws that you would like to impose on it? So who is there who believes that he has to observe an accord by which he becomes your slave and you become his lord?[73]

Gattinara did not think the French king would respect the treaty, and he imagined that a powerful show of force would only increase Italian opposition to Spain. His overall goals remained the same: the defeat of the French king and the conquest of Italy. However, he believed that doing so required an accurate estimation of one's opponents that would take their mental state into consideration. The set of speeches which illustrate both Gattinara's use of predatory empathy and Guicciardini's evaluation of it, is worth reading in its entirety as a brilliant commentary on Renaissance statecraft.[74]

The Venetian ambassador Gasparo Contarini regarded Gattinara as a potential saviour for Italy. In March 1525, he related that he had told the grand chancellor:

> I was sure the Almighty had made him the Emperor's prime minister, in order that being an Italian he might benefit Italy, in like manner as the Lord made Joseph the Hebrew great with Pharaoh King of Egypt for the benefit of his Hebrews.[75]

Indeed, this was the image Gattinara wanted to project. In July of the same year, three Venetian ambassadors, Contarini, Andrea Navagero and Lorenzo Priuli, reported a conversation with the grand chancellor in which he appeared to speak candidly about the plight of Italy. With his characteristic smile he confided:

> I will speak plainly to you, not as the Emperor's Chancellor, but as an Italian [. . .] You know that I am an Italian, and anxious for the welfare of Italy; once and for all, let us get these Spaniards (who go on plundering and destroying everything) out of the country. The way to get them out is to pay them, so let us find the money.[76]

The Venetian ambassadors, who wondered whether he aimed to liberate or enslave Italy, must have gained confidence from the statement. Throughout 1525 and 1526, the Venetian ambassadors had concluded that Gattinara was 'a good Italian'.

By 1527, however, Andrea Navagero had changed his opinion of the grand chancellor. In February he described him as standing in the way of peace during negotiations at the Spanish court. All representatives of the League of Cognac had been given powers by their states to finalise a peace treaty. Even the emperor seemed to support it, but Gattinara remained adamant. According to Navagero, he had heard from an astrologer that peace would be concluded in Italy by a jovial man (*un homo joviale*), whom he believed was himself. The frustrated Navagero reported:

> Amongst the Emperor's ministers many are well disposed towards peace, though everything is thwarted by the Chancellor [. . .] so that [Navagero] was much deceived in his original opinion of him. He does not know whether he acts thus because he is averse to peace, or to further his own personal interests, or because he desires to do everything himself. He asked leave of the Emperor to come to Italy, and obtained it; announces his intention to depart at the end of March, and quotes daily the prediction of an astrologer, that no valid peace or truce will be made in Italy before June, implying that he is the person to make this peace, as he will then be in Italy. With this vanity he embarrasses the whole world, and is most obstinate in any opinion he forms. The course pursued by him is much disapproved by his colleagues in the ministry, but he still pursues it. Gattinara is the person who rules everything.[77]

Gattinara seemed to think that the power of his own convictions, combined with careful planning, would outlast the coalition. And it did. By 1529, he had managed to detach several key players from the league. In 1528, negotiations had secured for Spain the Genoese admiral, Andrea Doria, as well as Genoa's fleet and banking families. In 1529, Clement VII, who by then faced not only the Lutheran revolt but also the defection of the English king, signed the Treaty of Barcelona establishing an accord between Spain and the papacy. The treaty stipulated the end of the Florentine republic. The pope's nephew, Alessandro de Medici, would rule Florence as the Duke of Tuscany. Also in that year, the 'Ladies' Peace' negotiated by Louise of Savoy and Margaret of Austria established peace between Spain and France. Charles V renounced his claims to Burgundy and released the two French princes held hostage according to the Treaty of Madrid. In exchange, Francis I paid the enormous sum of 900,000 *ecus*. With these questions of diplomacy settled, the emperor stood unencumbered on the eve of the Italian invasion.

One might ask what Italy really meant to Gattinara. He pursued the goal of Italian conquest single-mindedly throughout his career as grand chancellor. No problem or complication could side-track him from this objective. It provided a focus for his energy and guided his policies in a far-flung, disorganised and often unstable political environment. Despite the riches of Genoa and Milan, and the symbolic power of the Church, however, there was no great strategic advantage to be gained by Italian domination. Historians have disagreed on his motivation for the conquest. John Headley proposed that Gattinara, an idealist at heart, aimed for Italian domination as the necessary base on which a united Europe and a peaceful world order might be created.[78] More recently, Manuel Rivero suggested that the grand chancellor had more selfish interests and intended to lay the foundation for his own state in Italy. Supporting the latter view are Gattinara's own words from his autobiography:

> He was Italian, he held no properties outside of Italy, and whatever he had in Italy had been pillaged, occupied and reduced to ruin. Mercurino could have no hope of enjoying his property unless Caesar, by his Italian voyage, put an end to the wars.[79]

Rivero has pointed out that in his will and testament, Gattinara gave precise instructions for the development of his feudal domains. These included building projects and urban spaces designed according to Neoplatonic principles of universal harmony, whereby his 'state' might be aligned with celestial hierarchies.[80]

Historians might disagree on his motives, but not on his overall success as a statesman. His command of military and diplomatic intelligence, finances and law made him the most informed advisor at the court of Charles V. None of his contemporaries questioned his intelligence or prudence, despite his penchant for astrology and prophecy. But his exceptional grasp of information did not fully explain his ability to influence his ruler and direct policy. What distinguishes Gattinara from other contemporary statesmen was his emotional intelligence, which attuned him to personality, charisma and fear. Undoubtedly this was a natural talent further cultivated by extensive reading in literature, philosophy and history. In addition, his personal experience in the battleground of northern Italy, an area of continuous political contest, might have encouraged him to seek means of building consensus among disparate interests. Always striving to understand the motives of his subjects and adversaries, he found ways to entice or coerce them to support the Spanish empire. For the common people he offered a promise of peace, justice and reform; to the states of Italy, a promise that Spain would respect their political autonomy; to the pope, a promise of support against the Lutherans; to the emperor, assurance that imperial conquest was morally defensible in the eyes of God. For these constituencies, Spain failed to deliver exactly what the grand chancellor had promised. In the end, it seems that only Mercurino di Gattinara got what he wanted from the Spanish empire.

NOTES

1. Luis de Requesens to Gonzalo Perez, 3 March 1565 in Mark Levin, *Agents of Empire: Spanish Ambassadors in Sixteenth Century Italy* (Ithaca, NY: Cornell University Press, 2005), pp. 206–7.
2. The most recent work on Gattinara in English is Rebecca Ard Boone, *Mercurino di Gattinara and the Creation of the Spanish Empire* (London: Pickering and Chatto, 2014), which contains a translation of his autobiography in its appendix. The best discussion of Gattinara's political administration is in John Headley, *The Emperor and His Chancellor: A Study of the Imperial Chancellery under Gattinara* (Cambridge: Cambridge University Press, 1983). Gattinara also figures prominently in Headley, *Church, Empire and World: The Quest for Universal Order, 1520–1640* (Brookfield, VT: Ashgate/Variorum, 1997). The most recent biography of Gattinara is Manuel Rivero Rodríguez, *Gattinara. Carlos V y el sueño del Imperio* (Madrid: Sílex, 2005). See also Franco Ferretti, *Un maestro di politica. L'umana vicenda di Mercurino dei nobili Arborio di Gattinara* (Gattinara: Associazione Culturale di Gattinara, 1999). His autobiography appears in *Historia vite et gestorum per dominum magnum cancellarium Mercurino Arborio di Gattinara, con note, aggiunte e documenti*, ed. Carlo Bornate, in *Miscellanea di Storia Italiana*, vol. 48 (Turin: Fratelli Bocca Librai di S. M., 1915).
3. Francesco Guicciardini, *The History of Italy, Translated from the Italian of Francesco Guicciardini, by Austin Parke Goddard, Esq.; the Third Edition*, 10 vols, trans. A. Parke Goddard (London: Z. Stuart, 1763).
4. Headley viewed his conflict with the nobility in terms of state centralisation versus local interests. See Headley, 'The Conflict between Nobles and Magistrates in Franche-Comté, 1508–1518', *Journal of Medieval and Renaissance Studies* 9:1 (1979), pp. 49–80. For general information about Gattinara's early life, see Boone, *Mercurino di Gattinara*, pp. 7–23.
5. Mercurino Gattinara, *Oratio Supplicatoria somnium interserens de novissima orbis monarchia, ac futuro Christianorum triumph, late enuncians, quibus mediis ad id perveniri possit*, British Library, MS 18008.
6. The historiography relating to Charles V is enormous, but a beginning exploration might include Karl Brandi, *The Emperor Charles V: The Growth and Destiny of a Man and of a World-Empire*, trans. C. V. Wedgewood (London: Jonathan Cape, 1954), which was the first modern biography to highlight the role of Gattinara and his vision of world monarchy. See also Willem Pieter Blockmans, *The Emperor Charles V: 1500–1558* (London: Arnold, 2002); H. G. Koenigsberger, *The Habsburgs and Europe, 1516–1660* (Ithaca, NY: Cornell University Press, 1971); Pierre Chaunu and Michèle Escamilla, *Charles Quint* (Paris: Fayard,

2000). The best description of the financial situation of his reign is Charles Tracy, *Charles V: Impressario of War* (Cambridge: Cambridge University Press, 2002).

7. On France as the real enemy of Charles V, see Tracy, *Charles V*, p. 311. On France as champion of liberty, see Franz Bosbach, *Monarchia Universalis. Storia di un concetto cardine della politica europea (secoli XVI–XVIII)* (Milan: Vita e Pensiero, 1998), p. 74.

8. Gattinara, *Oratio Supplicatoria*, fo. 7r. The translation is from Boone, *Mercurino di Gattinara*, p. 26.

9. Gattinara, *Oratio Supplicatoria*, fos. 22v, 93v. See Boone, 'Empire and Medieval Simulacrum: A Political Project of Mercurino di Gattinara, Grand Chancellor of Charles V', *Sixteenth Century Journal* 42 (2011), p. 1037 (pp. 1027–49).

10. Boone, 'Empire and Medieval Simulacrum', pp. 1041–2. The full text of the prophecy in Latin appears in Josep Perarnau I Espelt, 'El text primitiu del *De mysterio cymbalorum ecclesiae* d'Arnau de Vilanova', *Arxiu de Textos Catalans Antics* 7/8 (1988–9), p. 103 (pp. 7–169).

11. Rebecca Boone, 'From Piedmont to Tenochtitlan: Social Conflict and Mercurino di Gattinara's Imperial Policies in New Spain', in Matthew Vester (ed.), *Sabaudian Studies: Political Culture, Dynasty, & Territory 1400–1700* (Kirksville, MO: Truman State University Press, 2013), p. 80 (pp. 79–91).

12. Juan Dantisco to Sigismundo I, 25 February 1523, in J. Dantisco, *Españoles y polacos en la Corte de Carlos V. Cartas del embajador Juan Dantisco*, ed. A. Fontán and J. Axer (Madrid: Alianza Editorial, 1994), p. 153.

13. Boone, 'Empire and Medieval Simulacrum', p. 1044.

14. Hilarius Bartel (ed.), *Epitaphia epigrammata et elegiae aliquot illustrium virorum in funere Mercurini Cardinalis, marchionis Gattinariae, Caesaris Caroli Quini Augusti supreme cancellarii* (Antwerp: Ioan. Graphei, 1531). For more on Agrippa, see Charles Nauert, *Agrippa and the Crisis of Renaissance Thought* (Urbana: University of Illinois Press, 1965), pp. 230–50.

15. A classic introduction to the Hermetic tradition in the Renaissance is Frances Yates, *Giordano Bruno and the Hermetic Tradition* (Chicago: University of Chicago Press, 1964). See also Florian Ebeling, *The Secret History of Hermes Trismegistus: Hermeticism from Ancient to Modern Times*, trans. David Lorton (Ithaca, NY: Cornell University Press, 2007).

16. Gattinara, 'Autobiography', in Boone, *Mercurino di Gattinara*, p. 109.

17. Andrea Navagero to the Signory, Bayonne 1 June 1528. 'Venice: June 1528', in Rawdon Brown (ed.), *Calendar of State Papers Relating to English Affairs in the Archives of Venice.* Vol. 4, *1527–1533* (London: Her Majesty's Stationery Office, 1871), pp. 140–58, available at <http://www.british-history.ac.uk/cal-state-papers/venice/vol4/pp140-158> (last accessed 18 June 2015).

18. Fontán and Axer, *Españoles y polacos*, letter from Juan Dantisco to Queen Bona of Poland, 6 May 1527, Valladolid.

19. Dante Alighieri, *Monarchy*, ed. Prue Shaw (Cambridge: Cambridge University Press, 1995), p. 11 (I, iv, 2–3), p. 15 (I, v, 9–10).

20. Ibid. p. 105.

21. Ibid. pp. xxvii–xxviii.

22. Boone, *Mercurino di Gattinara*, p. 21.

23. Ibid. p. 77.

24. Anthony Pagden, *Lords of All the World: Ideologies of Empire in Spain, Britain and France c. 1500–c. 1800* (New Haven, CT: Yale University Press, 1995), p. 28.

25. Gattinara, 'Apologiae Madritae conventionis . . . refutatio', in Bornate, *Vite*, p. 436.

26. Headley, *Church, Empire and World*, p. 99; John M. Headley, 'Rhetoric and Reality: Messianic, Humanist, and Civilian Themes in the Imperial Ethos of Gattinara', in Marjorie

Reeves (ed.), *Prophetic Rome in the High Renaissance Period* (Oxford: Clarendon Press, 1992), p. 242.

27. Gattinara, *Oratio*, fo. 34r–v.

28. Carina Johnson, *Cultural Hierarchy in Sixteenth-Century Europe: The Ottomans and Mexicans* (Cambridge: Cambridge University Press, 2011), p. 75.

29. Federico Chabod, 'Carlo V nell'opera del Brandi', *Studi Germanici* 4 (1940), p. 5 (pp. 1–34).

30. Gattinara, *Oratio*, fo. 101r.

31. Marcel Bataillon, *Erasmo y España. Estudios sobre la historia spiritual del siglo xvi*, trans. Antonio Alatorre (Mexico City: Fondo de Cultura Económica, 1950), pp. 155–65.

32. James Hankins, *Plato in the Renaissance* (Leiden: Brill, 1991), pp. 15, 294. See also Roy Strong, *Art and Power: Renaissance Festivals, 1450–1650* (Berkeley: University of California Press, 1984); Frances Yates, *Astraea: The Imperial Theme in the Sixteenth Century* (London: Routledge & Kegan Paul, 1975).

33. Thomas Dandelet, *The Renaissance of Empire in Early Modern Europe* (Cambridge: Cambridge University Press, 2014), p. 4. Dandelet calls Headley's book on Gattinara 'an important chapter in the Imperial Renaissance in his own right' (p. 14).

34. Boone, *Mercurino di Gattinara*, p. 17; translated from Rivero, *Gattinara*, p. 83.

35. For a detailed analysis of the institutions of the Spanish government and Gattinara's efforts to consolidate, reform and rationalise them, see Headley, *The Emperor and His Chancellor*, pp. 20–39. For Francisco de los Cobos, see Hayward Keniston, *Francisco de los Cobos: Secretary of the Emperor Charles V* (Pittsburgh: University of Pittsburgh Press, 1958).

36. Headley, *The Emperor and his Chancellor*, pp. 27–9.

37. Rivero, *Gattinara*, p. 84. Charles continued to sign documents simply as 'Yo el Rey', or 'I the King'.

38. Rebecca Ard Boone, *War, Domination, and the Monarchy of France: Claude de Seyssel and the Language of Politics in the Renaissance* (Leiden: Brill, 2007). A jurist from Turin, Seyssel rose to the position of Master of Requests under Louis XII. He advised the king on matters relating to the French invasion of Italy and the occupation of Milan. He also translated numerous ancient histories into French, including Appian and Thucydides. Seyssel shared with Gattinara a similar career path in the service of a foreign court, an interest in scholarship, and a concern with administration and predatory conquest. However, Seyssel's assessment of social mobility in the French state gives his thought an originality lacking in the works of Gattinara.

39. Koenigsberger, *The Habsburgs and Europe*, p. 11.

40. Ferdinand, Philip I, Juana the Mad, Cardinal Cisneros, Ferdinand again, then Cisneros again. Stephen Haliczer, *The Comuneros of Castile: The Forging of a Revolution, 1475–1521* (Madison: University of Wisconsin Press, 1981), p. 151.

41. J. B. Owens, *'By My Absolute Royal Authority': Justice and the Castilian Commonwealth at the Beginning of the First Global Age* (Rochester, NY: University of Rochester Press, 2005), pp. 81–2.

42. Haliczer, *Comuneros*, pp. 204–5.

43. Sara Nalle, 'Revisiting El Encubierto: Navigating between Visions of Heaven and Hell on Earth', in K. Edwards (ed.), *Werewolves, Witches, and Wandering Spirits: Traditional Belief and Folklore in Early Modern Europe* (Kirksville, MO: Truman State University Press, 2002), pp. 77–92. See also Ricardo García Cárcel, *Las Germanías de Valencia* (Barcelona: Ediciones Peninsula, 1981).

44. Peter Martyr d'Anghiera, *De Orbe Novo: The Eight Decades of Peter Martyr d'Anghiera*, trans. F. Augustus MacNutt (New York: G. P. Putnum's Sons, 1912); Peter Martyr d'Anghiera, *Pedro Mártir de Anglería Epistolario*, ed. and trans. J. López de Toro (Madrid: Góngora, 1957).

45. Peter Martyr d'Anghiera to the Grand Chancellor and Luigi Marliano, 13 December 1519, in López de Toro, *Epistolario*, p. 376.

46. Gattinara, *Historia*, pp. 417–19.

47. Boone, *Mercurino di Gattinara*, pp. 94–5.

48. Boone, 'From Piedmont to Tenochtitlan', pp. 79–91. Luigi Avonto, *Mercurino Arborio di Gattinara e l'America: Documenti inediti per la storia delle Indie Nuove nell'archivio del Gran Cancelliere di Carlo V* (Vercelli: Biblioteca della Società Storica Vercellese, 1981).

49. Manuel Giménez Fernández, 'Fray Bartolomé de Las Casas: A Biographical Sketch', in Juan Friede and Benjamin Keen (eds), *Bartolomé de las Casas in History: Toward an Understanding of the Man and His Work* (DeKalb: Northern Illinois University Press, 1971), pp. 67–125.

50. Specifically, he sought permission to penetrate the land of Cumanà, in present-day Venezuela, with fifty men to establish a peaceful settlement of ten thousand Native Americans, which would be both a base for future exploration and a source of tribute for the Crown. He wanted a grant of 1,000 leagues of coastline for settlement, and he estimated the revenue of this settlement to be at least 15,000 ducats by the third year, and 60,000 ducats by the end of the decade (Avonto, *Mercurino di Gattinara e l'America*, p. 26). A printed copy of the text, with Gattinara's recommendations attached at the end, is in the Biblioteca Nacional de España. See also Bartolomé de las Casas, *Carta del señor don Fray Bartolomé de las Casas al illustre . . . señor don Mercurino Arborio de Gattinara . . .* (London: Charles Whittingham, 1854).

51. Bartolomé de Las Casas, *History of the Indies*, ed. and trans. André Collard (New York: Harper and Row, 1971), p. 264: '"Sir, if you saw people mistreat Our Lord Christ, laying hands on him, insulting and reviling him, would you not try to have him handed over to you, that you might love him, serve and cherish him, and be unto him all that a true Christian should be?" He answered that of course he would. "What if they refused to give Him to you graciously but instead sold Him to you, would you not buy Him?" He said he would undoubtedly. The clergyman then said, "Well, Sir, that is what I have done."'

52. Ibid. pp. 265–9.

53. 'La gran ciudad de Tenustitan', Biblioteca Reale Torino, MS Storia d'Italia, no. 75, pp. 279–86.

54. Avonto, *Mercurino di Gattinara e l'America*, p. 93.

55. Fontán and Axer, *Españoles y polacos*, p. 336.

56. Luigi Avonto, 'Documenti sulle Indie Nuove nell'archivio di Mercurino Arborio di Gattinara, Gran Cancelliere di Carlo V', in L. Avonto (ed) *Mercurino Arborio di Gattinara Gran Cancelliere di Carlo V 450° Anniversario della Morte 1530–1980, Atti del convegno di studi storici* (Vercelli: Associazione Culturale di Gattinara, 1980), pp. 257–61.

57. Gattinara, *Consigli del gran Cancelliere all'Imperator* (September 1525) in Bornate, *Vite*, p. 469: 'La resolucion de la jda este secreta : y que se hagan los dichos preparativos con otra color : que me parece se podria muy bien colorar : mostrando que su Md quiere hazer armada ponderosa : para embiar a reduzir a su verdadera obedientia la tierra discubierta par cortes y poner orden en ella por gozar de tantas riquezas commo hay en ella : que por ser discubierta l jda del almirante : y siendo sobravenidas otras nuevas ya publicadas que requieren : de dar prompta remedia a la malicia del dicho cortes : creheran todos que por ello se disponga la dicha armada de mar : y no por la jda de su md en jtalia : y de esta color podra saccarse : otro fructo : que poniendo en temor : los : parientes aliados y amigos de cortes : saldran ellos : a tales medios que sin embiar armada asseguren la venida del dicho cortes con mayor provecho de su md : y lo reduzgan a ser buen ministro y a contentarse de la razon.'

58. Huguette and Pierre Chaunu, *Seville et l'Átlantique, 1504–1650*, 12 vols (Paris: SEVPEN, 1955–60). See also Roger Schlesinger, *In the Wake of Columbus: The Impact of the New World on Europe, 1492–1650*, 2nd edn (Wheeling, IL: Harlan Davidson, 2007), p. 14.

59. Gattinara, 'Discorso del gran Cancelliere sull'indirizzo della politica estera di Carlo V', in Bornate, *Vite*, p. 500.

60. Joachim Whaley, *Germany and the Holy Roman Empire* (Oxford: Oxford University Press, 2012), vol. I, p. 171.

61. Gattinara, 'Discorso', pp. 502–3: 'Con clemencia y con perdon de las dichas penas: se podran assegurar y mas facilmente retirarse de los dichos errores; especialmente dando les camino con que rectamente se pueda determiner la verdad de la doctrina evangelica en la qual principalmente se funda la dicha secta: y con esta reduction: y con la submission arriba dicha de mas del sossiego: y remedio de la dicha secta: creesse poderse saccar algun buen soccorro de gente de cavallo y de pied: por juntarse con el dicho senor jnfante: a qualquiere cosa que los quiera emplear: sea por soccorrer hungaria o por passer adelante a soccorrer las cosas de jtalia: con color del beneficio public de la Christiandad: y esto podra ser un torcedor al papa por traherlo mas facilmente a la razon: temiendo que tal reduction y ajunctamento no sea causa de dar mas prissa a la convocacion del concilio que es la cosa que mas teme.'

62. Boone, *War, Domination, and the Monarchy of France*, p. 64.

63. See Daniel Crews, *Twilight of the Renaissance: The Life of Juan de Valdés* (Toronto: University of Toronto Press, 2008).

64. Alfonso de Valdés, *Pro Divo Carolo eius nominis quinto Romanorum Imperatore Invictissimo* (Mainz: Schoeffer, 1527), sigs. Av–Avii, cited in John Headley, *The Emperor and His Chancellor*, p. 100.

65. Alfonso de Valdés, *Dialogue of Lactancio and an Archdeacon*, ed. and trans. J. E. Longhurst and R. R. MacCurdy (Albuquerque, NM: University of New Mexico Press, 1952), p. 70.

66. Ibid. p. 95.

67. Boone, *Mercurino di Gattinara*, p. 124.

68. Gasparo Contarini to the Senate, 16 November 1525, in Eugenio Albèri, *Relazioni degli ambasciatori veneti al Senato* (Florence: Tipografia e Calcografia al insegna di Clio, 1840), ser. 1, vol. 2, p. 55. See also Daniele Santarelli, 'Itinerari di ambasciatori veneziani alla corte di Carlo V', *Medioevo Adriatico* 2 (2008), pp. 121–52.

69. Contarini to the Senate, 16 November 1525, p. 56.

70. Albèri, *Relazioni degli ambasciatori*, p. 59, cited in Headley, *The Emperor and His Chancellor*, p. 12.

71. Ludovico Canossa to Clement VII, undated, in Gabriel Chappuys, *Le Secrettaire*, ed. V. Mellinghoff-Bourgerie (Geneva: Droz, 2014), pp. 499–501.

72. Francesco Guicciardini, *Storia d'Italia*, ed. E. Mazzali, vol. 3 (Milan: Garzani, 1988), p. 1855.

73. Ibid. pp. 1855–6.

74. Ibid. pp. 1855–6, cited in Boone, *Mercurino di Gattinara*, p. 65.

75. Gasparo Contarini to the Signory of Venice, 14 March 1525, in 'Venice: March 1525', in Brown, *Calendar of State Papers Venice*. Vol. 3, 1520–1526, pp. 410–19, available at <http://www.british-history.ac.uk/cal-state-papers/venice/vol3/pp 410-419> (last accessed 24 June 2015).

76. Gasparo Contarini, Andrea Navagero and Lorenzo Priuli to the Signory, 15 July 1525, in Brown, *Calendar of State Papers Venice*. Vol. 3, 1520–1526, pp. 455–67.

77. Andrea Navagero to the Signory, 16 Febuary 1527, Valladolid, in Brown, *Calendar of State Papers Venice*. Vol. 4, 1527–1533, pp. 24–34, available at <http://www.british-history.ac.uk/cal-state-papers/venice/vol4/pp24-34> (last accessed 29 June 2015).

78. See J. Weiss, 'Unifying Themes in the Oeuvre of John M. Headley', *Religions* 3 (2012), pp. 1094–102.

79. Boone, *Mercurino di Gattinara*, p. 133.

80. Rivero, *Gattinara*, pp. 153–4.

CHAPTER 4

'This continuous writing': The Paper Chancellery of Bernhard Cles

Megan K. Williams

At the height of his political influence in 1531/2, Austrian Habsburg chancellor Bernhard Cles (1485–1539) commissioned artist Girolamo Romanino to paint his portrait in the newly constructed Audience Chamber of the Castello del Buonconsiglio in his prince-bishopric of Trent. The large lunette of Cles in his recently acquired scarlet cardinal's robes dominates the room's gold and black frescoes of the Habsburg dynasty he served: Austrian Archduke Ferdinand I speaking to his brother the Emperor Charles V, their father Philip the Fair and their grandfather Maximilian I.[1] As *Gesamtkunstwerk*, the chamber celebrated Cles' 'exceptional credit and authority' with both ruling Habsburg brothers. He was, in the words of a contemporary, 'not only Bishop of Trent but also a temporal prince, and councillor and Grand Chancellor of all Germany, [enjoying] the greatest esteem and credit among all'.[2] It is Cles' office as statesman, advisor to the young Ferdinand, and above all chancellor which Girolamo Romanino's *Portrait of Cardinal Bernhard Cles, 1531/32* particularly captures. Set in a shadowy bed-chamber, the portrait suggests Cles' perpetual vigilance over the interests of the Casa d'Austria. Grave and calm, and with a packet of unopened letters in his left hand, Cles dictates to a soberly clad secretary, over whose epistolary production he casts an appraising gaze.

Cles' biographers have highlighted his pivotal role as princely advisor during a critical decade in European history, from 1526 to 1539. Due to his frequent absences from court, however, they have questioned the degree to which Cles was engaged in chancellery affairs and foreign policy-making on a daily basis.[3] A rich and growing body of literature on court culture has emphasised how imperative it was for early modern courtiers to remain in close physical proximity to the prince, should they wish to retain favour, access and ultimately influence, authority or reward. Although often absent from court, Cles' influence with his sovereign did not wane, and he did not eschew political engagement. Nor did his absences necessarily entail political crises or administrative delay; in Cles' case, distance does not appear to have been Fernand Braudel's 'public enemy number one' of sixteenth-century statecraft.[4] Instead, as this chapter argues, Cles' protracted absences meant that his was a paper-borne foreign policy-making apparatus and a chancellorship exercised by correspondence.

Cles' ability to direct Austrian Habsburg foreign policy from a distance, via correspondence, was feasible for three reasons: his unrivalled influence with his prince; his position as head of the Privy Council, combined with his close oversight of a functioning chancellery staffed by competent and loyal secretaries; and above all, his access to the most basic material artefact of early modern diplomacy and foreign policy-making processes – the paper which supported the era's voluminous correspondence. Among the more fruitful insights to emerge from the recent rehabilitation of materiality in the social sciences and humanities is the impossibility of abstracting a text's significance from the material and physical circumstances that allow readers to approach and use that text. Yet paper has been too often overlooked in studies of early modern diplomacy, politics or administrative institutions. To paraphrase aptly named paperwork ethnologist Ben Kafka, historians have tended to look *through* paper, at how it can be used to reconstruct events or processes, but rarely *at* it, as a material medium and communications technology around which coherent historical practices developed.[5] Cles' chancellorship by correspondence offers an excellent illustration of how paper, as material medium, not only supported early modern diplomacy's new reporting functions and the era's foreign policy-making processes, but also shaped them.

Paper historians generally agree that paper production arrived in Europe via China and the Muslim Mediterranean in the late twelfth or early thirteenth century. By the end of the fourteenth century, there were about thirty papermills on the Italian peninsula. But although Italian paper was extensively exported, it was only in the second half of the fifteenth century that papermills came to be widespread across the European continent, including in the Habsburgs' patrimony. The number of mills mushroomed in the first decades of the sixteenth century. This growth has usually been attributed to the spread of printing, but in fact long predated printing: by the fifteenth century, southern German and Austrian chancelleries, counting-houses and urban administrations had become eager purchasers of paper products.

The diplomatic and political implications of paper's wider availability and cheaper cost after about 1460 cannot be ignored: by the late fifteenth and early sixteenth centuries, European chancelleries, their ministers, and the diplomats and princes with whom they corresponded operated in what Francesco Senatore has termed 'a world of paper'.[6] By 1530, for example, the Austrian Court Chancellery was consuming at least twice as much paper per week as its larger predecessor, the Imperial Court Chancellery, had consumed in the 1470s; while towards the end of Ferdinand's reign, in 1555, the Court Chancellery consumed at least four times as much paper as it had in 1530.[7] The chancellery's increasing demand for paper reflected the expansion of 'state business' in the first half of the sixteenth century, and also contributed to it. Over the same period, moreover, European diplomatic relations intensified. It is likely no coincidence that paper became more widely available at the same time that the gathering and reporting of strategic information became the crucial, if not the primary, tasks of ambassadors abroad. Paper opened new opportunities and methods for acquiring, accessing and transmitting information. Ministers and princes soon became voracious consumers of information which they could analyse, deploy or file away in their burgeoning chancery archives.[8] At the same time, paper also enabled new methods of assimilating, redacting, manipulating and preserving that information. By the 1520s and 1530s, therefore, reading papers and writing on paper had become the daily condition for chancellery secretaries, ministers and diplomats.

This was certainly the case for Cles. Contemporaries recalled that he was never without paper, writing utensils, and correspondence awaiting his signature.[9] Indeed, the titles of the chief archival fonds upon which the 'Clesian' historiography rests – the *Grosse Korrespondenz*, *Römische Correspondenz* or the *Corrispondenza Clesiana* – attest to the importance Cles attached to managing paper information flows in the exercise of his political authority and influence.[10] The fine, white, northern-Italian paper that Cles favoured even possessed a further, representational function. Watermarked with a cardinal's broad-brimmed, tasselled hat, or *galero*, it projected the marriage of Cles' ecclesiastical ambitions with the temporal foreign policy initiatives that were inked across it.[11] As Cles' self-representation as energetic correspondent, together with his voluminous surviving correspondence suggest, paper was the primary medium through which Cles sought to obtain, control and deploy political advice and strategic information in the formulation of Ferdinand's foreign policy. Paper precluded the need for his physical presence by allowing Cles to engage in politicking and policy-making from a distance, via correspondence.

ALTER ES MANUS PRINCIPIS: BERNARD CLES' UNRIVALLED INFLUENCE

A precondition for Cles' ability to direct Austrian Habsburg foreign policy via paper correspondence was the unrivalled influence and trust he enjoyed with his sovereign, Ferdinand I. Cles' contemporaries and his biographers have long acknowledged Ferdinand's high regard for his chief minister. In 1521/2, the twenty-year-old Ferdinand inherited an incomplete and ambiguous authority over a deeply indebted, politically and confessionally riven territorial conglomerate on the Ottoman frontier. Particularly in his early years, Ferdinand repeatedly demonstrated his dependence upon his *lieben frundt* and correspondent for advice and counsel. He apologised when he could not answer Cles' letters personally or read through all of Cles' advice at once.[12] Diplomats and observers remarked on Cles' pre-eminence among Ferdinand's councillors: as early as 1525 Venetian observer Gasparo Contarini described Cles as 'the leading councillor of this prince and much esteemed by him, and a person of integrity'.[13] Cles' influence with Ferdinand had not waned by 1534, when the Venetian ambassador noted that 'when Cles is at court, he is truly first in His Majesty's eyes, and all others cede him the floor'. Later that year, Ferdinand's *Hofmeister* Wilhelm von Roggendorf observed that Cles could not live without his king, nor his king without him.[14]

Cles' counterparts in the Imperial Chancellery, Mercurino Gattinara or Antoine Perrenot de Granvelle, fought their way to their positions past rivals and survived repeated court intrigues.[15] By contrast, Cles ascended to the office of *magnus cancellarius* in 1528 largely unchallenged, and he encountered few rivals during his decade-long tenure. Lacking rivals, his influence remained largely undisputed even in his frequent absences from court. His authority rested instead on his political dexterity and perceived integrity, prudence and extraordinary capacity for work,[16] as well as on the guarantee he represented to the Emperor Charles and to Charles's advisors that he would guide Charles's younger brother and deputy, Ferdinand, in policies loyal to the dynasty and to the Church. Cles thus had the blessing of both Habsburg brothers.[17] In the eyes of the Austrian estates, moreover, Cles was an acceptable advisor to the Spanish-born archduke on account of his Tyrolean birth and kinship networks.

Cles was born in the Tridentine Val de Non in 1485 into a noble family with a long history of service to the prince-bishops of Trent and the archdukes of Tyrol. The third of seven sons, he was early on destined for an ecclesiastical career. Following his parents' premature deaths, Cles' eldest brother sent him to Verona and then Bologna to study rhetoric, the humanities, and civil and canon law.[18] While at Bologna, Cles came into contact with a number of figures who would play significant roles in his later career, among them Emperor Maximilian's private secretary and close advisor Cardinal Matthäus Lang von Wellenburg,[19] as whose familiar he received early diplomatic training; the papal legate in Bologna Giovanni de' Medici (from 1513 Leo X); and the jurist Antonio Quetta, whom Cles later employed as his Tridentine chancellor. Cles' contemporaries adjudged him a talented and personable young man, with a particular penchant for assessing personalities, inspiring confidences and winning allies.[20]

A year after graduating from Bologna, in 1512, Cles began his ecclesiastical career as protonotary apostolic, canon and archdeacon in Trent. Within two years, thanks to his political skills and good connections, he had won election to the prince-bishopric of Trent. Cles much preferred his bishopric to the court. Trent, and after 1530 his cardinalate, provided him with a secure base of power and a 'refuge' or 'nest' (*nido*) from which he could direct policy by post, and to which he could always return.[21] This combination of a largely unrivalled position and ecclesiastical dignities furnished Cles space for manoeuvre and an apparent autonomy that many of his counterparts lacked.

As the newly elected prince-bishop of Trent, Cles soon demonstrated himself an invaluable – if typically absent – member of the Tyrolean Diet and imperial council. In the emperor's Venetian campaigns (1514–17) he played a key role in organising the defence of Verona and imperial northern Italy, in part by leveraging his extended familial connections among the local nobility and in part through his tactical, logistical and diplomatic skills.[22] Though Cles moved frequently between Verona, Trent and Emperor Maximilian I's court at Innsbruck, and though his organisational talents and initiatives were prized and trusted by Maximilian as well as by Maximilian's grandsons, he did not enjoy a prominent position at court in this period.[23] Cles remained largely aloof from the political intrigue and factional infighting between 'old' and 'new' advisors which followed Maximilian's death and persisted into the first years of Ferdinand's government.[24]

This reserve did not mean eschewing political engagement altogether. Nearly all news from northern Italy passed through Trent en route to Innsbruck, making Cles a vital link in Maximilian's informational networks and later those of the emperor's grandsons. Cles also enjoyed a close personal relationship with the gossipy court at nearby Mantua and a considerable correspondence with the Sforza chancellery at Milan, providing him with valuable access to strategic political information.[25] Cles could analyse this information in Trent from the comforts of his own, aptly named Buonconsiglio palace, rather than from the peripatetic and often poorly housed Austrian court. In particular, from at least 1515 Cles maintained a familiar and frequent, sometimes daily, correspondence with Maximilian's most experienced diplomat, Andrea de Burgo of Cremona (1467–1533).[26] Burgo kept Cles well apprised of the shifting political situation at court as well as of the news from his embassies in the Italian states, Spain, France, England, the Netherlands and Hungary.[27] Burgo's letters to Cles repeatedly reference Cles' correspondence with leading political figures at court, their interest in his advice and counsel, and his intimate knowledge of state business.

In recognition of his political talents, Cles was nominated to the interim government upon Maximilian's death in 1519. He built trust with both Habsburg brothers through his active role in ensuring Charles V's election and coronation in 1519/20, and in negotiating the secret accords by which Charles granted Ferdinand governance of the Habsburgs' Austrian and German patrimonies in 1521/2. By retaining good ties to both Habsburg brothers, by not allying himself too closely to any faction, and by maintaining a lively political correspondence with Burgo and with other well-informed court officials,[28] Cles positioned himself as a trusted and objective councillor.

Cles came to play a more prominent role at court only in late 1525 and early 1526, as Ferdinand's early advisors were sidelined in the aftermath of the Peasants' Revolt. The first to retreat was Maximilian's powerful advisor and Cles' former patron, Cardinal Lang. More dramatic was the fall of Ferdinand's *obrister secretari*, treasurer, advisor and much-hated Castilian favourite, Gabriel von Salamanca. In December 1525 the Lower Austrian Estates convened a General Diet to resolve the financial and political crises facing the Habsburg dynasty's Austrian patrimony, many of which they blamed on Salamanca's tenure of multiple court offices. Their gravamina concluded in demands for the far-reaching reform of Austrian administrative organs and in particular the chancellery, since, they concluded, 'a chancellery must be esteemed as the heart of a prince, and is as much'.[29] In the following year, Ferdinand reorganised the complex of chancelleries and councils under his jurisdiction. Salamanca was replaced in early 1526 as head of the Court Chancellery by the Lower Austrian nobleman Lienhart (III) von Harrach, and in the Privy Council by Cles.[30] With Harrach's death in December 1527 and the addition of the kingdoms of Hungary and Bohemia to Ferdinand's territorial conglomerate in the course of that year, Cles was granted the title *magnus cancellarius* in February 1528 – possibly in imitation of Charles V's Imperial Chancellery,[31] but equally likely to mark his status vis-à-vis the Hungarian and Bohemian chancellors who had joined Ferdinand's administration. The title signified Cles' central authority over all paperwork emanating under Ferdinand's name and seal. He held this position until resigning on 28 January 1539, a few short months before his death.

'THE HEART OF A PRINCE': THE LATIN EXPEDITION

If the chancellery constituted the prince's heart, then that heart was largely a paper one. The secretaries who served under Cles experienced his statecraft in the form of unrelenting paperwork and 'continuous writing', as his Latin Secretary Johannes May (Johannes Maius (1502–36)) complained in a January 1530 letter to the absent Cles. 'Since [diplomatic correspondence] concerns secrets', May wrote,

> Up til now I myself alone have personally extracted everything from the letters which Your Illustrious & Most Reverend Lordship sent to His Majesty, being without any sort of assistant, and I alone have read and disclosed [the letters] to His Majesty and I alone, at his bidding, have written many responses to Your Illustrious and Most Reverend Lordship and to [ambassadors abroad] [. . .] I wish I could free myself from this continuous writing . . .[32]

Letters such as May's not only detail chancellery processes, but also demonstrate the centrality of paper to Cles' chancellorship: it was through correspondence that Cles provided policy direction and counsel, and through correspondence that secretaries like May kept Cles closely apprised of their actions in framing and communicating that policy. Cles' chancellorship by correspondence required loyal, competent secretaries like May to mediate his advice and promote his policies to Ferdinand.

Cles' oversight of a functioning, loyal chancellery, and his simultaneous position as head of the Privy Council, were also key factors enabling Cles to direct foreign policy from afar, via correspondence. The administrative reorganisation of 1526–8 has often been portrayed as Cles' handiwork.[33] As Austrian historian Gerhard Rill has argued, however, this reorganisation largely followed the administrative system instituted by Ferdinand's grandfather Maximilian after 1502, and showed, at least for the chancellery organs, substantial continuities in personnel and institutional practices.[34] The most visible innovation was the formal constitution of a separate Latin section, or Expedition, within the chancellery. This development, in essence, brought Maximilian's personal secretariat largely under the control of the chancellor, both physically and in terms of jurisdiction.[35] From at least 1526, therefore, the Latin Secretary was housed in the same busy chamber as the Court Chancellery's registrators, engrossers and scribes, although the Latin Secretary and his two engrossers enjoyed their own writing desk, budget and chancellery archives.[36] He was charged with handling all political and diplomatic correspondence in Latin or Italian not pertaining to the Empire's German lands. The Latin Expedition was consequently of particular importance to Cles, since it was chiefly through its correspondence that Cles established and maintained Ferdinand's diplomatic networks, and determined and represented his foreign policy.

The extensive literature on Austrian Habsburg administrative history published since the late nineteenth century, often dependent upon prescriptive chancellery ordinances and tending towards structural description rather than functional analysis, portrayed Ferdinand's chancellery as a secretarial organ (*Schreiborgan*) rather than as an active locus for policy-making.[37] Additionally, the most thorough studies of Ferdinand's chancelleries begin only with the establishment of his Imperial Chancellery in 1559, by which time the Latin Expedition's importance had declined substantially. Yet as Gerhard Rill's assiduous delving into archived political correspondence and court networks has shown for the earliest years of Ferdinand's reign up to 1526, the early sixteenth-century Austrian Habsburg Court Chancellery was far from a mere bureaucratic *Schreiborgan*; rather, it was an integral part of the prince's personal household (*Hofstaat*) and of his policy-making and governing apparatus.[38] Cles won the loyalty of his Latin Expedition secretaries through the influence he wielded over Ferdinand's distribution of princely and personal patronage within the *Hofstaat* and across his domains. Above all, Cles' leadership of chancellery and Privy Council ensured close ties between the chancellery's processing of paper and policy-making.

Because the Austrian Habsburg Latin Expedition secretaries' status in the Court Chancellery ordinances or royal household ranks was modest, they have remained inconsequential, often nameless figures in the historiography. Yet the Latin Expedition secretaries' roles in enabling Cles to direct Ferdinand's political decision-making were anything but modest. John Headley has labelled the sixteenth century 'an age of secretaries'.[39] With the proliferation of political correspondence among European rulers, he has argued, secretaries came to play leading roles in government and administration – not only in redacting the business of government but also as diplomats and councillors. This was certainly the case with the secretaries of the Latin Expedition, who despite their lowly status enjoyed privileged access to the king's person, to his secrets and to his papers.

Two additional factors enhanced the roles of Cles' Latin Secretaries in the 1520s and 1530s: Cles' pan-European campaign to affirm and defend Ferdinand's claims to the kingdoms of Bohemia and especially Hungary dramatically expanded their competencies; and, due to Cles' frequent absences, the secretaries actively participated in the court or privy councils where political decision-making occurred. The Austrian Habsburg Privy Council, of which Cles was from 1528 president, was tasked in Ferdinand's 1527 *Hofstaatsordnung* with meeting daily in the king's presence to deal with 'all sorts of the most important, weighty, and secret matters and threats [. . .] such as: how to conduct affairs with foreign potentates, [and] how foreign intrigues can be avoided'.[40] As we shall see, in Cles' absence it was typically Latin Secretary Johannes May who drafted and proposed the Privy Council agenda, read aloud and exhibited incoming diplomatic dispatches or extracted portions thereof, drafted minutes of responses, and maintained documentation or protocols of the council's proceedings.

Archival records allow us to reconstruct the backgrounds, training and careers of Cles' Latin Secretaries in ways that highlight the high degree of trust both Cles and Ferdinand reposed in them, and the substantial licence and political agency Cles' chancellorship by correspondence granted them in framing and transmitting Ferdinand's foreign policy decision-making. Johannes May was one of two individuals who filled the post of Latin Secretary under Cles; his successor was the less well-documented Adam Karl (Adamus Carolus; d. c. 1547). May served during the heyday of Cles' pan-European diplomacy. Karl's tenure from mid-1536 coincided with Cles' declining influence abroad and the reduced scope of his European poli-tics.[41] Both were considered highly competent secretaries by their contemporaries. Perhaps most important to Cles, however, was their personal and professional invest-ment in his policy-making success. Having been brought under Cles' oversight in the 1526–8 administrative reorganisation, the status of the Latin secretariat rose as the scope of Cles' diplomacy and foreign politicking expanded in the later 1520s and early 1530s, and declined as it diminished.

Johannes May's path to the Latin Expedition was shaped by personal and patriotic connections. He was raised, together with the older half-brother who preceded him as Latin Secretary, Jacob Spiegel (c. 1483–c. 1547),[42] in the Alsatian city of Sélestat (Schlettstadt) in a bracing humanist climate. Though from modest circumstances, their mother was the younger sister of humanist publicist, pedagogue and poet Jacob Wimpfeling. Wimpfeling, himself a student of Imperial Chancellor Konrad Stürtzel, promoted his nephews' educations at Sélestat's renowned grammar school and at the universities of Heidelburg and Freiburg. Wimpfeling also ensured their connec-tions with the important Alsatian humanist circles inhabited by Rudolf Agricola and Beatus Rhenanus.

In 1504, imperial treasurer Jacob Villinger, a former classmate of Spiegel's who also came from Sélestat's petit-bourgeoisie, recommended Spiegel to Maximilian's Imperial Chancellor Matthäus Lang. Spiegel was soon named Latin scribe in the Imperial Chancellery, under the leadership of elegant Latin stylist Pietro Bonomo, bishop of Trieste.[43] Spiegel's colleagues quickly came to appreciate his humanist connections and ability to give outgoing political correspondence 'colour and much honey'.[44] Spiegel soon rose to become Emperor Maximilian's personal secretary. With Maximilian's death in 1519, however, Spiegel retired to Sélestat in penury. To pay his debts and regain his status, he began a campaign of dedicating humanist works to prominent figures in the new administration. By 1520, he had succeeded in returning to Charles V's chancellery, this time bringing May in tow as amanu-ensis. In August 1523, in part thanks to a recommendation from Erasmus, Spiegel and May transitioned to the service of Charles's brother Ferdinand, under the pay and direction of Salamanca.[45] Following Salamanca's fall in early 1526, Spiegel, as Salamanca's 'closest colleague', found it expedient to withdraw again to Sélestat. He left his position, and the fruits of a 1525 campaign to ingratiate himself with Cles, the new chief figure at court, to his brother May.[46] Well trained by Spiegel,[47] May quickly made himself indispensable to Cles and to Ferdinand. May, Ferdinand noted in a 1531 extraordinary grant, was 'commended to us not via any second-hand testimony but through daily experience'.[48] Indeed, the secretary was kept busy at all hours, 'administering our Latin Chancellery and our secret, salient affairs at our court, sparing neither body nor any toil or effort', as Ferdinand phrased it in another, 1535 pension grant.[49]

Soon after May took over the Latin Expedition, its competencies expanded dra-matically. Following the intestate death of his brother-in-law at the Battle of Mohács in August 1526, Ferdinand laid claim to the Bohemian and Hungarian Crowns. Ferdinand's struggle to obtain the Hungarian throne entailed a diplomatic and propa-ganda campaign on two fronts: the first to press his royal claims over those of his

Hungarian rival, former Transylvanian voivoda János Szapolyai; and the second to obtain political, military and especially financial aid in repelling Ottoman offensives. By 1527, Szapolyai had succeeded in obtaining subsidies and political support from France, England, the Ottomans and Venice.[50] Moreover, in the years after Mohács German princes wary of overweening Habsburg predominance within the Empire repeatedly withheld or delayed the *Türkenhilfe* as a political and confessional bargaining chip.[51] Thus both aspects of Ferdinand's diplomatic and propaganda campaign overlapped with the Habsburg dynasty's broader political and military rivalries with Francis I of France, Henry VIII of England, the papacy and Ottoman sultan Süleyman. As a result, from 1526 Cles engaged Ferdinand in a pan-European diplomacy in which the Latin Chancellery played a central, coordinating role.

Cles' diplomatic initiatives in defence of Ferdinand's new titles and claims brought with them a substantial increase in diplomatic correspondence and paperwork, much of which fell upon the twenty-four-year-old May's shoulders. Since most Hungarian magnates (including the kingdom's regents) as well as their Ottoman foes corresponded chiefly in Latin or Italian, May became a crucial intermediary between Buda, Bratislava, Constantinople and Linz during the subsequent decade's succession conflict and repeated Ottoman invasions. Most of the incoming correspondence now found in the Vienna Haus-, Hof- und Staatarchiv's *Ungarische Akten* or *Turcica* bears May's annotation, and nearly all drafts of outgoing correspondence in the same fonds are in his small, neat script. May not only drafted but frequently also engrossed outgoing correspondence. Placed opposite that of Cles, his signature authenticates much of Ferdinand's Latin correspondence with foreign potentates and princes, and it is his Latin which communicated Cles' policies and Ferdinand's claims abroad. The redaction and production of well-written and well-ordered diplomatic papers played an important representational role in upholding Ferdinand's honour and governing authority among foreign diplomats and statesmen; its implications of orderly government and wise council could, as Francesco Senatore has suggested, almost be considered a fundamental pillar of the state.[52] In May's absence or illness diplomatic business and foreign policy-making at the court was often delayed – indicating May's centrality to these affairs.[53]

Following the exhausting whirlwind of paperwork related to the 1527–8 Hungarian campaigns and 1529 Ottoman invasion, May began to complain of weakness, tumours and other physical ailments. May concluded a January 1530 letter:

> I have myself written a long letter in cipher to [ambassador] Burgo, which has left me exhausted, sapped of energy, and weak, so that if I don't write more on those matters as Your Illustrious and Reverend Lordship desires, you will graciously excuse me.[54]

A few days later, having in one day received five letters from Cles (dated 17, 18, 19, 21 and 27 January), May again excused himself for responding 'as time and circumstance permits me' – which proved to be three letters within three days.[55] May's frequent correspondence was a valuable source of information for Cles about affairs at court, as his contemporaries acknowledged.[56] His surviving letters also provide the historian with an intimate view of how Cles' almost daily oversight of and close cooperation with the Latin Expedition was largely conducted via paper.

May was compensated for his 'continuous writing' – although never adequately, in his eyes[57] – with a series of benefices, annuities and expectancies. Cles played an important intercessionary role in helping May obtain these financial rewards, for which May repeatedly expressed his gratitude.[58] Neither May nor his successor came from affluent families, and their meagre, frequently delayed salaries were often insufficient to cover their living costs. The secretaries' debts particularly mounted when the court was on progress or when prices skyrocketed in the aftermath of political and military crises, such as the 1529 Ottoman siege of Vienna. By wielding his influence with the king and other court officials to assist his secretaries, Cles ensured their loyalty in the framing and execution of his policy initiatives, and their willingness to keep him promptly and fully informed of how these were received and discussed at court.

May's last, shaky signature on outgoing correspondence dates from April 1536.[59] In mid-July he died, leaving an annual pension to the nurse who had tended him for several years 'so that [he] could that much better continue in [Ferdinand's] service and important affairs'.[60] His brother erected a marble sepulchre in his honour in Hall (Tyrol), and more modest epitaphs in Sélestat and under the heading 'snatched away' (rapi) in the 1538 juridical lexicon he dedicated to May's successor.[61]

From 1533, May had been assisted in the Latin Expedition by Adam Karl. We know little about Karl's background beyond that he claimed to be 'of the German nation', came from a family ennobled under Emperor Frederick III, and had studied humanist letters under Ferdinand's court historian and royal preceptor Caspar Ursinus Velius, probably at Leipzig or Vienna.[62] Our best clue to Karl's career is the narratio to the 1534 patent which confirmed and augmented his noble status. There he is described as having served 'for many years first in our regimental chancellery in our province of Upper Austria in Innsbruck, then in Venice and later in Rome for our ambassadors in various and secret of our affairs and arduous negotiations, and now in our court . . .'.[63] Indeed, Karl's elegant hand can be detected in the dispatches of Ferdinand's ambassador at Venice from the summer of 1527.[64]

In early 1531, Cles recruited and dispatched Karl to Ferdinand's ambassador Andrea de Burgo in Rome, in whose service he remained until January 1533. Although Karl had been offered a higher salary elsewhere, Cles' powerful position as both Privy Council president and chancellor, and the patronage opportunities and honours Cles could offer him, proved decisive in Karl's decision to join Burgo.[65] Burgo was somewhat chagrined to receive so ambitious and well trained a young man: 'As Your Worshipful Lordship knows, I asked solely for a faithful subject of the King's who knows how to write in cipher, not for one who wishes to become royal secretary, as he deserves.'[66] Burgo urged Cles to have the king name Karl royal secretary so that Karl, who knew 'many secrets' and penned most of Burgo's correspondence, would not be tempted to join another prince's better-paid service. Cles' subsequent successful intercession with Ferdinand on Karl's behalf ensured that Karl remained indebted to Cles, and that the secretary continued to serve as Cles' eyes and ears in Rome.[67] Moreover, since Burgo's own hand was an atrocious scrawl in a 'bar-

baric' Latin, Karl acted as Burgo's chief communicator.[68] Karl's elegant script and his familiarity with diplomatic rhetorical conventions made Burgo's news, observations and advice usable and useful to the ambassador's correspondents.

Burgo died at Bologna in the first days of January 1533, and Karl returned to the Latin Expedition under Johannes May, now as a royal secretary. As May sickened, Karl took over many of May's duties. Despite his indebtedness to Cles, Karl's relationship with the chancellor was more formal than May's had been. Moreover, Cles' declining influence with the emperor during Karl's tenure meant that the Latin Expedition's ability to further Ferdinand's claims and secure political and financial support abroad was accordingly diminished. By 1533, Cles' relations with the emperor had begun to cool after a series of actions by Charles – including Charles's prematurely terminated 1532 Ottoman campaign, his undercutting of Ferdinand's dynastic ambitions in the duchy of Württemberg in 1534, his failure to support Cles' papal bid in the same year, and his interference in Ferdinand's financial housekeeping after that date – showed that Charles's policy concerns could not be easily harmonised with those of his younger brother.[69] Cles experienced these diplomatic disappointments as personal failures. In the same period, Ferdinand's near break with the papacy over Württemberg, and his conciliatory approach to Lutheranism in the wake of the territory's loss, meant that Cles began to perceive his dual roles as high priest of church and state as increasingly irreconcilable.[70] Likewise, after years of exhausting civil warfare and repeated Ottoman campaigns in Hungary, it had become abundantly clear that an accord between Ferdinand and Szapolyai was necessary to preserve peace not only in Hungary but also in Italy and Germany, where Szapolyai had many supporters. The possibility of an accord meant a winding down of Cles' broader European campaign to legitimate and realise Ferdinand's Hungarian claims. By 1534, Cles' health was also deteriorating, with what his doctors diagnosed as syphilis; in any event, his biographers perceive a growing pessimism in this period.[71] In the summer of 1534 matters came to a head as Cles sought permission to leave his court offices and retreat, apparently for good, to his bishopric in Trent.

Although Cles returned to court following the election of Pope Paul III, his relations with the emperor suffered a further blow during negotiations at Naples in early 1536, when Charles declined to endow Ferdinand with the duchy of Milan or offer Ferdinand his unconditional backing in the Hungarian peace talks.[72] In Cles' eyes, Charles's concessions to Szapolyai appeared as a rebuke to Ferdinand and to the chief architects of Ferdinand's Hungarian policy: they undermined Ferdinand's bargaining position in the ongoing negotiations. At Naples, moreover, Charles received Cles only twice. For the cardinal, who was used to politicking face-to-face at the highest levels, having his contact with the emperor filtered through Imperial Chancellor Granvelle was a humiliating rejection.[73] Cles saw these reverses as a demotion of Ferdinand's interests in the emperor's political programme, and as a further sign of his own diminishing diplomatic sway. Since his authority at the Austrian court had been largely predicated on his ability to mediate between the Habsburg brothers (and in particular his ability to obtain from Charles a suitable settlement for Ferdinand and for Ferdinand's now ten-year-old heir), Cles found his influence among Ferdinand's domestic advisors waning, too. Imperial political and confessional priorities were increasingly unpopular in the Austrian lands. Even the nephew whose political career Cles had most avidly promoted, Leonhard von Fels (d. 1545), had joined an ascendant court clique openly critical of the emperor.[74] Upon his return from Naples, therefore, Cles focused his remaining energy on ecclesiastical affairs: namely, the reform of his diocese and his long-standing dream of convening a church council. (His advocacy and efforts contributed to the convening of the Council of Trent in 1545.)

Cles' diminishing influence abroad reduced the scope and status of Latin Expedition business. His increasingly uncompromising views on confessional issues at home also may have contributed to a more distant relationship with his new Latin Secretary.[75] By 1539, when Cles resigned his political offices, Karl had already begun a campaign of dedicating his humanist compilations to prominently placed potential (Lutheran) patrons at the Austrian court.[76] Among Cles' last acts as chancellor and statesman, on 29 January 1539, was to collect, deposit in the Latin chancellery registry, and inventory, together with Karl, the paper heritage of his pan-European diplomatic and policy endeavours.[77]

FOREIGN POLICY-MAKING BY POST?

Incomplete as it is, the 1539 Latin Expedition inventory provides a striking sense of how important written, paper-borne correspondence had become to the business of foreign policy-making by the early sixteenth century. Through facilitating new means of collating, transmitting, manipulating and framing information, paper played a crucial role in enabling statesmen such as Cles to engage in political decision-making from a distance. Central to Cles' diplomatic and foreign policy initiatives at the height of his influence between 1526 and 1533 was his close correspondence with Andrea de Burgo, Ferdinand's dextrous, trustworthy and experienced *orator* at Europe's premier listening post and centre of information exchange, the Roman curia. Following the paper trail of their correspondence offers considerable insight into how Cles effected a paper-based foreign policy.

By the time Burgo arrived at Rome in 1529, he had over thirty years of diplomatic experience in Milanese, Imperial and Austrian service. Burgo was consequently one of the first generations of diplomats to engage in what diplomatic historian Garrett Mattingly labelled 'the new institution of permanent diplomacy' – the relatively novel practice by which princes established networks of resident ambassadors who were tasked with gathering politically relevant or strategic information which they dispatched in written reports from their host courts every few days.[78] Ferdinand expected Burgo to keep him 'continually apprised of the news in Rome'.[79] Indeed, Burgo dispatched his missives, typically comprising two or three closely written bifolios and as many postscripts, on average every two to four days.

In January 1530, for example, despite an attack of gout which impeded him from writing *manu propria*,[80] Burgo dispatched letters to Ferdinand on 1, 4 (three letters), 6/8, 14 (two letters, the second with postscripts of the 15th and 16th), 27, 28/29 and 30 (two letters) January. His abundant postscripts, penned while waiting for the departure of the postal courier, provided his correspondents with the most up-to-date news. In the same packets, Burgo also dispatched more informal letters to Cles on 1, 7, 8, 12/13, 17/20 and 30 January. While Burgo's letters to Ferdinand focused chiefly on his negotiations with the pope and emperor at Bologna, his dispatches to Cles included news, advice and also, '[t]o bother [Ferdinand] less', extended complaints about his poor health and dire financial straits.[81] This prodigious epistolary production highlights the degree to which the daily life of Burgo's embassy revolved around paper. Yet not all that paper was usable for Cles' political purposes. Tracing the ways in which Cles and his secretaries received, filtered information from and responded to Burgo's prolific and prolix dispatches, it becomes clear just how central paper was to the shaping and communicating of Ferdinand's foreign policy priorities.

Burgo posted his dispatches, folded into eighths and addressed with varying levels of urgency, via acquaintances and servants travelling to Trent, via the 'ordinary' postal system run by the Taxis family through Bologna, Mantua, Trent and Innsbruck, or, when speed was of the essence, via imperial 'extraordinary' couriers riding the same route. In 1530–1, the post in Italy constituted a 'great expense'.[82] Under Cles' direction, Ferdinand invested heavily, if unsystematically, in expanding and extending postal networks and improving roads to meet the growing need for effective political communications in managing his new territories and pursuing his pan-European diplomacy. As court postmaster Anton von Taxis remarked in 1526, 'your princely illustriousness' business grows from day to day, and has become much more diverse and is increasingly critical to all sorts of affairs of far-reaching and necessary import for your lands and subjects'.[83] The same era which saw paper become pervasive and diplomacy intensify also saw the dramatic expansion of the postal infrastructure which carried diplomats' and ministers' paper productions.[84]

When Cles was at court, Burgo's dispatches for Ferdinand were directed to be delivered into Cles' hands, to ensure their integrity and 'since [they] contain secrets'.[85] When Cles was in his bishopric of Trent, however, Burgo sent his letters for Ferdinand via Trent, as open letters that Cles could peruse, analyse, (re-)seal, and forward together with a dictated billet of advice (*meditatio*) on how to act or respond to the letter.[86] As a result, Burgo's letters often took a circuitous route to their primary addressee, passing through an additional chancellery and under at least two additional pairs of eyes and hands along the way. On 12 January 1530, for example, Cles received Burgo's letters of the 8th, addressed to both himself and to the king, 'which [latter] we diligently perused and considered, since it concerns affairs of the greatest moment'.[87] Cles responded immediately to Burgo with policy advice, in their shared Italian tongue.[88] The chancellor then composed letters to Ferdinand *pro consilio* outlining the issues Burgo had raised in his dispatches, recommending strategy or a line of action, and detailing the advice he had given Burgo. He added these to Burgo's letters and forwarded the now plump packet by post to Secretary May.[89] Thus when Cles' packet arrived in Budweis (České Budějovice) a week later, it contained not only Burgo's 29 December, 4 and 6/8 January dispatches, but also Cles' advices of 6, 7, 8 and 10 January. The packet materialised Cles' paper-based foreign policy-making by correspondence.

Once Cles' packet arrived in Budweis, the postmaster brought it to the Court

Chancellery. In Cles' absence, diplomatic dispatches were designated for delivery directly into the hands of Latin Secretary May, and were to be opened solely by him. Upon receipt of the packet, May sorted its contents, deciphered Burgo's coded dispatches and gave his letters their second close reading.[90] Whereas Cles had read the letters in order to prepare policy, May's reading was designed to help him communicate that policy and its urgency in Cles' absence. Paired with the 'continuous writing' of which May had complained only a few days earlier, May's reading left indexing marks such as underlining and sidebars as well as marginal rubricisation (such as 'quo. tractan. p. Ces. in dieta', 'Anglus sup. diuortio' and 'Tractatg Way[da] Turcg'). These marks assimilated, selected and highlighted certain items for discussion in the Privy Council, while dismissing others ('nihil'). May's annotations made Burgo's densely written dispatches more amenable to rapid scanning or repeat consultation, but also constituted an initial judgement about what topics were worthy of discussion, under what rubrics. Even as Cles' advisory letters highlighted particular priorities, objectives and strategies, this process nonetheless allowed May to exercise his discrimination, operational experience and political prudence. Paper (and pen) thus permitted May to redact and reframe Burgo's dispatches so that they better conformed to what he and Cles perceived as germane to Ferdinand's foreign policy-making priorities.

Since he adjudged Burgo's dispatches to concern issues 'of such importance that it won't do to give a superficial response, but rather a wholesome and solid and in all cases apt one', May presented the letters to Ferdinand promptly, and *in toto* rather than in part.[91] 'I read Burgo's three letters, of 29 December and the 4th and 6th of the present month, not once but more than thrice, word for word, to the king', he reported to Cles on 19 January. Certain aspects, such as Burgo's outstanding diets or a precedence conflict with the English ambassador, could be dealt with at once, in accordance with Cles' advice.[92] On more complicated and weighty matters, however, such as the precondition of Charles's coronation for Ferdinand's election as King of the Romans, or the pressing Ottoman threat to his Hungarian lands, Ferdinand wished to obtain further counsel from Cles before committing policy decisions to paper. In these cases, the king urged Cles to provide him 'immediately' with his opinion, point for point, about how he should respond and what threats or opportunities particular responses might entail.[93]

'Because [Burgo's] one letter is substantial and the other very detailed', and perhaps because May was visibly tired of rereading them to the king, Ferdinand directed the secretary to provide extracts or compose epitomes of Burgo's letters. May often drew up such extracts of diplomatic dispatches to facilitate decision-making.[94] His paper extracts collated notes on each of the diverse issues in Burgo's dispatches on one folio, leaving a wide margin for commentary and emendation. The extracts thus enhanced busy readers' ability to process the dispatches and to situate their content in a broader context. When annotated by May during Privy Council sessions, the extracts served as a sort of 'track-changes' record of foreign policy-making in action.

Even as Cles granted secretaries such as May wide discrimination in presenting, framing and recording Ferdinand's day-to-day foreign policy-making, he continued to exercise a powerful influence over policy through his paper-borne advice and oversight. May's reports to Cles and Cles' responses formed a written dialogue between secretary, minister and prince. As May noted in a detailed report to Cles on his receipt and processing of Cles' 12 January packet, the king had directed him to send the extract to Cles; Cles was to return it to May together with his advice, as he had done with Burgo's previous packet of letters.[95] Cles responded with additional counsel on 14, 18, 20 and 21 January.[96] On 29 January, May was finally able to send off a 'rather long and important', mostly ciphered response to Burgo, together with the king's 'barely legible and not much shorter' autograph letter to the emperor, as he described it to Cles.[97] The densely written fifteen-folio response involved specific policy points to raise with emperor and pope. Among other things, Burgo was to press the emperor on Ferdinand's imperial lieutenancy; to seek papal subsidies for the defence of the Slavonian borders; and to warn of the imminent Ottoman threat 'which we expect in our patrimonial lands any day', of Szapolyai's alleged ties to Lutherans in the Empire, and of Lutheran intrigues with France and England. Burgo received the letters on 5 February. After having them deciphered, he immediately presented the letters to the emperor, and successfully persuaded the pope to adopt Cles' policy recommendations regarding the Hungarian situation.[98] May's detailed reports of his activities were a key component in Cles' chancellorship by correspondence, but came at a high cost in paper, ink, post and physical exertion. As May complained to Cles, 'I end up writing to the very extremity of my being.'[99]

A CHANCELLORSHIP BY CORRESPONDENCE

May's pen and paper materialise the three key factors which made Cles' chancellorship by correspondence possible: the unrivalled trust and authority Cles enjoyed with Ferdinand; his oversight of a functioning Latin Expedition staffed by competent, loyal secretaries who were invested in the success of his policies; and above all, the availability of paper. With pen and paper at his service, Cles was able to direct Ferdinand's foreign policy and to engage in the policy-making process from a distance.

In the court of the paper prince, a courtier's physical proximity to the prince became less imperative. Far from being Braudel's 'public enemy number one', distance had its advantages. When Burgo's negotiations in Bologna over the emperor's progress through his brother's lands into Germany stalled for lack of policy direction, for example, Cles could attribute the problems to May's dilatoriness or illness; distance added a layer of executive deniability and diffused responsibility.[100] As Ferdinand's expressions of gratitude suggest, distance also enhanced the seeming value of Cles' advice. The incessant stream of Cles' plump packets and the sheaves of closely written paper they contained made physically and 'abundantly manifest to us how much zeal and good work you have expended in all our affairs'.[101] Cles' billets of advice materialised his policy-making efforts and fixed his advice to the page, making it available for repeated consultation and reflection; May could read, and reread, his letters to Ferdinand as often as necessary. Moreover distance, and the formality of the written form, lent Cles' advice that air of dispassionate impartiality which Ferdinand particularly prized in his chancellor: 'There is no one who deals with my affairs without that mixture of passions, hate or love or self-interest', he claimed, 'but Your Lordship.'[102]

Paper transformed chancellors such as Cles and chancellery secretaries such as May from amanuenses to privy councillors. Through the early modern secretary's access to and control over diplomatic correspondence, and particularly through his reframing, presentation and preservation of that correspondence, the secretary came to play a fundamental, powerful, but often neglected role in early modern foreign policy decision-making.[103] In the Spanish Habsburg realms, secretaries were not only considered as the metaphorical necks connecting the body of the state to the kingly head, but were also described as the stomach of the state,[104] digesting paper and paper-borne knowledge. This process of digestion altered power relations in ways that were not always legible in prescriptive ordinances. May's illnesses delayed decision-making, just as the regular arrival and departure of the postriders bearing Cles' policy memoranda between Trent and Innsbruck or Vienna set its beat. When power and knowledge are inscribed on paper, media ethnologist Ben Kafka has argued in his study of administrative writing during the French Revolution, they inevitably change their speed and shape: paperwork, he suggests, and those professionals who manipulate paperwork, can accelerate or decelerate power, syncopate its rhythms, or disrupt its cycles. As such paper becomes intensely political, negotiated and contested by various networks of people and other, especially paper, artefacts it generates as it circulates.[105] The role of secretary or chancellor was not merely discursive, therefore, but also deeply material: they wielded power through their manipulation of paper.

The late medieval expansion of European paper production and chancellery consumption enabled an extended infrastructure of collegial oversight, communications and information processing which could not help but shape sixteenth-century dynastic and inter-state relations. 'Earlier the prince was advised by councillors', preached the Portuguese Jesuit Antônio Vieira (1608–97); 'today he is wrapped up in paper.'[106] By the end of the sixteenth century, Philip II – suspicious of his ministers' motives, and determined to preserve his decision-making prerogative – had become a proverbial 'prince of paper(work)' (*el rey papelero*): he based his decisions on thick dossiers of papers, studies and reports. Philip, as Venetian ambassador Francesco Morosini observed in 1581, preferred written to oral petitions, as they gave him more time to prepare a well-considered response; and he often chose to present himself at audiences with a sheaf of papers in hand, suggesting his detailed background knowledge of the matter under discussion – even if the papers he shuffled during the audience were in fact irrelevant.[107]

As Paula Fichtner has pointed out, however, such a designation could not yet apply to Ferdinand, who was more willing to delegate the paper aspects of the decision-making process to well-chosen ministers such as Cles.[108] As we have seen, the papers presented in Ferdinand's councils were accompanied by memoranda and advices from Cles and were heavily marked up by secretaries like May – but they were not yet systematically linked to other papers to form files. The 1539 inventory of the Latin Expedition Archives is a rather haphazard listing of individual letters, petitions and reports; few constitute chronological, thematic or geographical dossiers. 'A single Turkish-language letter to the King of the Romans' Majesty, without translation; Item, another in the Turkish language' is more typical of this inventory than entries such as 'All sorts of writings related to the current Election as King of the Romans, 1533'.[109] This does not diminish the role of paper in Ferdinand's foreign policy decision-making, however. Ferdinand, who relied on a close paper-borne correspondence with Cles in his policy and decision-making, was rightly a 'prince of paper' – but unlike his nephew Philip II, whose decision-making rested on paper files, he was no 'prince of papers'.

And as for Cles? The volume and intensely political quality of the correspondence and counsel which Cles exchanged with Burgo and with Ferdinand and May in the course of a single month in 1530 must refute any notion that Cles eschewed political engagement or that his absences from court impeded political decision-making. Cles' world was a world of paper, of the political correspondence preserved in the *Grosse Korrespondenz* or *Corrispondenza Clesiana* which constitute his archival legacy today. And as his proud portrait with secretary in the Audience Chamber of the Buonconsiglio suggests, chancellorship by correspondence appears to have suited Cles.

NOTES

1. Roberto Festi, *Bernardo Cles. Iconografia* (Trent: QM Edizioni, 1985), pp. 78–82, fig. 15. By 1531/32, Ferdinand's titles also included King of Bohemia (1527), King of Hungary (1527) and King of the Romans (1531).
2. 'per essere esso Mon.re huomo di grandissimo credito et autorità appresso la M.ta Ces.a et appresso al Ser.mo Re d'Ongaria, et poi a tutti li Principi de Alemania, chè oltre che Vescovo di Trento è anche S.re dil Temporal, et è consiliario et Gran Cancellero di tutta l'Alemania et anchora di grandissima reputatione et estimatione appresso a tutti' (Giacinto Romano (ed.), [Luigi Gonzaga], *Cronaca del soggiorno di Carlo V in Italia (dal 26 luglio 1529 al 25 aprile 1530)* (Milan: Hoepli, 1892), p. 195).
3. The absences as 'wohl zu den auffallendsten Merkmalen seiner Karriere', Gerhard Rill and Christiane Thomas, *Bernhard Cles als Politiker. Kriterien für das Verhaltensbild eines frühneuzeitlichen Staatsmannes* (Graz: Schodl-Weiss, 1987), pp. 11–13, 26, 31.
4. Fernand Braudel, *The Mediterranean and the Mediterranean World in the Age of Philip II*, trans. Sian Reynolds (New York: Harper and Row, 1972), vol. I, pp. 354–94.
5. Ben Kafka, 'Paperwork: The State of the Discipline', *Book History* 12 (2009), p. 341 (pp. 340–53). On the importance of the material medium, see Roger Chartier, *Forms and Meanings: Texts, Performances, and Audiences from Codex to Computer* (Philadelphia: University of Pennsylvania Press, 1995).
6. Francesco Senatore, *'Uno mundo de carta'. Forme e strutture della diplomazia sforzesca* (Naples: Liguori, 1998), p. xii.
7. Calculated from purchasing patterns. For July–August 1471, see Gerhard Seeliger, 'Kanzleistudien', *Mitteilungen des Instituts für österreichische Geschichtsforschung* 8 (1887), pp. 55–64; from 4 September 1530 to 31 October 1531, see Vienna Haus-, Hof- und Staatsarchiv (hereafter HHStA), Reichskanzlei: Reichstaxbuch 720; and minimum figures for 1555, see ibid. Reichstaxbuch 2.

8. M. K. Williams, 'Unfolding Diplomatic Paper and Paper Practices in Early Modern Chancellery Archives', in Arndt Brendecke (ed.), *Praktiken der Frühen Neuzeit* (Vienna: Böhlau, 2015), pp. 496–508. On early modern archives more generally, see Markus Friedrich, *Die Geburt des Archivs. Eine Wissensgeschichte* (Munich: Oldenbourg, 2013); and the special issues of *Archival Science* 7:4 (2007) and 10.3 (2010).

9. 'Et mi racordo io vedere il Cardinal di Trento Bernardo da Cles, Canceliero dello presente Imperator Ferdinando, che era all'hora Re de Romani, portarci sempre un carniero di velutto all'arzone della sua mulla, con un calamaro, carta et scritture dentro per insegna et stendardo della nottaria' (Marino Cavalli, *Informatione dell'Offitio dell'Ambasciatore* [1550], ed. T. Bertelé (Florence: Olschki, 1935), pp. 90–1). I wish to thank Paul Dover for bringing this to my attention.

10. Cles' wide-ranging influence and multifaceted activity as chancellor, churchman, Renaissance prince and statesman during a critical decade in European history has left his own papers and sources regarding his statesmanship scattered in archives and libraries across Europe. Cles' political papers resided in the Prince-Bishopric of Trent prior to its 1802 secularisation. Subsequently at Innsbruck, they were transferred to Vienna in 1860. Their arrival in Vienna coincided with the great age of archivally derived administrative, diplomatic and political history initiated by Leopold von Ranke. Given Cles' central role in Ferdinand's government, and Ferdinand's own key role in laying the foundations for a future Habsburg Monarchy in Central Europe, Cles' papers attracted early interest among political historians. Scholarship on the statesman had just begun to emerge when, following Austria-Hungary's defeat in the First World War, most of Cles' prolific correspondence was transferred to Allied Italy between 1919 and 1921. There Cles constituted a figure of local and especially cultural interest, with rich contributions on his architectural, artistic and patronage legacy in Trent. Scholarship on Cles' political activities revived with improved Austrian–Italian relations in the 1970s to 1980s. His papers are today chiefly divided between the HHStA and the Archivio di Stato in Trent, Archivio del principato vescovile, Corrispondenza Clesiana (hereafter CC, busta, fascicle, and (where foliated) foliation). For the chief works on Cles: Renato Tisot, *Ricerche sulla vita e sull'epistolario del Cardinale Bernardo Cles (1485–1539)* (Trent: Società studi trentini di scienze storiche, 1969) particularly exploits Italian archives; Rill and Thomas, *Cles als Politiker*, and their 'Il Cardinale Clesio come politico – una carriera fra Trento e la Corte di re Ferdinando', in the essay collection P. Prodi (ed.), *Bernardo Clesio e il suo Tempo* (Rome: Bulzoni, 1987), pp. 45–102, focuses on Cles' political activity, as does Rill's biography of Cles in the *Dizionario biografico degli italiani (DBI)* (Rome: Istituto della Enciclopedia italiana, 1982), vol. 16, pp. 406–12; Alfred Strnad's recent biography *Bernhard von Cles (1485–1539). Herkunft, Umfeld und geistiges Profil eines Weltmannes der Renaissance. Zum Erscheinungsbild eines Trienter Kirchenfürsten im Cinquecento* (Innsbruck: StudienVerlag, 2004), follows Rill and Thomas nearly verbatim on political aspects but adds valuable social and ecclesiastical angles.

11. The *galero* watermark predated Cles' 1530 cardinalate. See Wasserzeichenkartei Piccard n. 32036, Hauptstaatsarchiv Stuttgart, available at <http://www.piccard-online.de> (last accessed 7 September 2014); or C.-L. Briquet, *Les Filigranes. Dictionnaire historique des marques du papier dès leur apparition vers 1282 jusqu'en 1600* (Geneva: Picard, 1907; Amsterdam: Paper Publications Society, 1968), vol. I, p. 225, nn. 3407–8, available at <http://www.ksbm.oeaw.ac.at/> (last accessed 7 September 2014).

12. For example, 'Recepimus insuper complures alias ab eodem Andrea [de Burgo] pro more longas, quas omnes cum ipsi Nos propter graua multaque negocia quibus nunc occupati sumus perlegere nequiuerimus. Nobis earundem substantia per Mag^{cum} fidelem nobis dilectum Leonardum ab harrach in Roraw Cancellarium Curie nostre pro maiori fieri potuit compendio relata est, sed inter hec gratissima nobis est assidua deuotionis V. cura et diligentia . . .' (Ferdinand [May] to Cles, Vienna, 20 July 1527, CC.2.1 fo. 86).

13. 'Lo episcopo di Trento è dei primi consieri di questo principe et molto da lui existimato et è degna persona' (Gasparo Contarini, cited in Marin Sanuto, *I diarii*, ed. N. Barozzi et al. (Venice: Visentini, 1879–1902), vol. 40, pp. 286–7, 370, 464).

14. 'Vero è ch' quando li il R^mo Car^l di Trento, lui è il primo apresso Sua M^tà et tutti li ciedono' (Francesco Contarini to the Signory, Vienna, 16 February 1534, Biblioteca Marciana (Venice), Mss. Ital. cl. VII cod. 802 fo. 42v). Roggendorf P. P. Vergerio to Cles, Prague, 20 July 1534, cited in Karl Ausserer, 'Kardinal Bernhard von Cles und die Papstwahl des Jahres 1534', *Mitteilungen des Instituts für österreichische Geschichte* 35 (1914), p. 116, n. 3. Cles' panegyrists captured this dependence: 'qui altera es manus principis et magnus Austriae ac omnium regium Australium Cancellarius, ac Curiae, ut merito secundo loco illi succedas . . .' (J. Cuspinian, *Austria . . . cum omnibus eiusdem marchionibus . . .* (Basel: J. Oporinus, 1553), p. 54); dedication to Cles, dated Vienna, 20 May 1528: 'nimirum ei, qui sua fide, prudentia, cordatoque iudicio, id vel omnium, consensum pridem meritus est, ut inter aulae proceres secundum regem primum esset . . .' (Vienna professor Claudius Cantiuncula, dedication (dated Prague, March 1534) to his *Paraphrasis in secundum librum institutionum imperialium Justiniani imperatoris* (Hagenau, 1534), fo. [iv]).

15. On Gattinara and his rivals, see Rebecca Ard Boone in this volume and her *Mercurino di Gattinara and the Creation of the Spanish Empire* (London: Pickering and Chatto, 2014). Other key works on Gattinara include Carlo Bornate, *Ricerche intorno alla vita di Mercurino Gattinara, gran cancelliere di Carlo V* (Novara: Miglio, 1899); Fritz Walser and Rainer Wohlfeil, *Die spanischen Zentralbehörden und der Staatsrat Karls V* (Göttingen: Vandenhoeck & Ruprecht, 1959), pp. 161–70, 242–64; John Headley, *The Emperor and His Chancellor: A Study of the Imperial Chancellery under Gattinara* (Cambridge: Cambridge University Press, 1983); Hayward Keniston, *Francisco de los Cobos: Secretary of the Emperor Charles V* (Pittsburgh: University of Pittsburgh Press, 1960), pp. 31–2, 99–103. On Granvelle, see Maurice van Durme, *El Cardenal Granvela: 1517–1586*, rev. edn. (Barcelona: Teide, 1957), exp. and rev. trans. of *Antoon Perrenot: Bisschop van Atrecht, Kardinaal van Granvelle, Minister van Karel V en van Filips II (1517–86)* (Brussels: Paleis der Academië 1953); Folkert Postma, *Viglius van Aytta: de jaren met Granvelle, 1549–1564* (Zutphen: Walburg, 2000).

16. Ferdinand praised Cles' 'fidem prudentiam et Integritatem . . . et eciam quia non que negocia mea tractat absque mixtione pasiones odius vel amoris vel proprio mody (que certe istis temporibus paruum est) vltra hoc que D. v. scit defectus personarus et quam deficile est Recuperan[d]o earum tam propter fidem erga demum quam eciam erga dominos suos et principaliter vby deproprio comodo agitur quo modo alias ego In curia cum personis sum prouisus D. v. scit melius quam nullis alius' (Ferdinand [manu propria] to Cles, undated, CC.3.1 fo. 456r). Legate Girolamo Aleandro recognised Cles' 'ingegno molto versatilo' ([1521], cited in Tisot, *Ricerche*, p. 75).

17. For example, 'Et quant est dud. evesque de Trente qu'avez trouvé tel experimenté personnaige que le reputies et affectionné à vostre service et au mien, certes, mons^r, je ne fais doubte que tousiours sera trouvé, comme il a esté jusques à present' (Ferdinand to Charles V, Prague, 27 March 1530, in Wilhelm Bauer (ed.), *Die Korrespondenz Ferdinands I* (Vienna: Holzhausen, 1937–8), vol. 1:2, n. 425§1).

18. Katherine Walsh, 'La formazione intellettuale del giovane Bernardo Clesio: Verona e Bologna', in Prodi, *Bernardo Clesio*, vol. 2, pp. 503–22; Strnad, *Cles*, pp. 31–6.

19. Having begun his career as Bishop of Gurk, Lang ended as Prince-Archbishop of Salzburg.

20. Helmut Goetz, 'Die Geheimen Ratgeber Ferdinands I. (1503–1564). Ihre Persönlichkeit im Urteil der Nuntien und Gesandten', *Quellen und Forschungen aus italienischen Archiven und Bibliotheken* 42/43 (1963), pp. 462–3 (pp. 453–94).

21. To judge by his annotations to his copy of Aeneas Silvio Piccolomini's 1444 *De curialium miseriis*, Cles largely agreed with Piccolomini's anti-curial diatribe (Rill and Thomas, *Cles*

als Politiker, p. 35). For Trent as refuge, see Tisot, *Ricerche*, n. 48 (4 July 1534); 'Postremo nos hic breui discedemus Tridentum versas, ubi post multos labores tandem quiescere cupimus, ut deo & ecclesio nostre inseruire possimus . . .' (Cles to Burgo, Innsbruck, 19 October 1532, CC.14.12 fos. 15v–16v).

22. Josef Marini, 'Beiträge zum Venezianerkrieg Maximilians I., 1515/1516, mit besonderer Berücksichtigung der Tätigkeit des Trienter Bischofs Bernhard II. von Cles', *Jahresbericht des k.k. Reform-Realgymnasiums in Bozen* 28 (1909/10), pp. 4–37, 1–30, 1–23.

23. Rill and Thomas, *Cles als Politiker*, pp. 12–13, 26, 31.

24. Ibid. pp. 31–2; Tisot, *Ricerche*, pp. 70–3, 76–9, 99–103; Gerhard Rill, *Fürst und Hof in Österreich von den habsburgischen Teilungsverträgen bis zur Schlacht von Mohács (1521/22 bis 1526).* Vol. 2, *Gabriel von Salamanca, Zentralverwaltung und Finanzen* (Vienna: Böhlau, 2003), pp. 231–4; Rill, 'Quecksilber aus Idria', *Mitteilungen des Österreichischen Staatsarchivs* 40 (1987), pp. 27–60.

25. Tisot, *Ricerche*, pp. 41 (Mantua), 161–214 (Milan).

26. For Burgo's biography, see Gerhard Rill, 'Borgo (Burgo), Andrea', in *Dizionario biografico degli italiani (DBI)* (Rome: Istituto della Enciclopedia italiana, 1970), vol. 12, pp. 749–53; Rill, *Fürst und Hof in Österreich: von den habsburgischen Teilungsverträgen bis zur Schlacht von Mohács (1521/22 bis 1526)*. Vol. 1, *Aussenpolitik und Diplomatie* (Vienna: Böhlau, 1993), pp. 141–50.

27. CC.8, *passim*; HHStA, Grosse Korrespondenz 8, *passim*.

28. Gerhard Rill, 'Die Hannart-Affäre. Eine Vertrauenskrise in der Casa de Austria 1524', *Mitteilungen des österreichischen Staatsarchivs* 34 (1981), pp. 89–146; Rill and Thomas, *Cles als Politiker*, p. 29. Cles also maintained a close correspondence with Saxon Elector Friedrick 'the Wise', whose advice both brothers esteemed.

29. 'ain cantzley aines fursten hertz geacht [werde] und also ist' (Complaint of the Lower Austrian Estates, 31 December 1525, Öst. Staatsarchiv, Finanz- und Hofkammerarchiv (HKA), NÖ. Landtagsakten r. Nr.53 fo. 71r). Background for this can be found in Rill, *Salamanca*, pp. 170–9.

30. For Cles' formal appointment as 'presidens privati et secreti concilii nostri' on 1 January 1526, see HHStA, Reichsregisterbücher [RRB] Ferd. I 1, fo. 46r–v. See also Karl Ausserer, 'Il decreto di nomina di Bernardo Clesio a presidente del Consiglio segreto', *Studi Trentini di Scienze Storiche* 3 (1922), pp. 173–5. That Cles headed this body and the Court Council as 'chancellor' or 'president' since May/June 1522, as Tisot, *Ricerche*, p. 78 and Wilhelm Bauer, *Die Anfänge Ferdinands I* (Vienna: Braumüller, 1907), p. 175 have suggested, is based in part on a faulty transcription in *Deutsche Reichstagsakten, jüngere Reihe* (Gotha: F. A. Perthes, 1901), vol. 3, p. 207, where 'Bishop of Trient' (Cles) should in fact read 'Bishop of Triest' (the ageing *magnus cancellarius* Pietro Bonomo (1458–1546), who withdrew to his bishopric in October 1523). See Rill and Thomas, *Cles als Politiker*, p. 44, n. 74; Rill, *Salamanca*, pp. 56–65. For Harrach's nomination as chancellor, 1 January 1526, see HKA, Gedenkbücher [GB] 25 fo. 114v.

31. Tisot, *Ricerche*, p. 104, gives a date of 12 February 1528; the first mention of Cles as 'Obrister Kanzler' occurs on 28 February 1528. Cles was congratulated (not confirmed) by Charles in a diploma issued at Toledo in November 1528 (AS-Trento, sez. Lat. cap. 17 n. 51). See Rill and Thomas, *Cles als Politiker*, n. 90; Rill, *DBI*, vol. 26, p. 408; Heinz Noflatscher, *Räte und Herrscher. Politische Eliten an den Habsburgerhöfen der österreichischen Länder 1480–1530* (Mainz: von Zabern, 1999), p. 343.

32. Jo. May to Cles, Budweis, 14 January 1530, CC.12.10, fos. 5–6.

33. See, for example, Tisot, *Ricerche*, pp. 100ff.

34. 'Die scheinbar so innovativen Akte ab 1526 bildeten nur zu einem bescheidenen Teil die Antwort auf ständische Ansprüche, sie stellten eher die Folge der Erweiterung des dynastischen Herrschaftsbereichs in Verbindung mit einer seit den Teilungsverträgen

nachweisbaren, intensiv betriebenen Behördenorganisation dar.' and 'Die These eines radikalen Umbaues in Folge ständischer Initiativen 1525/26 wird widerlegt' (Rill, *Salamanca*, pp. 79, 94–9); Rill and Thomas, *Cles als Politiker*, pp. 13–14.

35. Though Latin Secretaries with similar competencies were not unprecedented, though Ferdinand retained personal secretaries, and though the new Latin secretariat exhibited strong personnel continuities with the period prior to 1526, this ordinance brought it formally into the chancellery as a distinct section. See Rill, *Salamanca*, p. 91.

36. 'Kanzleiordnung des Erzherzogs Ferdinand I. Augsburg 1526 März 6', in Thomas Fellner and Heinrich Kretschmayr, *Die österreichische Zentralverwaltung*. Section I, *Von Maximilian I. bis zur Vereinigung der österreichischen und böhmischen Hofkanzlei (1749)* (Vienna: Adolf Holzhausen, 1907) (hereafter *ÖZV*), vol. 2, *Aktenstücke, 1491–1681*, n. 11§18, cf. n. 13§12. See also M. K. Williams, '"Zu Notdurfft der Schreiberey": Die Einrichtung der frühneuzeitlichen Kanzlei', in Dagmar Freist (ed.), *Diskurse-Körper-Artefakte. Historische Praxeologie in der Frühneuzeitforschung* (Bielefeld: Transkript, 2015), pp. 335–72.

37. Traditionally, the reigns of Maximilian and especially Ferdinand have been portrayed as laying the groundwork for a centralised Austrian state bureaucracy. Maximilian's reign, thanks to the research school around H. Wiesflecker, and the final years of Ferdinand's reign after he succeeded his brother as Holy Roman Emperor, have been well researched: building on Gerhard Seeliger, *Erzkanzler und Reichskanzleien. Ein Beitrag zur Geschichte des Deutschen Reiches* (Innsbruck: Wagner, 1889), Lothar Gross published a detailed and exceptionally valuable study of the personnel and organisation of the Imperial Court Chancellery after 1559, *Die Geschichte der deutschen Reichshofkanzlei von 1559 bis 1806* (Vienna: Selbstverlag des Haus-, Hof- und Staatsarchivs, 1933). Rill's equally magisterial *Salamanca* traced Ferdinand's administration up to 1526. For the interim period from 1526 to 1559, however, Ferdinand's chancelleries have attracted rather less attention. Depending upon ordinances, Fellner and Kretschmayr described Ferdinand's royal chancellery as a 'Schreiborgan' rather than a true governmental body. See *ÖZV*, vol. 1, *Geschichtliche Übersicht* (Vienna: Holzhausen, 1907), pp. 142–3. Eduard Rosenthal highlighted Ferdinand's administrative organs as model: 'Die Behördenorganisation Kaiser Ferdinands I. Das Vorbild der Verwaltungs-organisationen in den deutschen Territorien', *Archiv für österreichische Geschichte* 69 (1887), pp. 51–316, a theme which Otto Hintze has reiterated.

38. Rill, *Salamanca*; Paula S. Fichtner, 'Habsburg Household or Habsburg Government? A Sixteenth-Century Administrative Dilemma', *Austrian History Yearbook* 26 (1995), pp. 45–60.

39. Headley, *The Emperor and His Chancellor*, pp. 15–16. Whereas Headley, and more classically Otto Hintze, argue for an early modern chronology, Andreas Kraus has argued that the institution of the princely secretary emerged around the beginning of the fourteenth century – a period which, perhaps not coincidentally, also saw growing paper consumption in European chancelleries. See Kraus, 'Secretarius und Sekretariat: Der Ursprung der Institution des Staatssekretariats und ihr Einfluss auf die Entwicklung moderner Regierungsformen in Europa', *Römische Quartalschrift* 55:1–2 (1960), p. 53 (pp. 43–84); Hintze, 'Die Entwicklung der modernen Staatsministerien', *Historische Zeitschrift* 100 (1907), pp. 53–111. See also Isabella Lazzarini's contribution to this volume.

40. 1 January 1527 Hofordnung, in *ÖZV*, vol. 2, n. 12§1. Consisting of 'a very few persons' – the court's four pre-eminent officials and up to eight additional advisors, when they were at court – the Privy Council was intended to function more discreetly and efficiently than could the larger Court Council (*Hofrat*). Privy Council protocols survive, very spottily and in incomplete form, from 1561 to 1716. See Gross, *Geschichte*, pp. 237–47. On the body, see *ÖZV*, vol. 1, pp. 37–67; Rosenthal, *Behördenorganisation*, pp. 80–6; Rill, *Salamanca*, pp. 62–4.

41. This general impression of Karl's more distant relationship with Cles may derive from the paucity of surviving documentation. However, Karl's correspondence with Cles may have been filtered through Innsbruck, where both had long-standing connections.

42. On Spiegel, see Gustav Knod, *Jacob Spiegel aus Schlettstadt* (Strasbourg: DuMont-Schauberg, 1884–6); Thomas Burger, *Jacob Spiegel, Ein humanistischer Jurist des 16. Jh.* (JD dissertation, University of Freiburg, 1973) adds little to Knod.

43. Knod, *Jacob Spiegel*, vol. 1, p. 19. Spiegel on several occasions referred to Villinger as 'Maecenatem meum, praesidium meum', and dedicated his 1512 commentary on the *Staurostichon* to Villinger. On Lang and Bonomo, see *Antonii Panormitae De dictis et factis Alphonsi Regis Aragonum libri quatuor . . . adiecta sunt singulis libris Scholia per Jacobum Spiegelium* (Basel: Herugiana, 1538), p. 266, and Spiegel's edition of *Isocratis De regno gvbernando . . .* (Vienna: Alantsee, 1514).

44. 'novit docto Spiegel colorem et multum mellis litteris illis imponere' (Schneitpeck to Salamanca, 23 January 1524, HHStA, GK25b fo. 2r). See also Erasmus' praise: 'eleganter doctus et stilo felici' (P. S. Allen (ed.), *Opus epistolarum Des. Erasmus Roterdami (OE)* (Oxford: Clarendon Press, 1906–58), vol. 5, p. 142, n. 1323).

45. GB19 fo. 239v [nomination as secretary, 14 August 1523], on Erasmus' recommendation. Spiegel ascribed his position to Salamanca. See HKA, Niederösterreichisches Kammerakten [NÖK] 3 fos. 469–72. In 1525, Spiegel was granted a salary of 500 Rheinisch gulden per year, from which he was to pay the keep of a Latin *Ingrossist* (likely May). See GB25 fo. 30v; GB26 fos. 35v–36r [1527].

46. For example, Spiegel to Cles, 4 June 1525, CC12.45 fo. 2 or 13 July 1525: 'Quando ego totus quantusque sum Do. V. R^{me} sum & esse volo, sicut & debeo.' (ibid. fo. 6). May is named as Latin Secretary in Ferdinand's 6 March 1526 *Hofkanzleiordnung* (*ÖZV*, vol. 2, n. 11§18), and his 1535 pension described him as having served in the Latin Chancellery for 14 years (GB44 fo. 87r–v).

47. Spiegel wrote of having personally trained May in the dedicatory epistle of his *Lexicon iuris civilis* (Strasbourg: Johannes Hervagius, 1538), fo. 2v: 'Quod si fratrem ad hoc officium scite formassem, fieri posse videbam, ut mihi successor, faventibus Superis, aliquando daretur.'

48. Provision of 1,000 Hung. gulden for May 'quibus idem nobis non alieno testimonio sed quottidiana experientia merito commendatus est ac item attentis longis gratis fidelibus & utilibus seruitys que nobis idem Maius & Sacre Regni nostri Hungarie Corone multifariam hucusque exhibuit & impendit . . .' (Prague, 7 May 1531, GB37 fo. 87r–v).

49. Vienna, 17 July 1535, GB44 fo. 87r–v.

50. M. K. Williams, 'Dangerous Diplomacy and Dependable Kin: Transformations in European Statecraft 1526–1540' (PhD dissertation, Columbia University, 2009).

51. Alfred Kohler, *Antihabsburgische Politik in der Epoche Karls V* (Göttingen: Vandenhoeck & Ruprecht, 1982); Stephen Fischer-Galati, *Ottoman Imperialism and German Protestantism, 1521–1550* (Cambridge, MA: Harvard University Press, 1959); Christine Turetschek, *Die Türkenpolitik Ferdinands I. von 1529 bis 1532* (Vienna: Notring, 1968).

52. Senatore, *'Uno mundo de carta'*, p. 96.

53. For example, 'Postscripta xx huius applicuimus in insprugg ubi inuenimus nonnullas literas uras., quibus ad huc responsum non est propter aduersam Valetudine may secretary. Curabimus igitur ut quam primum possibile sit omnia expediamur' (Cles to Burgo, Innsbruck, 22 November 1531 – CC.14.6 fo. 9r).

54. May to Cles, Budweis, 29 January 1530, CC.12.10 fo. 8r.

55. May to Cles, Prague, 5, 5, and 8 February 1530, CC.12.10 fos. 11r, 13r, 14r.

56. 'Ich gedenck E.f.g. heben onzweyfel ain pessere kuntschafft zu hof dan was an mich langt' (Beatus Widmann, Tyrolean chancellor, to Cles, Vienna, 9 October 1534, CC.13.21 fo. 1v).

57. For example, May to Cles, Budweis, 29 January 1530, CC.12.10, fo. 8r; May to Cles, Prague, 29 April 1531, CC.12.10 fos. 20v–21r.

58. For example, May to Cles, Budweis, 14 January 1530, CC.12.10 fo. 5v. The most important of May's benefices was his provostship of the well-endowed Cistercian abbey at Zwettl.

59. May to Cles, Anaso[?], 16 January 1536 [addressed in Karl's hand], CC.12.10 fo. 28; 'Ideo de mea manu non multas amplius literas do. v. R^ma habebit' (May [in Karl's hand, with May postscript] to Cles, undated [likely February 1536], CC.12.10 fos. 34–5). Of Ferdinand's correspondence with Cles, the last letter May signed was dated 1 April 1536; thereafter Karl signed the Latin (CC.3.1 fos. 277–85).

60. 'dardurch dann yetzgedachter Johann May desster pass in unnsern diensten unnd treffenlichen geschäfften bisheer also erhalten werden mügen' (Innsbruck, 1 March 1536, GB45 fo. 28r).

61. The Hall and Sélestadt epitaphs are both printed in Spiegel, *Lexicon*. This work was dedicated to Adam Karl: 'In Lexicon Ivris Civilis per D. Iac. Spiegelivm Selestadien. Congestum, ad ornatiss. D. Adamum Carolum, Sacr. Latin. Scrin. in Aula sereniss. Regis Cesarisq. Ferdinandi prefectum Praefatio' (fos. 2r–3v).

62. See Karl's preface to the collection of elegaic poetry by his friends Johannes Lange, Johannes Rosinus (a fellow student), Georg Logau, the Brassicanae brothers and Lazaro Bonamico: *Elegia . . . de miserabili fato Casparis Ursini Velii Silesii, Poetae Oratoris & Historici Regii* (Vienna: Johannes Singrenius, 1539), which he dedicated to Lange. Velius taught at Leipzig from 1508 to 1510, from 1510 was secretary to Matthäus Lang, and taught at Vienna from 1515 to 1516 and 1524 to 1525/6; he drowned in the Danube, a likely suicide, in 1539.

63. 'Nobilitatio et saluaguardia cum Armorum auctario et melioratione pro Adamo Carolo', Vienna, 31 October 1534, RKB Ferd.2 fo. 182r–v; AVA.RAA.61.2 fos. 1–6 (concept, in Karl's own hand).

64. HHStA Venezia: Berichte 1, ins. 1.

65. 'Haud enim nescia est Amplitudo tua, quomodo Oeniponti primum, deinde mox Aulam secutus Augustae commendaticys scilicet Tirolensis Cancellary literis fulcitus, apud sese conditionem ambierim, relicto me hercule tum non vulgari Munere, propterea que pro certo mihi persuadebam, si in locum aliquem abs tua R^ma Celsitudine, quae merito summi Cancellary partes apud tam potentissimum Regem administraret, eiusque Secretioris Consily Praeces esset, sufficierer facile breuia fore, uti fortunis meis augendis commodius meliusque consulere possem. Itaque cum Amplitudo tua, voluntatem istam meam Mentisque decretum intellexisset, quo adiuuaret, mittendum me huc ad Oratorem Regium [Burgo] statuit ut apud se scribendarum uiuuem literarum prouinciam obirem, id quod libenter cupideque suscepi, meque statim sicuti iussit, in hanc vrbem contuli' (Karl to Cles, Rome, 4 June 1531, CC.9.2. fos. 86–7).

66. Burgo to Cles, Rome, 20 January 1531, CC.9.2 fo. 6r–v.

67. 'Adam Carolo secretario hogi me ha dicto che resta obligatissimo a V. Sig^ria R^ma de lopera facta per luj' (Burgo to Cles, Rome, 6 March 1532, CC.9.3 fo. 132r); Karl to Cles, Rome, 25 February 1532, CC.9.3 fos. 124–5.

68. On handwriting, see Rill, *Aussenpolitik*, p. 147.

69. On the campaign, corruption allegations and Cles' relationship with Charles at Bologna in 1532–3, see Rill and Thomas, *Cles als Politiker*, pp. 10, 19–20, 22. On the papal election of 1534, see Ausserer, 'Cles und die Papstwahl'. These events also suggested Cles' inability to persuade Charles to revisit the disappointing 1521–2 inheritance partition, which Ferdinand refused to consider as final.

70. Clement VII refused to condemn the territory's invasion by the exiled Duke Ulrich, who had developed strong Lutheran sympathies, in April 1534. For its impact on Cles, see Rill and Thomas, *Cles als Politiker*, p. 19; Strnad, *Cles*, pp. 83–4.

71. Celebrated Padua professor Benedetto Vettori diagnosed Cles as suffering from 'Gallica affectione' in September 1535 and May 1539: Benedetto Vettori, *Medicinalia consilia ad*

varia morborum genera (Venice: Stellae, 1551), fos. 5r–28v. See Tisot, *Ricerche*, p. 156; Strnad, *Cles*, pp. 94–5.

72. On the 1536 Naples summit, see Andreas Cornaro, 'Die Reise Kardinal Bernhards von Cles zu Kaiser Karl V. nach Neapel im Jahre 1536 nach seinen Briefen an Ferdinand I.' (PhD dissertation, University of Vienna, 1956).

73. Ibid. 94ff.; Rill and Thomas, *Cles als Politiker*, pp. 23–4.

74. Rill and Thomas, *Cles als Politiker*, p. 20.

75. Karl corresponded with religious reformers Philipp Melanchthon and Johannes Camerarius, and dedicated his *De Insigni Adventv Caroli V. Caesaris . . . per Adamum Carolum Regium Secretarium, ex Italica lingua translata* (Vienna: Johannes Singrenius, 1536), dated 24 December 1535, to Ferdinand's increasingly influential privy councillor Hans Hofmann von Grünpuchl, whom papal nuncio Morone considered an open Lutheran. See W. Friedensburg (ed.), *Nuntiatur des Morone 1536–1538*. Nuntiaturberichte aus Deutschland 2 (Gotha: Perthes, 1892), p. 123.

76. Adam Karl (ed.), *Joannis Langi Silesii, ad Jesum Christum Dei filium, pro Christianis contra Turcas elegia* (Vienna: Johannes Singrenius, 1539; 2nd edn, Antwerp: Johannes Gymnicus, 1540). In 1539, Karl was dispatched on a diplomatic mission to Kraków together with experienced diplomat and royal councillor Sigismund von Herberstein (1486–1566), to whom he turned as patron following Cles' death. See Öst. Nationalbibliothek, Bibl.Pal.Vind. Cod. 13598, *passim*. By 1546, Karl had been named 'councillor' (*Rat*) (HKA, Hofzahlamtsbücher 4 (1546), fo. 115r), and in July 1546 was granted a retirement pension of 200 Rhenish Gulden per year (HKA, GB60 fos. 89v–90r).

77. While Rill and Thomas, *Cles als Politiker*, p. 36, see this 'resignation' more in terms of an *Urlaub*, Karl's inventory of Latin Expedition papers received from Cles on 29 January 1539 suggests a more final step. See HKA, NÖHA, H83–4 fos. 2061–78. Most of the enumerated documents are now in the HHStA, Ungarische Akten or Turcica.

78. As Mattingly noted, 'no clause is more certain to appear in [Renaissance diplomats'] instructions than the injunction to report frequently and minutely everything of possible political importance' (Garrett Mattingly, *Renaissance Diplomacy* (Boston: Houghton Mifflin, 1955), p. 110).

79. For example, 'sua M^tas habeat gratum monendum continuo de occurrentibus Rome' (Burgo to Cles, Rome, 20 April 1531, CC.9.2 fo. 55r).

80. On gout's effects on early modern diplomacy, see M. K. Williams, 'Immobile Ambassadors: Gout and Early Modern Diplomacy', *Sixteenth Century Journal* (forthcoming).

81. 'de quibus aliqua scripsi M^ti Vestre que pro minore eius molestia scripseram particularius R^mo D^no Tridentino, qui plene est informatus' (Burgo to Ferdinand, Bologna, 4 January 1530, HHStA, Rom. Ber. 4 fo. 8r).

82. On the 'great expenses' for the post in Italy, and Cles' negotiations with the Tridentine and Mantuan postmasters, see Ferdinand to Cles, Linz, 19 December 1529, HHStA, ÖAT1.2 fo. 77; HKA, Alte Postakten 1.1, fos. 204–48. While at Bologna, Charles V laid on extra couriers as far as Trent to ensure swifter and more frequent communications with his brother: 'Poste posite sunt a Cesare usque Tridentum, possent nunc celerius que frequentius haberi litere' (Burgo to Ferdinand, Bologna, 4 January 1530, HHStA Rom. Ber. 2c fo. 9r).

83. Supplication of Hofpostmeister Antonj de Tassis, ad 24 October 1526, HKA, Alte Postakten 1.1 fos. 16–17.

84. On postal expansion, see Fritz Ohmann, *Der Anfänge des Postwesens und die Taxis* (Leipzig: Duncker & Humblot, 1909); Wolfgang Behringer, *Im Zeichen des Merkur: Reichspost und Kommunikationsrevolution in der Frühen Neuzeit* (Göttingen: Vandenhoeck & Ruprecht, 2003); and more generally, E. John B. Allen, *Post and Courier Service in the Diplomacy of Early Modern Europe* (The Hague: Nijhoff, 1973).

85. 'All und jede posten, si kommen aus Hispanien Frankreich Italien Hungern Behaimb

Teutschland oder von andern ortn aus unsern erblanden, dieselbigen sollen durch unsern hofpostmaister niemants andern dan gedachtem unserm obristen canzler oder wem er das bevilcht, zuebracht und überantwort und in seiner gegenwert geöfnet' ('König Ferdinands I. Instruktion für den obersten Kanzler. Gran 1528 Februar 12', in *ÖZV*, vol. 2, n. 13§3). See also Burgo's many letters marked with some variant of 'manibus R^{mi} Dni. Cardinalis Tridentini', in HHStA, Rom. Ber. 2–4, 6–7, *passim*.

86. Cles and Ferdinand praised Burgo's open letters: 'Cum his erit expeditio Regia, et alie litere que destribuentur aperturam literarum M^{tas} Regia videtur laudarum et vt a nobis continue fiat, expetere, approbareque consilium ad vestras datum, quod officium nobis in iunctum non intermittemus, quamuis aliquantulum graue futurum sit, quum alys quoque agendis implicemur, ut utrisque M^{bus} [Charles and Ferdinand] pro debito nostro satisfaciamus M^{tique} Regie presentium copiam pro consilio, quod desuper impetiri potuisset una cum vestris transmissimus' ('extractus Zifere Domini Tridentini ad D. Comitem Andream Burgum', Trent, 12 January 1530, CC.9.1 fo. 10r). Secretary May also considered this handling of Burgo's letters prudent, as it ensured clarity of communications between all parties and speedier responses. See May to Cles, Budweis, 19 January 1530, CC.12.10 fo. 9r. That Cles' reading of Burgo's letters was a regular practice is repeatedly demonstrated in the CC and HHStA, Rom. Ber., for example, 'Presentes inclusae litere mag^{ci} Domino burgj R.M.V. apud pontificem oratori mihi nuper allate fuerunt; quas de mandato E.R.M.V. aplici: sed nihil in his inueni, quod rescriptione aliqua indigenti . . .' (Cles to Ferdinand, Trent, 13 December 1532, CC.14.13 fo. 3r).

87. 'Extractus Zifere Dni. Tridentini ad D. Comitem Andream Burgum', Trent, 12 January 1530, CC.9.1 fo. 7r. Cles' chancellery, like the Court Chancellery, prepared and revised minutes of his advice for Ferdinand and his responses to Burgo in chronologically organised, thick paper booklets.

88. 'que ad literas prefati Burgi Italie Idiomate respondit optime placent nobis, sicut et cetera que prudenter et consulto agere solet' (Ferdinand [May] to Cles, Prague, 3 February 1530, HHStA, ÖAT1.2 fo. 85r).

89. 'Accepi binas literas do.v. R^{me} et Ill^{me} de viij et 10 huius quarum altere unacum bulla excommunicationis [for Ferdinand's rival Szapolyai] et compluribus alys adiuunctis ad me directe fuere, quas singulas singulis distribuj et inprimis Ser^{mo} d. Regi nostro domino meo clementiss^{mo} suas que decet reuerentia exhibui. [. . .] Ternas burgi literas de 29 Decembris ac de 4 et 6 presentis . . . ego legi regi . . .' (May to Cles, Budweis, 19 January 1530, CC.12.10 fo. 9r–v); 'Accepimus plures successiue literas dil. et deuo^{nis} vestre de vj, vij, 8 et 10 presentis et bines quas M^{cus} Andreas de Burgo orator noster ad eam dedit unacum tribus responsis per eam factis ad literas eiusdem burgj de 29 preteriti ac de iij et 8a eiusdem mensis, que nobis magnopere placent Intentionique vestre se conformant, atque ex eis abunde cognauimus qua diligentia et prudentia tractare soleat res illas arduas et grauas. . .' (Ferdinand [May] to Cles, Budweis, 19 January 1530, HHStA, ÖAT1.2 fo. 83).

90. On May's readings of diplomatic dispatches, see M. K. Williams, '"Ad regem": Diplomatic Documents as Artefacts of Early Modern Foreign Policymaking', in J. W. J. Burgers et al. (eds), *Medieval Documents as Artefacts, 1100–1600*. Schrift en Schriftdragers in de Nederlanden in de Middeleeuwen (Hilversum: Verloren, forthcoming).

91. 'hoc sit onus meum meaque diligentia confici debere, me reuiritur, ut literas cum diligentia m^{ti} regie proponeram legam et declaram' (May to Cles, Budweis, 14 January 1530, CC.12.10 fo. 5r; May to Cles, Budweis, 29 January 1530, CC.12.10 fo. 8r).

92. Ferdinand (concept) to Burgo, Budweis, 19 January 1530, HHStA, Rom. Weis. 5a fo. 16; 'Placet item nobis consilium eiusdem dilco^{nis} et deuo^{nis} vestre super precedentia cum oratore anglico . . .' (Ferdinand to Cles, Budweis, 19 January 1530, HHStA, ÖAT1.2, fo. 83r).

93. 'Hortantes eadem plurimum ut nos statim de opinione et apparere suo certificare velit quidnam per nos super eisdem sit respondendum, et quibus remedys occurrendum periculis

et motibus de quibus In eisdem fit mentio, Idque in ceteris quoque si que talia a burgo veniant, nostri et boni publici causa cui eandem deuo[ne] v. aeque ac nos intentam esse scimus, facere, literasque suas aperire et legere nosque super singulis de Iuditio suo separatim cetificare pergat, quod nobis erit contissimum' (Ferdinand to Cles, Budweis, 19 January 1530, HHStA, ÖAT1.2, fo. 83r).

94. Biographer Gerhard Rill has suggested that it was Burgo's excessive 'circuitousness and garrulity' which compelled the chancellery to produce extracts of his letters. See Rill, *Aussenpolitik*, pp. 147–8. However, May also drew up similar extracts for other, less effusive diplomats' dispatches.

95. 'tercium extractum de eisdem solus feci, quem mittit rex do. V. R[me] quem etiam cupio cum suo responso ad Regem remitti, quia locupletior est iste et copiosior alys'. As May rushed to add, though, 'non recusem legere Integras literas quoties petatur' (May to Cles, Budweis, 19 January 1530, CC.12.10 fo. 9v). For Ferdinand's gratitude for Cles' advice on Burgo's previous packet of letters, see Ferdinand [May] to Cles, Linz, 3 January 1530, CC.15b.1 fo. 5r.

96. Ferdinand [May] to Cles, Prague, 3 February 1530, HHStA, ÖAT1.2 fo. 84r.

97. Ferdinand [May] concept to Burgo and Salinas, Budweis, 29 January 1530, HHStA, Rom. Weis. 5a fos. 17–32; May to Cles, Budweis, 29 January 1530, CC.12.10 fo. 8.

98. Burgo and Salinas to Ferdinand, Bologna, 8 February 1532, HHStA, Rom. Ber. 2c fo. 42r–v.

99. 'scribo tandem usque ad aras, et tamen nihil recuso, aly vero Iam habunt latifundia ego quoque panem quotidianum egre nauiscet, patientia . . .' (May to Cles, Budweis, 19 January 1530, CC.12.10 fo. 9v).

100. May to Cles, Budweis, 14 January 1530, CC.12.10, fos. 5–6. On modern bureaucracies' diffusion of responsibility via file circulation and mediation techniques, see Bruno Latour, *The Making of Law: An Ethnography of the Conseil d'État*, trans. Marina Brilman and Alain Pottage (Cambridge: Polity, 2010); Matthew Hull, *Government of Paper: The Materiality of Bureaucracy in Urban Pakistan* (Berkeley: University of California Press, 2012), pp. 134–50.

101. For example, 'Accepimus ternas litteras dil[nis] et deuo[nis] Vestre de 29 et penultima mensis decembris proxime elapsi unacum copia responsiua ad litteras M[ci] andree de burgo oratoris nostrj quibus abunde nobis Innotuit quanto studio et opere rebus omnibus bene gerendis Intendat, et quod singula pro nobis prospere et commode geri cupiat, de quo eidem meritas agimus gratias, Placuitque nobis responsum dil[nis] et deuo[nis] Vestre prefato Andree velut prudenter et necessario datum, cui nos etiam nihil superaddendum esse censuimus . . . per alias nostras separatim respondebimus . . . Quoad consilium dil[nis] et deuo[nis] Vestre de mouementis armis hac hyeme . . .' (Ferdinand [May] to Cles, Budweis, 9 January 1530, HHStA, ÖAT1.2, fo. 81).

102. Ferdinand [manu propria] to Cles, s.d., CC.3.1 fo. 456r.

103. Behavioural international relations has repeatedly shown modern-day decision-makers' susceptibility to how information is framed and presented. See Robert Jervis, *Perception and Misperception in International Politics* (Princeton: Princeton University Press, 1967).

104. Arndt Brendecke, '"Diese Teufel, meine Papiere . . .": Philipp II. von Spanien und das Anwachsen administrativer Schriftlichkeit', *Aventinus nova* 5 (Winter 2006), available at <http://www.aventinus-online.de/no_cache/persistent/artikel/7785> (last accessed 21 July 2015). Here he is citing Diego de Saavedra Fajardo, *Idea de un príncipe político cristiano en cien empresas* (Antwerp: Juan Bautista Verdussen, 1678), pp. 56, 219.

105. Ben Kafka, *The Demon of Writing: Powers and Failures of Paperwork* (New York: Zone Books, 2012), p. 117; Hull, *Government of Paper*.

106. 'Agora estareis mais empapelado, mas nem po isso mais bem aconselhado' (Antônio Vieira, *Sermões*, ed. Alcir Pécora (São Paolo: Hedra, 2001), vol. 1, p. 307, cited in Arndt

Brendecke, 'Papierbarrieren. Über Ambivalenzen des Mediengebrauchs in der Vormoderne', *Mitteilungen des Sonderforschungsbereichs* 573.2 (2009), p. 13 (pp. 7–15)).

107. Brendecke, '"Diese Teufel"'; Brendecke, 'Papierbarrieren', pp. 13–14; Geoffrey Parker, *The Grand Strategy of Philip II* (New Haven, CT: Yale University Press, 1998), pp. 13–45; Lothar Müller, *Weisse Magie: Die Epoche des Papiers* (Munich: DTV, 2012), pp. 59–60.

108. Ferdinand made a special point of advising his sons to confer with good and sound councillors in decision-making. See Paula S. Fichtner, 'Of Christian Virtue and a Practicing Prince', *Catholic Historical Review* 61:3 (1975), pp. 409–16. On Maximilian II's policy-making, see Fichtner, 'To Rule Is Not to Govern: The Diary of Maximilian II', in Solomon Wank (ed.), *The Mirror of History: Essays in Honor of Fritz Fellner* (Santa Barbara, CA: ABC-Clio, 1988), pp. 255–64.

109. HKA, NÖHA, H83–4 fos. 2061–78.

CHAPTER 5

Parables and Dark Sentences: The Correspondence of Sir William Cecil and William Maitland (1559–73)

Rayne Allinson

[N]ow I will merely co[m]playne off yow to yo[ur] selff. yow write alwayes to me parables at least bref and derk sentences and yow have experience off my simplicity [. . .] I offer franknes on my p[ar]t and wishe yt by yo[ur] souerayg-nes co[m]mandement at least p[er]mission I may fynd the counterpayne w[ith] yow.

Maitland to Cecil, 29 January 1562

The relationship between Mary I of Scotland (1542–87) and Elizabeth I of England (1533–1603) was fraught with tension, suspicion and mutual distrust. Their personal misgivings had deep roots in the violence and antagonism that had characterised Anglo-Scottish relations for centuries, but also stemmed from more immediate religious and political anxieties. Like many of his predecessors, Henry VIII had a cunning plan to unite the two countries under one (English) crown, but just like other English kings who had 'behaved like bulls in the Scottish china shop', his attempts backfired.[1] The Scots refused to deliver up their infant Queen Mary for marriage to Henry's own son Prince Edward, driving them further into the arms of their 'Auld Alliance' with France, which for centuries had worked as a check on English dominance of Britain. As a result, the six-year-old Mary was spirited away to the French court and betrothed to the Dauphin François, whom she married on 24 April 1558. As the grand-daughter of Margaret Tudor (Henry VIII's older sister), Mary also had a strong claim to the English throne, and following Mary Tudor's death without an heir on 17 November 1558, the French seized the opportunity to assert her rights and cast suspicion on the legitimacy of the proclaimed Protestant Queen Elizabeth. Mary even incorporated the English arms into her royal iconog-raphy, a threatening move that increased in significance after she became queen of France on 10 July 1559. However, to the relief of English Protestants, Mary's political position was transformed again when François died on 5 December 1560, and she was forced to return to her native Scotland in August 1561. Despite her cousin's fall from fortune's favour, Elizabeth could not forget or forgive Mary's challenge to her crown, and refused to allow her safe passage overland through

England. The cycle of Anglo-Scottish hostility seemed doomed to repeat itself for another generation.

The burden of diplomacy fell heavily on the queens' principal secretaries, William Maitland of Lethington (1525/30–73) and Sir William Cecil, Lord Burghley (1520/1–98), who corresponded regularly with each other for fourteen years during one of the most tumultuous and formative periods in Anglo-Scottish relations. The similarities between these two men are striking. Both were precocious university-educated scholars who shared a Protestant faith (albeit more 'hot' on Cecil's side than Maitland's). Both had family origins among the 'middling sort' of lairds and minor gentry who became increasingly prominent in sixteenth-century government. Once in office, both saw the peace and security of a united, Protestant Britain as the chief objective of their deliberations. All of these commonalities allowed them to bond in a way their sovereigns, divided by conflicting faiths, divergent cultural upbringings and competing political ambitions, could not. Many of their letters reflected a playful familiarity; Maitland often referred to Cecil as his 'father', and asked him to treat him like his son. Nevertheless, their friendship was often tested over the years: Maitland was frequently frustrated by Cecil's reticence and 'bref and derk sentences', while Cecil grew impatient with Maitland's apparent lack of evangelical fervour.

Their letters – by turns humorous, philosophical and moving – not only provide insights into the development of Anglo-Scottish relations during one of its most formative periods, but also reveal how Maitland and Cecil viewed their roles as secretaries at a time when the office in both countries was rapidly evolving. As two of the most prominent politicians of their age, Cecil and Maitland have received a great deal of scholarly attention as separate individuals, yet few studies have examined their relationship in depth, or analysed their voluminous correspondence for insights into how they negotiated the complex relationships between themselves, their queens and countries over time.[2] Maitland and Cecil's exchanges show that they defined their secretarial roles according to classical, Ciceronian models of civic virtue, but also in terms of spiritual vocation. Despite the many institutional changes taking place around them, they saw themselves as links in a historical chain of public servants who had subjugated their personal fears and ambitions to the greater good. Ultimately, however, these letters show that despite their many common goals, Maitland and Cecil differed fundamentally on the role of religion in politics and the nature of political authority. Cecil believed the furtherance of the reformed religion trumped all other concerns, including one's loyalty to a monarch (especially a Catholic one), while Maitland argued that peace and stability could only be achieved through the unifying figure of the monarch, regardless of their religious persuasion. These differences eventually tore their friendship apart, with fatal consequences for Maitland who died shortly after English forces captured Edinburgh castle in 1573, ending the Queen's Party's hopes of restoring Mary to the Scottish throne following her forced abdication on 24 July 1567. Their correspondence provides the perfect lens through which to examine the role of the secretary in early modern Britain, and the personal costs the office often claimed.

An epistolary approach to Cecil and Maitland's relationship is not without its difficulties, however: the first being the huge disparity in the records. Unfortunately, while much (if not all) of Maitland's side of the correspondence is preserved in the British Library, the National Archives and the Cecil Papers at Hatfield House (which together house the bulk of Cecil's diplomatic 'in-tray'), nearly all of Cecil's letters to Maitland are no longer extant. One possibility is that Maitland's papers were seized or destroyed following his capture at Edinburgh Castle on 29 May 1573, which would not be surprising considering the earl of Morton refused Maitland a decent burial, so 'that the vermin from it [his body] came creeping out under the door of the house'.[3] Any papers Maitland had stored in his family house at Lethington would also likely have been seized after his death: much to his father's distress, the family furniture was sold off and the house itself allowed to fall into disrepair.[4] Any remaining papers would have passed to Maitland's younger brother John, later Lord Thirlestane (1543–95), and ultimately to his grand-nephew John Maitland, 1st Duke of Lauderdale (1616–82), whose archive represented 'one of the most important collections of Scottish historical documents of the sixteenth and seventeenth centuries'.[5] Sadly, most of Lauderdale's papers were dispersed in various private sales in the nineteenth century, and while many were purchased by the British Library, only a handful of Cecil's letters to Maitland appear to be among them.[6] Maitland's papers may also have been among the many state papers lost, stolen or destroyed during the Cromwellian siege of Stirling Castle in 1651, or their subsequent removal to the Tower of London. They may also have been among the 'eighty-five hogsheads' of Scottish records lost or plundered when the ship (ironically named *The Elizabeth*) returning them to Edinburgh following the Restoration in 1660 sank in a storm off the Northumbrian coast.[7]

Despite these unfortunate twists and turns of the Scottish historical records, the situation is not quite as dire as Conyers Read suggested when he claimed that *none* of Cecil's letters to Maitland were extant.[8] Against the roughly 106 surviving letters from Maitland, a precious four letters from Cecil are preserved in the British Library and National Archives.[9] Moreover, a fair amount of the content of Cecil's letters can be reconstructed through close analysis of Maitland's responses. In line with common practice, Maitland often summarised the main points of the letter he was answering. Moreover, one can assume that his relaxed, conversational tone (or what he called the 'private frendship intelligence and familiarity betwuix ws two') must have been reciprocated for it to be maintained so consistently over the years.[10] As will be shown, Maitland also repeatedly drew attention to what was *not* in Cecil's letters, or what he expected to find in them but could not. Despite the uneven nature of the sources, Read concluded that 'there can be little doubt that Cecil and Maitland spoke the same language'.[11] This shared language derived largely from their similar backgrounds, education, and the comparable structures of their secretarial offices – though, as will be shown later, there were times when their different personalities and divergent political views caused some ideas to be lost in translation.

Besides the striking fact that both Williams were the only (Cecil) and eldest (Maitland) sons of courtiers named Richard, both men came from families of the minor gentry with a history of court service, and shared similar educational paths and apprenticeships to reach their offices. The Maitland family had a longer pedigree, tracing their origins back to the twelfth century and acquiring the fortified family house at Lethington (now Lennoxlove) by royal charter in 1345. They had also distinguished themselves as courtiers and soldiers: Maitland's grandfather appeared briefly in Gavin Douglas's allegorical poem *The Palis of Honoure* (1501), and lived up to this chivalric ideal by dying heroically at Flodden in 1513.[12] Maitland's father Sir Richard (1496–1586) was a renowned poet, historian and high court judge, who continued the family tradition of royal service by serving as a councillor to Regent Moray and Keeper of the Privy Seal from 1562 to 1567. The Cecil family had humbler origins, but rose quickly over three generations to become one of the first families in England. Cecil's grandfather David raised himself from a yeoman of the Welsh marches to a prosperous country gentleman and, having won royal recognition for his service at the Battle of Bosworth, attained the position of Sergeant-at-Arms to Henry VIII. This opened the door for Cecil's father, Richard (d. 1553), to enter royal service first as Page of the Chamber and later as Yeoman of the Wardrobe. Richard also served as sheriff of Rutland and Justice of the Peace in Nottinghamshire, showing his interest in local politics.[13]

Thanks to their fathers' prosperous careers at court, both Cecil and Maitland received the finest educations available. Maitland was probably educated at Haddington Grammar School in East Lothian, where he likely experienced a similar curriculum to Cecil, who attended the Grantham and Stamford schools in south-west Lincolnshire. Most grammar schools of the time focused on the study of Latin language and literature, with perhaps a smattering of Greek (although this was less common).[14] Both young men showed great aptitude for learning, progressing to university in their early to mid-teens: Cecil went up to St John's College, Cambridge in May 1535 aged fifteen, while Maitland attended St Leonard's College at St Andrew's in 1540, possibly aged as young as twelve.[15] As reformed ideas began to percolate through the veins of Britain's intellectual elite, both St John's and St Leonard's became closely associated with the Protestant movement (to have 'drunk of St Leonard's well' became colloquial shorthand for having imbibed reformed opinions).[16] Cecil remained at St John's for six years before moving on (without taking his degree) to study the law at Gray's Inn, while Maitland left St Leonard's after only two years to study at the University of Paris along with fifty other Scots who chose to take advantage of the 'auld Parisiane kyndnes', one of the cultural benefits of the Franco-Scottish alliance.[17] Maitland's experience of studying abroad gave him a cosmopolitan perspective on Scottish politics, and may explain why he was later sent on several diplomatic trips to the French court during his career.[18] By contrast, Cecil's only experience of foreign travel was spent escorting Cardinal Pole from France to England in 1554.[19]

Cecil's and Maitland's educations raised them above the level of mere bureaucrats or household servants: they saw themselves firstly as scholars who drew on their extensive learning to further the public good. Cecil's love of classical literature, particularly Cicero, was well known, but he was equally conversant with contemporary literature.[20] No record of Maitland's library survives, but considering his reputation for learning, one assumes it must have rivalled Cecil's. In both his conversation and letters Maitland deftly demonstrated his familiarity with Italian and classical literature (especially Greek, the trademark of a true humanist), and he could 'commune well in Latin and French, as well as English and his native Scots'.[21] Maitland impressed his friends and enemies alike with his extraordinary range of intellect and his gifts of persuasion. According to George Buchanan, himself one of the most learned scholars in Scotland (and one of Maitland's severest critics), he was 'subtil to draw out the Secrets of every Man's Mind, and improve all to his own proper Interest'.[22] Cecil was similarly impressed by Maitland's abilities, which he observed first hand during his visit to inspect the English troops at Edinburgh in June 1560:

> I fynd ye Lord of Leddyngton disposed to work all the myndes of the nobilite to allow any thyng that your Ma[jesty] shall det[er]myne / he is of most creditt here for his witt, and almost susteneth the whole burden of forsight.[23]

Like Cecil, Maitland was as well versed in scripture as he was in the classics, and could trade rhetorical blows with the fiery-tongued Protestant reformer John Knox.[24] Interestingly, both Maitland and Cecil were accused of using their rhetorical gifts for Machiavellian ends.[25]

After several years at Gray's Inn, Cecil entered government service as chief clerk of the common pleas and caught the attention of Protector Somerset, who employed him as his personal secretary in 1548. Despite a two-month sojourn in the Tower following Somerset's first fall (November 1549–January 1550), Cecil was eventually promoted to privy councillor and junior third secretary of state, and used his apprenticeship to establish a valuable array of contacts at home and abroad. In 1551 he was knighted for his service, but narrowly avoided disaster when he signed the 'instrument' in favour of the Protestant Jane Grey's succession in 1553. Although Cecil made peace with the Catholic Queen Mary, outwardly conforming to the new religious status quo and maintaining an active life at court, it was not until the accession of her Protestant half-sister Elizabeth (with whom he had kept closely in touch) on 17 November 1558 that Cecil regained his place at the heart of government.[26] Meanwhile, after returning from Paris, Maitland began his secretarial apprenticeship in 1554 as clerk of the council and assistant secretary to David Paniter, Bishop of Ross. Paniter had studied with Erasmus and travelled widely through Europe as an ambassador, but towards the end of his life became 'extreme corpulent and unable of bodie and extreme seiklie and weake and altogether unable to exercise his office'.[27] Maitland, having all the necessary skills in Latin and French (as well as a wicked pack of cards to entertain the Queen Dowager, Mary of Guise, in the long winter evenings), was chosen to replace him. Despite some initial misgivings about overstepping his place, Maitland was officially appointed 'our souverane lord and ladies secretare and keipar of all thair signets all the dayis of his life' on 4 December 1558.[28]

Thus, both Cecil and Maitland became Principal Secretaries in their mid-twenties, and (amazingly) within a month of each other.[29] Cecil and Maitland represent the rise of a professional, educated elite in sixteenth-century government, but also the waxing importance of the Secretary as a central officer of state. G. R. Elton's argument that a bureaucratic 'revolution' took place in the 1530s in England was echoed by Maurice Lee's thesis that John Maitland of Thirlistane presided over a similarly transformative period in Scottish government in the 1580s and early 1590s.[30] Both arguments have been repeatedly contested over the last several decades, yet even taking into account the evolutionary rather than revolutionary nature of institutional developments, it is hard to ignore the extraordinary – and arguably unprecedented – influence both Cecil and Maitland came to wield in government affairs.[31] At a time when the early modern nation state was readapting itself to post-Reformation ideas and institutional parameters were in flux, their careers demonstrated how much individual personality, political circumstance and the temperament of the ruler could determine the limits of the office of Principal Secretary.

Although the Scottish secretariat was smaller than the English, structurally they were very much alike, both having grown out of the royal household during the medieval period when the Keeper of the Signet (Secretary) eventually became independent of the Office of the Privy Seal and Keeper of the Great Seal (Chancellor).[32] The English secretariat evolved more rapidly: the earliest reference to the office of 'Secretary' in England appears in 1253, while in Scotland it appears in 1360.[33] The formalities of government functions were also more fluid in the Scottish system than the English: in Scotland the Privy Council usually met in the Secretary's chambers, reinforcing his central importance as a minister and advisor as well as record-keeper, while the English Privy Council usually met in a specially designated 'Council Chamber' within the royal palace of Westminster.[34] Although the English Secretary was a prominent member of the Council, the more neutral location of the Council chambers emphasised (at least in formal terms) its separateness. As Secretary, Maitland held a prominent place in Parliament, acting as 'harangue-maker' (that is, Speaker) in 1560, 1564 and 1567, a position that allowed him significant control over legislative decisions.[35] Cecil, however, was never formally elected Speaker, since this position was not permitted for officers of the English Crown; nevertheless, he was allowed to *appoint* the speaker, and could therefore choose a sympathetic ally (usually from among the back benches or law offices) to guide parliamentary discussion in the direction he preferred.[36]

While much of the information about Maitland's and Cecil's secretariats is 'slight, tantalising and obscure', it is possible to note some interesting differences in their secretarial practices.[37] The English typically filed all official correspondence in chronologically arranged bundles of in-letters organised by geographical region.[38] The Scots, however, had followed the French *registre* system (in which both in and out letters were copied, summarised and recorded in large registers) since the late fifteenth century.[39] One of the effects of this system was that the Scots were less concerned about preserving original letters (another possible explanation for Cecil's missing letters). However, whether or not a letter was recorded in the official register also depended on whether it was considered private or public, which could evidently vary by circumstance as much as by correspondent. In September 1564 Cecil asked Maitland to double-check the wording of a letter Maitland had sent to Elizabeth, which had apparently upset her. 'In gude fayth', Maitland replied:

I know not yt [i.e. that] I reserved any copy off those l[ett]res to my selff at least I can not yet find any [and confess] my neglegence I seldome reserve copyes of any l[ett]res I privately write my selff. Mary the more fault is myne and I intend to amend it hereafter.[40]

This exchange suggests that Maitland was far more casual in his approach to recording letters than Cecil (whose record-keeping was notoriously assiduous), but more interestingly, it shows that he considered his holograph (that is, handwritten) correspondence with Cecil to be 'private' – the implications of which will be discussed further below.

The day-to-day responsibilities of both secretaries were vast, and required an encyclopaedic knowledge of legal, administrative, financial, ecclesiastical and mercantile affairs. With the expansion of diplomatic agents and permanent ambassadors in the mid-sixteenth century the volume of diplomatic correspondence increased, and the management of foreign policy became one of the Secretary's largest concerns.[41] In 1600 Cecil's younger son Sir Robert (1563–1612) wrote a treatise entitled *The State and Dignity of a Secretary of State's place with the care and peril thereof*, in which he enumerated the many tasks and responsibilities that fell to him, including (for example) knowledge of the queen's treaties with foreign princes, the actions and negotiations of ambassadors, the proceedings of the councils of Wales and the North, developments in Ireland, the costs of ongoing wars, overseeing the council and muster books, the custody of letters to and from foreign princes, and finally, collating 'intelligence abroad'.[42] Despite a similarly impressive burden of work, William Cecil kept his secretariat small: between 1558 and 1572 he 'had not above two or three [secretaries]', which won him the approval of secretaries Robert Beale and Nicholas Faunt, who thought more than this created confusion.[43] In Scotland, it is known that by 1538 the Secretary had 'a small legion of assistants including four chief clerks to the signet engaged under his direct supervision', though how many Maitland personally employed is less clear.[44]

Since early modern politics operated within and across networks of personal relationships bridged by kinship, friendship and clientage that transcended institutional boundaries, both Cecil and Maitland did their best to ensure that the secretariat and other important offices of state stayed within the family.[45] Sir Robert Cecil followed in his father's footsteps to serve as Elizabeth's Principal Secretary from 1590 until her death, and then in the same capacity for James VI/I until his own death in 1612. Maitland's father, Sir Richard, was appointed Keeper of the Privy Seal for life in 1562 (despite being completely blind), but resigned it to his younger son John following Mary's abdication in 1567.[46] Maitland's younger brother John (1543–95) shared many of his political instincts, and despite remaining loyal to the doomed cause of the Queen's Party during the Marian civil war, he managed to survive the fallout to become Secretary himself in 1584 and Chancellor in 1588.[47] The advantages of maintaining familial continuity within the office were emphasised by Cecil (then Lord Burghley) in December 1590, who fondly recalled to John Maitland the 'ould famyliar acquaintances in a verie strict amitye' he had shared with

yo[ur] elder brother the younge lard of Lethington, he a Secretary to that crowne, and I then to this crowne, [which] was so beneficiall to both these crownes, by restoringe them by o[ur] minestery to suche a brotherly peace, as never had bene in many hundred yeares before.[48]

Burghley, ever the expert diplomatist, went on to assure John that he intended to continue the same relationship with him, 'a Secretarye by Office, as he [Maitland] was, thoughe now also placed in an office being Chauncelor, w[hich] I accompte the principall Secretary of yt realme'.[49]

Another obvious (and unusual) commonality that Cecil and Maitland shared was that they both served female rulers. This was an unprecedented situation in the history of Anglo-Scottish relations, and further complicated ongoing plans to unite the two kingdoms, since in the past Anglo-Scottish amity was usually cemented through marriage of an English princess to a Scottish king.[50] The irony of this became the source of many jokes at court, especially during Mary's marriage negotiations in 1563. 'Randolphe', exclaimed Mary, 'wold have me marie in Englande', to which the earl of Argyle merrily replied, 'Is the Quene of Englaunde become a man?'[51] As well as limiting the diplomatic options for establishing peace between the realms, these unusual gender dynamics also influenced the way politics was conceptualised and practised during Elizabeth's and Mary's reigns. When John Aylmer answered John Knox's infamous *First Blast of the Trumpet Against the Monstrous Regiment of Women* (1558), he argued that God had singled out Elizabeth as an exceptional woman to rule, but had also provided England with a unique form of 'mixed monarchy' that meant she would be guided by male counsellors.[52] Elizabeth may have been tacitly acknowledging this when, in her first speech as queen, she charged Cecil to 'be faithful to the *state*, and that without respect of my private will, you will give me that counsel that you think best'.[53] Maitland recognised the young queen Mary's intelligence, which he described as 'far exceeding her age', and defended her against the vehement sermons of the evangelical reformer John Knox, whom he wished would 'deal with her more gently being a young princess unpersuaded [. . .] god grant her the assistance off his spirit'.[54]

Foreign ambassadors were quick to recognise Cecil's and Maitland's influence over their respective queens. On 19 March 1559 the Spanish ambassador, Count de Feria, informed Philip II that Maitland was rumoured to rule the Queen Dowager, Mary of Guise, 'body and soul', while on 5 May 1561 Álvaro de la Quadra noted that Cecil 'has so entire a control over the Queen and affairs, that, however much I wished I could not negotiate through any other channel'.[55] In practice, however, the gendered lines of power between queen and councillor were not so clear-cut as contemporary political theorists like Knox and Aylmer had assumed. Before she arrived in Scotland, Mary sent Maitland a stern letter of warning that dispelled any impression of her as a helpless young girl: 'Nothing passes amongst my nobility without your knowledge and advice. I will not conceal from you that if anything goes wrong after I have trusted you, you are the first one I will blame.'[56] Although Cecil tried on numerous occasions to pressure Elizabeth (both personally and through Parliament) on matters he considered to be vital to the public interest, such as her marriage and succession (and eventually, the condemnation of Mary for treason), she famously refused to allow discussion of points that touched on her prerogative. Elizabeth was especially reluctant to provide military support to the Protestant Lords of the Congregation in their attempt to oust French forces from Leith in 1560, and only relented because Cecil threatened to resign if she refused her consent.

In light of all Cecil and Maitland had in common, it is little wonder that when the Spanish ambassador Guzman de Silva asked his French counterpart Paul de Foix to describe what kind of man Maitland was, de Foix replied: 'A sort of Scotch Cecil.'[57] Even their mutual enemies saw them as two ends of the same political animal. In May 1569 the exiled James Hepburn, fourth earl of Bothwell (then stewing in captivity in Denmark) reportedly groaned that 'ther are two secreataryes, thone in Englande, and thother in Scotlande, and if they weare deade, both realmes should be the better'.[58] Cecil acknowledged that he and Maitland 'have many thynges common to us both, wherein our inentions ought to agree'.[59] Maitland himself repeatedly made clear how much he honoured and revered Cecil, and sought to emulate his example: 'sence the first begynning off o[ur] acquentance', he wrote in 1565, 'I have ever set yow before my eyes as a paterne wysshing I myght co[n]forme my selff and all my actions to the imitation off yo[urs]'.[60] Throughout their correspondence, both men drew on their many common bonds, experiences and objectives to preserve and further the amity between their two countries.

Although Maitland was only five to ten years younger than Cecil, he frequently referred to the older man in affectionately filial terms as his 'father'. '[Y]ow have always bene a father unto me', Maitland wrote in February 1562, 'and whatsoever good luck shall fall onto me is dew unto yow.'[61] Maitland's attempt to create a rhetorical bond of close kinship with Cecil was not unusual in political discourse of the time, yet this rhetoric had a greater utility beyond merely paying deference and respect to an elder colleague. Maitland most often invoked Cecil's paternal care in times of crisis. Two weeks after the murder of Mary's second husband, Henry Stuart, Lord Darnley, on 10 February 1567 (which Maitland was almost certainly involved in, if not directly responsible for), he concluded a hasty letter to Cecil by begging him 'to make alwayes accompt off me as off one who solong as I lyve will hono[ur] yow as my father'.[62] A week after Mary's dramatic defeat at the Battle of Langside on 13 May 1568 and subsequent escape into England, Maitland again excused the brevity of his letter, committing the rest of his news to the bearer: 'this onely I will add yt I do always remayne that sam man yow ever knew me & asfar at yo[ur] co[m]mandement as yo[ur] owne sone'.[63] Following the unravelling of Mary's complicity in the Ridolfi Plot against Elizabeth's life in the summer of 1571, Maitland's anxiety over losing Cecil's support was palpable:

> to few strangears yea rather to none at all have I ever so frankly utered my conceptions as to yo[ur] L. to whome from the begynning off o[ur] acquentance I have borne reverence as to my father & whose advises I have for the most p[ar]t followed as off the dearest friend I had.[64]

Maitland clearly used the language of filial duty and affection as an emotional lever to encourage Cecil's support when he needed it most. Whether Cecil ever reciprocated in kind is difficult to say, since so few of his letters survive: although he referred to him as 'the yong L. of Leddyngtone', this was because Maitland's father Sir Richard (the 'elder' Lord of Lethington) was still alive.[65] Nevertheless, Maitland's persistence in using this deferential language suggests much about the balance of power in their relationship – and how Maitland sought to tip the balance in his favour by emphasising Cecil's obligation to assist his political 'son'.

Another way Maitland sought to strengthen his alliance with the English Secretary was by striking up a friendly correspondence with Cecil's wife Mildred (1526–89). The eldest of five exceptionally learned daughters of the renowned scholar Sir Anthony Cooke, Mildred married Cecil in December 1545 and bore him five children, and in addition to supervising their sizeable household of wealthy wards and servants, she frequently acted as intermediary between her husband and various petitioners.[66] Maitland probably met Mildred during his first London embassy in 1558, and like many others was no doubt impressed by her erudition and learning.[67] Maitland drew heavily on his friendship with Mildred during the tumultuous months of 1559–60, when he risked his life and career by openly defecting to the Lords of the Congregation at the expense of the Queen Regent Mary of Guise, and struggled to oust the remaining French forces from Scotland with English support. Knowing that Mildred was reputed to be a strong advocate for godly reformers, Maitland repeatedly assured her that he and his friends intended to 'hazard lyves landes and all' for the Protestant cause.[68] After the conclusion of the Treaty of Edinburgh (6 July 1560) by which the French occupying forces agreed to evacuate Scotland (thus paving the way for the Reformation Parliament), Maitland thanked Mildred at length for her 'gentlenes' and 'moche favo[ur]', and reminded her that their 'co[m]mon caus' was only just beginning: 'Mary now shall we begynne to have most nede off yo[ur] help in the mater quharunto yow know I most earnestly prease. I beleve tyme is not able so to owercome yow yt yow will waxe cold in it.' He concluded with the hope that 'yow have ever opinion off me yt I shall esteme my selff happy if I may have occasion to do pleso[ur] or s[er]vice to Mr Secretary or yow to whom I owe more then I shall ever be able to pay'.[69] Maitland often ended his letters to Cecil with a request that he 'mak my most hasty reco[m] mendations to my Lady yo[ur] bedfellow to whom and yow I am more bound then I shall ever be able to descharg'.[70] Maitland invested much time and effort in cultivating his friendship with Mildred, whose influence with her husband provided further leverage in times of crisis.

Just as Mary and Elizabeth continually emphasised the ties they shared as cousins and queens to tighten their bonds of mutual obligation, so Maitland and Cecil frequently discussed the particular burdens they shared as Principal Secretaries to highlight the need for mutual support, honesty and directness. Although their positions gave them privileged access to the heart of government and the means to influence events as they unfolded, it also made them vulnerable to public criticism should things go wrong. Maitland was nervous in the months leading up to Mary's return to her native Scotland in 1561, since (like many others) he was unsure how she would react to the revolutionary constitutional and religious changes enacted in the Reformation Parliament, which had proceeded without her permission, and in which he had played a leading role. Yet if he seemed to side with Mary too much, he risked alienating his Anglophile allies among the Lords of the Congregation. On 26 February 1561 Maitland confided his fears to Cecil:

> I pray yow co[n]sidder what danger it is for me to write / many mens eyes loke upon me / any familiarity w[ith] that realme is knowne and sofar mislyked yt I feare at length it shalbe my ondoing onelesse the Q. maj[esty] be made favourable to Engl[and].[71]

Nevertheless, Maitland was philosophical about his predicament, since being the focus of other men's anger was the common lot of a secretary:

> for that I know this burden is co[m]mon to me w[ith] many others I beare it the more patiently / I will serve the Q. my soverayne truely and do wishe yt these two realmes may co[n]tinew in friendship and if by my laubors I could invent or procure the meane I wold thynk it wer good s[er]vice / yet p[er]haps will it not be so taken / this maketh me so oft to touche this poynt.[72]

As public servants, he and Cecil had to be ready to sacrifice their personal desires, security and prosperity for the common good: 'if by the meanes off ws two soche a co[n]iunction may be procured we shalbe estemed happy instrumentes for o[ur] countreyes'.[73]

The main obstacles to the Anglo-Scottish amity at this time were Elizabeth's reluctance to publicly acknowledge Mary as her successor, and Mary's corresponding refusal to ratify the Treaty of Edinburgh, which required her to relinquish her claim to the English throne. In September 1561 Maitland had three interviews with Elizabeth in which she utilised her characteristic tactics of prevarication and feint promises; yet Maitland came away with hopes for a compromise, and also with Elizabeth's blessing that he and Cecil use 'o[ur] co[n]ference by l[ettres]' to 'digest and put in some towardnes thaffaires betwixt theyr ma[jesties]'.[74] Maitland was enthusiastic about liaising with Cecil, 'for therupon me thynketh doth depend the felicity off both the countreyes [. . .] the litle moyen [means] I have shalbe employed to that end'.[75] Maitland hoped that 'yow and I be both off one mynd to direct all o[ur] actions and credit in the place off service w[hich] we occupy', and he encouraged Cecil:

> playnely write to me how my maistress shall deale w[ith] yo[urs] to come to that good accord w[hich] I trust both yow and I desyre / soche is my co[n]fidence in yow yt as yow counsall me so will I be bold to advise her ma[jesty] to do and so upon yo[ur] opinion haserd my credit w[ith] my maistress w[hich] I trust yow wold not be willing I shold lose / write amply unto me what answer yow think will be accepted in good p[ar]t.[76]

Maitland's exhortations are revealing of his own relationship with Mary, whose chief advisor at this time was ostensibly her half-brother, James Stewart (made earl of Moray in 1562). Moray and Maitland were close allies at this time, and it is likely they worked as a team – but Maitland had one key advantage over Moray: as

Secretary, he was responsible for drafting Mary's letters, and therefore had a certain degree of editorial authority in crafting her words on the page. On 15 January 1562 Maitland asked Cecil to let him know how Mary's last holograph letter to Elizabeth was received, for 'if any thing be mislyked the falt is myne'.[77] This suggests that Mary had either copied out a letter Maitland had written for her, or that she had relied heavily on his editorial suggestions. Maitland's requests for Cecil's advice in framing his own queen's letters were clearly intended to strengthen Cecil's trust and give the English at least the perception of directing the negotiations, but they also reveal a sophisticated, multilayered understanding of how diplomatic communication worked in practice:

> many things may pas betwix ws two upon theyr [Mary and Elizabeth's] knowlege w[hich] neither off them both will for the first face write to thother. ones agayne I pray yow write planely and directly onto me what farthar yow wold have spocken or done on o[ur] p[ar]t, to what end, and what hope yow have off the success.[78]

While the queens' correspondence was constrained by formulaic niceties, Maitland and Cecil could cut through the diplomatic double-speak and thereby advance their negotiations more speedily. Nevertheless, Maitland believed the best way for their queens to overcome their mutual suspicion was to write regularly to each other, preferably in their own handwriting: '[Elizabeth's] franknes in wryting may serve for a sufficient argument off a singular trust [. . .] I pray yow advise her ma[jesty] to an[swer] these [i.e. Mary's] l[etters] so playnely friendlie and w[ith] soche spede as the mater requireth.'[79]

Cecil, however, was far less willing to satisfy Maitland's pleas for 'plain and direct' conversation. Although he wanted Scottish support, he was all too aware of the benefits of allowing 'the Scottish Queen's affairs [to] hang in an uncertainty'.[80] Cecil, like Elizabeth, was well trained in the art of giving 'answers answerless', leaving Maitland and Mary frustrated by their enigmatic replies. On 29 January 1562 Maitland complained:

> yow write alwayes to me parables at least bref and derk sentences and yow have experience off my simplicity – *davus sum no[n] oedipus*[81] – I wold be glade yow shold uter yo[ur] selff onto me more playnly / I offer franknes on my p[ar]t and wishe yt by yo[ur] soueraygnes co[m]mandement at least p[er]mission I may fynd the counterpayne w[ith] yow [. . .] I pray yow keape on yo[ur] trade off wryting so oft as occa[sion] shalbe offred and yo[ur] leasure serve / for I had rather gess at dirk l[ett]res then have none.[82]

Cecil was aware of Maitland's frustrations. In the wake of the inconclusive conference at Berwick in November 1564, where the English commissioners made it clear that even if Mary accepted Elizabeth's proposal that she marry the Earl of Leicester, she would still not be guaranteed the succession, Cecil drafted a letter addressed to both Maitland and Moray, asking them to interpret his letters to ye best, and rather than to fynd any fault in me ether for obscurite, which many tymes yow ye L. of Leddyngton have noted in my ^formar^ wrytinges ^concerning^ this matter, I wish yt yow wold reckon to me your doutes or mis-lykynges, that I might enlarge [. . .] ^the same^.[83]

This sentence, however, is struck through in the draft; perhaps Cecil thought it wise to avoid accepting the fault of 'obscurite', lest it leave the door ajar for further accusations.[84]

Although he was exasperated by Cecil's obfuscations, Maitland acknowledged Cecil's excuse that 'the less yow medle in so greate maters the less is yo[ur] danger', since the concern 'is co[mm]on to ws both'. However, in order to break the diplomatic deadlock, he reminded Cecil they were not only working for 'o[ur] owne gryetnes yea and security', but for the greater good of their two kingdoms, even though 'the reward off o[ur] well meaning shalbe litle thank for o[ur] labo[ur]'. Maitland tried to persuade Cecil to cooperate by putting their situation into historical perspective:

> this hath bene and many tymes worse the reco[m]pense off those yt were cheefe ministers in co[mm]on wealthes as by the historyes off all ages may clearely appeare yet more to be feared in all other kyndes off gou[er]nement than in monarchyes, for yt the popular estate is a greate deale more ingrate than princes be. Mary the peple be alwayes lyke onto themselffs to misco[n]strue mens actions be theyr dealing never so oupryght. I trust neyther off ws both lacketh thexperience off this in o[ur] owne p[er]son. but serving two soche maistresses sofar different in iugement fro[m] the co[mm]en sort I think all this p[ar]t ought to be co[n]temned.[85]

So long as their actions met with the approval of their queens and were in accordance with their consciences, they had little to fear. Maitland agreed with Cecil's own sentiment that 'for the love off yo[ur] Countrey yow will set asyde yo[ur] owne p[er]ell'. He felt the same, and 'never did forbeare but when eyther yo[ur] silence or obscure and dark wryting gave me cause'.[86] In February 1565 Maitland invoked the classical ideal of civic virtue to bring his point home:

> if we did resemble the old romaynes for attayning theroff we wold not styck to sacrifice o[ur] selff and offer o[ur] veary lyves to what soever danger my[ght] occur [. . .] what greatar good luck could any off ws wyssh than to be called to this honorable office? [W]ere not this hono[ur] sufficient to satisfy the most ambitious hart in the world?[87]

Maitland then tied his history lesson from Ancient Rome back to the Anglo-Scottish context:

> more honorable shall the report be in the ages to come when the posterity shall tast the frute off o[ur] p[rese]nt laubo[urs] off those whose hap and good fortune

shalbe to be employed in this cause then off any whosoever thay were did most vailzeantly serve kyng Edward the first in his co[n]quest or kyng robert the bruce in the recovery off his countrey. go fordwart therfor I pray yow as yow haiff begone and suffer neyther the malice off fortoun nor envy off man to owerthrow the werk yow haiff already buylded upon so good a fundation suffer not yo[ur] selff and co[n]sequently yo[ur] frendes to be violently robbed off so greate an hono[ur].[88]

The implicit contrast Maitland draws here between Elizabeth and Edward I, and between Mary and Robert the Bruce, further illustrates the seriousness Maitland attached to their negotiations, yet it also hinted at a possible return to the violent hostilities of the past if the Anglo-Scottish union was not resolved.[89]

After several years of fruitless negotiation and stalling, both secretaries observed that the arduous process of letter-writing had frustrating limitations when it came to working out solutions to complex diplomatic problems. In September 1564 Maitland acknowledged Cecil's assertion that 'one halff ho[ur]s frank co[m]munication by mouth were more worth for those proposses than xx whole dayes wryting', and assured his friend that 'I have wisshed my selff w[ith] yow not halff an ho[ur] bot rather an whole day'.[90] Three years later Maitland again lamented that he had missed an opportunity to meet with Cecil in person, 'but being so lately maryed it wes not reasonable to mak a divorsement fro[m] my wyfe so soone'.[91] On 6 January 1567 Maitland had married his sweetheart, Mary Fleming (1542–1600), one of the 'four Maries' who had attended the queen throughout her childhood in France, and whom Kirkcaldy of Grange described as being as fit for Maitland as he was to be pope, on account of her youth and Catholicism.[92] Maitland had been courting Mary since 1564, and his giddy delight in her company occasionally bubbled over into his letters to Cecil:

the co[m]mon affaires do never so moche trouble me but yt at least I have one meary ho[ur] off the fo[ur] & twenty / and yow laubo[ur] co[n]tinually w[ith] out intermission nothing co[n]sidering yt the body yea and the mynd also must sometyme have recreation or els they can not long last. soche physik as I do minister onto my selff I appoynt for yow. Mary yow may p[er]haps reply yt as now the world doth go w[ith] me my body is better disposed to digest soche then yo[urs] is / for those yt be in love ar ever set upon a meary pyn.[93]

Such jovial digressions illustrate the affectionate friendship both men shared. '[H]owsoever the princes maters fall out', Maitland wrote to Cecil in June 1565,

I trust so far as we may reserving o[ur] dewtyes to o[ur] souereygnes o[ur] private frendship shall not be violated [. . .] hald hand I pray yow yt nothing breake out on yo[ur] p[ar]t as yow may co[n]veniently / I will do the like on this p[ar]t / the best off every thing must be made.[94]

Cecil and Maitland's friendship was firmly rooted in a common goal: the peace, prosperity and security of a united and Protestant Britain. They differed, however, in how they sought to achieve it. Cecil had a coherent 'British Policy' founded on an imperial vision of England's right to dominate Scotland and Ireland, and driven by an ideological commitment to furthering the Protestant cause.[95] Although Maitland once acknowledged in 1561 that, thanks to his association with Cecil, he was 'taken in ffrance to be a better englishman then other', he was, as Loughlin notes, 'always a unionist but only briefly an Anglophile'.[96] He was consistent in seeking acknowledgement of Mary's place in the English succession, which he believed was the most effective way to unite the kingdoms. Cecil, however, was unable to countenance the prospect of a Catholic Scottish queen on the English throne. The issue of religion was therefore the key point on which Maitland and Cecil diverged. When circumstances put their respective positions to the test during the Marian Civil War of 1568–73, their friendship – which had held fast for over a decade – quickly began to unravel.

Cecil was a much 'hotter' sort of Protestant than his Scottish counterpart, who seems to have shared his father Sir Richard's Erasmian attitude to religion.[97] As Stephen Alford has noted, Cecil was 'Pragmatic, tough and uncompromising [. . .] but he was also a conviction politician who acted with ideological purpose.'[98] Cecil's 'ideological purpose' was clearly articulated in one of his few extant letters to Maitland dated 20 August 1563, written shortly after news reached him that Mary was contemplating a marriage to Don Carlos of Spain, or possibly Charles IX of France (both Catholics) and in anticipation of the final session of the Council of Trent (or as he called it, the 'congregation of Antichristes soldyars'). The failure of the Le Havre expedition to support French Protestants in 1562–3 and Elizabeth's close encounter with smallpox in October 1562 had exposed England's vulnerability to attack, and if Scotland, France and Spain were to join forces, Cecil's nightmare of a grand alliance of Catholic powers united against an isolated Protestant England would come true. After reassuring Maitland of his intention to 'use a few sentences playnely and truely, nether curioosly nor collorably wrytten',[99] Cecil laid out with scholastic precision the three priorities he and Maitland should always hold before them in their negotiations:

> What so ever maye furder ye satlyng of ye Gospell of Christ and ye dissolution of Antichrist, ought to be cheeffly afore all regarded of us both and herin no wisedom of ye world, no affection to person, no care of our selves ought to blynd us. Next what so ever maye ether unyte the hartes of the people of this Ile, to gither in one, or preserve them from discord and hatred, ought to be regarded by us both afore ye affection to any nation and contry. Last what so ever might make ye accord betwixt our twoo soverayns perpetuall, ought to be sought by us bothe, and ye contrary, or any thyng to the same, ought to be w[ith]stand and bannished.[100]

Furthering the Gospel of Christ; preserving the unity of the British people; and ensuring amity between their respective sovereigns. These were Cecil's objectives – and the order of them is revealing. Although Cecil acknowledged that he and Maitland might differ on some things, such as the 'particular avancement of the honor or state of our Soveranys',[101] these three principles were paramount – but ultimately, the success of the last two depended on the first:

> My Lord, I require yow in Gods name befor who yow and I shall answer w[ith] out any advocate, lett no respect move yow to allow of th[at] which by good prooffe yow may see is intended to sett upp Antichrist [. . .] I onely feare, that your affection is so larg as it hath covered your judgment. God gyve yow his spyrit to discerne herin what shall be most to his honor [. . .].[102]

For his part, Cecil concluded,

> I will never be author, or assentor to that which I shall probably thynk will ether extinguish ye knowledg of ye Gospell in this Ile, or will diminish ye concord yt is presently betwixt the nations, for if I shall willingly so doo I shall syne ageynst my conscience.[103]

To bring the point home, he signed himself: 'Yours in God and the concord of this Ile insaparable.'[104]

Cecil had the same order of priorities in mind when he drafted his plan for a conciliar interregnum in 1563, in the event of Elizabeth's death without heir.[105] At the heart of Cecil's plan was an idea encapsulated by the Marian exile John Aylmer, whose *An Harborowe for faithfull and trewe subiectes* (1559) provided a blueprint for parliamentary monarchy: 'if the parliament vse their priuileges, the King can ordein nothing without them'.[106] This in turn influenced Thomas Smith's *De republica Anglorum* (written during the crisis of 1562–5 and published in 1583), which argued that the 'most high and absolute power of the realme of Englande, consisteth in the Parliament'.[107] As Patrick Collinson noted: 'when it came to the crunch, the realm took precedence over the ruler'.[108] However, Cecil's letter to Maitland quoted above suggests that religion ultimately took precedence over all.

The idea of parliamentary sovereignty also manifested in the political culture of Scotland, albeit a little later in the century.[109] By contrast, however, Maitland – who had served as secretary to two Catholic rulers, had been educated at the University of Paris, and had married the Catholic Mary Fleming in 1567 – had a very different outlook to Cecil.[110] His biographer Ernest Russell noted that Maitland's view on religion 'had never been that of Cecil, and partly under the influence of his relations to a Catholic sovereign, partly owing to his chronic warfare with Knox and his party, it was becoming less so every year'.[111] In the early years of his office Maitland had often strongly asserted his Calvinistic orthodoxy, and in September 1560 he even asked Cecil's advice on how the Scottish Confession of Faith ought to be framed.[112] In his 'harangue' (address) to the 1567 Parliament, Maitland pronounced that the bloodless triumph of Protestantism within the space of eight or nine years was 'a peculiar benefite grantit onlie to the realme of Scotland' and a sign of God's providential favour that 'the trew relligioun hes obtenit a frecourss univ[er]sallie throch the haill realme'.[113] But his tone was always far more conciliatory and latitudinarian than Cecil's. Indeed, Maitland lamented that some of the policies approved in the Reformation Parliament of 1560 were 'more vehement then I for my opinion at ane other tyme wold have allowed'.[114] At other times he felt obliged to counter the impassioned speeches of men like Knox, who were clamouring for a 'purer' reformation in Scotland: 'yow know the vehemency off Mr knox spreit w[hich] can not be brydled / and yet doth sometymes uter soche sentences as can not easely be dygested by a weake stomach'.[115] Nor was he keen to jeopardise his credit with his Catholic queen by preaching at her. In March 1567 he acknowledged Cecil's wish in his last letter 'yt her ma[jesty] wold allow off yo[ur] estate in relligion' and affirmed that 'it is one off the thinges in earth I most desyre', but still advocated a gentle approach:

> I dare be bold anough to uter my fansy in it to her ma[jesty] trusting yt she will not lyke me the worse for utering my opinion & knowlege in that is proffitable for her everyway / and I do not dispayre but althogh she will not yealde at the first yet w[ith] progress off tyme that poynt shalbe obteyned / I pray god it may be shortly.[116]

Like Cecil, Maitland viewed his secretarial work as a religious vocation as much as a secular office, and that its ultimate goal was peace. 'As to me', Maitland wrote on 15 January 1562,

> since I first entred in any trade off publik actions I have ever bene a minister off peax and alwayes bent my selff that way as a thing in my iugement pleasing god and most profitable to both he who searcheth the secrets off hartes knoweth the treuth off my meaning.[117]

More often, however, Maitland invoked God in fatalistic terms, in recognition of how much was out of his (and Cecil's) control. In June 1564 Maitland wondered aloud whether their failure to resolve the tensions between their two queens was the fault of the circumstances, their queens' own 'hum[ours] to be slowe in resoluing', the fault of those 'neerest about them' not working hard enough, or

> that w[hich] I most feare yt god by the ingratitude off both the nations being prouoked to anger will not suffer ws to attayne so great worldly felicity as the succes off that negociation must bring w[ith] it if it wer ones bro[ught] to an happy end.[118]

If this last possibility were 'so determyned in his [God's] secreit counsall', then 'shall all o[ur] counsalles tending to the contrary be frustrated w[ith] what soever care and diligence we do proceade'.[119] Maitland had fallen out with Mary over her sudden, unilateral decision to marry Henry Stewart, Lord Darnley in 1565, and as a result Mary began to rely more on her personal secretary, the Italian Catholic David Rizzio. Maitland was almost certainly the mastermind behind Rizzio's murder in March 1566, which took place in the presence of the pregnant Mary in her private chambers. Although Maitland was not officially dismissed from his duties, he lost

some lands and absented himself from court for six months. '[S]o shall it fall out',
Maitland confided to Cecil, 'as god his providence hath appoynted and no polecy
off man can alter that w[hich] he hath determyned.'[120] Even following his political
rehabilitation into Mary's favour that September, Maitland saw no resolution to the
business they were endlessly engaged in:

> ffor I think it is not the pleaso[ur] off god to have the subiectes off this isle
> throughly [sic] settled in theyr iugement. ffor w[hich] cause he dothe keape
> thinges most necessery ondetermyned so as thay shall alwayes have somewhat
> wherew[ith] to be exercised.[121]

Maitland's fatalism contrasted sharply with Cecil's idealism, and his moder-
ate religious views ultimately led his English allies to question his loyalty to the
reformed cause. This was especially so when, after playing a key role in Mary's
abdication (following the murder of Lord Darnley and Mary's subsequent marriage to Bothwell, which Maitland considered disastrous) and James's coronation
(which Maitland later described as a temporary 'fetch'), he switched his allegiance
back to the queen, believing only Mary had sufficient authority to reunite the realm.
Although Maitland sought out the support of Catholic powers during the ensuing
civil war, he assured Cecil in May 1570 that his decision to stand by Mary was
not determined by faith, but policy: he saw the King's Party as a 'factioun [. . .]
that asperrs to reule without reasone and can be content nether of fellowship nor
unione'.[122] In a lengthy letter justifying his actions to Thomas Radcliffe, third Earl of
Sussex in July, Maitland chose not to assert the ferocity of his religious convictions
or the orthodoxy of his beliefs, but instead declared himself to be

> a student in that schole wher it is taughte that wysemens myndes must be
> ledde by probable reasons, w[hich] doctrine the disciples of Plato and Aristotle
> have embraced. *That same firme, certane, unchangeable and undoubted p[er]*
> *swacion w[hich] is requisite in matters of faithe, must not be required of men*
> *in matters of pollicie* [. . .] The chief thinge we oughte moste to respecte is
> o[ur] countrie the co[m]mon parent of us all, and the quiette therof [. . .] in this
> I followe thaucthoritie of two moste notable philosophers, Plato emongeste the
> Greekes and Cicero emongeste the Romaines.[123]

That faith should be separated from politics is a striking statement in the context of
Reformation Europe. For Maitland, the 'quiette' of his country was the most important consideration, above and beyond the furtherance of any religious cause, and he
believed the restoration of the queen was the only means to achieve that end. Cecil,
however, who saw the forces of antichrist rallying at the gates of Britain, could all
too easily imagine a realm operating successfully without a queen, especially if it
ensured the triumph of the Gospel.[124]

The final years of Maitland's correspondence with Cecil mark the heartbreak-
ing dissolution of their long friendship. On 11 August 1570 Cecil drafted a letter
from Elizabeth to Thomas Radcliffe, third earl of Sussex, commending him for his

refutation of Maitland's arguments for Mary's restoration, from which the Queen took 'great plesure':

> we do certenly see [therin] such a sufficieny of wisdom mixed w[ith] good lerning, as we ar glad to thynk yt lyddy[n]gton who is acco[m]pted ye flowre of ye wyttes in Scotland, shall see hym self over matched, and as we surely iudg uppo[n] ye matter, much confounded.[125]

Maitland made several desperate appeals to Cecil (elevated to Lord Burghley in 1571) during the 'lang seige' of Edinburgh Castle (May 1571–May 1573). In January 1572 he lamented that 'yo[ur] L[ordship] hath a longtyme intermitted the accustomed offices whearby amity is entreteyned betwene p[er]sons absent I meane the entrecourss off l[ett]res', and reminded him that 'truely the tyme hath bene when yo[ur] sone wes nomore ready tobe directed by yow then I was'.[126] In July 1572 Maitland again tried to renew their former filial affection: 'I have reverenced yow as my father & I will still obey you as my good lord.'[127] Yet when the thousand English troops led by Sir William Drury finally succeeded in storming the castle on 29 May 1573, Burghley's own son Thomas witnessed the weary, haggard and fatally ill Maitland's surrender, yet refused to intercede with his father on Maitland's behalf.[128]

For many years, Maitland and Cecil had worked together towards a common goal: the unification of their two countries in peace and amity. As their lengthy correspondence shows, both men recognised parts of themselves in each other, and their friendship was founded on their similar upbringings, education and a mutual recognition of the difficult burdens they shared as secretaries. Although their disagreements on the role of religion and the nature of political authority ultimately destroyed their friendship, Burghley was right when he later recalled that 'by o[ur] minestery' they had restored both kingdoms 'to suche a brotherly peace, as never had bene in many hundred yeares before'.[129] Indeed, Maitland and Burghley's dream of a united Britain came true only decades after their correspondence ceased: on 24 March 1603 Elizabeth died, and was succeeded by Mary's son James VI and I, who became the first monarch to unite Scotland, England and Ireland under one crown. On 20 October 1604 James assumed the title of 'King of Great Britain' in a proclamation that went unratified by the English Parliament, which refused to accept the rebranding of their culture that had dominated the British Isles for so long.[130] It was not until the Acts of Union took effect on 1 May 1707 that the two Crowns and Parliaments were officially merged into one Kingdom of Great Britain, which Ireland later joined on 1 January 1801.

Nevertheless, it is not unreasonable to see Maitland and Cecil as the earliest architects of the union they believed would one day come to pass. For Maitland in particular, it was the legacy he most ardently hoped would be remembered by posterity:

> I have in a maner co[n]secrate my selff to the co[m]mon wealth / the uniting off this Ile in friendship hath in my co[n]cept bene a scope wherat I have long shot and wheronto all my actions have bene directed these five or six yeares [. . .] and ever as one occa[sion] doth fayle me I begyn to shuffle the cardes off

new alwayes keping the same grownd. I shall not weary solong as any hope remayneth.[131]

NOTES

1. Wallace T. MacCaffrey, *Queen Elizabeth and the Making of Policy, 1572–1588* (Princeton: Princeton University Press, 1981), p. 158.

2. Aside from the late Mark Loughlin's sadly unpublished PhD thesis, 'The Career of Maitland of Lethington, c.1526–1573' (University of Edinburgh, 1991), Maitland has not received a published biography since Edward Russell's *Maitland of Lethington, The Minister of Mary Stuart: A Study of His Life and Times* (London: James Nisbet & Co., 1912). By contrast, Cecil's historiography is voluminous: the most recent works of note include Norman Jones, *Governing by Virtue: Lord Burghley and the Management of Elizabethan England* (Oxford: Oxford University Press, 2015) and Stephen Alford, *Burghley: William Cecil at the Court of Elizabeth I* (New Haven, CT: Yale University Press, [2008] 2011).

3. Mark Loughlin, 'Maitland, William, of Lethington (1525x30–1573)', in *Oxford Dictionary of National Biography* (hereafter *ODNB*) (Oxford: Oxford University Press, 2004), available at <http://0-www.oxforddnb.com.wizard.umd.umich.edu/view/article/17838> (last accessed 23 June 2014). As the strongest fortress in Scotland, Edinburgh Castle was the place where all important documents were kept from earliest times. Matthew Livingstone, *A Guide to the Public Records of Scotland Deposited in H. M. General Register House, Edinburgh* (Edinburgh: H. M. General Register House, 1905), p. xvii.

4. 'Information for Killegrew of Sir Richard Maitland's affairs', 24 August 1574, N[ational] A[rchives], S[tate] P[apers] 52/26/2 fo. 113r–v. On 24 August 1574 Sir Richard wrote a pleading letter to Elizabeth asking for her help in restoring his family's house and lands. See NA SP 52/26/2 fo. 111. It was not unusual for secretaries to file their official papers at home: a large number of Cecil's papers were stored at Salisbury House. Simon Adams, 'The Papers of Robert Dudley, Earl of Leicester: II. The Atye-Cotton Collection', *Archives* 20:90 (1993), p. 140 (pp. 131–44).

5. Simon Adams, 'The Lauderdale Papers 1561–1570: The Maitland of Lethington State Papers and the Leicester Correspondence', *Scottish Historical Review* 67:183 (1988), part 1, p. 30 (pp. 28–35).

6. The Lauderdale Papers are now B[ritish] L[ibrary] Add[itional] MSS 23108–23138, 23240–23251 and 35125.

7. While many important papers escaped this disaster, '[t]he want of any inventory of the whole must leave us for ever in the dark as to the real extent of the loss which was then sustained', but it must have included 'the greater part of the original instruments of a public nature' up to 1651. Robert Chambers, *Domestic Annals of Scotland from the Reformation to the Restoration* (Edinburgh; London: W. & R. Chambers, 1858), II, p. 266. See also Livingstone, *A Guide to the Public Records of Scotland*, pp. xiv–xvi.

8. Conyers Read, *Mr Secretary Cecil and Queen Elizabeth* (New York: Alfred A. Knopf, 1955), pp. 218, 230.

9. These are: Cecil to Maitland, 16 April 1560, BL Add MS 33531, fo. 31; Cecil to Maitland, c. July 1563, BL Stowe MS 142 fo. 21; Cecil to Maitland, 20 August 1563, BL Add MS 32091 fos. 199r–200r; Cecil to Maitland and Murray, 16 December 1564, SP 52/9 fo. 187. I am grateful to Simon Adams for noting that although MSS Add 33531, 32091 and Stowe 142 are not catalogued with the other Lauderdale Papers, they have a probable provenance from that collection.

10. Maitland to Cecil, 1 February 1565, SP 52/10 fo. 12v.

11. Read, *Mr Secretary Cecil*, p. 158.
12. Gavin Douglas, *The Palis of Honoure*, ed. David J. Parkinson (Kalamazoo: Medieval Institute Publications, 1992), ll. 1717–18.
13. Read, *Mr Secretary Cecil*, pp. 19–21.
14. Joan Simon, *Education and Society in Tudor England* (Cambridge: Cambridge University Press, 1979), pp. 59ff.
15. Although there is some uncertainty about Maitland's year of birth, the generally accepted date is 1528, although Loughlin admits that twelve is almost incredibly young for Maitland to have entered university. Moreover, the 1544 statutes of St Leonard's College stipulated that 'No one shall be received under fifteen nor above twenty-one years of age.' Loughlin, 'Career of Maitland', p. 21; C. J. Lyon, *History of St Andrews, Episcopal, Monastic, Academic and Civil* (Edinburgh: William Tait, 1843), vol. II, p. 245.
16. Lyon, *History of St Andrews*, vol. II, p. 206. The famous Greek scholar, John Cheke, became Cecil's brother-in-law in 1541.
17. Anthony Ross, 'Reformation and Repression', in David McRoberts (ed.), *Essays on the Scottish Reformation, 1513–1625* (Glasgow: John S. Burns & Son, 1962), p. 409 (pp. 371–414).
18. Loughlin, 'Career of Maitland', p. 19.
19. Jones, *Governing by Virtue*, pp. 45–6.
20. Ibid. pp. 51–2; Mary Partridge, 'Lord Burghley and Il Cortegiano: Civil and Martial Modes of Courtliness in Elizabethan England', *Transactions of the Royal Historical Society* 19 (2009), pp. 95–116.
21. The Italian Humanist Pietro Bizzari even dedicated one of his works to Maitland. Mark Loughlin, 'Career of Maitland', pp. 20–1.
22. George Buchanan, 'The Chamaeleon or Crafty Statesman; in a Character of Mr Maitland of Lethington, Secretary of Scotland: By Mr George Buchanan; never before published', in *Miscellanea Antiqua: Containing First the Life and Death of King James the Vth of Scotland* (London: W. Taylor, 1710), p. 99.
23. Cecil to Elizabeth, 19 June 1560, SP 52/4 fo. 29v.
24. Jane Dawson, *John Knox* (New Haven, CT: Yale University Press, 2015), pp. 240, 318.
25. See Mark Loughlin, 'The Dialogue of the Twa Wyfeis: Maitland, Machiavelli and the Propaganda of the Scottish Civil War', in A. A. A. MacDonald, Michael Lynch and Ian Cowan (eds), *The Renaissance in Scotland: Studies in Literature, Religion, History and Culture Offered to John Durkan* (Leiden: Brill, 1994), pp. 226–45. John Leslie, Bishop of Ross, denounced Cecil as one of the masterminds behind Elizabeth's 'Machiavellian State'. 'The Preface to the Reader', in 'A Treatise of Treasons against Q. Elizabeth and the Croune of England' [1572], is attributed to John Leslie and is printed in Alfred C. Southern, *Elizabethan Recusant Prose, 1559–1582* (London; Glasgow: Sanda and Co., 1950), pp. 310–19.
26. Jones, *Governing by Virtue*, p. 45; Alford, *Burghley*, pp. 69–80.
27. James Maitland, *Maitland's Narrative of the Principal Acts of the Regency, during the minority; and other papers relating to the History of Mary, Queen of Scots*, ed. W. S. Finch (Ipswich: S. I. R. Root, 1842), pp. ci, ciii.
28. Loughlin, 'Career of Maitland', p. 1. Evidently, Maitland did not follow his father's Polonius-style advice to avoid card-playing, described in his poem, 'Counsel to my son being in the Court' (c. 1555), published in *Ancient Scottish Poems, never before in print, but now published from the MS collections of Sir Richard Maitland of Lethington* (London: C. Dilley, 1786), vol. I, pp. 275–8; John Skelton, *Maitland of Lethington and the Scotland of Mary Stuart: A History* (Edinburgh and London: William Blackwood and Sons, 1887), vol. I, p. 26.
29. As noted above, Cecil had been a junior secretary under Edward VI. Maitland's exact age is

difficult to determine with certainty, but this is the age his son James claims he was when he accepted the appointment. Maitland, *Maitland's Narrative*, pp. ci, ciii.

30. G. R. Elton, *The Tudor Revolution in Government: A Study of Administrative Changes in the Reign of Henry VIII* (Cambridge, Cambridge University Press, 1953); Maurice Lee, *John Maitland of Thirlestane and the Foundation of the Stewart Despotism in Scotland* (Princeton: Princeton University Press, 1959).

31. For an overview of English debates in response to Elton, see Stephen Alford, 'Politics and Political History in the Tudor Century', *The Historical Journal* 42:2 (1999), pp. 535–48; for Scottish debates in response to Lee, see Julian Goodare, *The Government of Scotland, 1560– 1625* (Oxford: Oxford University Press, 2004), pp. 276–97.

32. For a brief history of the evolution of the various royal seals, see Rayne Allinson, *A Monarchy of Letters: Royal Correspondence and English Diplomacy in the Reign of Elizabeth I* (New York: Palgrave Macmillan, 2012), pp. 3–4.

33. F. M. G. Higham, *The Principal Secretary of State; a survey of the office from 1558 to 1660* (Manchester: Manchester University Press, 1923), p. 12. In 1546 the Scottish Secretary's presence at Privy Council meetings became mandatory. Loughlin, 'Career of Maitland', pp. 2–3, 6.

34. In Scotland, Privy Council meetings were usually presided over by the Chancellor, the first minister of the state, while the council clerk managed the council's records. Goodare, *Government of Scotland*, p. 151.

35. In 1567 the position of Secretary was recognised as a distinct category of membership in the Scottish Parliament. Loughlin, 'Career of Maitland', pp. 2–3, 6.

36. The Scottish Parliament was also much smaller than the English, 'usually involving the assembly of about fifty or sixty members of the three estates – higher clergy, peers, and commissioners of royal burghs – plus the leading officers of state'. By contrast, in 1559 the size of the English Commons alone had risen 9 per cent to a total of 438. Julian Goodare, 'The First Parliament of Mary, Queen of Scots', *The Sixteenth Century Journal* 36:1 (2005), p. 56 (pp. 55–75).

37. Alan G. R. Smith, 'The Secretariats of the Cecils, circa 1580–1612', *English Historical Review* 83:328 (1968), p. 482 (pp. 481–504).

38. Adams, 'Leicester Papers II', p. 140.

39. This system can be seen at work in *Correspondence Diplomatique de Bertrand de Salignac de la Mothe Fénélon, ambassadeur de France en Angleterre de 1568 à 1575* (Paris, 1838). My thanks to Simon Adams for this observation.

40. Maitland to Cecil, 18 September 1564, SP 52/9 fos. 103v–104r.

41. For the Scottish secretary, this included the handling of Border policy. Goodare, *Government of Scotland*, p. 151.

42. Quoted in Higham, *Principal Secretary*, p. 59.

43. Smith, 'The Secretariats of the Cecils', p. 483.

44. Loughlin, 'Career of Maitland', pp. 2–3, 6. For more on the division of labour within the Elizabethan secretariat, see Allinson, *A Monarchy of Letters*, pp. 17–35.

45. For more on Cecil's use of patronage for political ends, see Pauline Croft (ed.), *Patronage, Culture and Power: The Early Cecils* (New Haven, CT: Paul Mellon Centre, 2002); Partridge, 'Lord Burghley and Il Cortegiano'.

46. There appears to be some confusion about whether Sir Richard was made Keeper of the Privy Seal or Great Seal, or both. See also the *ODNB* entries for Sir Richard, Sir William and Sir John Maitland.

47. Maurice Lee Jr., 'Maitland, John, First Lord Maitland of Thirlestane (1543–1595)', in *ODNB*, available at <http://0-www.oxforddnb.com.wizard.umd.umich.edu/view/ article/17826> (last accessed 10 June 2014).

48. Burghley to John Maitland (copy), December 1590, BL MS Lansdowne 115 fo. 66r.

49. Ibid.
50. Such pairings included: Margaret of Wessex to Malcom III (m. 1070–93), Ethelreda of Northumbria to Duncan II (m. 1093–4), Maud of Northumbria to David I (m. c. 1112–c. 1130), Joan I of England to Alexander II (m. 1221–38), Margaret of England to Alexander III (m. 1251–75), Joan II of England to David II (m. 1328–62) and Margaret Tudor to James IV (m. 1503–13).
51. Randolph to Cecil, 31 December 1563, NA SP 52/8, fo. 176r.
52. Aylmer argued that 'The regiment of England is not a mere Monarchie . . . but a rule mixed of all three [monarchy, oligarchy, democracy], wherein each one of these have or should have authority' (A. N. McLaren, *Political Culture in the Reign of Elizabeth I: Queen and Commonwealth, 1558–1585* (Cambridge: Cambridge University Press, 2004), p. 66).
53. 'Queen Elizabeth's First Speech' (my emphasis), Hatfield, 20 November 1558, quoted in Leah Marcus, Janel Mueller and Mary Beth Rose (eds), *Elizabeth I: Collected Works* (Chicago: Chicago University Press, 2000), p. 51.
54. Maitland to Cecil, 25 October 1561, SP 52/6 fo. 162r.
55. Count de Feria to Philip II, 19 March 1559, in Martin A. S. Hume (ed.), *Calendar of Letters and State Papers relating to English Affairs, preserved principally in the archives of Simancas* (hereafter *CSPSpan (Simancas)*), 4 vols (London: Public Record Office, 1896), vol. I, p. 38; De la Quadra to Philip II, 5 May 1561, in M. F. Navarete et al. (eds), *Colección de Documentos Inéditos para la Historia de España*, 113 vols (Madrid: Academia de la Historia, 1842–95), vol. lxxxvii, p. 350.
56. Mary to Maitland [translated from French], 29 June 1561, SP 52/6 fo. 98r.
57. Guzman de Silva to Philip II, 31 March 1565, *CSPSpan (Simancas)*, vol. I p. 412, no. 292.
58. Peter Adrian to Cecil, 12 May 1569, SP 70/107 fo. 30v.
59. Cecil to Maitland, 20 August 1563, quoted in Martin Philippson (ed.), *Histoire du règne de Marie Stuart* (Paris: É. Bouillon, 1891–2), vol. III, p. 465.
60. Maitland to Cecil, 1 February 1565, SP 52/10 fo. 12r.
61. Maitland to Cecil, 28 February 1562, SP 52/7 fo. 26r.
62. Maitland to Cecil, 23 February 1567, SP 52/13 fo. 15r.
63. Maitland to Cecil, 21 May 1568, SP 52/15 fo. 44r.
64. Maitland to Cecil, 20 October 1571, SP 52/21 fo. 182r.
65. Cecil to Maitland, 16 April 1560, BL Add MS 33531, fo. 31; Burghley to John Maitland (copy), December 1590, BL MS Lansdowne 115 fo. 66r. Elizabeth and Mary used the same filial rhetoric at different times to emphasise their close (and actual) bonds of kinship. Allinson, *A Monarchy of Letters*, pp. 73–92.
66. Caroline M. K. Bowden, 'Cecil [Cooke], Mildred, Lady Burghley (1526–1589)', in *ODNB*, available at <http://www.oxforddnb.com.wizard.umd.umich.edu/view/article/46675> (last accessed 19 November 2015).
67. In February 1558 Mary of Guise sent Maitland (along with Yves de Rubay) on an embassy to mediate peace between England and France, but since Mary Tudor was too enraged over the loss of Calais to negotiate, his mission was aborted before he got further than London. John Roche Dasent et al. (eds), *Acts of the Lords of Privy Council of England*, 46 vols (London: Her Majesty's Stationery Office, 1890), vol. VI, p. 275.
68. Maitland to Lady Cecil, 18 April 1560, C[ecil] P[apers] 152 fo. 136r; Maitland to Lady Cecil, 28 April 1560, CP 152/125.
69. Maitland to Lady Cecil, 19 July 1560, CP 153 fo. 42r.
70. Maitland to Cecil, 25 May 1560, SP 52/3 fo. 238v; Maitland to Cecil, 15 August 1560, SP 52/5 fo. 7v.
71. Maitland to Cecil, 26 February 1561, SP 52/6 fo. 49r.
72. Ibid.
73. Maitland to Cecil, 25 October 1561, SP 52/6 fo. 162r.

74. Maitland to Cecil, 29 January 1562, SP 52/7 fos. 14r–15r; Loughlin, 'Career of Maitland', p. 124.
75. Maitland to Cecil, 7 December 1561, SP 52/6 fo. 179r.
76. Maitland to Cecil, 15 December 1561, CP 153 fo. 95r.
77. Maitland to Cecil, 15 January 1562, SP 52/7 fo. 8r.
78. Ibid. fos. 8v–9r.
79. Maitland to Cecil, 7 December 1561, SP 52/6 fo. 178r.
80. Cecil to Nicholas Throckmorton, May 1561, in Philip Yorke of Hardwicke (ed.), *Miscellaneous State Papers: From 1501 to 1726*, 2 vols (London: W. Strahan, 1778), vol. I, p. 173.
81. 'I am Davus, not Oedipus'. Maitland is here quoting a character named Davus, a slave in Terence's comedy *Andria*, who explains that he is a simple man not used to unlocking riddles (like Oedipus).
82. Maitland to Cecil, 29 January 1562, SP 52/7 fos. 14v–15r.
83. Cecil to Maitland and Moray, 16 December 1564 (draft), SP 52/9 fo. 187r.
84. Ibid.
85. Maitland to Cecil, 18 September 1564, SP 52/9 fo. 102r.
86. Ibid. fo. 102r–v.
87. Maitland to Cecil, 1 February 1565, SP 52/10 fo. 12v.
88. Ibid. fo. 13r.
89. Edward I was nicknamed the 'Hammer of the Scots' because of the series of devastating military campaigns culminating in the Battle of Dunbar in 1296; Robert the Bruce (1274–1329) led the Scots to victory at the Battle of Bannockburn in 1314, thereby re-establishing an independent Scottish monarchy.
90. Maitland to Cecil, 18 September 1564, SP 52/9 fo. 103r–v.
91. Maitland to Cecil, 8 February 1567, SP 52/13 fo. 11r.
92. Loughlin, 'Career of Maitland', p. 238.
93. Maitland to Cecil, 28 February 1565, SP 52/10 fo. 31v.
94. Maitland to Cecil, 12 June 1565, SP 52/10 fo. 128r.
95. Jane E. A. Dawson, 'William Cecil and the British Dimension of Early Elizabethan Foreign Policy', *History* 74:241 (1989), pp. 196–216; Roger A. Mason, 'Scotland, Elizabethan England, and the Idea of Britain', *Transactions of the Royal Historical Society* 14 (2004), pp. 279–93.
96. Loughlin, 'Career of Maitland', p. 342.
97. Ibid. p. 340.
98. Alford, *Burghley*, p. 126.
99. Cecil to Maitland, 20 August 1563, quoted in Philippson, *Histoire du règne*, vol. III, pp. 465–8.
100. Ibid. p. 466.
101. Ibid. p. 466.
102. Ibid. p. 467.
103. Ibid. pp. 467–8.
104. Ibid. p. 468.
105. Stephen Alford, *The Early Elizabethan Polity: William Cecil and the British Succession Crisis, 1558–1569* (Cambridge: Cambridge University Press, 1998), pp. 109–19.
106. John Aylmer, *An Harborowe for faithfull and trewe subiectes* (London, 1559), H.3.
107. Thomas Smith, *De Republica Anglorum* [first published in London, 1583], ed. L. Alston (Cambridge: Cambridge University Press, 1906), p. 48. For further discussion, see Dale Hoak, 'Sir William Cecil, Sir Thomas Smith, and the Monarchical Republic of Tudor England', in John F. McDiarmid (ed.), *The Monarchical Republic of Tudor England: Essays in Response to Patrick Collinson* (Aldershot and Burlington: Ashgate, 2007), pp. 37–54.

108. Patrick Collinson, '*De republica Anglorum:* or, History with the Politics Put Back', in Collinson (ed.), *Elizabethan Essays* (London: Hambledon Press, 1994), p. 19.
109. This assertion of parliamentary power is usually traced to the 1580s (Goodare, *Government of Scotland*, pp. 278–9), although it is possible to see a similar idea reflected in the King's Party's declaration (likely drafted by George Buchanan) at the York–Westminster conference in 1568 that regency should be an elective office in the hands of the estates. Amy Blakeway, *Regency in Sixteenth-Century Scotland* (Woodbridge: The Boydell Press, 2015), pp. 17–53.
110. Maitland was not the only prominent Scottish politician to share this sentiment: James Stewart, Earl of Moray, also emphasised 'quyetnes' ahead of theological disputes in his letters to Elizabeth and Cecil. Theo van Heijnsbergen, 'Advice to a Princess: The Literary Articulation of a Religious, Political and Cultural Programme for Mary, Queen of Scots, 1562', in Goodare and Alasdair A. MacDonald (eds), *Sixteenth-Century Scotland: Essays in Honour of Michael Lynch* (Leiden and Boston: Brill, 2008), p. 107.
111. Russell, *Maitland of Lethington*, pp. 186–7.
112. Maitland to Cecil, 13 September 1560, SP 52/5 fo. 28r.
113. 'Maitland's Harangue to Parliament', 15 December 1567, SP 52/14 fo. 201v. Maitland was also trying to justify the legitimacy of the 1560 Reformation Parliament, which Mary never formally accepted.
114. Maitland to Cecil, 6 February 1561, SP 52/6 fo. 29r.
115. Maitland to Cecil, 25 October 1561, SP 52/6 fo. 162r.
116. Maitland to Cecil, 13 March 1567, SP 52/13 fo. 27r.
117. Maitland to Cecil, 15 January 1562, SP 52/7 fo. 8r.
118. Maitland to Cecil, 23 June 1564, SP 52/9 fo. 88r.
119. Ibid.
120. Maitland to Cecil, 27 July 1564, SP 52/9 fo. 99r.
121. Maitland to Cecil, 11 November 1566, SP 52/12 fo. 112r.
122. Maitland to Cecil, 17 May 1570, SP 52/18 fo. 72r.
123. Maitland to Sussex, 16 July 1570, SP 52/19 fo. 8r (my emphasis).
124. Cecil was also convinced of Mary's guilt following the production of the 'Casket Letters' at the Hampton Court Conference in October 1568. These letters (which no longer survive) purportedly proved her complicity in Darnley's muder and her secret love affair with Bothwell.
125. Elizabeth to Sussex (draft in Cecil's hand), 11 August 1570, SP 52/19 fo. 31r.
126. Maitland to Cecil, 3 January 1572, SP 52/22 fo. 1r.
127. Maitland to Cecil, 30 July 1572, BL Cotton MS Caligula C/III fo. 348r.
128. Loughlin, 'Career of Maitland', p. 332.
129. Burghley to John Maitland (copy), December 1590, BL MS Lansdowne 115 fo. 66r.
130. Jenny Wormald, 'James VI and I (1566–1625)', in *ODNB*, available at <http://0-www.oxforddnb.com.wizard.umd.umich.edu/view/article/14592> (last accessed 23 June 2014).
131. Maitland to Cecil, 28 February 1562, SP 52/7 fo. 26v.

CHAPTER 6

Axel Oxenstierna and Swedish Diplomacy in the Seventeenth Century

Erik Thomson

Viewed from a perspective unavailable to him, the Swedish Chancellor Axel Oxenstierna (1583–1654) appears to have played a minor role in what Victor Lieberman has suggested was a process of 'strangely parallel' state formations distinguished by increased interstate competition, administrative capacity, commercial exchange, and cultural and religious exclusivity that reshaped Eurasian polities from 1450 until 1830 from the Chao Phraya basin to the Vistula delta, from La Rochelle to Edo. Oxenstierna could serve as a textbook example of the 'ratchet-like' accumulation of administrative expertise, in which royal servants altered domestic practices by imitating foreign theories and practices.[1] From a narrower perspective, historians might depict Oxenstierna as a statesman playing a role in the elaboration of European diplomatic practice, or as one of the chief ministers that distinguished early seventeenth-century European governance such as Richelieu, Olivares, Buckingham and Mazarin.[2]

In Sweden, historians, government officials and even newspaper columnists invoke Oxenstierna as the founder of modern Swedish administration.[3] Unlike Richelieu, who tends to overshadow Louis XIII in the scholarship, Oxenstierna has been overshadowed by the monarchs he served, Gustavus Adolphus and Christina. Oxenstierna may have encouraged this focus, as he himself began to compose a biography of Gustavus Adolphus; Hugo Grotius had refused a request to write one, arguing that Oxenstierna was more suitable.[4] The major historical work Oxenstierna patronised, Bogislaw Philip von Chemnitz's *Königlich Schwedischer in Teutschland geführter Krieg* (*The Swedish Kingdom in the Recent War in Germany*), while featuring the chancellor, did not elevate him to the central figure of the day, nor did it organise the narrative around him and his actions.[5] Perhaps because of his importance to the history of Sweden and Europe more broadly, the volume of material was so overwhelming that the first biography to cover his entire lifespan was not completed until 2002.[6] Institutional historians in the first half of the twentieth century celebrated Oxenstierna's role in the founding of many central institutions of the Swedish state, including a system of regular diplomatic representation, the elaboration of a chancery and archive, and the establishment of a postal system.[7] Historians debated whether Sweden's Baltic expansion was motivated by hope of material gain, for defence and security, or, recently, in defence of a notion of identity.[8] Following the pioneering work by Arne Losman, many historians have broadened our understanding of diplomatic actors, focusing upon national, kin-based and confessional networks, the personal ambitions and aspirations of emissaries, and the cultures and personal relations that undergirded diplomacy.[9] These studies have tended to study the structures and practice of diplomacy, rather than the substance of negotiation or the formation of policy. They exemplify the New Diplomatic History, which attempts to revivify the field by studying a more complex blend of actors, motives, and cultural and social contexts in relations between states.[10]

Oxenstierna's formal control over the Chancery, his extensive relations with the Swedish elite and many clients, and his longevity meant that he played a predominant role in shaping many of Sweden's central institutions, including those involving foreign affairs. Before Oxenstierna's chancellorship, Sweden did not maintain formal permanent embassies in which the Crown paid employees directly to represent its interests, gather information and conduct negotiations. By the time of Oxenstierna's death, Sweden employed a number of permanent representatives abroad, who were paid salaries for a variety of duties. Why did this particular ratcheting up of representation take place, why did it take the particular form that it did, and why did Oxenstierna believe that such representatives were necessary, when his predecessors had not? Historical research has shown that early modern merchants and scholars were often better at collecting and distributing information than were members of state institutions, and economic and social theorists have suggested that informal networks can be more robust and resilient sources of information than more formal institutions, which accrue agency problems due to rent seeking and informational asymmetry.[11] For a kingdom as poor as Sweden, maintaining the personnel and correspondence required to carry out an active diplomacy demanded substantial investment.[12] First, Oxenstierna developed a system that employed permanent residents and other emissaries – whatever their costs and inefficiencies – in part because he believed it had become necessary for Sweden's reputation in a changing world. Such institutions were part of what distinguished, as he put it, 'other civil nations'.[13] Concern for reputation, as well as limited numbers of suitable and willing Swedish emissaries, initially often meant that Oxenstierna hired foreigners with excellent connections and humanist reputations. While such foreigners would never entirely disappear, Oxenstierna increasingly sought to have his own clients, whether Swedish or foreign-born, play a larger role in foreign relations. Without neglecting ceremony, Oxenstierna increasingly began to distinguish, as he put it in a letter to his son Erik, between 'courtesies and realities', and emphasise mercantile and financial abilities above humanist reputation in choosing emissaries.[14] As Oxenstierna came to view relations between princes less as personal relations between members of a society of princes, and more as an arena for contests of interests guided by reason of state, he tended to choose emissaries who could see to the fiscal and mercantile aspects of power. Yet Sweden's foreign emissaries always played multiple roles, and reflected multiple interests. If Oxenstierna can serve as a textbook example of the Eurasian ratcheting up of administrative capacity through imitation and emulation, his management of emissaries demonstrates how he had to respond to diverse interests, particular talents and the demands of distinct events.

BECOMING CHANCELLOR

Oxenstierna's background and education, as well as the political situation in Sweden when he first entered royal service, influenced the manner in which he approached foreign relations once he became chancellor.[15] Both sides of Oxenstierna's family were prominent members of Sweden's small and close-knit aristocracy, with traditions of royal service as well as noble descent, and connections to those who chose to serve Sigismund III (Vasa) of Poland, and to those who supported his paternal uncle Charles IX, who had eventually accepted the Swedish throne after securing Sigismund's deposition on the grounds that his Catholicism was incompatible with Sweden's fundamental laws. Unlike his father (who as a youth had fought at Prince Mauritz's side in the Netherlands and against the Ottoman Empire in Hungary before serving Swedish monarchs in a variety of ways) and his uncles, Oxenstierna did not volunteer to fight in foreign armies. Instead, he attended from 1599 to 1603 universities of northern Germany renowned for the purity of their Lutheran teaching: Rostock, Wittenberg and Jena. While making contacts with northern German and Swedish nobles and future clergymen, he received a thorough grounding in Lutheran theology while also exploring history, politics and law.[16]

After a few months' tour through the Rhine, Switzerland, Bavaria and Bohemia, Oxenstierna returned in October 1603 to a Sweden where disputes over political, legal and religious matters between noblemen, including some near kith and kin of his mother Barbro Bielke, and the new king Charles IX, had created for Oxenstierna a dangerous political environment. Despite, or perhaps because of, these controversies, Oxenstierna soon entered Charles IX's service, where he advanced quickly, such that by 1606 he was undertaking a mission to resolve various dynastic disputes in Mecklenburg. Though this mission proved unsuccessful, he was decently recompensed, and married Anna Bååt, whose father worked in the chancery, and who brought significant lands to the marriage, including what would become one of Oxenstierna's principal manors, Tidö.[17] Named to the *Riksråd* – the Council of the Realm – in 1609, he undertook a mission to Reval (modern Tallinn) in the company of the non-noble chief of the Chancery Nils Chesnecopherus, who had played a central role in organising the Chancery's work. As Charles IX's foreign policies stumbled from difficulty to difficulty, with war with Denmark added to conflicts in Russia and Poland, Oxenstierna rose to occupy a prominent place among the aristocrats on the Council, while still enjoying the trust of Charles IX, Queen Christina and other members of the royal family. After Charles IX's death on 30 October 1611, Oxenstierna played a crucial role mediating among the different political factions, crafting a compromise between the high aristocracy and the royal family, reflected in the royal oath and a series of noble privileges issued at a *Riksdag*, an assembly of estates required to approve taxation and major legislation, at the end of the year. As part of the compromise, Nils Chesnecopherus was removed from the Chancery, and Oxenstierna, at the age of twenty-eight, was named chancellor of the Swedish kingdom in early 1612. As Sven A. Nilsson has argued, Gustavus Adolphus and Oxenstierna may have initially regarded themselves as divided by differing views of royal and aristocratic power, but quickly developed a close working relationship and compatible views of the state.[18]

Oxenstierna's authority in foreign affairs rested upon several different foundations. First, he served the monarch and other members of the royal family as an advisor. Although Gustavus Adolphus may initially have resented Oxenstierna, the king quickly came to trust his chancellor's counsel. When the king and chancellor were not in the same place, Oxenstierna exchanged frequent letters with the king, discussing approaches to problems of government and describing and interpreting foreign and domestic news. When they were in the same place, everything indicates that the two men were regularly in conference. Oxenstierna also kept the Queen Mother Christina informed of the Crown's actions and other news, both out of respect to her position and because, as a wealthy landholder, she was in a position to loan the Crown significant sums.[19]

His role as an advisor extended to the *Riksråd*, the Council of the Realm, where Oxenstierna played a vital role. The Council served as a forum for the informal discussion of news and policies. On controversial or vital matters, however, the Council could adopt more formal procedures to deliberate over a particular matter, and even prepare a formal opinion, known as a *Rådslag*. During the first decade of Oxenstierna's chancellorship, the records of these formal opinions and occasional accounts in letters provide evidence of the Council's activity; from 1627, however, we have minutes that provide a record of the Council's deliberations and business. Foreign affairs formed a major part of the Council's business, including nearly daily reading and assessment of emissaries' letters, deliberations over the selection and revocation of agents, informal discussion of approaches to negotiation and strategy, and formal debates about making peace or declaring war. Oxenstierna's family and clients often made up most of the Council's members. According to Gustavus Adolphus's royal oath, the *Riksdag* had to be informed and consulted about foreign affairs. These consultations were often pro forma, little more than opportunities to present a view of the kingdom's relations with other powers that some historians have not hesitated to call propaganda. Nonetheless, meetings of the *Riksdag* often placed Oxenstierna in a position where he had to balance two roles, that of a governor, a royal official responsible for the Crown's actions, and that of a prominent nobleman dedicated to the interests of his estate.[20]

While the *Riksdrots*, or Marshall, was officially the highest office of the realm, Oxenstierna built upon earlier acts that made the Chancery the effective centre of administration, with the authority to act in very nearly every domain of government. In instructions for the Chancery, Oxenstierna attempted to delegate responsibilities among the secretaries according to their linguistic ability, knowledge of different regions and competence with different problems of statecraft, from the management of documents in archives to knowledge of laws and ordinances. Thus, in a 1618 instruction, Oxenstierna mandated that one secretary should keep charge of the archive, another should oversee writing laws and ordinances, and another should supervise the production of documents concerning the privileges of towns, estates and individuals. One secretary – Anders Bure – was responsible for both Russian affairs and instructions for *Ståthållare* – governors – and other officers within the kingdom. Three other secretaries had responsibilities for different foreign nations: one, with the aid of two scribes, drafted and organised documents concerning Denmark, Poland and Livonia; another secretary, also with the aid of two scribes, was responsible for relations with France, England and the Netherlands; and a third, with the help of one scribe, covered relations with German princes and Hansa towns.[21] The Chancery was also a vital component of Oxenstierna's patronage network, a place where young nobles and even commoners gained experience and proved their aptitude to advance to higher offices and assume greater responsibility.[22]

DIPLOMATIC ENTREPRENEURS IN THE BALTIC

Before the reign of Gustavus Adolphus, Sweden had not maintained an officially accredited permanent resident ambassador at any foreign court. Swedish monarchs dispatched embassies when relations demanded them, and most probably kept abreast of situations abroad by correspondence with friends, merchants or other correspondents. The horizon of Swedish monarchs had usually remained confined to a fairly small group of princes and towns surrounding the Baltic, but regional diplomacy was not without its own complexity. The Baltic Sea served as a vital shipping route, with the Baltic grain trade rightly viewed as the 'mother trade' of Dutch commerce.[23] It served as a crossroads linking a diverse group of polities, with different linguistic, confessional and cultural characters, which interacted with each other in complex and often unpredictable manners. Informal networks, often inflected by ties of ethnicity, kin and religion, could serve as the foundation of these interactions, and shaped the flow of people, goods and information. News and intelligence could be reported by local officials in seaside towns; even high officers of the realm went to the quays in Stockholm to discuss news with ship captains and merchants. Outside the Baltic, Charles IX had sought to grow closer to Protestant powers, often through dynastic marriage, particularly with those with significant interests in the Baltic, in order to shore up the legitimacy of his newly acquired throne. A prominent example is the marriage of Gustavus Adolphus's half-sister Katarina to Johan Casimir of the German state of Pfalz-Zweibrücken in 1615.[24]

Oxenstierna's accession to the chancellorship in many respects did not fundamentally alter the dual Baltic and Protestant focus of Sweden's diplomacy. He continued to draw upon special embassies of trusted noblemen and other royal officials to carry out significant negotiations. Oxenstierna himself directed the negotiations at Knäred in 1613, which ended the disastrous war against the Danes. Oxenstierna's methods of personal negotiation have not been scrutinised closely. At Knäred, faced with Danish military victories, Oxenstierna repeatedly marshalled arguments from customary law and history and used both legal and historical examples to try to make the best of a poor situation.[25] Given the reality of the Swedish defeat, he had to agree to pay a substantial ransom for the return of the fortress of Älvsborg, on the current site of the town of Gothenburg, Sweden's only important port to sit directly on the North Sea and thus free from the Danish control of the Sound.[26]

Oxenstierna drew upon the people and practices employed by Charles IX, but also began to expand the scope and reach of Swedish representation, and to arrange more comprehensive and regular sources of news and information. With few suitable and willing Swedish-born candidates with the connections and knowledge to serve as representatives abroad, Oxenstierna turned to foreigners with diplomatic experience, often as the representative of another power in Sweden. The use of such foreigners was not new for Sweden, and was common among other Baltic powers. Oxenstierna expected such foreigners to draw upon their own network of contacts, and was not offended if they took their own initiative, even on issues of great import. In a sense, these were diplomatic entrepreneurs, akin to the 'military entrepreneur' defined by Fritz Redlich and recently refined by David Parrott: men who drew upon private assets and organisational abilities to supplement the limited and weak organisational capacity of early modern states.[27] Like a modern consultancy, emissaries drew upon their expertise, knowledge and contacts in return for a fee. Sometimes the relationship was established using a formal contract, but the normal expectation that an ambassador would pay the members of the embassy as a part of his household in essence meant that one could consider the diplomatic household and other agents and informants as a firm, as Ronald Coase defined it, 'the system of relationships which comes into existence when the direction of resources is dependent on an entrepreneur'.[28]

Sometimes the categories of military and diplomatic entrepreneur overlapped. The Scottish military entrepreneur Sir James Spens had been employed by Charles IX to raise troops in Scotland, and command them in Sweden's wars.[29] In 1612, James VI and I of Scotland and England had sent him to mediate at the peace of Knäred, while his step-brother Sir James Anstruther was sent in a similar role to Christian IV of Denmark. Following the peace, Spens was sent as Gustavus Adolphus's ambassador to James in London, where, apart from carrying out specific negotiations for the Swedes, he relayed news available to him at the Stuart court and elsewhere in London. Spens, indeed, became the hub of a network of largely Scottish informants and spies that funnelled information not only about the British Isles, but also about other areas where Scottish troops were serving, such as Poland and Denmark.

In other cases, cultural savvy and good connections were among the primary attributes that prompted Oxenstierna to employ someone as a representative. As Heiko Droste has illuminated, in 1615 the Brandenburg native Hieronymus von Birckholtz, who had been intermittently in Swedish service for over a decade, was commissioned to establish a network of correspondents in northern Germany to inform, primarily, on Sigismund's activities.[30] Daniel Riches has argued that Birckholtz most likely initiated the discussions that led to Gustavus Adolphus's marriage to the Brandenburg princess Maria Eleanora in November 1620.[31] Relations with Brandenburg were not limited to connections through Birckholtz, but rested on a wide range of personal connections, particularly those formed during the king's and chancellor's visits to arrange the marriage.

COMMERCE AND INFORMATION

Major commercial centres quickly became the most important nodes in Sweden's information networks abroad. Oxenstierna's system for information was more dependent on commercial centres than on princely courts. The Crown's representatives or others ostensibly acting on its behalf could sell commodities, such as copper, vital to Swedish finances, and buy weapons, munitions and other goods, including books, art, wine and other luxuries. Swedish emissaries could negotiate loans and procure bills of exchange and other forms of financial instruments. Commercial centres also provided information networks, with easy access to postal services and handwritten newsletters as well as more exclusive news and rumour. Printing shops in such centres began to produce printed newspapers, which Oxenstierna received along with diplomatic correspondence, perhaps as early as 1617.[32] Great commercial cities offered large supplies of talent, as well, ranging from military entrepreneurs to professed experts in skills such as cannon-founding, shipbuilding, architecture and Latin poetry.

Some commercial centres had more political importance than others. The United Provinces became one of the most important destinations for Swedish emissaries for reasons that were simultaneously political, commercial and cultural. Members of the States General appreciated the importance of Baltic trade to their well-being, and sought to ally with powers such as the Hanseatic towns and Sweden which might serve as counterweights to Danish domination of the region. As a result, in 1614 the United Provinces extended to Sweden a treaty of alliance and mutual defence that they had signed with the Hanseatic towns; the treaty called for the exchange of ambassadors.

For this task, too, Oxenstierna initially appointed a foreigner, one who had entered into Swedish service during the reign of Charles IX. Born in Haarlem and a one-time law student at Leiden, Jacob van Dijck probably arrived in Sweden with a group of Dutchmen who in 1607 had hoped to obtain a charter from the king for a company to trade with Persia, perhaps as a means of breaking the monopoly of the Vereenigde Oostindische Compagnie (VOC), the Dutch East India Company. While the proposed company never came into operation, many of the intended participants entered Swedish service, some as governors of the city of Gothenburg. Van Dijck was sent as part of an embassy that should have gone to France, but as Henri IV's death rendered the trip fruitless, he stayed in the Netherlands, lobbying fruitlessly for the States General's support in Sweden's war against the Danes. After the peace of Knäred, however, van Dijck convinced the States General to loan Sweden money. He returned to Sweden in the company of a promising young humanist named Jan Rutgers, who had studied in Leiden with scholars such as Joseph Justus Scaliger and Daniel Heinsius, before training as a lawyer in Orléans. Van Dijck received accreditation as Swedish ambassador to the States General; Rutgers remained in Sweden somewhat longer, and would return to Holland both as van Dijck's secretary and as an emissary in his own right, conducting his own correspondence with Oxenstierna. Rutgers was regarded as a conduit to Oxenstierna independent of van Dijck, as, for example, when he was approached by some cannon merchants interested in setting up foundries in Sweden. They sought out Rutgers because they did not trust van Dijck, thinking he had his own competing commercial agenda in Sweden.[33] They were right to suspect van Dijck. Van Dijck's political negotiations about financial assistance from the States General went along with efforts to raise money and purchase munitions on behalf of the Swedish state with prominent merchants and bankers. While van Dijck was signing contracts on behalf of the Swedish Crown with the famous Dutch merchant Louis de Geer, Louis de Geer also acted for van Dijck's interests and helped him conceal those dealings from the Swedish king and chancellor.[34]

BOHEMIAN REVOLT, POLISH WAR AND THE INTENSIFICATION OF FOREIGN RELATIONS

Many factors influenced Oxenstierna's approach to selecting and managing Sweden's foreign emissaries during the 1620s. The Bohemian Revolt and the consequent outbreak of war in the Holy Roman Empire, combined with the expiry of the Twelve Years Truce, raised the prospect of the creation of broader confessional alliances. Oxenstierna and Gustavus Adolphus hoped, with little success, that other Protestant powers would recognise Sweden's war with Catholic King Sigismund of Poland, resumed after the expiration of a truce in 1620, as part of a broader Protestant cause.[35] The Polish war affected Oxenstierna's statecraft in other ways, as well. First, the practical demands of war finance quickly were among Oxenstierna's central concerns. Second, Oxenstierna increasingly resided outside of Sweden, particularly after the summer of 1626 when he became General Governor of Prussia, initiating a decade when he would not set foot in Sweden. On the one hand, this allowed him to participate in more negotiations personally. On the other, it denied him direct control of the Chancery in Stockholm, forced him to develop a field chancery, and also precluded him from playing a role in the Council or *Riksdag*. It also placed him in contact with individuals who would play important roles in his political programme in the years to come. The demands of the 1620s encouraged the growth of a yet more elaborate emissarial system, whose development revealed tensions in Oxenstierna's beliefs about government and the practical possibilities for Swedish politics. On the one hand, he hoped that Sweden would be able to educate, recruit and train Swedish-born nobles in sufficient numbers to fill roles in a rapidly expanding bureaucracy. Not only did Sweden fail to produce sufficient numbers of nobles with the skills necessary to take on such employment, but Oxenstierna also recognised that foreigners could offer Sweden symbolic and practical assets that no Swede possessed. Only slowly did Oxenstierna begin to employ young Swedes as residents, while continuing to employ foreigners of talent.

As early as the winter of 1620, Oxenstierna began to reconsider Sweden's role in Protestant politics, and to identify suitable correspondents. Gustavus Adolphus's brother-in-law Johan Casimir formed one important early connection with the Rhine Palatinate. Oxenstierna entered into a correspondence with the militantly Protestant Palatine Councillor Ludwig Camerarius, quickly offering him a yearly pension to serve as another Swedish correspondent in the Netherlands.[36] He served not only as a symbol of Sweden's attachment to the Protestant cause, but as a well-connected source within the pan-Protestant networks.[37] Jan Rutgers was dispatched on a tour of Denmark and north German Protestant courts and towns, trying to advance Swedish interests in meetings designed to shape a Protestant union, while at the same time recruiting agents such as the painter Peter Isaacsz as an informant at the Danish court and arranging a dedicated Swedish postal service in Hamburg through the Dutch merchant Leonard von Sorgen.[38] In the summer of 1620, Rutgers travelled to Prague, where he received appeals for help from Frederick V, who also gave him his portrait to forward to Gustavus Adolphus.[39] After the Battle of White Mountain, he returned to Hamburg, finding new correspondents for Oxenstierna, and keeping his eyes on evangelical politics. Van Dijck resigned his post in the United Provinces in 1620. Although Rutgers recommended Daniel Heinsius, who had dedicated an edition of Aristotle's *Politics* to the chancellor, as van Dijck's replacement, Oxenstierna chose Camerarius instead. The chancellor also dispatched Peter Falck, a young Swede who had acted as tutor supervising the peregrinations of two young noblemen who had been Oxenstierna's wards. Falck took on much of the negotiations with merchants, and much of the routine postal management. Eventually, however, Rutgers himself returned to the Netherlands as resident, where he performed tasks ranging from the political to the mercantile, arranging loans, munitions deals and credit transactions.[40]

This combination of supporting Protestant politics, gathering information, and transacting commercial and financial business was typical of Swedish agents in major commercial centres. Alongside Rutgers in Amsterdam, and von Sorgen in Hamburg, Oxenstierna appointed another of his clients as commissioner to Denmark. Anders Svensson was Swedish, the son of a tailor. Oxenstierna had arranged support for his foreign studies, which included a tour in the entourage of the famous English collector and ambassador Dudley Carleton on a trip to Italy and The Hague. Svensson was placed in Helsingör, the Danish port station where the Sound tolls were collected, rather than Copenhagen. Helsingör served as a vital hub in commercial, postal and news networks, and Svensson's presence there allowed him to arbitrate the grievances of Swedish merchants. Svensson collected commercial and political news, as well, and served as an intermediary with other correspondents in Denmark.[41]

Oxenstierna was satisfied enough by Svensson's service in Helsingör that, in October 1625, he had him replace Sorgen in Hamburg as resident and postmaster. His instruction not only noted that he was to provide general news about 'anything that could be of advantage or damaging to the king or the kingdom', but specified in detail what sorts of commercial information he should provide, including printed price currents, supplementary information about trade, and even information about specific merchants 'in Genoa, Venice, Milan, Lyons, Augsburg, Nuremburg, Amsterdam, Antwerp, London, Hamburg, Danzig, Lübeck, Poland, Copenhagen, and in other places', detailing their wealth, trade, contact, and, if things went badly, bankruptcies.[42] The instruction for his replacement in Helsingör, Jonas Bure, another Swedish client of Oxenstierna's and a long-time Chancery secretary, emphasised commercial information in similar terms.[43] After Rutgers died of an illness, Ludwig Camerarius replaced him. His instructions, too, emphasised the provision of commercial information, and asked him to establish, like Svensson before him, a network of commercial informants.[44]

With little fanfare, Oxenstierna had begun to shape diplomatic institutions in distinctive ways. Oxenstierna depended on his informal relations with emissaries, while hoping for a more reliable order of public servants, to continue to honour his bills of exchange so he did not go broke from paying Swedish military expenditures during his time as General Governor of Prussia, an office to which he had been appointed in October 1626. In addition to these financial pressures, Oxenstierna's ability to maintain his credit was complicated by differences with other counsellors and Gustavus Adolphus about the role of private merchants in state affairs.[45] These disagreements, combined with the king's favour for different people as well as basic confusion and incompetence, led the king to entrust significant resources to particular merchant groups.[46] Their transactions, above all in commodities such as copper, over which companies had been granted monopolies by the Crown, undermined the chancellor's effort to pay soldiers using bills of exchange issued on the security of deposits of copper. Oxenstierna's response to these difficulties was multifaceted. He wrote a memorandum to the king and council, criticising the king's use of monopoly as confusing the boundary of public and private interests, maintaining that merchants, unlike Crown officials, by the very nature of their estate, looked towards their own interests, and thus should not have public power.[47] At the same time, Sweden's war finances depended, to a great degree, on Crown officials known as 'factors' (agents dispatched specifically to engage in mercantile transactions on the Crown's behalf), and Oxenstierna complained that these emissaries failed to carry out such transactions as would merchants.[48]

Reconciling the need for mercantile savvy with the ideal of public service might have been impossible in any case, but was particularly difficult when the financial demands of the war with Germany necessitated the use of short-term mercantile expedients. Gustavus Adolphus instructed Oxenstierna, for example, to organise a monopoly on grain exports from Muscovy, with the cooperation of the Tsar, to help finance the Swedish war in Germany.[49] In order to keep factors from defrauding the Crown, Oxenstierna ordered audits and collected detailed information about the price of grain and details of credit arrangements, while at the same time relying on financial and commercial networks that he himself could control or which were dependent upon his own clients' resources. Although this search for control was logical, in the short term it served to add to financial confusion, as different networks of Swedish factors undermined each other's credit and transactions.[50]

THE GERMAN WAR

While overseeing the continuing campaigns against Prussia, Oxenstierna was also engaged in the negotiations and deliberations that would eventually lead to Sweden's involvement in the Thirty Years War. Since the Bohemian revolt, Oxenstierna had kept a wary eye on developments in the Holy Roman Empire, and argued that Sweden's war with Sigismund formed part of a broader struggle for Protestantism.

With the calamitous defeat of Christian IV's army, however, Oxenstierna feared that the emperor and the king of Spain might really become involved in Baltic affairs. The prospect of Imperial General Albrecht von Wallenstein's fleet being based in the Baltic, combined with the commercial company proposed by the Spanish emissary Gabriel le Roy and designed to exclude Dutch shipping from Hanseatic and Polish towns, caused Oxenstierna great alarm.[51] While he argued that Sweden should prepare to meet these threats, rather than get involved in war with the emperor, he thought that Sweden would be safer if it pursued its war against Poland and assured its dominion over the Baltic by building a strong navy for use in that sea, which would provide both safety and revenues from tolls.[52] By contrast, Gustavus Adolphus argued for active engagement in the war against the Empire and emphasised the need to restore German liberties to prevent the emperor from becoming a threat to Sweden. Gustavus Adolphus perhaps also perceived the opportunity to act as the protector of European Protestantism more favourably than did Oxenstierna, and viewed war as a chance to preserve and enhance his and his kingdom's reputation.[53]

In early January 1629, the Council in Stockholm consented to the king's desire to wage war on the emperor, and consequently to try to make a peace, or at least conclude a truce with Sigismund.[54] Oxenstierna's counsels had been rejected, but the chancellor immediately began to act in support of the king's plans. The small Prussian port of Elbing, where Oxenstierna resided, became a major hub of diplomatic activity as ambassadors and mediators arrived from near and far.[55] The Holy Roman Emperor and Maximilian of Bavaria attempted to be included in truce negotiations between the Poles and the Swedes, but their appeals were rebuffed. Thomas Roe arrived to mediate on behalf of Charles I, and Hercule de Charnacé on behalf of Louis XIII. More locally, Oxenstierna negotiated with representatives of Kurland, Brandenburg, Pomerania, and a whole host of Hansa towns and Polish cities. News of the negotiations, suitably tailored for different political needs, had to be relayed to correspondents in Hamburg, The Hague, Transylvania and elsewhere.

Negotiations with the Poles quickly focused upon terms for a truce, complicated by Sigismund's refusal to cede his dynastic claims to the Swedish Crown. Above all, Oxenstierna hoped to preserve fortresses controlling the sea-coast and Sweden's right to collect war tolls (also known as 'licences') on merchant shipping, claiming this right as spoils of war. These tolls raised significant revenues, but also brought the talented Spieringk family and, above all, Pieter Spieringk into Swedish service. Born in Delft, Spieringk's father François ran one of the premier tapestry workshops in the Netherlands, a trade that exposed Pieter to mercantile, artistic, learned, and courtly life.[56] Along with his four brothers, Spieringk had gone as a young man to Danzig, where he became embroiled in a dispute about some property in the town, and came into contact with Swedish authorities while seeking restitution. When, in 1627, the Swedes resolved to collect war tolls along the cost of Poland in ducal Prussia, the Spieringks devised the collection method and ran its administration.[57] Despite the complaints it engendered among Dutch merchants and eventually among some in the States General, Oxenstierna so admired Spieringk's toll regime that he would call it Sweden's 'foremost secret', and extend it to Livonia.[58] Spieringk quickly became a key figure in maintaining the Swedish Crown's fiscal networks. Thomas Roe, as mediator, promoted the interests of both English and Dutch merchants; his arrival gave them hope that the tolls might be eliminated altogether. However, Oxenstierna wrote Charnacé a blunt letter explaining that revenues from the tolls were the primary benefit that Sweden had gained from the Polish war, and were necessary for their participation in a war against the emperor. Five days later, the two parties agreed to a six-year truce which, as the chancellor jubilantly wrote to his brother, ensured that 'all the harbours of the Baltic sea from Kalmar through Livonia and Prussia to Danzig will be in his Majesty's hands'.[59] Beyond the Baltic, the decision to go to war with the Holy Roman Empire spawned Swedish diplomatic efforts to gain support that, while unprecedented in scope, built upon long-cultivated networks of emissaries. James Spens, newly ennobled as Baron of Orreholmen, succeeded in coordinating a levy of troops in Britain, if not in attracting Charles I's explicit political support.[60] In the Netherlands, Camerarius's efforts to secure an alliance with the States General were seconded by a number of agents, who combined politics with their mercantile missions.[61] Anders Svensson in Hamburg coordinated negotiations with northern German principalities such as Mecklenburg until his death in 1630, and was ennobled for his services by the king, who was by that time on German soil.

The scope of Swedish diplomacy extended further afield. Emissaries were sent to Moscow, not only to prompt the Tsar to act as a counterbalance to Polish power, but also to arrange the purchase of Russian grain that had been offered as a sort of subsidy for the Swedish war effort. The French alliance, formalised by the treaty of Bärwalde in January 1631, required representation in Paris. The French promise to pay the Swedes a subsidy of 400,000 *riksdaler* a year as long as Gustavus Adolphus maintained an army of 30,000 foot and 6,000 horsemen also required the development of a financial network capable of transferring the subsidies. Sweden solicited diplomatic and military support widely: in Transylvania, Switzerland and in Germany (especially the Protestant states of Brandenburg and Saxony). Initially, these efforts were largely unsuccessful, but as the king's armies pushed deeper into the Holy Roman Empire, Sweden rapidly accumulated allies. While some of this support took the form of military contracts with German princes, other alliances, such as that with Saxony, were formal treaties of mutual support between two sovereign powers.[62]

The expansion of the scale and scope of Sweden's diplomacy posed a number of challenges. Oxenstierna's workload expanded greatly. Although he had developed a second chancery while serving as General Governor of Prussia, he now employed German staff as he travelled more widely, posing further logistical difficulties. Not only did more letters need to be written, treaties drafted and negotiations conducted, but a much greater range of news, information and intelligence needed to be deciphered, read, analysed, and then organised and stored. The volume of both incoming and outgoing letters and papers increased; regular transfers of older materials back to Sweden had to be arranged. This expansion of Sweden's diplomacy tested the limits of Sweden's supply of skilled men of state, particularly as other tasks of governance associated with waging a major war also required educated and capable people. The separation of king, Oxenstierna and the central government in Stockholm necessitated secretaries and other personnel to maintain three separate chanceries, with the added burden of maintaining communication between them.

Those who possessed the requisite skills and connections could profit from these opportunities. After Anders Svensson's death, his duties in Hamburg were assumed by Johan Adler Salvius.[63] Son of a town secretary in Strängnäs, he had enrolled at Uppsala University in 1609; he had then served as a preceptor for a nobleman on a study tour that included the universities at Helmstedt, Strasbourg and Marburg. After returning briefly to Stockholm, Salvius received support from Oxenstierna for a second study tour to Montpellier and Valencia, during which he took a doctorate in law before returning to Stockholm. As a thirty-year-old, he married a rich gold-smith's widow twice his age – she would reach the age of ninety-seven, dying five years after Salvius. After early work organising the town government in Gothenburg and then time at court, Salvius served on foreign missions in Denmark and northern Germany, including levying troops and purchasing munitions in Hamburg. He then entered the Chancery, working closely with Gustavus Adolphus, and coordinating the king's relations with the chancellor while Oxenstierna was in Prussia. He travelled to Pomerania with the king in 1630, and en route wrote the Swedish war manifesto, justifying Sweden's invasion of the Empire. Salvius would combine Svensson's responsibility for news, communication and financial transactions with oversight of a broad range of other political and military tasks. Yet even though Salvius played a vital role during Gustavus Adolphus's campaign and after the king's death, his services were so desperately required in Stockholm that he returned there in 1634.

AFTER GUSTAVUS ADOLPHUS'S DEATH

Gustavus Adolphus's string of military victories and the rapid expansion of Swedish forces into western and southern Germany might well have been unsustainable, as David Parrott argues, because it was unlikely that future conquests would be sufficiently lucrative to pay for themselves.[64] Gustavus Adolphus's death, in any case, significantly altered the nature of Oxenstierna's diplomacy. Christina was six when her father died, and consequently the chancellor not only needed to replace a famous and charismatic military figure on the German scene, but he also had to ensure that Swedish legitimacy would not be contested by divisions over minority rule at home.[65]

Oxenstierna complained that 'he was overwhelmed by negotiations, and did not now have much help'.[66] Swedish relations abroad relied to an extraordinary degree on Oxenstierna's own negotiations, under powers that were on his request eventually formalised under the rubric of Sweden's 'legate'. He thus exercised quasi-sovereign powers which were accepted by many other sovereigns, but not by all. Oxenstierna, for example, performed many of the complicated negotiations that led to the League of Heilbronn. This League, formed ostensibly along lines suggested by the late king, drew upon the form of the constitution of the United Provinces in an attempt to bring into line Sweden's German allies, who combined the pretensions of sovereigns with the cupidity of military entrepreneurs.[67] Yet many northern German princes did not join the league, as they distrusted Sweden. Oxenstierna also personally conducted many important negotiations with the French, usually with French ambassadors but on one occasion meeting with Louis XIII and Richelieu at Compiègne in 1635.

While Oxenstierna's title of 'Legate' provided him with the authority to operate on the continent, a controversial constitutional charter cum administrative plan known as the 'Form of Government' formally established the minority government's authority in Sweden, and reinforced Oxenstierna's authority to act in the name of the Swedish Crown. The chancellor maintained that this arrangement, too, had been discussed with Gustavus Adolphus, but some historians have viewed it as Oxenstierna taking advantage of the king's death to fulfil the programme of the noble party in Sweden that dated back to the reign of Charles IX.[68] Oxenstierna organised the government into five main colleges – the Royal Court, the Chancery, the Treasury, the Admiralty and the Army. The five great officers of the realm were at the head of the colleges, and they or their deputies acted together as the Regency government. Oxenstierna's family and friends held many, if not all, of the five offices, and played guiding roles in the Council; despite this, the chancellor could not always rely upon the Council to do his bidding. After the Swedish defeat at Nördlingen in 1634 and even more so after the Peace of Prague in 1635, members of the Council began to worry that Sweden would lose the war. The councillors' doubts spawned differences with Oxenstierna, above all in negotiations over the renewal of the truce with Poland in 1635. In order to secure a long truce, Swedish negotiators – including Axel's own son Johan – were granted both the means to conciliate George William of Brandenburg by offering him Polish territory in compensation for the cession of Pomerania, and, more significantly, the right for the Swedes to collect the Prussian war tolls. When they subsequently abandoned the right to collect war tolls off Polish harbours, Oxenstierna judged that the negotiators had left 'Sweden [. . .] not half the kingdom that it was last fall'.[69]

Apart from the nearly impossible task of maintaining any sort of consensus among the Protestant princes and Swedish counsellors, Oxenstierna had to attend to more mundane matters. He had to find people to fill new diplomatic posts, despite complaints that there were too few suitable Swedes who had the education, experience and knowledge needed to fill them.[70] Consequently, suitable foreigners continued to be considered for service as Swedish resident ambassadors. The most famous of these was the exiled Dutch statesman and man of letters, Hugo Grotius. Oxenstierna had been aware of Grotius since early in his chancellorship; more or less desultory discussions about his entering Swedish service had occurred for the best part of a decade. After meeting Grotius in Frankfurt in May 1634, Oxenstierna considered employing him, perhaps to replace Salvius in Hamburg. However, Salvius himself thought others more suitable, and suggested that Grotius become resident in Paris, and perhaps at the same time serve as tutor for Oxenstierna's son Erik.[71] Oxenstierna agreed to this, and at the end of 1635, Grotius was engaged for the unprecedented sum of 8,000 *Reichsthaler* a year.[72] In addition to representing Sweden's political interests, the resident ambassadors in Paris were charged with transferring the war subsidies furnished by the French Crown. Grotius, however, was not asked to administer the subsidies, although he may have wanted to. This task remained in the hands of Pieter Spieringk and the French banker of Dutch descent Jan Hoeufft.

The long-serving agent in London Spens died shortly after Gustavus Adolphus. Departing from the convention of using Scots as agents in England, Oxenstierna contracted with Michel le Blon, an engraver, art collector, and acquaintance of the artists Pieter Paul Rubens and Anthony van Dyck, to serve as resident ambassador in England.[73] The choice seems to have been made because le Blon had served, with the help of the notorious Balthasar Gerbier, as an intermediary between Charles I's favourite George Villiers, Duke of Buckingham, and Gustavus Adolphus, as they explored a scheme to realise Walter Raleigh's outlandish plan to colonise the Oronoco.[74] Though ambassador to England, le Blon resided mostly in the Low Countries, providing a wide range of political intelligence and cultural information, including advice about painters.

HOMECOMING: OXENSTIERNA'S SYSTEM

In mid-July 1636, Oxenstierna returned to Sweden. He arrived in the midst of a *Riksdag*, and had a number of opportunities, formal and informal, to discuss his present and future activities as legate. During the autumn of that year, the chancellor brought the members of the Council to a seeming consensus, if not unanimity, about the course of Sweden's relations with other powers, as well as how to approach a wide range of domestic policies. Sweden's politics and institutional development from his homecoming until shortly after Christina reached her majority would be shaped chiefly by Oxenstierna. He enjoyed considerable success placing his clients in positions of importance. These included members of his family, as he sought to establish his sons in positions of influence.

Among other things, Oxenstierna established regular procedures for the post and the distribution of news within Sweden. In 1636, Anders Wechel, a German who had been manager of the Swedish post in Leipzig, was brought to Sweden and installed as the first postmaster general at a salary of 600 *Reichsthaler*.[75] He died after several months in the job, and his wife Gese took over the office for six years, until Salvius, the ambassador in Hamburg, complained that she had not paid money that she owed him for the post between Stockholm and Hamburg. She was relieved of her duties, received a pension and was replaced by Johan Beijer, another German who had been in Oxenstierna's German chancery. Beijer followed the chancellor to Stockholm, where he served in the Royal Chancery and nominally in a nascent College of Commerce whose instructions were drafted in 1637 but appears never to have met.[76] His instructions as postmaster called for him to correspond with emissaries through-out the continent, put together collections of extracts of the news, weighing them for their effect upon subjects' morale, and then sharing them with other postmasters across the realm. By 1645, Beijer was overseeing the publication of the *Ordinari Post Tijdender*, Sweden's first real newspaper.[77]

Upon his return, Oxenstierna also reorganised Swedish representation in the crucial financial and political centre of the Netherlands. As the Prussian tolls were no longer collected by the Swedish, the Spieringk brothers had only partial employment. Oxenstierna, however, believed that retaining the service of the brothers, and particularly Pieter, was of vital importance to the Swedish state, because their knowledge of the toll system, as well as their broader financial and political savvy, might prove valuable to other powers. While the Poles were able to employ some of the brothers – and did, ultimately, set up a toll system based on the Swedish model – Oxenstierna retained Pieter Spieringk by offering him a post as resident in the Netherlands, where he had already been an occasional agent in 1634, helping, among other things, to arrange the transfer of the French subsidies for the war effort. Spieringk returned to the Netherlands this second time under an awkward arrangement where he initially shared the post with Camerarius, who became convinced that Spieringk was plotting to undermine him.[78] Spieringk's appointment reflected not only Oxenstierna's high estimation of Spieringk's personal qualities, but the dissatisfaction of members of the Council with Camerarius's high salary and tendency for humanistic pedantry. Oxenstierna's brother Gabriel opined that 'the budget no longer allows Camerarius to be kept there, and he is of little use, as he cannot penetrate all the things that he should, and he does not understand merchants'.[79] For all that, Camerarius remained at his post until 1640. Grotius, too, provoked the ire of the Council; members of the Council complained of his high salary and ineptitude, and hoped that he could be replaced with a Swede.[80]

At least in the Netherlands, Oxenstierna valued commercial and mercantile savvy as much as any other factor when employing emissaries. While Spieringk performed functions typical of resident ambassadors, mercantile matters also occupied much of his time. He wrote bills of exchange, purchased arms, and procured legal advice to try to free the Crown from its obligations to a copper company. He rented a house in Amsterdam, where he spent time when he had no business in The Hague, the 'more diligently to inform myself about commerce'.[81] Indeed, even if money was short, enough was found to employ other agents to carry out the Crown's mercantile affairs in the Netherlands. An administrator of the Dutch West India Company named Samuel Blommaert was cajoled into leaving the Company's service to become a Swedish commissary. In this capacity, he helped organise Sweden's colonial company, which would found New Sweden on the Delaware River in North America. He was joined by others, who took on mercantile and fiscal errands, such as Louis de Geer's old bookkeeper Johan Le Thor, and a young Swede named Peter Trotzig.[82] When Blommaert left Swedish service, he was replaced by another young Swedish client of the chancellor, Harald Appelboom, who claimed on a study tour to Amsterdam to have 'learned the country's language, polity, and the course and value of all sorts of commerce'.[83] Oxenstierna also agreed to pay a pension to support the aged Willem Usselinx, who, after failing to create the Dutch West India Company, had worked tirelessly to raise capital for a colonial company for the Swedish Crown. The proliferation of Swedish agents and emissaries in the United Provinces reveals not only the importance of the Netherlands to Sweden's news and information network, but the high value that Oxenstierna placed upon mercantile counsel and information.

Mercantile information did not play a large role in the correspondence of every

Swedish ambassador. Although Salvius dealt with many financial and commercial matters in Hamburg, he did not dwell on such matters in his correspondence. Salvius had become an essential contact point in the complex negotiations regarding peace talks with the French and Imperial envoys, and while he still referred to Oxenstierna as a patron, he had established a degree of autonomy and personal authority. He had even, subtly, begun to build up his own client network, not only in Hamburg and northern Germany, but even inside the Swedish Chancery.[84] He may well have hoped to attract royal favour, in the event that Oxenstierna fell out of favour with the Queen.

More seriously, some agents turned out to be untrustworthy. The first resident in Portugal, Lars Skytte, had studied at Uppsala University and undertook a study tour to the United Provinces, and then participated in a number of short diplomatic missions, before being chosen for the embassy. In Amsterdam, however, he came into contact with a variety of Christian sects, and this made him doubt the truth of the Lutheran creed. Recalled to Sweden in 1647, he instead entered the Franciscan order. He may well have given advice to the Jesuit Antonio Macedo, who would play a role in Christina's conversion to Catholicism, before Macedo left for Sweden.[85]

SECURING THE FUTURE: CHRISTINA'S RULE

Oxenstierna might have concluded that his statecraft had secured both the kingdom's place in the Baltic and his family's reputation. Yet Christina's years of maturity (after 1644), while in some respects consolidating and extending Oxenstierna's earlier work, also threatened the future of both his progeny and the security of Sweden. Oxenstierna was growing old and was frequently ill, giving good reason for ambitious youth to seek out other patrons. Christina's assertions of independence also proved a challenge, coming to a head when the queen drew upon a party that included Salvius to stir up the non-noble estates against Oxenstierna and other members of the nobility who opposed her succession plans.[86] Her political goals sometimes differed from those of Oxenstierna. She emerged as an independent source of royal favour, further weakening Oxenstierna's stature as a patron. Christina calculated ways to reduce the authority of the chancellor and his sons, so as to increase her own autonomy. The period from 1647 until his death was a period of extraordinary political turbulence for Oxenstierna and he occasionally expressed worries in correspondence about the revolts and insurrections that historians have recently grouped under the rubric of 'the Crisis of the Seventeenth Century'. The assault on Denmark can be seen as inaugurating a new stage in Swedish policy, when the rhetorical force of Protestant allegiance withered in the face of political pragmatism. While the alliances with France might be construed as strategically aimed at Catholic Habsburg power, the instability of relations with Denmark, England and the Netherlands suggested that Protestant confessional allegiance had lost even its rhetorical allure as an organising principle in foreign affairs.

Even if Oxenstierna did much to secure the gains, territorial and otherwise, won in the Peace of Westphalia/Osnabrück, the Treaty did not constitute an unambiguous personal triumph. Oxenstierna had manoeuvred for years to make Johan, the older of his living sons, one of the Swedish plenipotentiaries at the negotiations, alongside Salvius. Oxenstierna's letters to Johan declare himself to be 'more jealous of your reputation than I am of my own', and anxious to provide advice and counsel that would help his son.[87] Johan's own pomposity and propensity to drink until he was incapable of negotiating contributed to a series of personal gaffes that undermined his legitimacy in the negotiations. Christina used allies in the Chancery to communicate directly with Salvius, and the circulation of a royal letter undermining Johan was a cause for deep humiliation.[88] What is more, while clearly favouring Salvius at the expense of Johan as her primary representative at the talks, she also proposed admitting Salvius to the Council, in the face of Oxenstierna's most vehement objections.[89] Over the next several years, Oxenstierna worried, too, that his other son, Erik, would be transferred to some unpromising post – such as a junior delegate to a peace conference with Poland in Lübeck – rather than a prominent domestic post that would allow him to exercise influence after his father's death.[90] After Christina secured a succession agreement that mandated that Carl Gustav, her first cousin on her father's side, would succeed the throne even in the case that she abdicated, Christina once again allowed Oxenstierna considerable latitude to advance his own family and clients. Oxenstierna was able to advance Erik into a position as head of the College of Commerce, which would smooth his succession into his father's job as chancellor.[91]

Yet even while Christina was putting pressure on Oxenstierna, many features of his system persisted; commercial information, for example, continued to be a major thread of many emissaries' correspondence.[92] Some young Swedes tried to make careers in foreign posts, even if Swedish noblemen such as Schering Rosenhane may have tried to avoid postings as resident ambassadors, so far from the political action at home.[93] At Oxenstierna's death, Sweden maintained a range of permanent residents. Cities of commercial importance – Helsingör, Hamburg and The Hague/ Amsterdam – were particularly important posts, both for their mercantile commodities and their access to broad streams of information. What is more, a certain specialisation had begun to take place, with dedicated commercial and postal employees, chosen and paid by the Swedish central authorities rather than the ambassador. The College of Commerce was instructed to maintain a set of special commercial correspondents, beginning with Moscow, Novogorod, continuing through Amsterdam, and more distant cities such as Venice, Florence and Livorno.[94]

Oxenstierna had been instrumental in shaping the institutions of Swedish diplomacy, and certainly oversaw a ratcheting up of bureaucratic capacity in the realm of foreign representation. Prompted both by practical demands and a belief that representation was expected of the great nations of his day, he supplemented temporary embassies and informal connections with foreign representatives who exchanged their expertise and connections for the salaries and career opportunities presented by Swedish service. The Thirty Years War prompted yet further expansion of Swedish foreign representation, with an even greater premium placed on commercial and fiscal information. While entrepreneurial diplomats would never disappear, with time, Oxenstierna's own clients, whether Swedish or foreign-born, played a growing role in Swedish diplomacy, and such service became a recognised method of social advancement within the kingdom. Swedish foreign policy was not always particularly well coordinated, with the chancellor not always acting completely in accord with the monarch or other members of the Council. Over his many years close to the centre of power, Oxenstierna shaped in meaningful ways a tradition of foreign representation, one that was distinctly Swedish but also reflected the Eurasian political, economic and cultural milieu in which Sweden operated.

NOTES

1. Victor Lieberman, *Strange Parallels: Southeast Asia in Global Context, c. 800–1830.* Vol. 2, *Mainland Mirrors: Europe, Japan, China, South Asia and the Islands* (Cambridge: Cambridge University Press, 2009), p. 44.
2. I. A. A. Thompson, 'The Institutional Background to the Rise of the Minister-Favourite', in J. H. Elliott and L. W. B. Brockliss (eds), *The World of the Favourite* (New Haven, CT: Yale University Press, 1999), p. 14; Heinz Schilling, *Konfessionalisierung und Staatsinteressen: Internationale Beziehungen, 1559–1660* (Paderborn: Ferdinand Schöningh, 2007), pp. 337, 566.
3. Björn Asker, *Hur Riket styrde: Förvaltning, politik och arkiv 1520–1920* (Stockholm: Riksarkivet, 2009), p. 80; Gunnar Wetterberg, *Axel Oxenstierna – Furstespegel för 2000-talet: Rapport till Expertgruppen för studier i offentlig ekonomi* (Stockholm: Regeringskansliet, 2003); Ardalan Shekarbi, 'Ny regionreform ska göra landstingen färre från 2019', *Dagens Nyheter*, 23 March 2015, available at <http://www.dn.se/debatt/ ny-regionreform-ska-gora-landstingen-farre-fran-2019/> (last accessed 8 July 2015).
4. The fragment of the history is in *Rikskansleren Axel Oxenstiernas Skrifter och Brefväxling* (hereafter *AOSB*), many editors (Stockholm: Kungliga Vitterhets, Historie och Antikvitets Akademien, 1888–), ser. I, vol. 1, pp. 246–50, and discussion of it in Salvius to Axel Oxenstierna, 23 May 1634, *AOSB*, ser. II, vol. 14, pp. 231–2.
5. Bogislaw Philipp von Chemnitz, *Königlichen Schwedischen in Teutschland geführten Kriegs* (Stettin: Georg Retten, 1648–53).
6. Gunnar Wetterberg, *Kanslern: Axel Oxenstierna i sin tid* (Stockholm: Atlantis, 2002). Since the appearance of the former volume, there has also been a German biography: Jörg-Peter Findeisen, *Axel Oxenstierna: Architekt der schwedischen Großmacht-Ära und Sieger des Dreißigjährigen Krieges* (Gernsbach: Katz, 2009), and a study of his statecraft: Alexander Zirr, *Axel Oxenstierna: Schwedens Reichskanzler während des Dreißigjährigen Krieges* (Leipzig: Meine Verlag, 2008).
7. For the chancery, see particularly Nils Edén, *Den svenska centralregeringens utveckling till kollegial organisation i början af sjuttonde Århundradet (1602–1634)* (Uppsala: Akademiska bokhandeln, 1902); Hjalmar Haralds, 'Kansliet – anima regni?', *Statsvetenskaplig tidskrift* 31 (1928), pp. 234–58, 300–23. For the Chancery's growing importance as a centre of cultural production and patronage, see Bo Bennich-Björkman, *Författaren i ämbetet: Studier i funktion och organisation av författarämbetet vid svenska hovet och kansliet, 1550–1850* (Uppsala: Scandinavian University Books, 1970); Svante Norrhem, *Uppkomlingarna: Kanslitjänstemännen i 1600-talets Sverige och Europa* (Stockholm: Almqvist & Wiksell, 1993). For early work on diplomacy's institutions, see Carl-Frederik Palmstierna, 'Utrikesförvaltningens historia, 1611–1648', in Sven Tunberg, Carl-Frederik Palmstierna, Arne Munthe, Torsten Gihl and Nils Wollin (eds), *Den Svenska Utrikesförvaltningens Historia* (Uppsala: Almqvist & Wiksell, 1935), pp. 41–107.
8. See Stefan Troebst, 'The Attman–Roberts Debate on the Mercantile Background to Swedish Empire-Building', in Aleksander Loit and Helmut Piirimäe (eds), *Die Schwedischen*

Ostseeprovinzen Estland und Livland im 16–18. Jahrhundert (Stockholm: Almqvist & Wiksell, 1993), pp. 33–52; Troebst, 'Debating the Mercantile Background to Early Modern Swedish Empire Building', *European History Quarterly* 24 (1994), pp. 485–509.

9. Arne Losman, *Carl Gustaf Wrangel och Europa: Studier i kulturförbindelser kring en 1600-talsmagnat* (Stockholm: Almqvist & Wiksell, 1980). See especially Heiko Droste, *Im Dienst der Krone: Schwedische Diplomaten im 17. Jahrhundert* (Berlin: LIT Verlag, 2006); Peter Lindström and Svante Norrhem, *Flattering Alliances: Scandinavia, Diplomacy and the Austrian–French Balance of Power, 1648–1740* (Lund: Nordic Academic Press, 2013).

10. See, most programmatically, John Watkins, 'Toward a New Diplomatic History of Medieval and Early Modern Europe', *Journal of Medieval and Early Modern Studies* 31:1 (2008), pp. 1–14 and also Sven Externbrink, 'Internationale Politik in der Frühen Neuzeit. Stand und Perspektiven der Forschung zu Diplomatie und Staatensystem', in Hans-Christof Kraus and Thomas Nicklas (eds), *Geschichte und Politik: Alte und Neue Wege: Beihefte der Historische Zeitschrift* 44 (München: De Gruyter, 2007), pp. 15–39; Michael Rohrschneider, 'Neue Tendenzen der diplomatie-geschichtlichen Erforschung des Westfälischen Friedenskongress', in Inken Schmidt-Voges, Siegrid Westphal, Volker Arnke and Tobias Bartke (eds), *Pax Perpetua: Neuere Forschungen zum Frieden in der Frühen Neuzeit* (Munich: R. Oldenbourg, 2010), pp. 103–21; Lucien Bély, *L'Art de la paix en Europe: Naissance de la diplomatie moderne XVIe–XVIIIe siècles* (Paris: Presses universitaires de France, 2007), pp. 1–23; Hillard von Theissen and Christian Windler, 'Außenbeziehungen in aktueurzentrierter Perspektive', in von Theissen and Windler (eds), *Akteure der Außenbeziehungen: Netzwerke und Interkulturalität im historischen Wandel* (Cologne: Bohlau, 2010), pp. 1–12.

11. See above all Wolfgang Behringer, *Im Zeichen des Merkur: Reichspost und Kommuikationsrevolution in der Frühen Neuzeit* (Göttingen: Vandenhoeck & Ruprecht, 2003); for informal network robustness, see Mark S. Granovetter, 'The Strength of Weak Ties', *American Journal of Sociology* 78:6 (1973), pp. 1360–80; for agent problems and information asymmetry, see Jean Tirole, 'Hierarchies and Bureaucracies: On the Role of Collusion in Organizations', *Journal of Law, Economics and Organization* 2:2 (1986), pp. 181–214, and Richard Waterman and Kenneth Meier, 'Principal Agent Models: An Expansion?', *Journal of Public Administration Research and Theory (J-PART)* 8:2 (1998), pp. 173–202.

12. For the material side of early modern correspondence, see James Daybell, *The Material Letter in Early Modern England: Manuscript Letters and the Culture and Practices of Letter Writing, 1512–1635* (Basingstoke: Palgrave Macmillan, 2012), pp. 1–108.

13. For 'civil nations', see Margareta Revera, 'The Making of a Civilized Nation: Nation-Building, Aristocratic Culture, and Social Change', in Arne Losman, Agneta Lundström and Margareta Revera (eds), *The Age of New Sweden* (Stockholm: Livrustkammaren, 1988), pp. 103–31.

14. Axel Oxenstierna to Erik Oxenstierna, 5 June 1645, Riksarkivet, Stockholm: Oxenstiernska Samlingen, E 1053.

15. In addition to Wetterberg, *Kanslern*, vol. I, pp. 89–150, see Wilhelm Tham, *Axel Oxenstierna: Hans ungdom och verksamhet intill år 1612* (Stockholm: Victor Petterson, 1935); Nils Ahnlund, *Axel Oxenstierna intill Gustav Adolfs död* (Stockholm: P. A. Norstedt, 1940), pp. 28–98.

16. See Erik Thomson, 'Axel Oxenstierna and Books', *Sixteenth Century Journal* 38:3 (2007), pp. 705–29; Lotte Kuras (ed.), *Axel Oxenstiernas Album amicorum und seine eigenen Stammbucheinträge* (Stockholm: Kungl. Vitterhets Historie och Antikvitets Akademien, 2004).

17. On elite women's roles, including Anna Bååt's political role, see Svante Norrhem, *Kvinnor vid maktens sida, 1632–1772* (Lund: Nordic Academic Press, 2007).

18. Sven A. Nilsson, 'Gustav II Adolf och Axel Oxenstierna: En studie i maktdelning och dess alternativ', *Scandia* 62:2 (1996), pp. 169–94.

19. Axel Oxenstierna to Christina, 25 March 1612, *AOSB*, ser. I, vol. 2, pp. 420–48.
20. Folke Lindberg, 'Axel Oxenstierna som riksdagstaktiker: ett bidrag till belysningen av Riksdagsdoktrin och Riksdagspraxis under förmyndartiden', *Statsvetenskaplig tidskrift* 34 (1931), pp. 251–69; Sven A. Nilsson, 'Politiskmobilisering i den svenska militärstaten', *Scandia* 60 (1994), pp. 115–54.
21. 'Riks-Kansleren Axel Oxenstjernas Kansli-Ordning, af den 16 Oct, 1618', in C. G. Styffe (ed.), *Samling af instructioner rörande den civila förvaltningen i Sverige och Finland* (Stockholm: Högberg, 1856), pp. 300–2.
22. Oxenstierna's patronage is underresearched, but see Björn Asker, 'Perspektiv på klientväsendet i svenskt 1600-tal', in Janne Backlund (ed.), *Historiska etyder: En vänbok till Stellan Dahlgren* (Uppsala: Historiska institutionen, 1997), pp. 21–30.
23. Milja van Tielhof, *The 'Mother of all Trades': The Baltic Grain Trade in Amsterdam from the Late 16th to the Early 19th Century* (Leiden: Brill, 2002), pp. 43–50.
24. 'Protokoll vid upprättandet af giftemålskontrakt mellan Prinsessan Katarina och Pfalzgrefven Casimir den 7, 8, 9, 10, 15, 18 och 19 Nov. 1614', *AOSB*, ser. I, vol. 1, pp. 85–96.
25. 'Dagbok öfver fredsunderhandlingen med Danska ombud på riksgränsen vid Sjöryd, Nov. 1612–Jan. 1613', *AOSB*, ser. I, vol. 1, pp. 49–84.
26. Michael Roberts, *Gustavus Adolphus: A History of Sweden, 1611–1632* (London: Longmans, 1953–8), vol. I, pp. 60–72, 122–9.
27. Fritz Redlich, *The German Military Enterpriser and His Workforce: A Study in European Economic and Social History* (Weisbaden: Franz Steiner, 1965); David Parrott, *The Business of War: Military Enterprise and Military Revolution in Early Modern Europe* (Cambridge: Cambridge University Press, 2012).
28. R. H. Coase, 'The Nature of the Firm (1937)', in Oliver E. Williamson and Sidney G. Winter (eds), *The Nature of the Firm: Origins, Evolution, and Development* (Oxford: Oxford University Press, 1991), p. 22. For an example of a contract with an emissary, see the two contracts for Michel le Blon from 1632 in the Riksarkivet, Oxenstiernska Samlingen, E 645.
29. His correspondence has been edited recently by Arne Jönsson, in *AOSB*, ser. II, vol. 13, pp. 23–224. See also Alexia Grosjean, *An Unofficial Alliance: Scotland and Sweden, 1569–1654* (Leiden: Brill, 2003), pp. 31–53; Steve Murdoch, *Network North: Scottish Kin, Commercial and Covert Associations in Northern Europe, 1603–1746* (Leiden: Brill, 2005), pp. 207–80; Murdoch, 'Oxenstierna's Spies: Sir James Spens and the Organisation of Covert Operations in the Early Seventeenth-century in Sweden', in Daniel Szechi (ed.), *The Dangerous Trade: Spies, Spymasters and the Making of Europe* (Dundee: Dundee University Press 2010), pp. 45–65.
30. Heiko Droste, 'Hieronymus von Birckholtz: Sveriges förste underrättelseman', *Personhistorisk tidskrift* 94 (1998), pp. 76–98.
31. Daniel Riches, *Protestant Cosmopolitanism and Diplomatic Culture: Brandenburg–Swedish Relations in the Seventeenth Century* (Leiden: Brill, 2012), pp. 141–2.
32. Clé Lesger, *The Rise of the Amsterdam Market and Information Exchange: Merchants, Commercial Expansion and Change in the Spatial Economy of the Low Countries, c. 1550–1630* (Aldershot: Ashgate, 2006), pp. 181–257. Though old, Folke Dahl's 'Amsterdam – Earliest Newspaper Centre of Western Europe: New Contributions to the History of the first Dutch and French Courantos', *Het Boek* 25 (1939), pp. 161–97, is useful, because many of the newspapers used by Dahl were taken from Oxenstierna's correspondence and transferred to the Kungliga Biblioteket.
33. Jan Rutgers to Axel Oxenstierna, 16 July 1618, *AOSB*, ser. II, vol. 13, pp. 296–7.
34. 'Kontrakt mellan J. van Dijck and Louis de Geer, samt hans participanter, om ett lån till svenska kronan, 's-Gravenhage, juli 1618, and Louis de Geer to Jacob van Dijck, 30 oktober 1620', in E. W. Dahlgren (ed.), *Louis de Geers brev och affärshandlingar, 1614–1652* (Stockholm: P. A. Norstedt, 1934), pp. 25–7, 43–4.

35. Axel Oxenstierna to Johan Caisimir, 4 February 1620, *AOSB*, ser. I, vol. 2, pp. 368–75.
36. Ibid. p. 373, particularly the excerpted letter from Camerarius in the footnote.
37. See Friedrich Schubert, *Ludwig Camerarius, 1573–1651: Eine Biographie* (Kallmünz: Lassleben, 1955), but note Brennan Pursell's estimation of him in his *Winter King: Frederick V of the Palatinate and the Coming of the Thirty Years' War* (Aldershot: Ashgate, 2003), p. 21.
38. Badeloch Noldus, 'Peter Isaacsz's Other Life – Legal and Illegal', in Noldus and Juliette Roding (eds), *Pieter Isaacsz (1568–1625): Court Painter, Art Dealer and Spy* (Turnhout: Brepols, 2007), pp. 151–63; Noldus, 'Loyalty and Betrayal: Artists-Agents Michel le Blon and Pieter Isaacsz and Chancellor Axel Oxenstierna', in Hans Cools, Marika Keblusek and Badeloch Noldus (eds), *Your Humble Servant: Agents in Early Modern Europe* (Hilverssum: Verloren, 2006), pp. 51–64.
39. Jan Rutgers to Axel Oxenstierna, 17 July 1620, *AOSB*, ser. II, vol. 13, pp. 347–54.
40. Jan Rutgers to Axel Oxenstierna, 12 October 1621 and 21 October 1621, *AOSB*, ser. II, vol. 13, pp. 382–5.
41. Leo Tandrup, *Svensk agent ved Sundet: Toldkommissaer og agent i Helsingør Anders Svenssons depecher til Gustav II Adolf og Axel Oxenstierna, 1621–1626* (Aarhus: Universitetsforlaget i Aarhus, 1971), pp. 15–73.
42. 'Instruction och underrättelse hwarefter Kon: M:tt vill att *Agenten* i Hamburg Anders Svänsson sigh rätta skall', 19 October 1625, Riksarkivet, Diplomatica, Germanica 746, D11, §15. For printed price currents, see John J. McKusker and Cora Gravensteijn, *The Beginnings of Commercial and Financial Journalism: The Commodity Price Currents, Exchange Rate Currents, and Money Rate Currents of Early Modern Europe* (Amsterdam: Nederlandisch Economisch-Historisch Archief, 1991).
43. Instruction for Jonas Bure, 19 October 1625, Riksarkivet, Riksregistaturet, fo. 601.
44. 'Instruction, ex mandato S:R: M:tis consignata', 20 June 1626, Riksarkivet, Diplomatica, Hollandica, 8, §16.
45. See Mats Hallenberg, *Statsmakt till Salu: Arrendesystemet och privatiseringen av skatteuppbörden i det svenska riket, 1618–1635* (Lund: Nordic Academic Press, 2008); Erik Thomson, 'Swedish Variations on Dutch Commercial Institutions, Practices, and Discourse, 1605–1655', *Scandinavian Studies* 77:3 (2005), pp. 331–46.
46. P. W. Klein, *De Trippen in de 17ᵉ Eeuw: Een Studie over het ondernemersgedrag op de Hollandse Stapelmarkt* (Assen: Van Gorcum, 1965), pp. 184–417.
47. See the discussion in Peter Englund, *Det hotade huset: adliga föreställningar om samhället under stormaktstiden* (Stockholm: Atlantis, 1989), pp. 49–69.
48. 'Betänkande om kopparhandeln och kopparmyntningen, dat. Fischhausen, d. 30 April 1630', in *AOSB*, ser. I, vol. 1, pp. 344–50, esp. p. 350.
49. See B. F. Porschnev, *Muscovy and Sweden in the Thirty Years War, 1630–1635* (Cambridge: Cambridge University Press, 1995); Lars Ekholm, 'Rysk spannmål och svenska krigsfinanser, 1629–1633', *Scandia* 40:1 (1974); Stefan Troebst, *Handelskontrolle – 'Derivation' – Eindämmung. Schwedische Moskaupolitik 1617–1661* (Wiesbaden: Harrassowitz Verlag, 1997), pp. 76–105.
50. For examples, see Conrad von Falkenberg to Axel Oxenstierna, 5 September 1629, 23 March 1629 and 2 July 1630, and Axel Oxenstierna to Gabriel Gustavsson Oxenstierna, P. S. to 16 June 1629, in *AOSB*, ser. II, vol. 11, pp. 570–1, 585, 588–90 and *AOSB*, ser. I, vol. 4, p. 545.
51. Axel Oxenstierna to Gabriel Gustafsson Oxenstierna, 1 November 1627, *AOSB*, ser. I, vol. 3, pp. 668–77.
52. Axel Oxenstierna to Gustaf Adolf, 19 April 1628, *AOSB*, ser. I, vol. 4, pp. 118–28.
53. Gustaf Adolf to Axel Oxenstierna, 1 April 1628, *AOSB*, ser. II, vol. 1, pp. 395–400.
54. The closest analysis of the debate is in Leif Åslund, '*Pro et contra* och *consultation* i 1600-talets svenska Riksråd, 1626–1658', *Samlaren* 110 (1989), pp. 7–25.

55. See the old account, Herman Brulin, 'Stilleståndet i Altmark', in Nils Edén (ed.), *Historiska studier tillägnande Professor Harald Hjärne på hans sextioårsdag den 2 maj 1908* (Uppsala: Almqvist & Wiksell, 1908), pp. 259–310.

56. Badeloch Noldus, 'An "Unvergleichbarer Leibhaber": Pieter Spierinck, the Art-Dealing Diplomat', *Scandinavian Journal of History* 31:2 (2006), pp. 173–85.

57. Einar Wendt, *Det svenska licent-väsendet i Preussen, 1627–1635* (Uppsala: Almqvist & Wiksell, 1933).

58. For 'secret', see Axel Oxenstierna to commissioners in Prussia, 21 August 1635, *AOSB*, ser. I, vol. 13, p. 534.

59. Axel Oxenstierna to Hercule de Charnacé, 11 September 1629, *AOSB*, ser. I, vol. 4, pp. 603–6; Axel Oxenstierna to Gabriel Gustafsson Oxenstierna, 25 September 1629, *AOSB*, ser. I, vol. 4, p. 523.

60. James Spens to Axel Oxenstierna, 17 April 1629 and 7 October 1629, *AOSB*, ser. II, vol. 13, pp. 217–22.

61. See Schubert, *Ludwig Camerarius*, pp. 360–86; Klein, *Trippen*, pp. 346–82.

62. For the often murky distinction between alliances and contracts, see Andrea Thiele, 'The Prince as Military Entrepreneur? Why Smaller Saxon Territories Sent "Holländische Regimenter" (Dutch Regiments) to the Dutch Republic', in Jeff Fynn-Paul (ed.), *War, Entrepreneurs, and the State in Europe and the Mediterranean, 1300–1800* (Leiden: Brill, 2014), pp. 170–92.

63. On Salvius, see Sune Lundgren, *Johan Adler Salvius: Problem kring Freden, Krigsekonomien och Maktkampen* (Lund: Lindstedt, 1945); Heiko Droste, 'Johan Adler Salvius i Hamburg: ett nätverksbygge i 1600-talets Sverige', in Kerstin Abukhanfusa (ed.), *Mare nostrum: Om Westfaliska freden och Östersjön som ett svenskt maktcentrum* (Stockholm: Riksarkivet, 1999), pp. 243–55; Droste, *Im Dienst der Krone*; and the new edition of his letters to Axel Oxenstierna, *AOSB*, ser. II, vol. 14.

64. Parrott, *The Business of War*, pp. 129–30.

65. See the excellent account by Michael Roberts, 'Oxenstierna in Germany, 1633–1636', in *From Oxenstierna to Charles XII: Four Studies* (Cambridge: Cambridge University Press, 1991), pp. 6–54.

66. Axel Oxenstierna to Gabriel Gustafsson Oxenstierna, *AOSB*, 6 December 1632, ser. I, vol. 7, p. 717.

67. Roberts, 'Oxenstierna in Germany', with additional literature mentioned there.

68. See most recently Johan Holm, 'Skyldig plicht och trohet: Militärstaten och 1634 års regeringsform', *Historisk tidskrift* 119 (1999), pp. 161–95.

69. Axel Oxenstierna to Gabriel Gustafsson Oxenstierna, 10 October 1636, *AOSB*, ser. I, vol. 14, p. 136. On the split, see Sverker Arnoldsson, *Svensk-Fransk Krigs- och Fredspolitik i Tyskland, 1634–1636* (Gothenburg: Elander, 1937).

70. Johan Adler Salvius to Axel Oxenstierna, 2 November 1633, P.S., *AOSB*, ser. II, vol. 14, pp. 206–7.

71. Johan Adler Salvius to Axel Oxenstierna, 23 May 1634, *AOSB*, II, 14, p. 231.

72. See Henk Nellen, *Hugo de Groot: Een leven in strijd om de vrede, 1583–1645* (Amsterdam: Balans, 2007), pp. 385–8.

73. For Michel le Blon, see Marika Keblusek, 'The Business of News: Michel le Blon and the Transmission of Political Information to Sweden in the 1630s', *Scandinavian Journal of History* 28 (2003), pp. 205–13; Badeloch Noldus, 'A Spider in Its Web: Agent and Artist Michel le Blon and His Northern European Network', in Marika Keblusek and Noldus (eds), *Double Agents: Cultural and Political Brokerage in Early Modern Europe* (Leiden: Brill, 2011), pp. 161–76; Noldus, 'Loyalty and Betrayal'; Paul Sellin, 'Michel Le Blon and England, 1632–1649: With Observations on van Dyck, Donne, and Vondel', *Dutch Crossing: A Journal of Low Countries Studies* 22:1 (1998), pp. 102–25.

138   ERIK THOMSON

74. Paul Sellin, 'Michel Le Blon III: Gustav II Adolf, Sir Walter Raleigh's Gold Mine, and the Perfidy of George Villiers, Duke of Buckingham', *Dutch Crossing: A Journal of Low Countries Studies* 23:1 (1999), pp. 102–32.
75. Magnus Linnarsson, *Postgång på växlande villkor: Det svenska postväsendets organisation under stormaktstiden* (Lund: Nordic Academic Press, 2010), pp. 82–92.
76. Ibid. pp. 95–103. See also Magnus Linnarsson, 'The Development of the Swedish Post Office, c. 1600–1721', in Heiko Droste (ed.), *Connecting the Baltic Area: The Swedish Postal System in the Seventeenth Century* (Huddinge: Södertörns högskola, 2011), pp. 25–43.
77. Claes-Göran Holmberg, 'Nästan bara posttidningar (tiden före 1732)', in Karl Erik Gustafsson and Per Rydén (eds), *Den svenska pressens historia I: I begynnelsen (tiden före 1830)* (Stockholm: Ekerlid, 2000); Per Ridderstad, 'Tryckpressens makt och makten över tryckpressen. Om tryckerietableringar i det svenska riket 1600–1650', in Sten Åke Nilson and Margareta Ramsay (eds), *1600-talets ansikte* (Nyhamnsläge: Gyllenstiernska, 1997), pp. 345–56.
78. See Schubert, *Ludwig Camerarius*, pp. 387–413.
79. 27 September 1636, in Severin Bergh (ed.), *Svenska Riksrådets Protokoll* (Stockholm: Norstedt, 1891), vol. VI, p. 611.
80. 18 December 1635, in Severin Bergh (ed.), *Svenska Riksrådets Protokoll* (Stockholm: Norstedt, 1888), vol. V, p. 385, and 4 November 1641, in Bergh (ed.), *Svenska Riksrådets Protokoll* (Stockholm: Norstedt, 1898), vol. VIII, p. 738; see, by contrast, Nellen, *Hugo de Groot*, pp. 532–44.
81. Pieter Spieringk to Axel Oxenstierna, 3 February 1637, Riksarkivet, Oxenstiernska Samlingen, E 727.
82. See, generally, Badeloch Noldus, 'Dealings in Politics and Art: Agents between Amsterdam, Stockholm and Copenhagen', *Scandinavian Journal of History* 28 (2003), pp. 215–25. G. W Kernkamp makes a number of mistakes about Appelboom's early career in his introduction to 'Memoriën van den Zweedschen Resident Harald Appelboom', *Bijdragen en Mededeelingen van het Historisch Genootschap* 26 (1905), pp. 290–375.
83. Harald Appelboom to Axel Oxenstierna, undated, Riksarkivet, Oxenstiernska Samlingen, E 558.
84. Droste, *Im Dienst der Krone*, pp. 265–73.
85. Magnus Nyman, 'Lars Skytte: Diplomat, Franciscan, Humanist', *Kyrkohistorisk Årsskrift* (1982), pp. 117–31.
86. For a recent biographical treatment of these issues, see Marie-Louise Rodén, *Drottning Christina: en biografi* (Stockholm: Prisma, 2008), pp. 69–139. See also Rodén, 'Ett ständigt skiftande porträtt: Kristinabilder i historieskrivningen, 1750–2000', in Per Sandén (ed.), *Bilder av Kristina: Drottning av Sverige – Drottning i Rom* (Stockholm: Livrustkammaren, 2013), pp. 39–59.
87. Axel Oxenstierna to Johan Oxenstierna, 30 September 1643, in Carl C. Gjörwell (ed.), *Bref ifrån Svea-Rikes Canceller Grefve Axel Oxenstierna til Grefve Johan Oxenstierna, Svea-Rikes Råd och Fullmyndig Kongl. Svensk Legat uti Tyskland åren 1642–1649* (Stockholm: Carlbohm, 1810), vol. I, p. 90.
88. Norrhem, *Uppkomlingarna*, pp. 91–3.
89. 27 March 1648, in N. A. Kullberg (ed.), *Svenska Riksrådets Protokoll* (Stockholm: Norstedt, 1908), vol. XII, pp. 304–7.
90. See Axel Oxenstierna to Erik Oxenstierna, 4 June 1652, Riksarkivet, Oxenstiernska samlingen, E 1053.
91. Patronage worries play a larger role in the biography by Ellen Fries, *Erik Oxenstierna: Biografisk studie* (Stockholm: Norstedt, 1889), pp. 43–54, 166–52 (mispagination in the original), than in the standard account of Swedish foreign relations in the last half-decade of Christina's reign. See Sven Ingemar Olofsson, *Efter Westfaliska freden: Sveriges Yttre*

Politik, 1650–1654 (Stockholm: Kungl. Vitterhets, historie och antikvitets akademi, 1957).

92. Bertil Rimborg, *Magnus Durell och Danmark*: *Studier i information* (Gothenburg: Historiska instituitonen, 1997).

93. Erik Thomson, 'Le Travail du diplomate et la diffusion des idées politiques à l'époque moderne: la Fronde vue par le résident suédois Schering Rosenhane (1648–1649)', *Histoire, Economie & Sociétés* (2010), pp. 5–15.

94. See Riksarkivet, Kommerskollegium, Huvudarkivet, Registratur, Huvudserien, 1651–1655, BI, a,1 s. 4–8. A copy of the list is also contained in Riksarkivet, Oxenstiernska samlingen, E 799.

CHAPTER 7

Statecraft and the Role of the Diplomat in Ducal Savoy: The Career of Alessandro Scaglia (1592–1641)

Toby Osborne

How was foreign policy made and conducted in early modern Europe? As this volume suggests, this is at once a very broad question and a multifaceted one. It belies a host of fundamental issues that touch on what even constituted 'foreign' policy; who was thought to have the right to decide policy; the logistics of actuating particular policies given the perennial early modern challenges of distance and time, coupled with the issue of how information was collected and digested; and how those serving as diplomats in the field might shape policy and the styles of diplomacy through their personal interests and character traits. While these questions naturally flow into each other, this chapter will principally address the last one, that of the role of the diplomat as a creative agency of foreign policy-making. More specifically, this chapter examines these issues through one ambassador, Alessandro Scaglia (1592–1641), who was in formal service to the ducal House of Savoy from 1614 until his self-imposed exile to the Spanish Netherlands in 1632. Importantly, in its early modern context, the question of 'foreign policy-making' both addresses and challenges a conception of international relations as a sphere of political activity monopolised by sovereign powers, and serviced by faceless bureaucrats. As we will see, the practice of diplomacy between states, or rather the practice of relations between princes given that dynastic states predominated, was profoundly influenced by its practitioners, who brought their social, cultural and family interests to their diplomatic activity.

This is more than evident in the case of Alessandro Scaglia, an individual of noble birth and a commendatory abbot of the Roman Church. He was the opposite of an anonymous bureaucrat, his recognisable image visually fixed by the series of portraits he commissioned from Anthony van Dyck, dating from the mid-1630s, and possibly one from 1627 or 1628. We should add that van Dyck planned to include one of the portraits for the *Iconographia* (posthumously published in 1645), his collection of engravings of leading figures in the realms of the court, politics and the arts based on his own paintings, meant for a commercial market interested in having images of the famous by an equally famous artist. This is testament to the extent to which a diplomat like Scaglia could become a figure of public interest around Europe, and a distinctive personality in his own right.[1] A less flattering, but equally revealing, pen-portrait was sketched by the leading late seventeenth-century diplomatic theorist, Abraham de Wicquefort. In his seminal treatise of 1681, *L'Ambassadeur et ses fonctions*, he included a section on well-known ambassadors of the seventeenth century, 'De quelques Ambassadeurs illustres de Nostre temps', possibly a reflection again of the interest in the reading public in the individuals who carried out diplomacy. According to de Wicquefort, Scaglia 'had spirit, but it was muddle-headed, again like his master, better at doing things than resolving them'.[2] It seemed to some that he and his ambitious prince, Duke Carlo Emanuele I (r. 1580–1630) were in effect one and the same – 'Like master, like servant. The duke, who was the most ambitious and unsettled of all princes, had him as his confidant, and he served him in the most delicate negotiations', as de Wicquefort wrote.[3] Not only does this evoke the notion of the ambassador as the embodiment of the prince, but also clearly implies that Scaglia was trusted to the extent that he was given considerable latitude while operating abroad, and that in effect he set the particulars of Savoy's foreign policies, within a framework of what he thought were Savoy's best interests.

Such an emphasis on Scaglia's 'iconography' – his recognisable personal agency as a diplomatic actor – is consonant with the recent historiographical interest in early modern diplomatic practice. Two significant issues in this respect deserve close scrutiny: first, that diplomacy was not necessarily a transparent set of political practices monopolised by sovereign powers alone; and second, that distinctions between 'foreign' and 'domestic' politics could be blurred. By considering both, we can gain a more nuanced understanding of the shape of Scaglia's diplomatic profile and of how early modern diplomats contributed to policy-making. In terms of the first question, the clear trend in recent scholarship on early modern diplomacy has been to downplay the importance of sovereigns and states in foreign policy-making. In practice, it is evident that up to the early sixteenth century, a variety of sub-national actors engaged in ambassadorial relations, and recent work has suggested that this was the case well into the seventeenth century, and even beyond. As André Kirscher has shown, during the seventeenth century imperial free cities, whose legal status as sovereign entities was at best uncertain, sent civic officials to neighbouring princely states in the Holy Roman Empire, who in turn received them with ambassadorial dignities, because of the 'symbolic capital' those officials could generate in appearing as diplomats.[4] To take a second example, mercantile companies operating beyond Europe through the seventeenth and eighteenth centuries, notably the Dutch and British East India Companies, also engaged in ambassadorial relations in order to secure their economic interests, acting with some of the markers of sovereignty as 'company-states'.[5]

The achievement of such work has been to suggest the messiness of early modern 'international relations' – there was no clear-cut inter-state 'system' monopolised by recognised sovereign states, even, it seems, after the supposed paradigm shift of the 1648 Westphalian peace. It is nonetheless easy to be carried away. By the seventeenth century, at least, a connection between sovereignty and the capacity to conduct formal diplomacy in Europe was largely established. That was evident when 'new' sovereign powers emerged, as their engagement in diplomacy was largely dependent on the reactions of established powers and their willingness to accept them. The clearest example of this can be seen in the protracted process by which the United Provinces acquired acceptance by existing sovereign powers in Europe, even after the 1609 Truce with the Spanish provided the notional pretext for some form of international legitimisation. It was not until the 1648 Treaty of Munster that the Spanish (reluctantly) accepted the legitimacy of the United Provinces, and by extension their capacity to engage in diplomacy. Even then, the papal representative at the peace talks, Fabio Chigi, famously refused to engage with the Dutch plenipotentiaries, and Pope Innocent X pronounced his hostility to negotiating with them.[6] In a second example, the recreation of the kingdom of Portugal in 1640, following sixty years of the dynastic union with Spain, was tested in a most practical way when the bishop of Lamego was dispatched to act as an ambassador in Rome. This led to violent opposition from the Spanish, who were determined to deny the bishop's right to act as a legitimate ambassador, to the point that blood was spilt in their efforts to block the ambassador's progress, as they confronted Portugal's French supporters in the city's streets – the French were just as determined, for obvious reasons, to support the ambassador's claims to legitimacy and the validity of Portugal's sovereign independence.[7] Sovereigns were undeniably assuming greater control of diplomacy, certainly by the seventeenth century, and as a corollary, sovereignty, as expressed through the practice of diplomacy, was to a significant degree underscored through the consent of already established sovereign authorities.

While it was generally sovereigns who practised diplomacy, or were deemed capable of practising diplomacy, we should nevertheless address the related issue about the demarcation of foreign and domestic policies, and what indeed constituted the prerogative of the sovereign. These are important, given this chapter's focus on Scaglia as an individual aristocrat-diplomat, and, by extension, the roles played by those below sovereign status in foreign policies. In the broadest terms, as suggested earlier, international relations, in a Europe largely dominated by dynastic states, can be conceived of as personal relations between princes, participating in an international society of princes – as we will see, a notion that was evident in the approach of the Duke of Savoy and Scaglia to international relations. Policies often directly concerned ruling dynasties and their patrimonies. Dynastic marriages, in particular, had been a customary staple of international relations, and remained so into the seventeenth century. Obviously, they could further territorial claims and guarantee the futures of princely lines, and since marriages – certainly in Catholic Europe – had sacramental power, they could also be employed to underscore peace-making between princes, even if in practice such unions did not necessarily guarantee lasting concord. Naturally, then, marriages were of great interest to princes.[8] Peace treaties into the seventeenth century too remained, in legal terms, bilateral agreements between princes as individuals, rather than between abstract states. While the formulaic language of treaties typically spoke of peace agreements lasting in perpetuity, for instance, legally it was generally accepted that this meant so long as the princely signatories were themselves alive. It was unclear whether international treaties remained binding once those signatories died.[9]

Understandably, though, sovereign princes typically sought advice on their foreign policies, at times from advisory councils, and they also delegated decision-making to favoured individuals, the classic cases being those of Richelieu in Louis XIII's France, Olivares in Philip IV's Spain, or Oxenstierna in mid-seventeenth-century Sweden. Foreign policies could also become the source of popular political engagement beyond the court, when it was felt that a 'public' or 'national' interest was at stake. This can be seen, for example, in the case of the 'mixed monarchy' of England, most strikingly during the 1620s, when the Stuart regime, whose foreign policies were being shaped by another notorious favourite, the Duke of Buckingham, was drawn into conflicts against both Spain and France. The twin issues of war and finance consequently involved Parliament in debates about the Crown's international policies. Popular sentiment beyond the palace and Parliament was correspondingly manipulated and animated by the highly sensitive questions surrounding the regime's relations with the two Catholic superpowers, though whether this constituted a pre-eighteenth-century 'public sphere', or set of 'public spheres', where a wider public was consciously involved in politics as a way of shaping decisions, remains open to debate.[10]

While this chapter's aim is not to examine the role of public opinion in shaping foreign policy-making, the interplay between the proprietary rights of princes and their wider responsibilities – of the need to listen to counsel and to respond on occasion to expressions of domestic opinion – draws attention to the ambiguous boundaries between 'foreign' and 'domestic' politics, a point of direct relevance to the case of Scaglia.[11] Where did one stop and the other begin? There is also the question, one that relates to Scaglia, of who influenced policy. Foreign policy-making might in essence have been the domain of sovereigns, but could be complicated by the involvement of sub-national and domestic interest groups. We need still to consider, however, the roles played by those who actually engaged in the diplomacy. Another trend in recent historical, literary and art historical scholarship emphasises the practices of 'unofficial' or 'informal' diplomatic actors, and brings into question the very categorisation of 'official' political activity. Thus artists, translators, missionaries and women (including ambassadors' wives who often travelled with their husbands on missions) could also perform functions of diplomacy, so long as 'diplomacy' is itself broadly conceived as something more than what happened in the settings of formal ambassadorial practice; such an actor-driven model expands the limits of what we might conceive of as international relations.[12] On this last point, the copious Venetian state archives offer extremely valuable insights into the different ways in which diplomatic interactions took place, thereby eroding clear boundaries between the formal and informal. The *Esposizioni principi*, an enormous and incredibly rich archival source running to some 316 *filze* (series) and registers, and covering the period 1541–1797, includes reports not just of the formal encounters between accredited ambassadors and the Doge and College in set-piece public audiences, but also voluminous records of preliminary and informal meetings in houses and on Venice's streets between ambassadors, their secretaries and lesser officials of the republic, who took it upon themselves to record those meetings. We might add to this list the dinners and social and ceremonial functions, and the encounters and passing conversations that took place in a wide range of spaces, beyond courts and palaces, where ambassadors and a range of satellite individuals, of official status and none, would have discussed politics.

In this methodological light, it seems as if almost anyone abroad involved in all kinds of social, cultural, religious or political engagements with those where they resided might be categorised as a diplomat, operating in some form or another for the sovereign. Of course, we should add that those 'unofficial' ambassadors still could not perform certain functions reserved for more formally accredited representatives, such as engaging in set-piece public entries and formal audiences, and might not necessarily enjoy the same legal rights and immunities which were becoming an increasingly important aspect of diplomatic practice by the seventeenth century. In the light of these historiographical points, then, how did official ambassadors, if they indeed represented a distinct category with uniquely defined and more systematised powers, also shape the style of early modern diplomacy?

This question can be answered through Scaglia, as an individual who represented, and indeed embodied, his sovereign, but who simultaneously brought to his office his personality and own diplomatic style. He encapsulates the understanding of diplomacy as a complex bundle of state service, personal interest, formality and informality – the very characteristics of the early modern sovereign state. After all, it was implicitly understood that the accredited ambassador, even as an idealised type, was not meant to be a faceless state official. According to the normative literature on the 'ambassador' that proliferated during the sixteenth and early seventeenth centuries, he was supposed to embody the virtues of his prince, acting not merely as the prince's representative but as his representation *in absentia*.[13] It was for that reason – of the consonance of prince and ambassador – that status competition, for instance, became so fierce and contentious from the sixteenth century. In an age when sovereigns, intensely jealous of their relative standing in the society of princes, did not meet frequently in person but increasingly engaged in permanent diplomacy, ambassadors competed for pre-eminence against rivals as their masters' surrogates.[14] More particularly, as representations of their princes, ambassadors were theoretically expected to demonstrate the qualities of the courtier and the moral virtues of their masters, assuming, as was probably accepted, that they did more than simply follow instructions to the letter.[15] Diplomacy, as a performative act of ambassadors embodying absent princes, was very much assumed to have a personal face. The Scaglia portraits, by van Dyck and de Wicquefort, only confirm this impression.

Scaglia's international reputation was made through his formal service to the House of Savoy, almost continuously from 1614 until 1632: as Savoy's ordinary ambassador in Rome from 1614 to 1623 (albeit with a brief interruption); as ordinary ambassador in Paris from 1624 to 1627, with an interlude as extraordinary ambassador in London in January 1626; as an informal ambassador without credentials in the Spanish Netherlands and United Provinces over the spring and summer of 1627; as extraordinary ambassador to London from November 1627 until September 1628, and then to Madrid; and finally, after returning to north Italy to mediate during the succession war in Mantua and Monferrato (1628–31), as extraordinary ambassador to London from November 1631 until March 1632, when he left Savoyard service for exile in the Spanish Netherlands, dying there in May 1641.[16] In this nearly uninterrupted diplomatic service (that Scaglia was almost permanently engaged abroad was unusual for an individual ambassador), we can discern three key themes that illuminate this chapter's core thread about the agency of non-sovereign individuals in foreign policy-making. First, ambassadorial service as a family enterprise; second, the particular skill set that Scaglia's background and training provided him, and the ways he drew on the specific dynastic power of Savoy to add to his ambassadorial leverage during the 1620s; and third, the limits of his service, revealed when he disobeyed his prince, Duke Vittorio Amedeo I (r. 1630–7), over what he thought were the better interests of his state against a backdrop of personalised attacks from Cardinal Richelieu. These thematic points need to be addressed in turn.

Turning to the first theme: Scaglia's career, both as an ambassador and as an ecclesiastic, was crafted by his father, Filiberto Gherardo Scaglia, the Count of Verrua (1564–1619). The Scaglia di Verrua clan had come from the Piedmontese city of Biella, north of Turin, the court capital of the Savoyard states from 1561. Filiberto himself stated that his family had been loyal to the Savoyard dynasty since it had first claimed lordship over its territories, in effect for hundreds of years, but the family committed itself to Turin and the ducal court permanently only at the end of sixteenth century.[17] During the early 1600s, under Filiberto Gherardo's direction, the Scaglia di Verrua was probably the most powerful family at court. Filiberto, certainly, can be characterised as the Duke Carlo Emanuele I's leading courtier. As Pietro Contarini, Venice's ordinary ambassador in Turin in 1607, wrote, Filiberto 'had always been employed by his highness in pretty much every policy, with the most serious and important matters passing through his hands'.[18]

Alessandro Scaglia, the younger of two sons, grew up in the world of the court, both in Turin and further afield, thanks to close connections with the ducal court and his father's service in a string of ambassadorial missions. For the Scaglia di Verrua, service to the ducal House was a family enterprise, one component in a strategy of maximising influence domestically and internationally. Indeed, just as we might characterise court history across Europe as the history of princely dynasties, with princes as the heads, so the histories of court families might be described in organisational terms where individuals were strategically assigned roles by the heads of their families and where families pooled their collective resources and skills.[19] Filiberto Gherardo Scaglia himself served in ambassadorial missions to Rome, Spain and Venice, while Alessandro's uncle had served as an ordinary ambassador in Venice. Filiberto was not immune to financial difficulties while serving as an ambassador, resorting on occasion to the perennial early modern complaint that he lacked the resources to represent his prince with appropriate dignity.[20] But while ambassadorial service was costly, its value was as a loss-leader, a form of social and political investment. Ambassadorial service, for instance, provided a means by which the Scaglia di Verrua educated their sons, serving as a way of introducing them to international court society, as fundamental experience for their own careers.[21]

The Count of Verrua also held some of the most significant offices at the ducal court, notably as *Maggiordomo* of the prince's household, and later within the ducal household itself, and his intimacy with the prince was confirmed by his promotion to Savoy's sovereign chivalric order of the *Annunziata* in 1608, the highest honour he could hold from his sovereign. Filiberto's closeness to the ducal family and court had clear benefits for his children, who in turn were used as assets to further the family's collective power. As mentioned, Alessandro was the younger of Verrua's two sons and the dynastic spare, and accordingly was placed in the Church both as a source of income and as a potential candidate for a cardinal's hat if the opportunity arose; his elder brother, Augusto Manfredo (1587–1637), married and followed their father's career path by combining diplomatic service, office holding within the court system and commands in the ducal army.[22]

Alessandro Scaglia's career trajectory as an ambassador and a commendatory abbot was thus plotted by his father, a piece in a jigsaw of family power that, across its various members (especially, though not only, the males), encompassed the key institutions of the Catholic dynastic state: the court, church, army and, of course, the diplomatic service. In this sense, the historian of early modern diplomacy should take account of the family histories of its practitioners, as fundamental for understanding their formative influences and the key terms of reference for their ambitions. By extension, we can view the diplomat as an individual whose role was to pursue not only the foreign policies of his prince, but also the ambitions of his family.[23] Such a family strategy was not peculiar to the Scaglia di Verrua. A similar cursus, for example, could be plotted of their closest court rivals in Turin, the S. Martino d'Agliè, another Piedmontese family whose rapid ascent in power from the end of the sixteenth century was marked by a combination of ambassadorial service and the acquisition of chivalric honours and heritable titles; they were to reach their apogee during the 1630s, when their most well-known, if not infamous, member, Filippo, emerged as the favourite of Marie Christine, the Duchess of Savoy. Such was the influence he was felt to hold over the duchess that Richelieu orchestrated his arrest in 1640 – he was to remain imprisoned until Richelieu's death in 1642, thereafter resuming service to the Savoyard dukes.[24]

Alessandro Scaglia emerged as an ambassadorial actor after his first formal mission in service to Savoy, to the papal court from 1614, leading us to the second strand of his diplomatic career: how he applied his distinctive skills set to enhance his diplomatic leverage. While scholars often assume that Rome and its papal monarchy were of declining importance on the international stage of early modern politics, the papal capital remained one of the only places where most Catholic sovereigns, at least, felt compelled to maintain a diplomatic presence. Rome – the 'Theatre of the World', as it was frequently styled – remained a venue of intense diplomatic activity, where rival ambassadors, embodying their sovereigns, engaged in constant struggles for pre-eminence.[25] Importantly, too, for the shape of Scaglia's career, his time in Rome attuned him to the value of collecting objects of art, principally on behalf of members of the Savoyard House, especially the ambitious and vain Cardinal Maurizio (1593–1657), Carlo Emanuele's fourth son.[26] Such art collecting was a means of affirming Savoy's importance on the international stage, and Scaglia was one of the principal instruments for conducting this diplomatic strategy.

Scaglia thus took from his first ambassadorial mission valuable experience in negotiating the complexities of an intensely competitive ritual and court system, and emerged with expertise as a patron and broker of the arts. We can gauge his growing reputation from a comment by Venice's ambassador in Turin, Alvise Morosini, when Alessandro had returned to Turin for an interlude during his mission to Rome in 1622. His description of Alessandro was nothing less than flattering, noting that he had served for a decade at the papal court and was a man of 'intelligence, ability and absolute sagacity without equal in this court'. Indeed, in a series of letters revealing the high standing of the Scaglia di Verrua family as a collective unit in service to the Savoyard house, Morosini reported how Alessandro's elder brother – the new head of the family following their father's death in 1619 – was acting as Duke Carlo Emanuele's representative to Louis XIII while the French king was in Toulouse, while Alessandro's uncle was operating as the duke's leading financial minister.[27]

The 1620s, especially the six-year period that followed his final departure from Rome in 1623 until November 1630, when England and Spain signed a peace treaty in which Scaglia was specifically named for his contribution to the peace process, along with the painter-diplomat Peter Paul Rubens and the English ambassador and secretary of state, Francis Cottington, marked the apogee of his diplomatic career.[28] In fact, we can discern two elements that fundamentally shaped Scaglia's emergence during the 1620s as a distinctive political figure on the stage of international power politics. The first relates to the nature of Savoyard power. Duke Carlo Emanuele I was determined to prove his family's importance as one of the top-ranking princely dynasties in Europe, with an appropriately modern court capital. If we recall de Wicquefort's disparaging characterisation of Scaglia and his sovereign prince, one of the supposed hallmarks of Savoyard diplomacy during these years was incessant ambition, which in practice meant the pursuit of territories in northern Italy, and the acquisition of royal status. How, then, could these be achieved, and how did Scaglia contribute to these policy aims? What leverage could he bring to bear? Such questions were especially acute for smaller European powers like Savoy; the duchy certainly had geo-strategic assets, such as its alpine passes that were so important for movement between Italy and northern Europe, but lacked the sheer power of France and Spain. Savoy's greatest asset was its dynastic pedigree: the ruling dynasty was one of Europe's oldest, dating back over six centuries. If diplomacy was largely about relations between princes, then it is unsurprising that Carlo Emanuele I and Scaglia played on that dynastic pedigree as their qualification for a place at the top table, though as a form of power it was certainly less tangible than mere material assets. The ties that bound Savoy with the Habsburgs, Bourbons and Stuarts gave Savoy, and Alessandro Scaglia, the means to operate in a particular dynastic and diplomatic nexus. Carlo Emanuele I's wife, Catalina Michaela, who had died in 1597, was the younger of Philip II's two daughters; together they had five sons and five daughters. During the 1610s he had tried unsuccessfully to arrange two marriage unions with the Stuarts, the first to Prince Henry Stuart, heir to James I, until Henry's death in 1612, and the second to Elizabeth, who eventually married the Palatine Elector. Despite the failure of these negotiations, Carlo Emanuele I had initiated an important relationship between Savoy and England, crossing the obvious confessional boundary, one that perceived common interests both as comparable states and as natural allies who might counterbalance France and Spain.[29] The Savoys and Stuarts were eventually dynastically connected through the Bourbons: in 1619, Carlo

Emanuele I's eventual heir, Vittorio Amedeo, married Marie Christine, a sister to Louis XIII of France, and this was followed in 1625 by Charles Stuart's marriage to Henrietta Maria, another of the Bourbon sisters.[30]

While Duke Carlo Emanuele I and Scaglia pursued Savoyard interests in dynastic terms, it was Scaglia as an individual who in effect shaped the specific style of Savoy's engagement with the Stuarts, Bourbons and Habsburgs, increasing his influence both with his prince and with other princes and courtiers through experience acquired earlier in his career. The duchy's capacity to extract benefits depended on playing France and Spain against each other, and Scaglia was astute enough to realise that during the 1620s England held the key to Savoy's interests, as Charles I, guided by his favourite the Duke of Buckingham, engaged in war with both Catholic superpowers. In shaping his relationship with the Stuart court, Scaglia employed his smooth manners and exceptional knowledge of the arts refined, as we have seen, in Rome – those were the very personal qualities that appealed to Charles I and Buckingham, who were both determined to prove themselves, according to the cultural standards of continental Europe, as modern and cosmopolitan. By its nature, Scaglia's influence was what we might call 'soft' power, not unlike the dynastic influence enjoyed by his prince. It was not grounded on the capacity to mobilise troops or to apply economic levers; it depended on friendships and contacts, and on working aside from more formal or institutional power structures. It was personal, and could not be replicated in any systematic way. Here, then, was the most intricate and intriguing aspect of Scaglia's diplomatic style: he inveigled himself into a position of exceptional favour in London largely through his smooth manners, and used England's wars with Spain and France as levers for extracting benefits for his home state, by offering mediation between England and either of the two leading powers.

We can also gain a sense of the latitude given to Scaglia by Carlo Emanuele I during this period, and of the ambassador's ability to operate beyond formal structures. In 1627, he left Paris without formal diplomatic credentials; he seems only to have had a passport that gave him permission to travel to The Hague, principally to further his involvement in a three-way Anglo-Spanish peace process also involving Buckingham's agent and art dealer, Balthasar Gerbier, and Peter Paul Rubens, two individuals whose own diplomatic strategies bear comparison with those of Scaglia. In one sense it would have been difficult to have had an accreditation, since, as we have seen, the broader issue of the legitimacy of the United Provinces was a live issue prior to 1648, especially for Catholic sovereigns. And yet Scaglia continued to negotiate, in effect side-stepping formal channels that might have complicated the talks, employing Brussels as a secondary channel between the English regime and Spain. By this stage of his career, Scaglia was experienced enough and equipped with the right kinds of skills to engage with the artist-diplomat Rubens and the cultural broker-diplomat Gerbier. A shared interest in the high arts provided the pretext for mediating an Anglo-Spanish peace that took place, it should be added, outside the centre stages of formal diplomacy, reminding us again of the multilayered character of early modern international relations.

This period, from Scaglia's departure from Paris in March 1627 until his formal accreditation in London in November 1627, is revealing in other ways. The logistics of diplomacy necessarily entailed a degree of autonomy for those in the field. While the day-to-day ambassadorial routines of observing and collecting information might not in themselves have entailed policy-making decisions, there were nonetheless moments and periods when ambassadors engaged in more substantive politicking that had a direct bearing on specific issues. What were they allowed to do? Were instructions binding in terms of an ambassador's room for manoeuvre, and how could ambassadors react to events given the time it might take to receive updated orders from their political masters? Such logistical challenges could in fact be turned themselves into diplomatic strategies. If a prince wished to facilitate relations with a given prince or state, he might naturally dispatch a sympathetic ambassador there. It is no surprise, for instance, that during the early seventeenth century, Endymion Porter was seen as a Spanish 'expert' and someone able to facilitate Anglo-Spanish relations, given the fact that he had a Spanish grandmother and – highly unusually for an Englishman – had spent part of his childhood in the household of a Spanish noble family. Conversely, a prince might dispatch an ambassador he knew to be hostile to his hosts in order to build into a mission a self-controlling mechanism, to ensure that the given ambassador would not concede much of significance. But what happened when an ambassador overstepped the mark, or indeed deliberately disobeyed his prince? One such instance, though one that occurred in specific circumstances, can be seen in the refusal of the French regime to ratify the treaty of Regensburg signed in October 1630 when the two French ambassadors sent to the negotiations went, according to Richelieu, beyond the powers granted by their instructions. This legal point gave the cardinal-minister the excuse to wriggle out of a treaty he viewed as unfavourable to France.[31]

Returning to Alessandro Scaglia as a case study, we have seen how during the 1620s he had acted on his own initiative, even when he lacked instructions or a formal accreditation. We might assume that his actions were tacitly approved by Carlo Emanuele, and that Scaglia himself was setting the tone and terms of Savoy's international strategies, of playing France and Spain against each other by aligning with England. However, while the 1630 Treaty of Madrid recorded Scaglia's personal influence at the Stuart court, it also presaged a period of rapidly changing fortunes that exposed the weaknesses of his diplomatic style. This brings us to the third and final strand of this chapter. By the time Charles I had settled with Spain, the war with France had also concluded (April 1629). Charles's relations with Parliament over the issues of war and taxation had deteriorated to the point that a bellicose foreign policy was no longer viable and – relevantly for Scaglia – Buckingham was dead, having been murdered by a disgruntled soldier in Portsmouth in September 1628. As we have seen, Scaglia's leverage was predicated on exploiting to the full Savoy's place in the web of dynastic relations, and was grounded fundamentally in the political friendships he himself had cultivated, especially with the English favourite. With his principal ally in London dead, and Charles I seemingly unwilling to continue an interventionist policy in Europe, Scaglia's influence predictably diminished.[32]

This was one side of the equation. 1630 also marked the death of Carlo Emanuele I, Duke of Savoy since 1580. His son and successor, Vittorio Amedeo, had known Scaglia since childhood, but like Charles I, the new Duke of Savoy wished to extricate his state from war, in this case the succession war over Mantua and Monferrato. This decision further weakened Scaglia, whose overarching strategy had been grounded on using force against France to secure what he perceived as Savoy's interests.[33] After all, the Duke of Savoy, with his Bourbon consort, had secured relatively favourable terms over the succession war from the French, whose own leverage was strengthened by their occupation of the key Piedmontese fortress at Pinerolo.[34] To Scaglia, the terms of settling with France, and their military presence in Savoy, were unacceptable, and he came to believe that it was in fact in Savoy's interests to perpetuate the war so as to force the French out of the Savoyard states: 'the abate tells me plainly that he hopes not for peace in Italy until the French be called from thence by a divertive war', the English representative in Madrid, Arthur Hopton, wrote when Scaglia was there.[35]

Behind Scaglia's hostility to France was a personalised animosity towards Richelieu, a striking inversion of the friendship with Buckingham cultivated during the 1620s. Scaglia held the cardinal-minister responsible for betraying Savoy's interests in 1626, by agreeing to the Treaty of Monzon, an agreement with Spain that sought to draw a line under their cold war in northern Italy. The abate's diplomacy thereafter was shaped largely by his efforts to pressurise Richelieu, increasingly, as mentioned above, through alliance with Spain. Richelieu correspondingly person-alised his attacks against Scaglia to exert his own leverage over Savoy, merging the known difficulties between the diplomat and cardinal-minister with bilateral relations between France and Savoy. That was evident immediately after Monzon, when Richelieu had accused Scaglia of complicity in the Chalais conspiracy (1626), a noble plot within France aimed at deposing the cardinal-minister – Richelieu was fully aware of Scaglia's dismay over Monzon, and the accusation, whether Scaglia was genuinely involved or not, had served to put the ambassador on the defensive.[36] At the moment when Vittorio Amedeo was seeking to withdraw from the war in north Italy over Mantua and Monferrato in the early 1630s, Richelieu once again resorted to personalising his attacks as the best way to neutralise the political threat posed by Scaglia. Sensationally, Richelieu claimed that Scaglia had tried to murder him.[37] As with the Chalais conspiracy, the veracity of the accusation is perhaps less important than the fact that the rumour was thought to be credible, given Scaglia's known loathing for the cardinal. Personalised animosity again had come to have a direct impact on relations between France and Savoy, and was used as a political tool to isolate Scaglia while he was in London agitating against Richelieu. This period of turbulence certainly took its toll on Scaglia. Physically and mentally exhausted with no clear official endorsement or set of mission objectives from Turin, and under pres-sure from Paris to return home, Scaglia experienced what we would now describe as a nervous breakdown. The tawdry conclusion to his London mission in the spring of 1632 brought to an end his career in formal service to Savoy.

This chapter began with some broad observations about what constituted foreign policy and what factors shaped its formulation. There is of course much more to be said, for instance about the logistics of information-gathering and transmission, and of how information was used, but the focus here has been less on the mechanics of doing diplomacy than on the very distinctive, and possibly representative, style of one diplomat of the seventeenth century. Diplomats like Alessandro Scaglia were not meant to be automatons, if that were in any way possible. Given the issues of time and distance, and more importantly given the character of diplomacy as an expression of princely identity – as a conversation amongst individual princes – it is entirely understandable that the personalities of the practitioners mattered, and they were often valued by princes precisely because of the distinctive contributions they could make to facilitate foreign policies, or even deliberately shape them.

What is more, 'foreign' policies could be inextricably linked with courtiers and families who competed with each other for princely favour, and for whom diplomatic service was but one component in their own strategies for acquiring power and prestige at home and abroad. The Scaglia di Verrua family are emblematic of this. In turn, Alessandro Scaglia's place as one of Europe's leading diplomats during the age of the Thirty Years War was partly the product of his courtly upbringing and of his experiences as an ambassador in Rome; his personality defined his career, as he skilfully cultivated a series of politically important friendships, especially with Stuart courtiers. But while his success during the 1620s was largely rooted in the exercise of informal types of power, it was this very style of diplomacy that also proved to be his undoing. Richelieu targeted Scaglia to exert his own leverage over Savoy: Scaglia himself became a subject of international politics precisely because of his personality, the stumbling block, so the cardinal-minister suggested, in relations between Savoy and France.

An actor-driven model of diplomatic practice adds texture and deeper understandings to the various ways in which policy-making was done and decisions arrived at. We need not deny that the practice of diplomacy in the early modern period was largely an expression of sovereign identity; at the same time, though, foreign policy-making was shaped by ambassadorial creativity and the multiple entanglements of families and individuals, both within states and between courts on the international stage.

NOTES

1. On the Scaglia portraits, see Arabella Cifani and Franco Monetti, 'New Light on the Abbé Scaglia and van Dyck', *The Burlington Magazine* 134 (1992), pp. 506–14; Toby Osborne, 'Anthony van Dyck: A Painter-Diplomat of the Thirty Years War?', in R. Malcolm Smuts and Luc Duerloo (eds), *The Age of Rubens: Diplomacy, Dynastic Politics and the Visual Arts in Early Seventeenth Century Europe* (Brussels: Brepols, forthcoming). On the *Iconographia*, see M. Mauquoy-Hendrickx, *L'Iconographie d'Antoine van Dyck: catalogue raisonné*, 2 vols (Brussels: Bibliothèque royale Albert I, 1991).

2. 'L'Abbé avoit de l'esprit; mais c'estoit un grand broüillon, aussi bien que son Maistre, & plus propre à faire des affaires q'à les démêler' (Abraham de Wicquefort, *L'Ambassadeur et ses fonctions*, 2 vols (The Hague: Maurice George Veneur, 1682), vol. II, p. 280).

3. 'tel Maistre tel Vallet. Le Duc qui estoit le plus ambitieux & le plus inquiet de tous les Princes, en avoit fait son confident, & se servoit de luy en ses plus delicates negotiations' (ibid. p. 280).

4. André Kirscher, *Reichsstädte in der Fürstengesellschaft. Zum politischen Zeichengebrauch in der Frühen Neuzeit* (Darmstadt: WGB, 2006).

5. On the semi-sovereign roles played by the East India Companies see, for example, Bhawan Ruangsilp, *Dutch East India Company Merchants at the Court of Ayuttaya: Dutch Perceptions of the Thai Kingdom, c. 1604–1765* (Leiden: Brill, 2007); Arthur Weststeijn, 'The VOC as a Company-State. Debating Seventeenth-Century Dutch Colonial Expansion', *Itinerario* 38:1 (2014), pp. 13–34; Philip J. Stern, *The Company-State: Corporate Sovereignty and the Early Modern Foundations of the British Empire in India* (Oxford: Oxford University Press, 2011).

6. Laura Manzano Baena, *Conflicting Words: The Peace Treaty of Münster (1648) and the Political Culture of the Dutch Republic and the Spanish Monarchy* (Leuven: Leuven University Press, 2011); Konrad Repgen, 'Der päpstliche Protest gegen den Westfälischen Frieden und die Friedenspolitik Urbans VIII', *Historisches Jahrbuch* 75 (1956), pp. 94–122.

7. Alessandro Ademollo, *La questione delle indipendenza portoghese a Roma dal 1640 al 1670* (Florence: Tipografia della Gazzetta d'Italia, 1878).

8. See, for example, Jocelyne G. Russell, *Peacemaking in the Renaissance* (London: Duckworth,1986), pp. 85–9; Lucien Bély, *La Société des princes. XVIe–XVIIIe siècle* (Paris: Fayard, 1999), especially chs 8 and 12; Sheila Ffolliott, 'Make Love, Not War: Imaging Peace through Marriage in Renaissance France', in Diane Wolfthal (ed.), *Peace and Negotiation: Strategies for Coexistence in the Middle Ages and the Renaissance* (Brussels: Brepols, 2000), pp. 212–31.

9. Randall Lesaffer, 'Peace Treaties from Lodi to Westphalia', in Lesaffer (ed.), *Peace Treaties and International Law in European History from the Late Middle Ages to World War One* (Cambridge: Cambridge University Press, 2004), pp. 17–22 (pp. 9–44).

10. The subject of domestic 'public' engagement in national and international politics is now an established historiographical trope, especially in an English context. See, for example, Peter Lake and Steven Pincus (eds), *The Politics of the Public Sphere in Early Modern England* (Manchester: Manchester University Press, 2007).

11. For a valuable study of princely rights and their limits, see Herbert H. Rowen, *The King's State: Proprietary Dynasticism in Early Modern France* (New Brunswick, NJ: Rutgers University Press, 1990).

12. There is a substantial and growing literature on these 'unofficial' agencies of diplomacy. See, for example, Hillard von Thiessen and Christian Windler (eds), *Akteure der Außenbeziehungen. Netzwerke und Interkulturalität im historischen Wandel* (Cologne: Böhlau-Verlag, 2010); Marika Keblusek and Badeloch Vera Noldus (eds), *Double Agents: Cultural and Political Brokerage in Early Modern Europe* (Leiden: Brill, 2011).

13. For example, Gasparo Bragaccia, *L'ambasciatore* (Padua: Francesco Bolzetta, 1627), pp. 35–6.

14. Toby Osborne, 'The Surrogate War between the Savoys and the Medici: Sovereignty and Precedence in Early Modern Italy', *International History Review* 29 (2007), pp. 1–21.

15. For some useful comments on the identity of the ambassador, see Ellen McClure, *Sunspots and the Sun King: Sovereignty and Mediation in Seventeenth-Century France* (Urbana and Chicago: University of Illinois Press, 2006), ch. 3. See also Joanna Craigwood, 'Diplomatic Metonymy and Antithesis in 3 Henry VI', *The Review of English Studies* 65 (2014), pp. 812–30.

16. For an overview of his formal career, see Toby Osborne, *Dynasty and Diplomacy in the Court of Savoy: Political Culture and the Thirty Years' War* (Cambridge: Cambridge University Press, 2002). See also Tobias Mörschel, *Buona amicitia?: Die romisch-savoyischen Beziehungen unter Paul V. (1605–1621). Studien zur fruhneuzeitlichen Mikropolitik in Italien* (Mainz: Verglag Philip von Zabern, 2002), pp. 119–25.

17. Archivio di Stato, Venice, Senato: dispacci degli ambasciatori [ASVen DA], Savoia, filza 37, Renier Zen to the Senate, 17 February 1615, enclosure.

18. 'è stato sempre incaricato da sua Altezza quasi d'ogni negotio, passando al presente per le sue

mani tutte le cose più gravi, et più importanti' (ASVen DA Savoia, filza 29, 56, Contarini to the Senate, 8 December 1607).

19. I am borrowing this image from Professor Luc Duerloo of the University of Antwerp.

20. For example, Archivio di Stato, Turin [AST] Lettere Ministri Roma, mazzo [m.] 18, fasciculo [fasc.] 3, Verrua to Carlo Emanuele I, 17, 18 January 1598.

21. For instance, Alessandro Scaglia oversaw all four of his nephews while serving as ambassador in Rome. Archivio Segreto Vaticano, Segreteria di Stato, Avvisi, 8, fo. 355v, Rome, 14 November 1618; fo. 372v, Rome, 21 November 1618.

22. For an overview of the Scaglia di Verrua's activities as a family unit at the Savoyard court and further afield, see Osborne, *Dynasty and Diplomacy*, ch. 2.

23. Certainly, the Scaglia di Verrua were accused of mixing personal interests with state politics. The family's aggressive support of Savoy's involvement in the first succession war for Mantua and Monferrato was motivated, some at the time claimed, by their desire to unify some of their territorial holdings which were outside the Savoyard duchy and in Monferrato. See, for example, Biblioteca Reale, Turin, Archivio Scarampi, 3755, 'Un volume di scritture riguard.ti il Conte di Verrua'.

24. While there is no systematic history of the San Martino d'Agliè, they naturally loom large in most narrative histories of Savoy. For example, consult *Augusto Bazzoni, La reggenza di Maria Cristina, duchessa di Savoia* (Turin: S. Franco e figli, 1865), especially chs 6, 9 and 27. Consult also C. Gallina, 'Le vicende di un grande favorito: Filippo San Martino d'Agliè', *Bollettino storico-bibiografico subalpino* 21 (1919), pp. 185–213, 292–305; 22 (1920), pp. 63–157. Moving beyond Savoy, there have been comparatively few studies of diplomacy in terms of family history, though consult Jean-François Labourdette, 'Le Recrutement des ambassadeurs sous les derniers Valois', in Lucien Bély (ed.), *L'Invention de la diplomatie: moyen âge, temps modernes* (Paris: Presses universitaires de France, 1998), pp. 99–114.

25. See, for example, Toby Osborne, 'The House of Savoy and the Theatre of the World: Performances of Sovereignty in Early-Modern Rome', in Matthew Vester (ed.), *Sabaudian Studies: Political Culture, Dynasty, & Territory 1400–1700* (Kirksville, MO: Truman State University Press, 2013), pp. 167–90; Maria Antonietta Visceglia, *La città rituale. Roma e le sue cerimonie in età moderna* (Rome: Viella, 2002).

26. Matthias Oberli, Magnificentia Principis: *Das Mäzenatentum des Prinzen und Kardinals Maurizio Von Savoyen (1593–1657)* (Weimar: Verlag und Datenbank für Geisteswiss, 1999).

27. 'che hà servitor per dice'anni l'Altezza Sua Amb.tor nella Corte di Roma, d'intelligenza, di maneggio, et di sagacità assolutam.te in questa Corte senza pare' (ASVen, Senato, DA Savoia, filza 56, Morosini to Senate, 27 June 1622). See also Morosini to Senate, 18 July 1622; Morosini to Senate, 1 August 1622.

28. For a text of the 1630 treaty, see Jean Dumont (ed.), *Corps universel diplomatique du droit des gens, contenant un recueil des traités de paix, d'alliance, &c., faits en Europe, depuis Charlemagne jusqu'à present* (Amsterdam: P. Brunel et al., 1726–31), vol. V, part II, p. 620.

29. Toby Osborne, 'England and Savoy: Dynastic Intimacy and Cultural Relations under the Early Stuarts', in Paola Bianchi and Karin Wolfe (eds), *Turin and the British in the Age of the Grand Tour* (Cambridge: Cambridge University Press, forthcoming). On the project involving Henry Stuart, see Andrea Pennini, 'Le missioni del conte di Cartignano (1611–1612): un progetto di matrimonio inglese per il principe di Piemonte', *Bollettino Storico Bibliografico Subalpino* 110.1 (2012), 141–73. In fact, the possibility of a Stuart–Savoyard marriage predated James I's accession to the English throne. See ASVen DA Savoia, filza, 24, 35, Simon Contarini to the Senate, 30 June 1601.

30. Osborne, *Dynasty and Diplomacy*, ch. 1.

31. D. P. O'Connell, 'A Cause Célèbre in the History of Treaty Making. The Refusal to Ratify the Peace Treaty of Regensburg in 1630', *British Yearbook of International Law* 42 (1967), pp. 71–90.

32. As was observed, 'che mancato il Duca di Bockinghem, che le servira di appoggio molto auttorevole presso il Re; le sue [Scaglia's] pratiche non faranno in tanto abbraciate' (ASVen DA Inghilterra, filza 36, fo. 105, Soranzo to the Senate, 18 July 1631).

33. Not only were they close in age, Scaglia born in 1592 and Vittorio Amedeo in 1587, but Scaglia's father may well have taken Alessandro with him when the count travelled to Spain with the ducal children, Vittorio Amedeo among them, in 1603. For background information, see G. B. Ansaldi, 'Giovanni Botero coi principi sabaudi in Ispagna', *Bolletino storico-bibliografico subalpino* 35 (1933), pp. 321–40.

34. For an interpretation of the Mantuan succession war that emphasises the underlying importance of Franco-Savoyard relations, see David Parrott, 'The Mantuan Succession: A Sovereignty Dispute in Early Modern Europe', *English Historical Review* 112 (1997), pp. 20–65.

35. British Library, Egerton MS 1820, fo. 21v, Hopton to Cottington, 14 April 1631. By contrast, the Savoyard duke emphasised to Scaglia the desirability of peace. See AST Lettere Ministri Milano, m. 18, 'Registro delle lettere del Duca', Vittorio Amedeo to Scaglia, 28 July 1631. The presence of French troops in Savoyard territories remained a contentious issue in the duchy throughout the 1630s.

36. Osborne, *Dynasty and Diplomacy*, pp. 109–11.

37. AST Lettere Ministri Francia, m. 31, fasc. 3, 2, Mazzarini to Vittorio Amedeo I, 17 May 1632.

CHAPTER 8

Richelieu, Mazarin and Italy (1635–59): Statesmanship in Context

David Parrott

Armand-Jean du Plessis, Cardinal Duc de Richelieu, and Giulio Mazzarino, Cardinal Mazarin, respectively first ministers of France from 1624 to 1642 and 1643 to 1661, might seem the personification of early modern statesmanship.[1] Undoubtedly some of the political achievements with which they were traditionally credited now appear anachronistic and questionable, such as the creation of Bourbon 'absolutism', the empowering of the secular nation-state or the establishment of a European system of collective security. Yet if statesmanship is essentially about articulating and building support to achieve clear and consistent political goals, then the cardinal-ministers still figure strongly. Their political goals were chiefly dynastic: both Richelieu and Mazarin represented themselves as servants of their kings and of the family policy of the House of Bourbon.[2] The aggressive pursuit of dynastic advantage was nonetheless accompanied by a broader appeal to the public interest, with a particular concern for French territorial security. Pointing to a Habsburg 'encirclement' of France by territories governed from Madrid and Vienna, the cardinals articulated and pursued policies which not only sought the glory of the Bourbon monarchy, but also aimed to roll back the supposed threat to France posed by Habsburg ambitions.[3]

Central to building a reputation for statesmanship was their status as 'first ministers'. Richelieu enjoyed the unmediated favour and support of Louis XIII; Mazarin that of his widow and Regent, Anne of Austria, and subsequently the young Louis XIV. Both ministers exercised a virtual monopoly of influence in determining policy. The other government ministers were their subordinates, and in many cases their appointees, and in no position to compete in offering an alternative perspective on policy. In this respect, Richelieu and Mazarin shared much in common with their Spanish counterparts and opponents, Gaspar de Gúzman, the Count-Duke of Olivares, and his successor from 1643, Don Luis de Haro.[4] All four built their predominance on an ability to combine official positions with what was effectively the status of royal favourite, and by doing so gained a remarkable degree of political initiative.[5]

Yet this wide scope for policy-making encountered numerous limitations when

it came to putting chosen policies into practice. Richelieu and Mazarin were statesmen in a time of war, and both of them recognised that their role was defined not
just by the political aims of the conflict, but by their management of the war effort.
Their enemies had no hesitation in arguing that both ministers saw the perpetuation
of warfare as a means to ensure their indispensability and to reinforce their arbitrary
authority, and claimed that they deliberately rejected opportunities to make peace.[6]
That these criticisms had broad currency was largely because the war that France
embarked on against both the Spanish and the Austrian Habsburgs from 1635 was
unprecedented both in scale and in duration. Richelieu and then Mazarin responded
to what they presented as the threat of Habsburg 'encirclement' by deciding to
wage war in up to six separate and simultaneous campaign theatres. This required a
mobilisation of military resources never before seen in France: as Richelieu boasted
to Louis XIII in his *Testament Politique*, 60 million *livres* had been spent each year
since 1635 in order to maintain 150,000 infantry and 30,000 cavalry under arms.[7]
But precisely this massive mobilisation, implying not just unprecedented troop
levies, but huge financial, logistical and administrative burdens, created new and
demanding challenges to their statesmanship, not just in raising resources but in
confronting or outmanoeuvring opposition.

The need to combine coherent military plans for the defeat of an enemy with the
practical challenges of mobilising resources, deploying them effectively and using
different means to achieve overall political aims, links statesmanship to what is generally referred to as 'grand strategy'. Since its initial formulation by Basil Liddell
Hart, grand strategy has been understood as the wide-ranging pursuit of the interests
of the state in a context that emphasises diplomacy as much as military capacity
and deployment. Significantly, it also implies an awareness of the state's available
resources, and the need to manage and deploy them towards the achievement of
prioritised objectives, to balance means against ends.[8] In this context, statesmanship
involves 'costing' the achievement of political and military objectives, especially
when these involve waging warfare which may place huge strains on the political
and social fabric of the state.[9]

The statesmanship of Richelieu and Mazarin thus needs to be assessed in terms of
a grand strategy deploying diplomacy as well as armies, and through innumerable
decisions concerning the availability, mobilisation and allocation of resources. In
understanding this decision-making, two additional factors are significant. The first
is the extent to which subordinate ministers, military commanders, and administrators in the campaign theatres, while unable to change the essential alignment of
policy decisions, can nonetheless have a major impact on the working-out of a grand
strategy, its prioritisation of resources and the success of individual initiatives. The
second is the personal agenda of the ministers themselves, whether a concern to
defend their authority and influence against rivals, to build up networks of clients and
allies, or to manage policies in order to pursue aims of personal or family aggrandisement. How far can this be reconciled with the statesmanlike pursuit of dynastic and
territorial objectives?

I

The aim of this chapter is to examine the reputation for statesmanship of Richelieu and Mazarin through their ability to prioritise and demonstrate flexibility in pursuit of coherent political goals during a twenty-five-year war. Rather than attempting such an evaluation over the full range of their strategic aims and political commitments from 1635 to 1659, it appears more practical and perhaps more illuminating to concentrate on one particular theatre of military and diplomatic activity.

The choice of theatre – the Italian peninsula and its constituent princely and republican states – may seem unexpected, for Italy has traditionally received little attention in accounts of the Franco-Spanish war. Historians might be forgiven for this, since the peace settlements concluded at Westphalia (1648) and on the Franco-Spanish frontier (1659), give modest attention to the Italian theatre, and brought about little or no territorial change in the peninsula.

However, this relative neglect fails to do justice to the contemporary understanding of the importance of Italy in political and strategic calculations. The political, economic and cultural vibrancy of Italy in the European state system was still widely acknowledged. If the majority of Italian states were, in military and demographic terms, of second rank, in every other respect they were influential actors in a complex network of dynastic politics, cultural representation and resource mobilisation.[10] It had been a huge boost to Spanish prestige to have achieved such a tight grip on the Italian states by the end of the sixteenth century, with direct control of Sicily, Naples and Milan, and with Genoa and Tuscany linked through close financial and political ties into the Spanish system.

For French policy-makers there was also the Valois legacy of the Italian Wars of the first half of the sixteenth century. Often dismissed as a futile struggle against the extension of Habsburg power, at several points throughout the six decades of war from 1500 to1559 it seemed probable that France would gain permanent control of the Milanese and/or Piedmont, and as a result would be able to exercise considerable influence over other Italian principalities.[11] No one, least of all their Bourbon successors, doubted that the Valois wars had come close to creating an entirely different geopolitical environment in Italy.

Other factors also made involvement in Italy an attractive proposition to Richelieu. His intervention during the War of the Mantuan Succession in 1629–31 on behalf of the French-born Charles de Gonzague-Nevers, which secured Charles's claim to the duchies of Mantua and Monferrato, also netted France the military-strategic prize of the fortress of Casale-Monferrato. Casale had been secretly occupied in contravention of the terms of the general settlement at Cherasco in 1631. But it was a *fait accompli* which left France in a considerably stronger position to play a continued role in Italian affairs. Moreover, as Richelieu had originally launched his military expedition against the Duke of Savoy, who had allied himself with Spain in order to occupy Monferrato, he was also able to retain the prize of the Savoyard fortress of Pinerolo, which had fallen to French troops after a short siege in March 1630.[12]

Yet while the Italian theatre might offer tempting possibilities for further French diplomatic and military action, there were particular challenges to operating in this theatre. Chief amongst these was the practical issue of supplying, arming and retaining troops across the Alpine barrier. The points made by Guy Rowlands in his essential article on the 'logistical geography' of France about the difficulty of sustaining the French war effort in Italy in the 1690s apply with redoubled force to the war of 1635–59.[13] The disjunction between riverine transport and French campaign theatres was especially evident when it came to military operations in north Italy. Moving supplies, munitions and artillery from the major production regions of France to muster points in Dauphiné and eastern Provence was already difficult. The problems were incomparably greater when the campaign theatre lay beyond the Alps, in Piedmont or Monferrato, where supply operations across the mountains were largely dependent on mules.[14] Though the war of the Mantuan Succession during 1629–30 had been a striking political success, the military operations nonetheless revealed the knife-edge on which military supply for a French army operating in Italy rested.[15] It was clear that any new military intervention in Italy would need to depend on the mobilisation of logistical resources from amongst France's Italian allies as much as on materiel from France.

II

Richelieu's decision to declare war on Spain in 1635 was not part of a premeditated grand strategy, taken after years in which military and financial resources had been carefully husbanded for an inevitable war with the Habsburgs. What for Richelieu had been a profitable few years of territorial and political opportunism while France stood on the sidelines of the European conflict, had come to an abrupt end with the overwhelming defeat of her main military ally, Sweden, at the battle of Nördlingen in September 1634.[16] Yet once the shock of this Habsburg victory had been absorbed, Richelieu regained composure and began planning for what he hoped would be a quick and decisive war.[17] Italy loomed large in both his diplomatic and military plans for the forthcoming campaigns. The possession of Pinerolo and Casale was a crucial part of this planning: these would be the key assembly and supply bases for all French operations in northern Italy, and potentially a way to mitigate the logistical problems of transalpine army supply.[18]

Richelieu, however, neither believed that it would be possible to rely exclusively on forward magazines to meet the logistical needs of a French army in Italy, nor did he intend that French forces should operate outside of a political and military alliance with Italian rulers. His diplomatic efforts to establish such an alliance had been in progress since 1632, and were brought to a rapid conclusion as France moved into war in the summer of 1635. The main challenge for Richelieu was that the Italian states had enjoyed a period of unprecedented peace and stability under Spanish hegemony since 1560. This had been briefly disturbed by the first and second Mantuan Succession crises of 1612–17 and 1627–31, and by France's short-lived attempt to wrest control of the Alpine passes of the Valtelline from the Habsburgs in 1625.[19] Faced with the apparently unending conflict raging elsewhere in Europe, the rational behaviour for Italian rulers and their subjects was to keep the peace and remain neutral. After Austrian troops had withdrawn following their brief and devastating assault on Mantua in 1629–30, the only potential threat to this peace appeared to be the ambitions of France, whose seizure of Pinerolo and Casale was easily perceived as evidence of a larger Valois-style design on Italian territory.

Richelieu therefore sought to draw the Italian rulers into political and military cooperation with France, while simultaneously reassuring them that France herself was not a threat to peace and stability. His approach was consistent with his presentation of the wider French struggle as a bid to avoid 'encirclement' by an ever-encroaching Habsburg 'universal monarchy'. The Italians, far from enjoying peace and prosperity, were the victims of 'Spanish tyranny', a century-long captivity which had enslaved rulers and subjects alike, whether in states directly under the yoke of Spanish rule, or those variously intimidated or coerced by Spanish power.[20] In contrast to the goals of the early sixteenth-century Valois, who had waged war in Italy to assert their dynastic claims on territory, French intervention in the peninsula was now presented as motivated by a disinterested concern to liberate the Italian rulers and peoples from their Spanish oppressor. But safeguarding the autonomy of the Italians meant destroying the power of Spain in Italy, and that would be achieved by the conquest and partitioning of the Spanish Milanese, the large and wealthy state at the centre of northern Italy, coveted by all the neighbouring rulers. So Richelieu's numerous diplomatic initiatives between 1632 and the outbreak of war aimed to enlist as many Italian states as possible in a French-directed League.[21] The League would provide both the resource base that French troops would need as they operated beyond the Alps, and a large part of the military force that would carry out the invasion of Spanish-held territory.

When these negotiations were rushed through to a final conclusion at the signing of the League of Rivoli in July 1635, the results fell far short of Richelieu's expectations.[22] Only the dukes of Savoy, Mantua and Parma were prepared to join France. Two of these were drawn into the League reluctantly. Vittorio Amedeo I of Savoy recognised that by resisting French blandishments he would sacrifice any hope of regaining Pinerolo, and was further threatened with the annexation of his transalpine duchy of Savoy.[23] The Duke of Mantua-Monferrato was similarly ill placed to resist French demands, given the occupation of Casale, and the threat that Richelieu would allow the Duke of Savoy to absorb the rest of Monferrato.[24] Only the callow Odoardo Farnese, Duke of Parma, appeared fully committed to the League. But his capricious rejection of the traditional Farnese alliance with Spain, together with his very limited resources, would give pause to anyone else receiving his support.[25]

Disappointing though the Italian rulers' response might have been, Richelieu was committed to war in 1635, and Italy was to be a key campaign theatre. The troops would be supplied and supported partly from France, and substantially from the resources of Piedmont and Monferrato, from where an attack would be launched into the Spanish Milanese.[26]

Logistical and diplomatic problems were not slow in developing. Richelieu had recognised the importance of the fortresses of Pinerolo and Casale, and the need to stockpile large quantities of grain, other food supplies and materiel, both for the garrisons of the two places and to meet the needs of a field army. Yet this stockpiling consistently failed to take place, not just in the opening years of the war but through the war into the 1650s.[27] Why the development of Pinerolo and Casale as forward magazines, and even their maintenance as properly garrisoned fortresses in good repair, should have proved so problematic is not entirely clear. Throughout the war, the cardinals' finance ministers compromised and created their own priorities: while providing funds for the provisioning of magazines at Pinerolo and Casale might seem more important than additional troop recruitment or the supply of armies closer to France's major centres of production, political exigency and special pleading frequently ensured that the latter concerns received priority.[28] A succession of military commanders, governors and intendants of Pinerolo and Casale complained about the dilapidated state of the fortresses, the desertion of unfed and unpaid garrison troops, and the crucial shortages of grain, powder and shot.[29] In return the central administrators asserted that substantial sums had been regularly remitted to both Casale and Pinerolo, and in turn alleged that these funds had been subject to large-scale misappropriation.[30] Precise blame is difficult to attribute beneath this series of accusations and counter-accusations, but the harsh reality was that the fortresses lacked any capacity to act as pivotal magazines, and they were scarcely able to defend themselves against opportunistic enemy attacks.[31] Despite a series of alarms in the 1630s, and having been saved from capitulation by the improvised, last-ditch intervention of the comte d'Harcourt in 1640, Casale finally fell to a force of Spanish and Mantuan troops in 1652.[32]

This festering issue of misappropriation of funds from the fortresses was to have larger consequences. If Richelieu saw the Italian theatre as a crucial part of his grand strategy to destroy Habsburg power in Europe, his finance and war ministers were deeply sceptical about the costs of fighting in this theatre. The *Surintendant des Finances*, Claude Bullion, was vocal in regarding Italy as a bottomless sink for expenditure, in which the management of the two fortresses was simply the tip of an iceberg of waste and misappropriation.[33] The disgrace of Abel Servien as Secretary for War in early 1636 removed a figure with a commitment to Italy based on earlier embassies and connections with the Court of Savoy, and saw him replaced with Sublet de Noyers, who sided with Bullion about the waste and corruption of the Italian theatre.[34] It was certainly the case that the central *munitionnaires* who contracted to supply bread to the armies charged a hefty premium for the army of Italy, some 42 *déniers* per ration compared with a typical army contract costing 24 *déniers*. [35] Equally contentious were the accounts drawn up by field commanders and governors to 'prove' how little they had received of the sums theoretically due to them, claims strongly disputed by the central authorities.[36] Amidst claims and counter-claims, Richelieu remained surprisingly passive.[37] Only when Surintendant Bullion's ad hoc methods of recouping 'lost' money by underpaying and delaying the accounts resulted in the collapse of the duc de Rohan's small army operating in the Valtelline during the winter of 1636–7, did Richelieu angrily intervene, threatening Bullion's disgrace.[38] But this was an isolated incident rather than the beginning of a fundamental policy change. The financing of the Italian theatre remained a low priority for Bullion, who continued to defend himself against complaints about shortfalls and delays in funds by alleging misappropriation amongst both officers and administrators.

These conflicts over financial priorities in the theatre had a number of operational effects. Year by year, right down to the late 1650s, the Army of Italy was always the slowest of the French campaign forces to mobilise and begin campaigning. Despite injunctions to draw the troops out of winter quarters and assemble the army in early spring, coordinated military activity rarely began before June or July each year, giving the Spanish a major advantage before the French were in a position to strike back with their own field forces.[39]

Rates of attrition amongst the soldiers were also astoundingly high. French soldiers' dislike of serving across the Alps was compounded by the weakness of supply and financial provisioning, which ensured high levels of desertion as campaigns continued.[40] Meanwhile the attempts to provide supplementary units later in the campaign to make good losses from desertion and sickness were even less likely to provide adequate reinforcements or maintain operational effectiveness.[41] Unsurprisingly, therefore, the armies operating in Italy were small, although the pre-campaign allocations of troops were comparable to or larger than those made to other theatres. In 1639 the army in Italy was allotted a respectable 13,400 infantry and 5,000 cavalry, yet in early April the number deployed only amounted to 4,500 men. A fresh allocation of troops was needed to raise the total to 7,000 infantry and what was described as 'a handful' of cavalry, so that campaigning could begin in June.[42]

These issues of inadequate logistical support, conflicts about funding the Italian theatre, and recruiting and maintaining adequate numbers of troops over a realistic length of campaign, might have been mitigated if Richelieu's diplomatic initiatives towards the Italian states had proved more successful. Had the cardinal been able to create a genuine 'coalition of the willing', and had the Italian rulers and their governing elites been enthused by the prospects of destroying Spanish power and redrawing the map of northern Italy, then both Italian soldiers and Italian resource bases might have done much to make military operations sustainable and successful.

But there was a deeper problem: the diplomacy of French-sponsored leagues and of overthrowing 'Spanish tyranny' did not rest on a realistic assessment of the interests of Italian rulers. If Richelieu and Mazarin were in some respects pragmatic statesmen, their diplomacy nonetheless reflected fashionable 'maxims of state' – the conviction that rulers and their peoples have immutable interests that will shape their policies.[43] The cardinals earnestly believed that the Italian states' fundamental concern lay in overthrowing Spanish power, and that this gave them a permanent interest in an alliance with France. Nearly two decades after the League of Rivoli, and after any number of twists and turns amongst France's Italian allies, Mazarin could still pronounce himself 'astonished' at the Duke of Mantua's shift back to a Spanish alliance in 1652, and simply refused to believe that it represented a considered decision on the duke's part, since his 'natural interests' must dispose him to a French alliance.[44]

Such *idées fixes* were challenged by the observable reality that the interests of the Italian princes were mutable, adapted rapidly to changing circumstances, and were strongly and dynamically shaped by rivalries within the peninsula.[45] Moreover, because the cardinals embraced the useful concept of 'Spanish tyranny' so whole-heartedly, they appear to have been naïve and unimaginative about the political benefits that Spanish hegemony brought the various Italian rulers and their governing elites. Venice was the prime example here of a state which was anything but ideologically pro-Spanish, but was alert to and realistic about the damaging consequences of destabilisation in Italy; her coolness towards all French attempts to draw her into military activity during these decades is evidence of a wider strand of thinking amongst the Italian rulers.[46]

Even when Italian rulers were prepared to enter into an alliance, their motives might be fundamentally different from those assumed by Richelieu. Italian princes as a group were both opportunistic and risk averse. In the absence of a decisive French challenge to Spanish power, those who had joined a French League could choose to remain almost entirely lukewarm in their military commitment, turning their support on and off as they saw fit, and tacking astutely in the light of military circumstances to avoid any breakdown of relations with Spain.[47] Most important of all, for the rulers of Savoy-Piedmont and Mantua-Monferrato, whose territories stood between France and the Spanish Milanese, entering a League that was explicitly presented as defending their autonomy against Spanish abuses of power meant that they could assert restrictions on French troop movements, billeting and campaigning across their territory, even when their own contribution to the war effort was negligible.

Richelieu's relationship with Vittorio Amedeo of Savoy between 1635 and his premature death in 1637 is instructive in all these respects. As we have seen, the duke entered reluctantly into the League of Rivoli. Although his brother, Tommaso di Carignano, signalled this ambiguity by leaving Turin to take command of Spanish troops in the Netherlands, Vittorio Amedeo's wife since 1619, Marie-Christine, was Louis XIII's sister, which ensured that he retained good lines of communication and influence at the French court even as he havered about his commitment to Richelieu's policies.

From the outset of the 1635 campaign it was clear to observers that Vittorio Amedeo was far from committed to military action against the Spanish.[48] Richelieu made him the overall commander of the allied army mustering in Piedmont, a virtually inevitable decision given the hierarchical assumptions governing precedence amongst senior military posts.[49] However, this antagonised both Odoardo Farnese, who lost no time in criticising Vittorio Amedeo's commitment and suitability for the command, and the French Maréchal Créqui, who as governor of Dauphiné had contributed heavily to the French army corps, which was substantially larger than the forces grudgingly being assembled by the duke.[50] Amidst supply difficulties and an army that was rapidly losing its effective strength, Créqui declined to wait for the duke to bring his forces to the army, and moved off in early September to besiege the town of Valenza, just within the Milanese.[51] When two weeks later Vittorio Amedeo arrived at the siege works to join Créqui and Odoardo Farnese, he offered a barrage of criticisms concerning the preparations for and feasibility of the siege, which, despite his objections, was dragged out for another six weeks. In late October the Spanish managed to force the French lines and threw reinforcements into the town, leading to the abandonment of the siege amidst acrimonious claims that Vittorio Amedeo had connived with the Spanish to allow them to break the siege.[52]

This lukewarm commitment to the military aims of the French was only one of the problems of depending on Savoy's support, however. As Particelli d'Hémery, ambassador in Turin, discovered, one of the reasons why it was proving so difficult to stockpile foodstuffs from local sources at Pinerolo was that Vittorio Amedeo had explicitly forbidden his subjects to trade with the French garrison, and instructed them to resist all attempts to requisition supplies in the vicinity.[53] Moving medium or heavy French artillery across the Alpine barrier was effectively impossible, and it had been agreed before the campaign that the artillery for the allied army would be provided, against French payments, from Piedmont. However, Vittorio Amedeo once again proved reluctant and obstructive, claiming that such artillery – vital for sieges in the second-most densely fortified area in Europe – would have to be taken from Piedmontese fortifications, dangerously weakening their defensive capability. This was to be an enduring problem for the future; complaints from French commanders through the 1630s into the 1650s highlighted the shortage of cannon and the constraints that this placed upon campaigning.[54]

If Vittorio Amedeo felt obliged to sanction the presence of French troops in Piedmont, and to accept some responsibility for their supply needs, he certainly intended to squeeze as much money as possible out of France for the privilege. A first 700,000 *livres* provided him by d'Hémery on his arrival as ambassador in September 1635 was dismissed as derisory compensation.[55] Both Vittorio Amedeo and his successor from 1637, the Regent Marie-Christine, sought to strike the toughest possible bargains for the provisioning of French troops en route through Piedmont, reinforcing their claims by arguing that the devastation of large areas of the country by French troops made it still less possible to provide foodstuffs, clothing and other necessary supplies for the soldiers.[56] To put this bargaining in wider perspective, a French army operating in Germany in those decades would simply have levied military taxes – 'contributions' – on its own authority or via conscripted local agents, taken without regard to the wishes of the local rulers or complaints about compensation.[57] As the dukes of Savoy and their agents well knew, adherence to the alliance with France provided an important safeguard against the danger of being treated in this way.

Most importantly of all, the status of Savoy as French ally virtually eliminated the possibility of quartering the main army of Italy in Piedmont over the winter months, when fighting stopped and the armies spent time recruiting additional troops and preparing for the next campaign. This refusal was at the root of many of the other French problems in the Italian theatre. If it had been possible to base significant French forces across the Alps over the winter months, then a core of experienced soldiers might have become habituated to military service in Italy and proved less likely to desert.[58] Campaigns could have begun earlier in the season, and there would have been a greater possibility of gaining the ultimate objective of French policy: projecting the army deep into the Milanese from where it could lodge itself, extract war contributions, and disrupt the Spanish military and economic system. The best means to facilitate this early start would have been to obtain agreement from the Duke of Savoy to billet French troops over the winter in Piedmont. But from the Savoyard viewpoint the overwhelming advantage of a treaty with France was precisely that they would not be compelled to accept such an arrangement, except at an exorbitant price and for a minimal number of troops. So as a result of a diplomatic decision, and despite huge efforts at persuasion, and a few moments when the military commanders came close to forcing the issue, the ministers acquiesced for the most part in withdrawing all French troops except garrison forces from Piedmont over the winter months.[59]

Much the same could be said of another foot-dragging League member, the Duke of Mantua, who was equally keen to use his status as ally to restrict the operation of French troops in Monferrato while gaining compensation for their presence, and otherwise doing as little as possible to antagonise the Habsburgs.[60] But even an apparently enthusiastic supporter of French policy like Odoardo Farnese revealed the limitations of his commitment. Odoardo stuck with the alliance into 1636, but his behaviour grew increasingly erratic and unmanageable, and he was seemingly unprepared for the prospect that his own territories would be counter-attacked by Spanish forces operating out of the Milanese. In late June 1636 as the allied campaign finally commenced and as troops moved towards a confrontation with the Spanish at the battle of Tornavento, Odoardo decided he had had enough of serving in the coalition; his army was fast disintegrating, and Spanish raiding parties were threatening Piacenza. Without warning, he simply abandoned the campaign and returned to Parma. Six months later, after a largely unsuccessful struggle to defend his duchies against the incursions of Spanish troops, he made peace with Spain, declared his military neutrality and handed over his key fortress of Sabbioneta to a Spanish garrison.[61]

As the impact of all these factors took its toll, Richelieu and his ministers grew disillusioned by the Italian theatre: heavy expenditure, a large military commitment, even a victory at Tornavento (22 June 1636), had achieved nothing. The limitations of the diplomatic side of the strategy became even more apparent. In the winter of 1636–7 Particelli d'Hémery returned to Paris to discuss with Richelieu and his fellow ministers whether France should simply abandon an offensive strategy in Italy, and either seek a local truce with the Spanish, or adopt a defensive stance, abandoning any plans for future assaults against the Milanese.[62] After heated debate it was reluctantly agreed that a purely defensive policy would fail to safeguard Casale and Pinerolo, and would allow the Spanish to carry the war deep into Piedmont. Added to this concern was the awareness of the reputational damage from abandoning the Bourbon dynasty's aspirations in Italy. The result was a compromise that was unlikely to satisfy any strategic goal: the key garrisons would be reinforced, but money would be saved by greatly reducing the numbers of French troops committed to the allied field army.[63]

Even as this scaled-down strategy for the Italian theatre took shape, news arrived of the dissolution of the last vestiges of the army that had been operating north of the Milanese in the Valtelline, where the failure to fund and supply had finally overwhelmed the army commander, Henri de Rohan.[64] Without the diversionary threat posed by Rohan's force, the Spanish were able to exploit the weakening of France's commitment to the Italian theatre with a major assault on Monferrato and Piedmont in the spring and summer of 1637.[65]

The military situation in Piedmont was already deteriorating under this Spanish military pressure when, in early October, Vittorio Amedeo died, leaving two young sons under the regency of his wife, Marie-Christine. The House of Savoy collapsed into civil war, as Tommaso and Maurizio, Vittorio Amedeo's brothers who had identified with the Habsburg cause, returned to Piedmont to lead Spanish forces and their Savoyard supporters in a bid to claim the regency from Marie-Christine. With the duchess-regent struggling to maintain any control in Piedmont, and ultimately being driven north into Savoy to take residence with the young duke in Chambéry, the political balance of the alliance with France shifted. The price of French support for the duchess was to be a French military occupation, of both the duchy of Savoy and whatever parts of Piedmont the French could hold or reconquer.[66] The previous safeguards against French military occupation and possible annexation were now swept away.[67] When the French commander, the comte d'Harcourt, managed to save Turin from falling to Tommaso in 1640, it began a period of French military occupation of the citadel in Turin that lasted until 1656, when it was finally returned to the Duke of Savoy by Mazarin as a goodwill gesture marking the marriage between his niece, Olympia Mancini, and Tommaso di Carignano's son, Eugène-Maurice.[68]

Yet while this situation greatly simplified the military-logistical issues for French troops operating in Piedmont, and offered the prospect of permanent French territorial gains as the price of propping up the regency of Marie-Christine, it was also one that presented considerable military dangers. Although Turin had been saved in 1640, almost every other city in Piedmont had fallen to the alliance of the princes and the Spanish.[69] The war continued through 1641 and 1642 with the French military effort concentrated on trying to win back a few cities while the Spanish consolidated their control deep into Piedmont. The solution to this impasse was achieved through the diplomatic efforts of Giulio Mazzarino, whose commitment to Richelieu's service had gained him a cardinal's hat in 1641.[70] Though Richelieu suspected Mazarin of being overly favourable to the Savoyards and their interests, Mazarin nonetheless managed to reconcile the feuding members of the ducal family. Tommaso and Maurizio were lured from their Spanish into a French alliance, and a new regency settlement was established, based on giving them a substantial stake in the overall direction of government in return for their acceptance of the succession and the titular regency of the dowager-duchess.[71]

However the price of this for France was a return to a formal alliance with Savoy-Piedmont, requiring sensitivity in matters of quartering, securing supplies and moving forces through Savoyard territory. Though French troops remained in control of cities that they had managed to prise back from the Spanish, the return of these places to Savoyard garrisons was a matter of protracted and potentially acrimonious debate. Meanwhile the issue of prohibiting French troops from wintering in Piedmont once again became a perennial issue, with the Savoyard government more intent than ever on excluding French troops.

III

The emergence of Cardinal Mazarin as First Minister in France from 1643 ensured that there would be a continued focus on Italy in French foreign policy. Indeed there was reason to think that Italy would occupy a still larger place in Mazarin's strategic thinking. Obviously Mazarin's family interests and knowledge, his background in Naples and then the Papal States, his employment by the Barberini family in the 1620s and early 1630s, all conditioned his political engagement with Italy.[72] Mazarin had worked closely with Richelieu to promote French interests in the peninsula ever since he had brokered the Franco-Spanish truce in 1630 which led to the Treaty of Cherasco. After Richelieu's death the prudent desire to defend the legitimacy of his new position by maintaining and upholding the policies of his predecessor, and the shared conviction that France could win the war against Spain in the Italian theatre, also contributed to a transalpine focus. Yet at the same time Mazarin brought a distinctive set of perspectives to the Italian theatre, which were to colour and shape French policy decisions in ways quite different from Richelieu.

As noted earlier, Richelieu was flanked by subordinate ministers who were sceptical about the costs and the management of military involvement in Italy, and sought to keep the scale of operations on a tight leash. Little had been achieved by the end of Richelieu's ministry, though the loss of Casale and a total Spanish occupation of Piedmont had been prevented. At the same time, this restricted military commitment had not drained resources from other campaign theatres in which greater progress had been made, such as the Flanders frontier and Roussillon-Catalonia, where intervention in the Catalan revolt from 1640 offered seemingly the most effective way to place pressure on Madrid. In grand strategic terms of effective resource management, the policy had some merit.

The advent of Mazarin led to several changes in these areas. In the first place, Mazarin believed that the military balance of power had irrevocably tipped in France's favour. The effects of the Catalan and Portuguese revolts, combined with Spain's apparent military exhaustion following the naval reverses of the late 1630s and the defeat of the Army of Flanders at Rocroi in 1643, persuaded him that the Spanish *monarquía* was close to military and political collapse, and that the aim should now be the short-term maximisation of military pressure.[73] Mazarin moreover had flanked himself with newly appointed ministers who had been his confidants and allies while in Italy: the *contrôleur général des finances*, Michel Particelli d'Hémery, had built close contacts with Mazarin while he was ambassador in Turin; the secretary for war, Michel Le Tellier, had been *intendant* of the army of Italy from 1640 to 1643. Both had direct experience of the Italian theatre, and even more significantly, both had been criticised, even humiliated, by Richelieu and his ministers for their lack of fiscal restraint.[74] The years from 1643 were thus in a sense the revenge of the 'Italian' party, hitherto regarded with suspicion but now at the centre of policy formulation and prioritisation. The commitment of troops and money to the Italian theatre rocketed upwards in 1645 and 1646.[75]

Such a shift might have brought favourable results: in 1643 the Franco-Savoyard army at last seemed to be achieving more than the recovery of lost ground, with the capture of Asti and Trino in the Milanese.[76] But higher expenditure did not necessarily translate into better maintenance and provisioning of the armies in the field. The poor management of funds for Italian military operations became even more acute under the new regime, partly because of the ministers' own direct or indirect involvement in the financing and supply of the troops. French officials in Italy who proposed contracting locally to undercut the excessive charges of the central provisioning companies were stonewalled or ignored by Mazarin and his fellow ministers. Instead a narrow group of Parisian-based *munitionnaires* and their agents gained what was effectively a monopoly of supply from the mid-1640s, and attempts to challenge their blatant profiteering – such as charging the same amount per ration regardless of whether the soldier was in garrison or on campaign – were simply brushed aside by the ministers.[77] Moreover, attempts by these same officials to draw attention to regimental and garrison commanders who were massively exaggerating the numbers of troops under their command to claim excess pay and rations, also encountered ambiguous and evasive responses from the ministers.[78] To generalise from this experience of the Italian theatre, it seems likely that the political culture that developed after 1643 was more openly tolerant of fraud and financial malpractice than had been the case during Richelieu's ministry.[79] Mazarin's government appeared to have lost even the aspiration to control and direct resources efficiently and economically.

Yet if this might suggest ever more entrenched interests pursuing the same campaign objectives with greater waste and less accountability, it soon became apparent that Mazarin's Italian policy was guided by a different set of strategic priorities and objectives. This shift reflected his conviction that his own experiences gave him a better understanding of the vulnerabilities of Spanish Italy, and an agenda which was as much shaped by personal and family ambitions in Italy as by the interests of Crown and state.

One consequence of these private concerns was Mazarin's support for, and excessive reliance upon, powerful figures in Italy he regarded as potentially useful to his ambitions. Tommaso di Carignano, the brother of Duke Vittorio Amedeo of Savoy, was an obvious case here, as Mazarin sought to construct a marital link with the House of Savoy.[80] But it was most characteristically evident in his unstinting support for the Barberini nephews of Pope Urban VIII, whose self-seeking and duplicitous behaviour was mitigated in Mazarin's eyes by the possibility of negotiating a marriage with the son of Taddeo Barberini for one of his nieces.[81] The two Barberini cardinals had double-crossed Mazarin at the papal conclave of 1644, where their sudden change of allegiance had ensured the election of the pro-Spanish Pamphilj pope, Innocent X, despite having previously agreed to support France's veto on Pamphilj's election.[82] In 1645 Innocent hit back at Mazarin by refusing to make his brother, Michele, a cardinal – an ambition dear to Mazarin's family interests, despite the laughable unworthiness of the candidate.[83] Moreover Innocent had repaid the naïve support of the Barberini nephews by launching an all-out attack on the political and social standing of the family, driving them into exile in France, where they were nonetheless received by Mazarin.

While family ambitions did not alone motivate Mazarin's decision to shift priorities in Italy, they formed a dangerous cocktail when combined with frustration at the slowing pace of the campaign in northern Italy in 1644, and the cardinal's personal conviction that the real key to defeating the Spanish in Italy lay not in attacking the 'garrison state' of the Milanese, but through the kingdom of Naples. Mazarin's network of Italian clients convinced him that Naples was a powder keg of festering unrest, requiring only the incursion of French troops to bring about sweeping revolts which would destroy Spain's power in Italy.[84] But a French attack on Naples would require naval support to underpin an amphibious operation, and Naples was outside the operational range of French galleys setting out from Toulon or Marseilles. Hence Mazarin's project in 1645 to launch an attack on Naples after an initial campaign that would conquer the Spanish military bases – the *presidios* – that stretched along the coast of the Grand Duchy of Tuscany, a state that was notionally independent but in practice an ally of Spain. The additional, and personal, advantage for Mazarin was that a French military presence in the *presidios* would pose a direct threat to the nearby Papal States, placing pressure on Innocent X.[85]

The decision to shift military priorities was hugely expensive and success was far from assured; it involved rebuilding the hitherto neglected Mediterranean fleet, largely via contracts with Dutch shipbuilders, and assembling a substantial combined force of soldiers, galleys, galleons and troop transports at Toulon. So substantial was the operation, and so lax its administration, that the expedition missed the campaigning season of 1645 altogether.[86] Despite this, its inevitable consequence was a massive refocusing of military resources from the north Italian theatre.[87] The expedition finally set out in February 1646, followed by the publication of a manifesto in which Mazarin set out his complaints against Innocent X.[88] The main campaign was a disaster. A drawn-out and unsuccessful siege of the main *presidio* at Orbetello was followed by a naval encounter in which the French admiral was killed, and which signalled the decision to abandon the campaign. The attack on Naples did not get beyond this first base. Faced with a crushing – and unnecessary – setback to France's reputation in Italy, a French fleet reassembled in the late summer, and achieved the surprise capture of the *presidio* of Piombino and of Porto Longone on Elba.[89]

The result of this military commitment and expenditure was not, as Mazarin had hoped, a transformation of France's situation in the Italian theatre. The attack on the *presidios* made no military sense unless Tuscany became an open ally of France, prepared to supply and support the installed garrisons rather than to blockade them, or unless France enjoyed a clear naval superiority in the western Mediterranean. Neither of these conditions prevailed, so maintaining the garrisons became a struggle against the virtual inevitability of logistical failure. Both locales fell back into Spanish hands in 1648.[90]

What the seizure of Piombino did achieve, given its proximity to the Papal States, was a degree of temporary tractability on the part of the pope towards Mazarin's personal demands. A cardinal's hat was found for Michele Mazarin, who reciprocated his brother's efforts by being an inept and absentee Viceroy of Catalonia until his death in 1648.[91] Innocent also agreed to suspend proceedings against the Roman property and interests of the Barberini nephews. As a result they recovered their influence in the Sacred College sufficiently to double-cross Mazarin at a second papal conclave, that of 1655: their support enabled the election of another pope whose name had originally been vetoed by France – Fabio Chigi, who became Alexander VII.[92]

The capture of the *presidios* had been intended to serve as a preliminary to an attack on Naples, which Mazarin had considered ready for revolt in 1645/6. Yet when revolt finally did break out in Naples, following the violent unrest in Palermo which had begun in May 1647, Mazarin's attitude was far more lukewarm and hesitant. In his correspondence, Mazarin showed indecisiveness about the character of the revolt: now that it had finally broken out, he worried that its composition was overwhelmingly popular, that it would not attract noble support and would have no staying power once the Spanish mustered their resources.[93] Moreover he had been burnt by the 1646 debacle, and was sceptical of the chances of organising any amphibious operation effective enough to shape the fast-moving events in Naples. Permitting Henri, duc de Guise, to launch his own bid to assume the popular leadership of the Naples revolt was to some extent a necessary recognition of the historic claims of the house of Guise-Lorraine over the kingdom. Moreover, as Mazarin's political opponents started to grow more outspoken during 1647 and early 1648, he was disinclined to add a volatile member of the house of Guise-Lorraine to the ranks of his domestic enemies. But Mazarin was also aware of the personal weaknesses and organisational incapacity of the duc de Guise, and he had no confidence that he would be able to transform the Naples revolt into a more serious base of resistance to the Spanish. The decision to permit this expedition seems to have been a symbolic gesture rather than a serious attempt to incorporate the revolt into a larger French strategy.[94] The two naval expeditions that were half-heartedly organised to support Guise, and in the second case arrived after the revolt had collapsed, simply put the seal on his failure since they demonstrated just how chimerical were his offers to bring in French military assistance. From a position at the centre of Mazarin's Italian strategy a few years earlier, the Naples revolt, now reduced to its dying embers, had been relegated to a minor and probably futile sideshow, and Mazarin's attentions refocused on the north Italian theatre.[95]

This shift of attention and resources to the north occurred partly because, for the first time since 1636, French diplomacy had succeeded in drawing a new ally into the Italian league. Francesco d'Este, Duke of Modena, entered into military alliance with France and Savoy in 1646, offended that his previous services to the Spanish had been insufficiently recognised.[96] He contributed limited military resources, but the alliance provided the opportunity to use the strategic position of Modena as a base for an attack on the Milanese from its eastern flank, opening up the possibility of a pincer movement against Milan itself. After a first campaign in 1647 which was badly coordinated and supplied, a combined force laid siege to Cremona in late July 1648. Without sufficient artillery and deploying an army that wasted away through desertion and illness, the siege was abandoned after three months. At this point Francesco emulated his predecessor in the League of a decade earlier, Odoardo Farnese, broke with the alliance and made unilateral terms with the Spanish, promising to disband his army and neutralise his territory.[97]

Unlike Odoardo Farnese, however, Francesco d'Este was once again beguiled by Mazarin's offers of support and alliance after France had re-emerged from the breakdown of the *Fronde*. From 1654 he made another opportunistic attempt to raise forces for combined operations. Yet this much-sought alliance turned out to be another liability for France: in 1655 Modena was occupied by Spanish troops, and the duke faced the threat of being placed under the Imperial ban and dispossessed.[98] Instead of being a useful launching pad for a new incursion into the Milanese, the invasion of the duchy by German troops enforcing the emperor's authority required the alliance to deploy common resources towards Modena's relief. In this fragile situation, Francesco considerably strengthened his bargaining position by agreeing to a marriage between his eldest son, Alfonso, and another of Mazarin's nieces, Laura Martinozzi. Mazarin reciprocated by granting Francesco command of a joint French–Modenese army, and allowing him to conduct a policy that was as concerned with safeguarding his own duchy as with pursuing the campaign in the Milanese.[99] A two-pronged attack by the French on the city of Pavia was heavily defeated in 1655 by Spanish troops and local militias.[100]

Setting aside Mazarin's reluctant sanctioning of the even more hopeless attempt by the duc de Guise to incite another revolt in Naples in 1654,[101] it seemed that the cardinal had returned belatedly to the strategy of his predecessor, recognising that the war in Italy would need to be fought on the Lombardy plain. In 1656 the allied army under Francesco d'Este finally captured the small town of Valenza, where the failed siege in 1635 had shown so clearly both the logistical and diplomatic limitations of Richelieu's policies. There were few achievements even of this modest sort in the remaining years of the war. Despite the evidence of Spain's collapsing military and financial position in Lombardy and the fragility of her entire military system, French armies failed to do much more than rampage through ill-defended countryside in the Milanese. With the death of Francesco d'Este in late 1658 the allies and Spanish finally agreed a truce which lasted until the peace of the Pyrenees was finally concluded a year later.[102]

What does this account of French policy in Italy tell us about the statesmanship of Richelieu and Mazarin? It certainly points to the need to think in grand strategic terms about the relationship of means to ends, above all in the deployment of scarce resources and in assessing the cost-effectiveness of goals. Neither minister seems to have demonstrated much concern with maintaining close control over the accumulation and allocation of troops and logistical support in this theatre, or to have adequately responded to the particular difficulties of maintaining military capability beyond the Alps. Mazarin in particular presided over what was, in retrospect, a reckless increase in overall French military expenditure in the mid-1640s; unwise shifts in policy and a general indifference to financial mismanagement and peculation ensured that the growth in spending provided no benefit to France's overall military position in Italy. Both ministers found it difficult to reconcile their military goals with their diplomatic initiatives, whether through wishful thinking about the aims and concerns of potential allies, or (especially in Mazarin's case) a willingness to allow personal and familial ambition to cloud political and military judgements.[103]

France's territorial and political presence in Italy after the Peace of the Pyrenees was reduced from that she had had enjoyed in 1631 at the Treaty of Cherasco. This setback might be attributed simply to the operational and logistical problems that were the nemesis of early modern warfare. Yet the contrast with the considerably more successful French military record in other campaign theatres, whether on the Flanders frontier, in Roussillon or across the Rhine in Germany, is nonetheless striking, even allowing for the particular logistical context of the Italian theatre.[104] More fundamental perhaps are questions about planning and resources, above all in the coordination of military and diplomatic strategy. And if the example of a single campaign theatre is insufficient to undermine the reputation for statesmanship of the two cardinal-ministers, it nonetheless raises important questions about their – and other early modern ministers' – success in reconciling those fundamental and enduring issues of political vision, governmental and personal interests, and the best use of limited resources.

NOTES

1. The author wishes to thank the Leverhulme Trust for the award of a Major Research Fellowship from 2013 to 2016 for a project to study French politics in the 1650s. Research conducted as part of that project has contributed significantly to the present chapter.
2. Richelieu, *Testament politique*, ed. Françoise Hildesheimer (Paris: Societé de l'Histoire de France, 1995), p. 43. Richelieu's proudest boast was that he had restored the king's name to the status it should enjoy amongst foreign nations.
3. Richelieu, *Mémoires*, in Claude-Bernard Petitot and Louis Jean Nicolas Monmerqué (eds), *Collection des mémoires relatifs à l'histoire de France . . .*, 52 vols (Paris: Foucault, 1819–26), vol. 24, pp. 46–7; Adolphe Chéruel and Georges d'Avenel (eds), *Lettres du Cardinal Mazarin pendant son ministère*, 9 vols (Paris: Imprimerie nationale, 1872–1906), vol. 1, p. 122, 9 March 1643, Mazarin to d'Aiguebonne. See also, for example, Loménie de Brienne on Spanish universalist ambitions in Italy: A(rchives des) A(ffaires) E(trangères), C(orrespondence) P(olitique) Sardaigne, 46, fos. 110–11, 18 April 1653, Brienne to Ennemond Servien.
4. See J. H. Elliott's classic comparative study, *Richelieu and Olivares* (Cambridge: Cambridge University Press, 1984).
5. The early modern phenomenon of the minister-favourite is extensively explored in J. H. Elliott and L. W. B. Brockliss (eds), *The World of the Favourite* (New Haven, CT: Yale University Press, 1999).
6. For example, Jouanna Arlette, *Le Devoir de révolte. La noblesse française et la gestion de l'État moderne, 1559–1661* (Paris: Fayard, 1989), pp. 359–61; Paul Sonnino, *Mazarin's Quest: The Congress of Westphalia and the Coming of the Fronde* (Cambridge, MA: Harvard University Press, 2008), pp. 169–71.
7. Richelieu, *Testament politique*, pp. 84–5.
8. Paul Kennedy, 'Introduction', in Kennedy (ed.), *Grand Strategies in War and Peace* (New Haven, CT: Yale University Press, 1991), pp. 1–7.
9. For two case studies where it is argued that these issues were not balanced, see Geoffrey Parker, *The Grand Strategy of Philip II* (New Haven, CT: Yale University Press, 1998), pp. 1–10; J. H. Elliott, 'Managing Decline: Olivares and the Grand Strategy of Imperial Spain', in Kennedy, *Grand Strategies*, pp. 87–104.
10. Sven Externbrink, *Le Coeur du monde. Frankreich und die norditalienischen Staaten (Mantua, Parma, Savoyen) im Zeitalter Richelieus 1624–1635* (Münster: Lit, 1999), pp. 339–47; Anna Blum, *La Diplomatie de la France en Italie du nord au temps de Richelieu et Mazarin* (Paris: Garnier, 2014), pp. 35–40.

11. Michael Mallett and Christine Shaw, *The Italian Wars, 1494–1559* (Harlow: Pearson, 2012), esp. pp. 250–88; M. M. Rabà, 'Ceresole (14 Aprile 1544): una grande, inutile vittoria. Conflitto tra potenze e Guerra di logoramento nella prima età moderna', in Alessandro Buono and Gianclaudio Civale (eds), *Battaglie. L'evento, l'individuo, la memoria* (Palermo: Associazione Mediterranea, 2014), pp. 101–40.

12. Externbrink, *Coeur du monde*, pp. 116–22; 190–201; David Parrott, 'The Utility of Fortifications in Early Modern Europe: Italian Princes and their Citadels, 1540–1640', *War in History* 7:2 (2000), pp. 127–53.

13. Guy Rowlands, 'Moving Mars: The Logistical Geography of Louis XIV's France', *French History* 25 (2011), pp. 492–514.

14. Pierre Grillon (ed.), *Les Papiers de Richelieu*, 6 vols (Paris: A Pedone, 1975–), vol. 5, pp. 393, 453–4, 481, 13 July, 30 July, 3 August 1630, Michel de Marillac to Richelieu – on the difficulties of requisitioning mules.

15. David Parrott, *Richelieu's Army: War, Government and Society in France, 1624–42* (Cambridge: Cambridge University Press, 2001), pp. 94–9.

16. David Parrott, 'The Origins of the Franco-Spanish War of 1635–59', in Jeremy Black (ed.), *The Origins of War in Early Modern Europe* (Edinburgh: Edinburgh University Press, 1987), pp. 72–111, 95–103.

17. D. L. M. Avenel (ed.), *Lettres, instructions diplomatiques et papiers d'état du cardinal de Richelieu*, 8 vols (Paris: Imprimerie impériale (nationale), 1853–76), vol. 4, p. 709, 18 April 1635, pp. 712–13, 20 April; AAE, M(émoires et) D(ocuments), 814, fo. 157, 1 June 1635, Richelieu to Bouthillier.

18. Avenel, *Lettres . . . de Richelieu*, vol. 4, pp. 666–7; AAE CP Mantoue, 5, fos. 15–16, 12 March 1635, *Mémoire* for conservation of Casale; AAE CP Sardaigne 24, fos. 25–8, [January] 1636, 'Estat de l'Armée' – on stockpiling at Casale.

19. R. Pithon, 'Les Débuts difficiles du ministère du Cardinal de Richelieu et la crise de Valtelline', *Revue d'histoire diplomatique* 74 (1960), pp. 298–322.

20. The instructions to the French ambassador, Louis de La Saludie, speak of the need 'to deprive the Spanish of their aim of making Italy the seat of their empire, thereby allowing them to achieve universal monarchy' (1633), cited in Externbrink, *Coeur du monde*, p. 289; Externbrink, '"Le Coeur du monde" et la "liberté de l'Italie." Aspects de la politique italienne de Richelieu, 1624–42', *Revue d'histoire diplomatique* 114 (2000), pp. 181–208, emphasises (pp. 186–9) that the Italians also had a rhetoric of Spanish 'enslavement', but this had limited practical implications, and few saw resolution in terms of French intervention.

21. Gabriel de Mun, *Richelieu et la maison de Savoie. L'Ambassade de Particelli d'Hémery en Piémont* (Paris: Librairie Plon, 1907), pp. 27–32; Externbrink, *Coeur du monde*, pp. 27–84.

22. Avenel, *Lettres . . . de Richelieu*, vol. 5, pp. 103–7, *Projet de Ligue . . .* , 11 July 1635.

23. Guido Amoretti, *Il Ducato di Savoia dal 1559 al 1713*, 4 vols (Turin: Famija Turinéisa, 1984–8), vol. 2, pp. 93–7; P. Merlin, 'La France et le duché de Savoie au début du XVIIe siècle', in Giuliano Ferretti (ed.), *De l'Ombre à la lumière: Les Servien et la monarchie de France, XVI et XVIIe siècle* (Paris: l'Harmattan, 2014), pp. 75–88.

24. Vittorio Siri, *Il Mercurio, overo Historia de' correnti Tempi*, 3 vols (Casale: Della Casa, 1644–7), vol. 1, p. 30.

25. Gregory Hanlon, *The Hero of Italy. Odoardo Farnese, Duke of Parma, His Soldiers and His Subjects in the Thirty Years' War* (Oxford: Oxford University Press, 2014), pp. 30–3.

26. Avenel, *Lettres . . . de Richelieu*, vol. 5, pp. 141–4, 4 August 1635, Instructions to d'Hémery.

27. See, for example, AAE CP Sardaigne 30, fo. 76, 15 February 1640, de La Court to de Noyers on the acute shortages in Pinerolo; Sardaigne 26, fo. 152, 25 April 1638, d'Hémery to Richelieu on the weakness and vulnerability of Casale.

28. Parrott, *Richelieu's Army*, pp. 260–8.

29. For example, AAE, CP Sardaigne 30, fo. 501, (mid June) 1640; Comte d'Harcourt to de Noyers, providing a detailed account of shortfalls; Sardaigne 45, fo. 279, 21 April 1652, de Piennes, governor of Pinerolo to Mazarin.

30. AAE CP Sardaigne 31, fo. 662, 17 December 1640, de Noyers to Mazarin.

31. Governors of both places were engaged in long-running disputes over the shortage of artillery, and anxious to resist further claims that guns should be commandeered for the field armies: AAE CP Sardaigne 26, fo. 152, 25 April 1638, d'Hémery to Richelieu: only 10 guns are in serviceable condition at the fortress of Casale.

32. Gregory Hanlon, *The Twilight of a Military Tradition: Italian Aristocrats and European Conflicts, 1560–1800* (New York: Holmes and Meier, 1988), pp. 124–5, 133; Robert Oresko and David Parrott, 'The Sovereignty of Monferato and the Citadel of Casale as European Problems in the Early Modern Period', in Daniela Ferrari (ed.), *Stefano Guazzo e Casale tra Cinque e Seicento* (Rome: Bulzoni, 1997), pp. 62–9 (pp. 11–86).

33. AAE CP Sardaigne 31, fos. 414, 662, 15 November/17 December 1640, de Noyers to Mazarin, reporting Bullion's complaints about Italian expenditure and suspicions of corruption.

34. For Abel Servien's previous roles as ambassador in Italy, see Externbrink, *Coeur du monde*, pp. 146–53, 208–12; Hélène Duccini, *Guerre et paix dans la France du Grand Siècle. Abel Servien: diplomate et serviteur de l'Etat (1593–1659)* (Paris: Champ Vallon, 2012), pp. 89–133. His brother, Ennemond Servien, served as ambassador at Turin from 1648 to 1676; see Sven Externbrink, 'La Politique de la France en Italie au XVIIe siècle. Le rôle d'Abel et Ennemond Servien', in Ferretti, *Les Servien*, pp. 63–73. For the disgrace of Servien, see Orest Ranum, *Richelieu and the Councillors of Louis XIII* (Oxford: Clarendon Press, 1963), pp. 100–1; Parrott, *Richelieu's Army*, p. 372.

35. Narcisse Léonard Caron (ed.), *Michel Le Tellier: son administration comme intendant d'armée en Piémont, 1640–43* (Paris: G. Pedone Lauriel, 1880), p. 50, 12 March 1641, De Noyers to Le Tellier. See also p. 69, 5 June 1641, de Noyers to Le Tellier on the 'insupportable costs' of supply to the army of Italy – 1,700,000 *livres* in the last year to the *munitionnaires*.

36. For example, AAE CP Sardaigne 30, fo. 501, 10 June 1640, Comte d'Harcourt to de Noyers, itemising the shortfalls in financial provision for the military costs in Italy over the previous two campaigns.

37. AAE CP Sardaigne 24, fo. 712, 2 September 1636, d'Hémery to Richelieu, making a last-ditch appeal to Richelieu to intervene to ensure funding.

38. Ranum, *Richelieu*, pp. 149–50.

39. Parrott, *Richelieu's Army*, pp. 117–60; for example, AAE CP Sardaigne, 46, fo. 119, 27 April 1654, Marquis Villa to Mazarin, reporting that the Spanish army is in the field, but the French have hardly assembled more than a few companies from Burgundy.

40. AAE CP Sardaigne, 26, fo. 422, 10 August 1638, La Valette to Chavigny on crisis levels of desertion.

41. AAE CP Sardaigne 28, fo. 319, 11 May 1639, Cardinal de La Valette to de Noyers.

42. Parrott, *Richelieu's Army*, pp. 208–9.

43. See, for example, H. de Rohan, *De l'Intérêt des princes et des États de la chrétienté*, ed. Christian Lazzeri (Paris: Presses universitaires de France, 1995), pp. 174–5, 'De l'intérêt des princes d'Italie'; Andrew Lossky, '"Maxims of State" in Louis XIV's Foreign Policy in the 1680s', in Ragnhild Hatton and John S. Bromley (eds), *William III and Louis XIV* (Liverpool: Liverpool University Press, 1968), pp. 7–23.

44. Chéruel, *Lettres . . . de Mazarin*, vol. 5, pp. 414–15, 19 October 1652, Mazarin to Le Tellier; for similar opinions voiced by Brienne in the preceding year, see AAE CP Sardaigne 45, fo. 110, 16 June 1651: the duke cannot forget 'ses propres interestz'.

45. See, for example, Toby Osborne, *Dynasty and Diplomacy in the Court of Savoy: Political*

Culture and the Thirty Years' War (Cambridge: Cambridge University Press, 2002).

46. Bernd Roeck, 'The Role of Venice in the War and during the Peace Negotiations', in Klaus Bussman and Heinz Schilling (eds), *1648. War and Peace in Europe*, 3 vols (Münster and Osnabrück: Westfälisches Landesmuseum für Kunst und Kulturgeschichte, 1998), vol. 1, pp. 161–8.

47. Avenel, *Lettres . . . de Richelieu*, vol. 5, pp. 104–5. In 1636 the French settled for 3,000 infantry and 800 cavalry from the duchy of Savoy, instead of the 6,000 infantry and 1,200 horse specified in the League. See AAE CP Sardaigne, 24, fo. 27, 12 January 1636.

48. AAE, CP Sardaigne 23, fo. 197, d'Hémery to Richelieu, 7 September 1635.

49. David Parrott, 'Richelieu, the *grands* and the French Army', in Joseph Bergin and Laurence Brockliss (eds), *Richelieu and His Age* (Oxford: Clarendon Press, 1992), pp. 135–73, 152–4.

50. Jacques Humbert, *Le Maréchal de Créquy. Gendre de Lesdiguières, 1573–1638* (Paris: Hachette, 1962), pp. 212–18.

51. Avenel, *Lettres . . . de Richelieu*, vol. 5, pp. 165–7, 30 August 1635, Richelieu to Créqui.

52. Humbert, *Créquy*, p. 225; Mun, *Particelli d'Hémery*, pp. 89–93 is more nuanced.

53. AAE CP Sardaigne 23, fo. 178, 29 August 1635, d'Hémery to Richelieu.

54. AAE CP Sardaigne, 26, fo. 236, 26 May 1638, d'Hémery to Richelieu: the army can muster only five cannon.

55. Mun, *Particelli d'Hémery*, pp. 54–5.

56. AAE CP Sardaigne 24, fo. 281, 20 April 1636, 'Estat des Affaires d'Italie', reports that the duke is charging 32 *sols* per day for the *logement* of French troops in Piedmont, whereas the French only allowed 19 *sols* for this. In 1640 the Duchess of Savoy's ministers claimed that quartering for the French forces remaining in Piedmont would cost at least 2 million *livres*. See AAE CP Sardaigne 31, fo. 795, undated (late 1640).

57. In late 1648 Turenne was congratulated by Mazarin on having managed to sustain his army in Germany for the whole of the campaign while hardly taking a shilling of funding from the French treasury. See Chéruel, *Lettres . . . de Mazarin*, vol. 2, p. 234, 6 November 1648; David Parrott, *The Business of War: Military Enterprise and Military Revolution in Early Modern Europe* (Cambridge: Cambridge University Press, 2012).

58. A point explicitly made by the commander in Italy, La Valette, to Richelieu: B(ibliothèque) N(ationale), M(anuscrit)s. F(rançais) 3770, fo. 3, 8 January 1639.

59. AAE CP Sardaigne 24, fo. 281, 20 April 1636, 'Estat des Affaires d'Italie' first raises the issue of evacuating the French troops from Piedmont during the winter of 1635–6 in what was to become a familiar demand, acquiesced in by the French ministers. The ministers seemed prepared to force the issue in the winter of 1653–4, arguing that the Savoyard forces would not be able to defend themselves adequately against Spanish incursions if the French pulled back across the Alps. See AAE CP Sardaigne 46, fos. 8–15, 7 January 1654, *et seq.* However, by 21 February they had backed down and agreed to withdraw all but a token force of troops from Piedmont. See AAE CP Sardaigne 46, fo. 117.

60. Externbrink, 'Politique italienne de Richelieu', p. 199; Blum, *Diplomatie de la France*, pp. 90–3.

61. Hanlon, *Hero of Italy*, pp. 157–60, 186–8; Mun, *Particelli d'Hémery*, pp. 170–2.

62. AAE CP Savoie 25, fos. 24–5, 30 January 1637, *mémoire* of d'Hémery; Mun, *Particelli d'Hémery*, pp. 173–7.

63. AAE CP Savoie 25, fos. 24–5, 30 January 1637, *mémoire* of d'Hémery. It was calculated that the semi-defensive policy would save France 2 million *livres* in the Italian theatre; Blum, *Diplomatie de la France*, pp. 73–83.

64. Jack A. Clarke, *Huguenot Warrior: The Life and Times of Henri de Rohan* (The Hague: Martinus Nijhoff, 1966), pp. 197–210; Pierre and Solange Deyon, *Henri de Rohan* (Paris: Perrin, 2000), pp. 156–81.

65. AAE CP Sardaigne 25, fo. 261, 22 July 1637, gives details of the Spanish army invading Piedmont; fo. 401, 22 August, d'Hémery to Richelieu; fo. 420, 9 September, d'Hémery to Richelieu on the grave threat to Casale, compounded by the weak garrison.

66. G. Quazza, 'Guerra civile in Piemonte, 1637–42 (nuove ricerche)', *Bolletino storico-bibliografico subalpino* 57 (1959), pp. 287–93 (pp. 281–321); BN, Msfr 3770, fo. 83, 5 April 1638, instructions to d'Hémery to obtain the transfer of remaining fortified towns in Piedmont into French hands.

67. Giuliano Ferretti, 'La France et la Savoie à la conférence de Grenoble (1639). Le duché au risqué de sa disparition', in Ferretti (ed.), *De Paris à Turin. Christine de France, duchesse de Savoie* (Paris: l'Harmattan, 2014), pp. 59–86.

68. Robert Oresko, 'The Marriages of the Nieces of Cardinal Mazarin. Public Policy and Private Strategy in Seventeenth-Century Europe', in Rainer Babel (ed.), *Frankreich im Europäischen Staatensystem der frühen Neuzeit* (Sigmaringen: Thorbecke, 1995), pp. 134–5 (pp. 109–51).

69. Avenel, *Correspondence de . . . Richelieu*, vol. 6, p. 338, 3 May 1639, Richelieu to Chavigny.

70. Madeleine Laurain-Portemer, *Une tête à gouverner quatre empires. Études Mazarines* (Paris: Diffusione de Boccard, 1997), pp. 607–93.

71. Robert Oresko, 'The House of Savoy and the Thirty Years' War', in Bussman and Schilling, *1648. War and Peace in Europe*, vol. 1, pp. 142–53; Amoretti, *Ducato di Savoia*, vol. 2, pp. 167–81.

72. Georges Dethan, *The Young Mazarin* (London: Thames and Hudson, 1977), pp. 13–88; Dethan, 'La Politique italienne de Mazarin', in Jean Serroy (ed.), *La France et l'Italie au temps de Mazarin* (Grenoble: Presses universitaires de Grenoble, 1986), pp. 27–32.

73. Chéruel, *Lettres . . . de Mazarin*, vol. 1, pp. 263, 300, 28 July and 26 August 1643, Mazarin to Nicolas Amontot (Resident at Genoa) and to Prince Tommaso of Savoy, speaking of the 'extraordinary prosperity' of French fortunes.

74. For de Noyers' criticism of Le Tellier in 1641–2, see Caron, *Michel Le Tellier*, pp. 37–8, 50, 69, 175, *passim*.

75. Richard J. Bonney, *The King's Debts: Finance and Politics in France, 1589–1661* (Oxford: Clarendon Press, 1981), pp. 195–201.

76. Jacques Humbert, 'Turenne en Italie (1630–1645)', in *Turenne et l'art militaire (Actes du Colloque International)* (Paris: les Belles Lettres, 1978), pp. 181–5.

77. The cartel was composed of members of the Falcombel family, Jean-Baptiste Paleologo and Jean-Baptiste Carrezzano; for the case for using local contractors see, for example, AAE CP Sardaigne 46, fo. 99, 12 April 1653, where Ennemond Servien asserts that he could supply the army with bread for 26 *déniers* per ration, massively undercutting the 42 *déniers* charged by the central *munitionnaires*.

78. AAE CP Sardaigne 46, fos. 170, 256, 12 July 1653 and 18 October 1653, accusation made to Le Tellier and his brother, the Surintendant Abel Servien, by Ennemond Servien concerning systematic corruption in the accounting of infantry regiments in garrison at Pinerolo.

79. Chéruel, *Lettres . . . de Mazarin*, vol. 6, p. 63, 23 October 1653, Mazarin to *Surintendants*, overlooking the likely overcharging for bread supply by the *munitionnaire* Falcombel; AAE CP Sardaigne 46, fo. 187, 1 August 1653, dismissal of E. Servien's accusations by Le Tellier.

80. For Mazarin's family strategies, see Oresko, 'The Marriages of the Nieces'.

81. Chéruel, *Lettres . . . de Mazarin*, vol. 3, pp. 990, 1017, 15 February and 30 April 1648; Géraud Poumarède, 'Mazarin, marieur de l'Europe. Stratégies familiales, enjeux dynastiques et géopolitiques au milieu du XVIIe siècle', *Dix-Septième Siècle* 243 (2009), p. 204 (pp. 201–18). The project was rejected by the Barberini.

82. Fontenay-Mareuil, M. du Val, marquis de, *Mémoires*, in Petitot, *Collection*, vol. 51, pp. 310–18; Irene Fosi, *All'ombra dei Barberini. Fedeltà e servizio nella Roma barocca* (Rome: Bulzoni, 1997), pp. 139–52.
83. Gabriel de Mun, 'Un frère de Mazarin, le cardinal de Sainte-Cécile', *Revue d'histoire diplomatique* 18 (1904), pp. 509–19 (pp. 497–530).
84. Adolphe Chéruel, *Histoire de France pendant la minorité de Louis XIV*, 4 vols (Paris, 1879–80), vol. 2, pp. 171–3.
85. Fontenay-Mareuil, *Mémoires*, vol. 51, pp. 320–2; Chéruel, *Lettres . . . de Mazarin*, vol. 2, pp. 267–70, 8 December 1645, Mazarin to Cardinal Grimaldi.
86. Chéruel, *Lettres . . . de Mazarin*, vol. 2, pp. xxii–xxiii.
87. Davide Maffi, *Il Baluardo della corona. Guerra, esercito, finanze e società nella Lombardia seicentesca (1630–60)* (Florence: Le Monnier università, 2007), pp. 42–3.
88. Chéruel, *Lettres . . . de Mazarin*, vol. 2, pp. xxiii–xxvii, 9 February 1646.
89. Chéruel, *Minorité de Louis XIV*, vol. 2, pp. 211–14, 293–301.
90. Hanlon, *Twilight of a Military Tradition*, pp. 132–3.
91. Mun, 'Cardinal de Sainte-Cécile', pp. 525–30.
92. Guy Joly, *Mémoires*, in Jean François Michaud and Jean Joseph François Poujoulat (eds), *Nouvelle collection des mémoires pour servir a l'histoire de France . . .* 3e série, 10 vols (Paris: Didier, 1838), vol. 2, pp. 115–21.
93. Chéruel, *Lettres . . . de Mazarin*, vol. 2, pp. 467, 26 July 1647, Mazarin to Cardinal Grimaldi (transcribed *in extenso*, vol. 2, pp. xliv–xlvii); vol. 2, pp. 475–7, 21 August 1647, Mazarin to Fontenay-Mareuil, anxious to avoid military commitments to Naples.
94. Chéruel, *Lettres . . . de Mazarin*, vol. 2, pp. 484–6, 6 September 1647 and 9 September 1647, Mazarin to Grimaldi, declaring reluctance to support Guise and scepticism about the outcome of the revolt; vol. 2, p. 524, 25 November 1647, Mazarin to Marquis de Fontenay, expressing grave doubts about the suitability of Guise for the expedition to Naples.
95. For a detailed account of the failure of the Naples expedition, see J. Loiseleur and G. Baguenault de Puchesse, *L'Expédition du duc de Guise à Naples. Lettres et instructions diplomatiques de la cour de France, 1647–48* (Paris: Didier, 1875).
96. Luigi Simeoni, *Francesco I d'Este e la politica italiana del Mazarino* (Bologna: N. Zanichelli, 1922).
97. Odoardo Rombaldi, *Il Duca Francesco I d'Este (1629–1658)* (Modena: Aedes Muratoriana, 1992), pp. 58–67; Chéruel, *Minorité de Louis XIV*, vol. 2, pp. 428–34; vol. 3, pp. 38–41.
98. Rombaldi, *Francesco d'Este*, pp. 77–85; Adolphe Chéruel, *Histoire de France sous le ministère de Mazarin (1651–1661)*, 3 vols (Paris: Hachetter, 1882), vol. 2, pp. 336–8.
99. Oresko, 'The Marriages of the Nieces', pp. 128–31; Poumarède, 'Mazarin, marieur de l'Europe', pp. 205–10.
100. Maffi, *Baluardo della corona*, pp. 55–7; Mario Rizzo, 'Demografia, sussistenza e governo dell'emergenza a Pavia durante l'assedio del 1655', in Buono and Civale, *Battaglie*, pp. 59–97.
101. Chéruel, *Lettres . . . de Mazarin*, vol. 6, pp. 403–4, 18 December 1654, Mazarin to Antonio Barberini. Chéruel cites Thévenot's damning critique of the expedition to Naples and of Guise.
102. Rombaldi, *Francesco d'Este*, pp. 81–6; Hanlon, *Twilight of a Military Tradition*, pp. 133–4.
103. In this respect, these conclusions are not dissimilar from those reached by Paul Sonnino in a recent study of Mazarin's crucial miscalculations and self-deception in the negotiations for the Peace of Westphalia. See Sonnino, *Mazarin's Quest*.
104. For a sensitive evaluation of the successes of French policy in the Empire during the mid-1640s, see Derek Croxton, *Peacemaking in Early Modern Europe: Cardinal Mazarin and the Congress of Westphalia, 1643–48* (Selinsgrove, NJ: Susquehanna University Press, 1999), pp. 72–94, 196–255.

CHAPTER 9

The Learned Ideal of the Mughal *Wazīr*: The Life and Intellectual World of Prime Minister Afzal Khan Shirazi (d. 1639)

Rajeev Kinra

The seventeenth century represented the zenith of the Mughal Empire's power, territorial reach and global influence. Best known for the construction of the Taj Mahal and other iconic monuments of early modern Indo-Islamic architecture, it was also an era when Mughal wealth, religious pluralism and cultural patronage inspired envy and awe practically the world over, including among many of the Europeans who travelled to the subcontinent and reported back on their experiences. Indeed, it was precisely in this period that the term 'Mogul' entered the English language as practically synonymous with conspicuous wealth and splendour. But beyond a merely superficial admiration for all the opulence that Mughal India had to offer, seventeenth-century European observers like Thomas Roe and François Bernier also expressed a keen appreciation for the openness and tolerance of the Mughals' distinct brand of political Islam, a pluralistic approach that used state policies to promote an ideology known at the time as 'universal civility' (*ṣulḥ-i kull*). It was through such policies, Roe argued in a 1640 speech to the English Parliament, that the Mughal emperors had been able to avail themselves of the talents of all of India's multiple ethnic, religious and linguistic communities, and even to attract skilled labour, administrators, literati, scholars and artists from all over the world to their courts. Tolerance, in other words, was good for business; and it was thanks to such policies, Roe pointed out to his fellow MPs, that the reigning emperor Shah Jahan (r. 1628–58) had managed to become the richest man in the world.[1]

Among the many who came to India and thrived under the Mughal dispensation of *ṣulḥ-i kull* was a Persian statesman named Mirza (or sometimes 'Mulla') Shukr Allah Shirazi, better known today by his official title of Afzal Khan (d. 1639). Afzal Khan came to India early in the seventeenth century during the reign of Jahangir (r. 1605–27), the fourth of the so-called Great Mughals whose courts dominated the culture and politics of much of the Indian subcontinent until the early eighteenth century. But it was under Jahangir's successor Shah Jahan, the celebrated builder of the Taj Mahal, that Afzal Khan reached the pinnacle of his career, serving as prime minister (*wazīr*, or *dīwān-i kull*) for nearly a decade.

There have been a number of fruitful studies of the Mughal nobility over the years.

But most of these investigations, a lot of them coming out of the twentieth-century Marxist and nationalist traditions of postcolonial Indian historiography, have also tended to view the Mughal nobility quite abstractly, whether as a military-political-administrative class acting to extract the agrarian surplus that was the Mughals' primary revenue stream, or as a set of nested family networks and ethnic blocs, or even simply as a series of hierarchical points on a litany of fluctuating ranks, titles and offices.[2] These works have taught us a great deal about how the nobility functioned as a kind of 'steel frame' of Mughal politics and administration. But they also tend to leave one with the distinct impression that such nobles operated in a virtual cultural vacuum, almost as mindless politico-military cogs in a vast 'apparatus of empire', as M. Athar Ali once characterised it. Very few works, by contrast, have examined the actual lives and careers of individual Mughal nobles, administrators or statesmen in any detail. There are of course a handful of important exceptions.[3] But most of these are quite dated, and in any case tend to focus primarily on the military and political exploits of Mughal grandees, rarely delving into the more intellectual or humanistic qualities that made some of the great Mughal *wazīr*s and statesmen highly successful in earning the admiration of their contemporaries: their learning, for instance, or their literary pursuits, their expertise in the secretarial arts, the norms of civility and ethics that they promoted, and the eclectic forms of spirituality and mysticism that they cultivated, to name just a few.

These features of the existing historiography on the Mughal nobility have been vigorously critiqued in recent years, most notably by Muzaffar Alam and Sanjay Subrahmanyam.[4] But the fact remains that there is still very little scholarship out there to help us understand what really made a great Mughal statesman like Afzal Khan Shirazi tick, intellectually speaking. This chapter, then, may be seen as a modest effort to address this lacuna, and attempts to show through Afzal Khan's example that for the seventeenth-century Mughal intelligentsia the ideals of good governance (*wizārat*) involved far more than a mere talent for military conquest and authority (*imārat*).

AFZAL KHAN'S EARLY LIFE AND CAREER

One thing to note at the outset is that this is not purely a 'Mughal' story, for Afzal Khan clearly began cultivating the qualities that would make him into one of the most eminent statesmen of his era long before he came to India. He was born in Shiraz (in south-west Iran) sometime around 1570, and over the next few decades he made quite a name for himself as a scholar, administrative savant, diplomat and linguist in various courts of Central and West Asia.[5] According to 'Abd al-Baqi Nahawandi, the author of the Mughal chronicle *Ma'āṣir-i Rahīmī* (1616), talent in administrative matters ran in Afzal Khan's family. His father, for instance, 'was among the great and noble men (*a'yān wa akābir*)' of that 'Abode of the Learned' (*dār al-afāzil*), Shiraz, and as a result 'consistently earned suitable ranks in the worldly courts of the *pādshāh*s of Iraq (i.e. Persia) by distinguishing himself among the specialists of the pen and men of accounts (*arbāb-i qalam wa ahl-i siyāq*)'.[6] According to Nahawandi,

Afzal Khan's father was so accomplished in the art of stylised prose, or *inshā'*, that, in an elegant turn of phrase, 'he routinely robbed the orb of expertise in that art away from the professional scribes and expert men of the pen' (*hamwāra dar ān fann gūy-i dānish az nawīsandagān wa arbāb-i qalam mīrubūd*). 'He had a special talent', Nahawandi adds, 'for keeping the imperial treasury in surplus and the royal affairs in order' (*dar kifāyat-i māl-i dīwān wa ẓabṭ-i mu'āmalāt-i sulṭānī ṭab'i-yi kāfī dāsht*).[7]

Initially following in his father's footsteps, Afzal Khan at an early age began his training in practical skills like calligraphy, accounts, prose composition and other branches of the standard curriculum in the secretarial arts (*fann-i dabīrī*).[8] Apparently, though, he was also a bit of a dreamer, exhibiting a 'worldliness, sensitivity, and inquisitiveness' that led him to reject the material opportunities afforded by his father's courtly connections because 'he saw in them the misfortunes of this world and the next, and did not want to become seduced by that environment'.[9] The implication, clearly, is that even as a youth Afzal Khan was no mere scrivener, but a man of uncommon intellectual and spiritual imagination. Thus, Nahawandi informs us, young Afzal Khan routinely 'sought out the company of seekers and sages'[10] – an early glimpse of the interest in Sufi mysticism and other spiritual pursuits that would colour Afzal Khan's views on the norms of governance and ministerial conduct for much of the rest of his career.

Nahawandi also tells us, significantly, that one of Afzal Khan's early teachers was the noted scholar Taqi al-Din Muhammad Shirazi, who was himself well connected to an influential network of sixteenth- and seventeenth-century intellectuals that has come to be known in modern scholarship as the 'Shiraz School' of scientists, philosophers and scholar-administrators. Broadly speaking, as Ali Anooshahr has recently outlined, those connected to the Shiraz School cultivated and debated amongst themselves an extensive and eclectic curriculum that went far beyond strictly religious or quasi-religious subjects like jurisprudence (*fiqh*), Qur'anic exegesis (*tafsīr*) and the traditional sayings of the Prophet (*hadīs̱*) in favour of subjects like logic, mathematics, astronomy, metaphysics, epistemology, political science and other 'practical sciences' (*'ilm-i amalī*).[11] Despite their polymathic and sometimes recondite interests, many of these Shirazi intellectuals also had important careers as administrators and courtly advisors throughout the Indian Ocean world, including Mughal India and the courts of Deccan Sultanates such as the 'Adil Shahi kingdom of Bijapur. A perfect example of such mobility is one of Taqi al-Din's own teachers, the noted polymath Fath Allah Shirazi (d. 1589), who would himself eventually emigrate to India, where he served for several years at the 'Adil Shahi court in Bijapur before becoming an influential scholar-administrator at the court of the Mughal emperor Akbar (r. 1556–1605).[12]

In their more worldly pursuits, as Anooshahr notes, the intellectuals of the Shiraz School also placed a heavy emphasis on cultivating knowledge in the domains of agricultural administration, irrigation, promoting the welfare of peasants and farmers, and so on – all areas, incidentally, in which Afzal Khan would eventually excel as the Mughal *wazīr* in later decades. To be considered an accomplished intellectual in this milieu, in other words, one was expected not only 'to perfect his "essence" and his mind, but also take on the task of managing a small state'.[13]

In any event, it was through Fath Allah Shirazi that Taqi al-Din Muhammad – and thus too his student, our own Afzal Khan Shirazi – had a direct link to this influential network of scholar-administrators.[14] One contemporary Safavid chronicle, Iskandar Beg Munshi's *Tārīkh-i ʿĀlam-Ārā-yi ʿAbbāsī* (1616), describes Taqi al-Din as having been 'extremely learned and wise' (*bisyār fāzil wa dānishmand*) even among this select company.[15] He is credited with having authored some twenty works in Persian and Arabic, both independent treatises and commentaries in subjects as diverse as mathematics, astronomy, medical science, ethics, statecraft, grammar, linguistics and the use of the astrolabe; he even composed poetry under the pen name 'Fahmi'.[16] Iskandar Beg adds that large crowds of scholars and students used to attend Taqi al-Din's lectures in Shiraz – and among these many disciples, Nahawandi tells us in *Maʾāsir-i Rahīmī*, Afzal Khan quickly distinguished himself for his own 'penetrating insight' (*nazr-i imʿān*).[17]

In short, even at a young age Afzal Khan was beginning to make a name for himself among the scholars and other learned elites (*ʿulamā*) of Shiraz, a community of intellectuals whose influence radiated out far across the Indian Ocean world. At some point in the late 1580s or early 1590s, though, Afzal Khan appears to have made a conscious decision to return to the worldly business of politics and court life, and made his way to Qazwin (then still the Safavid capital).[18] Once there, according to Nahawandi, 'he put his charisma and capabilities (*kaifiyat wa hālat-i khwud*) on display for the local *ʿulamā*", and eventually managed to enter the service of one of the most prominent political families of the era, that of the brothers Farhad Khan Qaramanlu (d. 1598) and Zulfiqar Khan Qaramanlu (d. 1610–11).[19]

The 1580s and 1590s were an especially turbulent period for the Safavid court. Shah Tahmasp's death in 1576 had led to a nearly decade-long struggle for the throne, a contest that ended only with the accession of Shah 'Abbas I (r. 1587–1629), who ended up ruling for a remarkable forty-two years. It was a period of shifting alliances and mutual suspicion at court, during which these internal tensions were exacerbated by some very real external threats to Safavid power, in particular the rising challenge from the Uzbek Khanate on their eastern frontier and the continuing rivalry with the Ottomans to the north and west. Many of these challenges lingered well into the tumultuous first decade of Shah 'Abbas's reign and thus, in the process of stabilising the political situation and reconsolidating Safavid territorial control over many parts of Iran, the Qaramanlu brothers proved to be stalwart allies of the court. Farhad Khan in particular emerged as one of Shah 'Abbas's most trusted and reliable military commanders, leading numerous campaigns across Iran over the course of the 1590s, most notably in strategically vital Caspian provinces like Azerbaijan, Gilan and Mazandaran. These regions were situated just north of the capital Qazwin, sandwiched between the frontiers with the Ottomans (to the west) and the Uzbek Khanate (to the east), and lay directly along the upper branch of the overland 'Silk Road' trade route from Central Asia to the Mediterranean. Besides leading these military campaigns, Farhad Khan also served several stints as governor of Shirvan, Azerbaijan, Gilan and Mazandaran during this period, growing so powerful that at least one contemporary observer remarked that the Safavid realm had been divided into two halves: one controlled by Farhad Khan Qaramanlu, and the other controlled by the rest of the nobility.[20]

We do not know exactly when Afzal Khan began working for Farhad Khan Qaramanlu, or in what capacity, but presumably he was involved in many of these activities, especially the campaigns of the early 1590s. Nahawandi does tell us that Afzal Khan's association with such a commanding presence at the Safavid court gave him yet another opportunity to display his learning and erudition 'among the [best] scholars and learned men of Iran' (*dar miyāna-yi 'ulamā wa fuzalā-yi īrān*).[21] Indeed, other sources describe Farhad Khan's court as lavishing patronage on literature and the arts. For instance, he built a library in the city of Simnan, where he employed the noted calligraphers Mir 'Imad Hasani and 'Ali Reza 'Abbasi Tabrizi.[22] He and his brother Zulfiqar also both served terms as warden of the shrine of Imam 'Ali Reza at Ardabil, one of the holiest sites in *shī'a* Islam, and a place of particular religio-political significance for the Safavid royal family.[23] It is perhaps in reference to this connection to the shrine at Ardabil that Nahawandi also mentions that, during his employment under Farhad Khan Qaramanlu, Afzal Khan 'worked to the best of his power and capabilities toward addressing the needs, affairs, and betterment of the pious and the needy' (*ba qadr-i imkān-o-maqdūr dar kār-sāzī wa muhimm-guzārī wa iṣlāḥ-kār-i ẓu'afā'-o-musalmānān mīkoshīd*).[24]

During this time Zulfiqar Khan Qaramanlu was also an important member of the Safavid political establishment and held several prominent posts including a stint as the governor (*beglar-begi*) of Azerbaijan, a position that his brother had once also held. Then, in 1595, at his brother Farhad's recommendation, Zulfiqar Khan was appointed to lead a diplomatic embassy to the Ottoman court, the main purpose of which was to convey a letter of condolence from Shah 'Abbas regarding the death of the Ottoman Sultan Murad III, along with congratulations on the accession of his successor, Muhammad III (r. 1595–1603).[25] Afzal Khan accompanied Zulfiqar Khan on this mission, and the assignment gave him an opportunity 'to demonstrate his knowledge and wisdom for the people of Rum [i.e. Anatolia]', as Nahawandi later put it.[26] Besides the chance to show off his learning and intellect to a new audience, this direct exposure to the Ottoman court would also pay great dividends for Afzal Khan later on during his years in Mughal service, as he became an important advisor on diplomatic relations between the two empires, especially under Emperor Shah Jahan (r. 1628–58). And even during the Ottoman embassy itself, Nahawandi tells us, Afzal Khan had begun to establish a reputation as an effective diplomat, upon whose 'rectitude and good advice' Zulfiqar Khan consistently relied throughout their sojourn in Anatolia.[27]

At this point Afzal Khan was still quite young, in his mid- to late twenties, but he was clearly moving up the career ladder of Safavid service elites, and beginning to forge connections with the upper echelons of the Safavid military and political establishment. But there was trouble lurking just on the horizon. Afzal Khan returned with the rest of Zulfiqar Khan's Ottoman embassy to the Safavid court in 1597 – incidentally, the same year that a pair of Mughal ambassadors was given leave to return to Akbar's court in India, accompanied by the Safavid envoy Manuchihr Beg bearing lavish gifts and expressions of friendship[28] – whereupon he appears to have rejoined Farhad Khan's inner circle. Barely a year later, however, Farhad Khan Qaramanlu himself came under a cloud of suspicion and was executed on Shah

'Abbas's orders in Herat in 1598. The exact circumstances and reasons for his execution are unclear, and have been a subject of debate among historians almost from the time of the events themselves.[29] But for our purposes the main point is that Farhad Khan's death meant that Afzal Khan had lost his main benefactor at court. Initially, at least, Zulfiqar Khan Qaramanlu somehow managed to avoid the suspicion that had doomed his brother and remained in the court's good graces for over a decade, in some cases even taking over some of his brother Farhad's duties. But this did nothing, apparently, to allay whatever concerns Afzal Khan may have had about his own security. Thus, Nahawandi explains, 'having decided it was no longer safe to remain at the royal court',[30] Afzal Khan withdrew once again from political life and relocated to the western city of Hamadan.[31]

Once in Hamadan, Nahawandi explains, Afzal Khan found himself once again enjoying the 'dialogue, counsel, and guidance' (*mubāḥaṣa wa ifāda wa istifāda*) of another of the great scholar-administrators of the era, Mirza Ibrahim Hamadani (d. 1616–17).[32] Mirza Ibrahim came from a notable family of Husaini Sayyids (those who claimed direct descent from the Prophet Muhammad's grandson Husain), and his father had served as the chief judge (*qāẓī*) of Hamadan during Shah Tahmasp's reign. In turn, Mirza Ibrahim himself held the same position under Shah 'Abbas I, although, according to the Safavid chronicler Iskandar Beg Munshi, 'his deputies [including perhaps our own Afzal Khan] took care of most of the work in the law courts . . . [so that he could] devote most of his time to study and research'.[33] Iskandar Beg refers to him several times as 'the most learned of the learned' (*'allāmat al-'ulamā'*), and notes that besides having studied with such intellectual luminaries of the previous generation as Mirza Makhdum Isfahani and Mir Fakhr al-Din Sammaki (who also taught the celebrated philosopher Mir Damad), Mirza Ibrahim himself also gave lectures and instructed students of his own, and 'produced a number of books and detailed glosses in the rational and philosophical sciences (*ma'qūlāt wa ḥukmiyāt*)', including several notable commentaries on the medical and philosophical works of the great medieval polymaths Nasir al-Din Tusi and Abu Ali Ibn Sina ('Avicenna').[34] It is perhaps in light of these intellectual pursuits that Nahawandi, among various other epithets and high praise, lauds Mirza Ibrahim as 'the Plato of the age (*aflāṭūn al-zamānī*)' and a latter-day 'Bu 'Ali [Ibn Sina] (*bū 'alī al-ṣānī*)'.[35]

It would appear, too, that Afzal Khan's relationship with Mirza Ibrahim involved a certain amount of what can only be described as spiritual tourism. 'Under his guidance', Nahawandi explains, '[Afzal Khan] made pilgrimages to the most eminent holy shrines (*ziyārat-i 'atabāt-i 'āliyāt*) and traveled throughout Mesopotamia (*'irāq-i 'arab*), after which he returned to Persia (*'irāq-i 'ajam*) in His Excellence's company.' This period of study, training and wandering via Hamadan appears to have lasted about six or seven years, after which, sometime in or around 1608, 'bearing a renowned legacy of learning this compassionate one decided to travel to India, and made his way via the port of Cambay to the provincial capital of Burhanpur'.[36]

AFZAL KHAN'S EARLY CAREER IN MUGHAL SERVICE

As a Persian emigré in India, Afzal Khan was hardly unique or out of place. Indeed, by Afzal Khan's lifetime South Asia had long been part of the larger Persianate world, and there was a rich history of traders, poets, intellectuals, religious divines, statesmen and conquerors from Central and West Asia coming to India for fame, fortune, adventure and asylum.[37] Certain skills, particularly literary talent, secretarial and administrative expertise, and spiritual wisdom were portable across this transregional Persianate ecumene – often referred to in contemporary sources as 'ajam, to distinguish it from the Arab world – and in high demand among the wealthy courts of South Asia where rulers, nobles and other patrons were eager to stake a claim to cultural and political pre-eminence in the wider Perso-Islamic world. The Mughal Empire is an especially dramatic example of this dynamic, famously attracting scores of poets, intellectuals and other prominent figures who for the most part found a welcoming, tolerant cultural and political atmosphere, and in turn helped to shape the Mughal cultural and political landscape throughout the sixteenth and seventeenth centuries.

When he arrived in Burhanpur, Afzal Khan's learning, administrative acumen and diplomatic experience helped him to make a quick impression on the Mughal nobility and royal family. In those days Burhanpur was a southern capital of sorts for the Mughal Empire, used as a staging area for campaigns into the Deccan Plateau and occasionally points further south. It was also the base of operations for one of the leading grandees of the Mughal court, 'Abd al-Rahim Khan-i Khanan (1556–1626), into whose circle Afzal Khan was soon introduced. 'Abd al-Rahim was renowned for his cultural patronage, and his court at Burhanpur was considered an outpost of refinement and good taste. Besides patronising some of the most accomplished early proponents of the new tarz-i tāza, or 'fresh style', that was then sweeping the early modern Indo-Persian literary scene, 'Abd al-Rahim was also a multilingual poet himself, well versed in the Indo-Persian literary canon, and fond of experimenting with poetry in Hindi and Sanskrit. He was also fluent in Turkish, and was said to be conversant in Portuguese. Meanwhile, his atelier of painters was rivalled perhaps only by that of the Mughal emperor himself.[38]

According to Ma'āṣir-i Raḥīmī, Afzal Khan quickly became one of 'Abd al-Rahim Khan-i Khanan's favourite companions, with the two men engaged in conversation 'day and night'.[39] He served 'Abd al-Rahim for some three years, during which time, according to Nahawandi, 'Abd al-Rahim repeatedly wrote to Jahangir boasting of the Shirazi émigré's wisdom and talents, and encouraging the emperor to offer him a ranked position (manṣab) in the Mughal administrative hierarchy. Jahangir eventually acquiesced, assigning Afzal Khan to 'an illustrious rank', but it was also around this time that Afzal Khan left 'Abd al-Rahim's service, for along with his new rank Jahangir also reassigned him to serve as dīwān, or chief executive officer, to the ambitious Prince Khurram (later known as Shah Jahan).[40]

The position of dīwān in Mughal governmental parlance typically combined two crucial administrative functions. In his primary role, the dīwān was a kind of 'chief fiscal officer' who oversaw the imperial revenue and record-keeping offices of the

Mughal chancery. He managed the veritable armies of clerks and accountants who produced and archived the voluminous bureaucratic records pertaining to the Mughal revenue system, land surveys, property records, taxation, charity, salaries, and so forth. But the role also included overseeing the Mughal 'office of correspondence' (*dār al-inshā'*), and its cadre of state secretaries, who were specifically tasked with drafting imperial orders, keeping diaries of day-to-day imperial business, and ghost-writing royal orders, correspondence and other kinds of official documents.

It was the Mughal *dīwān*'s responsibility for this last function that made him a crucial official in the domain of statesmanship, diplomacy and foreign policy. Like most early modern states the world over, virtually any time the Mughal government interacted with another state, whether a subordinate client state or a rival empire like the Ottomans or Safavids (or the Habsburgs, for that matter), it did so through official letters and other kinds of diplomatic correspondence. A good *dīwān* was able to manage this entire epistolary operation on behalf of the king (or in this case, prince), and, given the levels of delicacy and discretion that were sometimes involved in the diplomatic manoeuvring among rival early modern states and their clients, the *dīwān* had to be an extremely trustworthy and competent figure. Competent, that is, in the same ensemble of secretarial arts that were the stock and trade of the professional scribes and secretaries (also known as *munshīs*, *dabīrs* and *kātibs*) he was oversee-ing: expertise in the conventions of 'artful prose' (*inshā'*), knowledge of the literary canon, the ability to use coded language, and of course a mastery of the complex norms of Indo-Persian epistolary and diplomatic etiquette. Being fluent in multiple languages did not hurt either, and someone like Afzal Khan, who possessed not only a native mastery of Persian (the chief diplomatic language in most of South, Central and West Asia during this period), but also fluency in Arabic and Turkish, would have been a useful advisor to have around even without all the other skills, talents and wisdom that he brought with him. In short, the *dīwān* was an extremely important officer in Mughal imperial governance, and appointment as *dīwān* for any member of the royal house – much less one as prominent as Prince Khurram, who by the 1610s was already emerging as the crown prince and likely successor to the emperor – was a notable accomplishment, one that carried with it a great deal of authority and influence.

By 1615, Afzal Khan had emerged as one of Prince Khurram/Shah Jahan's chief diplomatic fixers. It was he, for instance, who led the delegation to negotiate a final peace settlement with Rana Amar Singh (d. 1620), the Hindu ruler of Mewar, one of the few houses of 'Rajput' (literally, 'descended from kings') chieftains in northern India that had yet to capitulate to Mughal imperial power. Led by Shah Jahan, the brutal three-year campaign against Mewar had greatly burnished the prince's reputa-tion as a military commander, and was one of the signal military-political achieve-ments of Emperor Jahangir's entire reign. It is noteworthy, then, that when the campaign was concluded it was none other than Afzal Khan who delivered the news of Rana Amar Singh's capitulation to Emperor Jahangir on the prince's behalf, and helped to broker the subsequent détente. In fact, it is precisely in connection with his contributions to the Mewar campaign and its resolution that Afzal Khan is first men-tioned in Jahangir's memoirs and identified by the official title of 'Afzal Khan' ('the

Learned Khan').[41] In conjunction with this elevation in title, Afzal Khan was also promoted in December 1616 to serve as deputy governor of the crucial north-western province of Lahore, even as he continued to serve as Prince Khurram's *dīwān*.[42]

It should be noted, too, that in the events of 1615 Afzal Khan worked in tandem with another close confidant of Prince Khurram/Shah Jahan, a Brahman aide named Sundar Das (d. 1623), who was himself promoted and awarded a lofty new title ('Ray-i Rayan') at the conclusion of the Mewar affair.[43] Sundar Das originally hailed from the class of landed gentry (*zamīndār*s) who were now being incorporated into the Mughal governing apparatus, and he emerged over the course of the 1610s as one of Prince Khurram's closest advisors, serving for much of that decade in the official capacity of the prince's steward (*mīr-i sāmān*), but also making a name for himself as an astute military strategist.[44] Indeed, his direct contributions to Prince Khurram's military successes over the course of the 1610s eventually earned him the lofty title of 'Raja Bikramajit' – 'an important title among the Hindus', as Jahangir notes in his memoir, adding that 'he is truly a suitable servant and worthy of patronage'.[45]

The duo of Afzal Khan and Sundar Das also teamed up for another signature diplomatic achievement of Jahangir's reign (and Shah Jahan's princely career), the negotiation of a peace settlement with the 'Adil Shahi Sultanate of Bijapur, a wealthy and powerful independent Deccan state on India's western coast. The complex historical background and web of shifting alliances that set the stage for this moment are far too complicated to recount here in any detail.[46] But as in the Mewar campaign – indeed, perhaps even more so in this case – Afzal Khan's diplomatic skills were crucial to the Deccan operation's successful outcome. While a major military operation led by Prince Khurram/Shah Jahan was launched, Afzal Khan and Sundar Das were sent to Bijapur at the start of the campaign to begin settlement negotiations, and by March 1617 they had already secured the 'Adil Shah's submission and reported the happy news back to Jahangir, who included their letter in his memoir.[47] Five months later, in August 1617, the duo personally escorted the 'Adil Shah's emissaries to Burhanpur, where they offered Bijapur's formal submission to Prince Khurram in person – having brought with them, as Jahangir notes, 'suitable offerings of gems, jeweled utensils, elephants, and horses – more than had ever come as an offering at any time before'.[48]

Thus, in the space of barely three years, Jahangir's forces had engineered arguably two of the most substantial Mughal military-political accomplishments in decades. That a good deal of the credit should go to Prince Khurram's strategic vision and determination is undeniable, a fact that was recognised even at the time. Indeed, it was precisely in the wake of the successful Deccan campaign that in October 1617 Jahangir officially gave his son the title by which he would be subsequently known to posterity – Shah Jahan, that is, 'King of the World' – and took the unprecedented step of placing a seat for the prince next to his own imperial throne.[49] But military might was not the sole factor in either of these campaigns. Indeed, savvy statesmanship and diplomacy played a crucial role in achieving the Mughals' imperial objectives in both Mewar and Bijapur, and in that domain arguably no one played a more critical role than Afzal Khan Shirazi.

In later years, Afzal Khan's long-time diplomatic partner Sundar Das began serving more exclusively as a military commander;[50] indeed, he would later be killed in battle during Shah Jahan's rebellion against Jahangir (see below). But Afzal Khan himself appears to have acted in a mostly administrative capacity. Throughout this period, for instance, he is referred to in Jahangir's memoir, and in other sources such as Khwaja Kamgar Husaini's *Ma'āṣir-i Jahāngīrī*, simply as Shah Jahan's '*dīwān*'.[51] A lot of that time was spent administering the new Deccan territories, over which the Mughals' actual control remained tentative throughout the seventeenth century. Meanwhile, at some point during the 1610s Afzal Khan's brother 'Abd al-Haqq Shirazi, or 'Amanat Khan' (about whom more below), also entered Mughal service, and in May 1619 he took a page from his older brother's book and undertook a diplomatic mission to Golconda, another independent sultanate of the Deccan.[52] Soon after, trouble was again stirring in the Deccan and Shah Jahan was once more dispatched to pacify a series of insurrections. These were mostly put down within a year, and in May 1621 it was Afzal Khan who once more travelled from Burhanpur to Agra as Shah Jahan's personal envoy to report the imperial victories to his father the emperor. As a reward for being the bearer of such happy news, Jahangir presented Afzal Khan with 'a robe of honor, an elephant, and a jeweled inkpot', and dispatched the *dīwān* back to the Deccan laden with gifts for Shah Jahan, including a 'ruby plume holder' (*sarpech*) valued at some 50,000 rupees that had been specially sent from Iran by the Safavid ruler Shah 'Abbas a few months earlier, and had once belonged to the celebrated Timurid ruler, mathematician and astronomer Ulugh Beg (d. 1449).[53]

Beginning in 1622, however, the relationship between Shah Jahan and his father began to fray, as a series of minor misunderstandings about the prince's privileges, responsibilities and assignments ballooned into outright hostility and mistrust. From Shah Jahan's perspective, it began increasingly to appear that outright rebellion was his only option. Despite this growing tension, however, it looked as though there might still be a chance for cooler heads to prevail, and it is telling that under these tense circumstances it was Afzal Khan whom Shah Jahan sent in October 1622 to plead with Jahangir in a last-ditch effort to resolve their disputes and avert a full-scale crisis. In the end, the *dīwān*'s mission was unsuccessful, and the language Jahangir uses to describe the audience in his memoir is strikingly dismissive and glib, especially given the high stakes involved. At the same time, Jahangir's remarks also betray a certain grudging respect for Afzal Khan's (usually) persuasive style, and are indicative of just how much Shah Jahan had come to rely on Afzal Khan's capabilities as a diplomatic fixer, and of the wider reputation the Khan had earned as an astute crisis manager:

> Khurram's divan Afzal Khan brought a letter from him. Cloaking his outrageous behavior in apologies, he had sent Afzal Khan in hopes that he might be able to advance his interests with slick talk and smooth over his rough spots. Paying not the slightest attention, I didn't even turn my face to him.[54]

This snub notwithstanding, Jahangir does note curtly that a couple of weeks later he 'gave Afzal Khan a robe of honor and dismissed him' with a stern warning to Shah

Jahan to focus on administering the territories for which he was responsible and demonstrating his obedience, or face the consequences. By that point, however, the strain in their relationship was clearly beyond repair, and the subsequent rebellion of Shah Jahan would convulse Mughal politics for nearly four years.

The exact circumstances and many plot twists that characterised Shah Jahan's rebellion are exceedingly complicated, and need not detain us here.[55] Suffice it to say, despite some modest successes, Shah Jahan and his partisans spent much of the next few years either thwarted or on the run, and ultimately, in 1626, he was forced to concede defeat and try to reconcile with his father. Concerning Afzal Khan, the main thing to note is that he remained loyal to Shah Jahan throughout this entire period, coordinating the prince's affairs as best he could. This included at least one more diplomatic mission to the Deccan in early 1624, a fruitless attempt to recruit the support of some of the same rulers in Bijapur and Ahmadnagar with whom Shah Jahan (on Jahangir's behalf) had been skirmishing off and on for nearly a decade.

Jahangir does a fair amount of crowing in his memoir about the Deccan rulers' refusal to rally behind the rebellious prince, but he also notes in passing another extremely important moment in Afzal Khan's life that was connected with these events. While Afzal Khan was away on his Deccan embassy, his son, Mirza Muhammad, had attempted to desert Shah Jahan's camp and flee 'with his mother and womenfolk'.[56] Embattled as he was at the time, Shah Jahan was predictably in no mood to tolerate even the slightest hint of treachery. He therefore immediately dispatched a team of officers to hunt Mirza Muhammad down and bring him back, dead or alive. When they caught up with him there was a scuffle, and Mirza Muhammad was killed and unceremoniously beheaded. The grim irony that Afzal Khan's only son had been cut down by Shah Jahan's agents even as Afzal Khan himself was steadfastly using every tool in his diplomatic arsenal to rally support for the prince's cause was not lost on Mughal observers. Even Jahangir, with a still detectable measure of respect and sympathy, makes a point of noting that 'Afzal Khan was still there [in Bijapur on Shah Jahan's business] when he received word that his son had been killed and his house destroyed, leaving him devastated.'[57]

One can only imagine how difficult this must have been for Afzal Khan, who had been so consistently loyal to Shah Jahan for over a decade, and might have hoped that his son would be shown some mercy, if only for his father's sake. The sources, oddly enough, are relatively silent on the fallout. But there are hints that Afzal Khan's loyalties may have begun to waver around this time, for Jahangir notes in his memoir that sometime in mid-1624, while Shah Jahan was still in rebellion, 'Afzal Khan, Shahjahan's divan who had remained in Bijapur, [came] to court, obtained an interview, and was showered with regal favour.'[58] Perhaps after his son's assassination Afzal Khan spent some time in Bijapur mulling over how to respond, and then decided to shift his allegiance toward the emperor. One might have assumed that a change of allegiance from one of Shah Jahan's most notable aides-de-camp would have been a newsworthy topic for contemporary chroniclers and other commentators, but unfortunately none of the available sources clarifies or elaborates on the exact circumstances. Indeed, interestingly enough, Jahangir and other sources like Khwaja Kamgar Husaini's *Ma'āṣir-i Jahāngīrī* continue to refer to Afzal Khan during this period as Shah Jahan's *dīwān*, despite his apparent defection from the prince's camp.

In any event, it appears that in the closing years of Jahangir's reign Afzal Khan began increasingly to work directly for the emperor, rather than in the prince's inner circle, as he had done for so many years. In 1626, as Shah Jahan's rebellion was finally coming to an end, Jahangir appointed Afzal Khan to the position of imperial steward (*mīr-i sāmān*), one of the most important posts in the Mughal military-administrative apparatus. And from that point until Jahangir's death in October 1627, Afzal Khan was based mainly in Lahore, rather than with Shah Jahan in Deccan, where the prince had returned after patching up his differences with Jahangir and re-entering the court's good graces.

Whatever resentment Afzal Khan may have harboured toward Shah Jahan over his son's death, however, he does not appear to have borne a lasting grudge. Quite the contrary, in the succession struggle that followed Jahangir's death Afzal Khan re-emerged as one of Shah Jahan's key allies, and even played a vital role in helping Shah Jahan to secure the throne.[59] Whether he did this out of a continuing sense of duty, honour and loyalty toward his estranged patron, or simply because he felt that Shah Jahan would make the best emperor, we do not know. But whatever Afzal Khan's underlying motivations were, it is clear that the war of succession after Jahangir's death provided an opportunity for him to mend his relationship with Shah Jahan, and even, it would seem, strengthen their bond. Indeed, Afzal Khan served Shah Jahan loyally for roughly another dozen years, including nearly a decade as the *wazīr* (also referred to in Mughal parlance as the *dīwān-i kull*, or 'prime minister') for the empire as a whole. It is to this late stage of Afzal Khan's career, and what it tells us about the theory, practice and ideals of Mughal governance, that we now turn.

MYSTICAL CIVILITY AND AFZAL KHAN'S CAREER AS PRIME MINISTER

At the beginning of Shah Jahan's reign Afzal Khan was initially assigned to share many of the chief executive duties with another nobleman by the name of Iradat Khan. Whether this is indicative of lingering mistrust between Afzal Khan and Shah Jahan is unclear. After barely a year, though, Afzal Khan 'was appointed *wazīr* in his own right', on account of what the contemporary observer Chandar Bhan Brahman describes as 'his intellect of Aristotelian genius' (*fahhāma-yi Arasṭo-manish*).[60] Several other sources record that the occasion was marked by a revealing chronogram that exalted both the king and his trusted advisor in grand historical terms: 'Plato has become the minister of Alexander' (*shud Falāṭūn wazīr-i Iskandar* = 1038 AH = 1629 CE).[61]

The 1630s were an eventful decade in Mughal politics and cultural life. It was, for instance, early in that decade – 17 June 1631 to be precise – that the beloved Queen Mumtaz Mahal died in childbirth, sending paroxysms of grief throughout not only the royal family, but also the court as a whole. Of course, Shah Jahan's commitment to build a tomb worthy of his love for Mumtaz would give rise to one of the world's great monuments, the Taj Mahal, most of which was built in the decade that followed – that is, in the same period that Afzal Khan served as chief minister, until his death in 1639. Mumtaz had died in Burhanpur, where Shah Jahan had established a camp during the early years of his reign, and from which the emperor directed yet another series of Deccan campaigns in 1631–2. The early 1630s also saw campaigns against the Portuguese at Hughly (1632) and internal challenges to Shah Jahan's authority in the form of rebellions by two former Mughal allies, Khan Jahan Lodi (1631) and Jujhar Singh Bundela (1635). But, on a more positive note, a détente with the Qutb Shahi Sultans of Golconda was successfully negotiated in 1636, while on the north-west frontier the Mughals were able to retake the crucial strategic fort of Qandahar from the Safavids in 1638 (though they would lose it again not long thereafter). The decade also saw several other massive new building projects besides the Taj Mahal, such as Jahangir's tomb complex in Lahore (completed in 1637) and the beginning of construction for the new capital of 'Shahjahanabad' in northern Delhi in 1639.

All of this took place while Afzal Khan was at the helm of the Mughal fiscal, logistical and diplomatic machine. Afzal Khan's varied experiences clearly contributed to his effectiveness as a manager of this vast administrative apparatus, and his shepherding of the Mughal imperial project more generally. As chief minister, one of his responsibilities was of course to review important imperial correspondence and official orders (*farmāns*) before they were circulated. Thus many of the surviving Mughal edicts from the first decade of Shah Jahan's reign bear his seal alongside that of the emperor.[62] But Afzal Khan did not just review and approve such documents. For especially sensitive matters, he was often tasked with composing them himself. Sometime in 1636–7, for instance, it was Afzal Khan who drafted the diplomatic correspondence and arranged the gifts for a Mughal embassy to the Ottoman court, a task for which he was presumably able to draw upon his own personal diplomatic experience in the Ottoman Empire. According to 'Abd al-Hamid Lahori's *Pādshāhnāma*, besides composing the official royal letters to the Ottoman Sultan Murad IV (r. 1623–40) on Shah Jahan's behalf, Afzal Khan also penned at least one courtesy letter to his personal counterpart at the Sublime Porte, the Ottoman grand *wazīr* (*wazīr-i a 'ẓam*).[63]

Being a master statesman in this cultural context, in other words, also meant being an expert in epistolary etiquette and the various other forms of artful prose (*inshā'*) that were the key mediums of discourse among learned Indo-Persian (and in this case, Turkish) elites. 'Official' government correspondence of this period was extremely stylised, and full of highly regimented and ornate codes, conventions and salutations that shifted in subtle ways depending on the difference in status (real or perceived) between the sender and recipient. And, while more everyday correspondence among Indo-Persian elites was usually far less regimented and formalised, it was nevertheless also typically written in an extremely learned idiom of Persian, however mundane the subject matter. Thus a true master of the epistolary arts like Afzal Khan would also have had to master the classical poetic canons and conventions that were staples of courtly Indo-Persian life and thus featured prominently in letter-writing and other forms of *inshā'*.[64]

The ideal Mughal *wazīr*, in short, had not only to embody certain norms of civility and comportment, but also display a broad range of classical learning in literature, rhetoric, history and composition, simply in order to do his job. Moreover, it was not just monarchs and other members of the military, political and diplomatic elite who valued such qualities in an ideal *wazīr*, but also members of the everyday civil service – the many clerks, accountants and secretaries who actually managed the business of empire, and who saw in someone like Afzal Khan a role model whose learning and civility they could emulate. In the Mughal context, these included the many Hindu secretaries who worked in the chancellery, fiscal office (*dīwānī*) or one of the other branches of bureaucracy that were under the *wazīr*'s supervision.

Indeed, sources tell us of a number of Hindu secretaries and other aides who worked directly with Afzal Khan during this period. We know, for instance, about a certain Nand Rai, who worked as a secretary (*munshī*) for Afzal Khan and was apparently very skilled in the art of composing extemporaneous Persian chronograms.[65] Even better known was another of Afzal Khan's *munshī*s by the name of Diyanat Rai Nagauri, who had been in the Mughal administrative service since Jahangir's time, and spent many of those years as one of Afzal Khan's most trusted assistants. Afzal Khan's dependence on Diyanat Ray became the stuff of minor legend, in fact, and for decades after his death an anecdote circulated in which a wag at his funeral had eulogised the Khan by suggesting that when the angels of death, Munkar and Nakir, appeared at his grave to ask him to account for his life and deeds, he had simply replied: 'Ask Diyanat Ray, he can answer' (*az Diyānat Rāy bapursad, ū jawāb khwāhad dād*).[66] Afzal Khan's mentorship clearly served Diyanat Ray well, too, because after the Khan's death Shah Jahan appointed Diyanat Ray to serve as interim *dīwān* for a period of nearly a year, before the post officially went to the nobleman Islam Khan Mashshadi.[67]

But far and away the most celebrated of Afzal Khan's Hindu protégés was *munshī* Chandar Bhan Brahman (d. c. 1670), one of the great Indo-Persian prose stylists and poets of the era. We do not know exactly when or how Chandar Bhan entered Afzal Khan's service, but it was definitely sometime during Jahangir's reign, and Chandar Bhan continued to work closely with the Khan all through the latter's tenure as prime minister, right up until Afzal Khan's death in 1639.[68] Chandar Bhan was thus in an excellent position to observe Afzal Khan's character and managerial style, and he offers numerous encomia to the Khan's learning and civility throughout his memoir of life at Shah Jahan's court, *Chahār Chaman* (*The Four Gardens*). Besides his administrative work, Chandar Bhan was a fixture at the Khan's literary salons, both as an audience member and as a participant, and the two also carried on a regular epistolary correspondence.[69]

One important thing that we learn from Chandar Bhan's account is that Mughal administration was far from static, and there were continual efforts to tweak and refine the system when necessary – an approach that, as mentioned above, hearkens back to Afzal Khan's decades-old connection to the Shiraz School of scholar-administrators. A good *wazīr*, in Chandar Bhan's view, had always to be open to new ways of improving the administration, and one of the things that distinguished Afzal Khan in his eyes was the *wazīr*'s willingness to innovate and update policies when necessary. This dedication to maximising 'economic productivity and the affluence of the people' (*kifāyat-i māl wa rafāhat-i ra'īyat*), Chandar Bhan was confident, would definitely earn Afzal Khan 'a good name for himself in this life and the next'.[70]

But it was not just Afzal Khan's administrative acumen and book learning that impressed Chandar Bhan. He also found his boss to be an astute literary mentor, noting at one point that

on many occasions [Afzal Khan] requested that the poems of this lowly author be conveyed to his forgiving ear, among which this couplet [of mine] was particularly dear to his heart: 'With the heart's eye I catch a glimpse of the witness to true Meaning / The veil is [actually] a looking glass for the man of real vision.'[71]

Years later, when Chandar Bhan was assigned to work for another of Shah Jahan's most eminent *wazīr*s, Sa'd Allah Khan (d. 1656), he wrote a letter to his new supervisor requesting literary guidance similar to what he used to receive from Afzal Khan, explaining that

when this humblest of servants had the good fortune to be employed in the service of that most eminent scholar and intellectual of the age, Afzal Khan, I used to send a fresh *ghazal* [i.e. short lyric poem] to him every day for suggestions, that it might be transformed under the examination of the late Khan's alchemical gaze.[72]

Clearly, then, if Chandar Bhan's account is any indication, Afzal Khan's literary expertise and patronage were important factors in his overall reputation for gentility and civility among contemporaries at the Mughal court. Chandar Bhan also marvelled at the *wazīr*'s sense of detachment (*bī-ta'alluqī*) from material concerns, and the uncanny mystical sensibility that Afzal Khan incorporated into his approach to governance. Thus, while Chandar Bhan consistently praises Afzal Khan's intellect and administrative abilities in *Chahār Chaman*, he also wonders at what he describes as 'the inner purity and compassionate heart of that knower of spiritual and universal mysteries'.[73] To illustrate these important aspects of Afzal Khan's character, Chandar Bhan narrates a string of anecdotes about the *wazīr*'s humility, lack of interest in material wealth, and ability to balance the concerns of governmental efficiency with a spiritual ethos reminiscent of a Sufi *darwesh*. In one of the anecdotes, the 'Plato-esque scholar' is suddenly transported to an almost trance-like state and 'overcome by compassion' upon hearing a single line of mystical text that Chandar Bhan had read to him. 'After he regained his senses', Chandar Bhan tells us, Afzal Khan immediately grabbed a pen and composed a letter replete with esoteric mystical aphorisms to the noted calligrapher Aqa Rashid Daylami (d. 1670–1), who, according to Chandar Bhan, 'was among the sagacious Khan's most trusted and intimate friends'.[74]

In another anecdote, Chandar Bhan tells of an occasion when Mu'izz al-Mulk, the magistrate of the port of Surat, sent Afzal Khan some sort of novel eye-glass (*'ainak*) as a gift. This may have been a telescope, many of which were brought to India by

Europeans in those days as diplomatic gifts, or perhaps it was some kind of kaleido-scope. The text does not quite specify, but Chandar Bhan does make clear that it was something that had the effect of either magnifying or multiplying objects for those who looked through it. He explains that while Afzal Khan was willing to accept the gift because it did not really have any material value (*chūn māliyatī nadāsht*), and thus could not be perceived as a bribe, the *wazīr* nevertheless had some doubts about the gadget's usefulness from a philosophical point of view, which he expressed in a terse reply to his colleague:

> Copy of the missive (*raqīma*) that the learned,
> Aristotle-like Afzal Khan had written to Muʿizz al-Mulk
>
> One can only hope that Allah on high will grant our ilk deliverance from the prison of this illusory existence (*hastī-yi mauhūm*) and from the contemplation of this ephemeral multiplicity. The viewing glass that you sent – which shows one thing as a multiplicity – has arrived. [But] this inmate of the prison of multiplicity is looking, rather, for a viewing glass that will turn such panoply into a unity. If you come across anyone who has such a glass, do give me some indication so that I can enlighten my eye by meeting him, and, having gotten hold of such a glass I can look through it and deliver myself from the prison of all this multiplicity.[75]

Even the most mundane transactions, it would seem, could be infused with a potent Sufi sensibility – in this case a meditation on the mystical concept of 'unity of being' (*waḥdat al-wujūd*) – in the hands of a learned administrator like Afzal Khan.

While Chandar Bhan's record of these conversations may seem somewhat recondite, in fact what we really see being articulated here is a distinct, if slightly idealised, Mughal attitude towards political power and the responsibilities of those who wielded it. In Chandar Bhan's view the ideal king, the ideal *wazīr*, and even the ideal secretary should not use their position for personal gain, but rather for the benefit of the general public. He makes this eminently clear later on in the text, when he records a dialogue with the *wazīr* Saʿd Allah Khan in which he asks the latter directly: 'should one's own interests (*irāda-yi khwud*) take precedence over the public interest (*irāda-yi khalq*), or should one rather give preference to the public interest over one's own?' The *wazīr* replies unequivocally that 'to the best of one's ability' (*tā maqdūr bāshad*) the public benefit should always override an adminis-trator's temptation to use his position for personal gain.[76] But how is a government official supposed to combat such temptations, in practice? The answer, Chandar Bhan suggests, lies in a commitment to an ethos of personal humility and detach-ment (*bī-taʿalluqī*) that is rooted in spiritual gnosis (*maʿrifat*), even while surrounded by the tremendous opulence of the Mughal court at the height of its power, wealth and splendour. Thus he says admiringly of Saʿd Allah Khan that 'even though his occupation was worldly, he also had a penchant for mystical introspection, and right there in the epicenter of worldly affairs he breathed an air of detachment (*dar ʿain-i taʿalluq dam az bī-taʿalluqī mīzad*)'.[77] And even though the sentiment is expressed in a slightly more oblique fashion, this notion that the ideal *wazīr* should embody a kind of 'mystical civility', as it were, permeates Chandar Bhan's various anecdotes about Afzal Khan's spiritualism and humility as well, even as he served as the managing director of one of the largest and most powerful empires of the early modern world.

AFZAL KHAN'S LEGACY IN MUGHAL CULTURE, POLITICS AND SOCIETY

Chandar Bhan follows these illustrations of Afzal Khan's humility and mystical civility with a lengthy discussion of Afzal Khan's advice on the art of governance (*wizārat*).[78] This part of *Chahār Chaman*, it should be noted, draws clearly on the deep traditions of Indo-Persian advice literature (*naṣīḥat-nāma*s), and the specific genre of treatises on political wisdom and ethical comportment known as *ādāb* and *akhlāq*. Such texts, many of which were themselves ultimately rooted in a mix of ancient Indian wisdom literature and the Greco-Hellenic tradition of political philosophy, circulated extensively in the medieval and early modern Indo-Persian world, and, as Muzaffar Alam has demonstrated, had an important influence on the Mughals' pluralistic form of political Islam.[79] Justice, wisdom, prudence, discretion and humility are the key themes that permeate this portion of *Chahār Chaman*, as Chandar Bhan is clearly trying to cast Afzal Khan as a modern incarnation of the great *wazīr*s of history, and to locate his own work within the grand tradition of Timurid 'manuals for *wazīr*s' (*dastūr al-wizārat*), in line with other noted works in the genre such as Saif al-Din Fadli's *Āṣār al-Wuzarā* (1478), Khwandamir's *Dastūr al-Wuzarā* (1509) and Qazi Ikhtiyar al-Din Hasan al-Husaini's sixteenth-century *Akhlāq-i Humāyūnī*.[80] Chandar Bhan's *Chahār Chaman*, in turn, was among the most widely read and emulated prose texts in early modern South Asia, so it is safe to say that his portrayal of Afzal Khan and other great Mughal *wazīr*s of the era had a lasting influence on norms of comportment and notions of civility among the Indo-Persian intelligentsia of the seventeenth and eighteenth centuries.

But before closing we should note too that Afzal Khan's legacy in Mughal culture and politics was also, in many ways, a family affair. We briefly mentioned above that both Afzal Khan's son (the ill-fated Mirza Muhammad) and brother 'Abd al-Haqq Shirazi (or 'Amanat Khan') had also come to India and become involved with Mughal politics as early as the 1610s. Amanat Khan is noteworthy especially for his artistic and architectural activities.[81] For instance, though he seems to have occasionally been tasked with administrative and diplomatic assignments, Amanat Khan is actually best known to posterity as an accomplished calligrapher. He had designed the decorative inscriptions (and possibly authored some of the poetic eulogies) for Akbar's tomb at Sikandra (Agra), completed in 1613, and for the Madrasa Shahi ('King's College') mosque, also in Agra. Like his brother, moreover, Amanat Khan was also extremely learned, and in addition to his calligraphic career, appears to have spent some time as a royal librarian. But most famously, it was he who crafted the exquisite Qur'anic and literary inscriptions inlaid on the Taj Mahal and its surrounding complex, arguably this legendary monument's 'single most important decorative feature'.[82] It is difficult to think of a more iconic symbol of the grandeur of Indo-Islamic imperial architecture – not to mention the cultural-historical imagination of modern South Asia generally – than the Taj, and Afzal Khan's brother Amanat Khan was, quite literally, the man who put the writing on the walls.

As it turned out, however, Afzal Khan died even before the finishing touches on the Taj Mahal were complete, and Amanat Khan was so distraught by his brother's passing in 1639 that, according to Chandar Bhan Brahman, he 'retired from service and gave up his rank (*manṣab*), betaking himself to a secluded corner and becoming a complete renunciant'.[83] Chandar Bhan does add, though, that Amanat Khan built a 'charming hostel' (*sarāy-i dilgushā*) about one day's journey from Lahore that became a notable architectural curiosity in its own right, and was where Amanat Khan himself was eventually buried when he died a few years later in 1644–5.[84] These curious architectural tastes appeared to run in the family, for Afzal Khan's own body was transported to Agra and buried in a tomb of his own design that also had a number of novel structural features, leading the locals to refer to it fondly as the 'Chinese Mausoleum' (*Chīnī kā Rauẓā*).[85] The calligraphic inscriptions on this tomb, too, appear to have been designed by his brother Amanat Khan. And more than one source notes that Afzal Khan also patronised the construction of a lovely garden complex and residence known as 'Afzalabad' in Kashmir, somewhere on the northern shore of Dal Lake.[86]

Meanwhile, Amanat Khan's own son 'Aqil Khan (d. 1649), who had actually been mentored and largely raised by Afzal Khan, also had a promising military and political career. He displayed his learning by serving for a time as the editor of royal petitions ('*arẓ-mukarrar*), and held a number of other distinguished administrative posts.[87] 'He was gifted in poetry and accounts' (*az naẓm wa siyāq bahrawar būd*), according to the *Ma'āṣir al-Umarā*,[88] and 'Aqil Khan was also married to the daughter of Sati al-Nisa Khanum (d. 1647), the noted grand dame of the ladies' quarter of the palace, and herself one of the most learned women in Mughal India (she was the sister of Jahangir's poet laureate Talib Amuli, and served as the personal tutor to Princess Jahan Ara).[89] In 1649 'Aqil Khan died suddenly on a diplomatic assignment in Afghanistan, when, as Chandar Bhan put it, 'while *en route* to Kabul, still in the prime of his youth, the tender shoot of his future success was cut down by the fierce winds of doom'.[90]

Afzal Khan's entire family, in other words, displayed a truly impressive range of cultural activities and expertise – poetry, stylised prose, calligraphy, architecture, accounting, diplomacy and mysticism – all of which were integral to the family's general success in Mughal politics. After noting 'Aqil Khan's sudden demise, however, Chandar Bhan Brahman's discussion of Afzal Khan and his family ends on a rather melancholy note, as he points out that 'now, apart from his good name there is no one to carry on the memory of the 'Allama [Afzal Khan]'s family line except for 'Aqil Khan's brother Faiz Allah'. The latter, though, was apparently an eccentric, or possibly even mentally disturbed. All Chandar Bhan will say about him, somewhat cryptically, is that 'he lives according to his own manner' (*ba ṭaur-i khwud zindagī mīkunad*).[91]

Chandar Bhan does, however, tell us some noteworthy things about his patron's final days. He tells us, for instance, that as his condition deteriorated Afzal Khan 'often spoke eloquently of the fickleness of fate', and among his final utterances he recited these two couplets:

> *gar ajal mard ast, gū pesh-i man ā'ī*
> *tā dar āghosh-ash bagīram tang tang*
> *man az ū jānī sitānam jāwidān*
> *ū zi man dalqī bagīrad rang rang*

> If Death himself shows up, tell him 'Come hither!'
> So that I can embrace him tightly, so tightly;
> From him I will receive a soul eternal,
> And from me he will get only this cloak patched brightly, so brightly[92]

The 'brightly patched cloak' (*dalq*) here refers to the typical garment of a Sufi mendicant (*darwesh*), which often had a colourful appearance on account of being stitched together from multiple scraps of cloth. Thus, reiterating the theme of mystical civility discussed above, the message of the two couplets is that Afzal Khan viewed all his worldly status and finery as nothing but the humble garb of a mendicant, and moreover, that when the appointed hour of his death arrived he would happily welcome it, giving up even this humble garb (that is, his worldly existence) in order to join with the cosmic soul. Needless to say, this is a stirring sentiment coming from one of the most powerful men in all of South Asia.

In another moving passage Chandar Bhan tells us that as his condition worsened Afzal Khan received personal visits from 'many elite nobles of the eternal empire', including none other than Emperor Shah Jahan himself, who at one point seems even to have taken personal charge of overseeing his old companion's medical care:

> The Emperor arranged whatever was necessary to tend to His convalescing servant. And when His Majesty the caliph of the age, out of an abundance of affection and respect, laid his blessed hand across the hand of that scholar of the world, and asked after the latter's condition, the gentle Khan was unable to muster the words. But, recalling their longstanding friendship and bond of service, he expressed his thanks for the favour His Highness had shown him and then suddenly lost control of his emotions and began to weep. Upon seeing this, the affectionate and considerate emperor used his inspired tongue to speak many words of encouragement for the improvement of that illustrious Khan's condition.[93]

Of course, even if the 'King of the World' himself is in charge of your medical care, time catches up with everyone – a sentiment that Chandar Bhan proceeds to express with quite a flourish:

> But, because it is a peculiar feature of the wine of destiny that ultimately it inebriates those who imbibe at the tavern of existence with the empty gulp of

nonexistence at the bottom of the cup, and then hurls the rock of fragmentation against the glass of desire, that wise man of the world abandoned the trappings of existence in this decentered world and became a sojourner on the path to eternal sanctity.[94]

Soon after, a royal proclamation bearing the sad news of the *wazīr*'s demise was read throughout the city of Lahore, where Afzal Khan had not only kept a private residence, but also served for a number of years as the provincial governor. According to Chandar Bhan:

> Since he had lived a well-fashioned life, indeed in every way, the Emperor of the world and its inhabitants, recalling the laudable ethics, habits, and manners (*ḥusn-i akhlāq wa auẓā' wa aṭwār*) of that scholar of the age, who had spent nearly a decade as the standard bearer for governance and administration (*imārat-o-wizārat*) in the land of Hindustan, earning fame for his kindness, wisdom, and good character, made known to the entire world the special esteem in which he had held his knowledgable *wazīr*.[95]

Meanwhile, during his funeral procession, Afzal Khan's bier was accompanied by a number of high-profile members of the Mughal nobility, including Wazir Khan, the governor of the Punjab; Mu'tamad Khan, the chief army paymaster (*mīr bakhshī*); Makramat Khan, the chief of equipment and materiel (*mīr sāmān*); and, *munshī* Chandar Bhan tells us, 'several other notables . . . who conveyed his corpse toward the eternal country, showing their grief in sobs amid the throng of onlookers who remained behind in this transient world'.[96]

We do not often hear much about basic human emotions like friendship, loss and grief in modern scholarship about the Mughal court. Chandar Bhan's reflections on these final weeks of Afzal Khan's life – as the Khan 'was making his way from this ephemeral abode (*dār-i fānī*) and turning his attention to the eternal world ('*ālam-i jāwidānī*)' – are thus especially noteworthy, and offer a brief yet powerful glimpse of the kinds of emotional ties and personal relationships cultivated within the Mughal political elite. But the virtual absence of such scenes, as well as the broader life and career of someone like Afzal Khan, in modern Mughal historiography also suggests that we have missed something very important about the inner lives of the Mughal courtly elite. Afzal Khan's reputation as a gentleman and a scholar was based neither on an especially distinguished record as a military commander, nor on any ruthless machinations at court, but rather almost entirely on his reputation as a statesman and the powerful example of learning and civility that he clearly tried to embody, and that those around him tried to emulate.

This is presumably why another source from the period, Muhammad Salih Kambuh's '*Amal-i Ṣāliḥ*, begins its biographical entry on Afzal Khan by introducing him as the 'Knower of the [esoteric] mysteries of both 'Ajam and Arabia' (*wāqif-i rumūz-i 'ajamī wa tāzi*).[97] Salih also reiterates many of the same types of praise for Afzal Khan that we have seen in the sources discussed above, for instance commending the Khan's devotion to using his status and influence to improve the lot of the common folk – a quality praised by 'Abd al-Baqi Nahawandi's *Ma'āsir-i Raḥīmī* all the way back in 1616. Salih also insists that Afzal Khan's learning, spiritual acumen and wisdom would 'gladden the spirits of Plato and Aristotle' (*rawān-i arasṭū wa aflāṭūn rā shād mīkard*), and that 'with the aid of his enlightened mind he could discourse with the best of the Ishraqi [illuminationist] philosophers' (*ham-gū-yi ishrāqiyān rā ba dastyārī-yi zamīr-i raushan mīgardānīd*).⁹⁸ Another contemporary source, Muhammad Sadiq Kashmiri Hamadani's *Ṭabaqāt-i Shāhjahānī*, lists Afzal Khan first among the 'scholars, wise men, and learned men' (*'ulamā wa ḥukamā wa fuzalā*) of the times. Like so many others, he showers praise on Afzal Khan's erudition, and says of him:

> he consistently shows great kindness to the [common] people of God on high, and oftentimes remains busy with matters related to the servants of God. He is unequalled in this era when it comes to agreeable manners and excellent qualities, and if the great *wazīr*s Nizam al-Mulk and Ibn 'Abbad, so renowned for their cultivation of learning, were alive today they would take lessons from him in the ways of *wizārat* and efficacious governance . . .⁹⁹

To his seventeenth-century contemporaries, then, Afzal Khan was seen as the embodiment of a particular ideal of learning, spirituality, tolerance and civility in action. A century later, he was still remembered in mostly similar fashion, with great fondness and reverence. For instance, perhaps the best-known compilation of Mughal political biographies of the eighteenth century, the *Ma'āsir al-Umarā*, repeats many of the same details regarding Afzal Khan's career as a statesman, and adds a telling observation: 'He had the most excellent manners (*fāzil-i muhazzab al-akhlāq būd*), and His Majesty [Shah Jahan] repeatedly used to say that in twenty-eight years of service he had never heard Afzal Khan say an unkind word about anyone.'¹⁰⁰

One can see quite clearly from many of the biographies and other accounts discussed above that the favour was usually returned, for it is difficult to find even a single early modern source with a negative word to say about Afzal Khan himself. This alone should give some indication that the learned ideals of civility, spirituality and tolerance that he cultivated and sought to promote were far more widespread and admired among a broad spectrum of Mughal nobles and other elites than most people today realise. Indeed, beginning toward the end of the eighteenth century, under the influence of British colonial historiography, the cultural memory of this strain of learned and tolerant intellectual life, as represented by Indo-Persian elites like Afzal Khan, began to fade in South Asia, as a new narrative of supposed 'Islamic orthodoxy' and inexorable 'decline' beginning under Shah Jahan began to take root, and has continued to dominate the popular image of the later Mughals almost to this very day. As a result, a number of prominent and powerful figures like Afzal Khan simply do not figure much in modern historiography on the Mughals, despite the great influence they wielded in their own day.¹⁰¹ The good news is that a number of specialists of the period have begun to offer a powerful corrective in recent years to such reductive narratives of seventeenth- and eighteenth-century Mughal cultural and political life, and of early modern India more generally. While there is still a great deal more work to do, this chapter may hopefully be viewed as another small step in that direction.

NOTES

1. Sir Thomas Roe, *Sir Thomas Roe his speech in Parliament, wherein he sheweth the cause of the decay of coyne and trade in this land, especially of merchants trade, and also propoundeth a vvay to the House, how they may be increased* (London: n.p., 1641). For a more detailed examination of seventeenth-century Mughal approaches to cultural pluralism and their global historical significance, see, for example, Muzaffar Alam and Sanjay Subrahmanyam, 'Frank Disputations: Catholics and Muslims in the Court of Jahangir (1608–11)', *Indian Economic and Social History Review* 46:4 (2009), pp. 457–511; Corinne Lefèvre, 'The *Majālis-i Jahāngīrī* (1608–11): Dialogue and Asiatic Otherness at the Mughal Court', *Journal of the Economic and Social History of the Orient* 55:2–3 (2012), pp. 255–86; Rahul Sapra, *The Limits of Orientalism: Seventeenth-Century Representations of India* (Newark, DE: University of Delaware Press, 2011), pp. 60–88; Paul Stevens and Rahul Sapra, 'Akbar's Dream: Moghul Toleration and English/British Orientalism', *Modern Philology* 104:3 (2007), pp. 379–411; Faith Beasley, 'Versailles Meets the Taj Mahal', in Christie McDonald and Susan Rubin Suleiman (eds), *French Global: A New Approach to Literary History* (New York: Columbia University Press, 2010), pp. 207–22; Rajeev Kinra, 'Handling Diversity with Absolute Civility: The Global Historical Legacy of Mughal *Ṣulḥ-i Kull*', *Medieval History Journal* 16:2 (2013), pp. 251–95; Kinra, *Writing Self, Writing Empire: Chandar Bhan Brahman and the Cultural World of the Indo-Persian State Secretary* (Berkeley: University of California Press, 2015).

2. On the revenue stream, see Irfan Habib, *The Agrarian System of Mughal India, 1556–1707*, 2nd rev. edn (Oxford: Oxford University Press, 1997). On family networks, see Afzal Husain, *The Nobility under Akbar and Jahāngīr: A Study of Family Groups* (New Delhi: Manohar, 1991); Firdos Anwar, *Nobility under the Mughals (1628–1658)* (New Delhi: Manohar, 2001). On ranks, titles and offices, see M. Athar Ali, *The Apparatus of Empire: Awards of Ranks, Offices and Titles to the Mughal Nobility (1574–1658)* (Oxford: Oxford University Press, 1985).

3. See, for example, Jagdish Sarkar, *Life of Mir Jumla: The General of Aurangzeb* (Calcutta: Thacker, Spink, 1951); Anil Kumar, *Asaf Khan and His Times* (Patna: Kashi Prasad Jayaswal Research Institute, 1986); Laiq Ahmed, *Prime Ministers of Aurangzeb* (Allahabad: Chugh Publications, 1976).

4. See, for example, Sanjay Subrahmanyam, 'The Mughal State—Structure or Process? Reflections on Recent Western Historiography', *Indian Economic and Social History Review* 29:3 (1992), pp. 291–321; Muzaffar Alam and Subrahmanyam (eds), *The Mughal State, 1526–1750* (Oxford: Oxford University Press, 1998), pp. 1–71; Alam and Subrahmanyam, *Writing the Mughal World: Studies on Culture and Politics* (New York: Columbia University Press, 2012), pp. 1–32.

5. I arrive at this approximate year of his birth simply by extrapolating from the information in *Ma'āṣir al-Umarā*, which tells us that he was seventy years old at the time of his death in January 1639. See Nawab Samsam al-Daula Shahnawaz Khan, *Ma'āṣir al-Umarā. Vol. 1*, ed. Maulavi Abd-ur-Rahim (Calcutta: The Asiatic Society, 1888), p. 150. Note, too, that although his given name was Shukr Allah Shirazi, and he did not receive the official Mughal title of 'Afzal Khan' until 1615, I have referred to him throughout this article as Afzal Khan to avoid confusion.

6. 'Abd al-Baqi Nahawandi, *Ma'āṣir-i Raḥīmī: Bakhsh-i Siwum: Zindagī-nāma-hā*, ed. 'Abd

al-Husain Nawa'i (Tehran: Anjuman-i Āsār wa Mufākhir-i Farhangī, 2002), p. 23. We learn from other sources that Afzal Khan's father was a certain Qasim al-Shirazi. The latter, according to W. E. Begley and Z. A. Desai, 'may be the calligrapher of the same name who achieved a certain renown in Shiraz around the last quarter of the sixteenth century' (W. E. Begley and Z. A. Desai, *Taj Mahal: The Illumined Tomb (An Anthology of Seventeenth-Century Mughal and European Documentary Sources)* (Cambridge, MA: Aga Khan Program for Islamic Architecture), p. xxxvii).

7. Nahawandi, *Ma'āṣir-i Raḥīmī*, p. 23.

8. For details on the refined secretarial culture of the Indo-Persian world in late antiquity and early modernity, see William Hanaway, 'Secretaries, Poets, and the Literary Language', in Brian Spooner and Hanaway (eds), *Literacy in the Persianate World: Writing and the Social Order* (Philadelphia: University of Pennsylvania Museum of Archaeology and Anthropology, 2012), pp. 95–142; Ishtiyaq Ahmed Zilli, 'Development of *Insha* Literature to the End of Akbar's Reign', in Muzaffar Alam, Françoise Delvoye and Marc Gaborieau (eds), *The Making of Indo-Persian Culture: Indian and French Studies* (New Delhi: Manohar, Centre de Sciences Humaines, 2000), pp. 309–50; Alam and Sanjay Subrahmanyam, 'The Making of a Munshi', *Comparative Studies in South Asia, Africa, and the Middle East* 24:2 (2004), pp. 61–72; Rajeev Kinra, 'Master and *Munshī*: A Brahman Secretary's Guide to Mughal Governance', *Indian Economic and Social History Review* 47:4 (2010), pp. 527–61; Kinra, *Writing Self, Writing Empire*.

9. Nahawandi, *Ma'āṣir-i Raḥīmī*, p. 23.

10. Ibid.

11. Ali Anooshahr, 'Shirazi Scholars and the Political Culture of the Sixteenth-Century Indo-Persian World', *Indian Economic and Social History Review* 51:3 (2014), pp. 331–52.

12. For overviews of Fath Allah Shirazi's impressive career, besides Anooshahr's article, see Altaf Ahmad Azmi, 'Shāh Fatḥullāh Shīrāzī – An Eminent Scholar of Mughal Period', *Studies in History of Medicine and Science* 18:2 (2002), pp. 39–57; S. M. Azizuddin Husain, 'Mir Fathullah Shirazi's Contribution for the Revision of the Syllabi of Indian *Madrasa*s during Akbar's Reign', in Husain (ed.), *Madrasa Education in India: Eleventh to Twenty-First Century* (Delhi: Kanishka, 2005), pp. 24–36; Sharif Husain Qasemi, 'Fatḥ-Allāh Šīrāzī, Sayyed Mīr; A Famous Sixteenth-Century Sufi, an Official in Mughal India, and One of the Most Learned Men of His Time', *Encyclopaedia Iranica* (online) (2012), available at <http://www.iranicaonline.org/articles/fath-allah-sirazi> (last accessed 21 August 2015). Most Mughal sources gush with praise for Fath Allah's learning, character and administrative acumen. Indeed, one gets some indication of just how greatly admired he was from the lament of Emperor Akbar himself upon learning of his death, as reported in the *Ma'āṣir al-Umarā*: 'He was my counselor, my philosopher, my physician, and my astrologer. Who can understand the extent of my sorrow? If he had fallen into the hands of the Franks, and they wanted my entire treasury as ransom, I would gladly have paid it and considered it a profitable transaction, that I had bought this precious gem so cheaply' (Shahnawaz Khan, *Ma'āṣir al-Umarā*, vol. 1, pp. 102–3 (Persian); in English, see *The Maāthir-ul-Umarā, being Biographies of the Muḥammadan and Hindu Officers of the Timurid Sovereigns of India from 1500 to about 1780 A.D.*, 2 vols, trans. H. Beveridge, revised, annotated and completed by Baini Prashad (Patna: Janaki Prakashan, 1979), vol. 1, p. 544).

13. Anooshahr, 'Shirazi Scholars', p. 337.

14. Note that while Qasemi, 'Fatḥ-Allāh Šīrāzī', describes Fath Allah Shirazi as 'a disciple of the Sufi shaikh Mīr Šāh Mīr Takīya Šīrāzī' (also known as Mir Taqi al-Din Muhammad), it was in fact the other way around. Iskandar Beg Munshi clearly states that Taqi al-Din was 'among the students/disciples (*talāmiẕa*) of Shah Fath Allah Shirazi' (*Tārīkh-i 'Ālam-Ārā-yi 'Abbāsī*, 2 vols, ed. Iraj Afshar (Tehran: Amir Kabir, 1971), vol. 1, p. 148).

15. Iskandar Beg, *Tārīkh-i 'Ālam-Ārā-yi 'Abbāsī*, p. 148 (Persian); in English, see Iskandar Beg Munshi, *History of Shah 'Abbas the Great (Tārīk-e 'Ālamārā-ye 'Abbāsī) by Eskandar Beg Monshi*, trans. Roger M. Savory, 2 vols, Persian Heritage Series, ed. Ehsan Yarshater, no. 28 (Boulder, CO: Westview Press, 1978), vol. 1, p. 236.

16. For details, see Farid Qasemlu, 'Taqī al-Dīn Fārsī', in *Dānishnāma-yi Jahān-i Islām* [Encyclopedia of the Islamic World] (1996?). Online version hosted by the *Kitābkhāna-yi Madrasa-yi Faqāhat* [Library of the College of Law], available at <http://lib.eshia. ir/23019/1/3770> (last accessed 19 August 2015).

17. Nahawandi, *Ma'āsir-i Raḥīmī*, p. 23.

18. Qazwin was the Safavid capital until 1598, when Shah 'Abbas moved it to Isfahan.

19. Nahawandi, *Ma'āsir-i Raḥīmī*, p. 24.

20. Quoted in Rudi Matthee, 'Farhād Khan Qaramānlū, Rokn-al-Salṭana; Military Commander of Shah 'Abbās I, Executed at the Shah's Orders in 1598', in *Encyclopaedia Iranica* (online) (1999), available at <http://www.iranicaonline.org/articles/farhad-khan-qaramanlu-rokn-al-saltana> (last accessed 24 April 2014), which also offers the most concise overview in English of Farhad Khan's military and political career generally. For more specific details, see the relevant chronicles of the period such as Iskandar Beg, *Tārīkh-i 'Ālam-Ārā* and Jalal al-Din Munajjim, *Tārīkh-i 'Abbāsī, yā Roznāma-yi Mullā Jalāl; Shāmil-i Waqāyi'-i Darbār-i Shāh 'Abbās Ṣafavī*, ed. Saif Allah Vahidniya (Tehran: Intisharat-i Wahid, 1987–8).

21. Nahawandi, *Ma'āsir-i Raḥīmī*, p. 24.

22. Matthee, 'Farhād Khan Qaramānlū'.

23. See Kishwar Rizvi, *The Safavid Dynastic Shrine: Architecture, Religion and Power in Early Modern Iran* (London: I. B. Tauris, 2011), pp. 128, 133–5, 140, 204.

24. Nahawandi, *Ma'āsir-i Raḥīmī*, p. 24.

25. Iskandar Beg, *Tārīkh-i 'Ālam-Ārā-yi 'Abbāsī*, vol. 2, pp. 512–13, 543 (Persian); *History of Shah 'Abbas the Great*, vol. 2, pp. 688–9, 723 (English).

26. Nahawandi, *Ma'āsir-i Raḥīmī*, p. 24.

27. Ibid.

28. Iskandar Beg, *Tārīkh-i 'Ālam-Ārā-yi 'Abbāsī*, vol. 2, pp. 543–4 (Persian); *History of Shah 'Abbas the Great*, vol. 2, p. 723 (English).

29. For an overview of the competing theories advanced in various Safavid sources, see Matthee, 'Farhād Khan Qaramānlū'.

30. Nahawandi, *Ma'āsir-i Raḥīmī*, p. 24.

31. Eventually, Zulfiqar Khan too ran afoul of Shah 'Abbas's suspicious nature, and was himself executed in 1610–11. After this several members of their family departed for India, where they enjoyed great success at the Mughal court for several generations. For details on these later descendants, see the entries on Asad Khan and Zulfiqar Khan Qaramanlu in Shahnawaz Khan, *Ma'āsir al-Umarā*, vol. 1, pp. 310–21 and Shahnawaz Khan, *Ma'āsir al-Umarā. Vol. 2*, ed. Maulavi Abd-ur-Rahim (Calcutta: The Asiatic Society, 1890), pp. 85–9. See also Satish Chandra, *Medieval India: From Sultanat to the Mughals – Part II: Mughal Empire (1526–1748)* (New Delhi: Har-Anand Publications, 2005), pp. 457–8; Laiq Ahmad, *The Prime Ministers of Aurangzeb* (Allahabad: Chugh Publications, 1976), pp. 100–43.

32. Nahawandi, *Ma'āsir-i Raḥīmī*, p. 24.

33. Iskandar Beg, *Tārīkh-i 'Ālam-Ārā-yi 'Abbāsī*, vol. 1, pp. 149–50 (Persian); *History of Shah 'Abbas the Great*, vol. 1, p. 239 (English).

34. Iskandar Beg, *Tārīkh-i 'Ālam-Ārā-yi 'Abbāsī*, vol. 1, pp. 149–50 and vol. 2, pp. 756, 914 (Persian); *History of Shah 'Abbas the Great*, vol. 1, p. 239 and vol. 2, pp. 949, 1130 (English). Incidentally, besides Afzal Khan, at least one other of Mirza Ibrahim Hamadani's students, a certain Hakim Mir Muhammad Hashim, went on to make a name for himself as a

doctor in Mughal India, eventually even serving as tutor to Emperor Aurangzeb while the latter was still a prince. O. P. Jaggi, *History of Science and Technology in Medieval India.* Vol. 8, *Medicine in Medieval India* (Delhi: Atma Ram and Sons), p. 183.

35. Nahawandi, *Ma'āṣir-i Raḥīmī*, p. 24.

36. Ibid. p. 24. Note that some sources, such as Shahnawaz Khan, *Ma'āṣir al-Umarā*, vol. 1, p. 145, report that Afzal Khan arrived in India via the port of Surat (just down the coast from Cambay).

37. See, for example, Aziz Ahmad, 'Ṣafawid Poets and India', *Iran* 14 (1976), pp. 117–32; Sanjay Subrahmanyam, 'Iranians Abroad: Intra-Asian Elite Migration and Early Modern State Formation', *Journal of Asian Studies* 51:2 (1992), pp. 340–63; Abolghasem Dadvar, *Iranians in Mughal Politics and Society, 1606–1658* (New Delhi: Gyan Publishing House, 1999); Richard Eaton, *A Social History of the Deccan, 1300–1761: Eight Indian Lives* (Cambridge: Cambridge University Press, 2005), pp. 59–77; Muzaffar Alam and Sanjay Subrahmanyam, *Indo-Persian Travels in the Age of Discoveries, 1400–1800* (Cambridge: Cambridge University Press, 2007); Finbarr Flood, *Objects of Translation: Material Culture and Medieval 'Hindu-Muslim' Encounter* (Princeton: Princeton University Press, 2009); Rajeev Kinra, 'Make It Fresh: Time, Tradition, and Indo-Persian Literary Modernity', in Anne C. Murphy (ed.), *Time, History, and the Religious Imaginary in South Asia* (London: Routledge, 2011), pp. 12–39; Kinra, *Writing Self, Writing Empire*, pp. 201–39.

38. The classic account of 'Abd al-Rahim Khan-i Khanan's court is 'Abd al-Baqi Nahawandi's *Ma'āṣir-i Raḥīmī*, from which we have also been drawing many of the details about Afzal Khan's early career. For overviews of 'Abd al-Rahim's career and patronage in English, see Annemarie Schimmel, 'A Dervish in the Guise of a Prince: Khān-i Khānān Abdur Rahīm as a Patron', in Barbara Stoler Miller (ed.), *The Powers of Art: Patronage in Indian Culture* (Oxford: Oxford University Press, 1992), pp. 202–18; Chhotubhai Ranchhodji Naik, *'Abdu'r Raḥīm Khān-i-Khānān and His Literary Circle* (Ahmedabad: Gujarat University Press, 1966). For a discussion of his stature as a prominent Hindi poet and patron, see Allison Busch, *Poetry of Kings: The Classical Hindi Literature of Mughal India* (Oxford: Oxford University Press, 2011), pp. 138–40. For his workshop of painters and calligraphers, see John Seyller, *Workshop and Patron in Mughal India: The Freer Ramayana and Other Illustrated Manuscripts of 'Abd al-Rahim* (Zurich and Washington, DC: Artibus Asiae Publishers, Museum Rietberg, in association with the Freer Gallery of Art, Smithsonian Institution, 1999). And for a discussion of the 'fresh' movement of early modern Indo-Persian poetry, see Paul E. Losensky, *Welcoming Fighānī: Imitation and Poetic Individuality in the Safavid-Mughal Ghazal* (Costa Mesa, CA: Mazda, 1998); Kinra, 'Make It Fresh'; Kinra, *Writing Self, Writing Empire*, pp. 201–39.

39. Nahawandi, *Ma'āṣir-i Raḥīmī*, p. 25.

40. Ibid. p. 25.

41. Nur al-Din Muhammad Jahangir, *The Jahangirnama: Memoirs of Jahangir, Emperor of India*, trans. Wheeler M. Thackston (Oxford: Oxford University Press,1999), pp. 164–5, 204; cf. Nahawandi, *Ma'āṣir-i Raḥīmī*, p. 25. Again, while we have been referring to him by his title of 'Afzal Khan' throughout this chapter for the sake of convenenience, his actual name prior to 1615 was Mirza (or sometimes 'Mulla') Shukr Allah Shirazi.

42. Jahangir, *The Jahangirnama*, p. 204; cf. also the discussion of these events in Khwaja Kamgar Husaini, *Ma'āṣir-i Jahāngīrī: A Contemporary Account of Jahangir*, ed. Azra Alavi (Bombay: Asia Publishing House, 1978), pp. 189–91, 195.

43. Jahangir, *The Jahangirnama*, pp. 164–5.

44. For details, see the lengthy entry on Sundar Das under the entry 'Raja Bikramajit Ray-i Rayan', in Shahnawaz Khan, *Ma'āṣir al-Umarā*, vol. 2, pp. 183–95. For a general discussion of the military-political organisation of Prince Khurram/Shah Jahan's household during this period, including the roles of Afzal Khan and Sundar Das, see also Munis

Faruqui, *The Princes of the Mughal Empire, 1504–1719* (Cambridge: Cambridge University Press, 2012), pp. 112–16.

45. Jahangir, *The Jahangirnama*, p. 233. 'Bikramajit' is a Hindi-Persian variation of the Sanskrit 'Vikramaditya', that is, the legendary ancient king.

46. For useful overviews, see Beni Prasad, *History of Jahangir* (Allahabad: The Indian Press, 1962), pp. 232–63; Banari Prasad Saksena, *History of Shahjahan of Dihli* (Allahabad: Central Book Depot, 1958), pp. 18–31.

47. Jahangir, *The Jahangirnama*, p. 216.

48. Ibid. p. 225; cf. also the discussion of these events in Kamgar Husaini, *Ma'āṣir-i Jahāngīrī*, pp. 229–30, 235–6, 242–5.

49. Jahangir, *The Jahangirnama*, p. 229. Both Afzal Khan and Sundar Das were also promoted that same month, and it was at that time (October 1617) that the latter was given the title 'Raja Bijramajit', as mentioned above.

50. As the *Ma'āṣir al-Umarā* colourfully puts it, 'having become the agent of glorious deeds through his lofty nature and great courage, he graduated from the pen to the sword' (*ba 'ulūw-i fiṭrat wa sumūw-i himmat maṣdar-i kār-hā-yi shigarf gashta az qalam ba shamshīr farāz-dastī namūd*) (Shahnawaz Khan, *Ma'āṣir al-Umarā*, vol. 2, pp. 183–95).

51. Jahangir, *The Jahangirnama*, pp. 303, 364, 381, 425.

52. Ibid. p. 303.

53. Ibid. pp. 364–5. Jahangir describes the ornament, and its particular historical-genealogical significance, in an earlier passage (p. 357); cf. also Kamgar Husaini, *Ma'āṣir-i Jahāngīrī*, pp. 243–4, 329, 334.

54. Jahangir, *The Jahangirnama*, p. 381; cf. also Kamgar Husaini, *Ma'āṣir-i Jahāngīrī*, pp. 352–4, 357, 361.

55. For details, see for example Saksena, *History of Shahjahan of Dihli*, pp. 32–65; Prasad, *History of Jahangir*, pp. 316–63; Faruqui, *Princes of the Mughal Empire*, pp. 181–234 (esp. pp. 208–17); Fergus Nicoll, *Shah Jahan: The Rise and Fall of the Mughal Emperor* (London: Haus Publishing, 2009), pp. 117–38; John Richards, *Mughal Empire* (Cambridge: Cambridge University Press, 1993), pp. 114–15. For Jahangir's version of these events, see Jahangir, *The Jahangirnama*, pp. 380–434.

56. Jahangir, *The Jahangirnama*, p. 414.

57. Ibid. p. 414. See also the descriptions of these events in Kamgar Husaini, *Ma'āṣir-i Jahāngīrī*, p. 388; Shahnawaz Khan, *Ma'āṣir al-Umarā*, vol. 1, pp. 147–8.

58. Jahangir, *The Jahangirnama*, p. 425; cf. Kamgar Husaini, *Ma'āṣir-i Jahāngīrī*, p. 404.

59. For some of the specific details regarding Afzal Khan's subterfuge on Shah Jahan's behalf during the war of succession, see Shahnawaz Khan, *Ma'āṣir al-Umarā*, vol. 1, pp. 148–9. For general overviews of the war of succession itself, see for example Prasad, *History of Jahangir*, pp. 396–402; Saksena, *History of Shahjahan of Dihli*, pp. 56–65.

60. Chandar Bhan Brahman, *Chahār Chaman*, ed. Syed Mohammad Yunus Ja'fery (New Delhi: Centre of Persian Research; Office of the Cultural Counsellor, Islamic Republic of Iran; distributed by Alhoda Publishers, 2007), pp. 51–2.

61. See Inayat Khan, *Mulakẖkẖaṣ-i Shāh Jahān Nāma*, ed. Jameel ur-Rehman (New Delhi: Centre for Persian Research; Office of the Cultural Counsellor, Embassy of the Islamic Republic of Iran, 2009), pp. 78–9; 'Abd al-Hamid Lahori, *Lahori's Pādshāh-nāma*, trans. Hamid Afaq Siddiqi, 2 vols (Delhi: Idarah-i Adabiyat-i Delli, 2010), vol. 1, p. 63; Shahnawaz Khan, *Ma'āṣir al-Umarā*, vol. 1, p. 149. A chronogram is a verse or short phrase used to mark the date of an important occasion, the talent for composing which was highly esteemed among Indo-Persian literati. Each letter in the Perso-Arabic alphabet also has a corresponding numerical value, thus, to find the value of a simple chronogrammatic phrase like this one requires one merely to add up the values of the various letters.

62. See, for instance, the examples collected in S. A. I . Tirmizi, *Mughal Documents (AD 1628–59). Volume 2* (New Delhi: Manohar, 1995), pp. 45, 49, 54, 56, 57, 60, 61.

63. Lahori, *Lahori's Pādshāh-nāma*, vol. 2, pp. 67–8; Inayat Khan, *Mulakhkhaṣ-i Shāh Jahān Nāma*, pp. 341–2 (Persian); Inayat Khan, *The Shah Jahan Nama of 'Inayat Khan, an Abridged History of the Mughal Emperor Shah Jahan, Compiled by His Royal Librarian; The Nineteenth-Century Manuscript Translation of A. R. Fuller (British Library, Add. 30,777)*, ed. and completed by W. A. Begley and Z. A. Desai (Delhi: Oxford University Press, 1990), p. 267 (English).

64. For an extended discussion of Mughal letter-writing practices during this period, and samples of such stylised prose, see Kinra, *Writing Self, Writing Empire*.

65. Cf., for example, the episode recounted in Brahman, *Chahār Chaman*, p. 70.

66. Shaikh Farid Bhakkari, *Zakhīrat al-Khawānīn*, ed. Syed Moinul Haq, 3 vols (Karachi: Pakistan Historical Society, 1961–74), vol. 2, pp. 255–6; Shahnawaz Khan, *Ma'āṣir al-Umarā*, vol. 1, p. 150. See also Muhammad Sa'id Ahmad Marahravi, *Umarā'-yi Hunūd: Ya'nī un Hindū Umarā ke Ḥālāt jo ki Salṭanat-i Mughaliya men Mumtāz 'Ahdon par Sarfarāz Rahe* (Kanpur: Nami Press, 1910), pp. 198–9.

67. Brahman, *Chahār Chaman*, pp. 57–8.

68. For a thorough overview of Chandar Bhan's career, including his relationship with Afzal Khan, see Kinra, 'Master and *Munshī*'; Kinra, *Writing Self, Writing Empire*.

69. See, for example, the letters included in Brahman, *Chahār Chaman*, p. 152; and Brahman, *Munsha'āt-i Brahman*, ed. S. H. Qasemi and Waqarul Hasan Siddiqi (Rampur: Raza Library, 2005), pp. 16–17, 55–7.

70. Brahman, *Chahār Chaman*, pp. 52–3.

71. Ibid. p. 147 (*naẓar ba shāhid-i ma'nī ba chashm-i dil dāram / ḥijāb 'ainak-i chashm ast mard-i bīnā rā*). In other words, to gain true spiritual insight one must use 'the heart's eye' (*chashm-i dil*) rather than ordinary physical perception, which from the mystical point of view is inevitably flawed. Thus the veil (*ḥijāb*), by occluding one's mundane faculty of sight, actually heightens one's access to esoteric Truth by forcing one to focus inward, and thus serves, paradoxically, almost as a magnifying glass (*'ainak*) for one who has real 'vision' (*bīnā*).

72. Brahman, *Chahār Chaman*, p. 154.

73. Ibid. p. 53.

74. Ibid. pp. 53–4. For further details, and a translation of the letter, see Kinra, *Writing Self, Writing Empire*, p. 72.

75. Brahman, *Chahār Chaman*, pp. 54–5.

76. Ibid. p. 62. See also Kinra, *Writing Self, Writing Empire*, pp. 78–80.

77. Brahman, *Chahār Chaman*, p. 60.

78. Ibid. pp. 55–7. For a translation and brief discussion of this discourse, see Kinra, *Writing Self, Writing Empire*, pp. 74–5.

79. Muzaffar Alam, '*Akhlāqī* Norms and Mughal Governance', in Alam et al., *The Making of Indo-Persian Culture*, pp. 67–95; Alam, *The Languages of Political Islam in India, c. 1200–1800* (Delhi: Permanent Black, 2004), pp. 26–80.

80. For details on *Āṣār al-Wuzarā* and *Dastūr al-Wuzarā*, see Hermann Ethé, *Catalogue of Persian Manuscripts in the Library of the India Office* (Oxford: India Office, 1903), vol. 1, p. 252 (no. 621), as well as Ethé, *Catalogue of the Persian, Turkish, Hindûstânî, and Pushtû Manuscripts in the Bodleian Library (Begun by Professor Ed. Sachau; Continued, Completed, and Edited by Hermann Ethé)*, Part 1, *The Persian Manuscripts* (Oxford: Clarendon Press, 1889), pp. 39–40 (no. 87); Charles Ambrose Storey, *Persian Literature: A Bio-Bibliographical Survey*, Vol. 1, *Qur'ānic Literature; History and Biography*. Part 2, *Biography, Additions and Corrections, Indexes* (London: Luzac, 1953), pp. 1090–1. On *Akhlāq-i Humāyūnī*, as well as general remarks on the place of such texts in medieval

and early modern Indo-Persian political culture, see Alam, *Languages of Political Islam*, pp. 51–4.

81.   Further information on Amanat Khan's life, career, and architectural contributions is available in Begley and Desai, *Taj Mahal*, pp. xxxii–xl, 247–57, from which many of the details in this paragraph are taken.

82.   Begley and Desai, *Taj Mahal*, p. xxxiii.

83.   Brahman, *Chahār Chaman*, p. 149.

84.   The complex is situated just outside Amritsar, and, though parts of it are crumbling, it is still standing and still known locally today as the 'Sarai Amanat Khan'. Begley and Desai date it to 1640–1, based on an inscribed colophon that bears Amanat Khan's signature. See Begley and Desai, *Taj Mahal*, p. xl.

85.   For details on its design and architectural significance, see Ebba Koch, *The Complete Taj Mahal and the Riverfront Gardens of Agra* (London: Thames and Hudson, 2006), pp. 43–5; and Koch, 'Mughal Agra: A Riverfront Garden City', in Salma K. Jayyusi, Renata Holod, Attilio Petruccioli and André Raymond (eds), *The City in the Islamic World* (Leiden: Brill, 2008), vol. 1, p. 573 (pp. 555–88).

86.   Wheeler Thackston, 'Mughal Gardens in Persian Poetry', in James L. Westcoat, Jr. and Joachim Wolschke-Bulmahn (eds), *Mughal Gardens: Sources, Places, Representations, and Prospects* (Washington, DC: Dumbarton Oaks Research Library and Collection, 1996), p. 255 (pp. 233–58).

87.   For an overview of 'Aqil Khan's career, see the entry in Shahnawaz Khan, *Ma'āṣir al-Umarā*, vol. 2, pp. 790–2.

88.   Ibid. p. 791.

89.   Shahnawaz Khan also credits her with being an expert in the arts of Qur'anic and poetic recitation, as well as practical skills like household management and medicine (*khāna-dārī wa 'ilm-i ṭibb*) (ibid. pp. 791–2).

90.   Brahman, *Chahār Chaman*, p. 149.

91.   Ibid. p. 149.

92.   Ibid. p. 148.

93.   Ibid. p. 148.

94.   Ibid. p. 148.

95.   Ibid. pp. 148–9.

96.   Ibid. p. 149.

97.   Muhammad Salih Kambuh, *'Amal-i Ṣāliḥ, al-Mausūm ba 'Shāh Jahān Nāma'*, ed. Ghulam Yazdani, rev. Wahid Qureshi, 3 vols (Lahore: Majlis-i Taraqqi-yi Adab, 1967–72), vol. 3, p. 296. As noted above, 'Ajam' was the medieval and early modern term for the larger Persianate world, that is, the vast transregional space of South, Central and West Asia east of the Arabian heartland where Persian (rather than Arabic) was the primary Islamicate language of culture and diplomacy.

98.   Salih, *'Amal-i Ṣāliḥ, al-Mausūm ba 'Shāh Jahān Nāma'*, vol. 3, p. 296.

99.   Muhammad Sadiq Kashmiri Hamadani, *Ṭabaqāt-i Shāhjahānī (Ṭabaqa-yi 'Āshira)*, ed. Mohammad Aslam Khan (Delhi: Department of Persian, University of Delhi, 1990), p. 34. Nizam al-Mulk refers to the celebrated Ghaznavid and Saljuq administrator Abu Ali Hasan 'Nizam al-Mulk' Tusi (1018–92), author of the influential *Treatise on Government (Siyāsat Nāma)*, as well as a manual on proper ministerial conduct known as *Dastūr al-Wuzarā (A Textbook for Wazirs)*. Ibn 'Abbad refers to Abu al-Qasim Isma'il ibn 'Abbad al-Talaqani (d. 990), the famed Buyid statesman, secretary, and polymath known for his patronage of arts and letters.

100.   Shahnawaz Khan, *Ma'āṣir al-Umarā*, vol. 1, p. 150.

101.   For instance, you will not find Afzal Khan Shirazi even mentioned in a lot of standard scholarship and textbooks on the period, even in the sections that deal specifically with Shah

Jahan's reign. He does not make a single appearance in Richards's *Mughal Empire*, Harbans Mukhia's *Mughals of India* (Malden, MA: Blackwell Publishing, 2004), Francis Robinson's *The Mughal Emperors and the Islamic Dynasties of India, Iran and Central Asia: 1206–1925* (London: Thames and Hudson, 2007), Stephen Dale's *Muslim Empires of the Ottomans, Safavids, and Mughals* (Cambridge: Cambridge University Press, 2010), Michael H. Fisher's *A Short History of the Mughal Empire* (London: I. B. Tauris, 2016), or in any of the essays assembled by Zeenut Ziad for her lavish edited volume, *The Magnificent Mughals* (Oxford: Oxford University Press, 2002). He does make a brief appearance in Annemarie Schimmel's magisterial *The Empire of the Great Mughals: History, Art and Culture*, trans. Corinne Attwood, ed. Burzine K. Waghmar (London: Reaktion Books, 2004), but only in connection with the architectural significance of his tomb.

CHAPTER 10

Reconsidering State and Constituency in Seventeenth-Century Safavid Iran: The Wax and Wane of the *Munshi*

Colin Mitchell

As noted by Rudi Matthee in his 2010 article 'Was Safavid Iran an Empire?', there is a conspicuous absence of comparative studies of early modern empires and political systems across Europe and Asia that engage the Safavid dynasty of Iran (r. 1501–1722).[1] However, what is particularly lacking within the field of Safavid studies is a conversation which addresses the thematic concerns that are currently shaping the study of the Mamluk, Ottoman and Mughal states.[2] Marshall Hodgson, in his seminal study *The Venture of Islam*, argued that the model of military patronage state best represented the political reality of the post-Mongol Islamic world. Indeed, this notion of military patronage state (MPS) served as the underpinning for the historiographical leviathan of the 'gunpowder empire' paradigm. Keen to nuance Hodgson's ideas for a Mamluk setting, Van Steenbergen argues that the model of the MPS does not accept the notion of a unitary state which exists independently of its surrounding constituencies, elite or otherwise. Rather, politics is not conducted on the basis of static institutions, but rather through constituency membership and the act of patronage.[3] Farhat Hasan argued similarly against overly structuralist approaches when examining the political landscape of Mughal India, and he explicitly rejected Stephen Blake's Weberian 'patrimonial-bureaucratic' model in favour of a methodology which understood state power in a much more reflexive and fluid manner.[4] In recent years, there have been lively debates regarding how we can look to seemingly quotidian institutions – chanceries, judiciaries, bureaucracies – to understand better the exercise and articulation of power in pre-modern settings.[5] This chapter contributes to these debates by examining the secretarial culture of the seventeenth-century Safavid Empire, in particular the changing roles and fortunes of the 'state-secretary' (*munshi al-mamalik*).

Admittedly, Safavid historians face a number of issues which prevent the ready acceptance of such military or household-specific models, which seem to thrive in Mamluk historiography and other contexts. First and foremost, the Safavid 'royal' dynasts came into existence as the spiritual leaders of a militarised millenarian Sufi Order. The basis of a ruler's authority in Safavid Iran was inherently religious; while 'secular' Ottoman, Mamluk and Mughal sultans were buttressed and endorsed by the clerical elite and the occasional caliphal testament (at least in the case of the Mamluks), the Safavid shahs wielded infallible spiritual credentials on the basis of both their status as Sufi masters (*murshid*s) and their genealogical lineage (*nasab*) which connected them to the Twelve Imams. Together these established their unimpeachable authority in the eyes of the Shi`ite community. While there were brief instances when the Qizilbash Turkish military elite used violence to interfere with and guide the Safavid state, the familiar challenges of military-political brinkmanship, household competition and the practice of tanistry – where succession was determined by military campaigns between familial contenders – were not as prominent in Iran as they may have been elsewhere.

This exceptionalism is also evident when one examines Safavid state formation, institutions and households. In the Safavid Iranian context, we have some unique factors to consider: namely, the adoption and promotion of Twelver Shi`ism, the rise of sayyid constituencies in this newly Shi`itised political space, the importing of an assertive class of Arab jurists into Iran, and the eventual use of *ghulam*s (converted slaves) from the Caucasus region. Said Arjomand was arguably the first historian to attempt a rationalisation of the Safavid state along socio-anthropological lines,[6] and most recently, he suggested that the military household model (and by association the moniker 'gunpowder empire') had little suitability in the case of Safavid Iran. Nonetheless, Arjomand supports the use of a Weberian patrimonial-bureaucratic model for understanding Safavid Iran, but only for the seventeenth and early eighteenth centuries, because the Safavid shahs practised 'systems of personal authority through delegation, with the royal court – the household of the ruler – at its centre'.[7] As Kathryn Babyan demonstrated, the dissolution of the traditional Qizilbash military elites and rise of the Shi`ite jurist classes were manifest in the decision by seventeenth-century Safavid shahs to arrange marriages with legal theorists and sayyids (descendants of the Prophet), rather than Turkmen Qizilbash families; most evocatively, the famous red Qizilbash headgear (*taj-i Qizilbash*) began to be referred to as *Taj-i Ithna `Ashari* ('The Crown of the Twelver Shi`is').[8] Court-household dynamics were profoundly changed by Shah `Abbas's (r. 1587–1629) decision to abandon the time-honoured practice of installing brothers, sons and nephews in gubernatorial positions across the empire in the care of senior Turkmen 'advisors' (*lala*s); henceforth, princes were ordered to remain in the Safavid harem. This ushered in a new era, whereby this *qafas* system (where power was privileged for those in the harem) enhanced the influence not only of kingly mothers, but also of those people who controlled access to the court: eunuchs, chamberlains and the *ishik aqasi bashi*.[9] To complicate the historiographical terrain, Safavid politics has traditionally been framed by the binomial of *turk o tajik* (Turk and Persian), which is often reified in medieval literature by the designation of a military class (men of the sword, or *ahl al-saif*) and bureaucratic class (men of the pen, *ahl al-qalam*). Such a Manichean approach, however, oversimplifies a very complex landscape which became increasingly nuanced throughout the sixteenth and seventeenth centuries as the Safavid state expanded. What constituted 'households' in Safavid political culture were composite assemblages of Qizilbash tribal chiefs, Iranian bureaucrat-scholars, sayyids, shaikhs, mystics, Arab jurists, Caucasian *ghulam*s (converted slave troops and officials) and numerous other elements.

This chapter examines traditional medieval conceptions of the secretarial arts and how these perceptions changed at the height of Safavid imperial power under Shah 'Abbas (r. 1587–1629), a time when 'systems of personal authority' became especially profound. By examining the shifting roles and functions of the *munshi al-mamalik*, and the degree to which bureaucratic classes were shuffled and recategorised during this period, we can better understand how patrimonial rule within different constituencies and households was negotiated in Safavid Iran. Moreover, by focusing on the secretarial classes, we will see how these bureaucrat-scholars chose to articulate authority in discursive spaces at a time when traditional divisions of authority and power were in serious flux.

RISE AND FALL OF THE *MUNSHI AL-MAMALIK* IN PERSO-ISLAMIC HISTORY

In the early modern period, Persian (Farsi) was undeniably the 'prestige language'[10] of choice for Muslim rulers, bureaucrats, scholars and poets from eastern Anatolia across to northern India. This broad swathe across the Middle East and South Asia – often referred to in scholarship as the 'Persianate world' – was an amalgam of political states and empires whose cultural matrices had been indelibly shaped by the Persian language. What are the roots of this notion of Persian as a 'prestige language'? The answer is long and complicated, but scholars of medieval Islamic history are in general agreement that Persian political and literary culture – initially subsumed after the conquest of the Sasanian Iranian empire by Muslim Arabs in the seventh and eighth centuries – enjoyed a renaissance in the ninth and tenth centuries thanks to its sponsorship and promotion by the Abbasid caliphs in Baghdad. For Abbasid caliphs like al-Ma'mun (r. 813–33), Persian scholar-bureaucrats were custodians of a political and administrative culture which had been shaping western Asia since the height of the Achaemenian empire in the fifth century BCE. Medieval Islamic society underwent significant reorientation whereby the epistemologies and socio-political patterns familiar to late antiquity – distinct notions of hierarchy, scriptural authority, elaborate judicial frameworks, confessional competition and above all, absolutist, divine kingship – re-emerged thanks to Abbasid caliphal patronage of Persian viziers and scholars. As the Abbasids were slowly displaced in Iran, Central Asia and India by a myriad of Turkish gubernatorial dynasties (Ghaznavids, Ghurids, Seljuks, Khwarazmshahs), Persian moved ahead of Arabic as the legitimising language of choice. Newly Islamicised and barely removed from their origins in the Inner Asian Steppe, Turkish tribal chiefs like Mahmud of Ghazna (r. 997–1030) and Alp Arslan (r. 1063–72) actively coveted the attention and input of Persian scholar-bureaucrats such as Firdausi (author of the epic poem *Shah namah*) and Nizam al-Mulk (prominent vizier and author of the masterful mirror-for-princes *Siyasat namah*) in order to gloss their profile as legitimate and divinely sanctioned rulers.

As I have argued elsewhere,[11] one of the chief discursive responsibilities of the medieval and early modern Persian bureaucrat-scholar was the epistolographic tradition (*insha*). *'Ilm-i insha*, or the science of epistolography, went well beyond literary ostentation and grandstanding. Practitioners of *insha* (known as *munshi*s, or 'styl-ists') were essential components of the quotidian exercise of governance in an Islamic dynasty, as their scribal habitus included the drafting of imperial tax assessments, land surveys, remissions/collections of dues, payments of salaries, assignments of titles, and other administrative duties. However, *munshi*s also employed the epistolo-graphic medium to offer commentary and input on some of the heated debates taking place in various literary and philosophical spheres regarding – for instance – the role and function of human reason in an Islamic society; the tension between natural and artificial language; the putative superiority of poetry for expressing the abstract and the ineffable; metaphysical implications regarding writing and revealed sacred texts; as well as the use of figurative language and literary devices to debate theosophy, mysticism and the eternality of God and His Creation. For your average *munshi*, the inkpot of bureaucracy and the inkpot of contemporary scholarly debate were one and the same. Thus, the epistolary arts stood at an epistemological point of intersection, and their practitioners were by necessity versed in a wide set of tools and operative languages. Mundane textual production tended towards formulas (used in decrees, petitions, tax documents, investitures and endowment deeds) and there are numerous didactic manuals by *munshi*s from the period which provide dozens of short 'model' and formulaic documents for emulation and inspiration.

However, the formal letter (often referred to as *maktub*, but also appearing in rubrics as *risala, namah* or *ruqaʿ*) was demonstrably different. In the discursive space of an epistle, the *munshi* flexed his strongest linguistic muscles as a 'master of two tongues' (*dhu al-lisanain* in Arabic), moving easily between poetry and prose, to embrace fully the Aristotelian notion of rhetoric as a way of exciting the imagina-tion (*khiyal*) to concretise abstract and ephemeral ideas such as sovereignty, author-ity, cooperation, enmity and submission. By conveying meaning through elaborate arrangements of figurative language, literary rhetoricians saw in the royal *maktub* (letter) an effective medium of persuasion (*iqnaʿ*) and staging of power which served directly the interests of sovereign rulers and notables of state. In this way, chancel-leries were tasked with drafting and physicalising the performative aspects of rule which, at least in the context of the Islamic world, had first been forged in the kiln of seventh-century Arabian orality. The association of performative utterances with authority and sovereignty is enshrined in Qur'anic revelation, and medieval Islamic chancellery scribes similarly saw themselves as transmitters of imperial verbal instructions and commands. This dynamic is clearly seen in the preliminary proto-cols of letters and decrees from the post-Mongol period (1300–1700), which often began with the phrase 'Our Word' (Mongol: *üge manu*; Turkish: *sözümïz*); it was readily understood that when such documents were read aloud, the invoking of 'Our Word' signalled a powerful transformation, whereby the document came to reify sovereignty and imperial will in the same existential spirit as the Qur'anic injunction: '"Be!" And it is' (Arabic: *kun fayakun*).[12] Official reciters and audiences understood in the increasingly spiritual climate of the post-Mongol Islamic world that an impe-rial order or document indeed 'unfolded its existence' with this utterance of 'Our Word'; thus, in an Ibn-Arabian sense, it is not necessarily the contents of the letter but the performative act of its creation which gives it power.[13]

Thus, the medieval and early modern Islamic world – like Europe – saw the emergence of an intricate bureaucratic machinery of 'papereality' whereby authority and sovereignty could not be enacted successfully without the use of symbols and written representation.[14] In the spirit of the medieval Latin maxim *quod non est in actis non est in mundo* ('what does not exist in the records does not exist in reality'), the Islamic world fused literacy with its formative seventh-century orality to constitute a new and profound hybridity. What particularly empowered the chancellery tradition and its reliance on epistolography was the growth of a network of literary and bureaucratic cultures across a vast area of the Middle East, Central Asia and South Asia which shared a common corpus of cognitive language and meaning;[15] in effect, this is what defined the 'Persianate world'. In her masterful study of bureaucracy, Cornelia Vismann traces the etymology of the term 'chancery' to the Latin *cancelli* (lattice) to describe how Roman-era courts of law were barricaded spaces; *cancellari*, those who worked to produce decrees and legal rulings, were in effect gatekeepers of a discursive tradition that was integral to the success of the Roman Empire.[16] This characterisation does not belong exclusively to the Western tradition, and there is good evidence to suggest that Perso-Islamic scribes and *munshi*s saw themselves likewise as custodians not only of the physical space of the chancellery, but also of a specialised and increasingly impenetrable language which energised and oiled the imperial organs of state. The profusion of epistolographic manuals in the fourteenth and fifteenth centuries, and the authors' defence of the importance and vaunted status of the epistolary arts in imperial projects, are reflections of this development.[17]

The highest bureaucratic station for epistolary stylists in a typical medieval Perso-Islamic chancellery (*dar al-insha*, or House of Epistolography) was the *munshi al-mamalik* (stylist of the kingdom). The origins of this *munshi al-mamalik* office are not entirely clear. Designated officials whose chief mandate was to oversee the production of state documents and missives have existed in the Persianate world since antiquity, and the Abbasid caliphate certainly revived many such elements of bureaucratic organisation in their imperial capital of Baghdad in the eighth and ninth centuries. The mandate of the *munshi al-mamalik* was to ensure that diplomatic correspondence, imperial decrees, diplomas of investiture and treaties were properly drafted in their content but also displayed an intricate layout of extra-textual signatures, seals and decorative calligraphy.[18] With respect to salary and sphere of influence, as an office, the *munshi al-mamalik* arguably reached its height during the Mongol period of the thirteenth and fourteenth centuries. Inheriting the Seljuk model, the ruling Mongols of the Persianate world (known as the Ilkhans) continued the long-standing dynamic of Inner Asian nomads adopting Persian as a 'language of prestige' whose rich literary traditions – in the form of panegyric court poetry (*qasidah*s), mirrors-of-princes (*siyasat namah*s), ethics literature (*akhlaq*) and other textual vehicles of legitimacy – were especially popular. It was in this milieu that Muhammad b. Hindushah Nakhjuvani chose to produce arguably one of the most impactful didactic manuals on epistolography, wherein the complexity of medieval administration and the hierarchy of Perso-Islamic society were rationalised and systemised. This 'Manual of the Scribe for the Affixing of Ranks' (*Dastur al-katib fi ta`yin al-maratib*) describes how the *munshi al-mamalik* is 'the keeper of the secrets of the kingdom' whose position alongside the ruler mediated access for audience seekers and could be a political barrier to other aspiring courtiers, bureaucrats and notables.[19] Moreover, his ceremonial task of finalising the multistaged ceremony of drafting and issuing formal chancellery documents by drawing the personal 'signature' (*tughra*) of the Mongol sultan – an intricate heraldic device containing the name of the ruler and the term *sözümïz* ('Our Word') – placed him as a scriptural anchor in the process of performative utterance and the 'routinisation' of authority and charisma which characterised pre-modern states and polities.[20] Such 'textual enunciations of power' were but one of many strategies by which sovereignty could by embodied and reified in medieval Islamic kingly courts, as noted by al-Azmeh in his seminal study.[21]

Turning to the Safavids, we discover that the *munshi al-mamalik* suffered a serious reversal of fortune during the reign of Shah `Abbas the Great (r. 1587–1629). Once a vaunted cog in the bureaucratic machinery of the Ilkhanate empire three centuries earlier, the *munshi al-mamalik* was paid the staggering annual wage of 20,000 gold *dinar*s,[22] but by the early eighteenth century the salary for this position had plummeted so far that it earned one tenth the salary of the *qurchi bashi* (chief military commander) and one eighth the salary of the *amir-i shikar* (lord of the hunt); the chief financial comptroller (*mustaufi al-mamalik*) and the market regulator (*muhtasib al-mamalik*) earned twice as much, while the *munshi*'s pay and status were equal to those of the master of the stable (*amirakhor-i jilau*).[23] Indeed, formal epistolographers became so undervalued that the anonymous *Tazkirah al-muluk* and Mirza Rafa'i's *Dastur al-muluk* – two key administrative manuals written in the early eighteenth century – describe how the *munshi al-mamalik* was no longer entrusted with the inscription of the royal *tughra*, and was relegated to ceremonially tracing (in red ink) formulaic *intitulatio*s for missives and decrees of lesser notables.[24] At the same time, many of the duties – including the drafting of important state letters – had been appropriated by another bureaucratic officer, the *majlis-nivis* (also known as *vaq`iah-nivis*), now a constant companion to the Safavid shah and whose approval and signature was expected and required for every important document.[25] As Vladimir Minorsky commented: 'among the civil officials (*arbab-i qalam*), there is no person, except the grand vizier, who stands higher in service and nearer to the throne [than the *majlis nivis*]'.[26] How could such a devolution have taken place, where a 'court reporter' had replaced the epistolographer laureate of the state as a major bureaucratic functionary and transmitter of royal authority? Was there something particular about the reign of Shah `Abbas that explains not only the extent of this change but also its suddenness? As this chapter will suggest, contextual politics did indeed play a critical role in the *munshi al-mamalik*'s loss of fortune, but there is sufficient evidence to suggest that *munshi*s of the 1620s and 1630s worked diligently to preserve their roles as promoters of religious and cultural alterity.

The only historian to shed any serious interpretative light on this transformation has been Klaus-Michael Röhrborn. For him, the fall of the *munshi al-mamalik* and the rise of the *majlis-nivis* were directly related to the personalising and centralising politics of the late sixteenth and early seventeenth centuries; as such, this interpretation is in line with the emphasis placed by Arjomand on the patrimonial nature of Safavid politics.[27]

The traditional offices of the *munshi al-mamalik* and his staff were marginalised while those of the *majlis-nivis*, which had hitherto been a relatively junior position, were extended.[28] Mirza Rafi'a's administrative manual, the *Dastur al-muluk*, mentions that the *munshi al-mamalik* had a staff of twenty-six persons under him who were issuing decrees and permits; the *Tadhkirat al-muluk* clarifies that there are technically places for twenty-seven *munshi*s in the administration 'but none of them actually exist' (*hich yek maujud nistand*).[29] A key development – in Röhrborn's estimation – was the decision to place the *majlis-nivis* in control of all documents relating to the nomination, installation and policies of provincial governors; the invigoration of this particular position came at a time when the monarchy was exerting more control over provincial centres and significant percentages of 'state' property (*mamalik*) were being converted to private royal property (*khassah*), the financial fruits of which went directly into the imperial treasury.[30] Such trends have been interpreted as hallmark features of the newly invigorated centralised Safavid state which emerged under Shah 'Abbas in the early seventeenth century. The nomadic military elite of the Qizilbash Turks was but one constituency among many to be directly challenged, controlled and threatened by these efforts. As Kathryn Babayan has pointed out, part of this narrative is interwoven with the development of the Nuqtavi 'heretical' mystical movement. The Nuqtavis, a fifteenth-century offshoot of the cabbalistic Hurufis, accorded humanity a divine status as the first and most important act of Creation; this anthropocentrism was deemed heretical by religious authorities. When certain Qizilbash groups were connected with this antinomian movement during the reign of 'Abbas, further ammunition was provided for their marginalisation and elimination.[31] Intriguingly, it is during this period of increased centralisation and crackdown on military tribal households that we find the aforementioned changes in the hierarchy of bureaucrats and important secretarial functionaries.

HATIM BEG URDUBADI AND BAHRAM'S BROOD

The recalibration of the secretarial positions is clearly located within the reign of Shah 'Abbas, but what has been perhaps less clear is the degree to which these changes were a product of the absolutist politics and the concomitant rise of a hierocratic order in Safavid Iran. By the early seventeenth century, certain extended family groups had positioned themselves strategically so as to play key roles in the Safavid imperial project as it morphed and changed under 'Abbas's leadership. The degradation of the *munshi al-mamalik* position was indeed part of a new ideological programme which promoted a multi-ethnic and increasingly orthopraxic Shi'ite state. The key figure here was Hatim Beg Urdubadi (d. 1611), who as grand vizier under Shah 'Abbas enjoyed the title of 'Pillar of the State' (*I'timad al-daulah*). It was during Hatim Beg's tenure as vizier that Shah 'Abbas introduced a number of sweeping centralising reforms in the military and court, not to mention renovating the central district of Isfahan and naming the city as the new capital. In many ways, Hatim Beg was Thomas Cromwell to Shah 'Abbas's Henry VIII: a scholar-bureaucrat who was charged to craft and execute a new imperial vision amidst dissent, organ-

ised state violence and institutional trauma. The bulk of `Abbas's 'innovative' poli-
cies as an absolutist ruler – the creation of a standing army, extensive importing of
*ghulam*s (military and courtly slaves) from the Caucasus, the centralisation of trade
routes through the new capital, a royal monopoly on specialised trade and industries
(such as silk), heightened appropriation of state land into royal hands – were all conceived and enacted during the two decades of Hatim Beg's administrative height of
power (1591–1611) and it seems reasonable to suggest that Shah `Abbas would have
worked with him to effect these changes.

Intriguingly, Shah `Abbas decided to visit Hatim Beg's home locale of Urdubad
– likely at the invitation of the vizier himself – on a number of occasions in the early
seventeenth century. The historian Iskandar Beg Munshi describes how, arriving for
the first time at Urdubad (now known as Ordubad, located on the Aras River in the
Nakhchivan Autonomous Republic of Azerbaijan) in 1607, the shah was struck by
the pleasant climate and agricultural abundance of the area.[32] Originally known as
Urdugah (military campground), which was likely a reference to its military frontier
status and function as a mustering location for troops since the eighth century, this
city was renamed in Mongol times to Urdubad to reflect the growth of a town with
buildings, roads, irrigation, agriculture and a distinct sense of urban space.[33] The
productivity of Urdubad, in Iskandar Beg's estimation, was not just a question of
agronomy, but also of bureaucracy and chancery tradition. The notable elites of
Urdubad were the Nasiriyyahs, who had dominated the political and religious landscape of the region in the post-Mongol era. The Nasiriyyah family claimed direct
descent from the thirteenth-century polymath scholar and Shi`ite *nom célèbre*, Nasir
al-Din al-Tusi (d. 1274). As both Sufi masters and Shi`ite emperors, the Safavids
(first of Ardabil, later based in Tabriz) were well connected with this region, and it
appears that the Nasiriyyah notables served the Safavids on a client basis as early
as the fourteenth century. The Nasiriyyah patriarch Malik Bahram was sponsored
in 1501 by Shah Isma`il, and was formally named *kalantar* (mayor) of Urdubad in
the 1530s by Shah Tahmasp (r. 1524–76).[34] Isma`il's support of the Nasiriyyahs
was undoubtedly a result of the fact that his first chancery official, Khvajah `Atiq
`Ali, had been a distant kinsman of Bahram's; indeed, `Atiq Ali had been the first to
design and draw the shah's *tughra*, along with the evocative and performative utterance of 'Our Word' (*sözümiz*).[35] Mirza Kafi, another member of Malik Bahram's
extended family, was also later named *munshi al-mamalik* in the 1530s.[36] These
nominations marked the beginning of a new role for the Nasiriyyahs of Urdubad:
serving as administrative guides for a new and ambitious dynasty which sought to
establish a Twelver Shi`ite polity.

It was Malik Bahram's personal brood which made arguably the largest contributions to the Safavid administration in the late sixteenth and early seventeenth centuries. As Iskandar Beg comments: 'Malik Bahram had five sons living, and I knew
them all. Although details of their life are not relevant to this history, nevertheless
. . . my close friendship and devotion to this family make me provide [these details]
here.'[37] All trained as secretaries and comptrollers, the five scions were (from oldest
to youngest): Mirak Beg,[38] Adham Beg,[39] Hatim Beg, Abu Turab Beg[40] and Abu
Talib Beg.[41] The middle son, Hatim Beg, became the most notable of Bahram's

progeny. Hatim Beg cut his administrative teeth in Azerbaijan by serving the governor of Khoy, Dalu Budaq Rumlu, for roughly a year, before relocating to the distant city of Kerman during the turbulent reign of Shah Isma'il II in 1576.[42] There, he became the vizier to governor Vali Khan Afshar, and later his son Biktash Khan, between 1576 and 1590.[43] His tenure as chief bureaucrat in Kerman came to a close when his patron and lord, Biktash Khan, was killed while rebelling against the newly enthroned Shah 'Abbas. 'Abbas – nineteen years old – spent the first two to three years of his reign moving around different parts of the Safavid empire to reinforce his royal authority and suppress a number of regional uprisings and rebellions.[44] It was not long after the death of Biktash Khan that Hatim Beg's vizierial reputation came to the attention of Shah 'Abbas. The young ruler seemed to have been particularly impressed by Hatim Beg – roughly ten years his senior – and within six months of his initial appointment as *mustaufi al-mamalik* (chief financial officer), he was named as grand vizier and 'pillar of the state' in March 1591.[45]

There is little doubt that Hatim Beg was an 'activist' vizier. In addition to presiding over an elaborate administration, he participated in a number of military campaigns, arbitrated several disputes between the Crown and regional notables, and oversaw diplomatic missions to the Ottomans and the Uzbeks. One of his chief contributions, however, was his restructuring (c. 1595) of the tax-collecting and land-tenuring systems in the silk-rich province of Gilan; this reorganisation was presented in a formal document, the 'Regulatory Ledger of Imperial Taxes' (the *Nuskhah-yi tashkhis-i jam' va kharaj-i mamalik-i mahrusah*, now lost), which so impressed the shah that he ordered that it be used as a template for the remaining provinces of the empire.[46] As an ambitious bureaucrat granted such royal permission and support, he then turned to the central administration to effect widespread change. It is the contention here that Hatim Beg Urdubadi's promotion and rise to power came at a crucial juncture in the early seventeenth century, as Shah 'Abbas was looking to promote a patrimonial, centralised order at the expense of constituencies which had traditionally positioned themselves as integral components in the execution and expression of Safavid authority and rule.

Until the 1580s, the importance of the *munshi al-mamalik* in Safavid Iran can be seen as a continuation of the power and esteem that secretarial classes, or 'men of the pen', had wielded in the post-Mongol Islamic world. During the earlier reigns of Shah Isma'il and Shah Tahmasp, secretaries and chancellery officials had largely come from well-established families of urban elites and bureaucrats who had been navigating a confessional landscape that was by no means uniformly orthodox Shi'ite.[47] I would argue that this chancery *Weltanschauung* was a composite of legacies and exigencies; older paradigms of Perso-Islamic literary and bureaucratic culture first formed in the Seljuk and Mongol periods were fused with the theological and judicial demands imposed by the Safavid ruling family as custodians of this new Twelver Shi'ite state. As we move into the reign (1587–1629) of Shah 'Abbas, the Nasiriyyahs of Urdubad were well positioned to promote 'Abbas's public role as both a traditional Perso-Islamic absolutist emperor and *na'ib* (deputy) and direct descendant (*sayyid*) of the Prophet's family. Boasting a genealogical connection with one of the greatest Shi'ite scholars of the age (al-Tusi), Hatim Beg Urdubadi and the *silsilah-yi Nasiriyyah* were heralding a new era in which the best men of the pen (*arbab-i qalam*) were those who could combine bureaucratic sensibility with a pedigree of piety. When he was promoted to be the shah's grand vizier, among his many initiatives was to name his nephew, Nasir Khan Beg, as *munshi al-mamalik*.[48] Hatim Beg's son Mirza Talib Khan served as grand vizier (*vazir-i divan-i a`la*) for a short time in 1632, while his nephew `Abd al-Husain (son of Adham Beg) was named by the shah at some point between 1629 and 1632 as the new *munshi al-mamalik* after the death of Nasir Khan;[49] other Nasiriyyahs (bearing the *nisbah* 'al-Tusi') would be named to the now-powerful position of *majlis nivis* later in the seventeenth century. Hatim Beg nonetheless took steps to undermine the prestige and power of the *munshi al-mamalik* position to allow for a reconfiguration of a Safavid administration which readily accepted and promoted a new hierocratic orientation.

The royal letters produced during Hatim Beg's tenure were not only shorter, but demonstrably less impressive as exercises in deliberative rhetoric and the use of literary devices and poetry than those from the preceding period. We can confidently attribute at least nine letters from 1590 to 1600 to Hatim Beg himself; another nine letters from this period exhibit structures, language and selective quotations that suggest he played a role in their drafting. In many of these letters, there are textual admonitions against excessive prose (for example, 'more hyperbole and prolixity is a violation of good custom!'), while certain short, formulaic components of these letters are clearly copied from a well-known Timurid epistolographic manual (*Makhzan al-insha*, c. 1501, by Husain Va`iz Kashifi), which provides thousands of concise *inscriptio*s, benedictions, prayers and titulatures.[50] These all combine to suggest that traditional perceptions of imperial epistolography – where letters could function as vehicles of debate regarding political philosophy, ethics, advice, as well as contemplative theology and theosophy – were being routinised with symbols, formulas and rhetorical expressions which conveyed – rather than argued – concepts like sovereignty (*daulat*), power (*qudrat*) and obeisance (*ta`at*). In essence, it constituted an epistemological recalibration whereby chancery missives were now formalised and bureaucratised to such an extent that their deliberative and rhetorical function of arguing and persuading – celebrated for half a millennium by poets, litterateurs and philosophers – was significantly reduced. For instance, *munshi*s prior to the reign of Shah `Abbas usually began formal letters with poetic quatrains (*ruba`i*s), or more sizeable excerpts of verse, often chosen from the classical Persian literary canon; with Hatim Beg's rise to administrative dominance, however, we find letters begun simply with the words 'a noble letter' (*namah-yi sharif*) or 'an honourable letter' (*namah-yi marhamat*).[51] Traditionally, *intitulatio*s, stylised epithets designed to identify and lionise the recipient, could be intimidating in their sophistication and length; here *munshi*s would indulge in sets of rhymed phrases (*musajja`*) to exalt addressees at length with a rich arsenal of similes, metaphors and exemplars. During Hatim Beg's tenure in the administration, such stylised *inscriptio*s and formal poetry were clearly being attenuated.[52]

While we encounter a linguistic downturn with respect to style and substance, certain components of letters – seals, formulas, prayers, benedictions, signatures – actually grew in prominence and complexity in the early seventeenth century. The *tughra* had been in Timurid (1370–1507) and Qara/Aq-Qoyunlu times (fifteenth century) at the top and centre of a chancellery missive. During the Safavid period it was replaced with a different performative utterance which was inked in gold and appeared as the beginning words in the first line of a document: 'a royal decree found the honour of being issued' (*farman-i humayun sharaf-i nafadh yaft*).[53] Different formulaic phrases were later introduced, and popularised during the period of Hatim Beg's vizierate; thus, *hukm-i jahan-muta` shud* ('the world-obeying order has happened') is a common feature in later Safavid documents, as is *farman-i humayun shud* ('a royal order has happened'). Interestingly, as Bert Fragner has demonstrated, the official Safavid seal was moved by chancery functionaries from the bottom of documents to the top; no longer round, the seal's pear-like shape was designed so as to better accommodate the name of the Safavid ruler, along with the names of the fourteen Immaculate Imams to which the dynasty boasted a familial connection.[54] Such proximity between the name of the Safavid shah and the Prophet's family was part and parcel of a larger genealogical programme by jurists and religious scholars designed to connect these early modern kings with the Prophet and his pre-eternal and infallible progeny.

Safavid seals became increasingly complex and varied in terms of their design and text, and as such, one could argue that their diversification and use in multiple chancery spaces reflected the degree to which agents of state could operate independently of the ruler but still enjoy the full symbolic weight of his sovereignty. In an absolutist monarchical context, a chancery without access to some form of visual and recognisable imperial sanction cannot do business. In this way, the 'Great Seal' (*muhr-i humayun*) was complemented by 'small' seals (*muhr-i asar*) which in turn could be affixed to signet rings (*muhr-i angushtar-i aftab asar*); less important documents could be validated with a specific Safavid seal which imprinted with ink the physical text of the imperial imperative itself: *hukm-i jahan-muta` shud* ('the world-obeying order has happened').[55] Two of our more valuable seventeenth-century sources which explicitly discuss the proliferation of seals, document typologies and their varying formulas were both written by Bahram Malik Urdubadi's descendants: `Abd al-Husain al-Tusi, *munshi al-mamalik* in the 1630s, and Abu al-Qasim b. Muhammad Riza Nasiri, who was the nephew of `Abd al-Husain al-Tusi and served as *majlis-nivis* in the late seventeenth century.[56] Their respective epistolary compilations – the *Munsha'at al-Tusi* (1633)[57] and the *Risalah-i davaran* (c. 1669–76)[58] – both contain explicit sections on the different seals used in the chancery. Hatim Beg himself designed a series of new seals to herald the new imperial profile in the early seventeenth century.

After a successful campaign against the Ottomans, Shah `Abbas chose to show his piety and gratitude by performing a pilgrimage across Iran to the massive Shi`ite shrine complex (boasting the mausoleum of the eighth Imam, Ali Riza) in the city of Mashhad. In the afterglow of this pilgrimage, `Abbas decreed that sizeable numbers of royal properties and businesses (primarily in Isfahan) were to be categorised as religious endowments (*waqf*).[59] Munajjim Yazdi (d. 1619) describes also various *waqf* deeds which were re-enacted from previous Safavid family members, such as Shah Tahmasp and Shah Isma`il, as well as other princely royals including Sultan-Muhammad Mirza, Sultan-Hasan Mirza, Hamza Mirza in cities like Qazvin, Kashan, Mahmudabad and Isfahan.[60] A prodigious amount of money was generated according to the terms of these trust deeds (drawn up by the well-known jurist, Shaikh Baha' al-Din), and monies in turn were divided into fourteen shares of various sizes; the largest share 'belonged' to the Prophet Muhammad (meaning it could only be used for buildings and projects somehow connected with him or his name), and the thirteen other shares were divided amongst the direct descendants (Imams) of the Prophet Muhammad, starting with his daughter Fatima and ending with the Hidden Twelfth Imam. It should be noted that this invigorated imperial piety came on the heels of `Abbas's visit to Urdubad and his interaction with the *silsilah-yi Nasiriyyah*. It was Hatim Beg and a chief religious overseer (*sadr*) named Mirza Riza who designed the fourteen specific seals to be used for these new legal endowments. Hatim Beg ordered his chancery staff to research appropriate histories and Shi`ite hagiographies so as to recreate the signet seals purportedly used by the fourteen Imams themselves. According to Hatim Beg, in the seventh and eighth centuries the daily transactions (*dad o sitad*) of each Imam (*sar kar*) were routinely blessed with their own personal seal; by recreating these seals, Hatim Beg claimed to be enacting the notion of deputyship (*niyabat*) on behalf of an Imam's holy spirit (*nafs-i nafis-i humayun*).[61] Indeed, the question of the pre-eternality of the Imams – a subject of central doctrinal importance to medieval Shi`ite thought – was directly connected with the issue of the Imams' official seals. The eleventh-century scholar al-Shaikh al-Mufid had quoted Imami traditions that the angel Gabriel had handed to the Prophet Muhammad a tablet (*lauh*) which contained the names of the twelve Imams; in another tradition, the angel delivered a folder containing twelve seals that had been created before time and were meant for each of the Imams.[62]

Hatim Beg's programme – whereby official chancellery material abandoned its traditional embrace of high-minded literary devices and programmatic philosophies of language for the promotion of pietistic slogans and visual symbols associated with an increasingly hierocratic order – had broader implications for state formation and praxis of rule in seventeenth-century Iran. On the one hand, the devaluing of the *munshi al-mamalik* position and the marginalisation of rival urban bureaucratic elites certainly served the careerist interests of Hatim Beg, but such changes also reflected a newly articulated Safavid state under `Abbas which was both territorially rapacious and confessionally unambiguous. This bureaucracy was tasked with ushering in a new era of centralisation, whereby extensive properties, cities and provinces were reclassified as private royal property; taxes and revenues reached unsurpassed levels in the 1590s and early 1600s. However, it was `Abbas's sustained military campaigns on numerous frontiers which truly recalibrated the Safavid state, and after twenty-five years of territorial gains at the expense of the Ottomans and Uzbeks, the Iranians were in control of parts of the Caucasus, eastern Anatolia, Iraq, Khurasan and Khwarazm. Post-bellum, it was often Hatim Beg who served as a diplomatic contact and mediator in many of these conflict zones, and for much of his career he oversaw negotiations and brokered reconciliations with many non-Persephone communities that were vassals of the shah: Turks, Kurds, Arabs, Gilakis, Turkmen, Uzbeks, as well as Bakhtiyaris and Qashqa'is. As an Azeri Turk from the south Caucasus – trained in Persian and Arabic – he was culturally and linguistically capable of handling the diversity of the frontier zones of Safavid Iran; he was repeatedly charged to negotiate with non-Persephone notables and tribal leaders. In 1594, he personally negotiated the reintegration of semi-autonomous Huvaiza in Arabistan, ruled by Sayyid Mubarak Arab, while also dealing directly with the rebellious Afshar tribesmen (agitated by the aforementioned Sayyid Mubarak) in Kuh-Giluya two years later.[63] In 1595, he took the lead in the reorganisation of Gilan province and its Gilaki-speaking population after its formal annexation. In 1598 and 1600 respectively, he was the chief bureaucrat appended to the shah's military during two campaigns in Khurasan and Khwarazm, and then brokered the surrender and vassal status of the Shibanid Uzbek claimant, Nur Muhammad Khan.[64] He played an important diplomatic role in the negotiated 1603 peace between the Ottomans and the Safavids, and his last service before dying in 1611 was an attempt to conciliate with rebelling Kurdish tribes in the region of Urumiya. Arguably one of most successful negotiations of this variety came at the end of his career in 1609 when some 20,000 Jalali Turkish tribesmen rebelled against the Ottoman Empire, and then decided to migrate eastward to formally ally themselves with the Safavid dynasty. 'It was royally decreed', writes Munajjim Yazdi, 'that I'timad al-Daulah Mirza Hatim Beg go to Tabriz for the winter season so as to rank and appoint that group.'[65] Along with notables, amirs and a team of bureaucrats, Hatim Beg welcomed thousands of Ottomanised Turks to Tabriz on behalf of the Safavid Iranian shah with royal letters and formal investitures in hand; he was also responsible for preparing roll lists of these newly included Turkish clans and their tribal leaders.[66]

Concurrent with Hatim Beg's activities in this regard, the Safavid state was also expanding its *ghulam* programme in the Caucasus. Throughout the early 1600s, thousands of Georgians, Circassians and Armenians were incorporated into the Safavid imperial project as new military leaders, governors, administrators and courtiers. As Sussan Babaie observed: 'uprooted from their indigenous socio-political networks, the slaves were transplanted into a reconfigured imperial court', where they were invested through conversion with 'a new Muslim identity predicated upon Shi'ite loyalty to the Safavid Shah'.[67] This 'ghulam-ification' clearly had an effect on the chancery, and the decision by Hatim Beg to simplify imperial documentary and epistolary language may have been a response to these new non-Persephone elements in the Safavid state. A cursory view of 'Abd al-Husain al-Tusi's *Munsha'at al-Tusi* – produced some two decades after Hatim Beg's death – underscores the chancery's recognition of these changes. In his fourth section (*fasl-i chahar*), 'Abd al-Husain focuses on the various imperial orders and decrees (*ahkam va arqam va nishan va parvanchat*) produced by the general administration (*divan-i a'la*); these were to be understood as 'administrative formulaic documents' (*dastur al-'amal-and*). Of the four short sample decrees (*parvanchat*) he provides, two deal explicitly with the *ghulam*-dominated Caucasus.[68] Many of the governors and lords installed here from the 1590s onward were either tributary vassals of the indigenous Bagratid line who had brokered arrangements with the Safavid ruling dynasty against the expanding Ottomans, or young Bagratids who had been raised and educated as diplomatic hostages in the Safavid court as Shi'ite *ghulam*s. The first 'model' document is addressed to Gargin Khan, the governor of the Georgian environs of Bashi Achuq.[69] The second 'model' document is written for the governor of Girjistan, Salim Khan Sharaf al-Dinlu; Iskandar Beg Munshi confirms that Salim Khan Sharaf al-Dinlu had been appointed as governor of Akhesqa in 1622 after its subjugation.[70] In this case, the clan of Sharaf al-Dinlus (part of the Zu al-Qadar tribe) had been settled in this region as part of the shah's programme of forced tribal resettlement; Georgians were being moved to parts of central Iran while large numbers of Turks were settled in southern and eastern Georgia. Moreover, provincial governorships which had normally been reserved for Safavid family members or ranking Qizilbash amirs were now being steered towards the *ghulam*s. By 1629, eight of the fourteen major provincial governorships were held by Caucasian elites.[71] Chancery configurations and documentary output may very well have been shifted to reflect these new geopolitical realities. As one scholar noted: 'the metamorphosis of Caucasian slaves into elite members of the Safavid household coincided with an official Shi`i language of authority that altered hierarchies of loyalty and consolidated a patriarchal family'.[72]

INSHA AND ALTERITY IN THE 1630s

One might be tempted to see these epistemological and ontological shifts in the chancellery as proof of the 'decline thesis' which characterises much of seventeenth-century Safavid studies. Indeed, the recalibration and effective marginalisation of traditional bureaucratic systems would appear to move in line with how other constituencies and households were either eliminated or overtly centralised during the reign of Shah `Abbas.[73] As many have pointed out, the short-term dividends of such reforms were indeed considerable for Shah `Abbas, but the dilution of traditional groups of elites – military, bureaucratic, religious – would ultimately have a corrosive effect on the Safavid polity, leaving it unable to respond to both internal and external challenges.[74] Such an interpretation has more than a whiff of teleology about it, and specialists point to the cultural and philosophical production in mid-seventeenth-century Safavid Iran by the likes of Mulla Sadra, Muhsin Faiz Kashani, Sa'ib Tabrizi, Mir Firindiski and Abd al-Razzaq Lahiji as evidence challenging the 'long decline' thesis.[75] Nor did stylised chancellery literature disappear, as a number of prominent *insha* texts were produced in the second half of the seventeenth century, including Muhammad Amin b. Abd al-Fattah Vaqqari Yazdi's *Goldastah-yi andishah*, Aqa Husain Khwansari's *Munsha'at*, Mir Abu al-Hasan Taj Husaini's correspondence and the famous *Insha-yi Tahiri* by Mirza Muhammad Tahir Vahidi Qazvini. Interestingly, however, there were contemporaries to Hatim Beg Urdubadi who were denied access to his controlled and reconfigured chancellery space who recognised the import of these new administrative priorities; indeed, they expressed anxiety and concern about the role and future of men of the pen in this new hierocratic Safavid Order.

Hatim Beg's own nephew `Abd al-Husain al-Tusi, a talented *munshi*, had been passed over for any ranking positions within the chancery during his uncle's tenure as grand vizier. At some point roughly twenty years after Hatim Beg's death, `Abd al-Husain earned entry into the central chancellery as the *munshi al-mamalik*, and in 1633, he compiled one of the most important *insha* collections of the Safavid era: the *Munsha'at al-Tusi*, a compendium of royal letters, state decrees and personal correspondences from both the pre-Safavid and Safavid periods. Of the over one hundred letters provided in the manual, only two of Hatim Beg's missives are formally included by his nephew, and a single letter by 'Sayyid Nasr', who may be the same Nasir Khan Beg (Hatim Beg's nephew) who served as the *munshi al-mamalik* during much of Shah `Abbas's reign. More interesting, however, is the *dibachah* (foreword) of the *Munsha'at al-Tusi*, which gives a diligent accounting of `Abd al-Husain's Nasiriyyah family in Urdubad without mentioning Hatim Beg even once.[76] What tension or misunderstanding existed between uncle and nephew is not clear from the sources, but `Abd al-Husain's lack of position until some two decades after Hatim Beg's death is telling. Moreover, his later decision as *munshi al-mamalik* to compile arguably the most comprehensive Safavid didactic and exemplary *insha* work since the collapse of the Timurids may have been an attempt to restore status and prestige to an office that had been systematically devalued since the early 1590s. The timing of `Abd al-Husain's compilation (1633) is also interesting given that it was a moment when Shah Safi was challenging openly the established hierocratic order of the jurists, and in turn appointing and supporting `irfan-inspired gnostics and mystical literati to positions of state. It was also in 1633 that the aspiring bureaucrat Saru Taqi, himself committed to the destruction of the Nasiriyyah Urdubadis on account of his father's being passed over for a position by Hatim Beg, came to the fore and arranged to have Mirza Talib Khan (Hatim Beg's son and current vizier) assassinated. Intriguingly, it may very well have been `Abd al-Husain's apparently fractured relationship with his uncle that allowed him to survive the purges of the old order after 1632.[77]

`Abd al-Husain al-Tusi was not the only notable *munshi* to have seized upon the shift in priorities in the Safavid state after the death of Shah `Abbas in 1629. Mir Muhammad Husain b. Fazl Allah Husaini Tafrishi was an acquaintance, if not a good friend, with a number of notables in the late sixteenth and early seventeenth centuries and was widely considered to be a man of scholarly repute.[78] Thanks to the editorial efforts of Mohsin Bahram-nejad, we now have access to Tafrishi's collected letters, the *Munsha'at-i Tafrishi*. Bahram-nejad believes that Tafrishi lived until 1632 (but this is not altogether clear from the sources), and that his father (Fazl Allah Husaini Tafrishi) had been responsible for training and educating not only Muhammad Husain, but also his brothers Mir Abu al-Baqa' and Mir Abu al-Mufakhir; Abu al-Baqa' (*takhallus*: Baqa'i) was a highly regarded poet in the time of Shah `Abbas before his death in 1621.[79] The contents of Mir Muhammad Husain's letters indicate that he was at least in regular 'friendly' (*ikhvani*) communication with highly placed individuals during a phase of great change in the Safavid bureaucracy. These included Hatim Beg Urdubadi himself, Mirza Talib Khan (Hatim Beg's son and prominent vizier), Khalifa Sultan (a grand vizier), Shaikh Baha' al-Din Muhammad (a prominent philosopher and jurist) and lastly, `Abd al-Husain al-Tusi, the aforementioned *munshi al-mamalik* and compiler of the *Munsha'at al-Tusi*. The letters' contents and addressees place the compilation date of this *Munsha'at* shortly before

Tafrishi's putative death in 1632. Indeed, `Abd al-Husain al-Tusi replicates episto-lary exchanges between himself and Tafrishi in his own compilation, while Tafrishi himself includes several letters to and from the *munshi al-mamalik*.[80] The content of these letters certainly suggest that both Tafrishi and `Abd al-Husain worked concur-rently from the inkpots of mystical philosophy, literary prose and scribal culture. It appears that Mirza Muhammad Husain Tafrishi was educated formally by none other than Ibrahim Hamadani, the well-known sayyid and scholar jurist who had served as chief *qadi* in Hamadan before joining the royal retinue of Shah `Abbas; indeed, the *Munsha'at al-Tusi* includes a letter from Shaikh Baha' al-Din to Tafrishi's formal instructor.[81]

With such elevated familial pedigree and well-heeled sponsorship, it is all the more surprising that Tafrishi's name does not appear as a chief Safavid functionary during the reign of Shah `Abbas. However, Bahram-nejad suggests that Tafrishi was dismissed and removed by Hatim Beg from his position as a courtly *munshi* and teacher 'on account of a jape' at the expense of the grand vizier; in one letter, Tafrishi describes himself as a *persona non grata* in the Safavid state, and it was only after the death of Hatim Beg in 1611 that he was able to recover any official standing.[82] According to decrees reproduced in the *Munsha'at-i Tafrishi*, Shah `Abbas's suc-cessor, Shah Safi, arranged for Tafrishi's daughter to be married to Haidar Beg, the son of the *ishik aqasi bashi*, Zainal Kham Shamlu (d. 1630), with the aim of exalting both families.[83] Moreover, Shah Safi was known for his antipathy toward jurists and Shi`ite orthopraxy, and not long after his accession he worked to promote a 'philo-sophical renaissance, heavily influenced by the currents in the intellectualized mysti-cism of the literati and the ascetic shaikhs, which produced the tradition of `*irfan*, or gnostic philosophy'.[84] A review of his correspondence with contemporaries certainly supports the notion that Tafrishi was a superlative practitioner of the epistolary arts, and as such, was out of character with Hatim Beg's chancellery and its embrace of the formulaic and prosaic. According to Bahram-nejad, Tafrishi's epistolary style was 'experimental in nature' (*tab`-i azma'i*), and for this reason `Abd al-Husain al-Tusi had chosen to include three of his letters in the *Munsha'at al-Tusi*.[85] It is my contention that Tafrishi's skill and mastery of `*ilm-i insha* also allowed for a nuanced and subtle challenge to the judicial orthopraxy advocated by Hatim Beg and his scribal staff, along with their endorsement of the Caucasian *ghulam*s.

In one of several letters to Mirza Talib Khan (Hatim Beg's son), who had been appointed as grand vizier in 1632, Tafrishi indulges in the literary ostentation associ-ated with traditional Perso-Islamic chancellery arts in his opening address:

> the sun-ray of hope appeared [with the arrival] of a letter [which is an] auspi-cious and ambergris-scented pastille from the royal *qiblah* and has made [my hopeless scribal] workshop the envy of the atelier of China as well as the Paradise and its houris.[86]

Tafrishi subsequently quotes a *ghazal* of the popular mystic poet Sa`di that invokes the motif of a letter's arrival via a bird (likely playing on the Qur'anic narrative of Queen Sheba's correspondence with Solomon through a hoopoe) to buttress his surprise and amazement.[87] 'I know and see better what has happened tonight to my mind', he waxes poetic, but 'what can be done when the palette of proper speech and proper deed has been rendered nonsensical with [this] delicacy?' Tafrishi pursues the point at some length: 'this sherbet [that is, the letter from Mirza Talib Khan] of truth, chivalry, civility, and honour is so sweet that it is indigestible'.[88] True to his dedication to the epistolary masters of the past, Tafrishi quotes a line of poetry from the staunchly Sunni Rashid al-Din Vatvat, who was a prominent twelfth-century scholar of chancellery craft, poetry and prosody: 'if the scent of honour was not in the world / then there would be no friendship among men'.

The most significant section of this letter, however, is Tafrishi's short section of advice and admonition to Mirza Talib Khan; it is possible that this letter was written to commemorate his nomination as grand vizier in 1632. As a professional epistolary stylist, Tafrishi would have been aware of the broad mandate of *insha* literature, and he employs here the traditional vocabulary and sentiments associated with Perso-Islamic advice manuals (*nasihah namahs*). Specifically, Tafrishi discusses how Mirza Talib is appointed in his position of governance (*maqam-i intizam*) so that he can observe 'the chain of generation and corruption' (*silsilah-yi kaun va fasad*) to ensure God's goodwill, the tranquility of mankind, and the maintenance of property and prayer. The reference to 'generation and corruption' (*kaun va fasad*) is an invocation of Aristotle's philosophical treatise of the same name, which was regularly referenced in classical Islamic metaphysical philosophy and cosmology.[89] 'Subsequently your position', Tafrishi clarifies, 'is to gather powers and senses day and night' (*jami`-i quva' va masha`ir-i ruz va shab*) towards attaining this goal (*tahsil-i in matlab*).[90] Making reference to his status as a revered *munshi* and to the presence of his own enemies in court, Tafrishi reminds Mirza Talib that there are those who indulge in sedition and disruption but it is the vizier's duty to be dedicated to the advising (*maslahat*) with 'kinsmen and relations' (*aqarib va khishan*) and communicating (*guftagu*) with old functionaries and servants (*khidmat-karan-i qadim va bandagan*).[91] Tafrishi – quoting Sa`di – declares to Mirza Talib Khan: 'I stand here for diligent service / whether this service will be received well or not.'[92]

There are, in fact, a total of fourteen letters addressed to Mirza Talib Khan in the *Munsha'at-i Tafrishi*, and the quantity and the quality of these suggest a close and deep relationship between the two men. These missives express not only Tafrishi's support both before and after Mirza Talib's nomination as grand vizier in 1632, but they occasionally offer advice regarding the role of viziers and bureaucrats, as well as the function of epistolography and chancelleries. In one letter, Tafrishi writes how rulers want the preservation of those 'stories of beneficences and good qualities' (*asar-i ahsan va afzal-ishan*) which have flowed for many years over the paths of the elite and the poor (*bar al-sunnah-yi khvas va `avam jari budah*). However, Tafrishi also realised that his predilection for Gnostic `*irfan* and Sufism – at least in theory – meant a certain separation from the secular world: 'it is not hidden that [gaining] happiness by serving a king is beyond the custom of [this] powerless beggar'.[93] Nonetheless, Tafrishi invokes the reign of Shah Safi as the beginning of a new era. After collecting (*talfiq*) and scrutinising (*tadqiq*) the phrases, metaphors and tropes of past writings from scholars like the Timurid polymath Sharaf al-Din

Yazdi, the Ottoman scholar Khvajah Sa`d al-Din Efendi, and the great Mughal vizier Shaikh Abu al-Fazl, he realises that encomiums like 'the exalted station of Khusrau' (*shayastah-yi makan-khusrau*) and 'Lord of the Auspicious Age' (*sahib-qiran*) are not suitable.[94] For Tafrishi, this reign is 'another order' (*samani-yi digar*) which requires an entirely different language, or set of tropes (*zabani-yi digar*). Thus, he hails this epoch as 'the spring equinox of knowledge and the best age of God's creation' (*nauruz-i bahar-i danish va khulasah-yi zaman-i afarin-ash ast*). With the grace of the kings of the age, and towards assisting ministers like Mirza Talib Khan, Tafrishi is presenting 'some phrases' (*harfi-chand*) here which should be suitable 'to cast among the holy congregation [around] the world's king of kings' (*nisar-i mahfal-i muqaddis-i shahinshah-i `alam*).[95] In another letter to Mirza Talib Khan, Tafrishi describes how the arrival of this great dynastic recycling (*daulat-i `uzmi*) is an auspicious event, while adding that divine decree (*hisb-i taqdir*) stipulates that some epochs of God's special honour are currently happening, and that those eras which had previously been divided 'are now being reassembled in a short time period' (*in azmina dar andak-i zamani farahim mi-ayad*), namely Shah Safi's reign.[96] Until Safi's accession, Tafrishi was stranded in social and spiritual desolation – as in the spirit of the Arabic saying 'loneliness has become his beast' (*al-wahshat washuhu*) – but now he cannot wait to stand in the shah's exalted retinue (*dar rikab-i `ali sarf shavad*).

The thematic emphasis here on cyclical time and rebirth is particularly intriguing in light of a number of instances where Tafrishi makes specific reference to how various individuals and groups are flirting with *hayulani*. *Hayulani* – meaning 'primordial matter' – was often understood as a euphemism for the Nuqtavi 'heresy' which had emerged in the late sixteenth century as a powerful socio-religious phenomenon in central Iran, Gilan and Mazandaran. Nuqtavis in the fifteenth to seventeenth centuries were gnostics who argued that all existent things on earth were transmutations of the same primordial matter (*hayula*), and that all humans are part of an ongoing, never-ending process of birth, growth, death and regeneration.[97] Nuqtavis were usually associated with antinomian elements who used coded and secretive cosmological language to critique stridently what they perceived to be corrosive social norms: increased orthopraxy, decreased spirituality, heightened materialism, and the refusal to recognise the greater cosmological cycle which explained the history of humankind and the universe.[98] Shah Tahmasp had some high-profiled Nuqtavis punished dramatically in the 1560s, while Shah `Abbas flirted with Nuqtavi discipleship (strictly for propagandistic and ideological purposes) before ordering a wide-scale persecution in 1593.[99] Continued Nuqtavi activity – or at least the perception of it – continued into the seventeenth century, and Tafrishi refers to *hayulani* devotees in several letters to both Mirza Talib Khan and `Abd al-Husain al-Tusi.

In a letter to Mirza Talib Khan, written likely in 1632, Tafrishi describes 'how lamentable it is to be preoccupied with the movements of the *ghulam-zadeh*s who – as a group – have moved from the path of reasonable ideas and, contrary to *muruvvat* (manliness), have now passed into the rank of `*aql-i hayulani*'.[100] Intriguingly, Tafrishi states that if Mirza Talib Khan was inclined to help resolve this situation, a person could be sent among these dissenters, but this could only happen with a little diligence from the ministers of the court. The *ghulam* princes (or *ghulam-zades*) mentioned here may be Tahmurs Khan and Davud Khan, who had been kept in the royal court of Isfahan as hostages, but later returned to Georgia and rebelled against the shah. Whether or not Caucasian *ghulam* elements were associating with Nuqtavi preachers and advocates is difficult to say, but it is certain that designating individuals or groups as *hayulani* would have been a common strategy to undermine support and confidence in an era of divisive court politics.

At the same time, Tafrishi's writings appear to reflect a personal connection with Nuqtavi thought. In one letter to `Abd al-Husain, the *munshi al-mamalik*, Tafrishi argues how God's presence in the elemental state (*nishat-i `unsuri*) and the physical world (`*alam-i jismani*) empowers the Sufis until the Day of Resurrection (*qiyam-i qiyamat*). 'Woe is me!' Tafrishi exclaims, 'that there are ignorant ones who will not know the power of those days' (*qadr-i an ayam na-danast*) on account of the deficiency and limitations of the human race (*nuqsan-i bashariyat*). He describes how religious scholars ordered the spiritual investigation (*istakshaf-i ahval mi-namudah-and*) of a group based in Qom who had initially been serving the Safavid state.[101] He theorises on the relative ease of determining a Muslim's external state (*hal-i suri*), but if one orders an investigation and report on the internal state (*hal-i darun istakshaf va istakhbar*), then the following needs to be considered: 'It is known – on account of the first cause (`*illat*) – that the elemental state (*nishat-i unsuri*) and the created world (`*alam-i tarkib-zadi*) are measured with regard to the wide and far journey of the state of abstraction (*nishat-i tajarrud*).' It becomes evident here that Tafrishi is explaining how such mystics could find themselves professing primordialism, or *hayulani*. 'Friendless, strange, wretched, and dishonest', these putative Nuqtavis now live in a 'jungle of beasts of different truths' (*jangal-i siba`-i mukhtilafah al-haqa'iq*).[102] In other letters, there are references to accusations against *hayulani*, and it would appear that Safavid religious authorities were regularly investigating individual Sufis and various cloisters that were known to Tafrishi.[103]

Tafrishi clearly belonged to a circle of bureaucrats and scholars who were comfortable with debating and discussing `*irfan*, mysticism, and various topics such as philosophies of language, body and the mind. In an undated letter to `Abd al-Husain al-Tusi, Tafrishi shows his literary-mystical proclivities and closeness with the addressee by opening the letter with a stanza from Sa`di: 'O! Your face is a treasury filled with gems of meaning / I have a mark of love for you buried in my heart.'[104] This letter proceeds immediately to a discussion of how 'lords of knowledge and mystical philosophy' (*arbab-i `ilm va `irfan*) and 'masters of discernment and discovery' (*ashab-i zauq va vajdan*) operate on elevated plains of cognition thanks to knowledge from the 'seas of Malakut' (*bihar-i malakuti*) and the 'coastline of Jabarut' (*savahil-i jabaruti*) which provide 'precious pearls' that are the basis for 'earrings of intellect' (*halqah-gush-i hush*).[105] In the spirit of the typical Avicennan metaphysics so popular in the medieval Perso-Islamic world, Tafrishi states it is the connection of 'subtleties of intellect' (*lizzat-i `aqliyyah*) to our human 'subtleties of senses' (*mustalazzat-i hisiyyah*), or the meeting of spiritual cognitions (*qiyas-i mudrakat-i ruhaniyyah*) with corporeal revelations (*mushahadat-i jismani*), that the finite becomes infinite (*muntanahi bi ghair-i muntanahi*).[106] This is followed by a lengthy exposition which details the ontological proximity between love and longing (*'ishq va shauq*) and includes an Arabic phrase 'he is in love with his own delights, he is beloved for his delights and for others' – from Ibn Sina's *Al-Isharat wa'l-tan-bihat* (*Remarks and Admonitions*). However, this passage is quoted by Tafrishi from Khvajah Nasir al-Din al-Tusi's (ancestor of the addressee, `Abd al-Husain al-Tusi) own commentary on Ibn Sina, the *Sharh-i isharat*.

Muhammad Husain Tafrishi also wrote two letters to Hatim Beg Urdubadi at some point soon after his exile from the Safavid chancellery. Given that Hatim Beg passed away in 1611, it is likely that these missives were written at some point in the first decade of the seventeenth century. In the first letter, there is none of the sycophantic prefatory language normally included for an addressee of the grand vizier's stature, but rather a short discussion of post-Avicennan metaphysics. After God's theophany (*ba'd az ada-yi ma huwa al-wajib*), Tafrishi explains, it was incumbent upon sages (*danayan*) and wise ones (*binayan*) to end their dependency on the physical world (*qat'-i ta'alluqat-i badani*) by drawing forth exalted wise secrets (*rumuz-i hikmat-i muta'aliyyah*) and great hidden truths (*haqa'iq-i asrar-i khufiyah-yi 'aliyah*) from the 'dark altars' (*hayakil-i zulmaniyyah*), the latter likely being a playful reference to Suhravardi's *Hayakil al-nur* ('The Altars of Light').[107] Indeed, what follows is unmistakably Illuminationist in its outlook, stating that it was these scholars who commanded that 'every kind of stars, constellations, elements, and compounds' (*har nu'i-yi aflak va kawakib va basa'it va 'anasir va marakibat*) is a 'directing light' (*nur-i mudiri*), which in turn is the 'lord of that kind' (*rabb-i an nu'*), or the Divine. This is a sensory world, Tafrishi informs Hatim Beg, where it has been 'fixed and commanded' (*sabit va mahkum*) that the thirsty truth-seekers (*muta'attishan*) move in the desert of corporeal dependence (*wadi-yi ta'alluqat-i jismani*).[108] It is for this reason (*li-hadha*), that 'great scholars' (*buzurgan-i danish*) and 'subtle sagacious ones' (*zirakan-i barik*) are incapable of constructing even one atom of God's benefi-cence and qualities, but their clustering together of powers of perception and senses towards understanding this subtlety (*daqiqah*) elevates them as the 'most exalted of the spiritual, perfect ranks' (*a'la-yi maratib-i kamalat-i nafsani*).[109]

In light of these comments, the second half of Tafrishi's letter to Hatim Beg is especially interesting. He notes – perhaps caustically – that the grand vizier has not been made aware of his condition, or he has simply been too busy to care. Tafrishi narrates how he, described as this abject one (*kaminah*), was compelled to leave on account of an insult (*zillat*), and was forced to travel endlessly in the desert of stupor and bewilderment (*badiyah-yi hairat va hayman*).[110] The tenor of the letter turns sententious when he writes:

Regarding the beneficence and kindness of great lords (*khudaigan*), it is hoped that moral duty (*zimmat-i muruvvat*) would require them to provide 2–3 days of sustenance. If there are those who do not approve of this notion, namely that the bounties of the emperor, the divine shadow, [are a] limitless sea and an endless ocean which are shared by the infidel (*kafir*), the Muslim, the believer, the unbeliever (*bi-aiman*), the Zoroastrian, the Christian, the Jew, the Nazarene, the ignorant one (*jahil*), the labourer (*amil*), the cautious one (*hushyar*), and the prudent one (*ghafil*), then this slave is without hope.[111]

The censorious tone here toward the 'great lords' and their violation of *zimmat-i muruvvat* is consistent with the tenor of anti-statist sixteenth-century writings of the Nuqtavis and their promotion of social justice and equity. Moreover, Tafrishi provides a schema of Safavid society that makes no special reference to Shi`ism, but instead invokes those constituencies normally marginalised by the Muslim majority: the *kafir*, the Zoroastrian, the Jew, the Christian. Tafrishi's emphasis here and elsewhere on *futuvvat* (chivalry) and *muruvvat*, as well as his references to a wide array of religious communities are consistent with Nuqtavi social bases: 'the arts and crafts dominate the professional occupations of most of the known non-Qizilbash Nuqtavi devotees. Craftsmen were linked to chivalric circles, which . . . were arenas of resistance where Muslim, Mazdeans, Armenians, and Jews created communal bonds of solidarity.'[112] Particularly enlightening is the ultimatum which follows this jeremiad:

and for the purposes of attaining immortal sustenance, I will go begging for this and that [like] a mendicant in India. Regarding [such] a trifling means of living – after the eternal, fortunate reward of serving the lordly court – [people] will know about [you] men of the age.[113]

It was common knowledge that many of the Nuqtavis – under threat of punishment and execution – had fled to Mughal India and secured employment and sponsorship in the ecumenical courts of Akbar (r. 1556–1605) and Jahangir (1605–27).[114] Moreover, Tafrishi's connection between 'immortal sustenance' (*faut al-yamaut*) and 'begging' (*bi-darvaizah*) was also likely a coy reference to the preaching of Safavid Iran's famous contemporary antinomian Nuqtavis like Dervish Khusrau and Dervish Kamal.

Tafrishi was undoubtedly a talented *munshi*, litterateur and philosophical thinker, but the reasons for his professional catastrophe at the hands of Hatim Beg Urdubadi need to be revisited. Rather than an inopportune 'joke' – as suggested by Bahramnejad – Tafrishi's connection to and flirtation with Nuqtavi thought and practice were likely grounds for his exile from the Safavid chancery and the court. A number of his letters from the early phase of Shah Safi's reign (1629–32) – when his friend and colleague Mirza Talib Khan enjoyed vizierial status in the Safavid court – embrace enthusiastic discussion of spiritual metaphysics and Gnostic thought (`*irfan*) while also explicitly highlighting this period as the best in a series of cyclical ages. His references to the unfortunate souls who sit in 'the rank of primordial intellect' (*martabah-yi `aql-i hayulani*) are surprisingly accommodating in tone and tenor, and we do not encounter any of the censorious and heresiographical language often used by Safavid religious authorities regarding the Nuqtavis. His response to these *hayulani*s and their spiritual interrogation by the state betrays more dispiritedness than moral outrage. Indeed, the only evidence of moral opprobrium we have comes from a letter to Hatim Beg Urdubadi written some twenty years earlier, when Tafrishi roundly condemned the behaviour of the worldly and affluent Safavid court while invoking the Nuqtavi themes of social equity and justice. Urdubadi's promotion of Shi`ite orthopraxy and the corresponding sponsorship of the *ghulam* Caucasus elite would certainly have been contrary to Tafrishi's ecumenical and spiritual worldview. It is likely that Tafrishi's unwillingness to accept these convictions of the Safavid court and administration guaranteed exile and marginalisation. His later extensive correspondence with fellow litterateurs-cum-bureaucrats like `Abd al-Husain al-Tusi and Mirza Talib Khan reveals an older and wiser scholar who had learned to temper his indignation while also placing hope in the change in dynastic leadership that came with the death of `Abbas and the accession of Safi.

Interestingly, as the Georgian, Circassian and Armenian *ghulam*s were being incorporated into the empire, many Iranian secretaries, bureaucrats, scholars and poets were leaving it, and here Tafrishi's threat to move to India makes sense. That this exodus was directly a result of the influx of the *ghulam*s, or the rise in power of families like the Shi`ite Nasiriyyahs of Urdubad, is unlikely. The exodus of Iranian literati, poets and *adib*s to more ecumenical lodestars like Mughal and Deccan India began in the sixteenth century with Shah Isma`il's privations against Iranian urban centres and Shah Tahmasp's sanctimonious policies against musicians, dancers and other *bons vivants*. To be sure, the siren call of India had been sounding for centuries for aspiring Iranian and Central Asian mystics, scholars and adventurers. It is possible that there was 'a second wave' into India of Iranian scholar-bureaucrats in the 1590s as a result of Safavid persecution of the Nuqtavis and the open-door policy that Akbar enacted; those who felt marginalised by the religious, ethno-political and social changes in Safavid Iran were occasionally sought out and recruited by the Mughals, and these individuals included some of the more accomplished minds of the age in the contemporary Persianate world.[115] If the grand epistolographic tradition was under threat during the reign of `Abbas in Iran, it certainly thrived and bloomed during the rule of Akbar and his successors in India. As Muzaffar Alam has shown, the Persianate intellectual and administration tradition became a defining feature for the Mughal Indian court in the early modern period.[116] Cities like Lahore and Agra became hubs of patronage for free-thinking and free-styling Persian poets and litterateurs – some of whom were *ksatriya* Hindus who had embraced Persian as a language of prestige and employment. Mid-seventeenth-century Mughal India played host to a flourishing epistolographic tradition that endorsed a 'whole range of normative Indo-Persian principles concerning ethical behavior, administration, competence, and idealized masculine conduct'.[117] Indeed, as Rajeev Kinra has further observed, the literary and administrative elites of Mughal India were inspired by the *munshi* exemplar of the twelfth- and thirteenth-century Islamo-Iranian world: 'penmanship, accounting, prose writing, social etiquette, diplomatic savvy, political discretion, literary flair, scholarly erudition and even mystical sensibility came to be associated with great *munshis*'.[118]

In the case of Safavid Iran, the *munshi*s no longer enjoyed a position of social and professional exclusivity in the shah's court and administration, as sayyids, jurists and shaikhs entrenched themselves, but we do find evidence to suggest that *munshi*s were able to survive these lean, captious times without necessarily opting en masse for the greener pastures of Mughal India. The period following the accession of Shah

Safi witnessed an intense articulation of *munshi* identity, which appears to have been a component of the larger fluorescence of spiritual philosophy and `*irfan* of the 1630s and 1640s. Indeed, Safi likely drew from such constituencies as part of a bigger challenge to the entrenched jurist networks and households of notables who had flourished during the reign of his father. But Safi was incapable of replicating the absolutist style of rule – and the extended patrimonial system which flowed from it – which `Abbas and Hatim Beg had developed. Indeed, the policies of promoting *ghulam*s and Shi`ite jurists while marginalising Qizilbash tribes and other traditional groups could only be effective alongside a healthy and committed personalised approach to sovereignty. The narrative of the early phase of Safi's rule (1629–33) suggests that he began with a comparable sense of conviction. And while he certainly played off competing *ghulam* and Qizilbash networks, evidence from *munshi*s and Persian bureaucrat-scholars of the day indicate that – for at least a brief period – they seized upon this opportunity to reverse Hatim Beg's privation and marginalisation of the literary and philosophically minded bureaucrat-scholars to contribute actively to the maintenance of the state. They comfortably operated in the discourse which had emerged as a Sufi–Shi`ite synthesis in the fifteenth and sixteenth centuries, and indeed many were likely comfortable with the orthopraxic Shi`ite Safavid state that was emerging. However, there were some exceptions – notably Mir Muhammad Tafrishi – who drew upon the epistolary arts to challenge the established hierocracy of the sayyids and the jurists in profound and provocative ways.

NOTES

1. R. Matthee, 'Was Safavid Iran an Empire?' *Journal of the Economic and Social History of the Orient* 53 (2010), p. 234 (pp. 233–65).
2. Jo Van Steenbergen, *Order Out of Chaos: Patronage, Conflict and Mamluk Socio-Political Culture, 1341–1382* (Leiden: Brill, 2006); Michael Chamberlain, 'Military Patronage States and the Political Economy of the Frontier, 1000–1250', in Youssef Choueiri (ed.), *A Companion to the History of the Middle East* (London: Blackwell, 2005), pp. 141–52. See also Rifa'at Ali ABou-El-Haj, *Formation of the Modern State: The Ottoman Empire, Sixteenth to Eighteenth Centuries* (Syracuse, NY: Syracuse University Press, 2006); Muzaffar Alam, 'State Building under the Mughals: Religion, Culture, and Politics', in Alam and Sanjay Subrahmanyam (eds), *The Mughal State, 1526–1750* (Oxford: Oxford University Press, 1998), pp. 105–28; Farhat Hasan, *State and Locality in Mughal India: Power Relations in Western India, c. 1572–1730* (Cambridge: Cambridge University Press, 2004).
3. Jo Van Steenbergen, 'The Mamluk Sultanate as a Military Patronage State: Household Politics and the Case of the Qalawunid Bayt (1279–1382)', *Journal of the Economic and Social History of the Orient* 56 (2013), p. 194 (pp. 189–217).
4. Hasan, *State and Locality in Mughal India*, pp. 4–7.
5. Bhavani Raman, *Document Raj: Writing and Scribes in Early Colonial South India* (Chicago: University of Chicago Press, 2012).
6. Said Amir Arjomand, *The Shadow of God and the Hidden Imam: Religion, Political Order, and Societal Change in Shi`ite Iran from the Beginning to 1890* (Chicago: University of Chicago Press, 1984).

7. Said Arjomand, 'Legitimacy and Political Organisation: Caliphs, Kings, and Regimes', in Robert Irwin and Michael Cook (eds), *New Cambridge History of Islam*, 6 vols (Cambridge: Cambridge University Press, 2010), vol. 4, p. 272.

8. Kathryn Babayan, 'The Safavid Synthesis: From Qizilbash Islam to Imamite Shi'ism', *Iranian Studies* 47:1–4 (1994), p. 157 (pp. 135–61).

9. Kathryn Babayan, *Mystics, Monarchs, and Messiahs: Cultural Landscapes of Early Modern Iran* (Cambridge, MA: Harvard University Press, 2002), pp. 99–100.

10. Muzaffar Alam, 'The Culture and Politics of Persian in Pre-Colonial Hindustan', in Sheldon Pollock (ed.), *Literary Cultures in History: Reconstructions from South Asia* (Berkeley: University of California Press, 2003), pp. 157–8 (pp. 131–98). This term 'prestige language' was actually coined by Kumkum Chaterjee in her discussion of Muzaffar Alam's article. See Chaterjee, 'Scribal Elites in Sultanate and Mughal Bengal', *The Indian Economic and Social History Review* 47:4 (2010), p. 459 (pp. 445–72).

11. Colin Mitchell, 'A Medieval Nexus: Locating *Enshâ*' and its Ontology in the Persianate Intellectual Tradition, 1000–1500', forthcoming in Bo Utas (ed.), *History of Persian Literature*, vol. 5 (Prose) (London: I. B. Tauris).

12. Lajos Fekete (ed. and trans.), *Einführung in die persische Paläographie: 101 persische Dokumente* (Budapest: Akadémiai Kiadó, 1977), p. 28.

13. Cornelia Vismann, *Files: Law and Media Technology*, trans. G. Winthrop-Young (Stanford: Stanford University Press, 2008), p. 49.

14. Raman, *Document Raj*, p. 3. See also David Dery, '"Papereality" and Learning in Bureaucratic Organizations', *Administration and Society* 29:6 (1998), pp. 677–89.

15. Dery, '"Papereality"', p. 681.

16. Vismann, *Files*, p. 17.

17. Notable examples include *Dastur al-katib fi ta'yyin al-maratib* ('The Manual of the Scribe and the Affixing of Rank') by Muhammad b. Hindushah Nakhjuvani, the *Tuhfah-yi Jalaliyyah* ('The August Gift') by Hakim al-Din Mohammad b. Ali al-Namus Khwari and the *Risalah-yi Qavanin* ('The Treatise of Regulations') by Mo'in-al-Din Mohammad Zamchi Esfezari.

18. Fekete, *Einführung in die persische Paläographie*, pp. 19–21.

19. Muhammad b. Hindushah Nakhjavani, *Dastur al-katib fi ta'yyin al-maratib*, ed. A. A. Ali-zade (Moscow: Nauka, 1964–76), vol. 2, p. 117, quoted in Ann Lambton, *Continuity and Change in Medieval Persia* (Albany: State University of New York Press, 1988), p. 58.

20. Michael Clanchy, 'Does Writing Construct the State?', *Journal of Historical Sociology* 15 (2002), p. 68 (pp. 68–70).

21. Aziz al-Azmeh, *Muslim Kingship: Power and the Sacred in Muslim, Christian and Pagan Polities* (London: I. B. Tauris, 2001).

22. Nakhjavani, *Dastur al-katib*, vol. 2, p. 121.

23. Vladimir Minorsky (ed. and trans.), *Tadhkirat al-muluk: A Manual of Safavid Administration, circa 1137/1725* (London: Luzac, 1943), pp. 158, 154.

24. Ibid. p. 61; Christoph Marcinkowski (ed. and trans.), *Mirza Rafi'a's Dastur al-Muluk: A Manual of Later Safavid Administration* (Kuala Lumpur: ISTAC, 2002), p. 213.

25. Minorsky, *Tadhkirat al-muluk*, p. 53.

26. Ibid. p. 53.

27. When 'Abbas was the crown prince (*vali 'ahd*) in the city of Herat, the Safavid ruler of the day – a thoroughly unhinged Isma'il II (r. 1576–7) – had ordered his nephew's execution along with dozens of other extended family members; the orders for this family murder spree likely would have been drafted and formalised by the *munshi al-mamalik*. The prince managed to earn a reprieve, but Röhrborn argues that 'Abbas never forgot this, and after his accession saw in the bureaucracy an opportunity to align and shape organs of state so as to settle old scores and implement his centralising agenda. See Klaus-Michael Röhrborn,

'Staatskanzlei und Absolutismus im safawidischen Persien', *Zeitschrift der Deutschen morgenlandischer Gesellschaft* 127 (1977), pp. 315–16 (pp. 313–43).

28. Ibid. pp. 315–16.
29. Marcinkowski, *Mirza Rafi`a's* Dastur al-Muluk, p. 213; Minorsky, *Tadhkirat al-muluk*, p. 62 (fo. 40b. in Persian text).
30. Röhrborn, 'Staatskanzlei und Absolutismus', p. 315.
31. Babayan, *Mystics, Monarchs, and Messiahs*, pp. 83–4.
32. Curiously, the bottom of page 912 of Savory's translation does not match the beginning of the text on page 913. See Iskandar Beg, *History of Shah 'Abbas the Great*, vol. 2, pp. 911–18; Iskandar Beg, *Tarikh-i `alam-ara-yi `Abbasi*, ed. I. Afshar, 3rd edn (Tehran: Intisharat-i Amir Kabir, 2003), vol. 2, pp. 722–3.
33. Rasul Ja`fariyan, 'Urdubad va ahamiyyat-i farhangi-yi an dar daurah-yi ahkir-i Safavi' ('Urdubad and its Cultural Significance in the Late Safavid Era'), *Payam-i Baharistan* 11 (2011), p. 14 (pp. 14–34).
34. Iskandar Beg, *Tarikh-i `alam-ara-yi `Abbasi*, vol. 2, p. 723.
35. Ibid. p. 723; A. H. Morton, 'An Introductory Note on a Safawid *Munshi*'s Manual in the Library of the School of Oriental and African Studies', *Bulletin of the School of Oriental and African Studies* 33:2 (1970), p. 357, n. 29 (pp. 352–8).
36. Erroneously, I referred to Mirza Kafi as a 'Khurasani' in my earlier book, Colin Mitchell, *The Practice of Politics in Safavid Iran: Power, Religion and Rhetoric* (London: I. B. Tauris, 2009), p. 90.
37. Iskandar Beg, *Tarikh-i `alam-ara-yi `Abbasi*, vol. 2, p. 724.
38. Mirak Beg served initially as a *munshi*, and later as vizier, to Tahmasp's *vakil* (plenipotentiary) Ma`sum Beg Safavi, but when the *vakil* was killed in 1568, Mirak was nominated to serve in the imperial court of Qazvin as the *majlis-nivis* (court reporter).
39. Adham Beg served as chief financial accountant (*mustaufi*) and vizier to one of the Safavid princes, Mustafa Mirza, who fell victim to Isma`il's bloodletting in 1576. Adham retired from administrative service, but returned to serve as vizier to the governor of Tabriz in 1584. When `Abbas ascended the throne, he retired to Ardabil to serve in the Safavid familial shrine; however, when his brother, Hatim Beg, was named as grand vizier, he was given a robust annual pension of 100 *tuman*s to live quietly in Shiraz until his death in 1608.
40. Abu Turab Beg served as a secretary in Mashhad, but was killed during the turbulent reign of Isma`il II (1576–7).
41. Abu Talib served as a secretary in Herat, but was killed in 1587 during hostilities with the Uzbeks to the east.
42. Fahimah Ali Begi, 'Hatim Beg Urdubadi', in *Danish-namah-yi jahan-i Islam* (*Encyclopaedia of the World of Islam*) (online), vol. 12, available at <http://www.encyclopaediaislamica.com/> (in Persian) (last accessed 10 November 2015).
43. Iskandar Beg, *Tarikh-i `alam-ara-yi `Abbasi*, vol. 2, p. 725.
44. Charles Melville, 'From Qars to Qandahar: The Itineraries of Shah 'Abbas I (995–1038/1587–1629)', in Jean Calmard (ed.), *Études Safavides* (Paris: Institut français de recherche en Iran, 1995), pp. 193–207.
45. Iskandar Beg, *Tarikh-i `alam-ara-yi `Abbasi*, vol. 2, p. 724. See also Mitchell, *The Practice of Politics in Safavid Iran*, p. 166.
46. Mitchell, *The Practice of Politics in Safavid Iran*, p. 180; Iskandar Beg, *Tarikh-i `alam-ara-yi `Abbasi*, vol. 2, p 633.
47. The seminal work on such topics is still Jean Aubin's 'Etudes Safavides. I. Shah Isma`il et les notables de l'Iraq persan', *Journal of the Economic and Social History of the Orient* 2:1 (1959), pp. 37–81.
48. Charles Melville, 'New Light on the Reign of Shah `Abbas: Volume III of the *Afzal*

al-tavarikh', in Andrew Newman (ed.), *Society and Culture in the Early Modern Middle East: Studies on Iran in the Safavid Period* (Leiden: Brill, 2003), p. 86 (pp. 63–96).

49. Muhammad Husain Tafrishi, a scholar active during the early reign of Shah Safi, wrote a letter where he extended condolences to ʿAbd al-Husain al-Nasir after the death of 'Mir Nasir', and this appears to have taken place at some point between 1629 and 1632. See Muhammad Husain b. Fazl Allah Husaini Tafrishi, *Munsha'at-i Tafrishi: Majmu'ah-i az namah-ha-yi ikhvani va divani-yi dauran-i Safaviyyah*, ed. Mohsin Bahram-nejad (Tehran: Kitabkhanah-yi Muza va Markaz-i Asnad-i Majlis-i Shura-yi Islami, 2011), p. 28.

50. Mitchell, *The Practice of Politics in Safavid Iran*, p. 181.

51. Colin Mitchell, 'Safavid Imperial *Tarassul* and the Persian *Insha'* Tradition', *Studia Iranica* 26:2 (1997), p. 197 (pp. 173–209).

52. Ibid. pp. 201–3.

53. Herbert Busse, 'Diplomatic: III. Persia', in *Encyclopedia of Islam*, 2nd edn (Leiden: Brill, 1960–2009), vol. 2, p. 311. See also Busse, 'Persische Diplomatik im Überblick: Ergebnisse und Probleme', *Der Islam* 37 (1961), pp. 202–45.

54. Bert Fragner, 'Tradition, Legitimität und Abgrenzung: formale Symbolaussagen persischsprachiger Herrscherurkunden', in Walter Slaje and Christian Zinko (eds), *Akten des Melzer-Symposiums 1991. Veranstaltet aus Anlaß der Hundertjahrfeier indo-iranistischer Forschung in Graz (13.–14. November 1991)* (Graz: Leykam, 1993), pp. 84–113. See also his excellent entry on decrees entitled 'Farman', in *Encyclopaedia Iranica*, ed. E. Yarshater (New York: Columbia University Press, 1999), vol. 9, pp. 282–95.

55. See Hyacinth Louis Rabino di Borgomale, *Coins, Medals, and Seals of the Shahs of Iran, 1500–1941* (Hertford: S. Austin and Sons, 1945).

56. Röhrborn, 'Staatskanzlei und Absolutismus', p. 322.

57. ʿAbd al-Husain al-Tusi, *Munsha'at al-Tusi*, MS Paris, Bibliothèque nationale, Supplément persan 1888, fos. 300a–301b.

58. Morton, 'An Introductory Note on a Safawid *Munshi*'s Manual', p. 357.

59. Iskandar Beg, *Tarikh-i ʿalam-ara-yi ʿAbbasi*, vol. 2, pp. 760–1.

60. Munajjim Yazdi, *Tarikh-i ʿAbbasi*, MS London, British Library, Or. 6263, fo. 158a–b.

61. Iskandar Beg, *Tarikh-i ʿalam-ara-yi ʿAbbasi*, vol. 2, p. 670.

62. al-Azmeh, *Muslim Kingship*, p. 193.

63. Iskandar Beg, *Tarikh-i ʿalam-ara-yi ʿAbbasi*, vol. 2, pp. 675–7, 699–701.

64. R. G. Mukminova, 'The Khanate (Emirate) of Bukhara', in Ahmad Hasan Dani and V. Masson (eds), *History of Civilizations of Central Asia*. Vol. 5, *Development in Contrast: From the Sixteenth to the Mid-Nineteenth Century* (Paris: UNESCO, 2003), p. 45 (pp. 33–62).

65. Munajjim Yazdi, *Tarikh-i ʿAbbasi*, fo. 162a.

66. Iskandar Beg Munshi has an entire section on Hatim Beg's reception of the Jalalis (*zikr-i raftan-i ʿali-janab I'timad al-dawlah Hatim Beg bi-istiqbal-i Jajaliyan bi-dar al-saltanat Tabriz va avardan-i sardaran-i an tabaqah-ra bi-dar al-saltanat Isfahan bi-ʿatabah-busi-yi dargah-i jahan-panah shahinshah-zaman*). See Iskandar Beg, *Tarikh-i ʿalam-ara-yi ʿAbbasi*, vol. 2, pp. 772–7.

67. Sussan Babaie, Kathryn Babayan, Ina McCabe and Massumeh Farhad, *Slaves of the Shah: New Elites of Safavid Iran* (London: I. B. Tauris, 2004), p. 7.

68. It should be noted that there are many other types of documents (*ruqa*ʿs, *ʿariza dasht*s) which are provided, but they do not appear in this explicit fourth section.

69. ʿAbd al-Husain al-Tusi, *Munsha'at al-Tusi*, fos. 305a–306a. Two possibilities exist as to the identity of Gargin (George) Khan. Either he was George X, who had ruled as the local dynast of Kartili in eastern Georgia from 1599 until 1606, or he was George III, who had ruled in Imereti from 1605 to 1635; in either case, both were part of the extended royal Bagratid family. Nasrullah Falsafi states that George X, son of Simon, ruled Kartili. See

Nasrullah Falsafi, *Zindagani-yi Shah `Abbas* (Tehran: Danishgah-i Tehran, 1953), vol. 5, p. 31. Röhrborn, however, states that Bashi Achuq is not in the Karteli kingdom, but to the west in the kingdom of Imereti; if this is the case, the Gorgin of this document refers to George III. See Klaus-Michael Röhrborn, *Provinzen und Zentralgewalt Persiens im 16. Und 17. Jahrhundert* (Berlin: De Gruyter, 1966), p. 76.

70. Iskandar Beg, *Tarikh-i `alam-ara-yi `Abbasi*, vol. 2, p. 1229.

71. Ilhan Niaz, *Old World Empires: Cultures of Power and Governance in Eurasia* (New York: Routledge, 2014), p. 121.

72. Babaie et al., *Slaves of the Shah*, pp. 47–8.

73. Regarding the Qizilbash, see Kathryn Babayan, 'The Waning of the Qizilbash: The Spiritual and the Temporal in Seventeenth-Century Iran' (PhD dissertation, Princeton University, 1993).

74. John Foran, 'The Long Fall of the Safavid Dynasty: Moving Beyond the Standard Views', *International Journal of Middle East Studies* 24:2 (1992), pp. 281–304.

75. For recent work on Mir Damad and Mulla Sadra, see the following works by Sajjad Rizvi: *Mir Damad* (Oxford: Oneworld, 2013); *Mulla Sadra Shirazi: His Life and Works and the Sources for Safavid Philosophy* (Oxford: Oxford University Press, 2007); *Mulla Sadra and the Later Islamic Philosophical Tradition* (Edinburgh: Edinburgh University Press, 2013). The seventeenth-century Iranian focus on `irfan has been recently examined by Ata Anzali in his dissertation, 'Safavid Shi`ism, the Eclipse of Sufism and the Emergence of `Irfan' (PhD dissertation, Rice University, 2013). For a general overview, see S. H. Nasr and M. Aminrazavi (eds), *An Anthology of Philosophy in Persia*. Vol. 5, *From the School of Shiraz to the Twentieth Century* (London: I. B. Tauris, 2015). Sa'ib Tabrizi is the subject of Paul Losensky's detailed entry, 'Sa'eb Tabrizi', in *Encyclopaedia Iranica* (online) (2003), available at <http://www.iranicaonline.org/articles/saeb-tabrizi> (last accessed 17 December 2015). The historiographical implications of the 'long decline' of the Safavids has most recently been examined by Rudi Matthee in *Persia in Crisis: Safavid Decline and the Fall of Isfahan* (London: I. B. Tauris, 2011).

76. `Abd al-Husain does take time to contextualise the role of his family in regards to the Safavids: 'my ancestors arranged themselves among the string of disciples and supporters of this family – defined as a pure embodiment of spiritual authority (*dudman-i vilayat-makan-i safiyyah-i safavi*) – who are a branch (*munsha'ab*, perhaps a coy allusion to *munsha'at*, or "letters") of the Prophetic and Imami family'. `Abd al-Husain describes how one of his Nasiriyyah ancestors – Qazi Imad al-Din al-Tusi – had demonstrated his loyalty to the Safavid shaikh Sadr al-Din by delivering (and possibly drafting) a letter to the Mongol ruler Sultan Ahmad Jala'ir during the 1380s; in this way, the Nasiriyyahs of Urdubad had always been in bureaucratic service on behalf of the Safavids, be they shaikhs or shahs. See `Abd al-Husain al-Tusi, *Munsha'at al-Tusi*, fos. 8b–9a.

77. The most detailed exploration of court politics during the reign of Shah Safi is Babayan's 'The Waning of the Qizilbash'.

78. Mohsen Bahram-nejad, 'Munsha'at-i Mir Muhammad Husain Tafrishi: Kandokavi dar zandagani-yi farhangi va divani-yi u' ('The Letters of Mir Muhammad Husain Tafrishi: A Study on a Cultural Life and His Administration'), *Ayinah-i Miras* 43:4 (2009), pp. 93–124.

79. Mohsen Bahram-nejad, 'Moqaddimah (Introduction)', in Tafrishi, *Munsha'at-i Tafrishi*, p. xxxv.

80. `Abd al-Husain al-Tusi, *Munsha'at al-Tusi*, fos. 327b–343b.

81. Ibid. fos. 308a–312a.

82. Bahram-nejad, 'Moqaddimah', p. xlii.

83. Ibid. p. xlviii.

84. Arjomand, *The Shadow of God*, 1984, p. 148.

85. Bahram-nejad, 'Moqaddimah', p. xliv.
86. Tafrishi, *Munsha'at-i Tafrishi*, p. 1.
87. Sa'di, *Kulliyat-i Sa'di*, ed. Muhammad Ali Furughi (Tehran: Nashr-i Hastan, 1993), p. 431.
88. Tafrishi, *Munsha'at-i Tafrishi*, p. 2.
89. Seyyed Hossein Nasr, *An Introduction to Islamic Cosmological Doctrines* (Albany: State University of New York Press, 1993), p. 84; Gerhard Endress, 'Aristotle and Aristotelianism', in Josef W. Meri (ed.), *Medieval Islamic Civilization: An Encyclopedia* (New York: Routledge, 2006), vol. 1, p. 68 (pp. 66–70).
90. Tafrishi, *Munsha'at-i Tafrishi*, p. 3.
91. Ibid. p. 3.
92. Ibid. p. 3; Sa'di, *Kulliyat-i Sa'di*, p. 414.
93. Tafrishi, *Munsha'at-i Tafrishi*, p. 36.
94. Ibid. p. 36.
95. Ibid. p. 36.
96. Ibid. p. 16.
97. Nuqtavis erased the line between Creator and created, arguing that humans themselves played a key role in their own genesis and later regeneration; thus, there is a doctrinal link between the Nuqtavis and the Hurufi doctrine of metempsychosis (*tanasukh*). The primacy ascribed by Nuqtavis to *hayulani* was deemed by orthodox Muslims to be a violation of God's eternality, while philosophers (following Ibn Sina and al-Tusi) worked with notions of *`illat, wajib al-wujud* and *mumkin al-wujud* (First Cause, Necessary Existence and Contingent Existence) to argue for a more rational explanation of God's creation. See Babayan, *Mystics, Monarchs, and Messiahs*, pp. 57–8.
98. Nuqtavis looked for evidence of this cosmological cycle in a variety of ways, including geomancy by letters (*`ilm-i huruf*), alchemy (*kimiya*) and magic (*sihr*); their focus on pre-Islamic Iranian religious traditions (Zoroastrianism, Mazdaism) also resulted in a particular emphasis on the Iranian solar calendar as well as those specific Persian letters (in Arabic script) which contain three dots – hence the name 'Nuqtavi', roughly meaning 'pointilist'. See Babayan, *Mystics, Monarchs, and Messiahs*, pp. 74–5.
99. Azfar Moin, *The Millennial Sovereign: Sacred Kingship and Sainthood in Islam* (New York: Columbia University Press, 2012), pp. 163–4.
100. Tafrishi, *Munsha'at-i Tafrishi*, p. 17.
101. Ibid. p. 26.
102. Ibid. p. 27.
103. Ibid. pp. 43–4, 45–6, 46–7, 53–5.
104. Ibid. p. 11; Sa'di, *Kulliyat-i Sa'di*, p. 661.
105. Tafrishi, *Munsha'at-i Tafrishi*, p. 11.
106. Ibid. p. 11.
107. Ibid. p. 12. On Suhravardi, see Annemarie Schimmel, *The Mystical Dimension of Islam* (Chapel Hill: University of North Carolina Press, 1975), p. 260.
108. Tafrishi, *Munsha'at-i Tafrishi*, p. 12.
109. Ibid. p. 13.
110. Ibid. p. 13.
111. Ibid. p. 13.
112. Babayan, *Mystics, Monarchs, and Messiahs*, p. 102.
113. Tafrishi, *Munsha'at-i Tafrishi*, p. 13.
114. Moin, *The Millennial Sovereign*, pp. 166–9.
115. Amir Rahimy and Sebastian Joseph, 'Causes of Migration of Iranians to India during the Mughal Period', *Indo-Iranica* 61:3–4 (2008), pp. 1–43; Masashi Haneda, 'Emigration of Iranian Elites to India During the 16th–18th Centuries', *Cahiers d'Asie Centrale* 3–4 (1997), pp. 129–43.

116. Alam, 'The Culture and Politics of Persian in Pre-Colonial Hindustan', pp. 163–6.
117. Rajeev Kinra, 'Master and *Munshī*: A Brahman Secretary's Guide to Mughal Governance', *Indian Economic and Social History Review* 47:4 (2010), p. 530 (pp. 527–61).
118. Kinra, 'Master and *Munshī*', p. 530.

CHAPTER 11

Choreographers of Power: Grigorii Kotoshikhin, State Secretaries and the Muscovite Royal Wedding Ritual

Russell E. Martin

Sometime before 1 September 1664, Grigorii Karpovich Kotoshikhin, a middle-level chancery clerk (*pod'iachii*) in the Russian Foreign Office (*Posol'skii prikaz*), fled his homeland for the West. He went first to Vilna, which was then part of the Polish–Lithuanian Commonwealth (the so-called *Rzeczpospolita*), then to Poland proper, and then on to Silesia, Prussia, Lübeck and, by the autumn of 1665, to Sweden. Kotoshikhin fled for several possible reasons, all of them good, though historians remain unclear which, if any, was the most important. He fled, according to one view, because he and his father had made powerful enemies at court and their property and other possessions had been (apparently unjustly) confiscated. Kotoshikhin feared additional reprisals and found escape the best alternative in his predicament. Or Kotoshikhin fled, as he himself would later claim, because he had inadvertently manoeuvred himself into the hopeless position of being a pawn in the intrigues of powerful men over him, each trying to cajole him into supporting their feud against the other. Or, what is most likely, Kotoshikhin fled his homeland and made a break for Russia's western neighbours and rivals because he had been passing secret information to the Swedes off and on since the summer of 1663 and feared that his treason was about to be discovered.[1]

Kotoshikhin was therefore one of the earliest and most famous of Russia's defectors. But his name may not have become so well known to us were it not for the account he wrote for his new Swedish masters in the late spring and summer of 1666, in which he described 'the whole Muscovite state'. This account, entitled *On Russia in the Reign of Aleksei Mikhailovich* (*O Rossii v tsarstvovanie Alekseia Mikhailovicha*), is a broad yet penetrating description of how seventeenth-century Muscovy was run. It is divided into thirteen thematic chapters, each treating what Kotoshikhin considered to be a key element of the Muscovite government and political culture, though he surely would not have used these terms to describe them. He begins in chapter 1 with a detailed description of the tsar's family and of important moments in the life cycle of the tsar and his kin, including a lengthy explanation of royal wedding ceremonies. Subsequent chapters treat the ranks and titles of officials at court (chapters 2 and 3); Muscovite diplomatic practice (chapters 4 and 5); the administrative divisions of the tsar's court, a topic Kotoshikhin knew well, being a well-placed scribe in the court (chapters 6 and 7); provincial administration (chapter 8); military levies (chapter 9); trade, commerce and state revenues (chapters 10–12); and the private lives of the tsar's boyars, the leading servitors at court – including, again, a detailed description of their wedding rituals (chapter 13).[2] He likely assumed that he and his text would fade into oblivion and out of the historical record, and that is what happened for a time.[3] His account was translated into Swedish and circulated for 'a generation or two' after his death,[4] but it eventually fell into obscurity in Sweden and was entirely unknown in Russia. But *On Russia* was rediscovered in the 1830s and its importance was immediately grasped by historians and philologists, being published in four competent editions between 1840, when the first Russian edition appeared, and 1906, followed by the definitive edition and study produced by A. E. Pennington in 1980.[5] An English translation appeared for the first time in 1970, but has been broadly accessible only since 2014.[6] On its publication in 1840, *On Russia* was greeted by scholars as a kind of Muscovite Dead Sea Scrolls. Early commentators called the text 'priceless', 'masterful', a 'rare phenomenon' and 'in places truly a classic'.[7] Kotoshikhin's account has since then been rightly considered a unique and indispensable source for early modern Russian court life, chancery practice and political culture inside the Kremlin. As Nancy Shields Kollmann put it, *On Russia* is an 'accurate and insightful description of the Muscovite court'.[8]

Kotoshikhin was in a good position to write this description of the Muscovite court. Born around 1630 and entering service in the Foreign Office around 1645 as a scribe (*pisets*) and later promoted (around 1658) to clerk (*pod'iachii*), Kotoshikhin worked in the one chancery that would give him the most exposure to the most important people and diplomatic and administrative procedures of the Muscovite state. The Foreign Office, like other central chanceries in the mid-seventeenth century, was headed by a *dumnyi d'iak* – a state or 'consular' secretary – who oversaw a large and competent staff of secretaries (*d'iaki*), clerks (*pod'iachie*) and scribes (*pistsy*).[9] Kotoshikhin was thus a fast riser among a relatively large and competent staff of professionals. He was evidently able and hardworking, and as a result had an extensive and varied diplomatic career before his defection. He served as a member of the team of scribes attached to embassies conducting treaty negotiations in Vilna (1658), in Pöhestekule (1659) and in Dorpat (1659–60), and he was a member of the Russian embassy that negotiated the Peace of Cardis with Sweden in June 1661. Later that year he was in Stockholm as a diplomatic courier, and in 1662 (and probably for much of the next two years leading up to his defection) he served as a diplomat attached to regional commanders of Russian forces fighting the Poles (in the Russo-Polish War of 1654–67).[10] When not off on diplomatic assignments, Kotoshikhin was in Moscow handling the everyday business of the Foreign Office, which included a range of diplomatic and dynastic matters. Among these matters was probably the preparation of royal wedding documents, which were drafted by the scribes and secretaries, and then, after the wedding was over, deposited in the chancery's archive, which doubled as the tsar's personal archive.[11] Thus the Foreign Office was not only the place that engaged in all manner of diplomatic matters we might expect to be within its purview – including treaty negotiations, diplomatic correspondence, ambassadorial receptions, and so on – it was also the centre for the production and preservation of all dynastic documentation, such as that related to royal wills and weddings.[12] In Muscovy, matters of dynasty and diplomacy were handled by the same cohort of scribes, clerks and secretaries.

It is therefore no accident that Kotoshikhin begins and ends *On Russia* with weddings. His goal in writing the text was to provide his new master, King Charles XI of Sweden (r. 1660–97), a useful exposé of aspects of court life that were not typically known by outsiders, or even by Muscovites outside the walls of the Kremlin. Such information would be invaluable to the Swedes as they negotiated war and peace with the Russians. The tsar's wedding rituals were glittering and precisely choreographed spectacles meant to project an image of royal power and nuptial contentment. They thus provide clues into the inner workings of the tsar's court and its chanceries. Tsars married in elaborate ceremonies that extended over four days (in the sixteenth century, it had been three days), which included several formal banquets, processions, gift exchanges, ritual baths and formulaic speeches. The bulk of the Muscovite court participated, filling a range of honorific duties traditional at Muscovite weddings (whether royal or not).[13] Which courtiers filled which ceremonial positions, who sat next to whom at the banquets, who marched in procession to the church and to the banquet hall, who held the ceremonial loaves of bread, the cheese, sables and torches – all these aspects of royal wedding rituals are seen by historians today, and by Kotoshikhin in his time, as vital clues to the nature and operation of high politics in the Kremlin.[14] Understanding the wedding ritual is key to understanding the inner structure of the Muscovite ruler's court: who was who, not just in terms of the ranks and titles of courtiers, which imperfectly reflected power relations at court anyway, but also in terms of the real and informal influence that men at court enjoyed by virtue of their proximity to the person of the ruler. These informal relationships are revealed by rituals, and Kotoshikhin shows us in his arrangement of topics in *On Russia* that he believed no court ritual revealed those informal relationships better than a royal wedding.

Though Kotoshikhin's *On Russia* has now appeared in excellent modern Slavonic and English editions, there have been only a handful of major studies of its contents and sources. The first, by A. I. Markevich, was published in 1895 and is as much a biography of Kotoshikhin as it is an analysis of his text. The second, by A. N. Pypin, appeared shortly after Markevich's book and examined (and challenged) some of his conclusions.[15] A third major study (and translation), by Benjamin Uroff, appeared in 1970 as an unpublished doctoral dissertation, which updated and expanded what Markevich and Pypin achieved more than half a century before.[16] In 2014, Uroff's dissertation was finally published by Marshall Poe, along with a new survey of Kotoshikhin's career and biography, an updated bibliography and a new appreciation of the contents of *On Russia*.[17] But, as Harvard historian Edward Keenan wrote in 1986, *On Russia* 'still awaits a modern evaluation': a glum assessment of the state of research thirty years ago that remains true even today.[18] The description of royal weddings in *On Russia*, which was so important to Kotoshikhin that he placed it in the very first chapter, reveals more than just information about weddings. It shows how scribes, clerks and state secretaries acted as choreographers of power in seventeenth-century Muscovy.

THE ROYAL CHANCERY AND ROYAL WEDDINGS

In early modern Russia, dynasty and diplomacy were linked, but not for the usual reasons. In most other European monarchies in the sixteenth and seventeenth centuries, dynasties were joined in crisscrossing lines of intermarriage that had been arranged by extensive diplomatic negotiations, often with the goal of ending wars or forging alliances.[19] But in Muscovy from about 1500 on, the ruling dynasty rarely entered the European-wide marriage market, preferring to avoid the exorbitant costs and confessional complexities of marrying a foreigner. Instead, Russia's rulers married the daughters of mid-level courtiers or provincial nobles, and they created (or, more accurately, borrowed from Byzantium) an elaborate bride-show ritual to facilitate the selection of a native-born bride. This bride-show was adopted to mask the inherent inequality of the match by artificially elevating the socially inferior bride to an 'equal' status with the grand prince or tsar through a number of symbolic steps. But the bride-show was a rather new practice in Muscovite marriage policy: for centuries before 1500, the rulers of the East Slavic principalities frequently *did* marry foreigners.[20] This long tradition had created a link between dynastic concerns and diplomacy among secretaries, clerks and scribes that specialised in matters of dynasty and foreign policy – a link that long outlived the change in marriage policy in 1500 away from marrying the Heterodox. The scribes who drafted the ruler's wills, letters and treaties were the same lot that drafted his wedding documents: these were all matters of the highest importance to the ruler personally. This group of secretaries, then, became skilled experts on the high politics of their realm, able to negotiate treaties, craft formal correspondence and lay out the seating chart for a royal wedding.

The Foreign Office emerged out of the grand-princely chancery, the earliest scriptorium that had formed around the Muscovite ruler in the late fourteenth century. In its earliest decades, the chancery engaged in a range of undifferentiated duties, handling essentially all of the grand prince's scribal needs, apart from those taken up by scriptoria in monasteries, large churches or in apanage courts scattered across north-eastern Rus'. When exactly the grand-princely chancery formed separate and specialised cells of scribes working on specific areas of documentation – military muster rolls, land charters, treasury records, and so on – is still uncertain, but most agree that by the 1540s, during the reign of Ivan IV the Terrible (r. 1533–84), there was a staff of scribes and secretaries already in place handling exclusively diplomatic and dynastic matters, the precursor to the Foreign Office.[21] The range of their responsibilities is evident in the case of the 1533 wedding of Prince Andrei Staritskii, the younger brother of Grand Prince Vasilii III (r. 1505–33). The draft of the wedding ceremonial (*svadebnyi chin*), which describes the sequence of rituals at the wedding, is written on the verso of a draft letter from Vasilii III to Khan Islam-Girei of Crimea (r. 1532). Both documents use the same scribal conventions and were evidently written and edited by the same secretaries.[22]

State secretaries and the ranks of scribes working underneath them, like Kotoshikhin, assumed enormous responsibility in choreographing the rulers' weddings, events that came to be known, euphemistically, as the 'sovereign's happy occasions' (*gosudarevy radosti*).[23] With very few exceptions, secretaries and scribes from the Foreign Office were charged with drafting and editing the documents related to dynastic weddings over the course of the sixteenth and seventeenth centuries. These documents included the wedding ceremonial (*svadebnyi chin*), which describes the rituals that took place over the course of a three-day (and the in the seventeenth century, four-day) wedding. Ceremonials (*chiny*) were arranged chronologically – describing in sequence events as they happened, with the names of courtiers mentioned as needed to complete the narrative descriptions. A second document, the wedding muster (*svadebnyi razriad*), was also compiled, which consisted merely of the names of the courtiers who held honorific posts at the wedding – best men (*druzhki*), matchmakers (*svakhi*, their wives), the master of ceremonies (the *tysiatskii*), and so on – all arranged in descending order of importance. Scribes used both documents to help them manage the wedding: the ceremonial (to tell them what rituals needed to take place next) and the muster (to tell them who was to perform them).[24] In the seventeenth century (and perhaps earlier), scribes from the Military Muster Chancery (*Razriadnyi prikaz*) also came to be involved in the work of compiling wedding documentation, which was an improvement on the previous procedure because the wedding muster (*svadebnyi razriad*) was drawn from lists of courtiers maintained by the Muster Chancery.[25] Scribes from other chanceries and from the Treasury were also called upon to carry out specific assignments related to weddings.[26] But even as the tasks expanded and came to involve more and more members of the court's scribal staffs, the Foreign Office ultimately remained in charge of the entire process. The only occasions between 1500 and 1671 when state secretaries of the Foreign Office (or its precursor, the grand-princely chancery) did not manage a royal wedding were during the later weddings of Tsar Ivan IV the Terrible, who eschewed the usual structures of Muscovite administration during the so-called *oprichnina* (Ivan IV's ruthless 'privy domain'),[27] and at the second wedding of Tsar Aleksei Mikhailovich in 1671, when the tsar reassigned the responsibilities from the state secretary in charge of the Foreign Office, who had fallen into disfavour.[28]

Secretaries and scribes from the Foreign Office were on hand at royal weddings, directing traffic, as it were, among the hundreds of servitors attending to the tsar. An important task of secretaries and scribes at royal weddings was to handle the wedding rosters (*vedali spiski*) and to move people about from venue to venue. Most surviving sources indicate that they had other important assignments, as well. Sometimes they walked in procession to and from the church alongside the boyars and other high-ranking courtiers, could be seated in a place of honour at the banquet table, and sometimes even oversaw arrangements for the wedding bed, making sure that everything about the couple's wedding night was in order. The latter might include hanging the appropriate icons on the walls, placing sables on the bed and sheaths of grain under it, or posting guards outside the bedchamber.[29]

Perhaps the most important role played by state secretaries and their scribal staffs was composing and editing the wedding texts themselves. While Muscovite weddings followed a standard and prescribed format, significant editing of these rubrics was nonetheless required each time a grand prince or tsar married. For every wedding, secretaries needed to create new versions of the documents (both the ceremonial and muster) because the cast of characters changed, not just the names of the bride and groom, of course, but also the names of those who would perform honorific and ceremonial duties. Even more important, state secretaries and scribes continuously introduced small but important changes to the texts of the wedding descriptions, such as composing increasingly fuller, more detailed descriptions of rituals so that it would be much easier to replicate the ritual the next time a tsar married, or improving the literary quality of the narrative overall by including the texts of speeches or prayers delivered at key moments in the wedding. Over the course of the sixteenth and seventeenth centuries, the choreographers of the tsars' weddings relied less and less on memory and skeletal textual descriptions to make sure they got the wedding 'right'. By the 1670s, they had in hand very detailed and serviceable manuals for choreographing a royal wedding.

The editing work of state secretaries was particularly important when the first ruler of the new Romanov dynasty, Tsar Mikhail Feodorovich (r. 1613–45), married for the first time in 1624. The need to 'get the wedding right' was particularly imperative because the wedding afforded the new regime the opportunity to say something about itself through the media of symbol and ritual. The *dumnyi d'iak* choreographing Tsar Mikhail's wedding, named Ivan Taras'evich Gramotin, was well aware of this opportunity and had his staff of secretaries, clerks and scribes investigate previous royal wedding rituals in order to make the wedding seem as traditional as possible, even as he was adding new elements to emphasise the new dynasty's claims of legitimacy. On the basis of research into previous royal weddings, Gramotin and his staff made significant changes to the ritual, changes which were designed to project an image of the new Romanov dynasty as a continuation of the Old Dynasty.[30] Similar strategic editing happened again in the reign of the second Romanov tsar, the devout Aleksei Mikhailovich (r. 1645–76), who eliminated many of the pre-Christian fertility rites and raucous entertainments that filled wedding celebrations in the previous century.[31] These changes – increasingly more detailed textual descriptions of rituals, the alteration of rituals for dynastic purposes, the fine-tuning of the ritual to emphasise the groom's religiosity – were the responsibility of the scribal staff in the Foreign Office: men whose control of the court's rituals (and the texts that described them) effectively made them choreographers of power. Or, as Keenan put it, '[t]here is much that is still unclear about the origins and rules of [the Muscovite political] system, but it is apparent that the keepers of the rulebook, the non-participant referees, were the *d'iaki*' – the secretaries.[32]

KOTOSHIKHIN AND THE MUSCOVITE ROYAL WEDDING RITUAL

Kotoshikhin understood as well as anyone the political system in Muscovy and how much it depended on marriage – that of the tsar, first and foremost, but also the marriages between and among the boyars who occupied the inner circles of power and privilege in the Kremlin.[33] The clusters of kinship that resulted from these marriages were the building blocks of high politics in Muscovy. The contents of *On Russia* provide a wealth of useful insights into what Muscovites themselves may have thought about their own political world. Still, scholars who have examined Kotoshikhin's text have wondered how he knew so much about so many different topics, and this question is all the more vital when it comes to his description of royal wedding rituals. His account of weddings is not without mistakes, which become apparent when we compare it with the original manuscripts of royal ceremonials (*chiny*) and musters (*razriady*) preserved in Russian archives today. But *On Russia* also gets a lot right, which suggests a deep familiarity with the chancery sources (and an equally remarkable memory, given the fact that he composed his description of them hundreds of miles away from Moscow and without access to the manuscripts in the Foreign Office's archive).

Kotoshikhin was born after the weddings of the first Romanov tsar in 1624 and 1626. He joined the scribal staff of the Foreign Office probably shortly after the ascension of Tsar Aleksei Mikhailovich in 1645; and he was on staff at the Foreign Office when the scribes, clerks and secretaries there were working busily on the documentation for the tsar's first planned wedding in 1647 (to Evfimiia Vsevolozhskaia), and his actual first wedding in 1648 (to Mariia Miloslavskaia).[34] In the course of that scribal work, Kotoshikhin may have handled documents from Tsar Mikhail Feodorovich's weddings since we know that copies of them were made and used as models for the documentation of the 1647 and 1648 wedding projects.[35] Thus, even though nothing in the surviving sources tell us directly that he worked on Tsar Aleksei Mikhailovich's wedding (his name is not mentioned as a scribe who worked on the texts, probably because of his low rank), it stands to reason that he may have done so and that his detailed knowledge of Muscovite royal wedding ritual so readily on display in *On Russia* derives from his many months of working on the wedding ceremonial and muster.

The likelihood that Kotoshikhin worked on wedding documentation occurred to A. I. Markevich, the first serious scholar of Kotoshikhin's life and text, who suggested that the source for the description of royal weddings in chapter 1 of *On Russia* was Kotoshikhin's own experience working on Tsar Aleksei Mikhailovich's wedding in 1648.[36] The problem, which even Markevich realised at the time, is that there are numerous small but telling discrepancies between Kotoshikhin's description of how a royal wedding works and the way the wedding of Tsar Aleksei Mikhailovich was actually performed in 1648. For example, Kotoshikhin reports that the royal groom received the patriarch's blessing to marry on the morning of the nuptials, and that right afterward he went on a mini-pilgrimage to monasteries and churches in the Kremlin to pray and to venerate the tombs of Russia's former rulers, but in fact Tsar Aleksei performed these traditional ritual actions on the eve of the wedding, which was a departure from previous practice. Markevich explains away the discrepancies by suggesting that Kotoshikhin was attempting to produce a generalised description of royal wedding customs in Muscovy, not to describe the wedding of Tsar Aleksei Mikhailovich. 'Kotoshikhin's description of the royal wedding ritual', Markevich writes, 'reflects, of course, the wedding of the tsar with Mariia Miloslavskaia, but it is presented so as to describe royal weddings in general, omitting the unique features of that particular wedding.'[37] Benjamin Uroff questioned this conclusion. Using the same sources that Markevich had at his disposal, Uroff compared Kotoshikhin's description not only with Aleksei Mikhailovich's wedding in 1648, as had Markevich, but with Mikhail Feodorovich's wedding of 1626.[38] Uroff found a much better match in the 1626 wedding. 'In a number of details', Uroff concluded, 'Kotoshikhin's account corresponds to the ceremonial not of Alexis's wedding but of Michael's in 1626.'[39] But even Uroff admitted that there still were discrepancies with the 1626 wedding, and he accounted for them less charitably (though more plausibly) than did Markevich, seeing them more likely as mistakes rather than a helpful and conscious effort on Kotoshikhin's part to produce a generic description of the royal wedding ritual.[40]

What Uroff does not explain is how Kotoshikhin would have had cause to examine Mikhail Feodorovich's wedding documents well enough to be able to write a reasonably good description of the royal nuptial rituals years later in Sweden. While it is conceivable that Kotoshikhin might have been tasked to venture into the Foreign Office's archive to retrieve documents or may have even learned his trade as a scribe by studying and perhaps copying old documents, it strains credulity to think that he would have acquired what amounts to an expert-level understanding of the royal wedding ritual without having actually worked intimately and extensively on the documents themselves. Of course, there was the opportunity to do so in the run-up to the wedding of Aleksei Mikhailovich in 1648, but as both Markevich and Uroff note, Kotoshikhin's description does not match the 1648 ritual either. It is much closer to the 1626 ritual of Mikhail Feodorovich. Why is Kotoshikhin's account closer to the earlier text, which was composed before he was even born?

The puzzle is perhaps solved by considering the sources available to Kotoshikhin and to Markevich and Uroff. Judging from their citations of sources, the latter two had access to published versions of wedding documentation, including wedding compilations, which began to appear in print in the late eighteenth century.[41] These compilations are problematic on a number of levels, however. They are based on later copies, not original manuscripts, and so they exhibit many of the errors that are typically made during complex copying and editing projects. They are also incomplete. Included in none of these compilations (nor published anywhere else) is the set of draft documents for the planned wedding of Tsar Aleksei Mikhailovich and Evfimiia Vsevolozhskaia in 1647.[42] These Vsevolozhskaia documents have never been published and remain largely unstudied (except for their palaeographical and textological features), and they have not attracted the attention of scholars because, simply, they describe a wedding that never took place.[43] A careful reading of the Vsevolozhskaia texts, however, reveals that the wedding being planned in 1647 was essentially identical to Tsar Mikhail Feodorovich's in 1626. In fact, the first draft of the Vsevolozhskaia wedding ceremonial is little more than a clean copy of the final version of the 1626 ceremonial, with blank spaces left for the names of the bride, her family members, and courtiers who would perform honorific duties at the wedding. Thus a vital piece of data for considering Kotoshikhin's activities in the Foreign Office and his sources for chapter 1 of *On Russia* have been overlooked.[44]

When Kotoshikhin's description of royal weddings is lined up against the original manuscript sources for Mikhail Fedorovich's wedding (1626), Aleksei Mikhailovich's first planned wedding (1647) and the latter's first actual wedding (1648), it becomes abundantly clear that Kotoshikhin, sitting in Stockholm in 1666, was not remembering the ritual of the one dynastic wedding that took place during his time in the Foreign Office (Aleksei Mikhailovich's in 1648). Nor was he attempting to produce a generic description of royal weddings, as Markevich suggested.

Table 11.1 (see p. 244), which compares selected moments in rituals common to most royal weddings, demonstrates that Kotoshikhin was recollecting as best he could either Mikhail Feodorovich's wedding in 1626 or Aleksei Mikhailovich's planned wedding of 1647. His treatment of the patriarch's blessing of the groom, the groom's processions to the Kremlin's monasteries, the banquet on the second day of the wedding, and the music and other entertainment – all these suggest that Kotoshikhin had extensive experience handling the texts describing the earlier weddings, rather than those describing the 1648 wedding of Tsar Aleksei Mikhailovich. When Kotoshikhin diverges from these earlier texts (1626 and 1647) he also diverges from the later text (1648), suggesting that he was misremembering a fact about the ritual, not that he was borrowing from the later source or attempting to reconcile different versions of the ritual.

It remains to explain why Kotoshikhin might be more familiar with the Vsevolozhskaia wedding ritual (1647) than with the Miloslavskaia ritual (1648), especially when it is so clear from the surviving manuscripts that the two were worked on in rapid succession (as one prospective bride, Evfimiia Vsevolozhskaia, was dismissed and quickly replaced by another, Mariia Miloslavskaia). We can only speculate, but it seems most plausible to think that Kotoshikhin's low rank as a novice scribe (he had entered service in the Foreign Office as a *pisets* only two years before) meant that he was assigned the tedious entry-level task of copying documents which would later be edited by more senior secretaries. Such a task would give him detailed familiarity with the rituals themselves, to be sure, but not with the changes that were introduced in them later. Alternatively, perhaps he was pulled from the job for some unknown reason and reassigned to other duties within the scriptorium before the final textual revisions were made. Whatever the case, it is likely that Kotoshikhin did not handle the reworked versions of the texts that were produced for the tsar's marriage to Mariia Miloslavskaia. And since we know he was not in attendance at the wedding itself and therefore saw none of it with his own eyes (his name appears in none of the musters[45]), he could have had little knowledge of the wedding ritual other than that which he had learned from reading and copying documents at his desk in the Foreign Office. Which was, in any case, apparently quite a lot.

MISSING SOURCES

If it is clearer now what royal wedding documents Kotoshikhin handled and read, it is also clear that he had other sources in mind and memory when he sat down to write chapter 1 of *On Russia*. Kotoshikhin's text includes additional information that is not included in any of the official royal wedding ceremonials (*chiny*) that he handled and

Table 11.1 Comparison of wedding rituals in manuscript descriptions and Kotoshikhin's *On Russia*

Moment in ritual	Mikhail Feodorovich, 1626	Kotoshikhin	Aleksei Mikhailovich, 1647	Aleksei Mikhailovich, 1648
Betrothal	At wedding, joined with crowning	Eve of wedding	At wedding, joined with crowning	Eve of wedding
Blessing of patriarch	Morning of wedding	Morning of wedding	Morning of wedding	Eve of wedding
Procession to monasteries and churches	Morning of wedding	Morning of wedding	Morning of wedding	Eve of wedding
Which church for the wedding?	Dormition Cathedral	Annunciation Cathedral	Dormition Cathedral	Dormition Cathedral
Eating after consummation	Heavy meal	Light meal	Heavy meal	Light meal
Day 2 banquet	Couple dine together	Couple dine together	Couple dine together	Separate banquets
Music	Secular, with other entertainment	Secular, with other entertainment	Secular, with other entertainment	Solemn Church hymns only

Sources: RGADA, *fond* 135, sec. IV, rub. II, nos. 16, 17 (Mikhail Feodorovich); nos. 21, 22 (Aleksei Mikhailovich and Evfimiia Vsevolozhskaia); nos. 21, 22, 23, 24 (Aleksei Mikhailovich and Mariia Miloslavskaia). Kotoshikhin, *O Rossii v carstvovanie Alekseja Mixajloviča*, pp. 36–52.

knew. The extra bits of information are, however, found in the descriptions of the weddings of members of the lower ranks of the Muscovite court. These texts date to the first quarter of the seventeenth century, and survive either as parts of manuscript miscellanies, or as additions to the famous sixteenth-century Muscovite manual for households called the *Domostroi*.[46] The *Domostroi*'s textual history is complex, but the wedding descriptions in its last chapter may be a product of the same flurry of scribal activity – led by the *dumnyi d'iak* Gramotin – that occurred in advance of the wedding of the first Romanov tsar, Mikhail Feodorovich, in 1624. It will be remembered that Gramotin ordered his scribes and clerks to copy and analyse the rituals of previous royal weddings so he could produce a wedding for the first tsar of the new dynasty that was both traditional and new – an effort that seems to have succeeded as planned. Afterward, as I have argued elsewhere, these copied texts found their way into compilations of wedding documents – compendia of wedding descriptions starting from 1526, mentioned above – or singly into various manuscript miscellanea. The wedding documents from 1624 therefore likely found their way into the last chapter of the *Domostroi*.[47] These wedding descriptions – both the compilations and the additions to the *Domostroi* – were probably generated by copyists working in the Foreign Office or other central chanceries (the resident experts on wedding texts), and then were copied yet again (and again) in private hands and made part of family archives. But in whatever fashion they were made and copied, they clearly circulated among a group of scribes and clerks who knew what royal wedding documentation looked like. Had Kotoshikhin seen these texts as well and did he draw upon them, at least from memory, in writing *On Russia*?

Again, we can only speculate, but two examples suggest that Kotoshikhin may have drawn from sources associated with the *Domostroi*. The first is the description of the sermon by the officiating priest that was delivered immediately after the crowning ceremony (the liturgical rite that seals the marriage). At the weddings of both Mikhail Feodorovich in 1626 and Aleksei Mikhailovich in 1648, the texts baldly report that the officiating archpriest 'instructed them in accordance with holy tradition'.[48] Kotoshikhin goes into much greater detail, however. He reports that the 'archpriest instructs them how to live together':

> The wife should be obedient to her husband, and they should not become angry at one another, except that for certain faults the husband should punish her a little with a rod: for the husband is to the wife as Christ is head of the church; and they should live in purity and fear of God, and fast on Sundays and Wednesdays and Fridays and during all the periods of fast; and on the Lord's holy days and any days that commemorate the apostles and evangelists and other designated saints they should not fall into sin and should go to God's temple and give offerings; and they should consult often with their spiritual advisor, for he will instruct them in all good things.[49]

This passage – which is not so much a quotation from the sermon as it is a summary of its contents – is, as Uroff has already noted, 'very similar to Kotoshikhin's account'.[50] Chapter 33 of the *Domostroi* contains a set of instructions comparable to these, written in the same prescriptive tone and including the same admonitions to husbands to 'instruct' their wives through corporal punishment.[51] Nowhere is this admonition for husbands to beat their wives found in official royal wedding documentation. In fact, much of what went on in the church during the wedding is ignored in the official ceremonials and musters – presumably because the Church had its own manuals (the *Book of Needs*, or *Trebnik*) that prescribed what was supposed to happen there.

Another example of Kotoshikhin providing information that goes beyond the contents of the official wedding documentation is his treatment of the wedding night – specifically, how the couple is visited after a time to verify that the union has been consummated. Again, the official documentation is discreet, merely mentioning that the couple was led at the appointed time to their bedchamber, after which the narrative immediately jumps to the morning of the next day of the wedding, when the couple separately took purifying baths.[52] There is no mention in the official documentation of the couple being visited by anyone to confirm that the marriage had been consummated. Kotoshikhin's account, however, fills in the missing pieces, drawing again from documents that may be related to the wedding texts in the *Domostroi*:

> And when an hour by the clock has passed, the father and mother and *tysiatskii* [master of ceremonies] send to the tsar and Tsaritsa to inquire of their health. And when the *druzhka* [best man] comes and inquires of their health, the tsar then answers that they are in good health, if the good thing has taken place between them; but if it has not taken place, the tsar orders him to return a second time, or a third; and the *druzhka* likewise comes and inquires. And if the good thing has taken place between them, the tsar says that they are in good health, and orders the entire wedding party and fathers and mothers to appear before him, though the archpriest does not appear; but if the good thing does not take place, then all the boyars and the wedding party disperse in sadness, without appearing before the tsar.[53]

The similarity between Kotoshikhin's account here and versions of the wedding ritual in the *Domostroi* is striking:

> The bridegroom goes about that business from which children are born. And after waiting a half hour a *druzhka* goes to the bridegroom and inquires of his health, and goes from the bridegroom to the father and mother to greet them and inquire of their health. And the father and mother send the *druzhka* to the bridegroom with order to announce their arrival.[54]

Kotoshikhin's phrasing is not identical to the *Domostroi*'s, but one must remember that this passage, like the whole of *On Russia*, derives from memory alone (a remarkable memory, to be sure). But the content of the royal wedding descriptions in *On Russia* suggests a relationship between it, the *Domostroi* (or the source texts for its chapter on weddings) and the manuscripts in the Foreign Office's archive.

Kotoshikhin clearly relied on a palette of sources to create his description of Muscovite royal weddings: sources both official (chancery documents in the Foreign Office) and unofficial (circulating copies of wedding documents made in 1624, which probably gave rise to the *Domostroi* and other texts like it). Both of these manuscript traditions are present in Kotoshikhin's *On Russia*. The relationship between these traditions and Kotoshikhin's text is depicted in the stemma in Figure 11.1.

Traitor though he was, Kotoshikhin was a remarkable man of letters whose range of experiences and skills (and memory!) helped him produce one of the most important texts of early modern Russia.

CONCLUSION

This study of Kotoshikhin's description of Muscovite royal wedding rituals reveals the important role that secretaries of various ranks in the central chanceries played in high court politics. Even low- and middle-level scribes and clerks were assigned great responsibility by the state secretaries running the chanceries, and for good reason. If Kotoshikhin is in any way representative of his peers, then the Foreign Office was staffed with remarkably intelligent and reasonably well-trained scribes, clerks and secretaries. That training may have been on-the-job and informal, but it was no less effective. To quote Keenan again:

> By the middle of the sixteenth century, leading clerks, called *d'iaki*, were commonly second- and even third-generation professional administrators; they were intermarrying within their profession, and were passing on to their sons and in-laws' sons the skills of their chanceries . . . and their influence, both in the sphere of bureaucratic routine and in higher councils of government, was considerable.[55]

Very little is known about Kotoshikhin's family, but it seems his father had been an 'official of some sort',[56] and that background may have been enough to gain him entry into chancery service; but his career was evidently propelled forward by his own merit.

One area in which the considerable influence in 'higher councils of government' was plainly apparent was the remarkable control state secretaries (*dumnye d'iaki*) and their staffs had over royal wedding rituals and the texts that described them. That these secretaries exercised editorial control over the texts is amply visible in the sources: their handwriting is all over them, and their names are inscribed in them as the clerks and secretaries who composed and handled these documents. But it is also clear from these same sources that state secretaries did much more than mechanically line edit texts. They were choreographers as much as they were editors and archivists. While Kotoshikhin was probably never highly enough ranked himself to choreograph the ritual movements of courtiers at weddings (or at any other court event), he worked with state secretaries who were. The accuracy of his account in chapter 1 of *On Russia* reveals him to be an expert on the matters handed by the Foreign Office at the time of his defection.

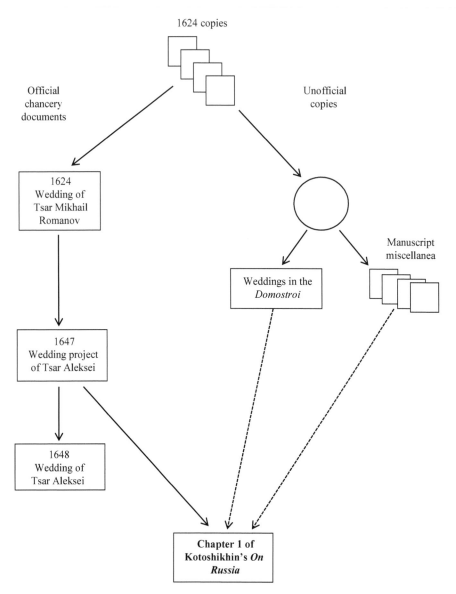

Figure 11.1 Textual relationships between chancery documents, the *Domostroi* and Kotoshikhin's *On Russia*

This study also reveals the continuing importance of Kotoshikhin's text as a source for Muscovite history in the seventeenth century: 'priceless', 'masterful', a 'rare phenomenon' and 'a classic'. But it remains, alas, an understudied text. The analysis here has identified the sources for one of its chapters on a particularly vital topic, and that analysis sheds light not only on the lives and work of scribes and clerks like Kotoshikhin, but also on the fascinating origin of the text of *On Russia* itself. But there are other chapters in the work that must have drawn on still other sources – or, more accurately, on Kotoshikhin's own recollection of those other sources – which remain unidentified. What sources did Kotoshikhin have in mind and memory when he wrote on the tsar's private life and that of his daughters and sisters, or on diplomatic practice, or on fiscal and military affairs, or on the private lives of boyars? This study of Kotoshikhin's account of royal marriage suggests that *On Russia* has still more to tell us about Muscovite political culture. And more to tell us about Kotoshikhin and the cohort of scribes to which he belonged.

Things did not end well for Grigorii Karpovich Kotoshikhin. His fortunes after his defection rose and fell, as also likely did his spirits. His financial woes in exile evidently compelled him by December 1666 to rent a room from Daniel Anastasius, a translator who worked in the chancery in Sweden that paralleled the Foreign Office in Moscow. The arrangement, which started out well enough, soured quickly. Kotoshikhin failed to pay his rent dutifully and he may have been a little too attentive to his landlord's wife. On 25 August 1667, in the midst of a drunken brawl, Kotoshikhin stabbed Anastasius, killing him. Kotoshikhin was tried for the murder and convicted, and he was executed in November 1667, having first converted to Lutheranism. Kotoshikhin seems in the end only to have wanted an anonymous death – Pennington says he may have 'welcome[d] death as a way of expiating his crime'[57] – but centuries later his name and his work have assumed great importance for historians of early modern Russia. He may very well have seen this fame as yet another cruel punishment for his betrayal and defection.

NOTES

1. On the biography of Grigorii Kotoshikhin, see Anne E. Pennington, 'Introduction', to Pennington (ed. and trans.), *O Rossii v carstvovanie Alekseja Mixajloviča* (Oxford: Oxford University Press, 1980), pp. 1–7; Pennington, 'An Unpublished Letter by Grigory Kotoshikhin', *Slavonic and East European Review* 46:114 (1971), pp. 113–24; A. N. Pypin, 'Grigorii Kotoshikhin', *Vestnik Evropy* (September 1896), pp. 245–95; A. I. Markevich, *G. K. Kotoshikhin i ego sochinenie o Moskovskom gosudarstve v polovine XVII v.* (Odessa: Tipografiia Shtaba okruga, 1895), pp. 19–20; A. Barsukov (ed.), *O Rossii v tsarstvovanie Alekseia Mikhailovicha, sochinenie Grigoriia Kotoshikhina*, 4th edn (St Petersburg: Tipografiia Glavnogo upravleniia udelov, 1906), pp. xiv–xix.

2. Pennington, *O Rossii v carstvovanie Alekseja Mixajloviča*, pp. 171–83; Benjamin Phillip Uroff, 'Grigorii Karpovich Kotoshikhin, "On Russia in the Reign of Alexis Mikhailovich": An Annotated Translation' (PhD dissertation, Columbia University, 1970), pp. 286–304; Grigorii Karpovich Kotoshikhin, *On Russia in the Reign of Alexis Mikhailovich*, trans. Benjamin Phillip Uroff, ed. Marshall Poe, managing editor, Katarzyna Ślusarska (Warsaw and Berlin: De Gruyter, 2014), available at <http://www.degruyter.com/view/product/212901> (last accessed 26 December 2015) (hereafter, Poe, *On Russia*), pp. 18–28.

3. Pennington, *O Rossii v carstvovanie Alekseja Mixajloviča*, pp. 6–7.

4. Uroff, '"On Russia in the Reign of Alexis Mikhailovich"', p. 5.

5. Ibid. p. 5. For published editions of *On Russia* in the original language, see Pennington's

O Rossii v carstvovanie Alekseja Mixajloviča and the titles she lists on p. 763. For a brief description of the other (earlier) editions, see Barsukov, *O Rossii*, pp. i–xxxvi.

6. For the English translation, see Uroff, '"On Russia in the Reign of Alexis Mikhailovich"'; Poe, *On Russia*.

7. These quotes are taken from Uroff, '"On Russia in the Reign of Alexis Mikhailovich"', p. 7; N. Barsukov, *Zhizn' i Trudy P. M. Stroeva* (St Petersburg: Tipografiia V. S. Balasheva, 1878), p. 360.

8. Nancy Shields Kollmann, *Kinship and Politics: The Making of the Muscovite Political System, 1345–1547* (Stanford: Stanford University Press, 1987), p. 125.

9. The ranks of the Muscovite chanceries evolved over time and the translations of these ranks into English varies, but the usual usage is as follows (from junior-most to senior-most position): scribe (*pisets*), clerk (*pod'iachii*), secretary (*d'iak*) and state or conciliar secretary (*dumnyi d'iak*). Within these gradations, especially in the *pod'iachii* rank, one could have appended to one's title 'junior' (*mladshii*), 'middle' (*srednii*) or 'senior' (*starshii*). See D. V. Liseitsev, N. M. Rogozhin and Iu. M. Eskin (eds), *Prikazy Moskovskogo gosudareva XVI–XVII vv.: Slovar'-spravochnik* (Moscow: Institute Rossiiskogo istorii RAN, Rossiiskii gosudarstvenyi arkhiv drevnikh aktov, Tsentr gumanitarnykh initsiativ, 2015); Marshal Poe, 'The Central Government and its Institutions', in Maureen Perrie (ed.), *The Cambridge History of Russia*. Vol. 1, *From Early Rus to 1689* (Cambridge: Cambridge University Press, 2003), pp. 435–63; N. F. Demidova, *Sluzhilaia biurokratiia v Rossii XVII v. i ee rol' v formirovanii absoliutizma* (Moscow: Nauka, 1987); Peter B. Brown, 'Muscovite Government Bureaus', *Russian History* 10:3 (1983), pp. 269–330; Borivoj Plavsic, 'Seventeenth-Century Chanceries and Their Staffs', in Don K. Rowney and Walter M. Pintner (eds), *Russian Officialdom: The Bureaucratization of Russian Society from the 17th to the 20th Century* (Chapel Hill: University of North Carolina Press, 1980), pp. 19–45; S. B. Veselovskii, *D'iaki i pod'iachie v XV–XVII vv.* (Moscow: Nauka, 1973); N. P. Eroshkin, *Ocherki istorii gosudarstvennykh uchrezhdenii dorevoliutsionnoi Rossii* (Moscow: Gosudarstvennoe Uchebno-Pedagogicheskoe izdatel'stvo Ministerstva prosveshcheniia RSFSR, 1960).

10. These details are drawn from Pennington, *O Rossii v carstvovanie Alekseja Mixajloviča*, pp. 1–3.

11. On the Foreign Office as the royal archive, see V. I. Gal'tsov (ed.), *Opis' arkhiva Posol'skogo prikaza 1626 goda*, 2 vols (Moscow: Glavnoe arkhivnoe upravlenie pri SM SSSR, 1977), vol. 1, pp. 255, 312–13, 314–15, 322, 328–9, 367–9, 404; Gal'tsov (ed.), *Opis' arkhiva Posol'skogo prikaza 1673 goda*, 2 vols (Moscow: Glavnoe arkhivnoe upravlenie pri SM SSSR, 1990), vol. 1, pp. 33, 34–5, 36–7; S. O. Shmidt (ed.), *Opisi Tsarskogo arkiva XVI v. i Arkhiva Posol'skogo prikaza 1614 g.* (Moscow: Izdatel'stvo vostochnoi literatury, 1960), pp. 32, 36, 40–1, 44, 48, 60–1; V. D. Nazarov, 'O strukture "Gosudareva dvora" v seredine XVI v.', in V. T. Pashuto (ed.), *Obshchestvo i gosudarstvo feudal'noi Rossii. Sbornik statei posviashchennyi 70-letiiu akademika L'va Vladimirovicha Cherepnina* (Moscow: Nauka, 1975), pp. 40–54.

12. On the use and preservation of wedding documentation, see V. D. Nazarov, 'Svadebnye dela XVI v.', *Voprosy istorii* 10 (1976), pp. 110–23; M. E. Bychkova, *Sostav klassa feodalov Rossii XVI veka: istoriko-genealogicheskoe issledovanie* (Moscow: Nauka, 1986), pp. 104–43; Russell Martin, 'Muscovite Royal Weddings: A Descriptive Inventory of Manuscript Holdings in the Treasure Room of the Russian State Archive of Ancient Acts, Moscow', *Manuscripta* 50:1 (2006), pp. 77–189.

13. On the honorific duties, see I. P. Sakharov (ed.), *Skazaniia russkogo naroda* (St Petersburg: Guttenburgovaia Tipografiia, 1849), vol. 2, book 6, pp. 5–25.

14. See Russell Martin, *A Bride for the Tsar: Bride-Shows and Marriage Politics in Early Modern Russia* (DeKalb, IL: Northern Illinois University Press, 2012); Ivan Egorovich Zabelin, *Domashnii byt russkikh tsarits v XVI i XVII st.*, vol. 2 of *Domashnii byt russkogo*

naroda v XVI i XVII st., reprint of 1901 edn, with additions (Moscow: Iazyki russkoi kul'tury, 2003).

15. Pypin, 'Grigorii Kotoshikhin'.
16. Uroff, '"On Russia in the Reign of Alexis Mikhailovich"'.
17. Poe, *On Russia*.
18. Edward L. Keenan, 'Muscovite Political Folkways', *Russian Review* 45 (1986), p. 158 (pp. 115–81).
19. See, for a start, Margaret M. McGowan (ed.), *Dynastic Marriages 1612/1615: A Celebration of the Habsburg and Bourbon Unions* (Farnham: Ashgate, 2013); John Watkins, 'Marriage à la Mode, 1559: Elisabeth de Valois, Elizabeth I, and the Changing Practice of Dynastic Marriage', in Carole Levin and Robert Bucholz (eds), *Queens and Power in Medieval and Early Modern England* (Lincoln, NE: University of Nebraska Press, 2009), pp. 76–97; Paula Sutter Fichtner, 'Dynastic Marriage in Sixteenth-Century Habsburg Diplomacy and Statecraft: An Interdisciplinary Approach', *American Historical Review* 81:2 (1976), pp. 243–65.
20. On this change in dynastic marriage policy, see Russell Martin, *A Bride for the Tsar,* pp. 31–56, 87–93, 107–12, 242–6; Martin, 'Dowries, Diplomacy, and Dynastic Marriage in Muscovy', *Journal of Medieval and Early Modern Studies* 38:1 (2008), pp. 119–45. See also Christian Raffensperger, *Reimagining Europe: Kievan Rus' in the Medieval World* (Cambridge, MA: Harvard University Press, 2012), pp. 47–114; Nikolaus de Baumgarten, 'Généalogies et mariages Occidentaux des Rurikides Russes du Xe au XIIIe siècle', *Orientalia Christiana* 9:25 (1927), pp. 5–95; Baumgarten, 'Généalogies des branches régnantes de Rurikides du XIIIe au XVIe siècle', *Orientalia Christiana* 35:94 (1934), pp. 1–152; Kollmann, *Kinship and Politics*, pp. 125–8.
21. See S. M. Kashtanov, *Issledovaniia po istorii kniazheskikh kantseliarii srednevekovoi Rusi* (Moscow: Nauka, 2014); S. O. Shmidt, *Rossiiskoe gosudarstvo v seredine XVI stoletiia* (Moscow: Nauka, 1984), pp. 44–90; A. K. Leont'ev, *Obrazovanie prikaznoi sistemy upravleniia v Russkom gosudarstve: iz istorii sozdaniiq tsentralizovannogo gosudarstvennogo apparata v kontse XV – pervoi polovine XVI v.* (Moscow: Izdatel'stvo Moskovskogo universiteta, 1961); S. A. Belokurov, *O Posol'skom prikaze* (Moscow: Izdanie Imperatorskogo Obshchestva istorii i drevnostei Rossiiskikh, 1906).
22. Russell Martin, 'Royal Weddings and Crimean Diplomacy: New Sources on Muscovite Chancery Practice during the Reign of Vasilii III', *Harvard Ukrainian Studies* 19 (1995), pp. 389–427.
23. For the term, see, for a start Russian State Archive of Ancient Acts (Rossiiskii gosudarstvennyi arkhiv drevnikh aktov, hereafter RGADA), *fond* 135, section IV, rubric II, number 3, fo. 1; no. 14, fos. 48, 120, 121; no. 16, fo. 5v; no. 18, fo. 123; no. 22, fo. 21v; no. 25, fos. 1, 35, 36, 53v.
24. On these documents, see Russell Martin, 'Archival Sleuths and Documentary Transpositions: Notes on the Typology and Textology of Muscovite Royal Wedding Descriptions in the Sixteenth and Seventeenth Centuries', *Russian History* 30:3 (Fall 2003), pp. 253–300.
25. See Iu. V. Ankhimiuk, *Chastnye Razriadnye knigi s zapisami za posledniuiu chetvert' XV–nachalo XVII vekov* (Moscow: Drevlekhranilishche, 2005); V. I. Buganov, *Razriadnye knigi poslednei chetverti XV–nachale XVII v.* (Moscow: Izdatel'stvo Akademii nauk SSSR, 1962); N. P. Likhachev, *Razriadnye d'iaki XVI v.* (St Petersburg: V. S. Balashev, 1888). Some copies of wedding documents ended up in the Muster Chancery in the seventeenth century, probably sent there from the Foreign Office during the drafting of these documents and never subsequently returned. See K. V. Petrov (ed.), *Opisi arkhiva Razriadnogo prikaza XVII v.* (St Petersburg: Dmitrii Bulanin, 2001), p. 32.
26. See Iu. M. Eskin, *Ocherki istorii mestnichestva v Rossii XVI–XVII vv.* (Moscow: Kvadriga, 2009), pp. 233–9.

27. On the *oprichnina*, see Edward Keenan, 'The Privy Domain of Ivan Vasil'evich', in Chester S. L. Dunning, Russell E. Martin and Daniel Rowland (eds), *The Rude and Barbarous Kingdom Revisited: Essays in Russian History and Culture in Honor of Robert O. Crummey* (Columbus, OH: Slavica, 2008), pp. 73–88.

28. RGADA, *fond* 135, sec. IV, rub. II, no. 29, fos. 8–8v; no. 30, fos. 5–6v. See also P. V. Sedov, *Zakat Moskovskogo tsartva* (St Petersburg: Dmitrii Bulanin, 2006), pp. 113–22.

29. See, for example, RGADA, *fond* 135, sec. IV, rub. II, no. 5, fo. 20; no 15, fos. 13, 23, 32; no. 16, fo. 19v; no. 17, fos. 21, 74; Nikolai [Ivanovich] Novikov (ed.), *Drevniaia rossiiskaia vivliofika. Soderzhashchaia v sebe sobranie drevnostei rossiiskikh, do istorii geografii, i genealogii rossiiskoi kasaiushchikhsia* (hereafter *DRV*), 2nd edn, 20 vols (Moscow: V tipografii Kompanii tipograficheskoi, 1788–1791), vol. 13, pp. 31, 38, 45.

30. Russell E. Martin, 'Choreographing the "Tsar's Happy Occasion": Tradition, Change, and Dynastic Continuity in the Weddings of Tsar Mikhail Romanov', *Slavic Review* 63:4 (2004), pp. 794–817.

31. See RGADA, *fond* 135, sec. IV, rub. II, no. 24, fos. 45v–46; no. 30, fos. 13v, 15.

32. Keenan, 'Muscovite Political Folkways', p. 143.

33. On the marriage-based political system in Muscovy, see, for a start, Kollmann, *Kinship and Politics*; Keenan, 'Muscovite Political Folkways'; Daniel Rowland, 'Did Muscovite Literary Ideology Place Limits on the Power of the Tsar (1540s–1660s)?', *Russian Review* 49 (1990), pp. 125–55; Rowland, 'The Problem of Advice in Muscovite Tales about the Time of Troubles', *Russian History* 6:2 (1979), pp. 259–83; Michael Flier, 'Court Ceremony in an Age of Reform: Patriarch Nikon and the Palm Sunday Ritual', in Samuel H. Baron and Nancy Shields Kollmann (eds), *Religion and Culture in Early Modern Russia and Ukraine* (DeKalb, IL: Northern Illinois University Press, 1997), pp. 73–95.

34. Evfimiia Vsevolozhshaia fell victim to a plot organised by courtiers who disapproved of her choice as the tsar's bride. See Russell Martin, 'Political Folkways and Praying for the Dead in Muscovy: Reconsidering Edward Keenan's "Slight" Against the Church', *Canadian Slavonic Papers* 48:3–4 (2006), pp. 283–305; Zabelin, *Domashnii byt russkikh tsarits*, pp. 244–51. Kotoshikhin mentions the plot, though not the name of the disappointed bride and he gets some details wrong. See Pennington, *O Rossii v carstvovanie Alekseja Mixajloviča*, p. 19.

35. RGADA, *fond* 135, sec. IV, rub. II, no. 22, fos. 1–8, 9–13, 14–19, 20, 49–51. See also Martin, 'Muscovite Royal Weddings: A Descriptive Inventory', no. 20.

36. Markevich, *G. K. Kotoshikhin i ego sochinenie o Moskovskom gosudarstve*, pp. 106–7.

37. Ibid. p. 107.

38. Among the sources Markevich surely had available to him were, among others, *DRV*, vol. 13, pp. 137–232; *Sobranie gosudarstvennykh gramot i dogovorov, khraniashchikhsia v gosudarstvennoi kollegii inostrannykh del*, 5 vols (Moscow: Tipografiia N. S. Vsevolozhskogo, 1813–1894), vol. 3, no. 72; Sakharov, *Skazaniia russkogo naroda*, vol. 2, book 6, pp. 74–98; Archimandrite Leonid, 'Razriadnye zapiski o likhakh byvshikh na vtorykh svad'bakh tsaria i velikogo kniazia Mikahila Fedorovicha v 1622 godu i tsaria i velikogo kniazia Alekseia Mikhailovicha v 1671 godu', in *Pamiatniki drevei pis'mennosti i iskusstva* (St Petersburg: Tipografiia V. S. Valasheva, 1885). The sources – manuscript and published – for Mikhail Feodorovich's first wedding (in 1624) are fragmentary or merely musters (*svadebnye razriady*) and therefore do not provide enough detail of the ceremony for useful comparison.

39. Uroff, '"On Russia in the Reign of Alexis Mikhailovich"', pp. 321–2.

40. See, for example, his treatment of discrepancies in ibid. pp. 321–9 (nn. 45–84).

41. Principally *DRV*, but probably also other sources listed above in note 38. On these compilations, see Bychkova, *Sostav klassa feodalov*, pp. 104–43; Martin, 'Archival Sleuths and Documentary Transpositions'.

42. RGADA, *fond* 135, sec. IV, rub. II, no. 21, fos. 1–71; no. 22, fos. 1–8, 9–13, 14–19, 20, 62, 63–77.

43. These manuscripts are described palaeographically and textologically in Martin, 'Muscovite Royal Weddings: A Descriptive Inventory', nos. 19, 20; L. V. Cherpnin (ed.), *Gosudarstvennoe drevlekhranilishche khartii i rukopisei: Opis' documental'nykh materialov fonda № 135* (Moscow: Glavnoe arkhivnoe upravlenie pri Sovete Ministrov SSSR, Tsentral'nyi gosudarstvennyi arkhiv drenikh aktov, 1971), p. 135, nos. 311, 312. Zabelin was one of the few to handle and use these manuscripts, as can be deduced from his account of the so-called Vsevolozhskaia Affair. See his *Domashnii byt russkikh tsarits*, pp. 244–51.

44. A. V. Shunkov noticed the similarities between Kotoshikhin's description and the Vsevolozhskaia wedding project of 1647, but does not analyse them in detail. See A. V. Shunkov, 'Dokumental'nyi tekst v literaturnoi traditskii perekhodnogo vremeni (k voprosu ob evoliutsii dokumental'nykh zhanrov v istoriko-literaturnykh usloviiakh vtoroi poloviny XVII v.)', *Vestnik Tomskogo gosudarstvennogo universiteta* 388 (2014), p. 44 (pp. 42–6).

45. RGADA, *fond* 135, sec. IV, rub. II, nos. 21, 22.

46. On the *Domostroi*, see Carolyn Johnston Pouncy, 'The Origins of the "Domostroi": A Study in Manuscript History', *Russian Review* 46 (1987), pp. 357–73; Pouncy, *The "Domostroi": Rules for Russian Households in the Time of Ivan the Terrible* (Ithaca, NY: Cornell University Press, 1994).

47. Martin, 'Choreographing the "Tsar's Happy Occasion"'.

48. *DRV*, vol. 13, p. 164 (Mikhail Feodorovich), p. 206 (Aleksei Mikhailovich).

49. Uroff, '"On Russia in the Reign of Alexis Mikhailovich"', p. 45.

50. Ibid. p. 327 (n. 68).

51. V. V. Kolesova (ed.), *Domostroi* (Moscow: Sovetskaia Rossiia, 1990), pp. 60, 146; Pouncy, *Rules for Russian Households*, ch. 33.

52. *DRV*, vol. 13, p. 170 (Mikhail Feodorovich), p. 211 (Aleksei Mikhailovich).

53. Uroff, '"On Russia in the Reign of Alexis Mikhailovich"', p. 47.

54. Ibid. pp. 327–38 (n. 71).

55. Keenan, 'Muscovite Political Folkways', p. 137.

56. Pennington, *O Rossii v carstvovanie Alekseja Mixajloviča*, p. 1.

57. Ibid. p. 7.

CHAPTER 12

Eberhard von Danckelman and Brandenburg's Foreign Policy (1688–97)

Daniel Riches

The scholarship on Eberhard von Danckelman (1643–1722), chief minister of Elector Friedrich III of Brandenburg from 1688 to 1697, is a curious lot. Nearly all historians who have worked on this period grant that Danckelman had a leading, and at times preponderant, role in crafting state policy – especially foreign policy – at a time when Brandenburg was deeply involved in matters of continental importance, including active support of William III's seizure of the British throne in the Glorious Revolution and significant participation in the Nine Years' War against Louis XIV and the emperor's struggle with the Ottomans in Hungary. Furthermore, those who have studied Danckelman have held him in almost uniformly high regard, not least the paragons of nineteenth- and early twentieth-century Prusso-German nationalist historiography, who have portrayed him as the exemplary Prussian civil servant and worthy steward of the legacy of Friedrich III's father, the 'Great Elector' Friedrich Wilhelm.[1] As an exemplar of that most despised and critiqued political species, the princely favourite, Danckelman has enjoyed remarkably good press.[2]

All of this makes it that much more surprising that the actual body of writing focused on Danckelman is unexpectedly thin. The Brandenburg minister has been the subject of no full-length biography and scarcely a handful of shorter studies and article-length treatments, and the majority of those have focused almost exclusively on his dramatic fall from power in 1697.[3] In most works examining Friedrich's reign, the longest sustained discussion of Danckelman is dedicated to the story of his fall.[4] As the bulk of documentary material related to his removal from office and subsequent imprisonment consists of the accusations and testimony of his many enemies, the historiographical record rests on relatively few of Danckelman's own words, despite the fact that he spent the better part of a decade sifting through enormous mountains of paperwork on a nearly daily basis.[5] The ironic upshot is that an effort to understand Danckelman's period of influence has much the feel of an exercise in microhistory, reading against the grain of often hostile legal records to discern the actual nature and substance of Danckelman's power.[6]

But Danckelman was no Menocchio. He was instead a leading statesman in a rising European power on its way to becoming what many of the same historians who praise, but do not examine carefully, his service hold up as the prototypical *Machtstaat*. So why has his period of ascendancy not received more substantial treatment? Three explanations come to mind. First, the study of princely favourites has garnered relatively little attention in German historiography, and in turn favourites from German-speaking lands have played lesser roles in broader and comparative studies of the phenomenon.[7] Danckelman, like many other German favourites, arrived on the scene comparatively late, his period in power falling decades after the heyday of the European minister-favourite came to an end around 1660.[8] He therefore falls outside of the geographic and chronological scope of most scholarship on favourites, and his position as minister-favourite was of a sort not usually investigated in German scholarship. He does not fit the model.[9]

Next, Danckelman's service under Friedrich III links him with a ruler consistently outshone by his 'Great Elector' father and 'Soldier King' son.[10] Despite its twenty-five-year duration, Friedrich's reign is often treated as a mere stopgap between eras of greater significance, and an inglorious one at that. The volume of scholarship on Friedrich accordingly amounts to only a fraction of that dedicated to his father or son.[11] Insufficient investigation of Danckelman's time in office may be the collateral damage of this broader historiographical neglect.

Finally, the tenor of what has been written about Danckelman leaves much of the actual substance of his power and impact on political affairs obscure. Danckelman is often portrayed less as a distinct historical actor and personality and more as an exaggerated prototype of 'good Prussian' values, the antithesis of the indecision and wasteful pomp and display associated with Friedrich's reign.[12] Discussions of Danckelman are replete with references to his honesty, discipline, austerity, work ethic, sense of duty, seriousness of purpose and dedication to reason of state, while giving little sense of how these traits translated into policy formation and the direction of governmental activity. Already in Danckelman's own lifetime he was being put forth as the laudable opposite of his extravagant and broadly hated successor as favourite, Count Kolbe von Wartenberg, a comparison that has persisted into the modern historiography.[13] Depictions of Danckelman as the valorised negation of others' shortcomings provide us with little more than a caricature of the man himself, and indeed understanding Danckelman is not really their point.

For all of these reasons, we know surprisingly little about the texture and mechanics of Danckelman's ascendancy over Brandenburg politics and the actual means through which he influenced policy and exercised power. The aim of the current chapter is to offer an overview of Danckelman's statecraft, with a particular eye towards issues of foreign policy, culminating in a brief case study of Danckelman's handling of a specific diplomatic relationship (that with Sweden) which will provide a window onto the challenges that he faced and the diplomatic methods he used to tackle them.

BIOGRAPHICAL BACKGROUND AND RISE TO POWER

Danckelman was born in 1643 in the Westphalian County of Lingen, a territory ruled by the Princes of Orange. His father Silvester served as an official in the local Orange government, and ties between the Danckelman family and the House of Orange proved enduring.[14] Eberhard was the fourth of seven academically accomplished brothers, all of whom eventually entered the service of the Brandenburg electors. A child prodigy, Eberhard received his law degree from the University of Utrecht at the age of twelve after publishing a dissertation and holding a public disputation.[15] Extensive travels throughout Western Europe followed. In 1663 Otto von Schwerin, chief minister of Elector Friedrich Wilhelm and supervisor of the education of the elector's sons, selected the now twenty-year-old Danckelman as tutor for the elector's second son, Prince Friedrich, then aged six.[16] When Friedrich's older brother Karl Aemil died in 1674, Danckelman's pupil became crown prince.[17]

Danckelman's demanding style of instruction prompted complaints from Friedrich's relatives that he was pushing the young prince too hard.[18] Nevertheless, a close relationship between teacher and student developed over the years, and Danckelman was able to win Friedrich's complete trust. This personal, trusting relationship with Friedrich formed the cornerstone of Danckelman's subsequent career. When Friedrich found himself in sensitive and challenging situations, Danckelman came forward time and again with loyal service, sage counsel and effective intervention, whether it be in smoothing the path for Friedrich's marriage to Sophie Charlotte of Hannover against Friedrich Wilhelm's objections; providing money from his personal funds to help the prince meet his expenses; serving as Friedrich's representative at the inquest into the sudden and unexpected death of his younger brother Ludwig; or mediating rapprochement in the strained relationship between Friedrich and his father shortly before the latter's death.[19] Friedrich even credited Danckelman with saving his life, not once, but twice.[20] Friedrich came to rely on Danckelman like no one else.

Such loyal and trusted service did not go unrewarded. In 1674 Danckelman was appointed the crown prince's counsellor, and when Friedrich came to the electoral throne in 1688 he immediately offered Danckelman rapid promotion and a collection of offices and titles that marked him as the most powerful official in the Brandenburg government. Within weeks of his ascension Friedrich placed Danckelman into the leading position on the Privy Council, the main governing body in Brandenburg, with unique powers (discussed below) that set him apart from his much more senior and experienced colleagues. Additional responsibilities and offices followed, in Brandenburg itself as well as in the elector's other provinces.[21] Although it was not until 1695 that Friedrich was able to insist that Danckelman accept the formal title of *Oberpräsident* to designate his official leadership of all bodies in the elector's government, his status as chief minister and Friedrich's personal favourite was clear to all long before that.[22]

Friedrich and Danckelman enjoyed what appeared to be an ideal relationship between a prince and his chosen favourite. Writing while Friedrich was still crown prince, Gregorio Leti claimed that 'there are few examples of a favourite so zealous in the service of his prince, or of a prince with so much fondness for a favourite'.[23] Danckelman possessed a monopoly on Friedrich's trust, and repaid the favour shown him with dedicated and competent service.[24]

DANCKELMAN'S ASCENDANCY

Danckelman's power was grounded first and foremost in this personal relationship with Friedrich and in his continuous access to and ability to maintain the trust of his prince: this was entirely typical of the other minister-favourites of early modern Europe. His ascendancy did, however, have distinctive contours and characteristics. The institutional anchor of his authority lay in the *Geheimer Rat*, or Privy Council, the highest deliberative and consultative body in the realm that came together several times a week for meetings routinely several hours in duration to discuss all important matters of state.[25] The council met in palace chambers not far from the prince's personal apartment, with the prince himself often in attendance.[26] Danckelman's power was always regarded as residing within the confines of the Privy Council, a body which, according to some historians, reached its apogee under his direction.[27] His position in the Privy Council was one of hegemonic leadership rather than formalised dominance, though from the outset of his reign Friedrich entrusted him with two functions that demonstrated his elevation above the other counsellors, despite his comparative lack of experience. The first was the ability to countersign all of Friedrich's edicts.[28] Although this did not necessarily imply a determining influence over the content of policy – Danckelman himself stressed that he would dutifully sign off on decisions once taken even when he had advocated against them in council – it did mean that all official acts would have to pass through his hands, and would emerge with his signature affixed below that of his prince.[29] This was an innovation in Brandenburg practice and a privilege that not even Danckelman's mentor Otto von Schwerin had enjoyed as the first minister to Friedrich Wilhelm, and it was bitterly resented by Danckelman's senior colleagues on the council.[30]

The other special capacity Friedrich granted Danckelman was the allocation of assignments within the council.[31] This allowed Danckelman to manage the flow of business and determine the specific personnel tasked to deal with each particular issue brought before the body. Danckelman thus possessed a practical lever with which to influence the outcomes of the council's deliberations, one that symbolically confirmed that the newcomer to the council was the new prince's man, and he was now in ascendance. It is no surprise then that a foreign observer once remarked that while matters were discussed and concluded in the Privy Council, it appeared that Friedrich 'had to a large extent already deliberated and decided upon them with Danckelman'.[32]

Danckelman also deployed other, less formal means alongside those assigned him by the elector to secure his predominance over the Privy Council. Although their accusations were likely overblown, many of his enemies – including a number who were themselves members of the council – complained that Danckelman jealously controlled the circulation of information and purposely excluded them from access to knowledge of the most sensitive and important matters. Otto von Schwerin the younger, the son of Danckelman's mentor and one who joined the camp of Danckelman's opponents, repeated the punning observation of a foreign diplomat that 'the secret [privy] counsellors are only called such because everything is kept secret from them'.[33] The British diplomat George Stepney called Kolbe von Wartenberg Danckelman's 'most violent Adversary', in part because 'he fancied himself capable of State affairs and thought himself injurd by Mr. Dankelmans excluding him from those secrets'.[34] Those opposed to Danckelman's preeminence in the council believed he was systematically and intentionally limiting and manipulating news flows at their expense.

Danckelman's drive to keep matters in his own hands may have been motivated in part by a jealous desire to preserve his own power. Equally responsible were Danckelman's own almost impossibly exacting standards. He did not suffer fools, and refused to tolerate the presence of those who would not or could not live up to his expected levels of intelligence, competence and commitment to their work. In many cases he appears to have thought that the only way to get something done correctly was to do it himself, and he therefore loaded himself with an extreme burden of work while at the same time incurring the resentment of those who felt cut out of state affairs.[35]

He did, however, maintain a sense of his own limitations, and an openness to working with those who had talents and expertise he lacked. This was particularly true in the realm of finance. Danckelman refused Friedrich's offer to assume leadership of Brandenburg's finances, remarking that his skills lay elsewhere.[36] His delegation of fiscal responsibilities to others met with mixed results. He was a warm supporter of Dodo von Knyphausen, given charge of administration of the princely domains, and placed his own brother Daniel Ludolf Danckelman as *Generalkriegskommissar*, the head of military finance and administration. Both were highly successful in their roles.[37] Other decisions by Danckelman, however, such as his promotion of Christian Friedrich Kraut (to whom he also entrusted some of his personal finances), bring Danckelman's judgement into question.[38]

Either through his own actions or those of his small cadre of clients, Danckelman pursued a varied domestic agenda during the nine years of his ascendancy. To mention but a sampling of his initiatives to give a sense of their range: he developed plans to weed out incompetent judges through a system of written examinations; he assumed direction and reform of Brandenburg's postal system; he supported the development of more effective and centralised means of poor relief; he stood behind Knyphausen's aggressive and insightful programme of fiscal reform; and he pursued a lively agenda of patronage of learning and the arts, including the foundation of the University of Halle (1694) and the Berlin Academy of Arts (1696) as well as the foundational work that would eventually lead to the famous Prussian Academy of Sciences (1700).[39] His efforts were not always successful, but his impact on Brandenburg-Prussia's development was substantial.

Danckelman knew from the beginning that his status as princely favourite would make him enemies, and he took certain steps to avoid enflaming the resentment of those he would be leaping over to preeminence.[40] When Friedrich came to the throne Danckelman worked to dissuade the new elector from his plan of releasing his father's experienced counsellors, especially Paul von Fuchs, Franz von Meinders and Joachim Ernst von Grumbkow, so that Danckelman could immediately assume the position of senior counsellor with its attendant precedence in council.[41] He similarly resisted efforts to have his leading position recognised with a special title. He was able to stave off Friedrich's intention of naming him *Großkanzler*, and it was not until 1695 that Friedrich surprised him with Schwerin's old title of *Oberpräsident* in a manner that left Danckelman little room to decline.[42] Friedrich's letter of appointment stressed that 'We would have conferred this position on him long ago, if he had not out of extreme modesty begged repeatedly and relentlessly to be spared it.'[43] Rather than emphasising the outward trappings of authority, Danckelman appears instead to have placed trust in his seemingly rock-solid hold on Friedrich's favour and exhibited great confidence in his own irreproachable conduct. These, he believed, would assure him continuing access to power and protection against the animosity engendered by his position.

This calculation, combined with Danckelman's personality traits and leadership style, prevented him from building an adequate base of support. As a foreigner in Brandenburg whose family possessed no meaningful long-term connections to the local elites, Danckelman needed to build a network of support on his own, and he proved singularly ill-suited to this task. Gruff, abrasive, impatient, doctrinaire, ever quick to point out the faults in others' abilities and the flaws in their plans – Danckelman possessed neither the art of the courtier nor the guile of the politician in attracting confidants and constructing coalitions. Stepney wrote from Germany that Danckelman's 'too rough behaviour . . . has, I fear, generally disobliged all sorts of People from the highest to the lowest'.[44] The eighteenth-century memoirist Karl Ludwig Freiherr von Pöllnitz remarked that Danckelman had never been seen to laugh.[45] Leopold von Ranke questioned whether he had the capacity or even the desire to make friends.[46] When he did make efforts to win opponents like Christoph zu Dohna over to his side, the attempt was so ham-fisted as to be rendered fully ineffectual.[47] Michael Kaiser, in the best recent study on Danckelman, declares that he was simply 'uncourtly', and that this contributed fundamentally to his undoing.[48]

Unlike most favourites, Danckelman therefore was never able to build up a robust clientele outside of his six brothers (each of whom occupied important governmental positions) and a scarce few others.[49] This left him entirely dependent on Friedrich's favour for his survival against the cabal of opponents who began conspiring as early as 1690 to throw off what Dohna referred to as 'the imperious yoke'.[50] By the time of Danckelman's fall in 1697 the accusations levelled by this group had grown into an enormous catalogue, centred on claims of tyrannical conduct and the usurpation of princely authority: altogether typical complaints against early modern favourites.[51] Danckelman's power remained secure in the face of such opposition as long as he was able to retain Friedrich's trust, but by 1697 the elector's faith in his chief minister had begun to falter.[52] Opponents noted with glee when Friedrich did not defend Danckelman from criticism in his presence and even at his table, a sharp contrast with previous practice.[53] Friedrich's decision to revoke his support of Danckelman was not easy – he spoke of sleepless nights and of the agony of 'having to take such hard resolution against my oldest servant' – but once he decided to do so things moved quickly.[54] Danckelman was released from office in November 1697; arrested a few weeks later; imprisoned without trial until 1707 (a planned trial was aborted for lack of evidence in 1702); and not fully pardoned until Friedrich was dead and his son Friedrich Wilhelm I was on the throne in 1713.[55] Danckelman's complete dependence on Friedrich left him with no one to break his fall when the elector's support went away, and his eclipse was rapid and complete. He spent the final years of life in quiet scholarly pursuits, far from the concourses of power he had once commanded, until his death in 1722.[56]

FOREIGN POLICY IN THE ERA OF DANCKELMAN

During the 1680s and 1690s, Brandenburg's foreign policy, like much of the rest of Europe's, revolved around concerns over Louis XIV's aggressive policies and efforts to form broad coalitions to resist them. The electorate had fought against Louis in the Franco-Dutch War in the 1670s, and from the mid-1680s returned to the fundamentally anti-French political and military orientation it would maintain for the remainder of the Sun King's reign. Motivated both by the desire to secure the elector's vulnerable Rhenish territories (Cleves, Mark and Ravensberg) as well as a legitimate concern for the well-being of European Protestantism, Brandenburg's diplomats as well as her army were active participants in the complex efforts to halt Louis's advance that included the Nine Years' War (1688–97), which corresponded almost exactly with the period of Danckelman's ascendancy. These efforts necessitated good relations not only with other Protestant powers, but also with the Catholic emperor, an important member of the anti-French coalition. Friedrich wished to cultivate the emperor's goodwill for another reason as well, since from the early 1690s he had his eye cast towards obtaining a royal title for his Prussian lands and knew this could only happen with the emperor's acquiescence. International power politics, dynastic ambitions, religious concerns and internal imperial politics thus flowed together in complicated and overlapping ways, creating substantial challenges for Brandenburg's statesmen to navigate.

During his nine years in power, foreign policy issues lay closest to Danckelman's heart.[57] Scholars have long acknowledged his central role both in shaping Brandenburg's foreign policy and in managing the operations of its diplomacy during this period.[58] The French diplomat de la Rosière referred to Danckelman as 'the Grand Vizier of Brandenburg' in charge of everything, indicating that foreign representatives at court believed that all important business ran through Danckelman.[59] As was true with his power in general, Danckelman exercised his influence over foreign policy primarily through the Privy Council. He included other counsellors in deliberation over the most important issues, and only rarely circumvented procedure by bringing matters to the elector privately.[60] Most diplomatic documents were drafted by Paul von Fuchs after consultation with Danckelman.[61] Nevertheless, a man of unquestioned talent and experience like Fuchs, who agreed with Danckelman on most important foreign policy issues, could still feel as if Danckelman's domineering leadership marginalised his own contributions. Shortly after Danckelman fell from power, Stepney wrote that Fuchs was 'perhaps . . . not displeased to have Mr. Dankelman removed, because of his insufferable behaviour especially to [Fuchs] . . . whom he used rather as Clerk, than as a fellow Minister'.[62]

In addition to hegemony in council, Danckelman had other means available to him with which to mould the conduct of foreign policy. His ability to influence appointments helped ensure that a trusted figure like his brother Nicolaus Bartholomäus retained the critical diplomatic post at Vienna for many years.[63] His own appointment as *Oberpräsident* in 1695 carried with it the directive that the elector's provincial governments as well as all diplomats stationed abroad were to correspond with Danckelman directly, though in practice this step changed little as previous correspondence addressed to Friedrich had already been channelled through Danckelman to the Privy Council in his capacity as distributing member.[64] Finally, foreign representatives like de la Rosière, who recognised that Danckelman held the real levers of influence, chose to work through him to carry out their charges. In short, Danckelman wielded disproportional influence over foreign policy. Historians have therefore marked his fall as exemplary of a fundamental transition in the history of Brandenburg-Prussian foreign policy administration, from a system dominated by individual personalities to one that worked through institutional structures.[65]

Danckelman and Friedrich did not always agree on foreign policy issues. Danckelman did not disguise his bitter disappointment when he learned many years after the fact of Friedrich's secret and independent decision made while crown prince to return the territory of Schwiebus in Silesia to Imperial control.[66] He also openly expressed his resistance to the elector's plan to pursue a royal crown, arguing that what became the leading project of his prince would result in wasteful expenditure and unnecessary diplomatic complications, especially with the emperor.[67] Friedrich in turn unfairly held Danckelman personally responsible for the disappointing results of the Treaty of Ryswick (1697) that concluded the Nine Years' War, as well as for the fact that the main allies continued to treat Brandenburg as a decidedly junior partner despite its substantial contributions to the war effort.[68] Tensions over these final two issues contributed to Friedrich's fateful turn against Danckelman.

Despite such rocky moments, the overarching trajectory of Brandenburg's foreign policy during Danckelman's ascendancy was one of continuity. Friedrich's foreign policy remained largely unchanged from that pursued by his father at the very end of his reign, and even after Danckelman's fall the reorientation of priorities expected by many (with the exception of intensified focus on procuring the royal title, which was eventually secured in 1701) did not materialise.[69] Resistance to French hegemony and the concomitant desire for Protestant cooperation formed the foundation of the elector's foreign policy agenda.[70] For Danckelman in particular these issues were united powerfully in his consistent and passionate support for William III of Orange.

Danckelman was born a subject of the Princes of Orange, his family had a history of service to that House, and his education and intellectual formation had been fundamentally Dutch in orientation.[71] He was also deeply interested in questions of Protestant union in both their religious and political aspects.[72] He was convinced of the intrinsic merit of William's seizure of the British throne and of the struggle against Louis XIV, and believed equally strongly that each served the best interests of Protestantism and Brandenburg as well. While Friedrich was still crown prince Danckelman was one of the very small number introduced into the inner circle made familiar with William's plans for an invasion of England.[73] During his ascendancy he worked tirelessly to provide William with diplomatic and military support, and to secure Brandenburg's position in the anti-French coalition.[74] De la Rosière reported back to France that Danckelman 'hates us, precisely because it is in William's interest'.[75] Contemporary documents note that accusations levelled against Danckelman's foreign policy focused on the claim that 'he paid more attention to the common [Protestant/anti-French] cause than to the Elector's private interests'.[76] William himself later remarked to the Brandenburg diplomat Dobrzenski that Danckelman's disgrace had been caused by the belief 'that he was too attached to my interests, which are nevertheless the same as the elector's'.[77] Danckelman's fall provoked a vigorous response from English and Dutch officials and forced the elector to go into damage control to convince William he was not about to switch to a pro-French stance.[78]

An additional foreign policy objective of Friedrich and Danckelman, related both to the struggle against France as well as the desire for Protestant cooperation, was the interest in maintaining stability in the north. Key to this matter was Brandenburg's relationship with Sweden, which I will now examine in some detail.

BRANDENBURG AND SWEDEN: A BRIEF CASE STUDY

In the late seventeenth century Brandenburg sought to diffuse regional tensions in northern and north-eastern Europe in order to protect its own holdings and interests in the region as well as to prevent a northern conflict from draining resources from the ongoing struggle against France.[79] In the case of Brandenburg's relationship with Sweden this took the form of a sincere attempt to improve bilateral relations set against an ongoing backdrop of suspicion that Sweden might be induced to return to its traditional pro-French orientation.[80] Efforts at reconciliation between Brandenburg and Sweden following the war years of 1674–9 had begun under Friedrich Wilhelm, culminating with the exchange of ambassadors and the conclusion of a defensive alliance in 1686, driven by a common desire for cooperation against the French threat and an interest in broader Protestant unity. Danckelman became actively involved in managing this relationship when Friedrich came to the throne in 1688.

Danckelman was perfectly suited to the anti-French, pro-Protestant mode of politics that characterised the Brandenburg–Swedish relationship at this time, and his Swedish counterparts found him an admirable partner with whom they could work. Peter Macklier, Sweden's representative in Berlin in the months surrounding the transition from Friedrich Wilhelm's to Friedrich's reign, referred to Danckelman as 'a man of probity' and took efforts to cultivate a relationship with him even before Friedrich Wilhelm's death, noting that Danckelman 'would become great' once Friedrich was in power.[81] Danckelman in turn gave Macklier assurances of his commitment to work for Brandenburg–Swedish friendship. After Friedrich assumed the throne subsequent Swedish diplomats continued to work closely with Danckelman and viewed him as their primary contact at court, often describing their relations in terms of personal friendship.[82]

The improvement in relations between Brandenburg and Sweden to which Danckelman had contributed and that served his own anti-French/pro-Protestant politics as well as the elector's interests suffered a significant setback in 1691 when Brandenburg's ambassador in Sweden, Alexander von Dohna, was angrily recalled from Stockholm following a scandal regarding the conversion of his wife (a native-born Swede) to Calvinism that resulted in Karl XI banishing her from appearing at court, a deeply insulting gesture that left Friedrich seething.[83] The reaction of both governments to this incident was so intense that high-level diplomatic contact between them was broken off for the following three and a half years. Despite Danckelman's disappointment over this disastrous turn in relations, which threatened to undo three years of his labours, and the fact that the aggrieved diplomat (Dohna) numbered amongst his recognised enemies, Danckelman defended the honour of his prince and state so vigorously in this incident that years later he would be accused of having mistreated the Swedish diplomat whom he took to task over the matter.[84] As statesman, Danckelman's sense of obligation to uphold Friedrich's reputation at all costs clearly outweighed any proprietary interest in preserving the fruits of his own diplomatic efforts for warm relations with Sweden, as well as any personal agenda in seeing his enemy Dohna publicly humiliated.

When the time came to rebuild relations with Sweden in 1694 Danckelman was once again a driving force.[85] He participated in a discussion designed to put the Dohna affair behind the two countries, and entered into an extended partnership with the Swedish official Nils Bielke aimed at renewing the defensive alliance of 1686, which faced significant resistance in both Brandenburg and Sweden.[86] This improved climate paved the way for cooperation on several important regional issues, including Sweden's long-running dispute with Denmark over the succession in Holstein-Gottorp and the looming Polish royal election.[87] Efforts to cooperate in a dispute over the dynastic succession in the north German duchy of Mecklenburg-Güstrow met with less happy results when the Swedish military commander on the ground overstepped his bounds, creating tensions for both Sweden and Brandenburg with the emperor, but their willingness to work together endured.[88] By the end of his ascendancy Danckelman was facing accusations from his opponents that he had worked too closely with the Swedes.[89]

This quick review of Brandenburg's relationship with Sweden during Danckelman's time in power provides insights into his methods as statesman. A broad commitment to pro-Orange, pro-Protestant and anti-French politics provided the overarching framework for his policy but did not necessarily determine its details. The necessity to defend the honour of his prince took its place alongside other imperatives of state as determining factors of his conduct. A willingness to take risky action involving independent initiative (such as his work with Bielke) marked his style in pursuing objectives he believed worthwhile. Above all, cultivating trusting personal relationships with foreign diplomats formed the backbone of his diplomatic method, and foreign diplomats in turn sought him out as their point of access to power. Ironically, Danckelman may have been better at forming friendships with foreigners than with those in his adopted home-land, who bristled at his brusque and domineering manner.[90]

For now these observations must remain tentative suggestions rather than fleshed-out conclusions, awaiting further research into Danckelman's statecraft.

CONCLUDING REMARKS

Writing with satisfaction on the totality of Danckelman's decline, Christoph zu Dohna noted that 'a man of that sort seldom falls half-way'.[91] Indeed, scholars of early modern favourites have argued that such men could not simply be removed from their positions by prosaic means, but rather must fall, usually dramatically and irrevocably.[92] Danckelman's intimate knowledge of the mechanisms of power in Brandenburg was too complete for him to be allowed to walk away quietly from service, his previous ties to the elector too intense to be able to dissolve peace-fully.[93] Such human drama exerts an understandable pull of fascination over scholars working on Danckelman, with the unintended consequence that those elements of his nine years in power not chiefly implicated in his fall are neglected. This unfortu-nately includes the great bulk of his activity in shaping Brandenburg's foreign policy for almost a decade.

An analogous claim can be made regarding his personality. Danckelman's reputa-tion for uncompromising, single-minded, iron-willed commitment to the political needs of state may seem unattractive to many scholars today. But to the classical historians of the Prusso-German tradition who continue to exert profound influence over our understanding of Brandenburg-Prussian history these traits were precisely what made Danckelman worthy of attention in the first place, especially given his service to a prince found lacking in those same characteristics. Their focus rests on the character rather than the specific actions of this man of 'free and noble mind' whose departure from office marked the unhappy day in which 'the spirit of the Great Elector disappeared from his state!'[94] Much like the disproportionate emphasis on Danckelman's fall, the exaggerated celebration of his character leaves us with a flat and uninformative image of his time in power that obscures what he wished to get done and how he went about accomplishing it.

Any full attempt to remedy these shortcomings and provide a new interpretation of Danckelman as statesman must be grounded in painstaking archival excavation. If the current chapter serves merely as encouragement to take up such work, it will have accomplished its own more modest task.

NOTES

1. See Johann Gustav Droysen, *Friedrich I. König von Preußen*, 3rd edn (Berlin: De Gruyter, 2001), pp. 17–19; Otto Hintze, *Die Hohenzollern und ihr Werk: fünfhundert Jahre vaterländischer Geschichte* (Berlin: Paul Parey, 1915), pp. 257, 260.

2. A fact noted by Michael Kaiser, 'Der unhöfische Favorit: Eberhard von Danckelman (1643–1722), Oberpräsident in Brandenburg unter Kurfürst Friedrich III.', in Kaiser and Andreas Pečar (eds), *Der zweite Mann im Staat: Oberste Amtsträger und Favoriten im Umkreis der Reichsfürsten in der Frühen Neuzeit* (Berlin: Duncker & Humblot, 2003), p. 271 (pp. 271–94). Kaiser's work is the best recent study of Danckelman. On the sharply negative reputation of favourites, see J. H. Elliott, 'Introduction', in Elliott and L. W. B. Brockliss (eds), *The World of the Favourite* (New Haven, CT: Yale University Press, 1999), p. 1 (pp. 1–10); Brockliss, 'Concluding Remarks: The Anatomy of the Minister-Favourite', in Elliott and Brockliss, *World of the Favourite*, pp. 288–90 (pp. 279–309); Kaiser and Pečar, 'Reichsfürsten und ihre Favoriten. Die Ausprägung eines europäischen Strukturphänomens unter den politischen Bedingungen des Alten Reiches', in Kaiser and Pečar, *Der zweite Mann*, p. 17 (pp. 9–19). Jean Bérenger, 'Pour une enquête européenne: le problème du ministériat au XVIIe siècle', *Annales* 29:1 (1974), pp. 166–92, remains foundational for work on favourites (and their negative reputations).

3. See Curt Breysig, *Der Prozess gegen Eberhard Danckelmann. Ein Beitrag zur brandenburgischen Verwaltungsgeschichte* (Leipzig: Duncker & Humblot, 1889); Harry Bresslau, 'Der Sturz des Oberpräsidenten Eberhard von Danckelmann (December 1697)', in Bresslau and Siegfried Isaacsohn, *Der Fall zweier Preussischen Minister des Oberpräsidenten Eberhard von Danckelmann 1697 und des Grosskanzlers C. J. M. von Fürst 1779* (Berlin: Weidmannsche Buchhandlung, 1878), pp. 5–74; Leopold von Ranke, 'Ueber den Fall des brandenburgischen Ministers Eberhard von Danckelmann. 1697. 1698.', in Ranke, *Sämtliche Werke* (Leipzig: Duncker & Humblot, 1872), vol. 24, pp. 71–113; Friedrich Meinecke, 'Danckelman's Sturz. Briefe Friedrich's III. an die Kurfürstin Sophie von Hannover', *Historische Zeitschrift* 62:2 (1889), pp. 279–85. Wider in scope is the curious but interesting *Sophie Charlotte und Danckelmann: eine preußische Historie* (Wiesbaden: Limes, 1949) by Bernard von Brentano, an author known more for his creative fiction and essays and as the brother of the political figures Clemens and Heinrich von Brentano. For biographical information, see the entries for Danckelman in *Westfälische Lebensbilder* (Münster: Aschendorff, 1933), vol. 4, pp. 162–79 (by Johannes Schulze); *Allgemeine Deutsche Biographie* (Leipzig: Duncker & Humblot, 1876), vol. 4, pp. 720–5 (by Bernhard Erdmannsdörffer); *Neue Deutsche Biographie* (Berlin: Duncker & Humblot, 1957), vol. 3, pp. 503–4 (by Hans Saring); Friedrich Beck and Eckart Henning (eds), *Brandenburgisches Biographisches Lexikon* (Potsdam: Verlag für Berlin-Brandenburg, 2002), p. 85 (by Meta Kohnke).

4. See the sections on Danckelman's fall in Droysen, *Friedrich I.*, pp. 123–33; Frank Göse, *Friedrich I. (1657–1713). Ein König in Preußen* (Regensburg: Friedrich Pustet, 2012), pp. 115–21; Linda and Marsha Frey, *Frederick I: The Man and His Times* (Boulder, CO: East European Monographs, 1984), pp. 75–85.

5. Breysig calls Danckelman 'Einem Manne, der nach dem Zeugnis seiner Sekretäre Cunow und Bergius von frühen Morgen bis spät abends beschäftigt war, dem Tausende von Akten durch die Hände ging' (Breysig, *Der Prozess*, p. 50). Brockliss notes that 'Favourites, even in the twentieth century, have seldom left their own account of their time at the top; they are primarily known through their detractors' (Brockliss, 'Concluding Remarks', p. 304, n. 4).

6. On the inverse relationship between the mass of legal material and its utility in understanding Danckelman, see Ranke, 'Ueber den Fall', pp. 76–7.

7. Kaiser and Pečar, 'Reichsfürsten und ihre Favoriten', p. 11; Ronald G. Asch, '"Lumine solis." Der Favorit und die politische Kultur des Hofes in Westeuropa', in Kaiser and Pečar *Der zweite Mann*, pp. 21–2 (pp. 21–38). Kaiser and Pečar's volume is the most concerted effort to remedy this situation.

8. An end date proposed by Jean Bérenger in 'Pour une enquête européenne', repeated in his 'The Demise of the Minister-Favourite, or a Political Model at Dusk: The Austrian Case', in

Elliott and Brockliss, *World of the Favourite*, pp. 256–68, and confirmed (though with a different explanation) in Brockliss's 'Concluding Remarks' in the same volume.

9. Although Danckelman stretches the chronological limits of prevailing discussions of the age of the European favourite, characteristics of his power align in important ways with the definition of the 'minister-favourite' put forth in Brockliss, 'Concluding Remarks', esp. pp. 280–5. The personal favour Danckelman received from his prince, largely for the colourless administrative competence and hands-on work ethic that made him indispensable for Brandenburg's governance, allowed him to exert disproportionate (and essentially unaccountable) personal power over state affairs until that princely favour was lost. He was also notably identified as Friedrich's favourite by contemporaries. See, for example, the quotation from Gregorio Leti in note 23 below. For an extended discussion of Danckelman as favourite, see Kaiser, 'Der unhöfische Favorit'.

10. Elector Friedrich Wilhelm of Brandenburg reigned 1640–88; King Friedrich Wilhelm I of Prussia reigned 1713–40.

11. See Göse, *Friedrich I.*, pp. 9–12; Frey and Frey, *Frederick I*, pp. 1–7.

12. On Danckelman as antithesis of Friedrich's reign, see Kaiser, 'Der unhöfische Favorit', pp. 271–2.

13. A comparison made in Danckelman's resounding favour in *Fall und Ungnade zweyer Staats-Ministres des Königl. Preußischen Hofes aus dem Frantzösischen Original ins Teutsche übersetzet* (1712). See also Kaiser, 'Der unhöfische Favorit', p. 272; Göse, *Friedrich I.*, p. 163; Leopold von Ranke, *Memoirs of the House of Brandenburg, and History of Prussia, during the Seventeenth and Eighteenth Centuries*, trans. Sir Alexander and Lady Duff Gordon, 3 vols (New York: Greenwood Press, 1968), vol. 1, p. 123.

14. Silvester Danckelman, a trained jurist, served primarily in legal offices (Landrichter; Gograf), but was also used by the Princes of Orange on a number of diplomatic missions, including to the Westphalia peace talks.

15. Eberhard von Danckleman, *Dissertatio juridica de contractu emphyteutico* (Ultrajecti: Pro Petro Baart, 1656). On contemporary amazement over Danckelman's intellectual precociousness, see Breysig, *Der Prozess*, p. 19, n. 1.

16. Danckelman's father, who had recently entered Brandenburg service and got to know Schwerin, was instrumental in securing Danckelman's appointment. On Schwerin's role in the education of Friedrich Wilhelm's sons, see Ferdinand Hirsch, 'Die Erziehung der älteren Söhne des Großen Kurfürsten', *Forschungen zur Brandenburgischen und Preußischen Geschichte* 7 (1894), pp. 141–71.

17. In addition to the biographical dictionary entries cited in note 3 above, information on Danckelman's background and early career can be found in Breysig, *Der Prozess*, pp. 14–23; Kaiser, 'Der unhöfische Favorit', pp. 274–6; Frey and Frey, *Frederick I*, pp. 25–6; Göse, *Friedrich I.*, p. 23; Brentano, *Sophie Charlotte und Danckelmann*, pp. 12–23, 29–31; Ranke, 'Ueber den Fall', pp. 74–5.

18. His mother, grandmother and step-mother all raised these concerns. See Breysig, *Der Prozess*, pp. 21–2; Ranke, 'Ueber den Fall', p. 75; Brentano, *Sophie Charlotte und Danckelmann*, p. 30; Göse, *Friedrich I.*, pp. 23–4; Kaiser, 'Der unhöfische Favorit', p. 275; Frey and Frey, *Frederick I*, p. 26.

19. On the marriage, see Frey and Frey, *Frederick I*, p. 34. On providing funds, see Breysig, *Der Prozess*, p. 23; Bresslau, 'Der Sturz', p. 33. On the inquest into Ludwig's death, see Göse, *Friedrich I.*, pp. 75–6; Kaiser, 'Der unhöfische Favorit', p. 278; Frey and Frey, *Frederick I*, pp. 37–9. On Danckelman's mediation between Friedrich and Friedrich Wilhelm, see Göse, *Friedrich I.*, p. 79; Kaiser, 'Der unhöfische Favorit', p. 279; Breysig, *Der Prozess*, p. 23; Brentano, *Sophie Charlotte und Danckelmann*, pp. 41–2; Frey and Frey, *Frederick I*, pp. 38–9.

20. Friedrich believed that Danckelman had saved him once from choking, once from poisoning.

See Kaiser, 'Der unhöfische Favorit', p. 278; Frey and Frey, *Frederick I*, pp. 26, 32, 36–7; Breysig, *Der Prozess*, p. 22.

21. This included Danckelman's appointment as president of the government of Cleve in 1692.

22. Kaiser, 'Der unhöfische Favorit', pp. 276–7; Breysig, *Der Prozess*, pp. 23–7; Göse, *Friedrich I.*, pp. 108–9, 115–16.

23. 'Im Vorübergehen will ich nur so viel sagen, daß man wenig Beispiele von einem Günstling hat, der so eifrig für den Dienst seines Fürsten wäre oder auch von einem Fürsten, der so viel Vorliebe für einen Günstling hätte, wie das bei den Kurprinzen und dem Herrn Danckelmann der Fall ist' (Gregorio Leti, *Abrégé de l'Histoire de la maison sérénissime et électorale de Brandenbourg* (Amsterdam: Robert Roger, 1687), quoted (in German translation) in Ranke, 'Ueber den Fall', p. 74). See also Brentano, *Sophie Charlotte und Danckelmann*, p. 47.

24. On Friedrich placing his trust in Danckelman alone, see Kaiser, 'Der unhöfische Favorit', p. 279.

25. The best work on the early history of the *Geheimer Rat* remains Gerhard Oestreich, *Der brandenburg-preußische Geheime Rat vom Regierungsantritt des Großen Kurfürsten bis zu der Neuordnung im Jahre 1651. Eine behördengeschichtliche Studie* (Würzburg-Aumühle: Konrad Triltsch, 1937).

26. On the *Geheimer Rat* during the first years of Friedrich's reign, and his active participation in its meetings, see Göse, *Friedrich I.*, pp. 93–4, 110–15.

27. Frey and Frey, *Frederick I*, p. 74. On Danckelman's power residing within the *Geheimer Rat*, see Breysig, *Der Prozess*, p. 27.

28. Friedrich's appointment of Danckelman reads: 'Absonderlich aber haben wir ihm [Danckelman] gnädigst aufgetragen, Alles, was von uns zu unterzeichnen ist, zu Verhütung aller Irrungen, so dabei vorgehen könnten, und fürnehmlich, dass Uns nichts so eines dem anderen zuwider oder Unserer Intention und Willen nicht gemäss ist, zur Unterschrift präsentiret werde, zu kontrasigniren' (quoted in Breysig, *Der Prozess*, p. 24). See also Göse, *Friedrich I*, p. 109; Kaiser, 'Der unhöfische Favorit', p. 276; Droysen, *Friedrich I.*, pp. 16–17; Brentano, *Sophie Charlotte und Danckelmann*, p. 81.

29. Breysig, *Der Prozess*, p. 27; Frey and Frey, *Frederick I*, p. 82.

30. On Schwerin as Friedrich Wilhelm's chief minister, see Michael Rohrschneider, '". . . vndt keine favoritten ahn Euerem hoffe haltet": Zur Stellung Ottos von Schwerin im Regierungssystem des Großen Kurfürsten', in Kaiser and Pečar, *Der zweite Mann*, pp. 253–69.

31. Breysig, *Der Prozess*, p. 24; Droysen, *Friedrich I.*, p. 16.

32. 'mit dem Geheimen Rat Danckelman sie mehrenteils vorher schon überleget und beschlossen' (quoted in Göse, *Friedrich I.*, p. 111). Göse himself challenges this assumption.

33. 'dass die Geheimen Räte nur deshalb also genannt wären, weil ihnen alles geheim gehalten würde' (Otto von Schwerin the younger, report of 31 January 1698, quoted in Bresslau, 'Der Sturz', p. 25). *Geheim* means 'secret' in German. See also Breysig, *Der Prozess*, p. 28; Droysen, *Friedrich I.*, p. 125; Frey and Frey, *Frederick I*, p. 79; Brentano, *Sophie Charlotte und Danckelmann*, p. 147.

34. Stepney to J. Vernon, Hamburg, 25 February 1698, printed in Ranke, 'Ueber den Fall', pp. 95–6 (pp. 95–8).

35. See Brentano, *Sophie Charlotte und Danckelmann*, p. 196.

36. Bresslau, 'Der Sturz', p. 34; Droysen, *Friedrich I.*, pp. 82–3; Brentano, *Sophie Charlotte und Danckelmann*, p. 147. Brockliss notes that minister-favourites often lacked personal financial wherewithal. See Brockliss, 'Concluding Remarks', p. 303.

37. Göse, *Friedrich I.*, pp. 122–5; Breysig, *Der Prozess*, pp. 28–9; Frey and Frey, *Frederick I*, pp. 85, 155–8; Kaiser, 'Der unhöfische Favorit', pp. 282–3; Hintze, *Hohenzollern und ihr Werk*, p. 260; Sidney Bradshaw Fay, *The Rise of Brandenburg-Prussia to 1786* (New York: Henry Holt, 1937), pp. 84–5.

38. Breysig, *Der Prozess*, pp. 66–8; Kaiser, 'Der unhöfische Favorit', p. 284; Frey and Frey, *Frederick I*, p. 85.

39. On legal exams, see Frey and Frey, *Frederick I*, p. 148; Brentano, *Sophie Charlotte und Danckelmann*, p. 148. On Danckelman's leadership of the postal system, see Frey and Frey, *Frederick I*, pp. 159–60; Breysig, *Der Prozess*, p. 30; Brentano, *Sophie Charlotte und Danckelmann*, pp. 147–8; Droysen, *Friedrich I.*, p. 80. On poor relief, see Göse, *Friedrich I.*, p. 326; Brentano, *Sophie Charlotte und Danckelmann*, p. 148. On intellectual and cultural life during Friedrich's reign, including mention of Danckelman's role, see Göse, *Friedrich I.*, pp. 292–8; Frey and Frey, *Frederick I*, pp. 92–118. For Danckelman's specific contributions, see also Konrad Grau, *Die Preußische Akademie der Wissenschaften zu Berlin: eine deutsche Gelehrtengesellschaft in drei Jahrhunderten* (Heidelberg: Spektrum Akademischer Verlag, 1993), pp. 57–60; Rudolf Greiser's introduction to Christoph zu Dohna, *Die Denkwürdigkeiten des Burggrafen und Grafen Christoph zu Dohna (1665–1733)*, ed. and trans. Greiser (Göttingen: Vandenhoeck & Ruprecht, 1974), pp. 14–15; Ranke, 'Ueber den Fall', pp. 75–6; Droysen, *Friedrich I.*, p. 131.

40. On the inevitable resentment favourites faced, especially from the native nobility, see especially Bérenger, 'Pour une enquête européenne'. Some scholars have suggested that the favourite's role as a magnet for hostility was at least partially by design since it could shield the prince himself from public wrath. See Brockliss, 'Concluding Remarks', especially pp. 288–91. See also Asch, '"Lumine solis"', p. 38. Along similar lines, Pauline Croft has written that 'one aspect of the traditional function of the favourite was to serve as political whipping-boy' (Croft, 'Can a Bureaucrat Be a Favourite? Robert Cecil and the Strategies of Power', in Elliott and Brockliss, *World of the Favourite*, p. 93 (pp. 81–95)).

41. Danckelman instead was able to convince Friedrich 'Das alles auf dem vorigen Fuß quoad formam regiminis bleibe' (Danckelman, quoted in Droysen, *Friedrich I.*, p. 297, n. 7, as well as pp. 15–16). See also Breysig, *Der Prozess*, p. 25; Göse, *Friedrich I.*, p. 109; Kaiser, 'Der unhöfische Favorit', p. 280; Frey and Frey, *Frederick I*, p. 71; Brentano, *Sophie Charlotte und Danckelmann*, p. 82.

42. Droysen, *Friedrich I.*, pp. 85, 109; Bresslau, 'Der Sturz', pp. 26–9; Kaiser, 'Der unhöfische Favorit', p. 280; Breysig, *Der Prozess*, p. 25; Brentano, *Sophie Charlotte und Danckelmann*, pp. 143–5.

43. Danckelman 'von unserm ganzen Estat und Interesse eine vollkommene Wissenschaft und Erfahrung erlangt hat und dessen Treue, Redlichkeit, Capacität, große Application und Desinteressement uns von unserer Wiege an dergestalt bekannt ist, daß wir von nichts mehr und besser als eben davon persuadirt sind; wir hätten ihm auch vorlängst solche Function conferirt, wenn er nicht aus einer sonderbaren Modestie ihn damit zu verschonen vielfältig und unablässig gebeten hätte' (Danckelman's letter of appointment as *Oberpräsident*, 23 July/2 August 1695, quoted in Droysen, *Friedrich I.*, p. 314, n. 176).

44. Stepney to J. Vernon, Hamburg, 25 February 1698, printed in Ranke, 'Ueber den Fall', p. 95 (pp. 95–8).

45. 'j'ai oui dire à des personnes qui avoient eu part à sa familiarité, que jamais elles ne l'avoient vu rire' (Karl Ludwig Freiherr von Pöllnitz, *Mémoires pour servir à l'histoire des quatre derniers souverains de la Maison de Brandebourg* (1791), quoted in Breysig, *Der Prozess*, p. 21, n. 2).

46. 'Freunde sich zu machen, hatte er vielleicht nicht das Talent, vielleicht auch nicht den Willen' (Ranke, 'Ueber den Fall', p. 88).

47. Dohna, *Denkwürdigkeiten*, pp. 109, 137–8.

48. Kaiser, 'Der unhöfische Favorit'. For the interesting parallel claim that Danckelman was incapable of seeing things like a politician, see Brentano, *Sophie Charlotte und Danckelmann*, pp. 102–4.

49. Kaiser, 'Der unhöfische Favorit', pp. 282–4; Göse, *Friedrich I.*, p. 117. For a description of

the positions held by Danckelman's brothers, see Breysig, *Der Prozess*, p. 54, n. 2. Breysig notes that following his arrest Danckelman defended himself against accusations of nepotism by arguing that each of his brothers had already entered Brandenburg service before his ascendancy and only two received marked advancement during it. On the centrality of patronage distribution to the careers of most favourites, see Brockliss, 'Concluding Remarks'; I. A. A. Thompson, 'The Institutional Background to the Rise of the Minister-Favourite', in Elliott and Brockliss, *World of the Favourite*, pp. 13–25; Asch, '"Lumine solis"'.

50. 'Ich erinnere mich, mehr als einmal zu Verhandlungen herangezogen worden zu sein, die keineswegs dazu dienten, seine Autorität zu festigen. Da ich mich in keiner Weise in ministerielle Angelegenheiten eingemischt hatte und daher weniger verdächtig erschien, war ich geeigneter als ein anderer, gewisse häufige Zusammenkünfte mehrerer anderer bedeutender Persönlichkeiten herbeizuführen, die sehr ungeduldig das herrische Joch dieses Ministers ertrugen' (Dohna, *Denkwürdigkeiten*, p. 110). On Danckelman's complete dependence on Friedrich, see esp. Kaiser, 'Der unhöfische Favorit'. On Danckelman's opponents enjoying a dense network of familial and friendship connections of the sort that he himself so notably lacked, see Bresslau, 'Der Sturz', pp. 25–6.

51. The final list of formal accusations drawn up against Danckelman in 1700 numbered 290 articles. See Breysig, *Der Prozess*, pp. 46ff. On usurpation and tyranny as the standard accusations against early modern favourites, see Bérenger, 'Pour une enquête européenne'.

52. Göse, who sees Danckelman's fall not only as the result of court intrigue but also as part of a natural process of Friedrich's maturation and liberation from his former tutor, argues that the relationship between the elector and Danckelman had begun to change earlier. See Göse, *Friedrich I.*, pp. 115–21.

53. 'hielt ich mich nicht zurück, ihn [Danckelman] an der Tafel aufzuziehen und ihn sehr lebhaft zu reizen, woran, wie ich sah, der Herr [Friedrich] Spaß hatte und selbst von einem zum anderen Mal dazu Gelegenheit bot: deutliches Zeichen, wie ich ihn kannte, daß die Dinge nicht mehr so standen wie früher, da der Fürst es nicht liebte, daß man sich im geringsten auf Kosten seiner Günstlinge belustigte' (Dohna, *Denkwürdigkeiten*, p. 152). See also Bresslau, 'Der Sturz', p. 36; Göse, *Friedrich I.*, p. 118; Brentano, *Sophie Charlotte und Danckelmann*, p. 154. On the tremendous importance of gesture in symbolising favour and its loss, see Brockliss, 'Concluding Remarks', p. 299. Once Danckelman was released from office, Friedrich's refusal to grant him a farewell audience carried even greater symbolic weight.

54. 'die verenderung, so ich an meinem hoffe gemacht . . . ich wil hoffen, daß solches zu vielem nützlich sein werde, dan ich gewiß nicht mehr herr, sondern diener war und also höchst nöthig hatte, dieses zu thun, ob es mir zwahr sehr schwehr ankam, daß ich gegen meinen Eltesten diener eine solche harte *resolution* faßen muste' (Friedrich to Sophie von Hannover, Berlin, 4 December 1697, printed in Meinecke, 'Danckelman's Sturz', p. 280). Note also the language of Danckelman's usurpation of Friedrich's authority here. See also Kaiser, 'Der unhöfische Favorit', p. 287; Bresslau, 'Der Sturz', p. 42.

55. The details of Danckelman's fall are covered extensively in the works/sections cited in notes 3 and 4 above.

56. Breysig, *Der Prozess*, p. 100; Brentano, *Sophie Charlotte und Danckelmann*, p. 222.

57. Breysig, *Der Prozess*, p. 28.

58. Typical is Jeannette Falcke, *Studien zum diplomatischen Geschenkwesen am brandenburgisch-preußischen Hof im 17. und 18. Jahrhundert* (Berlin: Duncker & Humblot, 2006), p. 35: 'Bis zu seinem Sturz im Jahre 1697 wurde die Außenpolitik und die Bearbeitung der auswärtigen Angelegenheiten im wesentlichen von Danckelmann geprägt.'

59. 'Herr Danckelmann macht darum alles, was er will; er ist *der* Minister'; 'Herr Danckelmann ist der Großwesir von Brandenburg; er regiert alles . . .' (quoted in Brentano, *Sophie Charlotte und Danckelmann*, pp. 116, 117; original emphasis).

60. Breysig, *Der Prozess*, p. 28.

61. Droysen, *Friedrich I.*, p. 59.
62. Stepney to J. Vernon, Hamburg, 25 February 1698, printed in Ranke, 'Ueber den Fall', p. 97 (pp. 95–8). See also Bresslau, 'Der Sturz', p. 25.
63. Kaiser, 'Der unhöfische Favorit', p. 283. A systematic study of Brandenburg's diplomatic appointments during Danckelman's ascendancy would be a welcome addition to our understanding of his influence over foreign policy.
64. Breysig, *Der Prozess*, p. 26.
65. Ulrike Müller-Weil, *Absolutismus und Aussenpolitik in Preussen: ein Beitrag zur Strukturgeschichte des preussischen Absolutismus* (Stuttgart: Franz Steiner, 1992), pp. 162–3.
66. Droysen, *Friedrich I.*, pp. 54–65; Frey and Frey, *Frederick I*, pp. 41–4; Göse, *Friedrich I.*, pp. 68–70, 180–1; Hintze, *Hohenzollern und ihr Werk*, p. 261; Bresslau, 'Der Sturz', pp. 12–14; Breysig, *Der Prozess*, pp. 5–6, 83–5; Brentano, *Sophie Charlotte und Danckelmann*, pp. 100–4.
67. Droysen, *Friedrich I.*, pp. 102–3; Breysig, *Der Prozess*, pp. 6–7, 35; Bresslau, 'Der Sturz', pp. 14–17; Frey and Frey, *Frederick I*, pp. 56, 77; Göse, *Friedrich I.*, pp. 118, 202; Kaiser, 'Der unhöfische Favorit', pp. 289, 294; Brentano, *Sophie Charlotte und Danckelmann*, pp. 106–10.
68. Frey and Frey, *Frederick I*, pp. 77, 83–4; Kaiser, 'Der unhöfische Favorit', pp. 288–9; Droysen, *Friedrich I.*, pp. 119ff.; Bresslau, 'Der Sturz', pp. 34–5; Hintze, *Hohenzollern und ihr Werk*, pp. 258–9; Breysig, *Der Prozess*, p. 35; Göse, *Friedrich I.*, p. 118; Brentano, *Sophie Charlotte und Danckelmann*, pp. 158–61.
69. On continuities in foreign policy following Danckelman's fall, see Ranke, 'Ueber den Fall', p. 78. For discussions of Brandenburg-Prussia's foreign policy during Friedrich's reign, see Göse, *Friedrich I.*, esp. pp. 170–201, 261–82; Droysen, *Friedrich I.*; Frey and Frey, *Frederick I*, pp. 184–243. It is interesting to note that the fault lines between Danckelman's opponents and his much smaller cluster of supporters did not fall in any meaningful way along patterns of disagreement over foreign policy. The accusations relating to foreign policy in the 290 articles compiled for his planned trial were also clearly of second-order importance. See Breysig, *Der Prozess*, p. 58.
70. On Friedrich's commitment to the Protestant cause as 'one of the guiding principles of his foreign policy', see Göse, *Friedrich I.*, pp. 299–308, here p. 301.
71. See Breysig, *Der Prozess*, p. 20.
72. Droysen, *Friedrich I.*, p. 131; Brentano, *Sophie Charlotte und Danckelmann*, pp. 165–6.
73. Droysen, *Friedrich I.*, p. 14; Ranke, 'Ueber den Fall', p. 75; Brentano, *Sophie Charlotte und Danckelmann*, p. 47.
74. On Danckelman's pro-Orange orientation, see Droysen, *Friedrich I.*, pp. 113, 124–5; Ranke, 'Ueber den Fall'; Göse, *Friedrich I.*, p. 176; Breysig, *Der Prozess*, p. 20; Hintze, *Hohenzollern und ihr Werk*, p. 258; Frey and Frey, *Frederick I*, pp. 77, 82–3; Brentano, *Sophie Charlotte und Danckelmann*, pp. 47, 118–19.
75. 'Uns haßt er, und zwar genau so, wie es im Interesse des Oraniers liegt' (quoted in Brentano, *Sophie Charlotte und Danckelmann*, p. 118).
76. 'desshalb umb chargen und ehre gekommen, dass er mehr auf das publicum gesehen, alss auf E. Ch. Durchl. privatinteresse' (Wolfgang von Schmettau, 11 February 1698, quoted in Bresslau, 'Der Sturz', pp. 34–5, n. 59).
77. 'qu'il se trouve des gens qui croyent, que sa disgrâce vient en parti de ce qu'il a été trop attaché à mes intérests, qui sont pourtant les mesmes que ceux de M. l'Electeur' (Dobrzenski's report out of London, 18/28 February 1698, quoted in Droysen, *Friedrich I.*, p. 317, n. 203).
78. The Earl of Portland in particular made his rage over Danckelman's dismissal and arrest known to Christoph zu Dohna in London. See Dohna, *Denkwürdigkeiten*, p. 166. On William's own more measured words to Dohna, see ibid. pp. 170–1. On George Stepney's

mission to Berlin on Danckelman's behalf, see Ranke, 'Ueber den Fall', and Stepney's correspondence printed therein. On Friedrich's negative reaction to Stepney's intervention and desire that William 'finally' stop speaking about Danckelman for the sake of their friendship, see Friedrich to Sophie von Hannover, Berlin, 19 March 1698, and Oranienburg, 15 August 1698, printed in Meinecke, 'Danckelman's Sturz', pp. 280–1. On the English and Dutch response in general, see in addition Droysen, *Friedrich I.*, pp. 129, 131; Göse, *Friedrich I.*, p. 120; Frey and Frey, *Frederick I*, p. 83; Brentano, *Sophie Charlotte und Danckelmann*, pp. 185–90.

79. Göse, *Friedrich I.*, pp. 181–5.
80. On Brandenburg–Swedish relations during this period, see Daniel Riches, *Protestant Cosmopolitanism and Diplomatic Culture: Brandenburg–Swedish Relations in the Seventeenth Century* (Leiden: Brill, 2013), esp. pp. 208–9, 225–84. Brandenburg's reaction to Swedish plans to send troops to support the emperor against the Ottomans in 1690 – a time when Brandenburg and Sweden were officially allies – displays the ongoing suspicion of Swedish motives in the Empire. See Göse, *Friedrich I.*, p. 188; Droysen, *Friedrich I.*, pp. 72–8.
81. 'hwilcken *passerar* för een Man af *probite*' (Peter Macklier to Karl XI, Berlin, 3 March 1688. RA, Diplomatica, Brandenburgico-Borussica, vol. 30); 'Ich habe beŷ allen gelegenheiten beŷ Sr: Churprintzl. Durchl. mich best möglichst zu *recommendir*en Gesücht, Auch mit dero Geheimbten Raht Hrn. Danckelmann, (der Alß dan Groß werden würde) gute Freüntschafft gemacht' (Macklier to Karl XI, Berlin, 18 April 1688. RA, Diplomatica, Brandenburgico-Borussica, vol. 30).
82. See the reports of Friedrich Wilhelm Horn (RA, Diplomatica, Brandenburgico-Borussica, vol. 31); Justus Heinrich Storren (RA, Diplomatica, Brandenburgico-Borussica, vol. 32); Friedrich Christoph von Dohna (RA, Diplomatica, Germanica, vol. 311).
83. See Daniel Riches, 'Conversion and Diplomacy in Absolutist Northern Europe', in David M. Luebke, Jared Poley, Daniel C. Ryan and David Warren Sabean (eds), *Conversion and the Politics of Religion in Early Modern Germany* (New York and Oxford: Berghahn, 2012), pp. 87–100; Riches, *Protestant Cosmopolitanism*, pp. 252–9.
84. Breysig, *Der Prozess*, p. 53.
85. On Danckelman's leadership of the movement in Brandenburg to improve relations with Sweden in the mid-1690s, see Georg Wittrock, 'Nils Bielkes Underhandling i Brandenburg 1696', *Karolinska Förbundets Årsbok* 1918 (Lund: Berlingksa Boktryckeriet, 1918).
86. Notes from the conversation, dated 25 June 1694, are contained in GStA PK, I. HA, Rep. 11, Nr. 247I Schweden, fasc. 47. On Danckelman's dealings with Bielke, see Wittrock, 'Nils Bielkes Underhandling'; Riches, *Protestant Cosmopolitanism*, pp. 275–81. The renewal of the 1686 defensive alliance was negotiated by Danckelman, Fuchs and Bielke and is dated Berlin, 11 July 1696. See Nr. 396 in Theodor von Moerner (ed.), *Kurbrandenburgs Staatsverträge von 1601 bis 1700* (Berlin: Georg Reimer, 1867), pp. 618–20.
87. See Droysen, *Friedrich I.*, p. 120.
88. Ibid. pp. 117–19; Göse, *Friedrich I.*, pp. 183–4; Georg Landberg, *Den Svenska Utrikespolitikens Historia I:3 1648–1697* (Stockholm: P. A. Norstedt & Söner, 1952), pp. 256–7; Frey and Frey, *Frederick I*, pp. 56–7.
89. Droysen, *Friedrich I.*, p. 120.
90. Ranke referred to the Dutch diplomat Ham as one of Danckelman's most trusted friends. See Ranke, 'Ueber den Fall', p. 77. Dohna described Portland as Danckelman's 'avowed friend'. See Dohna, *Denkwürdigkeiten*, p. 166.
91. 'denn ein Mann dieser Art fällt selten halb' (Dohna, *Denkwürdigkeiten*, p. 154).
92. Kaiser and Pečar, 'Reichsfürsten und ihre Favoriten', p. 16; Brockliss, 'Concluding Remarks', pp. 283–4. Brockliss notes that 'Courtier opponents found them annoyingly hard to remove by the usual methods.'

93. On concerns over Danckelman's potential betrayal of state secrets following his release from service contributing to his arrest, see Dohna, *Denkwürdigkeiten*, pp. 154–5; Droysen, *Friedrich I.*, p. 128; Ranke, 'Ueber den Fall', p. 77; Frey and Frey, *Frederick I*, p. 80.

94. 'eine Befugnis, die mehr alles andere den hohen und freien Geist zeigte, in dem Danckelmann seine Stellung und die Führung des Staates betrachtete' (Droysen, *Friedrich I.*, p. 82); 'Wahrlich, es war doch, als sei erst nach jenem unseligen 24. November des Jahres 1697 der Geist des Grossen Kurfürsten von seinem Staate gewichen!' (Breysig, *Der Prozess*, p. 99).

CHAPTER 13

Chancellor of State: Prince Wenzel Anton Kaunitz, the Habsburg Foreign Office and Foreign Policy in the Era of Enlightened Absolutism

Franz A. J. Szabo

Count, and later Prince Wenzel Anton Kaunitz-Rietberg[1] was a leading statesman in the eighteenth-century Habsburg Monarchy for over fifty years, for some forty of which he was its Foreign Minister and the principal minister of the Crown. During his tenure in office he fundamentally transformed the foreign policy priorities of the Monarchy, was instrumental in professionalising and modernising both his own ministry as well as the administrative structure of the state as a whole, and played a leading role in the implementation of the ambitious reform programme of Habsburg enlightened absolutism. His career spanned the reign of five monarchs and three major cultural epochs, during which he contributed significantly to redefining the normative framework of aristocratic career-making in the state that he served. He was the longest-serving and most influential minister of any government in eighteenth-century Europe, and his position in time grew to such significance that historians have been tempted to call him 'the third Head of State' in the Habsburg Monarchy after Maria Theresia and Joseph II.[2] Above all, he set the premises of the foreign policy of the Habsburg Monarchy from the War of the Austrian Succession to the French Revolution.

In traditional diplomatic histories the Central European state-complex of the Habsburgs is frequently simply referred to as 'Austria'.[3] However, in the eighteenth century the term 'Austria' had various meanings and different geographical radii,[4] and the various lands of the House of Habsburg were still, in Evans's felicitous phrase, 'a complex and subtly balanced organism, not a state but a mildly centripetal agglutination of bewilderingly heterogeneous elements'.[5] Yet at the same time these lands did constitute a powerful 'political geographic center' that defined it as one of the great powers of Europe.[6] The dynasty's titular sovereignty over the Holy Roman Empire made matters more complex still, for the imperial title and the territorial basis of Habsburg hereditary holdings were not conterminous. It is thus not surprising that for centuries the conduct of Habsburg foreign policy reflected these complexities.

Despite having been pressured into appointing an Imperial Advisory Council (*Reichs-Hofrat*) in 1498, Holy Roman Emperor Maximilian I explicitly affirmed that 'the personal, confidential, great matters of the Emperor' were to remain his exclusive preserve, and that he would make decisions in this area either by himself or in consultation with a few hand-picked advisors.[7] In the 1520s these consultations became institutionalised by the formation of a Privy Council (*Geheimer Rat*) to advise the monarch on 'confidential great matters', with diplomatic correspondence and other relevant paperwork being handled by the Imperial Chancellery (*Reichskanzlei*) in Vienna, whose head, the Imperial Vice-Chancellor (*Reichsvizekanzler*), came to be regarded as the functional Habsburg Foreign Minister. During the seventeenth century increased awareness on the part of the dynasty that its main claim to great power status rested on its hereditary lands and not on the imperial title led to the transfer of the conduct of the private affairs of the dynasty to one of its three territorial chancelleries, the Austrian Court Chancellery (*Österreichische Hofkanzlei*).[8] As a result a rivalry soon grew up between the Imperial and Austrian Chancelleries over conduct and control of diplomatic correspondence that lasted well over a century. Initially the advantage swung from the former to the latter, but the unimpeachable loyalty of three successive Imperial Vice-Chancellors at the end of the century – Leopold Wilhelm Königsegg (1669–94), Gottlieb Windischgraetz (1694–5) and Dominik Andreas Kaunitz (1698–1705) – managed to reverse this trend and regain firm control of the administration of foreign affairs.[9]

All this changed dramatically in 1705 when the Archbishop and Elector of Mainz and titular Imperial Chancellor, Lothar Franz von Schönborn, managed to secure the position of Imperial Vice-Chancellor for his nephew, Friedrich Karl. The Habsburgs had no intention of entrusting their diplomatic correspondence to a 'foreigner', and the incumbent Austrian Court Chancellor Philipp Ludwig Sinzendorf was quick to seize the opportunity. In October 1706 he secured an imperial order giving his chancellery full control of all diplomatic matters except those dealing with the Holy Roman Empire. In 1720 the whole chancellery was reorganised and a separate department for foreign affairs was created.[10] However, due to the centuries of conflict with the Ottoman Turks, diplomatic correspondence with the Porte continued to be handled by the War Ministry (*Hofkriegsrat*), to which in time those with Russia were added as well.[11] Of course, decision-making still rested in the first instance with the emperor and his advisory council. Here, too, major changes had occurred. In the course of the seventeenth century the Privy Council had grown so large (reaching a total of 150 members by 1700) that as early as 1665 substantive discussions were confined to a smaller 'inner council' subsequently called the Privy Conference (*Geheime Konferenz*), whose membership was in due course limited to a maximum of nine.[12]

In the early eighteenth century the Department for Foreign Affairs within the Austrian Court Chancellery continued to develop. In 1726 a new aide was appointed with the upgraded title of Secretary of State (*Staatssekretär*), Johann Christoph von Bartenstein. He not only took on additional staff, enlarging his department, but even more significantly became the permanent secretary of the Privy Conference, from which position he gradually rose to be the commanding figure of Habsburg foreign policy until the arrival of Kaunitz in 1753.[13] The measure of Bartenstein's dominance became apparent upon the death of Sinzendorf in February 1742, when the Department of Foreign Affairs was formally severed from the Austrian Court Chancellery and raised to the status of a Court Chancellery in its own right, now explicitly responsible for the personal and confidential matters of the dynasty (the *Haus*) and for international relations, which in eighteenth-century terminology were called 'matters of state' (*Staatssachen*). This gave the new ministry the unwieldy title of House, Court and State Chancellery (*Haus-, Hof- und Staatskanzlei*). Almost from the beginning this was generally abbreviated to State Chancellery (*Staatskanzlei*) in everyday usage, and the minister himself was generally referred to as Chancellor of State (*Staatskanzler*). The minister appointed to this position was the former ambassador to Constantinople, Count Corfiz Anton Ulfeld, who was Bartenstein's candidate for the job, less because of Ulfeld's abilities and more because of his perceived mediocrity and malleability. In short, Bartenstein remained the dominant voice in foreign policy discussions for the subsequent eleven years.[14]

To occupy a position of predominance in the foreign policy counsels of the Habsburg Monarchy had been the principal ambition of the Moravian magnate family, the Kaunitzes, ever since the Imperial Vice-Chancellor, Dominik Andreas Kaunitz, first held it. Unfortunately Dominik Andreas was a spendthrift who left his family's finances in tatters, so that his son, Maximilian Ulrich Kaunitz, could only rise to the position of Governor of Moravia. The latter, however, had high ambitions for his own gifted eldest surviving son, Wenzel Anton (born in Vienna in 1711). As a particularly forward-looking seigneur, who understood that a career in state service for his son was not just a birthright but required a thorough modern education, Maximilian Ulrich chose the University of Leipzig for his son's post-secondary education, since an institution of similar quality simply did not exist within the boundaries of the Habsburg Monarchy. But it was his father's stern injunction that 'time at university should not be spent on anything but the acquisition of knowledge (*Scienzien*)'[15] which prescribed an intellectual vigour that was indeed unusual, but that Maximilian Ulrich saw as absolutely vital in the pursuit of the avowed objective of his son following in the footsteps of his own father. The attempt, as soon as young Wenzel reached the canonic age of consent, to secure revenue-producing ecclesiastical prebends in the lower Rhine region for him, where family connections of his mother, Maria Ernestine von Rietberg, could be brought to bear, as Grete Klingenstein has convincingly shown, were part of a larger family strategy not uncommon for the period to keep career options open for younger siblings, and no indication that an ecclesiastical career was ever intended for Wenzel Anton.[16]

Upon his return from the customary grand tour, the twenty-three-year-old Kaunitz's entrée into the political and social life of the monarchy also bore all the signs of future success one would expect from a young member of the magnate elite. Being named a member of the Lower Austrian *Regimentsrat* in June 1734, even if it was as a *Supernumerarius*, gave him the advantage of holding a position in the imperial capital and therefore being close to the court. This meant more than just proximity to the sovereign, for the court as a whole was a site of a 'maze of interconnections and influences'[17] that could be drawn upon for a successful career, as court nobles formed a power elite where social capital played a central role in access to that power.[18] In this respect the career of the young Kaunitz was exemplary. His induction as an Actual Aulic Councillor (*wirklicher Reichshofrat*) in January 1735 may have entailed limited duties but placed him in a smaller pool of promising young nobles for whom this largely titular position was a springboard to higher office at court. Finally his marriage in May 1736 to Maria Ernestine Starhemberg, the grand-daughter of the powerful long-serving President of the Finance Conference (*Finanz Conferenz*) and member of the Privy Conference, Gundaker Thomas Starhemberg, enhanced the already formidable family connections, which virtually assured that opportunities for advancement would certainly not be lacking.[19]

Indeed, if one were to regard any aspect of Kaunitz's rise as remarkable, it would be that it took as long as it did to develop. The years from 1735 to 1741 were years of frustration for the young Kaunitz as his career progress seemed stifled. The poor state of the family's finances was a factor that would continue to plague him and limit his career opportunities well into the 1740s. One of the most important stepping-stones for young nobles with ambitions for senior court or government positions was a dip-lomatic mission. More than half of the senior office holders under Charles VI had at one time or another served in this capacity, but the problem was that salaries in the diplomatic service were low, often in arrears or simply unpaid. Hence an embassy had largely to be financed from personal fortunes and was essentially regarded as a career investment.[20] Inability to cover such an investment and to meet the required expenses was the reason prospective embassies in both Copenhagen and London that were offered to the young Kaunitz had to be turned down. In fact, only the extraordi-nary royal consent to take out loans on entailed properties provided Kaunitz adequate sums to accept the offer to be made ambassador to Sardinia in 1742, in the midst of the War of the Austrian Succession.[21]

In the Turin Embassy Kaunitz finally had an opportunity to display his remarkable intellectual gifts and his far-reaching diplomatic vision. His first two important posi-tion papers, written at a critical point in the war and submitted with a diplomatic report in March 1743, already revealed both in style and content the elements that were increasingly to captivate his sovereign. On the one hand, there was the clarity and lucidity of expression as well as the inexorable logic of the construction of his argu-ments; on the other hand, we see manifest already at this stage a clear formulation of the notions which were to characterise his subsequent foreign policy – above all, the reorientation of the foreign policy priorities from the largely non-contiguous periph-eries of the Monarchy to the central core of hereditary lands within the Holy Roman Empire. During the years that Kaunitz's career seemed to be on hold the Habsburg Monarchy had suffered serious set-backs both in the War of the Polish Succession and in the brief Turkish War of 1738–9, which helped drain resources and build up debt to the point where it was vulnerable to complete dissolution by a predatory coalition at the accession of Charles VI's young daughter, Maria Theresia, in 1740. Frederick II of Prussia's assault on Silesia struck at the very core of the Monarchy and weakened its position in the Holy Roman Empire. This established a life-long premise of Kaunitz's foreign policy – that Prussia was the Monarchy's most dangerous foe – and confirmed that her traditional ally, England, would do little to help in this struggle.[22]

These observations made a decisive impression on Kaunitz's new young sovereign; in part because they mirrored so well her own instinctive feelings on the matter. His appointment as Minister Plenipotentiary for the Austrian Netherlands in February 1745 confirmed that Kaunitz had become one of the young queen's favourites amongst her diplomatic servants. The new position was, however, short-lived, due to the French conquest of the Austrian Netherlands during the War of the Austrian Succession. Upon his return to Vienna it was nevertheless clear that Kaunitz's stock had risen dramatically: in 1747 he was a finalist for the position of Governor of Milan and the next year he was selected as plenipotentiary to the peace conference that was assembled at Aachen (Aix-la-Chapelle) when the War of the Austrian Succession finally came to an end. His experiences at Aachen confirmed the conclusions he had already drawn at Turin, though it left little hope that French hostility could be diffused.[23]

Upon his return to Vienna, Kaunitz was appointed to the Privy Conference, where Habsburg policies were now subjected to a thorough review in light of the bitter experiences of the previous decade. In a series of conferences in the spring of 1749, Kaunitz soon distinguished himself by focusing on the new Prussian threat that had emerged. Considering this the primary problem of Habsburg foreign policy, he suggested other policies had to be tailored to this reality. He underlined that the basis of Habsburg power lay in its central European lands and its dominant position in Germany. Consequently the interests of the contiguous Austrian-Bohemian-Hungarian core triad of the Habsburg state complex had to take precedence over the peripheral possessions in south-western Germany, the Low Countries, Italy or elsewhere. Precisely because Silesia was one of the most important links and one of the wealthiest resource bases of this central triad, its loss merited the subordination of all other diplomatic considerations to its recovery – or else the acquisition of an equally central and significant alternative such as Bavaria. With this premise the principal foreign threat to the Habsburgs was now Prussia, not the Bourbons. The old enmities, Kaunitz suggested, were outdated, and the traditional alliance system was no longer efficacious. It followed that an effort should be made to diffuse time-worn Bourbon hostility to Austria, even at the price of territorial concessions from the peripheral holdings of the Habsburgs.[24]

The triumph of Kaunitz's ideas was signalled at the end of 1749 by his promotion to the exclusive Order of the Golden Fleece and by his appointment as ambassador to Paris.[25] But even before his actual departure for France in the autumn of 1750, there is reason to believe that Maria Theresia had already decided to make Kaunitz her Chancellor of State at the first suitable opportunity. When that opportunity arose and the offer was formally made to Kaunitz, it is a measure of his now well-nigh indispensable status that he was able to set preconditions on both personnel changes – above all the 'promotion' of Bartenstein out of the ministry because there could not be 'two pipers in the same tavern' – and the complete reorganisation of the ministry to his acceptance of a position he had desired and for which he had been trained.[26]

With his formal appointment as House, Court and State Chancellor in May 1753 Kaunitz had fulfilled his career ambition. In less than a decade he had risen to be not only a leading minister, but *the* leading minister at the Habsburg court. This is best illustrated by his relationship to the heretofore most influential body in all policy matters, the Privy Conference. When first made a full member of the Privy Conference in February 1749, Kaunitz astonished and silenced its senior members by the 'judiciousness' of his comments, and soon asserted his intellectual dominance over the body.[27] Once State Chancellor, he assumed the responsibility of chairing the Privy Conference. In a dramatic break with precedent, meetings were now no longer called in the usual manner, by the senior member's official 'council announcer', but by an impersonal memo containing time, place and agenda, circulated by Kaunitz. Subordinate professionals from the Foreign Ministry were regularly brought into the meetings when dealing with areas of their expertise, and the file subsequently forwarded to the monarch now included the minutes of the meeting itself, all relevant supporting documents, as well as the personal recommendations of the minister. Meetings took place in the palace, not in private residences, and Kaunitz determined when these meetings would occur. As the number of Privy Conference meetings began to decline, its members soon found occasion to complain bitterly about the growing 'despotism' of the State Chancellor, and by the time of the Seven Years War it was becoming obvious that the Privy Conference was becoming marginalised. For the next thirty-five years it met increasingly infrequently and the Chancellery of State became the exclusive ministry for foreign affairs.[28]

Kaunitz's shift of diplomatic priorities from the peripheral Habsburg possessions in the Low Countries and Italy to the central core of the Monarchy ironically added another dimension to the responsibilities of his ministry. Since their acquisition as a result of the War of the Spanish Succession these peripheral territories were administered from Vienna by the so-called Italian–Spanish Council, and at the local level by Authorised Ministers appointed by the Crown. With Kaunitz's appointment as State Chancellor, a process set in that within four years transformed the responsible ministry in Vienna into mere 'Italian and Belgian Departments' of the Foreign Ministry. Two Kaunitz protégés played a key role in that process: Karl Philipp Cobenzl, who as Authorised Minister to various German courts had done much to keep major German princes on a pro-Habsburg course, and Beltrame Cristiani, who had been a Habsburg troubleshooter for Italian affairs – the Habsburg–Este marriage negotiations being his biggest accomplishment. As the terms of both the Authorised Ministers in Belgium and Milan were about to expire in 1753, Kaunitz now argued in favour of appointing Cobenzl and Cristiani respectively to these posts. Once appointed, the new Authorised Ministers were ordered to enter into a correspondence with the Chancellor of State in order to keep the latter informed on 'affairs in general' and diplomatic matters touching on neighbouring powers in particular. All domestic matters were to be reported to the nominal minister, Don Manoel Tellez de Menez e Castro, Duke of Sylva, Count of Tarouca. Secret unofficial instructions, however, also bade the two ministers to report every domestic matter to Kaunitz as well.[29] The new dual jurisdiction inevitably created difficulties for Cobenzl and Cristiani, precisely because Sylva-Tarouca was kept in the dark about these developments. The instructions they received from their nominal minister often conflicted with the unofficial instructions they were receiving from Kaunitz. Kaunitz soon became impatient and urged that the administrative anomaly be rectified:[30] in March

1757 the transfer of the administrative responsibilities for these provinces to the Foreign Ministry was formally announced.[31]

In Kaunitz's diplomatic calculations the peripheral lands of the Habsburg Monarchy assumed importance to the central core primarily in their foreign policy context. Having hitherto enjoyed relatively high priority as domestic possessions, but being much more difficult to defend than the contiguous central core, Belgium and Italy tended to drain resources from the Austrian-Bohemian-Hungarian triad far out of proportion to their relative contributions to the commonweal. As such, Kaunitz diagnosed them as domestic as well as foreign policy liabilities. An integral aspect of shifting the diplomatic focus from the Rhine and Italy to Bavaria, Prussia and Germany in general, therefore, was a shift in domestic priorities as well. If Belgium and Italy were to be transformed from domestic liabilities into domestic assets, they would have to be handled *sui generis*, not as integral domestic provinces – certainly reformed and modernised, but not integrated into the central core. In principle the shift in foreign policy priorities did not absolutely require any substantial alteration in the administrative status quo. Demoting the Italian–Spanish and Netherlands Councils from the ministerial rank, however, gave institutional meaning and structure to the shift in policy. The new diplomatic context made the Foreign Ministry the most logical candidate to absorb these councils, and the formal announcement of the change by Maria Theresia in 1757 stressed this logical connection. The Belgian and Italian Councils would henceforth be subordinated to the Chancellery of State, the announcement stated, 'because of the existing connection between foreign policy and the domestic affairs of these two lands'.[32] While this statement was essentially true, it did not tell the whole story. More than to the Foreign Ministry, Belgium and Milan were being subordinated to the Foreign Minister, *qua persona*. And this was true less because Kaunitz had been the prime mover of the diplomatic shift ultimately responsible for this demotion, but instead because Kaunitz held out the promise that under him these lands would prove to be assets – especially in times of war – not only diplomatically, but militarily and financially as well.[33] In Milan the advent of Kaunitz inaugurated a decade or so of what Capra has called the 'heroic moment' of enlightened reform in Milan, marked by the defeat of the traditional patrician oligarchy, the arrival of a new class of government and the diffusion of Enlightenment ideas.[34] A similar turning point in the history of the Austrian Netherlands came with the appointment of Cobenzl, which inaugurated an era of economic growth and prosperity.[35]

That this political rise to power, which can be ascribed in the first instance to Kaunitz's professional capacities, was cemented by other dimensions of the relationship with his sovereign, however, is also quite clear. Access to the power elite of the court may have required demonstrated capacity in lesser positions such as an embassy, social capital to accelerate networking, and financial resources to support both, but remaining within the court elite also required what has been aptly called 'cultural capital'.[36] This meant above all the ability to demonstrate a certain level of intellectual, social and cultural polish and sophistication.[37] That Kaunitz's rigorous education had given him the appropriate intellectual tools had already been displayed in his reports from Turin. What impressed about Kaunitz, however, was not only how articulate he was, but also his level of cultural sophistication and engagement. Shortly after his return from the Austrian Netherlands we find him among the young nobles who were intimates of the imperial couple in the social and cultural life of the court. In particular we find Kaunitz participating in the amateur theatrical productions of this 'young court',[38] and making a reputation for himself in the cultural field as much as in the political. Indeed, it was his report of March 1750 urging the introduction of the French stage at the Court Theatre[39] that led to Gluck's opera reform, of which Kaunitz was the political lynchpin.[40]

If Kaunitz was prepared to defuse traditional Austrian hostility to the Bourbons of both France and Spain, his brief period as ambassador in Paris made it clear there was little reciprocal inclination to be found there. Despite his deep disenchantment with Britain, he recommended keeping all options open, 'to proceed with extreme caution . . . [and] be guided by circumstances, keeping in mind that these cannot be forced but only prepared and introduced'.[41] However, Kaunitz's assessment that Britain had little concern for the Habsburg Monarchy's German priorities was soon confirmed when in January 1756 Britain signed the Convention of Westminster with Prussia, by which the two courts agreed not to attack each other's territories and to preserve the peace in Germany by preventing any other power from entering it. France, angered at Prussian duplicity and afraid of isolation in its already blazing colonial war with Britain, saw that a compromise with the Habsburgs was now necessary. Kaunitz, long soured by Britain's almost callous indifference to the Habsburgs' primary concern with Silesia in the previous war, could now abandon the British option. The result was a dramatic realignment of alliances that is generally known as the Diplomatic Revolution.[42] In February France decided not to renew its alliance with Prussia (due to expire in June) and on 1 May 1756 Austria and France signed a neutrality pact and a defensive alliance, which are collectively known as the First Treaty of Versailles. The most significant part of the treaty, however, was the secret provision to assist each other if attacked by an ally of Britain and, in such a case, to begin negotiations for an offensive alliance.[43] Securing French neutrality in any future Austro-Prussian conflict certainly met Kaunitz's immediate objective, for Russia under Empress Elizabeth not only had remained consistent in its hostility to Prussia since the last war and prepared to renew the alliance it had concluded with the Habsburgs as early as 1726 and again in 1746, but was anxious to initiate the conflict as early as the spring of 1756.[44] However, Kaunitz had to tread carefully, as he was well aware of French suspicions of Russian expansionist motives. His long-range agenda, already articulated clearly in 1755, was the elimination of Prussia as a great power and its reversion to a middle-sized German principality, and then to reach a broad continental understanding among the Bourbons of France, Spain and Naples, the Habsburg Monarchy and Russia.[45]

Fortunately for Kaunitz, his bitterest foe, Frederick II of Prussia, played into his hands. Realising that the Convention of Westminster had not been a brilliant stroke to buy him time but a fatal diplomatic error, Frederick sought to rescue the situation with a military option. Looming encirclement, he calculated, could be broken before the mould set with a lightning strike against what he perceived to be the lynchpin of the Alliance: the Habsburg Monarchy. Unaware of how eager the Russians were to attack him, he calculated Russia's weight in the international system only as an auxiliary of Austria, which would be cowed by the defeat of the latter. This was already mistaken in 1756 and would grow to be ever more so as the Seven Years War progressed. Frederick's gamble to launch a preventative war had indeed misfired, as it now cemented the very alliance he hoped to forestall by it. His action not only triggered the defensive alliance between Austria and France, but also the secret clause to begin negotiations on an offensive alliance. On 1 May 1757, exactly one year after the signing of the First Treaty of Versailles, a second treaty of the same name was signed. France agreed to participate in offensive measures against Prussia and not to lay down arms until Silesia had been reconquered and Austria had received additional territorial compensations. Upon the successful termination of the war, Austria would cede a number of districts in the Austrian Netherlands directly to France, while the remainder would be exchanged with Infanta Don Philip of Parma, husband of Louis XV's daughter, for his Italian territories.[46] The provision for the transfer of the Austrian Netherlands to the Duke of Parma really meant its transfer to his strong-willed spouse and Louis XV's favourite daughter, Princess Louise Élisabeth, thus creating what amounted to a functional French secundogeniture. At one fell swoop the Austrian Netherlands would have been transformed from barrier to French expansion to French buffer and client. It must be kept in mind how important the Austrian Netherlands were to British commercial interests, and the notion that this territory was virtually a British outpost is clear from Newcastle's famous comment that the Austrian Netherlands was, in fact, 'a kind of common country' shared by Austria, Britain and the Dutch.[47]

What is clear from all this is that a continental consensus settlement lay within reach in the early years of the war, which would have not only substantially enhanced France's position but left her completely free to devote her energies and resources to the global conflict with Britain. The permanent removal of the Southern (Austrian) Netherlands from the British orbit would certainly have redounded not only to France's geo-political but also commercial advantage. Further, a French conquest of Hannover, now within reach, would have provided France with such a significant pawn that it could make good substantial reverses elsewhere. Of course, there is no doubt that one way or the other this conflict would have definitively brought Russia into the recognised ranks of the great powers, but the real key issue is the position the Polish–Lithuanian Commonwealth would have held in this new state system. For most of the Seven Years War Russia had no direct territorial designs on Poland and continued to support the succession of the Saxon dynasty as the most effective instrument of the Austro-Russian condominium in this buffer state. What is more, given the Saxon dynasty's connections to the French royal house and France's subsequent endorsement of a Saxon candidature, it was the best compromise for all concerned. The continued existence of Poland as a benign buffer agreeable to all three continental great powers was key to a stable European state system. Indeed, the territorial compensations foreseen for Saxony and Poland at the expense of Prussia would only have enhanced this role. Certainly a Habsburg reconquest of Silesia and the reduction of Brandenburg to its original status as a mid-sized German principality would have restored Austrian primacy in the Holy Roman Empire. But in light of what recent historiography has shown about the continued vitality and functionality of the organs of the Holy Roman Empire in the eighteenth century, and indeed, Austria's relation to these mechanisms,[48] it is clear that Austrian primacy did not equate to Austrian hegemony, in that its primary objectives were defensive and status quo-oriented rather than offensive. To this should be added the one factor that did survive the Seven Years War – namely, the Habsburg détente with the Bourbons of Spain and the stabilisation and pacification of the Italian peninsula through a complex series of dynastic intermarriages. In short, the European state system envisioned by the Austro-French-Russian entente had the potential to be closer to a stable consensus-oriented framework rather than the volatile mixture of fear and opportunism that characterised balance-of-power politics after the Seven Years War.

Nor can it be argued that Allied defeats at the end of 1757 – above all, the battles of Rossbach and Leuthen – definitively ended any hope that such a system could be put in place. These two spectacular Prussian victories did not change but merely delayed these fundamental realities: France retained its numerical superiority over the Anglo-Hanoverians and still had the opportunity to conquer Hannover both in 1758 and 1759, and Frederick II's scope for successful initiatives shrank and the grip of the Austro-Russian vice tightened with every passing year. By the end of 1761 even he had to concede that the war was lost.[49] The real failure of any potential construction of a new consensual European state system came with a French collapse of nerve in 1758. Military setbacks led to defeatism and to certain thoroughly unrealistic policy decisions (such as a planned invasion of England), which made the French want to back out of the Second Treaty of Versailles. By a third treaty of the same name, signed in March 1759 but backdated to December 1758, France no longer committed herself not to lay down arms until Silesia had been reconquered, but in return no part of the Austrian Netherlands was to be ceded, either to France or to the Duke of Parma. This led Kaunitz to doubt seriously whether a French alliance was worth signing at all,[50] but he ultimately agreed that the French contribution to the war effort could be restricted to the obligations under the First Treaty of Versailles as long as Prussia's reduction to a secondary power and the Habsburg reacquisition of Silesia remained an explicit war aim.[51] French pressure, escalating war costs and failure to achieve war-ending victories in 1760 then led Kaunitz to the reluctant conclusion that a reconquest of Silesia was now virtually impossible and that only modest territorial compensations could be hoped for.[52] What also changed was that Russia became increasingly assertive and determined to win some territorial concessions for its military sacrifices in the war. In its negotiations with Austria on its accession to the Third Treaty of Versailles, Russia demanded and received a commitment for further territorial compensation,[53] leading Kaunitz to fear that Russian expansionism might in time prove to be an even greater concern than Prussian ambitions.[54]

In the event, Austria came agonisingly close to victory over Prussia at the beginning of 1762, when the death of Empress Elizabeth of Russia and the accession of the Prussophile Peter III, who switched sides long enough to scuttle any such prospects, forced Kaunitz to accept a peace on the basis of the status quo. It might have been expected that failure to achieve the principal objective of the Seven Years War – the reconquest of Silesia and the reduction of Prussia to its earlier status as a secondary power – would have shaken Kaunitz's position and put an end to his career. Yet the opposite proved to be the case. While developments in the Seven Years War emphasised the degree to which Kaunitz was the most powerful and influential minister at the Habsburg court, the crises of the war solidified rather than shook his position, so that, in fact, not only did his foreign policy premises remained uncontested, but he could also spearhead major domestic reform in the post-war period.[55]

The ministerial primacy of Kaunitz was underscored when, at the outbreak of the Seven Years War he was effectively given the position, though not the title, of a prime minister in the modern sense of the word of presiding over an assembly of other ministers. Historians have generally overlooked this important development, as meetings of what may be appropriately termed a War Cabinet were confused with the separate and different meetings of the Privy Conference. Though the royal order to assemble such a cabinet was published as early as 1875,[56] historians have since largely ignored it and failed to appreciate its significance. Matters were complicated even more when in 1757 members of the War Cabinet were briefly ordered to meet with members of the Privy Conference in a so-called *Conferenz in mixtis*, while a parallel but overlapping Military Conference dealt with military strategy. All these bodies were chaired by Kaunitz with most of the secretarial support coming from subordinates of his ministry.[57] The institutional basis of the power of the Chancellor of State was thus so enhanced that to all appearances he had reached the apogee of his career. Yet to Kaunitz this represented an unsatisfactory state of affairs, less with respect to his own position than to the structure of government as such. In his view rivalry rather than cooperation tended to characterise the War Cabinet, and inter-ministerial wrangles made the ministers less inclined to see the interests of the whole. This, in his assessment, so debilitated the war effort that a new and completely neutral domestic advisory body, whose members had no other ministerial function, needed to be created. These efforts led to the creation of the Council of State in 1760, and while it is certainly true that the one exception Kaunitz made to the principle of ministerial exclusion from this body was for the Chancellor of State himself, it is noteworthy that he also retreated from the kind of directing role he had played in the War Cabinet, and for the remainder of his life the role of First Directing Minister or chairman of the Council of State was to be filled by others.[58]

Nevertheless, the Council of State now gave Kaunitz a formal institutional position through which to influence domestic reform – a position, moreover, which he retained to the end, even after he had resigned from the Foreign Ministry. Already in 1749 Kaunitz had argued, 'the domestic condition of a monarchy is the first and most important consideration, which affects all foreign policy deliberations'.[59] After the Seven Years War his foreign policy aimed at what he called 'a genuine peace system', which had as its basis the maintenance of general peace, good relations with all other powers, including Prussia if possible, no offensive alliances, and doing the best to diffuse any international tensions. Instead he urged the state to focus its attention on domestic reforms and the 'improvement of agriculture, industry, commerce and the financial infrastructure'.[60] As Lothar Schilling has pointed out, Kaunitz's policies were based on a clear assessment of both qualitative and quantitative factors determining power relationships,[61] and these in turn were as dependent on domestic socio-economic vibrancy and strength as they were on geopolitics and military power. Throughout his life Kaunitz was recognised as the leading minister of the Enlightenment party in the Habsburg Monarchy,[62] and for over a generation he played a key role in the acceleration of the reform dynamic of 'enlightened absolutism' within it. In Kaunitz's view an enlightened state required 'a government based on reason, justice and equity',[63] which encouraged 'a freedom-loving entrepreneurial spirit'.[64] As he put it, it was far better 'to reign over free and thinking individuals than to rule over base slaves'.[65]

In general terms, the domestic reforms that Kaunitz advocated and played a significant role in implementing had two broad and inherently related objectives: the first was to replace the patterns of thought and culture and the concomitant social and political infrastructure associated with the Counter-Reformation polity that was the Habsburg Monarchy in the Baroque era; the second was to introduce measures to metamorphose tightly controlled subjects into dynamic autonomous citizens. It is not surprising that Kaunitz played a key role in the confessional dimension of this reform process – the establishment of a state Church only loosely tied to Rome, the elimination of various Counter-Reformations pieties, the reduction of holy days, the dissolution of about one third of the monarchy's monastic institutions with its concomitant confiscation of Church property, the proclamations of confessional tolerance for Protestants and Jews, the effective establishment of a civil constitution for the Austrian clergy through state control of seminaries and the wide-ranging reorganisation of parishes, and the promulgation of civil marriage and austere burial ordinances – because all these issues involved diplomatic negotiations with the papacy, which fell within the purview of his ministry. Kaunitz's was by no means the most radical in the chorus of voices demanding such reforms.[66] The primary, though not exclusive, vehicle through which Kaunitz influenced and often spearheaded domestic reform was the Council of State. Here Kaunitz supported and strongly urged measures that would lead to a more liberal economy, as well as measures that would change the pattern of landholding and transform the bonded serf into a self-sufficient and enterprising yeoman. He supported efforts to reform and codify civil and criminal law, to abolish judicial torture, to dramatically loosen censorship laws, to overhaul the whole education system – including the introduction of compulsory primary education for both boys and girls – and, above all, and to revolutionise the value system, to create an open society that encouraged and supported the development of the arts and letters.[67]

Despite the enormous progress made, and despite the success of the reforms of 'enlightened absolutism', Kaunitz was nevertheless painfully aware that in many respects the Habsburg Monarchy was the most vulnerable of the great powers, chiefly due to its geographic position, which could offer little security from any direction.[68] This became especially critical after the accession of Catherine II in Russia in the last months of the Seven Years War. She withdrew Russia's previous support for a Saxon prince on the throne of Courland, and, indeed, made it clear that upon the death of its Saxon king, Augustus III, she intended to turn the entire Polish–Lithuanian Commonwealth into a Russian client state by placing her personal candidate and former lover on its throne.[69] Russian expansionist dynamism became evident to all during Russia's successful war with the Ottoman Empire during 1768–74. Kaunitz initially attempted to restrain Russian ambitions with armed mediation, but when Maria Theresia inadvertently revealed to the Prussian ambassador that Habsburg military preparations were a pure bluff, he felt he had little choice but to participate in the Prussian solution of moderating Russian demands on Turkey by granting territorial compensations at the expense of Poland.[70] This resulted in the 1772 Partition of Poland, by which the Habsburg Monarchy acquired the new province of Galicia, followed shortly by the province of Bukovina from the Ottoman Empire in 1774 as a sort of reward for having limited Russian territorial demands on the Porte at the conclusion of the Russo-Turkish War. After the first partition of Poland, however, Kaunitz came to the pessimistic conclusion that Russian expansionism, particularly at the expense of the Ottoman Empire, could not be stopped. As a result, the Habsburg Monarchy only had three options: she could resist Russia militarily, which Austria could not afford either financially or diplomatically; she could remain neutral, which would simply lead to unilateral Russian expansion; or she could ally herself with Russia in the hope of moderating its ambitions and sharing in the spoils. This last option was in Kaunitz's view 'certainly not the most desirable' but the 'least hazardous' one, and it was the policy pursued in the reign of Joseph II.[71]

Kaunitz's relations with Maria Theresia's son and successor, Joseph II, were uneasy at best but did not shake his position. Kaunitz had already had a serious disagreement with the young crown prince over the reduction in the size of the army at the end of 1761, at the very height of the Seven Years War. This issue revealed a major divergence of opinion between the Chancellor of State and the young heir on whether security through maximum military power or fiscal solvency and economic development ought to have priority in the policies of the Habsburg state.[72] When, after the sudden death of his father, Francis I, in 1765, Joseph became Holy Roman Emperor and as 'Co-Regent' of the Habsburg family domains, the differences with Kaunitz escalated. From Joseph's first great memorandum in his new capacity in 1765, the military tone of which Kaunitz criticised, through Joseph's vetoing of fiscal and agrarian reforms backed by Kaunitz in 1767, through Kaunitz's determined opposition to Joseph's plans to introduce conscription in the Habsburg Monarchy, through the emperor's expressed dissatisfaction with the State Chancellor's administration of the Italian and Belgian provinces, through Joseph's increasingly trenchant criticisms of Kaunitz's creation, the Council of State, through Kaunitz's opposition to Joseph's ambition to be given dictatorial powers to ride roughshod over the Monarchy's problems in 1771 and 1772, through fundamental disagreements over the future status of the newly acquired province of Galicia, to serious disputes over foreign policy both in the Polish partition crisis and the War of the Bavarian Succession, Kaunitz could hardly be blamed for seeing what appeared to be the handwriting on the wall. In the face of these disagreements Kaunitz offered to resign no fewer than four times during the Co-Regency period, and while these resignations were not devoid of strategic manoeuvring, there is little doubt that he could sense that his career was coming to an end. Certainly the appointment of Joseph's intimate and exact contemporary, Philipp Cobenzl, as Vice-Chancellor of the Foreign Ministry in July 1779 seemed to presage the imminent retirement of the old Chancellor, who was now already approaching his seventieth birthday.[73]

By 1780 it could be argued that Kaunitz had had as illustrious, full and successful a career as any European statesman of his century, and that with the death of Maria Theresia it was likely in any case to come to an end. Yet within an hour of his mother's death Joseph dispatched a personable note to Kaunitz asking him to stay on.[74] For all their disagreements the emperor's respect for the ageing Kaunitz bordered on the paternal, while Kaunitz, for his part, was imbued with an unshakable loyalty to the dynasty that transcended all personality conflicts. As he put it to one of his closest aides, 'I have always held to this principle: A good citizen must strive as long and as hard as he can to serve the state and his sovereign, often even despite him.'[75] The actual relationship between the emperor and the Chancellor of State, however, was far from harmonious. That tensions between the two men over both the style and substance of policy continued throughout the reign of Joseph is evident from Kaunitz's complaints to his intimates about Joseph's 'despotic obstinacy',[76] and the brutally frank assessments of the late monarch that he offered the emperor's successor, Leopold, in 1790,[77] but the position of the Chancellor of State seemed nevertheless unshakable. Thus, whatever disagreements might have clouded the relationship with Joseph, as his brother noted during a visit to Vienna in 1784, Kaunitz enjoyed his entire confidence,[78] and during the periods of the emperor's absence from Vienna it was Kaunitz who was repeatedly left in effective charge of the state.[79]

Although Joseph II occasionally considered proposals for a rapprochement with Prussia in the 1780s, he retained the main outlines of Kaunitz's anti-Prussian foreign policy. This was characterised in the first instance by adherence to the French alliance. Though everyone in Vienna was perfectly aware that French policies were frequently spiteful and duplicitous toward the Habsburg Monarchy[80] – a point on which Joseph and Kaunitz were in full agreement[81] – and that France could not be counted on to support any Austrian initiatives, for the geographically vulnerable Habsburg Monarchy the alliance had the value of neutralising traditional conflict zones in Italy and the Low Countries. The second cornerstone of foreign policy in the 1780s was the alliance with Russia. Secretly concluded in 1781, it was eventually to draw Austria into the Turkish war of 1788–91.[82] Both Joseph and Kaunitz were well aware that this alliance was a two-edged sword, as it required some degree of acquiescence to Russian territorial ambitions. Though Austria was doomed to play second fiddle in this partnership, drawing Russia away from its previous (and from the Austrian point of view, dangerous) alliance with Prussia did offer Austria a greater degree of security.

For Kaunitz the basis of Habsburg power lay in its central European lands and its dominant position in Germany – what McGill calls 'the core of Austria's great power status'.[83] Under the circumstances the struggle with Prussia for primacy in the Holy Roman Empire was bound to remain the centrepiece of policy and dominate all other considerations. The loss of the German province of Silesia had weakened Austria's position in the Empire, and Kaunitz had argued as early as 1743 that only the exchange of one of Austria's peripheral possessions for a contiguous German principality such as Bavaria could redress this situation. As a consequence he was certainly in favour in principle of the Bavarian exchange projects initiated by Joseph in 1778 and 1783, but in both cases he found the emperor's radical and confrontational approach to the project counterproductive, and he certainly could not have been pleased with how many of these imperial initiatives were undertaken behind the Chancellor's back.[84] Other aspects of Joseph's foreign policy, such as attempting to force the opening of the Scheldt estuary to international (that is, Austrian) shipping, his contempt for the Imperial Constitution, or his high-handed treatment of the ecclesiastical princes of the Empire, met with serious objections from Kaunitz.[85]

However, Kaunitz had much stronger differences with Joseph over his ministry's administration of the Belgian and Italian provinces. Having found men who enjoyed his confidence, Kaunitz was prepared to allow his authorised ministers considerable freedom of action. These ministers, Kaunitz insisted, should be 'honoured, respected and even feared' in their respective provinces.[86] Nor were they to be regarded as simple executors of Vienna's will. In Kaunitz's view the relationship between the central government and local administrators had to be reciprocal. Not only was informed input necessary from the local level; measures often also had to be adapted to local conditions if a genuine change in the social fabric were to be effected.[87] As has been pointed out, the relationship of Kaunitz to Cobenzl and Cristiani and their eventual successors – and for that matter to all the senior staff of his ministry – was one that treated them more as partners than subordinates,[88] and thus Austria's rational approach to Lombard and Belgian political culture was undertaken with a clear sense of their separate status. Of course, there was every intent that the peripheral provinces should be useful to the central core,[89] but no intent that they should be assimilated into it or patterned after it. This was precisely the reverse of Joseph's vision of turning all the diverse possessions of the Monarchy into 'just one body, uniformly governed'.[90] In 1785 Joseph began implementing his centralising plans for Milan, and though he asked for Kaunitz's input, he largely ignored the advice proffered and relegated both the Chancellor and his Italian Department officials to minor roles. The emperor then moved to impose a similar set of decrees on the Austrian Netherlands, again largely against the advice of Kaunitz. This led to open popular resistance in Belgium in 1787 and eventually to outright rebellion. With Kaunitz's backing the regents – Joseph's sister Marie Christine and her husband Duke Albert of Saxe-Teschen – tried to forestall the crisis by suspending Joseph's decrees, only to incur the full fury of the emperor's wrath.[91]

With the outbreak of the Turkish war in 1788 resistance to Joseph's centralising policies also began to reach crisis point in Hungary. By the end of 1789 the kingdom was on the verge of open rebellion. At the end of January 1790 Kaunitz confronted Joseph with brutal frankness: he reminded the emperor that he had 'already lost the Netherlands, perhaps lost them irrevocably', because he had not heeded his advice in 1787. Now, Kaunitz feared, 'the same misfortune will befall the Monarchy with Hungary' if Joseph did not rescind all his decrees for that kingdom.[92] The emperor gave in, but the very day after approving the Hungarian demarche he informed Kaunitz that he was reinstituting the Privy Conference, which Kaunitz's ministry had effectively marginalised during the Seven Years War, and which played no significant role thereafter. Joseph himself had been communicating with Kaunitz only in writing for two years before his death, so that it was Vice-Chancellor Philipp Cobenzl who had frequent personal contact with the emperor, and who availed himself of the opportunity to propose policy options contrary to those of his chief.[93] Kaunitz clearly was not entirely blind to the fact that important policy discussions were taking place behind his back, and the reanimation of the Privy Conference was only further evidence of this truth.[94]

With the accession of Leopold II the mandates that left Kaunitz in charge of government during the monarch's absence from the capital were repeated, though by this point they clearly reflected more the public stature of Kaunitz than the unreserved trust of the monarch. While Kaunitz and Leopold saw eye to eye on domestic policies, in foreign policy the new emperor, faced with a major international and domestic crisis upon his succession, was inclined to seek an accommodation with Prussia, while Kaunitz remained deeply suspicious of the Monarchy's old rival – as it turned out, with good cause. Under these circumstances the recently appointed deputy minister (*Referendar*) of the Foreign Ministry, Anton Spielmann, quickly found favour with Leopold and spearheaded the talks at the Convention of Reichenbach that eventually culminated in a new alliance with Prussia. And once Philipp Cobenzl had reingratiated himself with Leopold after the monarch's initial distrust of him, the two conspired to pursue foreign policies at odds with their chief. By then the eighty-one-year-old Kaunitz, while still venerated, appeared to be the embodiment of bygone days and bygone policies for whose Cassandra-like injunctions the confident expectations of the new generation had little patience.[95]

Cobenzl and Spielmann continued to play this role, after the sudden and unexpected death of Leopold in March 1792, under his successor, Francis II. With confident expectations of significant territorial compensations in a complex balance of power compensation arrangement proposed by Prussia, both a war with revolutionary France and naïve participation in the second partition of Poland, for which Austria was promised but failed to acquire Bavaria, were confidently pursued against the advice of Kaunitz. He had long argued that a policy of territorial aggrandisement with equitable territorial compensation for each great power in the name of maintaining a putative 'balance of power' was not in the interest of the Habsburg Monarchy, for 'every enlargement of the Monarchy loses its relative value, as soon as the Court of Berlin acquires an equivalent'.[96] In his later years he argued explicitly that such 'balance of power' ideas were little more than a rationalisation of naked aggression – 'in truth an expression void of sense, and at the same time an idea of something that is as unjust as it is impossible' – and that it was time once and for all to abandon this 'unjust illusion'.[97] Seeking to avoid war with France, and once it had broken out, to end it as quickly as possible,[98] and totally opposed to the policies which led to the second partition of Poland as 'a political morality not in accord with my principles, and one that should never be adopted by a great power that has any self-respect and recognizes the value of its good name',[99] a now embittered Kaunitz resigned. This time his resignation was accepted and his career as Foreign Minister of the Habsburg Monarchy came to an end.[100] In accepting his resignation, Emperor Francis urged Kaunitz to continue to give his advice as he saw fit, and documents from the Foreign Ministry continued to be sent to him when requested, but after August 1792 Kaunitz's voice disappeared from foreign policy discussions, except for an unsolicited and unheeded appeal to all belligerents in October 1792 to bring the war to an end.[101]

The old Chancellor, however, retained his seat on the Council of State, where he continued to participate in the discussions until only days before his death at the age of eighty-three on 27 June 1794. In these last two years of his life, which coincided with the Reign of Terror in France, and, in response, with an onset of political reaction in the Habsburg Monarchy, Kaunitz devoted his last energies to combating this abandonment of the path of the Enlightenment, of which he had been such a staunch adherent. 'Civil liberties and property rights are not French fantasies;' he wrote in September 1793, 'they are deeply embedded in any just monarchical constitution.'[102] Under the circumstances, he argued, 'coercive measures can never be a means to change people's opinions'.[103] In his view 'a wise and benevolent government' must recognise that '*Enlightenment* is the surest means to maintain civic order and to guarantee the loyalty of its subjects'.[104]

NOTES

1. Count Kaunitz was raised to the status of a Prince of the Holy Roman Empire in 1764 and to that of a Prince of the Habsburg Hereditary lands in 1776.
2. For example, see P. G. M. Dickson, *Finance and Government under Maria Theresia, 1740–1780*, 2 vols (Oxford: Oxford University Press, 1987), vol. I, p. 255.
3. See, for example, Derek McKay and H. M. Scott, *The Rise of the Great Powers, 1648–1815* (London and New York: Longman, 1983); Scott, *The Emergence of the Eastern Powers, 1756–1775* (Cambridge: Cambridge University Press, 2001); Michael Hochedlinger, *Austria's Wars of Emergence, 1683–1797* (Harlow: Longman, 2003); Scott, *The Birth of a Great Power System, 1740–1815* (Harlow: Longman, 2006).
4. Grete Klingenstein, 'The Meanings of "Austria" and "Austrian" in the Eighteenth Century', in Robert Oresko, G. C. Gibbs and Hamish Scott (eds), *Royal and Republican Sovereignty in Early Modern Europe: Essays in Memory of Ragnhild Hatton* (Cambridge: Cambridge University Press, 1997), pp. 423–78.
5. R. J. W. Evans, *The Making of the Habsburg Monarchy, 1550–1700* (Oxford: Oxford University Press, 1979), p. 447.
6. Samuel Clark has astutely observed that in the early modern period states emerged in Western Europe as powerful 'political-geographical centers' rather than 'nation-states' or 'national states', and that these states in turn shaped the aristocracy and transformed its political, economic, cultural and status power. See Samuel Clark, *State and Status: The Rise of the State and Aristocratic Power in Western Europe* (Montreal: McGill-Queens University Press, 1995).
7. Thomas Fellner and Heinrich Kretschmayr (eds), *Die österreichische Zentralverwaltung* (hereafter *ÖZV*). Section I, *Von Maximilian I. bis zur Vereinigung der österreichischen und böhmischen Hofkanzlei (1749)*, vol. 1, *Geschichtliche Übersicht* (Vienna: Holzhausen, 1907), pp. 23–9; vol. 2, *Aktenstücke, 1491–1681* (Vienna: Holzhausen, 1907), pp. 84–91.
8. Ibid. sec. I, vol. 1, pp. 150–60. The other two territorial chancelleries were the Bohemian Court Chancellery and the Hungarian Court Chancellery.
9. Lothar Gross, 'Der Kampf zwischen Reichskanzlei und österreichischer Hofkanzlei um die Führung der auswärtigen Geschäfte', *Historische Vierteljahrschrift* 22 (1924–5), pp. 279–312; Gross, *Die Geschichte der deutschen Reichshofkanzlei von 1559 bis 1806* (Vienna: Selbstverlag des Haus-, Hof- und Staatsarchivs, 1933), pp. 58–62. On the evolution of the Habsburg Foreign Office in general, see Franz A. J. Szabo, *Kaunitz and Enlightened Absolutism, 1753–1780* (Cambridge: Cambridge University Press, 1994), pp. 38–51.

10. *ÖZV*, sec. I, vol. 1, pp. 43–9, 167–9. See also Erwin Matsch, *Der Auswärtige Dienst von Österreich (-Ungarn), 1720–1920* (Vienna, Cologne and Graz: Böhlau, 1986), pp. 47–50.

11. Klaus Müller, *Das kaiserliche Gesandtschaftswesen im Jahrhundert nach dem Westfälischen Frieden (1648–1740)* (Bonn: Ludwig Röhrschneid Verlag, 1976), pp. 24, 30–1; *ÖZV*, sec. I, vol. 1, pp. 169, 268; *ÖZV*. Section II, *Von der Vereinigung der österreichischen und böhmischen Hofkanzlei bis zur Einrichtung der Ministerialverfassung (1749–1848)*, vol. 1, part 1, Friedrich Walter, *Die Geschichte der österreichischen Zentralverwaltung in der Zeit Maria Theresias* (Vienna: Holzhausen, 1938), pp. 78–9; *ÖZV*, sec. II, vol. 2, Joseph Kallbrunner and Melitta Winkler (eds), *Die Zeit des Directoriums in Publicis et Cameralibus. (Vorstadien 1743–1749. Das Directorium 1749–1760): Aktenstücke* (Vienna: Holzhausen, 1925), pp. 421–2.

12. Stefan Sienell, *Die Geheime Konferenz unter Kaiser Leopold I.: Personelle Strukturen und Methoden zur politischen Entscheidungsfindung am Wiener Hof* (Frankfurt: Peter Lang, 2001); *ÖZV*, sec. I, vol. 1, pp. 53–67; *ÖZV*, sec. I, vol. 3, *Aktenstücke, 1683–1749* (Vienna: Holzhausen, 1907), pp. 52–5; Jean Bérenger, *Finances et absolutisme autrichien dans la seconde moitié du XVIIe siècle* (Paris: Imprimerie nationale, 1975), pp. 37–42.

13. Grete Klingenstein, 'Institutionelle Aspekte der österreichischen Aussenpolitik im 18. Jahrhundert', in Erich Zöllner (ed.), *Diplomatie und Aussenpolitik Österreichs: Elf Beitrage zu ihrer Geschichte* (Vienna: Österreichischer Bundesverlag, 1977), p. 20.

14. *ÖZV*, sec. II, vol. 1, part 1, pp. 77–9; *ÖZV*, sec. II, vol. 3, Friedrich Walter (ed.), *Vom Sturz des Directoriums in Publicis et Cameralibus (1760/1761) bis zum Ausgang der Regierung Maria Theresias: Aktenstücke* (Vienna: Holzhausen, 1934), pp. 479–85; Klingenstein, 'Institutionelle Aspekte', pp. 82–6; Matsch, *Auswärtige Dienst*, pp. 51, 181.

15. Grete Klingenstein, *Der Aufstieg des Hauses Kaunitz: Studien zur Herkunft und Bildung des Staatskanzlers Wenzel Anton* (Göttingen: Vandenhoeck & Ruprecht, 1975), p. 112.

16. On the youth and family background of Kaunitz, see ibid. pp. 41–219. The earlier Alfred Ritter von Arneth, 'Biographie des Fürsten Kaunitz: Ein Fragment', *Archiv für österreichische Geschichte* (hereafter *AÖG*) 88 (1900), pp. 1–201, contains a number of errors and should be read only in conjunction with Klingenstein. The story that Kaunitz was originally intended for an ecclesiastical career is still widely repeated.

17. Jeroen Duindam, *Vienna and Versailles: The Courts of Europe's Dynastic Rivals, 1550–1780* (Cambridge: Cambridge University Press, 2003), p. 296.

18. Ibid.; Andreas Pečar, *Die Ökonomie der Ehre: Der höfische Adel am Kaiserhof Karls VI. (1711–1740)* (Darmstadt: Wissenschaftliche Buchgesellschaft, 2003).

19. Klingenstein, *Aufstieg*, pp. 254–65.

20. Pečar, *Ökonomie der Ehre*, pp. 41–53.

21. Klingenstein, *Aufstieg*, pp. 269–83.

22. Vienna, Haus- Hof- und Staatsarchiv (hereafter HHStA), Staatenabteilung: Sardinien Berichte, Faszikel 4, Kaunitz's 'Rohe Gedancken und Reflexionen über den Zustand von Italien', and 'fernere Gedancken', submitted with his report of 18 March 1743. See the discussion and analysis of these memoranda in Arneth, 'Biographie des Fürsten Kaunitz', pp. 52–5; William J. McGill, 'The Roots of Policy: Kaunitz in Italy and the Netherlands, 1742–1746', *Central European History* 1 (1968), pp. 137–8 (pp. 131–49); Elisabeth Garms-Cornides, 'Kaunitz und die habsburgische Italienpolitik während des Österreichischen Erbforgekrieges', in Grete Klingenstein and Franz A. J. Szabo (eds), *Staatskanzler Wenzel Anton von Kaunitz-Rietberg, 1711–1794: Neue Perspektiven zu Politik und Kultur der europäischen Aufklärung* (Graz, Esztergom, Paris and New York: Andreas-Schnider-Verlagsatelier, 1996), pp. 29–46; Harm Klueting, *Die Lehre von der Macht der Staaten: Das Außenpolitische Machtproblem in der 'politischen Wissenschaft' und in der praktischen Politik im 18. Jahrhundert* (Berlin: Duncker & Humbolt, 1986), pp. 174–6; Lothar Schilling,

Kaunitz und das Renversement des alliances: *Studien zur außenpolitischen Konzeption Wenzel Antons von Kaunitz* (Berlin: Duncker & Humbolt, 1994), pp. 20–2.

23. On Kaunitz in Aachen, see William J. McGill, 'Wenzel Anton von Kaunitz-Rittberg and the Conference of Aix-la-Chapelle, 1748', *Duquesne Review* 14 (1969), pp. 154–67; Arneth, 'Biographie des Fürsten Kaunitz', pp. 112–53; Adolf Beer, 'Zur Geschichte des Friedens von Aachen im Jahre 1748', *AÖG* 47 (1871), pp. 72–93; Schilling, *Kaunitz*, pp. 122–45.

24. This famous comprehensive analysis, which has been the centrepiece of all discussions of the Diplomatic Revolution, has been published in its entirety in Reiner Pommerin and Lothar Schilling (eds), 'Denkschrift des Grafen Kaunitz zur mächtepolitischen Konstellation nach dem Aachner Frieden von 1748', in Johannes Kunisch (ed.), *Expansion und Gleichgewicht: Studien zur europäischen Mächtepolitik des ancien régime* (Berlin: Duncker & Humblot, 1986), pp. 165–239. See the discussion and analysis in William J. McGill, 'The Roots of Policy: Kaunitz in Vienna and Versailles, 1749–1753', *Journal of Modern History* 43 (1971), pp. 228–44; Alfred Ritter von Arneth, *Geschichte Maria Theresias*, 10 vols (Vienna: Wilhelm Braumüller, 1863–79), vol. 4, pp. 272–80; Arneth, 'Biographie des Fürsten Kaunitz', pp. 164–79; Klueting, *Die Lehre von der Macht*, pp. 176–9; Schilling, *Kaunitz*, pp. 145–59; Franz A. J. Szabo, 'Wenzel Anton Kaunitz-Rietberg und Seine Zeit: Bemerkungen zum 200. Todestag des Staatskanzlers', in Klingenstein and Szabo, *Staatskanzler Wenzel Anton von Kaunitz-Rietberg*, pp. 12–13 (pp. 11–28).

25. Kaunitz was raised to the Order of the Golden Fleece on 30 September 1749. See Rudolf Khevenhüller-Metsch and Hanns Schlitter (eds), *Aus der Zeit Maria Theresias: Tagebuch des Fürsten Johann Josef Khevenhüller-Metsch, Kaiserlichen Obersthofmeisters*, 8 vols (Vienna and Leipzig: Holzhausen, 1907–72), vol. 2, p. 371. He was known to be ambassador designate as early as June 1749. See Gaston von Pettenegg (ed.), *Ludwig und Karl, Grafen und Herren von Zinzendorf: Ihre Selbstbiographien* (Vienna: Wilhelm Braumueller, 1879), p. 58.

26. Hanns Schlitter (ed.), *Correspondance secrète entre le Comte A.W. Kaunitz-Rietberg, Ambassadeur impérial à Paris, et le Baron Ignaz de Koch, Secrétaire de l'Impératrice Marie-Thérèse, 1750 – 1752* (Paris: E. Plon, 1899), pp. 155–62; Grete Klingenstein, 'Kaunitz kontra Bartenstein: Zur Geschichte der Staatskanzlei in den Jahren 1749–1753', in Heinrich Fichtenau and Erich Zöllner (eds), *Beiträge zur neueren Geschichte Österreichs* (Vienna: Holzhausen, 1974), pp. 243–63; Klingenstein, *Aufstieg*, pp. 284–301.

27. Khevenhüller-Metsch and Schlitter, *Aus der Zeit Maria Theresias*, vol. II, pp. 296–8, 303–4.

28. Ibid. vol. III, pp. 114–15, 119,123; vol. IV, pp. 138, 143–4; vol. V, p. 103.

29. The official and unofficial instructions were originally framed for Cobenzl (whose term began a few months earlier than Cristiani's) and then applied to Cristiani. HHStA, Belgien: Vorträge, Faszikel 5, Maria Theresia to Cobenzl, 19 May and 6 August 1753; 'Puncten, So dem Herrn Graffen Cobenzl zu Seiner Geheimen Instruction zu dienen hätten', 9 August 1753; Maria Theresia to Kaunitz, undated [6–9 August 1753].

30. Ibid. Faszikel 6, Kaunitz to Maria Theresia, 20 November 1754.

31. On the changes in the administrative structure of the Austrian Netherlands, see Renate Zedinger, *Die Verwaltung der Österreichischen Niederlande in Wien (1714–1795): Studien zu den Zentralisierungstendenzen des Wiener Hofes im Staatswerdungsprozeß der Habsburgermonarchie* (Vienna, Cologne and Weimar: Böhlau, 2000), pp. 78–95.

32. *ÖZV*, sec. II, vol. 2, pp. 422–3; Khevenhüller-Metsch and Schlitter, *Aus der Zeit Maria Theresias*, vol. 4, pp. 319–21.

33. Cf. Franz A. J. Szabo, 'The Center and the Periphery: Echoes of the Diplomatic Revolution in the Administration of the Habsburg Monarchy, 1753–1773', in Marija Wakounig, Wolfgang Mueller and Michael Portmann (eds), *Nation, Nationalitäten und Nationalismus im östlichen Europa: Festschrift für Arnold Suppan zum 65. Geburtstag* (Vienna: LIT Verlag, 2010), pp. 473–90.

34. Carlo Capra, 'Il Settecento', in Giuseppe Galasso (ed.), *Storia d'Italia*. Vol. 11, Domenico Sella and Carlo Capra, *Il Ducato di Milano dal 1535 al 1796* (Turin: UTET, 1984), pp. 151–663. The work was also issued as a separate volume, *La Lombardia Austriaca nell'età delle riforme (1706–1796)* (Turin: UTET, 1987). Cf. Capra, 'Kaunitz and Austrian Lombardy', in Klingenstein and Szabo, *Staatskanzler Wenzel Anton von Kaunitz-Rietberg*, pp. 245–60; Capra, 'Luigi Giusti e il dipartimento d'Italia a Vienna, 1757–1766', *Società e storia* 15 (1982), pp. 61–85.

35. Piet Lenders, 'Vienne et Bruxelles: une tutelle qui n'exclut pas une large autonomie', in *La Belgique autrichienne, 1713–1794: les Pays-Bas méridionaux sous les Habsbourg d'Autriche* (Brussels: Crédit Communal de Belgique, 1987), pp. 37–70; cf. Henri Pirenne, *Histoire de Belgique*, 7 vols (Brussels: Henri Lamertin, 1922–32), vol. 5, pp. 219–324.

36. Pierre Bourdieu, 'Ökonomisches Kapital, kuturelles Kapital, soziales Kapital', in Reinhard Kreckel (ed.), *Soziale Ungleichheiten* (Göttingen: Schwarz, 1983), pp. 185–90.

37. Pečar, *Ökonomie der Ehre*, pp. 126–38.

38. Khevenhüller-Metsch and Schlitter, *Aus der Zeit Maria Theresias*, vol. 2, pp. 160–1.

39. Gustav Zechmeiter, *Die Wiener Theater nächst der Burg und nächst dem Kärntnerthor von 1747 bis 1776* (Vienna: Österreichische Akademie der Wissenschaften, 1971), p. 46; Robert Haas, *Gluck und Durazzo im Burgtheater (Die Opera comique in Wien)* (Zürich, Vienna and Leipzig: Amalthea-Verlag, 1925), p. 5.

40. The literature on these developments is enormous, but has been mostly supplanted by Bruce Alan Brown, *Gluck and the French Theatre in Vienna* (Oxford: Oxford University Press, 1991).

41. Adolf Beer (ed.), 'Denkschriften des Fürsten Kaunitz', *AÖG* 48 (1892), p. 38 (pp. 1–162).

42. The best introductions to the Diplomatic Revolution are Scott, *The Birth*, pp. 72–95; D. B. Horn, 'The Diplomatic Revolution', in J. O. Lindsay (ed.), *The New Cambridge Modern History*. Vol. VII, *The Old Regime, 1713–63* (Cambridge: Cambridge University Press, 1957), pp. 440–64. See also Schilling, *Kaunitz*, pp. 189–213; Franz A. J. Szabo, *The Seven Years War in Europe, 1756–1763* (Harlow: Longman, 2008), pp. 11–16.

43. While Richard Waddington, *Louis XV et le reversement des alliances* (Paris: Firmin, 1896) and Albert Broglie, *L'Alliance autrichienne* (Paris: C. Lévy, 1897), remain the standard works on these negotiations and on the First Treaty of Versailles, the most important modern corrective is the unpublished John Charles Batzel, 'Austria and the First Three Treaties of Versailles, 1755–1758' (PhD dissertation, Brown University, 1974), pp. 82–150.

44. Walther Mediger, *Moskaus Weg nach Europa: Der Aufstieg Russlands zum Europäischen Machtstaat im Zeitalter Friedrichs des Grossen* (Berlin: Georg Westermann Verlag, 1952), pp. 181–329; Michael G. Müller, 'Rußland und der Siebenjährige Krieg', *Jahrbücher für die Geschichte Osteuropas* 28 (1980), pp. 202–8; Müller, 'Das "Petrinische Erbe": Russische Grossmachtpolitik bis 1762', in M. Hellmann, K. Zernack and G. Schramm (eds), *Handbuch der Geschichte Russlands*. Vol. 2, Zernack (ed.), *Vom Randstaat zur Hegemonialmacht* (Stuttgart: A. Hiersemann, 1985), pp. 433–7. On the alliances of 1726 and 1746, see Walter Leitsch, 'Der Wander der österreichischen Russlandspolitik in den Jahren 1724–1726', *Jahrbuch für Geschichte Osteuropas* 6 (1958), pp. 33–92; Paul Karge, *Die russisch-österreichische Allianz von 1746 und ihre Vorgeschichte* (Göttingen: R. Peppmüller, 1887).

45. Beer, 'Denkschriften', p. 42.

46. Richard Waddington, *La Guerre de sept ans: Histoire diplomatique et militaire*, 5 vols (Paris: Librairie de Paris, 1899–1914), vol. 1, pp. 52–156; Arneth, *Maria Theresia*, vol. 5, pp. 97–153; Batzel, 'Austria', pp. 147–294.

47. D. B. Horn, 'The Duke of Newcastle and the Origins of the Diplomatic Revolution', in J. H. Elliott and H. G. Koenigsberger (eds), *The Diversity of History: Essays in Honour of Sir Herbert Butterfield* (London: Blackwell, 1970), p. 257 (pp. 245–68).

48. Most recently, R. J. W. Evans, Michael Schaich and Peter H. Wilson (eds), *The Holy Roman Empire, 1495–1806* (London: German Historical Institute, and Oxford: Oxford University Press, 2011); R. J. W. Evans and Peter H. Wilson (eds), *The Holy Roman Empire, 1495– 1806: A European Perspective* (Leiden: Brill, 2012). See also Michael Rohrschneider, *Österreich und der Immerwährende Reichstag: Studien zur Klientelpolitik und Parteibildung (1745–1763)*. (Göttingen: Vandenhoeck & Ruprecht, 2014).

49. Frederick to Finkenstein, 6 January 1762, in Johann Gustav Droysen et al. (eds), *Politische Correspondenz Friedrichs des Grossen*, 47 vols (Berlin: various publishers, 1879–), vol. 31, pp. 165–6; vol. 13, p. 383.

50. HHStA, Staatskanzlei: Vorträge, Karton 83, Kaunitz to Maria Theresia, 6 November 1758.

51. Waddington, *La Guerre de sept ans*, vol. 2, pp. 461–70.

52. HHStA, Staatskanzlei: Vorträge, Karton 83, Kaunitz to Maria Theresia, 31 October and 30 December 1760. Brief summaries are given in Arneth, *Maria Theresia*, vol. 6, pp. 201–17.

53. Article separé et secret de la Convention, 21 March [1 April], 1760, Arnold Schaefer, *Geschichte des siebenjährigen Krieges*, 2 vols (Berlin: Wilhelm Hertz, 1867–74), vol. 2, part i, pp. 522–3, no. 11.

54. HHStA, Staatskanzlei: Vorträge, Karton 83, Kaunitz to Maria Theresia, 30 December 1760. Discussion in Arneth, *Maria Theresia*, vol. 6, pp. 207–14; Schaefer, *Geschichte*, vol. 2, part ii, pp. 186–9; Schilling, *Kaunitz*, pp. 250–1; Reiner Pommerin, 'Bündnispolitik und Mächtesystem: Österreich und der Aufstieg Russlands im 18. Jahrhundert', in Kunisch, *Expansion und Gleichgewicht*, pp. 150–2; Szabo, *Seven Years War*, p. 274.

55. On Kaunitz's role in domestic affairs, see Szabo, *Kaunitz and Enlightened Absolutism.*

56. Arneth, *Maria Theresia*, vol. 5, p. 467.

57. Khevenhüller-Metsch and Schlitter, *Aus der Zeit Maria Theresias*, vol. 4, pp. 91, 302–12.

58. On the Council of State, see Carl Freiherr von Hock and Hermann Ignaz Bidermann, *Der österreichische Staatsrath (1760–1848)* (Vienna: Wilhelm Braumüller, 1879). For a detailed discussion of the Council's establishment and the historiographical controversies surrounding it, see Szabo, *Kaunitz and Enlightened Absolutism*, pp. 51–60.

59. Pommerin and Schilling, 'Denkschrift des Grafen Kaunitz', p. 206.

60. Beer, 'Denkschriften', pp. 67–8.

61. Schilling, *Kaunitz*, pp. 302–80; Schilling, 'Ohne Leidenschaft und Vorurteil? Prämissen außenpolitischer Urteilsbildung bei Kaunitz', in Klingenstein and Szabo, *Staatskanzler Wenzel Anton von Kaunitz-Rietberg*, pp. 142–67.

62. His protegé, Ludwig von Zinzendorf, explicitly called the adherents of enlightened reform with Kaunitz at their head 'un espèce de parti'. See Vienna, Deutscher Orden, Zentralarchiv, Handschriften, vol. 64, Ludwig Zinzendorf to Karl Zinzendorf, 18 December 1768. Voltaire himself wrote to Kaunitz: 'Nous ne demandons qu'à faire voir à l'Europe combien la vraie philosophie, c'est à dire la philosophie bienfaisante, fait de progrès dans ce siècle. Vous êtes Monsieur à la tête de ceux qui l'encouragent' (Voltaire to Kaunitz, 3 July 1766, in *The Complete Works of Voltaire* (Banbury: Voltaire Foundation, 1973), vol. 114, pp. 295–6).

63. HHStA, Kabinettsarchiv: Kaunitz Voten, Karton 6, 1793/3203, Kaunitz Staatsratvotum, 15 September 1793.

64. HHStA, Österreichische Akten: Österreich Staat, Fasz. 5, Kaunitz to Maria Theresia, 21 April 1767.

65. Beer, 'Denkschriften', p. 157.

66. On this point, see Franz A. J. Szabo, 'Intorno alle origini del giuseppinismo: motivi economico-sociali e aspetti ideologici', *Società e storia* 4 (1979), pp. 155–74; Szabo, 'Fürst Kaunitz und die Anfänge des Josephinismus', in Richard Georg Plaschka, Grete Klingenstein, et al. (eds), *Österreich im Europa der Aufklärung: Kontinuität und Zäsur in Europa zur Zeit Maria Theresias und Josephs II.*, 2 vols (Vienna: Österreichische Akademie der Wissenschaften, 1985), vol. 1, pp. 525–45.

67. Kaunitz's role in the domestic reforms of the Habsburg Monarchy in the era of enlightened absolutism is the subject of Szabo, *Kaunitz and Enlightened Absolutism, 1753–1780* and Szabo, *Kaunitz and Enlightened Absolutism, 1780–1794* (forthcoming).
68. HHStA, Staatskanzlei: Vorträge, Karton 121, Kaunitz to Joseph II, 22 December 1776.
69. Martin Schulze Wessel, 'Die Restitution Birons zum kurländischen Herzog 1762 als Zäsur in der russischen Ostmitteleuropapolitik des 18. Jahrhunderts', in Claus Scharf (ed.), *Katharina II., Rußland und Europa: Beiträge zur internationalen Forschung* (Mainz: Philipp von Zabern, 2001), pp. 59–73; Karl Elias, 'Die preussisch-russischen Beziehungen von der Tronbesteigung Peters III. bis zum Abschluss des preussisch-russischen Bündnisses vom 11. April 1764' (PhD dissertation, University of Göttingen, 1900), pp. 62–119; Sergei M. Soloviev, *History of Russia*, ed. and trans. Peter von Wahlde et al., 48 vols (Gulf Breeze, FL: Academic International Press, 1976–), vol. 42, pp. 166–76; Scott, *Emergence of the Eastern Powers*, pp. 103–6.
70. Saul K. Padover, 'Prince Kaunitz' Résumé of His Eastern Policy, 1763–71', *Journal of Modern History* 5 (1933), pp. 352–65.
71. HHStA, Staatskanzlei: Vorträge, Karton 136, Kaunitz to Joseph II, 26 October 1782. On Kaunitz's reaction to the rise of Russia, see Harvey L. Dyck, 'Pondering the Russian Fact: Kaunitz and the Catherinian Empire in the 1770s', *Canadian Slavonic Papers/Revue Canadienne des Slavistes* 22:4 (1980), pp. 451–69. See also Karl A. Roider, *Austria's Eastern Question, 1700–1790* (Princeton: Princeton University Press, 1982), pp. 151–88; Adolf Beer, *Die Orientalische Politik Oesterreichs seit 1774* (Prague: Temsky, and Leipzig: Freytag, 1883), pp. 30–145.
72. Franz A. J. Szabo, 'Competing Visions of Enlightened Absolutism: Security and Economic Development in the Reform Priorities of the Habsburg Monarchy after the Seven Years War', in János Kalmár (ed.), *Miscellanea fontium historiae Europaeae: Emlékkönyv H. Balázs Éva történészprofesszor 80. születésnapjára* (Budapest: ELTE, 1997), pp. 191–200.
73. The disputes with Joseph are covered in detail, from Kaunitz's perspective in Szabo, *Kaunitz and Enlightened Absolutism*, *passim*, and from Joseph's perspective in Derek Beales, *Joseph II.* Vol. 1, *In the Shadow of Maria Theresa, 1741–1780* (Cambridge: Cambridge University Press 1987), *passim*. See also Franz A. J. Szabo, 'Prolegomena to an Enlightened Despot? Text and Subtext in Joseph II's Co-Regency Memoranda', in Szabo, Antal Szantáy and István György Tóth (eds), *Politics and Culture in the Age of Joseph II* (Budapest: Hungarian Academy of Sciences, 2005), pp. 11–21. Philipp Cobenzl was the nephew of Karl Philipp Cobenzl.
74. Adolf Beer (ed.), *Joseph II., Leopold II. und Kaunitz: Ihr Briefwechsel* (Vienna: Wilhelm Braumüller, 1873), pp. 20–1.
75. HHStA, Staatskanzlei: Vorträge, Karton 110. Kaunitz to Binder, 14 September 1772.
76. Alfred Ritter von Arneth and Jules Flammermont (eds), *Correspondance secrète du comte de Mercy-Argenteau avec l'Empereur Joseph II et le prince de Kaunitz*, 2 vols (Paris: Imprimerie Nationale, 1889–91), vol. 2, p. 294.
77. HHStA, Kabinettsarchiv: Voten des Fürsten Kaunitz zu Staatsratakten, Karton 6, No. 1662 of 1791, Kaunitz Votum, 20 July 1791. Partially cited in Michael Hochedlinger, *Krise und Wiederherstellung: Österreichische Großmachtpolitik zwischen Türkenkrieh und 'Zweiter Diplomatischer Revolution' 1787–1791* (Berlin: Duncker & Humblot, 2000), p. 317. For other critiques, see Karl Otmar Freiherr von Aretin, *Heiliges Römisches Reich, 1776–1806: Reichsverfassung und Staatssouveränität.* Part II, *Ausgewählte Aktenstücke, Bibliographie, Register* (Wiesbaden: F. Steiner, 1967), p. 204; Elemér Mályusz, 'Kaunitz über die Kulturpolitik der Habsburgermonarchie', *Südostdeutsche Forschungen* [now *Südostforschungen*] 2 (1937), p. 11 (pp. 1–16).
78. HHStA, Hausarchiv: Sammelbände, vol. 16, Leopold's 'Relazione di Sua Altezza Reale del Viaggio, e Soggiorno fatto a Vienna nel Luglio 1784', p. 77.

79. HHStA, Staatskanzlei: Vorträge, Kartons 133–45, Joseph to Kaunitz, 20 May 1781, 21 April 1783, 2 December 1783, 12 June 1786, 31 March 1787 and 13 February 1788.

80. Leopold's 'Relazione', p. 298.

81. Alfred Ritter von Arneth (ed.), *Maria Theresia und Joseph II: Ihre Correspondenz sammt Briefen Joseph's an seinen Bruder Leopold*, 3 vols (Vienna: Braumüller, 1867–8), vol. 2, pp. 184–9; Arneth and Flammermont, *Correspondance secrète*, vol. 2, p. 535.

82. For the most recent discussion of the Russian alliance, with full reference to the older literature, see Derek Beales, *Joseph II*. Vol. 2, *Against the World, 1780–1790* (Cambridge: Cambridge University Press, 2009), pp. 104–32, 376–88, 555–77. For the secret alliance of 1781, see Isabel de Madariaga, 'The Secret Austro-Russian Treaty of 1781', *Slavonic and East European Review* 38 (1959–60), pp. 114–45. See also Roider, *Austria's Eastern Question*, pp. 160–88; Beer, *Orientalische Politik*, pp. 3–145; Hochedlinger, *Austria's Wars of Emergence*, pp. 376–86. The standard military account of the Turkish war remains Oskar Criste, *Kriege unter Kaiser Josef II.* (Vienna: L. W. Seidel, 1904), pp. 143–251. For the most recent assessment of the war as a whole, see Matthew Z. Mayer, 'The Price for Austria's Security: Part I. Joseph II, the Russian Alliance, and the Ottoman War, 1787–1789', *International History Review*, 26:2 (2004), pp. 257–99; Mayer, 'The Price for Austria's Security: Part II. Leopold II, the Prussian Threat, and the Peace of Sistova, 1790–1791', *International History Review* 26:3 (2004), pp. 473–514. Karl A. Roider, 'Kaunitz, Joseph II and the Turkish War', *Slavonic and East European Review* 54 (1979), pp. 538–45 and Paul P. Bernard, 'Austria's Last Turkish War', *Austrian History Yearbook* 19–20 (1983–4), pp. 15–31, contain major errors and are unreliable. The war was begun by Russia in 1787 and though Joseph II agreed to join his ally, his formal declaration of war did not occur until February 1788; similarly Austria agreed to end the war largely on the basis of the status quo in June 1790, but did not sign the formal peace treaty until August 1791.

83. McGill, 'Kaunitz in Italy and the Netherlands', p. 138.

84. On the Bavarian exchange projects, see Paul P. Bernard, *Joseph II and Bavaria: Two Eighteenth-Century Attempts at German Unification* (The Hague: Martinus Nijhoff, 1965), which underrates the differences between Kaunitz and Joseph. For a corrective, see Beales, *Joseph II*, vol. 1, pp. 386–422; vol. 2, pp. 388–90, 393–8. Cf. Karl Otmar von Aretin, 'Kurfürst Karl Theodor, 1778–1799, und das Bayerische Tauschprojekt', *Zeitschrift für Bayerische Landesgeschichte* 25 (1962), pp. 745–800; Peter Schmid, 'Joseph II, Kaunitz und die bayerische Erbfolgfrage', in Dieter Albrecht (ed.), *Forschungen zur bayerischen Geschichte: Festschrift für Wilhelm Volkert zum 65. Geburtstag* (Frankfurt am Main: Peter Lang, 1993), pp. 135–57; Angela Kulenkampff, *Österreich und das Alte Reich: Die Reichspolitik des Staatskanzlers Kaunitz unter Maria Theresia und Joseph II.* (Cologne, Weimar and Vienna: Böhlau Verlag, 2005), pp. 68–123.

85. On Joseph as Holy Roman Emperor, see Beales, *Joseph II*, vol. 1, pp. 110–33; vol. 2, pp. 403–24; Kulenkampff, *Österreich und das Alte Reich*, pp. 56–131, both with full reference to the older literature.

86. HHStA, Belgien: Vorträge, Faszikel 6, Kaunitz to Maria Theresia, 12 December 1754. Cf. Szabo, 'The Center and the Periphery', pp. 485–6; Renate Zedinger, 'Kaunitz und Johann Karl Cobenzl. Zu den Zentralisierungstendenzen des Staatskanzlers im Wiener Verwaltungsapparat der Österreichischen Niederlande, 1753–1757', in Klingenstein and Szabo, *Staatskanzler Wenzel Anton von Kaunitz-Rietberg*, pp. 197–217.

87. HHStA, Staatskanzlei: Vorträge, Karton 112, Kaunitz's 'Allergnädigst anbefohlenes Gutachten über die Verbesserung des systematis in Internis', 1 May 1773.

88. Antal Szántay, *Regionalpolitik im Alten Europa: Die Verwaltungsreformen Joseph II. in Ungarn, in der Lombardei und in den österreichischen Niederlanden, 1785–1790* (Budapest: Akadémiai Kiadó, 2005), p. 39; cf. Beer, 'Denkschriften', pp. 155–6.

89. Michele Galand, 'Kaunitz et les Pays-Bas autrichiens: la centralisation administrative', in Klingenstein and Szabo, *Staatskanzler Wenzel Anton von Kaunitz-Rietberg*, pp. 218–31.

90. Alfred Ritter von Arneth (ed.), *Joseph II. und Leopold von Toscana: Ihr Briefwechsel von 1781 bis 1790*, 2 vols (Vienna: Wilhelm Braumüller, 1872), vol. 2, p. 17. I am using the translation of Derek Beales, who has used this quotation as a chapter heading for describing Joseph's centralising ambition. See Beales, *Joseph II*, vol. 2, pp. 477–525.

91. The most recent analyses of these policies, with full refence to the extensive older literature, are to be found in Szántay, *Regionalpolitik*, pp. 105–202; Beales, *Joseph II*, vol. 2, pp. 494–512.

92. HHStA, Staatskanzlei: Vorträge, Karton 147, Kaunitz to Joseph, 28 January 1790, printed in Leopold von Ranke, *Die deutschen Mächte und der Fürstenbund: Deutsche Geschichte von 1780 bis 1790*, 2nd edn (Leipzig: Duncker & Humblot, 1875), pp. 541–2; Henrik Marczali, *Magyarország története II. József korában*, 3 vols (Budapest, Pfeifer F. Kiadása,1885–8), vol. 3, pp. 563, 605–6; Hanns Schlitter (ed.), *Kaunitz, Philipp Cobenzl, und Spielmann. Ihr Briefwechsel, 1779–1792* (Vienna: Adolf Holzhausen, 1899), pp. xxxiv–xxxv. Cf. Franz A. J. Szabo, 'Prince Kaunitz and the Hungarian Diet of 1790–1791', in Helmut Wohnout, Ursula Mindler and George Kastner (eds), *Auf der Suche nach Identität: Festschrift für Dieter Anton Binder zum Sechzigsten Geburtstag* (Vienna: LIT Verlag, 2014), pp. 265–6 (pp. 255–87).

93. Sebastian Brunner (ed.), *Correspondances intimes de l'Empereur Joseph II. avec son ami le comte de Cobenzl et son premier ministre le prince de Kaunitz* (Paris, Mainz and Brussels: F. Kirchheim, 1871), pp. 60–1.

94. HHStA, Staatskanzlei: Vorträge, Karton 147, Joseph to Kaunitz, 29 January 1790. On the re-establishment of the Privy Conference, see Hochedlinger, *Krise und Wiederherstellung*, pp. 309–14.

95. Hochedlinger, *Krise und Wiederherstellung*, pp. 315–461. See also Hochedlinger, 'Das Ende der Ära Kaunitz in der Staatskanzlei', in Klingenstein and Szabo, *Staatskanzler Wenzel Anton von Kaunitz-Rietberg*, pp. 117–30.

96. HHStA, Staatskanzlei: Vorträge, Karton 136, Kaunitz to Joseph II, 26 October 1782.

97. Kaunitz's 'Reflexions sur l'idée de ce que l'on appelle l'Equilibre des Puissances de l'Europe', in Franz A. J. Szabo, 'Prince Kaunitz and the Balance of Power', *International History Review* 1:3 (1979), pp. 406–8 (pp. 399–408).

98. Ernst Wangermann, 'Kaunitz und der Krieg gegen das revolutionäre Frankreich', in Klingenstein and Szabo, *Staatskanzler Wenzel Anton von Kaunitz-Rietberg*, pp. 131–41. See also T. C. W. Blanning, *The Origins of the French Revolutionary Wars* (London: Longman, 1986), pp. 87–8.

99. Alfred Ritter von Vivenot (ed.), *Quellen zur Geschichte der Deutschen Kaiserpolitik Oesterreichs während der französischen Revolutionskriege, 1970–1801.* Vol. 2, *Die Politik des oesterr. Vice-Staatskanzlers Grafen Philipp von Cobenzl unter Kaiser Franz II. von der französischen Kriegserklärung und dem Rücktritt des Fürsten Kaunitz bis zur zweiten Theilung Polens. April 1792 – März 1793* (Vienna: Wilhelm Braumüller, 1874), p. 115.

100. Ibid. pp. 157–9.

101. Ibid. pp. 283–8; Wangermann, 'Kaunitz und der Krieg', pp. 139–40; Hochedlinger, 'Das Ende der Ära Kaunitz', pp. 127–8.

102. Szabo, 'Wenzel Anton Kaunitz-Rietberg und Seine Zeit', p. 26.

103. Ibid. p. 26.

104. Ibid. pp. 26–7. Cf. Szabo, 'Staatskanzler Fürst Kaunitz und die Aufklärungspolitik Österreichs', in Walter Koschatzky (ed.), *Maria Theresia und Ihre Zeit: Eine Darstellung der Epoche von 1740–1780 aus Anlaß der 200. Wiederkehr des Todestages der Kaiserin* (Salzburg and Vienna: Residenz Verlag, 1979), p. 44; Michael Hochedlinger, '". . . Dass Aufklärung das sicherste Mittel ist, die Ruhe und Anhängichkeit der Unterthanen zu

befestigen": Staatskanzler Kaunitz und die "franziszeische Reaktion" 1792–1794', in Helmut Reinalter (ed.), *Aufklärung – Vormärz – Revolution: Jahrbuch der 'Internationalen Forschungsstelle Demokratische Bewegungen in Mitteleuropa von 1770–1850' an der Universität Insbruck* 16/17 (1996/97), pp. 62–79; original emphasis.

Index